CW01649949

wYork

Tort and Insurance Law
Yearbook

European Tort Law 2004

Edited by the
European Centre of Tort
and Insurance Law

together with the

Research Unit for European Tort Law
of the Austrian Academy of Sciences

Helmut Koziol
Barbara C. Steininger (eds.)

European Tort Law 2004

With Contributions by

Håkan Andersson
Bjarte Askeland
Ewa Bagińska
Elena Bargelli
Agris Bitāns
Michel Cannarsa
Eugenia Dacoronia
Anton Dulak
Isabelle C. Durant
Michael Faure
Jörg Fedtke
Herkus Gabartas
Israel Gilead
Suvianna Hakalehto-Wainio
Ton Hartlief
Jiří Hrádek
Denis N. Kelliher
Bernhard A. Koch
Helmut Koziol
Irene Kull
Fabien Lafay
Rok Lampe
Milda Laučienė
Peter Loser
Meinhard Lukas
Attila Menyhárd
Olivier Moréteau
Emanuela Navarretta
Kunihiko Okubo
Ken Oliphant
Caroline Pellerin-Rugliano
André G. Dias Pereira
Eoin Quill
Jordi Ribot
Geneviève Schamps
Barbara C. Steininger
Vibe Ulfbeck

SpringerWienNewYork

European Centre of Tort and Insurance Law
Landesgerichtsstraße 11
A-1080 Vienna
Tel.: +43 1 40127 1688
Fax: +43 1 40127 1685
E-Mail: ectil@ectil.org

Austrian Academy of Sciences
Research Unit for European Tort Law
Landesgerichtsstraße 11
A-1080 Vienna
Tel.: +43 1 40127 1687
Fax: +43 1 40127 1685
E-Mail: etl@oeaw.ac.at

This work is published with the financial support of the
Austrian Ministry of Education, Science and Culture,
Munich Re and Freshfields Bruckhaus Deringer.

Gedruckt mit Förderung des Bundesministeriums für Bildung, Wissenschaft
und Kultur in Wien.

Printed in Austria

SpringerWienNewYork is a part of
Springer Science + Business Media
springeronline.com

Typesetting: Composition & Design Services, Minsk, Belarus
Printing and binding: Ferdinand Berger & Söhne Gesellschaft m.b.H., 3580 Horn, Austria

Printed on acid-free and chlorine-free bleached paper
SPIN: 11382744

CIP data applied for

ISSN 1616-8623
ISBN-10 3-211-24479-4 SpringerWienNewYork
ISBN-13 978-3-211-24479-1 SpringerWienNewYork

Preface

A harmonisation of European law presupposes sound mutual knowledge of the jurisdictions involved in the harmonisation process. However, partly due to language problems it is not always easy to obtain information about all these jurisdictions, especially as far as new developments are concerned. Against this background, the European Centre of Tort and Insurance Law and the Research Unit for European Tort Law decided to publish a Yearbook on European Tort Law containing reports on the most interesting new developments in the field of tort law in different European countries.

The present Yearbook on European Tort law includes reports on most EU Member States, including the new Member States the Czech Republic, Estonis, Hungary, Latvia, Lithuania, Poland, Slovakia and Slovenia. Contributions from Switzerland and Norway, an overview of the developments in the field of EC law as well as a brief note on Japanese tort law are also included. Furthermore, the Yearbook includes a comparative overview and several essays on key issues of tort law, most of which focus on questions of strict liability. Those essays, as well as the most important results of the country reports and the comparative overview, were presented and discussed at the 4th Annual Conference on European Tort Law in Vienna from 31 March to 2 April 2005. The 5th Annual Conference on European Tort Law will again take place in Vienna from 20 to 22 April 2006.

In publishing the Yearbook we pursue the idea of providing a comprehensive overview of the latest developments in the law of torts of many European countries thereby enabling scholars as well as practitioners from different national backgrounds to keep abreast of questions concerning tort law. Furthermore, we do hope that the Yearbook will enhance and promote a greater understanding of the respective national legal and judicial systems which is essential for a successful harmonisation of European tort law.

At this point, we would like to express our gratitude for the support of this project by the Austrian Ministry of Education, Science and Culture; the Austrian Ministry of Justice; Freshfields Bruckhaus Deringer; the Kulturabteilung der Stadt Wien, Wissenschafts- und Forschungsförderung; Munich Re and Wiener Städtische Allgemeine Versicherung AG. Without their support this project could never have been realised. Moreover, we would like to thank the staff of the Research Unit for European Tort Law and the European Centre of Tort and Insurance Law. Special thanks go to Mag. Lisa Zeiler for making the Conference such a success and Donna Stockenhuber M.A. for once again taking on the delicate and time-consuming task of proof-reading the entire manuscript. Moreover, we would like to thank Mag. Julia Dörfel, Mag. Kathrin Karner, Denis Kelliher B.L., Simone Sartor and Mag. Nora Wallner for their help and Mag. Alexander Warzilek for the compilation of the Index.

Helmut Koziol and Barbara C. Steininger Vienna, September 2005

Table of Contents

Essays 1

I. Financial Compensation in Case of Catastrophes: A European Law and Economics Perspective
(Michael Faure) 2

II. On the Justifications of Strict Liability
(Israel Gilead) 28

III. Strict Liability in the New Austrian Draft on Liability Law
(Helmut Koziol) 50

IV. Revisiting the Grey Zone Between Contract and Tort: The Role of Estoppel and Reliance in Mapping out the Law of Obligations
(Olivier Moréteau) 60

- *A. Introduction* 60
- *B. Exploring the Grey Zone* 63
- *C. The Taxonomic Nature of the Problem* 66
- *D. The Four Corners of Civil Obligations* 69
- *E. Reliance as a Driving Force* 78
- *F. Conclusion: Mapping out the Hidden Side of the Planet Obligations* 79

V. *Rylands v Fletcher* and the Emergence of Enterprise Liability in the Common Law
(Ken Oliphant) 81

- *A. Introduction* 81
- *B. Rylands v Fletcher (1868)* 86
- *C. Rylands v Fletcher, Strict Liability and the Rise of the Fault Principle* 99
- *D. Rylands v Fletcher and the Theory of Enterprise Liability* 107
- *E. Conclusion* 118

VI. The Precautionary Principle versus a General Principle for Compensation of Victims of Dangerous Activities in Belgian Law
(Geneviève Schamps) ... 121

A. Introduction ... 121
B. The Existence of the Precautionary Principle in Belgian Law ... 126
C. Is the Precautionary Principle a new Basis for Belgian Tort Law? ... 128
D. The Advantage of Creating a General Principle Based on a Specific Danger ... 132
E. Conclusion ... 138

Reports ... 141

I. Austria
(Barbara C. Steininger) ... 142

A. Legislation ... 142
B. Cases ... 143
C. Literature ... 161

II. Belgium
(Isabelle C. Durant) ... 166

A. Legislation ... 166
B. Cases ... 170
C. Literature ... 191

III. Czech Republic
(Jiří Hrádek) ... 195

A. Legislation ... 195
B. Cases ... 201
C. Literature ... 214

IV. Denmark
(Vibe Ulfbeck) ... 218

A. Legislation ... 218
B. Cases ... 218
C. Literature ... 225

V. England and Wales
(Ken Oliphant) ... 227

A. Legislation and Official Reports ... 227
B. Cases ... 230
C. Literature ... 243

VI. Estonia
(Irene Kull) ... 248

A. Legislation ... 248
B. Cases ... 254
C. Literature ... 260

VII. Finland
(Suvianna Hakalehto-Wainio) ... 264

A. Legislation ... 264
B. Cases ... 266
C. Literature ... 272

VIII. France
(Michel Cannarsa, Fabien Lafay, Olivier Moréteau and Caroline Pellerin-Rugliano) ... 274

A. Legislation ... 274
B. Cases ... 282

IX. Germany
(Jörg Fedtke) ... 300

A. Legislation ... 300
B. Cases ... 304
C. Literature ... 321

X. Greece
(Eugenia Dacoronia) ... 327

A. Legislation ... 327
B. Cases ... 327
C. Books and Articles ... 346

XI. Hungary
(Attila Menyhárd) ... 349

A. Legislation ... 349
B. Cases ... 349
C. Literature ... 360

XII. Ireland
(Eoin Quill) ... 363

A. Legislation ... 363
B. Cases ... 367
C. Literature ... 379

XIII. Italy
(Emanuela Navarretta and Elena Bargelli) 382

A. Cases 382
B. Literature 392

XIV. Latvia
(Agris Bitāns) 395

A. Legislation 395
B. Cases 399
C. Literature 403

XV. Lithuania
(Herkus Gabartas and Milda Laučienė) 405

A. Introduction 405
B. Legislation 405
C. Cases 408
D. Literature 417

XVI. The Netherlands
(Michael Faure and Ton Hartlief) 420

A. Introduction 420
B. Legislation and Evolutions at Policy Level 421
C. Case Law 423
D. Doctrine 445
E. Concluding Remarks 449

XVII. Norway
(Bjarte Askeland) 451

A. Legislation 451
B. Cases 451
C. Literature 458

XVIII. Poland
(Ewa Bagińska) 462

A. Legislation 462
B. Cases 464
C. Literature 475

XIX. Portugal
(André G. Dias Pereira) 479

A. Legislation 479
B. Cases 489
C. Literature 501

tion justification. This consideration would militate *against* strict liability in situations where first-party insurance is a better loss spreader than third-party/ liability insurance, or where the activity that incurs the harm is better positioned to spread it through price rise or has a deeper pocket.

But even where fairness or loss-spreading do justify strict liability, there are two major considerations that may point in the opposite direction. One consideration is the concern of overdeterrence. Imposition of strict liability on a desirable activity raises its price to the actor, as we have seen, and that may induce the actor to render the activity too safe or to reduce its level below the desired level. In this regard, fairness and deterrence may conflict. Another consideration against strict liability is the extra costs – administrative and other – that may be involved in strict liability when compared to the costs of fault-based liability.[52] 55

5. Applying the "Justification Analysis"– Strict Liability for Abnormally Dangerous Activities

The above discussion of the different kinds of strict liability and their respective justifications has sketched the lines of a "justification analysis"of strict liability arrangements. The analysis distinguishes between two kinds of strict liability. Activity-based strict liability is predicated on a rebuttable or non-rebuttable presumption that the activity is undesirable either because it is careless, or because it should be avoided or reduced in extent, and is justified on these grounds. Outcome-based strict liability is imposed on desirable activities and is justified by the need to change the outcomes of a collision between activities in order to increase fairness in its various aspects and to avoid unwanted secondary harms. 56

a) The Question

To examine how this "justification analysis" works it would be a natural choice to apply it to a major area of strict liability, liability for abnormally dangerous activities. The elements of this liability, under Sec. 20 of the Third Restatement[53] and Art. 5:105 of the European Principles,[54] are a) dangerousness – activity that creates a "highly significant risk" b) foreseeability of the 57

Fairness and Utility in Tort Theory, 85 *Harvard Law Review* (Harvard L. Rev.), 537. "Reciprocity of reasonable risk imposition thus defines a circumstance where risk is fairly distributed" – G.C. Keating, [2000] 74 So Cal L Rev, 207. Yet, Keating argues that fairness requires not only ex ante reciprocity of risk but also ex post reciprocity of harm in the sense that both sides share the burden of the materialized risk. According to this view, fairness may justify strict liability where the risk is reciprocal but the harm is not – ibid., at 208.

[52] The relative costs of a given strict liability arrangement when compared to a corresponding fault-based arrangement depend on the number of litigated claims under any regime, the number of settlements, and the private and public resources consumed by litigation and settlements under the alternative liability regimes.

[53] Supra fn. 3, 293–355.

[54] PETL (supra fn. 2), 101–111.

risk and c) the fact that the activity "is not a matter of common usage".[55] It is often argued that this liability is "the paradigm of strict liability",[56] and that justifying it would not be a "demanding task" as it is "the lowest common denominator of all legal systems under survey".[57] So what are the underlying justifications of this form of strict liability? Is it really self evident?

b) The Presumed Undesirability of the Activity as a Justification

58 Is strict liability for abnormally dangerous activity justified by a non-rebuttable presumption of undesirable, careless, conduct? Is it, at least to some degree, *activity-based* strict liability? Well, there are some strong indicators to that effect. First – the requirement of dangerousness. As we have seen, where dangerousness renders the due care standard very demanding it may become more probable than not that this demanding standard has not been met. Second – the requirement of "uncommon usage". Where an activity is a matter of uncommon usage its risks and the ways to prevent them may not be sufficiently known and ascertainable, so it may well be that there is no way to persuade the court that due care has been taken. This may justify a non-rebuttable presumption that the abnormally dangerous activity was not sufficiently careful as there is no way to establish otherwise. Furthermore, such a non-rebuttable presumption may be justified on the ground that the costs of such rebuttal are prohibitive. Third – the requirement of foreseeability, which is a precondition to liability, is, as we have seen, a fault-oriented requirement. The foreseeability of the harm may render it more probable than not that the actor was at fault.

59 The Third Restatement indeed supports the conclusion that strict liability for abnormally dangerous activity is, at least to some extent, activity-based liability justified by a presumption that the activity is undesirable. It refers to "safety incentives" as a justification for its imposition.[58] Moreover, an economic analysis of law also supports this conclusion. It justifies strict liability for abnormally dangerous activity on the grounds that such activity is undesirable (inefficient) in the sense that it should be avoided or reduced in extent.[59]

[55] Sec. 20 of the Third Restatement (supra fn. 3) states:
a) A defendant who carries on abnormally dangerous activity is subject to strict liability for physical harm resulting from the activity.
b) The activity is abnormally dangerous if:
1) the activity creates a foreseeable and highly significant risk of physical harm even when reasonable care is exercised by all actors: and
2) The activity is not a matter of common usage.
Article 5:105 of the PETL, (supra fn. 2), 101–111 essentially uses the same language but there are some differences – it is not limited to physical harm, it explicitly requires that the damage should be "characteristic to the risk presented by the activity" and it further adds that "A risk of a damage may be significant having regard to the seriousness or the likelihood of the damage".

[56] F. Werro/V. Palmer (supra fn. 4), 400.

[57] PETL (supra fn. 2), 109.

[58] Supra fn. 3, 296, 306 – Comments b and i to §20. For justifying strict liability for abnormally dangerous activity as being an extension of fault liability, see E.J. Weinrib, *The Idea of Private Law* (1995), 185 – 196.

[59] S. Shavell (supra fn. 15), 31–32.

Although the requirements of dangerousness, foreseeability and uncommon usage do indicate that strict liability for abnormally dangerous activities is to some degree activity-based liability justified on grounds of its presumed undesirability, it is obvious that in its essence this liability is perceived as liability imposed on *desirable* activities. Both the Restatement and the Principles stress that an activity would be considered "abnormally dangerous" even when reasonable care is exercised".[60] The Restatement notes that "this section's discussion of strict liability tends to assume that … the advantages of the activity are sufficient to justify all its risks."[61] The commentaries to the Principles emphasize that "Liability under this Article is not based on any sense of fault".[62] The question, then, is what are the justifications for imposing strict liability on *desirable* abnormally dangerous activities? 60

c) "Causation *per se*" and "Dangerousness" as Justifications

The Third Restatement's answer to the above question is essentially "causation *per se*". Although it recognizes that the reciprocal nature of causation "makes causation indeterminate and insufficient as strict liability criterion",[63] it is nevertheless argued that with regard to abnormally dangerous activities causation "is sufficiently exclusive to render the imposition of liability appropriate."[64] This justification, however, is questionable. Once it is acknowledged that causation is reciprocal, namely, that harm is caused by the collision of two or more voluntary activities, each of which is avoidable or reducible, it is unclear how the "degree of causation" is determined and what renders one cause "almost" or "nearly" exclusive and the other cause only a marginal cause. When a surgeon makes a reasonable mistake that harms her unconscious patient, is this mistake a "sufficiently exclusive" cause? Does it justify strict liability? Notably, an economic analysis of law also does not support the argument that "causation *per se*" justifies strict liability for abnormally dangerous activities.[65] 61

The European Principles' answer to the question of what justifies strict liability for *desirable* abnormally dangerous activities focuses on the dangerousness of such activities. Danger, we are told, is the "first test".[66] But why? Dangerousness may indeed indicate that the activity is undesirable, but the issue here is to justify liability for *desirable* conduct. That the danger cannot be controlled is a characteristic of danger, not a justification for imposing strict liability on a desirable activity that created it. One may argue that dangerousness 62

[60] Supra fn. 55.
[61] Third Restatement (supra fn. 3), 295 – Comment b to §20.
[62] PETL (supra fn. 2), 105.
[63] Supra fn. 3, 300 – Comment f to §20.
[64] Ibid., 301.
[65] S. Shavell (supra fn. 15), 30–31, refers to strict liability for abnormally dangerous activities as liability which is imposed in order to lower undesirable levels of such activities and not as liability imposed on grounds of causation. Regarding the distinction between unilateral accidents and bilateral accidents, see supra fn. 33.
[66] B.A. Koch/H. Koziol (supra fn. 5), 408.

implies severe harm to basic and vital interests that deserve special protection. But if severity of harm is the justification, why is this liability limited to uncommon usage? Some common activities may be even more dangerous. Moreover, neither Art. 5:101 of the Principles nor Sec. 20 of the Restatement require severe harm to a vital interest. Both impose strict liability for harm which is not severe but which is highly probable.[67] In fact, the Principles do not even require physical harm. Furthermore, if the harm is severe and should not be left uncompensated, why should costs be levied on the desirable activity? Why should they not be borne by society at large?

63 It therefore appears that the justifications offered by the Restatement (causation *per se*) and by the Principles (dangerousness) for imposing strict liability on *desirable* abnormally dangerous activities are questionable. Can such liability be nevertheless warranted by other justifications of strict liability?

d) Allocative Fairness as a Justification

64 Can strict liability for desirable and yet abnormally dangerous activities be justified on grounds of allocative justice? This would be the case if such activities lead to unfair distribution of benefits and burdens among all the affected parties and strict liability would rectify this unfairness or increase fairness. Where, for example, an abnormally dangerous activity generates significant benefits to those engaged in it, imposes significant burdens on colliding activities and generates no benefits to thirds parties or society at large, considerations of allocative fairness may justify strict liability that shifts the full burden of the harm to the harm inflicting activity.

65 Indeed, it may be argued that the requirement of *uncommon usage*, which is a pre-condition to liability under both the Restatement and the Principles, points to allocative justice as a justification. If commonness means that "the activity's benefits are distributed widely among the community",[68] and activity is accordingly uncommon "when its risks are imposed on third parties while its benefits are concentrated among a few",[69] then there is indeed a close relation between the uncommonness requirement and allocative fairness.[70]

66 Yet, it appears that neither the Restatement nor the Principles predicate liability for abnormally dangerous activities on this ground of allocative fairness. Although the social value of an activity is an important consideration in as-

[67] "The risk can be highly significant because the likelihood of the harm is unusually high, even though the severity of the expected harm is no more than ordinary" – Third Restatement (supra fn. 3), 301 – Comment f to §20. "If chances are high that somebody is injured, strict liability might make sense even though the harm to be expected is only minor" – B.A. Koch/H. Koziol (supra fn. 5), 408.

[68] Restatement Third (supra fn. 3), 308 (Comment j). See also PETL (supra fn. 2), 107.

[69] Restatement Third (supra fn. 3), 308.

[70] See also the observation that "the wide recognition of liability for ultra-hazardous activities is based on the idea that whoever derives benefits from such an activity should also bear the related loss"– F. Werro/V. Palmer (supra fn. 4), 400.

sessing whether its outcomes are fair in terms of allocative fairness, the Third Restatement insists that the activity's social value is *not* a factor that should be counted against liability, although it has been such under the *Second* Restatement.[71] As to the Principles, the commentaries do refer to the old principle "cuius commodum, eius et incommode" and to the comparison of benefits and profits with the distribution of risk, but it is later stated that this weighing process and rationale is applicable to other areas of strict liability, and the major rationale of strict liability for abnormally dangerous activity is dangerousness.[72] It therefore follows that, under the Principles and the Restatement, strict liability may be imposed on desirable abnormally dangerous activities even where their benefits lie mainly with the colliding activities, third parties or society at large and not with those who are engaged in the dangerous activity. Such liability can hardly be justified on grounds of allocative fairness.[73]

e) Loss Spreading or Deep Pocket?

Can strict liability for abnormally dangerous activities be justified on grounds 67
of loss spreading or "deep pocket" considerations? It may be argued that such activities are better "loss spreaders" than the colliding activities or that they have more resources than the latter and are therefore better suited to bear the losses. Neither the Restatement nor the Principles, however, support this argument. On the contrary, the Restatement explicitly rejects this justification of loss spreading by stating that "the appeal of strict liability ... does not depend on any notion that the defendant is in a better position than the plaintiff to allocate or distribute the risk of harm."[74] This should not come as a surprise given that this kind of liability originates in times in which loss spreading through liability insurance was less extensive than it is today.

f) Conclusion

The application of the "justification analysis" to strict liability for abnormally 68
dangerous activities suggests that this is a "mixed strict liability". On the one hand, it can be justified on the grounds that such an activity is presumed to be undesirable – careless or too extensive – given its dangerousness, its uncommon nature and the foreseeability of the risk. In this respect it is *activity-based* strict liability. On the other hand, it can be justified on the grounds of allocative fairness. The uncommonness of the activity and its dangerousness also indicate that its benefits and burdens are not fairly allocated between the colliding activities and that the imposition of strict liability is needed to increase

[71] See the discussion of this factor in 341–349 – Reporters' Notes to §20.
[72] PETL (supra fn. 2), 108–109.
[73] The Third Restatement suggests a different kind of fairness justification, one which is embodied in the foreseeability requirement. It is argued that where a person is engaged in an abnormally dangerous activity although reasonably aware of its risks, it is fair to make her strictly liable – supra fn. 3, 305–306 – Comment i to §20. But if the activity is a desirable one, why does the foreseeability of its outcome justify liability? "Foreseeable *per se*" does not justify strict liability as there are many foreseeable risks that do not involve tort liability because they are generated by desirable, reasonable activities.
[74] Ibid., 300 – Comment e.

allocative fairness. In this regard, strict liability for abnormally dangerous activities liability is *outcome-based* strict liability.

69 Given its mixed nature, this liability can hardly be characterized as self-evident, as "the paradigm of strict liability", or as liability located on the strictest zone of the continuum.[75]

70 Yet, Sec. 20 of Third Restatement and Art. 5:101 of the European Principles not only downplay the activity-based aspects of strict liability but also focus on the questionable justifications of "causation *per se*" (the Restatement) and "dangerousness *per se*" (the Principles) rather than on allocative fairness. One may therefore be left with the overall impression that the foundations of strict liability for abnormally dangerous activities are somewhat shaky.[76] This may explain the English tendency to narrow the scope of this distinct principle of strict liability.[77]

6. Concluding Remarks

71 1. The above "justification analysis" suggests that strict liability arrangements may often be "mixed" in the sense that they are a combination of activity-based and outcome-based strict liabilities. Such mixed arrangements are justified by a presumption that a given activity is undesirable, on the one hand, and, on the other hand, by considerations that support changes in the outcomes of desirable activities.[78] This has been exemplified by the above analysis of strict liability for abnormally dangerous activity. This also seems to be the case with regard to strict liability for animals, where the presumed undesirability of the "keeper's" conduct in controlling the animals' risk is obviously a major factor and a justification.[79] Vicarious strict liability also seems to be such a mixed liability although it appears to be more outcome-based than activity-based. It is justified, to some extent, by a non-rebuttable presumption that the employer's conduct in controlling the risks was undesirable in some aspects and, on the other hand, by a variety of outcome-based justifications: the fairness of making the employer liable for the costs that his agents impose on others when pursuing the employer's benefits and the employer's ability to

[75] For the observation that this liability is a "far cry" from a concept of "absolute liability" see F. Werro/V. Palmer (supra fn. 4), 409.

[76] For a criticism of this form of strict liability as being too vague, see ibid., 20. The authors conclude that it "remained a controversial concept" – at 400.

[77] See W.V.H. Rogers, Winfield and Jolowitcz on Tort (16th edn., 2002), 548–553.

[78] "'absolute liability' in the sense of liability resting on a merely factual test of causation and comprising responsibility for utterly unforeseeable harm, is extremely rare in European tort law" – F. Werro/V. Palmer (supra fn. 4), 456–7.

[79] It appears that under the Third Restatement strict liability for intruding livestock, wild animals and abnormally dangerous animals is mainly justified by a non-rebuttable presumption of undesirable conduct. See Comment e to Sec. 21 (intruding livestock), 361–363; Comment d to Sec. 22 (wild animals), 387–388; Comment b to Sec. 23 (Abnormally dangerous animals), 398–399. For the deterrence function of strict liability for animals in Europe see B.A. Koch/H. Koziol (supra fn. 5), 396–398, F. Werro/V. Palmer (supra fn. 4), 8.

spread losses or her "deep pocket".[80] Notably, all these justifications lose ground where the harm is caused not by an employee but by an independent contractor and strict vicarious liability is usually avoided in such circumstances.[81] Strict product liability for manufacturing defects may also be justified by a non-rebuttable presumption of fault.[82]

2. The justification-analysis explains and supports the *diversity* of strict liability arrangements and the absence in most European jurisdictions of a general rule of strict liability.[83] The difference between activity-based and outcome-based strict liabilities, the variety of justifications that back outcome-based strict liability and their complex interrelation, and especially the need to conduct a separate "benefits/burdens" for each collision of activities, all clearly indicate that strict liability arrangements should be fine-tuned and tailored to the specific collision of activities to which they apply. Strict liability may be justified with regard to one product or service but not with regard to another product or service.[84] It may be justified, for example, with regard to *manufacturing* defects in products but not with regard to defects in *design* or in *warnings and instructions*.[85] It therefore appears that blanket rules of strict liability that cover a wide range of activities or risks, such as the famous Art. 1384 of the French Civil Code (strict liability for things in one's keeping), are questionable. 72

3. Finally, the imposition of tort liability on desirable conducts – activity-based strict liability – should not be considered an anomaly or an illegitimate child of tort law. It is a powerful tool that, through the reallocation of benefits and burdens and loss spreading, can promote fairness and justice in society and mitigate the unavoidable misfortunes of modern life. 73

[80] See F. Werro/V. Palmer (supra fn. 4), 393–394.
[81] Ibid., 397.
[82] Supra fn. 22.
[83] B.A. Koch/H. Koziol (supra fn. 5), 395–6. F. Werro/V. Palmer (supra fn. 4), 401–403, 405. The major exceptions are Austria and France.
[84] See supra 4.d).
[85] For the distinction between these defects and its underlying justifications, see The Third Restatement on the Law of Tort: Products Liability, Sec. 2, comment a.

III. Strict Liability in the New Austrian Draft on Liability Law

Helmut Koziol

1. Introduction

1 The drafting commission was set up by the Austrian Ministry of Justice four years ago on 16 January 2001. The members of the commission are two high officials of the Ministry; five professors; three members of the Supreme Court and one representative from the insurance sector. The draft was completed on 14 January 2005 and the last details of phrasing were decided upon on 4 March 2005.

2 First I would like to cast a quick glance at the present Austrian liability law. The Austrian Code, the *Allgemeines bürgerliches Gesetzbuch* (ABGB) dates from the beginning of the 19th century (1811) and is strongly influenced by the Natural law school. Contrary to the German Code, the Austrian provision is extremely broad, as it covers not only tortious but also contractual liability. The second part of the first sentence in § 1295 reads: "The harm may be caused by breach of contract or may have no relation to a contract." Furthermore, the beginning of § 1295 rules that everyone is entitled to demand compensation of the person who did harm him through fault. But the Code does not or only to a very small extent contain provisions on strict liability; this area is covered almost exclusively by quite a number of special acts outside the Code.

2. General Remarks on the New Draft

3 I thought this brief glance would be useful as the new draft – to some extent – continues the Austrian tradition: The draft covers both, tortious and contractual liability as the unity brings many advantages[1]; it prefers more general provisions and it attempts to retain a degree of flexibility. But it also tries to move on, especially in regard of strict liability.

[1] Cf. H. Koziol, Die Vereinheitlichung der Delikts- und Vertragshaftung im Schweizer Vorentwurf für einen Allgemeinen Teil des Haftpflichtrechts, [1998] *Zeitschrift des Bernischen Juristenvereins* (ZBJV), 517 et seq.

In drafting the new liability law, the following ideas regarding the relevant factors in establishing liability were important: If we take a look at the present European tort law systems, we can observe that there is more than just one relevant factor in attributing damage to the tortfeasor[2]. Above all, aside from misbehaviour of the tortfeasor, the special dangerousness of the tortfeasor's sphere is a decisive factor in establishing liability. As to *misbehaviour*, we can say that objective wrongfulness alone does not have enough weight to transfer the burden of the damage from the injured party to the tortfeasor[3]. However, in combination with subjective fault, objective wrongfulness is in a position to establish liability. Factors other than fault can be decisive: Minors and insane persons who wrongfully caused damage have to indemnify the victim if this seems reasonable considering their financial capacity to bear the damage. Not only is the financial capacity important but also the special dangerousness of minors or insane persons. Therefore, we can observe that, instead of one weighty factor, two other factors together may have the same weight in establishing liability. 4

As to *dangerousness*, in the last century this factor became nearly as relevant as misbehaviour in establishing liability[4]. The greater part of strict liability is based on this factor and this type of liability is increasingly gaining importance. Usually, one only mentions this function of dangerousness. But I would like to point out that not only is dangerousness the decisive factor in the area of strict liability, it also has a strong influence in establishing wrongfulness: The greater the danger of damaging another person, the more diligence has to be demanded[5]. 5

Furthermore, increased dangerousness leads to tightening liability based on fault by shifting the burden of proof to the injuring party[6]. As a result, the defendant may be held liable even if his behaviour was not faulty but he is unable to prove this. Therefore, his liability is merely based on presumed fault. For example: Under the effective Austrian law, the keeper of an animal has to compensate the damage caused by his animal unless he is able to prove that he has not been negligent (§ 1320 ABGB). 6

What I would like to demonstrate is that a low degree of dangerousness will only be able to establish liability in combination with other factors, such as 7

[2] In more detail W. Wilburg, *Die Elemente des Schadensrechts* (1941); W. Wilburg, *Entwicklung eines beweglichen Systems im bürgerlichen Recht* (1950); further F. Bydlinski, *Juristische Methodenlehre und Rechtsbegriff* (2nd edn. 1991), 529 et seq.

[3] Cf. H. Koziol, Rechtswidrigkeit, bewegliches System und Rechtsangleichung, [1998] *Juristische Blätter* (JBl), 619 et seq.

[4] See B.A. Koch/H. Koziol (eds.), *Unification of Tort Law: Strict Liability* (2002).

[5] Cf. OGH (*Oberster Gerichtshof*, Austrian Supreme Court) in *Entscheidungen des Österreichischen OGH*, *Zivilsachen* (SZ) 63/166; B.A. Koch/H. Koziol, Comparative Conclusions, in: B.A. Koch/H. Koziol (supra fn. 4), no. 158; B.C. Steininger, *Verschärfung der Verschuldenshaftung* (in preparation), III. A, B and H.

[6] See B.A. Koch/H. Koziol, Austria no. 6, in: B.A. Koch/H. Koziol (supra fn. 4); B.C. Steininger (supra fn. 5), III. E.

misbehaviour; a high degree of dangerousness, however, is sufficient to establish liability on its own. It follows that liability based on fault and strict liability based on dangerousness are not completely separate categories but – in their pure form – represent the ends of a continuum[7].

3. Some Important Provisions

8 The understanding for the position of strict liability in the new Austrian system of liability law demands having a look not only at the provisions on strict liability but also at some other important provisions.

a) Fundamental Norm

9 § 1292 sec. 1 points out that liability law strives for compensation of the damage, thereby also providing an incentive to avoid damage. According to § 1292 sec. 2, a person has to compensate a damage only if it is attributable to the person. As such, the draft expresses the fundamental principle that anyone who suffers a loss has to bear it himself, because everyone has to bear the risks of his own goods. *Holmes*[8], a common law lawyer, expressed this idea as follows: "Sound policy lets losses lie where they fall, except where a special reason can be shown for interference." But the injured person is entitled to claim compensation if another person is – so to speak – closer to the damage than the victim. The decisive question is: Under which conditions is it reasonable that the injured person be allowed to shift the harm to another person?

10 This question is roughly answered by § 1292 sec. 3: Attribution requires not only that the person caused the damage but also that one of the bases of liability is given. Therefore, the damage has to be caused by his faulty or otherwise incorrect behaviour; by a source of special danger in his sphere; by his auxiliary. These two sections are similar to Art. 1:101 of the Principles of European Tort Law drafted by the European Group on Tort Law (European Principles) and show that the authors of both drafts are of the opinion that liability for the source of special danger, i.e. strict liability, is on the same level as liability based on fault. Strict liability is no longer seen solely as an exception to fault-based liability.

b) Liability Based on Fault

11 To make clear the position of strict liability in the draft's liability system first we have to cast a glance at fault-based liability. There is neither the time nor the need to discuss all the details; therefore, I would only like to mention some points which are relevant for our topic. Remarkable is § 1296: The required standard of conduct is the conduct which can be expected in the circumstances

[7] OGH in [1996] JBl, 446 with commentary by P. Jabornegg; C. von Bar, *Verkehrspflichten* (1980), 144; E. Deutsch, Gefährdungshaftung und Verschuldenshaftung, [1981] JBl, 450; H. Koziol, Bewegliches System und Gefährdungshaftung, in: F. Bydlinski/H. Krejci/B. Schilcher, *Das Bewegliche System im geltenden und künftigen Recht* (1986), 51.

[8] O.W. Holmes, *The Common Law* (1881).

of a reasonable person who takes into regard the interests of others. Similar to the European Principles (Art. 4:102), rank and value of the endangered interests, the dangerousness of the situation, the proximity, the possibility of avoiding the danger, and the costs of precautionary steps have to be taken into regard. What I would like to point out is that dangerousness is a decisive factor in establishing the required standard of conduct and thus also of fault: The higher the dangerousness of the situation, the higher the required standard of care.

A fundamental question[9] is solved by § 1300: According to traditional opinion in Austria[10], the assessment of negligence of the tortfeasor has to be based on the subjective blameworthiness of lack of willpower. Therefore, a person can only be accused of negligence if he himself, by proper effort of willpower, was able to recognise that he was acting dangerously and illegally and could have behaved differently. As a subjective yardstick has to be used, one has to examine whether the abilities of the actual actor were sufficient to avoid the damage. Sec. 2 of § 1300 provides a presumption: Persons older than 14 years of age are supposed to have the ordinary abilities, the contrary is supposed if the person is below this age. 12

As we have seen, Austrian law avoids the consequence of the widespread objective doctrine, which leads to a sort of strict liability[11] based on the special danger posed by persons with limited abilities. Nevertheless, in case of violating the objective duties of care, such persons with abilities below average may be liable even without subjective fault: The judge is allowed to impose on the tortfeasor liability either for the whole damage or only for an equitable part thereof. In determining liability and its extent, the judge has to consider, above all, the financial position of the wrongdoer and that of the injured party. The tortfeasor has to indemnify the victim if the judge ascertains that it is much easier for the tortfeasor than for the victim to bear the whole loss or part of the loss. Further, the judge has to consider the advantage which the defendant gained from the wrongful activity. 13

According to Sec. 3, there is an exception to the rule of using a subjective yardstick: Someone who has, by contract, promised a certain performance is liable if he does not possess the required abilities, the idea being that the defendant has guaranteed that he has the necessary abilities. Further, an expert is liable if he lacks the abilities required for the profession carried out by him; thus a normative standard of fault has to be applied. The exception with experts can be justified by the following consideration: a person who takes on an occupation which requires particular knowledge and intelligence even though 14

[9] See in detail H. Koziol, Liability Based on Fault: Subjective or Objective Yardstick? [1998] *Maastricht Journal of European and Comparative Law*, 111.

[10] Cf. P. Apathy, in: P. Apathy/A. Riedler, *Schuldrecht, Besonderer Teil* (2000), no. 13/31 et seq. Regarding Switzerland, P. Widmer, Die Vereinheitlichung des Schweizerischen Haftpflichtrechts – Brennpunkte eines Projekts, [1994] ZBJV, 410.

[11] Cf. I. Gilead, Israel, in: B.A. Koch/H. Koziol (supra fn. 4), no. 4.

he does not have such abilities causes, in so doing, a special danger, e.g., the structural engineer who incorrectly calculates a bridge so that it is in danger of collapsing or the hospital doctor who treats patients incorrectly so that they suffer harm.

4. Liability for Sources of High Danger

15 So far legislators have enacted a great many supplementary statutes providing strict liability of the keepers of dangerous objects[12]. It does seem fair that someone who pursues an activity or makes use of an object in his own personal interest also has to bear possible external costs thereof. Benefit and risk should fall on the same side. However, the choice of dangerous objects by the legislator gives the impression of being rather accidental. For example, motor boats, dams and factories making explosives are not included.

16 Therefore, one of the most remarkable aspects of the draft is the general provision for strict liability based on dangerousness and, as such, the draft follows the Swiss example[13]. § 1302 provides that the keeper of a source of *high danger* is liable for the harm resulting from such danger. A source of high danger is given if the mere existence of an object or its ordinary use or an activity creates the risk of frequent or serious damage, notwithstanding all required care. The provision cites examples of sources of great danger, e.g., nuclear power stations, aeroplanes, trains, motor vehicles, mining activities, explosive activities. The duty to compensate harm can be reduced or excluded, among others, if the injury was caused by *force majeure* or an unavoidable event, that means that all due diligence according to the circumstances has been employed and the object was not defective. I have to point out that the defence of *force majeure* not only always excludes liability but also can only lead to a reduction of compensation. The reason is that even in case of *force majeure* the seriousness of the harm has to be attributed to the source of danger. For example, if a nuclear power station is damaged by an earthquake the fact that the harm caused is so enormous has to be attributed to the high dangerousness of the plant.

17 § 1303 concerns sources of danger which bring about *heightened risk*, but not to the extent required by § 1302. Examples are animals, buildings, riding a bicycle or alpine skiing at high speed. In such cases the keeper's liability is not strict but a tightened fault based liability: He is liable if he cannot prove that he has exercised the required care.

18 §§ 1302 and 1303 are explained by the idea that – as already mentioned – strict liability based on dangerousness and fault-based liability are really to be

[12] See the country reports in: B.A. Koch/H. Koziol (supra fn. 4).

[13] Swiss draft Art. 50. Art. 5:101 of the European Principles only grasps sources of extraordinary danger. As to the discussions of the European Group on Tort Law see B.A. Koch/H. Koziol, Generalklausel für die Gefährdungshaftung, [2002] *Haftung und Versicherung* (HAVE), 368 et seq.

found on a continuum rather than as being two distinct categories. Of course, fault liability and strict liability are based on very different ideas: Liability based on fault goes back to the fundamental thought that the tortfeasor has to be liable because of his incorrect, wrongful behaviour. In the area of strict liability such behaviour is not decisive: Taking the abstract possibility of endangering others, e.g. by running a railway or a nuclear plant, is not prohibited by law, on the contrary, the enterprise is even welcome. The decisive idea is that those who enjoy the benefit of a dangerous activity also have to bear the risk.

In the final analysis, nevertheless, one has to admit that the areas of liability 19 based on fault and the areas of strict liability do not form homogenous blocs, but that there are many differentiations.[14] For example, greater care is required where someone is working with things that are inherently dangerous. Of course, in such cases one is still concerned with the question whether the wrongdoer's behaviour was in accordance with the standard of the reasonable man and, therefore, with the question of fault. But nevertheless, one has to conclude that in such cases liability is stricter because of the dangerousness of the things the tortfeasor has been working with.

Corresponding to the degrees of "strictness" of liability based on fault, the 20 strictness of no-fault liability can also be very different. The lowest degree of strictness and, therefore, next to liability based on fault, is liability which is established by the violation of an objective duty of care, while subjective fault is no prerequisite. If fault is assessed in an objective way, there is in substance almost no difference to fault liability. Liability is even stricter if the failure to perform an abstract statutory duty is sufficient to establish liability and violation of a concrete duty of care is of no relevance at all: The decisive behaviour of the concrete tortfeasor does not necessarily have to be incorrect. For example: The keeper of a building is liable if he does not take the necessary measures to repair the defective building, independently of whether he was not able to take them because of a sudden illness.

Furthermore, even strict liability based on dangerousness, independent of any 21 violations of some duty of care, vary with regard to strictness: On the one hand, there may be no excuse at all, or "Act of God" or unavoidable event may be the only exemption; on the other hand, the excuses can be far-reaching and come very close to the defence that the defendant acted without fault.

Thus it can be seen that both fault liability as well as strict liability can be 22 more or less strict. This leads to the conclusion that – as mentioned above – one could theoretically draw a line between the two areas at stake, with liability based on fault on the one side and no-fault liability on the other. But in substance the stricter part of liability based on fault passes over without any clear-cut borderline to that part of strict liability based on dangerousness

[14] Cf. B.C. Steininger (supra fn. 5), III. H, V.

which is less strict. Furthermore, the borderline depends on whether fault is assessed by a – more or less – subjective or objective yardstick.

5. Liability of Enterprises

23 One who pursues an enterprise for economic or professional purposes can be held liable if damage is caused by a defect of the enterprise, or its products or services (§ 1304)[15]. Liability is barred if the entrepreneur can prove that he took all necessary care. The ideas behind this provision are[16], on the one hand, that benefits and risks should fall on the same side, and, on the other hand, that both the producer and customers should share the risk involved: Lower production costs due to reduced safety standards are reflected in a cheaper price of the product; while all buyers profit therefrom, the few amongst them who suffer harm due to a defect should not be left alone with that loss; their damage should be compensated by the producer who is in a position to re-distribute such loss back to all consumers by adjusting the product price.

24 As we can see, the Austrian draft does not generally provide strict liability for entrepreneurs, but on the other hand also not an ordinary fault based liability: The entrepreneur's liability is tightened up in so far as he bears the burden of proving that he took all necessary care. Therefore, you can say that he already is liable because of assumed fault.

6. Liability for Technical Devices

25 I do feel that § 1305 sec. 2 will be of special interest: In the area of contract the parties are also liable for the failure of the technical devices which one party uses similar to a vicarious agent. Furthermore, § 1306 sec. 4 rules for the area of delict: A person is liable for the failure of technical devices which he uses in the same way as employees if the victim proves that the device was unsuited or that the defendant did not select them with proper care or did not supervise them carefully. Entrepreneurs are liable if they cannot prove the absence of these prerequisites.

26 This provision is not based on the idea of liability because of high dangerousness but the reaction to the fact that nowadays computers or computer-controlled installations frequently take the place of ancillary staff[17]. Special features of these technical devices are that they work independently and that their

[15] Cf. Art 4:202 European Principles.

[16] See W. Wilburg, *Elemente* (supra fn. 2), 32; W. Wilburg, Zusammenspiel der Kräfte im Aufbau des Schuldrechts, [1964] *Archiv für die civilistische Praxis* (AcP), 163, 346; A.A. Ehrenzweig, *Negligence without Fault. Trends towards an Enterprise Liability for Insurable Loss* (1951); C.-W. Canaris, Die Gefährdungshaftung im Lichte der neueren Rechtsentwicklung, [1995] JBl, 6 et seq.; G. Brüggemeier, Unternehmenshaftung – Enterprise Liability. Eine europäische Perspektive? [2004] HAVE, 162 et seq.

[17] See, in particular, C.-W. Canaris, *Bankvertragsrecht* I (3rd edn. 1988), no. 367; H. Koziol, Die Haftung der Banken bei Versagen technischer Hilfsmittel, [1987] *Österreichisches Bankarchiv* (ÖBA), 3; K. Spiro, *Die Haftung für Erfüllungsgehilfen* (1984), 209 et seq.

activity is not sufficiently verifiable. Therefore, we feel that in analogy to the provisions on vicarious liability for persons employed, the person who uses computers has to be responsible for the failure of these technical devices. The same basic idea that governs vicarious liability also applies here. Nevertheless, this is a sort of stricter liability, particularly in case that the device was unsuited.

7. Provisions on Strict Liability in the Special Part of the Draft

As § 1302 provides a general clause on strict liability for the keeper of a source of high danger there is no longer an urgent demand for special rules on strict liability. Nevertheless, the commission is of the opinion that the most important areas of strict liability which are of relevance for a great part of the population should be mentioned explicitly in a general code. Therefore, the special part contains provisions on the liability of the holder of a mass media and the keeper of means of transportation (motor cars, railways); on product liability and on environmental liability. 27

a) Liability of Mass Media

In the special part the draft initially deals with some important kinds of damage, among others in § 1320, invasion of honour. It is in this context that the draft provides for strict liability of the holder of a media. I feel this is a very interesting innovation. According to § 1320 sec. 4, holders of mass media are liable for spreading false statements of facts unless they prove that the damage occurred in spite of compliance with the utmost standard of care or else by an unavoidable event. The utmost standard of care is beyond the standard of conduct which is normally expected and which is the basis of fault; therefore, the holder of mass media are liable even if they are not at fault but only neglected to act with the utmost care. 28

There are already evident hints of strict liability under present Austrian media law[18]. Further, one argument weighs heavily in favour of introducing strict liability of the holder of the media: the *special dangerousness* of the mass media[19]. However, the dangerousness concerned here differs from the cases for which strict liability is provided for today, e.g. nuclear power plants, airplanes, motor vehicles or pipe lines. What is similar, however, is the high probability that damage occurs and the particular severity of the potential damage caused, which is a result of the wide circulation of information by the 29

[18] Under Artt. 6 and 7 of the Austrian Media Law, the victim of defamation, abuse, mockery or slander has a claim against the holder of the media for compensation of non-pecuniary damage, the amount of which is limited. Since the media holder can justify his behaviour only by proving the truth of the statement, he becomes liable even if the false information did not occur at his fault. Cf. M. Graff, Das neue Medienrecht – Vorzüge und Schwächen, [1981] *Richterzeitung* (RZ), 213; H. Koziol, Die Haftung für kreditschädigende Berichte in Massenmedien, [1993] JBl, 617 et seq.

[19] H. Koziol, [1993] JBl, 618 et seq. See also H. Koziol/A. Warzilek (eds.), *Protection of Personality Rights against Invasions by Mass Media* (2005, forthcoming).

mass media. The reason for this is not only that the number of those who receive the information is large but also that they regard the mass media as very reliable[20], a fact that might be surprising. Thus, the danger is high that the readers or listeners adjust their behaviour towards the person who is the subject of the false information. Furthermore, information is – in the public interest – required to be up-to-date and thus reports have to be published very quickly[21]. Lack of time, however, limits the possibility to verify the information so that the risk of false information is high. This raises a further important argument in favour of strict liability, i.e. that damage cannot be avoided even if due care is applied. Thus, significant factors, on which strict liability is generally based, apply also in the case of the mass media: high probability of damage, great severity of damage and unavoidability of damage even if due care is applied.

b) Liability for Means of Transportation

30 § 1324 sec. 1 provides that the keeper of a vehicle is liable according to § 1302 if a person is killed or injured (§ 1319) or property is damaged by an accident while the vehicle is in operation. Vehicle is defined as a railway, a cable car or a motor car. Liability is – according to the general rules – excluded if the accident has been caused by an unavoidable event, that means that all due diligence according to the circumstances of the case had been employed and that the vehicle was not defective.

31 Insofar there is no change in substance to the present situation. It is also in accordance with the existing law that pecuniary and non-pecuniary losses have to be compensated as in case of fault-based liability. The innovation in substance is that – according to the general rule – damages are no longer limited by maximum amounts.

c) Product Liability

32 Compared with the current Product Liability Act, the provisions of the draft do not bring any change in substance as the provisions have to conform with the EU-Directive. As a result there is a discrepancy between the liability of entrepreneurs in general and liability of the producer of goods. As we have seen before, the liability of entrepreneurs is still based on fault, although liability is stricter because of a reversal of the burden of proof in regard of fault.

33 The drafting commission feels that the EU-Directive on product liability goes too far in providing a very strict liability of the producer and, therefore, that it would be unreasonable to generalize this far-reaching liability. As a result there exists an inconsistency in the new draft between product liability and the general rules on enterprise liability.

[20] So the Austrian OGH in SZ 60/93 and SZ 64/36 with reference to J. Helle, *Der Schutz der Persönlichkeit, der Ehre und des wirtschaftlichen Rufes im Privatrecht* (2nd edn. 1969), 158 et seq.

[21] Cf. OGH in SZ 44/45.

d) Environmental Liability

§ 1334 provides strict liability according to § 1302 in case someone keeps an installation or exercises an activity involving the risk of frequent or serious damage to the environment. A person is liable in the same way for serious damage to the environment if he keeps an installation or exercises an activity although their risk to the environment obviously cannot be estimated. Thus liability is established even if the keeper does not know about the dangerousness but, on the other hand, also if he cannot be sure that the installation or the activity is not dangerous. 34

IV. Revisiting the Grey Zone Between Contract and Tort: The Role of Estoppel and Reliance in Mapping out the Law of Obligations

Olivier Moréteau

A. Introduction
B. Exploring the Grey Zone
  1. Cross-Border Problems
  2. Cross-Border Similarities
    a) Breaking Contractual Negotiations
    b) Non-Performance of Contractual Obligations
    c) Negligence in the Performance of Contractual Duties
C. The Taxonomic Nature of the Problem
  1. Conceptual Categories as Obstacles
  2. The Heuristic Value of Functional Categories
D. The Four Corners of Civil Obligations
  1. A Three-Corner Game
  2. Estoppel and Reliance
  3. Back to Pre-Contractual Liability
  4. A Four-Corner Analysis
  5. The Contract Corner
  6. The Tort Corner
  7. The Restitution Corner
  8. The Estoppel Corner
E. Reliance as a Driving Force
F. Conclusion: Mapping out the Hidden Side of the Planet Obligations

A. Introduction

1 This paper is not intended to supply a full and detailed survey of some obscure and sometimes neglected areas of what civilians call the law of obligations, a term sometimes used by common lawyers themselves.[1] The purpose is rather to give an overview of the law relating to civil obligations in a general perspective, yet focusing on side issues, which tend to be much more informative as to the contours of familiar concepts. I propose to look at problems not

[1] See the first attempts to offer such an overview in A.M. Tettenborn, *An Introduction to the Law of Obligations* (1984); D. Harris, *Remedies in Contract and Tort* (1988).

through the local lenses of the traditional conceptual categories but through new lenses shaped by informed comparative methodology. Like many other terms used in this article, the phrase "law of obligations" will be used in its widest sense, and will include obligations to perform or to compensate victims of breach of contractual promises, to compensate victims of torts as well as restitution in cases of unjust enrichment. Interferences with the law of property will be left aside, the focus being on the borderline between contract and tort, often described as a grey zone or area.[2]

The present study is part of an ambitious project.[3] It is based on more complete and in-depth research made over a long period of years when I was researching the origins, purpose and uses of estoppels in English law and exploring French law in the light of what could then be described as a concept almost alien to the civil law. In *L'estoppel et la protection de la confiance légitime*, a doctorate dissertation defended in Lyon in 1990 but never published,[4] I proposed to redefine some time-honoured concepts viewed as the cornerstones of civil obligations, so that we may compare what happens in civil law and common law jurisdictions. This attempt is the core idea of the present paper, and it may be regarded as a sketch, preparing a more elaborate fresco. It was presented orally at the opening of the 4th Annual Conference on European Tort Law, held in Vienna in the spring 2005 and I am very grateful to my friend Professor Helmut Koziol for his kind invitation. In the magnificent baroque hall of Palais Trautson, I used PowerPoint and therefore do not have a written text on which I may elaborate. Due to shortage in time and assistance, I will just unroll the flow of ideas as I did orally. Referenced footnotes will be scarce. I may indeed rewrite and develop this text in the future, after more comprehensive research. 2

Every sophisticated legal system is challenged by claims made by parties complaining of sudden breach of advanced contractual negotiations. Claims in damages for personal injury or economic loss suffered in the course of performance of a contract are likewise common, as well as claims based on an agreement to which the claimant is not a party. Every time the following questions come up: 3

- Should the defendant be made liable or not?
- Is the cause of action in tort or in contract?
- Is negligence required to make that party liable?

[2] P.S. Atiyah, Recent Judicial Developments in Private Law, in: D. Mendes da Costa (ed.), *The Cambridge Lectures* (1981), 8. Grant Gilmore described it as a "no-man's-land": *The Death of Contract* (1970), 15.

[3] It is conducted within the ambit of the Research Network "Uniform Terminology for European Private Law". The member universities are Torino (Co-ordinator), Barcelona, Lyon, Münster, Nijmegen, Oxford and Warsaw. The research network is part of the *Improving Human Potential* (IHP) Programme financed by the European Commission (Contract no. HPRN-CT-2002-00229).

[4] It will be updated and published in French in a series of articles in *Revue de la common law en français*, starting with the historical part, in 2006.

4 A substantial part of the problem lies in the definition of contract and tort, which differs in civil law and common law systems. As a result, comparative lawyers themselves happen to be lost. These cases may be described as borderline issues between contract and tort, but how may we tackle them in the perspective of comparison and harmonisation if we do not agree on the scope of contract and tort in various legal systems?

5 The Principles of European Contract Law (PECL) and the newly published Principles of European Tort Law (PETL)[5] may govern such borderline issues, yet with overlaps:

- There is a *culpa in contrahendo* provision in the PECL;[6]
- The PETL are broad enough to cover all borderline issues;
- The PETL may even take over the PECL on all contract liability issues, as demonstrated by Prof. R. Zimmermann in his lecture at the 3rd Annual Conference on European Tort Law last year;[7]
- The newly published third part of the PECL may also govern a number of tort issues, a point also pointed out by Prof. Zimmermann.[8]

6 This is one more European paradox we are left to live with, following the publication of these two doctrinal instruments aiming at the harmonisation of the law. The PECL and PETL are based on fine comparative studies, and yet they do not define the scope of contract and tort. The consequence is that grey zones may be as grey as before and there is a need for clarification.

7 The grey zone needs to be revisited. The problem we are facing is linked to existing categories. Despite the huge efforts mentioned above, we remain prisoners of conceptual categories developed in national legal cultures. In my view, there is a need to transcend these categories. Comparative law may help define new categories based not on concepts but on functional analysis. Here is the approach I propose to help solve the problem:

- Let us first quickly explore part of the grey zone, like rushing tourists concentrating on landmarks;
- I will then point out the taxonomic nature of the problem;
- Some time will be spent to identify what I will describe as the four corners of the law of obligations;
- Reliance will be identified as a driving force in western legal systems;
- We may eventually start mapping out the hidden side of the law of obligations.

[5] European Group on Tort Law, *Principles of European Tort Law, Text and Commentary* (2005).
[6] Art. 2:301, cited in its full terms below.
[7] R. Zimmermann, Principles of European Contract Law and Principles of European Tort Law: Comparison and Points of Contact, in: H. Koziol/B.C. Steininger (eds.), *European Tort Law 2003* (2004), 2.
[8] Ibid.

B. Exploring the Grey Zone

This paragraph aims at defining cross-border problems and cross-border similarities. 8

1. Cross-Border Problems

All domestic legal galaxies have a star called "contract". Yet, depending on the systems we look at, this star may have a different size, position and composition. We may list the conventional names as they appear on national maps: *contrat et convention*, *Vertrag*, *Rechtsgeschäft*, *contratto e convenzione*, *negozio giuridico*, *contract* ... We may try to translate them. All these stars may at times differ or be similar. For the sake of convenience, I will use the term "contract" in a loose sense, to describe binding agreements of all kinds. They may occupy a different place at different times, hence the importance of looking at things in a historical perspective. They may look bigger or smaller depending on where they are, hence the importance of defining a clear perspective and keeping to it when engaging in a comparative study. They are sometimes hidden by other stars, which does not mean that they disappear. All specialists remember the eclipse of the star contract described by Grant Gilmore in *The Death of Contract*[9]. 9

Every legal system adjusts the concept of contract with an answer of its own. French law may be cited as a system stretching it to the utmost, giving it a strong gravitational force. The common law and particularly English law gives a very narrow definition, lowering the gravitational force of contracts. 10

Let us observe what I may describe as the size of the star "contract". In civil law systems, most types of legally binding agreements fall into the category of contract. Contracts may be gratuitous and donations are viewed as categories of contracts. In the common law, a contract means an agreement, which may be described as an exchange of promises. A promise may only be contractually binding if supported by a consideration, namely something promised or given by the promisee in return for the promise. Therefore, gifts or donations are not viewed as contracts. The civil law contract is therefore a much larger star that the common law one. 11

We may now turn to the gravity of the star "contract", concentrating on two national legal systems. In French law, the contract is a big star with a very strong gravitational force. The French contract easily creates rights to the benefit of third parties. French law has developed a concept of chain of contract allowing direct action by a party at the end of the chain as against the one at the beginning. For instance, where sold goods are defective, the final purchaser may sue the manufacturer even where he received the goods from a retailer who purchased from a distributor who got them from the manufacturer. In ad- 12

[9] Supra fn. 2. See also P.S. Atiyah, *The Rise and Fall of Freedom of Contract* (1979).

dition, many contracts are said to contain an implied contractual *obligation de sécurité*, whereby carriers, medical doctors or suppliers of goods must compensate victims of personal injury and collateral losses. On the other end of the spectrum, English law has developed a very strict doctrine of privity of contract, making the star third party proof. It took an Act of Parliament in 1999 to allow satellite action by third parties. The concept of chain of contract is unknown and compensation claims for physical injury caused in the course of performance of what may be regarded as a contract are based on tort rather than on contract. The planet tort therefore has a much stronger gravity.

13 One may also note that inside the stars, one may find different molecule arrangements. The civil law views the contract as an agreement and insists on the common intention of the parties. Interpreting the contract means searching this common intention of the parties, which may be pure fiction. The common law views the contract as a bargain, an exchange of two promises traded one against the other. In this context, interpretation requires an examination of the intention of the promisor. The difference in approach may not be ignored but should not be dramatised. After all, both systems also apply similar techniques such as, for instance, the *contra proferentem* interpretation.

2. Cross-Border Similarities

14 National legal galaxies may be different, yet they follow similar laws. Most systems allow action or compensation in the case of abusive breach of contractual negotiations, although there are some English exceptions. All legal systems agree that non-performance of a typical contractual obligation like delivering goods or carrying a passenger presents a claim for damages. Most legal systems allow a claim for compensation to victims of negligence in the performance of contractual duties, yet with nuances. Let us consider these three points in turn.

a) Breaking Contractual Negotiations

15 Legal systems do not speak with one voice regarding the question of the revocability of a contractual offer. Offers may be irrevocable under German law, Italian Law or the American Uniform Commercial Code (UCC). They are revocable at English law, unless supported by a consideration. The French Civil Code does not even use the terms offer and acceptance and is completely silent on the point. Yet, pre-contractual liability is usually recognised, exceptionally at English law under the torts of fraud or negligence and sometimes lavishly in other systems. The Germans call it contractual liability and the French, despite the formidable gravity of contract, regard the action as based on tort liability where they do not manage, by way of interpretation, to infer the existence of a binding contract.

16 Researching the gist of pre-contractual liability is an interesting but challenging exercise. May we stick to traditional explanations? We find reasons based on contract there: existence of pre-contractual agreements (see the French no-

tions of *avant-contrat, engagement unilatéral de volonté*), *culpa in contrahendo*, and liability based on negligence or malicious intent such as in English law. As will be explained below, a true reason seems to lie in the protection of reasonable or legitimate reliance, sometimes confusingly termed expectation.

b) Non-Performance of Contractual Obligations

Where actual performance is promised, all legal systems agree that non-performance generates liability. Liability may in some cases coincide with termination of the contract and can also be replaced by performance in kind. This seems to be the lowest common denominator of contractual liability, which always lies inside the boundaries of contract. 17

c) Negligence in the Performance of Contractual Duties

Some legal systems recognise the existence of collateral duties to what may appear as the main obligations stemming from the contract between the parties. Carriers must ensure the safe transportation of their passengers, medical practitioners must make sure they give proper information to their patients and must perform their art with due care. What will happen in case of improper performance of such duties or obligations? On which legal ground and under which conditions may the defaulting party be made liable? 18

French law distinguishes two types of contractual obligations. The *obligation de résultat* is a typical contractual obligation where the party must perform and achieve the promised result. The duty for the seller to deliver the goods falls within this category, as well as the duty to transport the goods from the point of departure to the point of arrival in a contract of carriage of goods. The party in breach of such a duty is liable and there is no need to prove negligence. However, in some cases, a party is not bound to reach a promised outcome but to act with due care, in which case the obligation is called *obligation de moyens*. The carrier of passengers can be made liable for the breach of such an obligation where a passenger slips on a snowy platform when boarding the train. In such cases, it is necessary to prove negligence; for instance, the defective maintenance of the railway platform.[10] 19

Liability for medical malpractice offers a good example. Such liability is based on contract in French law. As a rule, the practitioner is not bound by an *obligation de résultat* since in most cases, there is no obligation to cure patients. In medical contracts, such an obligation may only exist where for instance a dentist promises to adjust and fix a cap on a tooth. Doctors are said to owe an *obligation de moyens*, whereby they must act with due care according to established scientific knowledge, as the courts repeatedly hold, following a 20

[10] Such an obligation, called *obligation de sécurité*, is analysed by the courts as an *obligation de résultat* when the damage occurs from the time the passenger has boarded the train to the moment where he has stepped off. All these rules have been devised by the courts on minimal (if any) Code support. See O. Moréteau, Codes as Straight-Jackets, Safeguards and Alibis, [1995] 20 *North Carolina Journal of International Law*, 273, at 285.

landmark *Cour de cassation* case, the *Mercier* case, decided in 1936.[11] As a rule, the victim must prove negligence. In some cases, however, the courts reverse the burden of proof and hold that negligence is presumed. Interestingly, in England, similar cases are decided not on the basis of contract but under the tort of negligence. The patient will have no difficulty to prove the existence of a duty of care, given the special relationship stemming from the contract between the patient and the practitioner. However, it may be quite difficult to establish that the doctor breached such duty and acted negligently.

21 May we compare these solutions? Let us first take the case of the typical contractual obligation, the one the French call *obligation de résultat*. Breach of such an obligation triggers contractual liability both at English law and French law. There is no need to prove negligence, it is strict liability. Let us then take the case of the breach of a contractual duty that the French would call *obligation de moyens*. In the same case, liability will be based on contract at French law and in tort at English law. And yet we see that it roughly follows the same rules in both systems. There must be some pre-existing duty, an implied contractual *obligation de moyens* at French law, or a duty of care based on the proximity between the parties at English law. And negligence must be established in both legal systems. The French prohibition to sue in tort where a contractual action is possible (*règle du non-cumul*) does not make a difference. The French judge would not apply a much different standard if the action was based on Article 1382 of the Civil Code, the general provision founding tort liability on fault or negligence.

22 Differences do not lie in solutions (despite some nuances) but in the categories used to justify the solution. The problem we face is taxonomic in nature.

C. The Taxonomic Nature of the Problem

23 It is crucial to stress that the problems we face when comparing systems and trying to harmonise them do not lie in the solution, but in legal categories. Conceptual categories are an obstacle to harmonisation and clarification (1). They should be abandoned, at least for the sake of comparison, to be replaced by functional categories, which have a great heuristic value (2).

1. Conceptual Categories as Obstacles

24 Domestic legal systems make large use of categories, which are based on concepts. These categories are so traditional and engrained in the lawyers' minds at such an early stage of their legal education or training that little effort is made to clarify them. Yet, they cause headaches to comparatists. They are often described by the use of similar terms and yet do not coincide when one moves from one system to another. For this reason, it has been suggested that

[11] Cass. Civ. 30 May 1936, [1936] *Dalloz* (D), I, 88.

it is best to take cases as a starting point when engaging in comparative studies.[12] And for the same reason, the drafters of the PECL and PETL refrained from defining the scope of leading concepts and categories such as "contract" and "tort".

Whilst liability may be based in "contract" or in "tort", the border may not be called "natural" since all legal systems do not agree as to where it should be drawn: 25

- pre-contractual liability is based here on contract and there on tort;
- some duties stemming from the performance of a contract are contractual here and tortious there;
- third parties may enforce contractual rights here and may only sue in tort there.

Such distinctions are as artificial as the French doctrine of "natural borders". 26 King Louis XIV insisted that the kingdom of France should be delineated by *frontières naturelles*. And yet, to those insisting that the Rhine separates two different regions, one may reply that Germanic languages are spoken on both banks, including Alsace. Likewise, looking at the high mountainous barrier separating France and Italy, it is to be noted that many people speak French on both sides and certainly share a common Alpine culture.[13]

Although liability may be based in "contract" or in "tort", this does not solve 27 the "no-man's land" or "grey zone" problems identified in most jurisdictions. Not surprisingly, the distinction is disregarded for the sake of harmonisation. The European directive of 1985 on product liability affords a good example. Very wisely so, the drafters concentrated on the solutions and avoided as much as possible any reference to contract or to tort. Likewise, the distinction is largely set aside in the PECL and PETL.

The traditional conceptual categories may be found suitable for the domestic 28 lawyer and yet it may be argued that they are often more confusing than helpful. One thing is sure, they are not suitable for comparative law:

- National concepts are not tools for comparatists and legal scientists.
- National concepts may be objects to be observed and assessed.
- National concepts are obstacles to harmonisation.

If categories are needed for the sake of comparing and, why not, harmonising 29 the law, they should be of a wholly different nature.

[12] See B.S. Markesinis, *Comparative Law in the Courtroom and Classroom: The Story of the Last Thirty-Five Years* (2003).

[13] When visiting Bhutan in 1999, I noted that the Himalayas did not prevent the Tibetan religion and language to spread there, economic and cultural exchanges criss-crossing over the highest summits.

2. The Heuristic Value of Functional Categories

30 Categories should be defined by their function rather than related to a sometimes very abstract concept. Reference to the function helps to devise a *neutral language* that is essential for the sake of comparing legal rules or systems.[14] We may not use a normative language where the meaning of it is changing from jurisdiction to jurisdiction. Strangely enough, academic lawyers have a hard time to accept these very simple ideas. It is probably due to the fact that the law itself is made of words. It is a language and it may only be described with words, hence the confusion between what we describe, on the one hand, and the words we use for the description, on the other hand.[15] These words often have a normative meaning in the legal system they come from. Translation itself is a problem, the meaning of the word in one language being too often polluted by another legal meaning in another language.

31 Comparative science may be easier in fields where the observed object is not made of words but for instance of flesh and bones. Let's see how one operates in a totally different, non legal context.

32 Take the example of comparative anatomy. Human beings have arms and legs. Cats and dogs have paws, which may be described as front paws and back paws. Nobody would use the words "arms" and "legs" or "paws" when comparing the anatomy of human beings to that of other mammals. One is using such neutral terms as "limbs". The terms "upper limbs" and "lower limbs" are indeed suitable to all earthly mammals.

33 To compare legal rules or systems, one also needs a neutral language, focusing on the function rather than on some abstract idea.[16] The difficulty is to create terms that may be appealing to the lawyer's mind. The world of practice is often more creative than the academic sphere. For instance, international trade specialists are using existing legal terms yet detached from domestic laws, giving these words a neutral meaning. Various languages may even be combined to that effect. For instance, a "force majeure" clause and "hardship" clause may be stipulated in the same contract, with one term in French and another one in English, regardless of the language used in drafting the contract.[17]

[14] See O. Moréteau, Can English become the Common Legal Language in Europe?, in: R. Schulze/G. Ajani (eds.), *Common Principles of European Private Law* (2003), 405; Boissonade revisité: de la codification doctrinale à une langue juridique commune, in: *De tous horizons, Mélanges Xavier Blanc-Jouvan* (2005), 103 at 120–127.

[15] See O. Moréteau, Conclusions, in: J. Du Bois de Gaudusson (ed.), *Le devenir du droit comparé en France* (2005).

[16] See O. Moréteau, Premiers pas dans la comparaison des lois, in: Jean-Claude Gémar/Nicholas Kasirer (eds.), *Jurilinguistique: entre langues et droits; Jurilinguistics: Between Law and Language* (2005), 407 at 425–428.

[17] See O. Moréteau, Le prototype, clé de l'interprétation uniforme: la standardisation des notions floues en droit du commerce international, in: R. Sacco (ed.), *L'interprétation des textes juridiques rédigés en plus d'une langue* (2002), 183 at 195–197; Le raisonnable et le droit: standards, prototypes et interprétation uniforme, [2002] 7 *Ars Interpretandi, Jahrbuch für Juristische Hermeneutik/Journal of Legal Hermeneutics*, Vol. 7, 221 at 234–237.

Latin may be seen as an excellent tool to describe functional categories and create such a neutral language. Good examples are to be found in private international law, with terms such as *lex contractus*, *lex rei sitae*, *lex loci delicti*, *lex fori* or *forum non conveniens* to cite but a few. 34

A dead language is very useful indeed since the meaning no longer changes. Botanists and zoologists made a wise and unchallenged choice when using Latin in their taxonomy. 35

It is best to avoid terms having too specific a meaning in any given jurisdiction and yet we do need concrete terms calling the attention to the reality we attempt to describe. Contemporary comparative law scholarship has gone quite far in that direction, in projects such as the Trento Common Core, the drafting of the Vienna Convention on International Sale of Goods, the Unidroit Principles, the PECL and PETL. And yet, no significant project has looked at the law of obligations as a whole field. One might expect this to be done by the von Bar Groups and yet they work as a galaxy of smaller groups where the work is broken down into specialised units. The following paragraphs aim at providing such an overall picture, based on functional categories. 36

D. The Four Corners of Civil Obligations

So far, civil obligations are viewed as a "three-corner game", featuring three basic categories, usually referred to in English as "contract", "tort" and "restitution". The word restitution was substituted to the category of "quasi-contract" inherited from Roman law and adopted in common law jurisdictions as well as in the civil law. "Restitution" is a functional category, most fortunately substituted to "quasi-contract", which is a conceptual category. 37

To this "three-corner" game (1), a new player may be added, under the name of "estoppel" (2). Pre-contractual liability may then be revisited (3), showing the interest of a "four-corner" analysis (4). Each corner will then be briefly explored in relation to the other three (5 to 8). 38

1. A Three-Corner Game

A law of obligations based on the aforementioned three corners leaves a dark corner in the area of pre-contractual liability. If it is tort, one should emphasise the existence of a fault or negligence every time a party complains that negotiations break down. If it is contract, the importance of intention and the possible existence of a unilateral agreement should be stressed. There is however a shared intuition that pre-contractual liability is often (if not always) based on reasonable reliance. 39

An illustration may be found in an American case, *Hoffman v. Red Owl Stores*, decided some forty years ago by the Supreme Court of Wisconsin.[18] 40

[18] 26 Wis. 2d 683, 133 N.W.2d 267 (1965).

The plaintiff, who owned a bakery, sought a franchise from Red Owl, the owner of a supermarket chain well known in the Midwest. The latter assured him that he would be granted a franchise if he took steps to gain experience and that the sum he had to invest, $ 18,000, would be sufficient. Over the course of two years, he made a number of significant steps, including the sale of his bakery, a move to another town and the purchase of a lot, each time upon the representation by Red Owl's representative that he would get the franchise. A much larger financial contribution was eventually requested, which he could not afford, and his refusal caused the collapse of the negotiation. He sued to recover his expenses and won his case. All details of the proposed transaction had not been agreed on but this was not regarded as an obstacle to compensation. The Court said "that injustice would result here if plaintiffs were not granted some relief because of the failure of defendants to keep their promises which induced plaintiffs to act to their detriment"[19].

41 The judgment was based on *promissory estoppel*, a rule preventing a promisor to deny the terms of a promise where this promise has been relied on by the promisee. The denial causing a detriment, the somehow intriguing phrase "detrimental reliance" is commonly used.

2. Estoppel and Reliance

42 The term "estoppel" is one of the most mysterious legal terms, not only for civilians but to common lawyers themselves. The meaning of the term has indeed fluctuated over the centuries. The old French word *estouper* gave to "estop", "stop" and "estoppel".[20] In medieval days, the word described a procedural rule, forbidding to deny the content of a judgment of a royal court (*estoppel by record*), the content of a formal document under seal (*estoppel by deed*) or the findings of the people living in the country, later on to become jury members (*estoppel by matter in pais*).[21] Estoppels by deed and by matter in pais gradually developed into a rule of substantive law preventing the denial of any statement or representation of fact, to become *estoppel by representation* with a sub-category of *estoppel by convention*.

43 In a system shaped by the judiciary rather than by academics, this caused overlaps and conflicts of meaning, making this area of the law particularly difficult to grasp. Estoppel is nevertheless a very powerful and potentially fruitful legal technique.[22] Two great English authors wrote: "Few doctrines are at once so potentially fruitful and so practically unsatisfying. It is more often cit-

[19] At 274–275.

[20] O. Moréteau, *L'estoppel et la protection de la confiance légitime* (1990), at 13.

[21] For a full survey of the historical development, see O. Moréteau (supra fn. 20), at 29–96. This chapter will soon be published in French in *Revue de la common law en français*.

[22] Two thoughts on estoppel: "A simple and wholly untechnical conception, perhaps the most powerful and flexible instrument to be found in any system of court jurisprudence", Sir Frederick Pollock, [1937] 53 *Law Quarterly Review* (L.Q.R.) 161; "The doctrine of estoppel is one of the most flexible and useful in the armoury of law", Lord Denning, *Texas Bank case* [1982] *Queen's Bench* (Q.B.) 84, 122.

ed than applied, and more often applied than understood"[23]. This is quite a challenge for a non-English lawyer studying this complex doctrine: when I met Lord Denning in 1982, he preferred to comment on his French gastronomic experience than on the many estoppel cases he had decided in the past 35 years. He did not believe a young French scholar could ever clarify the matter!

To make a long story short, in contemporary English law, estoppel means a preclusion to deny a statement where such a denial would harm a party who relied and acted on it. The following conditions must be met: 44

- A party (the *representor*) makes a clear and unambiguous statement (*representation*). This representation may be express (words) or implied (conduct).
- Another party (the *representee*), led to believe in the truth of the representation, reasonably acts on the basis of it. This condition is often referred to as "alteration of position", meaning that he changes his position in so relying on the representation.
- A denial of the representation by the representor would cause the representee some kind of detriment, meaning that, due to the denial, the alteration of his original position by the representee puts him in a worse position.

The estoppel therefore has a preventive effect. Would the representor be allowed to deny his representation, the representee would suffer a detriment and may possibly recover in damages if having a cause of action, probably in tort. The preclusion prevents the occurrence of the damage. 45

The traditional estoppel, called "estoppel by representation", prevents to deny a statement of fact (representation). A modern version, said to be based not on the common law but on equity, prevents to deny a statement of intention, a promise. It is called "promissory estoppel". In England, promissory estoppel appeared shortly after World War II, in the famous controversial *High Trees* case decided by Lord Denning, then a judge in the High Court.[24] Subsequent to the bombings of London, a landlord had accepted to reduce the rent of a leased building by half. The tenant had contracted in order to sublet the apartments for profit. The lease was signed in 1939 but, due to the Blitz, more than half the apartments were left empty. The landlord sued the tenant shortly after the war. The Court held that he was entitled to the full rent for the future but as to the war period, he was "estopped" from denying the promise to accept a reduced rent and was therefore not entitled to arrears. Such a denial would have caused a detriment to the tenant who remained in occupancy on the faith of the promise. Without the reduced rent, he would indeed have terminated the lease at the beginning of the war. In the United States, promissory estoppel is 46

[23] G.C. Cheshire/C.H.S. Fifoot, [1947] 63 L.Q.R. 283, 286.

[24] *Central London Property Trust Ltd. v. High Trees House Ltd.* [1947] 1 *King's Bench* (K.B.) 130.

expressed in rather loose and general terms at § 90 of the Restatement of Contract.[25]

47 Looking at the relationship of estoppel and contract, estoppel prevents a party from denying:

- a statement made in the course of concluding a contract, such as the recognition by a principal that A has authority to act as his agent, or a representation by the owner that A has a power to sell;
- a promise made in the course of performance of a contract, like the waiver or abandonment of the right of having the contract performed by a certain date, this sort of indulgence being quite common in commercial life.

48 The potentialities of estoppel have never been fully explored at English law.[26] Judges and authors are more interested in investigating the precedents so as to be able to predict circumstances where estoppel may be pleaded successfully. Also, there is always this big concern that estoppel may have a subversive effect: it may interfere with established tort or contract doctrines. The consistency of English law must be preserved, often at the cost of clear-cut doctrinal lines. For this reason, it was decided that promissory estoppel could only be used as a defence and not a cause of action, as a shield and not a sword.[27] Indeed, only a promise supported by a consideration may serve as a cause of action at English law. Enlarging the scope of promissory estoppel may have the effect of interfering with the time-honoured doctrine of consideration.[28]

49 For instance, estoppels have been largely excluded from the formation of contracts, an area where the technique could be very useful and powerful. There is too much insistence on the non-existence of pre-contractual liability, due to the fact that a contractual offer is revocable, as long as it has not been accepted. There is one famous case where estoppel was envisaged in this context, but eventually rejected. In *Queen's Gardens,*[29] two parties had agreed to exchange two pieces of land in Hong Kong. Before signing the final documents, they proceeded to the exchange and one party even knocked down the building on the land received from the other. One party refused to sign. It was held

[25] *Restatement of the Law of Contract, 2nd*, § 90: "A promise which the promisor should really expect to induce action or forbearance on the part of the promisee or a third person and which does induce such action or forbearance is binding if injustice can be avoided only by enforcement of the promise. The remedy granted for breach may be limited as justice requires."

[26] The specialised literature on the subject is very descriptive, like for instance G. Spencer Bower/A. Turner, *The Law Relating to Estoppel by Representation* (1977). Yet, see M. Spence, *Protecting Reliance: The Emergent Doctrine of Equitable Estoppel* (1999).

[27] *Combe v. Combe* [1951] 2 K.B. 215, Birkett L.J., 224.

[28] In *Combe v. Combe*, 220, Lord Justice Denning admitted, though reluctantly, that: "The doctrine of consideration is too firmly fixed to be overthrown by a side-wind." American law shows a greater flexibility. § 90 Restatement of Contract allows promissory estoppel to be used as a cause of action. It is therefore accepted in most States that a promise may be binding either if supported by consideration or if relied on by the other party.

[29] *Attorney-General of Hong Kong v. Humphreys Estates (Queen's Gardens) Ltd.* [1987] *Appeal Cases* (A.C.) 114 (Privy Council).

that no contract existed and restitution had to take place. The parties were not estopped from denying the existence of an agreement because throughout the whole negotiation and even after the actual exchange they always agreed "subject to contract", meaning that there was no intention to enter into a binding agreement.

Yet, estoppel offers the appropriate tool to solve pre-contractual liability cases. It protects reliance wherever reasonable or legitimate, and prevents the harmful consequences of what would otherwise be a tort. 50

3. Back to Pre-Contractual Liability

The traditional analysis of pre-contractual liability has a number of shortcomings, that may be elucidated by an "estoppel" or "reliance based analysis". 51

Let us look at the apparent drastic opposition between French law and German law. In German law, based on the doctrine of *culpa in contrahendo*, breach of a contractual negotiation is traditionally regarded as triggering contractual liability. At French law, on similar facts, liability will be based on tort. However, the difference is only on the surface. What matters is to look at the way the compensation is calculated. Analysis shows that, in such cases, compensation is limited to the actual losses and does not cover the gain or benefit that a party may expect from a contract had the contract been concluded. The compensation is limited to the *damnum emergens*, to the reliance interest or *negatives Interesse* as the Germans would call it. In that sense, it is not pure contract liability. 52

The international teams working at harmonising this tricky area of the law resort to the loose concept of good faith to phrase a solution. The problem is that nobody in Europe and in the world agrees on the meaning of good faith, which varies from intimate belief to fair dealing. It is worth citing the Unidroit Principles and the PECL. 53

Unidroit Principles 2004, Art. 2.1.15 (Negotiations in bad faith) 54

(1) A party is free to negotiate and is not liable for failure to reach an agreement.
(2) However, a party who negotiates or breaks off negotiations in bad faith is liable for the losses caused to the other party.

The PECL associate the words good faith with fair dealing, giving more substance to its meaning: 55

PECL, Article 2:301: Negotiations Contrary to Good Faith 56

(1) A party is free to negotiate and is not liable for failure to reach an agreement.
(2) However, a party who has negotiated or broken off negotiations contrary to good faith and fair dealing is liable for the losses caused to the other party.

57 In addition to the use of good faith, the same instruments also use intention. According to the Unidroit Principles, Article 2.1.15(3) "[i]t is bad faith, in particular, for a party to enter into or continue negotiations when intending not to reach an agreement with the other party". Likewise, the PECL, at Article 2:301(3), provide that "[i]t is contrary to good faith and fair dealing, in particular, for a party to enter into or continue negotiations with no real intention of reaching an agreement with the other party".

58 Yet, in all European and western jurisdictions, it appears that most pre-contractual liability cases are decided on the basis of reliance or may be explained if reliance was used as a key to justify or understand the solution. Breaking off a contract negotiation is "against good faith" where the other party could reasonably rely on a *declared* intention to move on with the negotiation. It is clear too that compensation is limited to the actual loss, which would be termed "reliance damages" by common law scholars.

59 An estoppel- or reliance-based explanation would offer, it is submitted, a much more predictable and clearer solution. Compensation, in the form of reliance damages, would be allowed only in those cases where the defendant has made, by words or conduct, clear and unambiguous statements showing a willingness to contract, provided that these statements have been relied on by the plaintiff. The idea is not totally new. Estoppels and their equivalents in civil law jurisdictions[30] have been studied. What may be new is the idea to use it in a different way, to explain what judges are doing and to allow them to step on firm ground when they venture on the marshland borderline between contract and tort. We may even go one step further and propose to view estoppel as the fourth corner of the law of obligations.

4. A Four-Corner Analysis

60 The proposal is to move from a three-corner analysis, featuring "contract", "tort" and "restitution" as the three pillars of the law of obligations, to a four-corner analysis, adding one more and fourth corner under the name of "estoppel". The proposal should not be misunderstood. The point is not to force estoppel into legal systems where it does not exist,[31] but to add and use the functional category of estoppel to improve the reading, understanding and comparison of the various legal systems. This attempt is doctrinal in essence, but may help to clarify and solve a number of practical difficulties, as exemplified above in the field of pre-contractual liability.

[30] *Vertrauensprinzip, venire contra factum proprium, Verwirkung, confiance légitime, doctrina de los actos proprios, preclusione, apparenza del diritto, théorie de l'apparence* are all doctrines that have been compared to estoppel by others before me: see O. Moréteau (supra fn. 20), at 20–24.

[31] Yet, see M. Behar-Touchais (ed.), *L'interdiction de se contredire au détriment d'autrui* (2001), concluding that there may be an estoppel principle in French law.

Attempts have been made in the past to read the law of obligations in the light of reliance. The French Emmanuel Lévy offered to explain the whole law of obligation through the concept of legitimate reliance (*confiance légitime*)[32] and, in a celebrated article, Fuller and Perdue revisited the whole field in the light of the protection of the "reliance interest".[33] 61

Reliance may be described as the core element of contract and tort. In the law of contract, the creditor relies on performance by the debtor, the terms creditor and debtor being used there in their continental sense. In the law of tort, pedestrians and other motorists rely on cars stopping at red lights, others on parents looking after their children and employers controlling the activity of their employees. In the grey zone between contract and tort, it may be reasonable to rely on some pre-contractual statements, promises or documents. However, my agenda is not to treat reliance as a paramount rule controlling all the others. One should rather try to identify a specific place for the functional category of estoppel as defined in the previous sub-paragraph. 62

The four corners of the law of obligations may be described by the following words used here in a very loose sense, followed by an indication of their basic function: 63

- Contracts: referring to an obligation to perform;
- Torts: referring to an obligation to compensate;
- Restitution: referring to an obligation to give back;
- Estoppel: referring to an obligation not to deny.

All four terms are meant to designate a basic function of the law of obligations, for the sake of comparison. Each corner may interfere with the other three (hence a formidable confusion in the literature and the terminology), as will be observed, when considering them in turn. 64

5. The Contract Corner

From a functional point of view, contract means an agreement, supposedly based on the parties' intentions, creating some obligations to which the law recognises a binding force. Breach of contract triggers an obligation to compensate the reliance interest (*damnum emergens*) but also the expectation interest (*lucrum cessans*). Some confusion was generated in the literature subsequent to the article by Fuller and Perdue. Samuel Stoljar put it right in an article[34] where he rejects the contention by Fuller and others that compensation in cases of breach of contract is enlarged to expectation damages (*lucrum cessans*) just because it is impossible to assess reliance damages (*damnum emergens*) in such cases. Stoljar rightly points out that the very existence of a 65

32 Responsabilité et contrat, [1899] *Revue critique de législation et jurisprudence*, 361; La confiance légitime, [1910] *Revue trimestrielle de droit civil*, 178.
33 The Reliance Interest in Contract Damages, [1936] 46 *Yale Law Journal*, 52, 373.
34 Promise, Expectation and Agreement, [1988] *Cambridge Law Journal*, 193.

contract justifies "passive reliance" (usually called expectation) whereas, where no contract exists, the protection should be limited to "active reliance" (usually called reliance). This is the fullest possible compensation in the law of obligations and it may be used as a marker, perhaps more efficient than intention or will, of what a contract is. It may under some conditions be substituted by performance in kind.

66 In some cases however, the liability of the party causing the breach may be limited to the reliance interest, in cases for instance of reliance on a pre-contractual statement. A party may also be estopped from denying a fact held true during the negotiation and also in the descriptive clauses of a contract, a field largely explored in my doctorate thesis.[35] If no contract was formed, claims in tort might be possible as well as restitution of part or full performance. Restitution may take place where the contract is avoided or where it is terminated following on a breach. It may also include the compensation of a loss of a chance where there is a breach of a duty, like in cases of medical malpractice but, then, we are shifting to tort liability.

6. The Tort Corner

67 This is a major corner as well, and its scope may not be described in such a limited space. Let us just note that tort interferes with the other three corners:

- with contract where there is a breach of duty within the ambit of a contractual relationship; breach of contract may functionally be described as a tort,[36] as it was in the early common law;[37]
- with estoppel in a number of pure economic loss cases, where the loss is caused by the reliance on pre-contractual or post-contractual representations as well as on professional expertise;
- with restitution wherever the victim is deprived of some property interest and therefore entitled to get it back.

7. The Restitution Corner

68 This corner has attracted a lot of attention in the past few years or decades, initiated by the famous book by Lord Goff and Professor Jones[38] and the works of the late Peter Birks[39]. There is even a *Restitution Law Review*. Restitution interferes with contract where a contract is avoided or terminated, and with tort where there property is displaced or removed.

[35] O. Moréteau (supra fn. 20), at 514–580.

[36] Yet with an extended compensation encompassing the expectation interest, as explained above.

[37] I did insist on this in my earlier work (O. Moréteau (supra fn. 20), at 338–342) but noticed how upsetting the view is when addressing an audience of first-class English and Italian specialists at a conference in Milan in 2002. This controversial point may be left aside for present purposes.

[38] R. Goff/G. Jones, *The Law of Restitution* (6th edn. 2004).

[39] P. Birks, *An Introduction to the Law of Restitution* (1989); in *Unjust Enrichment* (2nd edn. 2005), Birks preferred this term, describing the cause of action, to that of restitution.

There is a special case traditionally associated to tort where the fault of the impoverished party is set off against a restitution claim. However, this may be analysed as an estoppel case. Restitution may occasionally be paralysed by the effect of an estoppel, as illustrated in *Avon County Council v. Howlett.*[40] A teacher was on a two year leave from work for health reasons. Sums were paid to him by mistake by his employer. The employee inquired whether these sums were owed to him. Upon the assurance received from the employer that he was eligible to these payments, he spent the money so far kept aside. The employer's claim in restitution was successfully paralysed by the estoppel opposed by the employee. He had reasonably relied on the statements made by the employer that the money was his and he had altered his position on the faith of these statements. He had spent the money that he had previously kept aside in case repayment was required. In French law, the employer may in such a case be regarded as liable in tort and the claim in damages would be set off against the restitution claim. Estoppel nonetheless offers a more satisfactory analysis for these cases where the impoverished party's conduct is taken into account in order to reduce or paralyse the restitution claim. 69

8. The Estoppel Corner

We reach the final and least visited corner, which has not attracted all the attention it deserves. I will not restate what has been explained above. Let us just stress the relationship of estoppel with the other three corners. 70

First, estoppel has the effect of preventing the occurrence of a damage that would be caused by the denial of the representation or promise in the case of promissory estoppel (tort dimension). 71

Secondly, estoppel strengthens the basis of a contract and promotes good faith and fair dealing, yet with a more precise analysis: facts that have been acknowledged by one party may not be denied and will serve as the contextual basis of the contractual relationship; clear promises altering the original contract may not be denied when they are acted on, even when they are not binding according to the original contract. This solution may apply in a common law context where the promise is unilateral and not supported by a consideration, but it may also explain solutions in contracts governed by the civil law. Let's take the example of a contract in writing stipulating that it may only be varied by a written agreement. If parties vary the contract orally, it may be regarded as contrary to good faith to use the clause imposing the written form for any variation. In estoppel parlance, this party will be prevented from denying a representation that oral variation was acceptable in the circumstances, a solution inspiring Article 29 of the CISG, which will be cited below in its full terms. 72

Thirdly, estoppel may prevent restitution where the plaintiff clearly acknowledged and represented that there was no unjust enrichment. 73

[40] [1983] 1 *Weekly Law Reports* (W.L.R.) 605.

74 From all these comments, it appears that reliance is a driving force of the entire law of obligations.

E. Reliance as a Driving Force

75 The importance of reliance in modern life has been clearly emphasised by Lord Reid in a formula also stressing the importance of the standard of the reasonable person: "Life would be impossible in modern conditions unless on the highway and in the market place we were entitled to rely on the other man behaving like a reasonable man"[41]. However, the recognition of the fundamental importance of reliance in the law of obligations should not undermine other doctrines, which are also central to this area of the law:

- contract remains based on will,
- tort is chiefly based on fault and negligence,
- restitution remedies unjust enrichment.

76 The interference of will and reliance needs further exploration, the one not excluding the other. For instance, it is generally admitted that a promise is to be interpreted according to the actual intention of the promisor where this intention is known. Likewise, at least in civil law jurisdictions, an agreement is to be interpreted according to the common intention of the parties. However, where the actual intention is not known, a contractual promise will be interpreted as understood by reasonable persons of the same kinds as the parties in the same circumstances.[42] There is no doubt that the use of linguistics, including sociolinguistics, may help towards a better understanding of this area of the law. Another illustration of the interference of will and reliance is provided for in Article 29 of the CISG:

(1) A contract may be modified or terminated by the mere agreement of the parties.
(2) A contract in writing which contains a provision requiring any modification or termination by agreement to be in writing may not be otherwise modified or terminated by agreement. However, a party may be precluded by his conduct from asserting such a provision to the extent that the other party has relied on that conduct.

77 Let us now consider the interference between fault and reliance. The denial of a statement relied upon by another party may be regarded as a fault generating liability. Reliance, together with the idea of estoppel, offers a proper answer to the *théorie de l'apparence*, *apparenza del diritto*. The French *Cour de cassation*, in the famous *Banque canadienne* case, insisted on the legitimate belief (*croyance légitime*) generated by the *apparence* as being the gist of the protec-

[41] *Gollins v. Gollins* [1964] A.C. 644.
[42] CISG, art. 8; Unidroit Principles, art. 4.1; PECL, art. 5:101.

tion.[43] Estoppel and reliance add a new dimension and more predictability to the *théorie de l'apparence*. It is not enough to insist on the "legitimate belief" or reasonable reliance. It ought to have been created by the words or attitude of the party to whom *apparence* is opposed, like in an estoppel case.

Reasonable reliance is also a useful test to check the existence of some duties. 78
It was promoted as a test of the duty of care in a landmark English case. In *Hedley Byrne*, the House of Lords held that a banker accepting to give some information to a company as to the state of affairs of a client was in a situation to owe this company a duty of care.[44] Lord Morris explained that in the circumstances, the company could reasonably rely on the banker's skill and ability to check the client's state of business.[45] Not surprisingly, the "expertise to be expected" and "special reliance" are criteria for the determination of the required standard of conduct in the PETL[46], proving that it is not just a fanciful English idea but that it is shared by other European legal systems.

Once again, but it is worth insisting, what matters is the combination (in deci- 79
sion making) or deconstruction (in explaining existing solutions) of the appropriate elements, the four corners offering a framework applicable to any legal system, whether it originates in the civil law or the common law or is a combination of both.

F. Conclusion: Mapping out the Hidden Side of the Planet Obligations

This conclusion is not the end of the story but rather a beginning. The whole 80
law of obligations in European and western (or westernised) countries may be revisited in the light of these few simple ideas. They may help explain the existing instruments aiming at the harmonisation or unification of the law and offer an aid for the drafting of new instruments.

The ideas proposed here are not ideological but are purely functional, techni- 81
cal. Adopting this framework is not a political agenda, but rather a scientific choice. The possibility is regained to have an overall view of the law of obli-

[43] Cass. Ass. Plén., 13 December 1962, [1963] D 277, note J. Calais-Auloy.

[44] *Hedley Byrne & Co. Ltd. v. Heller & Partners* [1964] A.C. 65.

[45] Relying on the positive statements made by the bank, the plaintiff, an advertising company, lost a large amount of money following the liquidation of the client. However, the banker was not made liable due to a disclaimer in the letter where the positive impression on the client's standing was confirmed.

[46] PETL, art. 4:102(1): "The required standard of conduct is that of the reasonable person in the circumstances, and depends, in particular, on the nature and value of the protected interest involved, the dangerousness of the activity, the expertise to be expected of a person carrying it on, the foreseeability of the damage, the relationship of proximity or special reliance between those involved, as well as the availability and the costs of precautionary or alternative methods."

gations in a European or more universal context, casting light on some dark corners. The approach is transsystemic and cuts across the dividing line between civil law and common law. It does not contradict traditional or contemporary doctrines but brings new perspectives and some enrichment in the perception we have of complex phenomena.

82 The key to all this identifies with modern comparative scholarship:

- We should look at things from an outside perspective, an ability developed only by those being conversant with several legal systems;
- We should use the tools shaped in various legal systems wherever appropriate, benefiting from the circulation of legal ideas;
- We should free our minds from the limits imposed by nationally defined concepts and categories, intellectual limits being the most difficult to remove;
- We should identify the functions behind the rules and develop a more informed analysis;
- We should pay attention to the words we use and develop a neutral or detached terminology when comparing legal systems and drafting international instruments.

83 This is a cross-cultural approach, favouring the dialogue among the various people. It makes human diversity intelligible and proves that unity may exist within diversity.

V. *Rylands v Fletcher* and the Emergence of Enterprise Liability in the Common Law

Ken Oliphant

A. Introduction

Sooner or later, or so it appears, every writer on tort in the common law world falls victim to the condition of *rylandsandfletcheritis*, whose main symptom is the irresistible compulsion to offer yet another interpretation – or re-interpretation – of the famous decision.[1] It can hardly be said that the world needs any more. From the time of Holmes and Pollock on, the case has attracted the attention of the greatest common law minds.[2] And the volume of commentary has hardly abated in more recent years.[3] As early as 1911, Bohlen was concerned that another analysis of the case might seem "a thrashing out of old straw".[4] So why tax the reader's patience with a further traverse of such familiar territory? The only excuse I can offer is that I believe there still to be new things to say. 1

[1] *Rylands v Fletcher* (1868) *Law Reports* (LR) 3 *House of Lords* (HL) 330.

[2] See, especially, O.W. Holmes, *The Common Law* (1881), 116–7; F. Pollock, Duties of Insuring Safety: The Rule in Rylands v. Fletcher (1886) 2 *Law Quarterly Review* (LQR) 52; F.H. Bohlen, The Rule in Rylands v Fletcher (1911) 59 *University of Pennsylvania Law Review* (U Pa L Rev) 298, 373 and 423; E.R. Thayer, Liability without Fault (1916) 29 *Harvard Law Review* (Harv L Rev) 801; P.H. Winfield, Nuisance as a Tort (1931) 4 *Cambridge Law Journal* (CLJ) 189; F.V. Harper, Liability Without Fault and Proximate Cause (1932) 30 *Michigan Law Review* (Mich L Rev) 1001; W.L. Prosser, Nuisance without Fault (1942) 20 *Texas Law Review* (Tex L Rev) 399; C. Morris, Hazardous Enterprises and Risk Bearing Capacity (1952) 61 *Yale Law Journal* (Yale LJ) 1172; and P. Keeton, Trespass, Nuisance, and Strict Liability (1959) 59 *Columbia Law Review* (Colum L Rev) 457.

[3] See C. Dalton, *Losing History: Tort Liability in the Nineteenth Century and the Case of Rylands v Fletcher* (unpublished typescript dated 1987); A.W.B. Simpson, Bursting Reservoirs and Victorian Tort Law: *Rylands and Horrocks v. Fletcher* (1868), in: *Leading Cases in the Common Law* (1995); G.T. Schwartz, *Rylands v Fletcher*, Negligence and Strict Liability, in: P. Cane/J. Stapleton (eds.), *Essays in Celebration of John Fleming* (1998); K. Stanton, The Legacy of *Rylands v Fletcher*, in: N.J. Mullany/A.M. Linden (eds.), *Torts Tomorrow: A Tribute to John Fleming* (1998); J. Murphy, The Merits of *Rylands v Fletcher* (2004) 24 *Oxford Journal of Legal Studies* (OJLS) 643; and D. Nolan, The Distinctiveness of *Rylands v Fletcher* (2005) 120 LQR 421.

[4] F.H. Bohlen (supra fn. 2), 298.

2 Interpretations of *Rylands v Fletcher* have veered, sometimes violently, between two poles.[5] Some consign it to the past, dismissing it as an anachronistic relic of a primitive legal system that has been wholly transformed by the rise of the fault principle. Others see in it a glimpse of the future, specifically, the theory of enterprise liability that shaped much of twentieth-century tort law, especially in the United States of America. This paper seeks to evaluate the competing claims. The thesis it advances is that the old principle of "action at peril" had not been fully displaced by the fault standard by the 1860s when *Rylands v Fletcher* was decided, and that the institutional changes in the legal system that were then underway, which culminated in the abolition of the writ system and the forms of action in 1875,[6] required the judges to address for the first time the *substantive* merits of fault-based and strict liability, and to define the proper role of each. Strict liability was part of a living legal tradition, not a relic of the past. But it was now possible to consider it afresh, and advance new justifications for it to reflect the demands of nineteenth-century industrial society. In legal and political debates around the time that *Rylands v Fletcher* was decided, an embryonic theory of enterprise liability was developing, and in many ways the case represented the perfect testing ground for it. So was *Rylands v Fletcher* the first example of enterprise liability in the common law? That is the question I seek to answer at the end of this paper.

3 I take "enterprise liability" to refer to a cluster of theories which provide a contemporary justification for the imposition of strict liability on those pursuing activities of (usually) a commercial nature.[7] Though the details of different accounts vary, the following may be considered key elements. The starting premise is that the responsibility to compensate is based on the defendant's engagement in a specified activity (the "enterprise") rather than actual fault. Though some accounts consider that the term embraces liabilities where there is *legal* fault, the attribution of fault in such cases is taken to be something of a

[5] See, e.g., C.A. Wright, The Adequacy of the Law of Torts [1961] CLJ 44, 52 ("a storm centre").

[6] On the forms of action and the writ system, see J.H. Baker, *An Introduction to English Legal History* (4th edn. 2002), ch. 4.

[7] The classic accounts include: F. James, Contribution among Joint Tortfeasors: A Pragmatic Criticism (1941) 54 Harv L Rev 1156; W.G. Friedmann, Social Insurance and the Principles of Tort Liability (1949) 63 Harv L Rev 241; A.A. Ehrenzweig, *Negligence Without Fault: Trends toward an Enterprise Liability for Insurable Loss* (1951); C.O. Gregory, Trespass to Negligence to Absolute Liability (1951) 37 *Virginia Law Review* (Va L Rev) 359; R.E. Keeton, Conditional Fault in the Law of Torts (1959) 72 Harv L Rev 401; G. Calabresi, Some Thoughts on Risk Distribution and the Law of Torts (1961) 70 Yale LJ 499; and J.G. Fleming, The Role of Negligence in Modern Tort Law (1967) 53 Va L Rev 815, especially 837–40. Important recent contributions include: G.L. Priest, The Invention of Enterprise Liability: A Critical History of the Intellectual Foundations of Modern Tort Law (1985) 14 *Journal of Legal Studies* (J Leg Stud) 461; V.E. Nolan/E. Ursin, *Understanding Enterprise Liability: Rethinking Tort Reform for the Twenty-first Century* (1995); R.L. Rabin, Some Thoughts on the Ideology of Enterprise Liability (1996) 55 *Maryland Law Review* (Md L Rev) 1190; and G.C. Keating, The Theory of Enterprise Liability and Common Law Strict Liability (2001) 54 *Vanderbilt Law Review* (Vand L Rev) 1285. See also American Law Institute, *Reporters' Study on Enterprise Responsibility for Personal Injury* (1991). Much of the literature has focussed on product liability, but that is too big a topic to address here.

fiction – consider Ehrenzweig's famous analysis of "negligence without fault"[8] – and to be a second-best solution as compared with *strict* enterprise liability.[9] In fact, most writers use the term to refer to a strict liability, even "*[t]he distinctive modern form* of strict liability."[10] It is not a liability for wrongdoing, the judicial righting of a wrong – more like "an overhead operating cost",[11] a licence fee for engaging in hazardous activities,[12] or a disguised form of indirect taxation.[13] The theory recognises that modern industrial technologies and methods of production create risks of injury that we are unable or unwilling to eliminate completely, and exact an inevitable toll on a randomly-selected class of victims. The defendant's activity is admitted to be "not only legal, but generally highly desirable: indeed so highly desirable that its utility alone justifies incurring a substantial, if irreducible level of risk."[14] It is above all the nonreciprocal nature of this risk that warrants the imposition of strict liability by way of exception to the predominant fault-based approach,[15] though considerations of social solidarity also often play a role.[16] As enterprise liability carries with it no imputation of wrongdoing, the exclusive remedy is damages, and there is no place for injunctions which expressly prohibit, or effectively require the defendant to desist from, the activity in question. In Calabresi and Melamed's famous formulation, the approach is one based on "liability rules" rather than "property rules".[17] Additionally, most proponents of the theory advocate the limitation of damages to foreseeable risks, both for reasons of fairness to entrepreneurs, who should have fair notice of their potential liabilities when embarking upon (and continuing) their venture, and so as not to deter enterprise.[18]

Enterprise liability justifies the imposition of accident costs on the defendant both as a means of loss distribution and because of its deterrent effects. Individual writers may emphasise one of these considerations over the other – to 4

[8] A.A. Ehrenzweig (supra fn. 7). Cf. R.E. Keeton's concept of "conditional fault" (supra fn. 7).
[9] See, e.g., J.G. Fleming (supra fn. 7), 839.
[10] G.C. Keating (supra fn. 7), 1286 (emphasis added). See also, e.g., C.O. Gregory (supra fn. 7), 383, G. Calabresi (supra fn. 7), 500.
[11] C.O. Gregory (supra fn. 7), 383.
[12] A.A. Ehrenzweig (supra fn. 7), 53–4.
[13] C.O. Gregory (supra fn. 7), 383.
[14] J.G. Fleming (supra fn. 7), 822.
[15] See, especially, G.P. Fletcher, Fairness and Utility in Tort Theory (1972) 65 Harv L Rev 537; K.N. Hylton, The Theory of Tort Doctrine and the Restatement (Third) of Torts (2001) 54 Vand L Rev 1413, 1433–6.
[16] See, e.g., F. James (supra fn. 7), 1156–7; R. Pound, The End of Law as Developed in Legal Rules and Doctrines (1914) 27 Harv L Rev 195, 233.
[17] G. Calabresi/A.D. Melamed, Property Rules, Liability Rules, and Inalienability: One View of the Cathedral (1972) 85 Harv L Rev 1089. This does not preclude the prohibition, whether by injunction or regulation, of activities that present an unreasonable risk of danger, but this is not enterprise liability but an application of the normal fault principle. See R.E. Keeton (supra fn. 7), 427–8.
[18] A.A. Ehrenzweig (supra fn. 7), 52–4; W.L. Prosser, The Assault Upon the Citadel (Strict Liability to the Consumer) (1960) 69 Yale LJ 1099, 1143–46. G. Calabresi (supra fn. 7), 529 finds that liability for unforeseeable losses, though inconsistent with the loss-spreading justification for enterprise, is required by the resource-allocation justification that he prefers.

such an extent, in fact, that it is legitimate to talk of two versions or variants of enterprise liability, one focussed on loss distribution, the other on deterrence or resource allocation.[19] "Loss distribution" may be contrasted with the cruder theory of loss shifting:[20] whereas the latter contents itself with the search for a "deep pocket",[21] the former points to the defendant's ability to spread liability costs by way of adjustments to product pricing, share dividends, wages and salaries, investment in research and development, and the like.[22] It also considers the extent to which the defendant can pool residual financial risks via insurance techniques, whether by purchase from a commercial provider or by the spreading of costs over time (*intertemporal*, as opposed to *interpersonal*, loss-distribution).[23] In short, the attraction of enterprise liability is that "the risk of injury can be insured by the manufacturer and distributed among the public as a cost of doing business."[24] The deterrence justification for holding the defendant liable is that prospective liability awards act as an economic incentive to encourage cost-effective investments in safety, and a switch from non-cost-justified activities to those whose benefits outweigh their costs.[25] Though some proponents of economic analysis of law argue that the same, or better, incentive effects can be achieved by the fault principle,[26] enterprise liability theory generally views strict liability as superior because of its ability to affect activity levels as well as marginal safety precautions.[27] As transaction costs and other market imperfections may prevent the parties from achieving the optimal allocation of resources by negotiation and agreement, enterprise liability theory characteristically seeks to mimic the result of market processes

[19] See, e.g., G. Calabresi (supra fn. 7), 500-01; G.L. Priest (supra fn. 7), 466.

[20] F. James (supra fn. 7), 1156. See further R.E. Keeton (supra fn. 7), 405–7; A. Tunc, *International Encyclopaedia of Comparative Law, vol XI, Torts* (1983), paras. 1.168–171; W.P. Keeton et al., *Prosser and Keeton on Torts* (5th edn. 1984), 24–5; P. Cane, *Atiyah's Accidents, Compensation and the Law* (6th edn. 1999), 353–6.

[21] In fact, it is hard to find unequivocal support for the pure loss-shifting thesis, but cf. R. Pound (supra fn. 16), 233: "There is a strong and growing tendency, where there is no blame on either side, to ask, in view of the exigencies of social justice who can best bear the loss, and hence to shift the loss by creating liability where there has been no fault." L.W. Feezer, Capacity to Bear Loss as a Factor in the Decision of Certain Types of Tort Cases (1930) 78 U Pa L Rev 805 and (1931) 79 U Pa L Rev 742 is sometimes cited as a proponent, but it is in fact clear that he regarded loss-shifting only as a means of loss-distribution. However, G. Calabresi, *The Costs of Accidents: A Legal and Economic Analysis* (1970), 40-2 offers a partial defence of the "deep pockets" approach, arguing that it can be combined with loss-spreading to reduce secondary accident costs further than is possible by pure loss-spreading. (This passage may be compared with G. Calabresi (supra fn. 7), 527–8.)

[22] C.O. Gregory (supra fn. 7), 383–4, G. Calabresi (supra fn. 7), 519–27.

[23] G. Calabresi (supra fn. 7), 518. See further A.A. Ehrenzweig, Assurance Oblige – A Comparative Study (1950) 15 *Law & Contemporary Problems* 450.

[24] *Escola v Coca Cola Bottling Co of Fresno* (1944) 150 *Pacific Reporter. Second Series* (P 2d) 436, 441, per Traynor J (considering strict liability for defective products). On Traynor's influence, see further P. Keeton, Roger Traynor and the Law of Torts (1971) 44 *Southern California Law Review* 1045.

[25] G. Calabresi (supra fn. 21), ch. 5.

[26] See, especially, R.A. Posner, A Theory of Negligence (1972) 1 J Leg Stud 29.

[27] The classic analysis is S. Shavell, Strict Liability Versus Negligence (1980) 9 J Leg Stud 1 (concluding that strict liability is superior to negligence in this respect in the case of "unilateral" accidents where only injurer activity levels are relevant).

by placing accident costs on the party who derives the chief benefit from pursuit of the activity in question. Liability rules are a means of internalising what would otherwise be external costs.

The origins of the theory of enterprise liability have been much debated. Fleming James,[28] Karl Llewellyn[29] and Leon Green[30] have all be named as decisive influences, and the propagation of the term has been attributed to Ehrenzweig,[31] though I have found it employed as early as 1921.[32] Indeed, even earlier writers evidently grasped key aspects of the theory, and employed very similar terminology. Pound wrote in 1914 of "placing upon an enterprise the burden of repairing injuries without fault of him who conducts it, which are incident to the undertaking."[33] Going further back in time, to the closing decades of the nineteenth century, we find Oliver Wendell Holmes writing that the modern law of torts was mainly concerned with injuries that were "the incidents of certain well known businesses," whose liability in damages "sooner or later goes into the price paid by the public."[34] Recognising therefore the loss-distributing effect of tort, he proceeded to identify the underlying issue of public policy:[35]

> the question of liability, if pressed far enough, is really the question how far it is desirable that the public should insure the safety of those whose work it uses.

Holmes also anticipated the modern theory of enterprise liability when he acknowledged that damages may be considered a tax on lawful activity, and not necessarily a remedy for wrongdoing:[36]

[28] By G.L. Priest (supra fn. 7), 465. See F. James (supra fn. 7).

[29] By J.B. Clutterbuck, Karl Llewellyn and the Intellectual Foundations of Enterprise Liability Theory (1988) 97 Yale LJ 1131.

[30] By V. Nolan/E. Ursin (supra fn. 7), 30 highlighting in particular Green's two-part article, The Duty Problem in Negligence Cases (1928) 28 Colum L Rev 1014 and (1929) 29 Colum L Rev 255 (see, e.g., 270: "The risks of physical harms could be distributed as well as could wages and other costs.").

[31] F. James, Social Insurance and Tort Liability: The Problem of Alternative Remedies (1952) 27 *New York University Law Review* (NYU L Rev) 537, 540n. It seems that Albert A. Ehrenzweig first used the term in his (anonymous) student note, Loss-Shifting and Quasi-Negligence: A New Interpretation of the *Palsgraf* case (1941) 8 *University of Chicago Law Review* (U Chi L Rev 72), 744. This usage was picked up later the same year by Charles O. Gregory in his review of W.L. Prosser's *Handbook of the Law of Torts* in the same journal: (1941) 9 U Chi L Rev 196, 198.

[32] K. Takayanagi, Liability Without Fault in the Modern Civil and Common Law—II (1921) 16 *Illinois Law Review* (Ill L Rev) 268, 270 and passim. From the 1920s onwards, a number of writers also began employing the term "entrepreneur theory" in connection with vicarious liability: see, e.g., W.O. Douglas, Vicarious Liability and Administration of Risk (1929) 38 Yale LJ 584 and 720, and C. Morris, The Torts of an Independent Contractor (1934) 29 Ill L Rev 339.

[33] R. Pound (supra fn. 16), 233. See also E.R. Thayer (supra fn. 2), 802–3 (who notes (803) that "ultimately, like any other overhead charge … [liability costs] would fall on the consumer") and F.H. Bohlen (supra fn. 2), 431–2 and 441–6.

[34] O.W. Holmes, The Path of the Law (1897) 10 Harv L Rev 457, 467.

[35] Ibid.

[36] O.W. Holmes (supra fn. 2), 148.

> It cannot be inferred, from the mere circumstance that certain conduct is made actionable, that therefore the law regards it as wrong, or seeks to prevent it … If we accept the test of liability alone … how do we distinguish between conduct which is prohibited, and that which is merely taxed?

In fact, many of these ideas were quite familiar by this time, being exactly those that had been advanced by advocates of workers' compensation statutes[37] and statutory compensation plans in other areas.[38] Such statutory innovation, it has been claimed, gave "a terrific impetus" to the recognition of enterprise liability in the common law.[39]

6 This paper consists of three principal sections. In the first, I analyse the decision in *Rylands v Fletcher* to see whether it represented, as some have claimed, merely the application or extension of an existing cause of action, or alternatively a demonstrably new principle of liability. Having come down in favour of the latter interpretation, I then – in the second main section of the paper – consider the new principle of strict liability in the context of the universally-acknowledged historical trend towards a generalised liability for fault. Although *Rylands v Fletcher* appeared to some later writers as an anachronism, I argue that strict liability was still a living part of the law at the time, and that the decision can be viewed in part as an attempt to define the proper roles of strict liability and fault in a legal world no longer governed by the old forms of action. Finally, I place the case in the context of an emerging theory of enterprise liability, and explain why it represented in some respects an ideal testing ground for the new theory, before considering what evidence there is to suggest that the judges in *Rylands v Fletcher* themselves conceived of their decision in enterprise liability terms.

B. *Rylands v Fletcher* (1868)

1. Overview

7 The facts of the case are too well-known to require full restatement here.[40] In brief, the defendants' reservoir flooded the plaintiff's mine without fault on their part. The defendants had commissioned the reservoir's construction in order to provide water for their mill. After the work was begun, their contrac-

[37] See, e.g., for England, P. Bartrip/S. Burman, *The Wounded Soldiers of Industry: Industrial Compensation Policy*, 1833–97 (1983) and, for the United States, J.F. Witt, The Transformation of Work and the Law of Workplace Accidents, 1842–1910 (1998) 107 Yale LJ 1467.

[38] See, e.g., A.A. Ballantine, A Compensation Plan for Railway Accident Claims (1916) 29 Harv L Rev 705 (1916).

[39] C.O. Gregory (supra fn. 7), 388. See also V.E. Nolan/E. Ursin (supra fn. 7), 21–9 and W.S. Malone, Damage Suits and the Contagious Principle of Workmen's Compensation (1952) 12 *Loyola Law Review* (Loy L Rev) 231.

[40] For a detailed account, using archival material as well as the reports, see A.W.B. Simpson (supra fn. 3).

tors came across certain disused mine-shafts in the reservoir bed and filled them with earth. It seems that the defendants were unaware of their existence at all material times. When the reservoir was filled, one of the shafts burst downwards and the water flowed into abandoned coal workings underneath, which (unbeknownst to everyone) were connected to the plaintiff's mine by underground passages. The flooding ensued. The contractors were negligent, but the general rule of English law then and now is to attribute to the employer only the fault of employees, not independent contractors. For reasons about which we can only speculate, the contractors played no part in the litigation that followed – perhaps because they were insolvent – and their identity remains unknown. The plaintiff proceeded only against the defendants, from whom he sought damages, and the claim was referred to arbitration. The arbitrator subsequently sought the opinion of the Court of Exchequer as to whether on the facts as he had found them the defendants were liable. By a majority of 2-1, the Court ruled that no liability arose (Baron Bramwell dissenting).[41] On appeal to the Exchequer Chamber, Bramwell's dissent was upheld, and a verdict entered in the plaintiff's favour.[42] Delivering the Exchequer Chamber's judgment, Blackburn J laid down what has become known as the rule in *Rylands v Fletcher*:[43]

> We think that the true rule of law is, that the person who, for his own purposes, brings on his land, and collects and keeps there anything likely to do mischief if it escapes, must keep it in at his peril, and, if he does not do so, he is prima facie responsible for all the damage which is the natural consequence of its escape. He can excuse himself by showing that the escape was owing to the plaintiff's default, or, perhaps, that the escape was the consequence of vis major, or the act of God.

On the defendants' further appeal to the House of Lords,[44] the Law Lords ex- 8
pressly endorsed Blackburn's statement of principle, though Lord Cairns' own summary of the relevant law seems to differ from Blackburn's in a number of respects, and is the source of the now generally-accepted requirement that the defendant's use of land must be "non-natural".[45] Blackburn nowhere uses this phrase himself, but he does elsewhere in his judgment state the doctrine as applying to the person "who has brought something on his own property which was not naturally there", and the phrase "non-natural user" may be considered Lord Cairns' paraphrase of Blackburn's words "not naturally there". Neverthe-

[41] *Fletcher v Rylands* (1875) 3 *Hurlstone & Coltman's Exchequer Reports* (H&C) 774, 159 *English Reports* (ER) 737.

[42] *Fletcher v Rylands* (1866) LR 1 *Exchequer Cases* (Exch) 265.

[43] (1866) LR 1 Exch 265, 279–80.

[44] *Rylands v Fletcher* (1868) LR 3 HL 330.

[45] (1868) LR 3 HL 330, 339. It may be doubted whether Cairns in fact conceived of this as adding anything to Blackburn's statement of principle: see F.H. Newark, Non-Natural User and Rylands v. Fletcher (1961) 24 *Modern Law Review* (MLR) 557. Further analysis of the non-natural user requirement may be found in W.T.S. Stallybrass, Dangerous Things and the Non-Natural User of Land (1929) 3 CLJ 376 and D.W. Williams, Non-Natural Use of Land [1973] CLJ 310.

less, non-natural user has come to be regarded as an essential element of the tort, and perhaps its most significant limiting factor.[46]

2. Judicial Reasoning

9 A good deal of debate has focused on the question of the decision's true doctrinal basis. To assess the various contentions, it is necessary to consider in some detail the reasoning in each of the three courts that heard the case.

a) Court of Exchequer (1965)

10 In the Court of Exchequer, Baron Bramwell (dissenting) would have found for the plaintiff on the basis that he had a right to be free from "foreign" (i.e. artificially diverted) water, and the defendants had no right to divert it to the plaintiff's land, whether wittingly or unwittingly.[47] In his view, it was not necessary to prove that there had been a trespass, a nuisance or negligence, but he considered that the flooding was in any case both a trespass (because of the physical invasion of the plaintiff's land) and a nuisance. In connection with the latter, he noted that "[t]he nuisance is not in the reservoir, but in the water escaping."[48] In neither trespass nor nuisance was it necessary to show negligence. This, he admitted, was the appropriate standard for highway collisions, but only because "[w]here two carriages come in collision, if there is no negligence in either it is as much the act of the one driver as of the other that they meet."[49] Where this difficulty of causal attribution did not arise, it seems that he considered liability to be strict: *sic utere tuo ut alienum non laedas*.[50] In case he had got this wrong, however, Bramwell concluded with the observation that the defendants could be held liable for the tort of their independent contractor, though to him this made no difference on the facts, given his view that the defendants had in any case been acting at their peril.[51]

11 The other judges in the Court of Exchequer, whose view prevailed on the day but not in the long run, were opposed to Bramwell in different ways. Baron Martin stated that there was no trespass, because the damage resulting from the defendants' acts was consequential rather than immediate, and no nuisance in the sense of "something hurtful or injurious to the senses."[52] There being no liability under these specific causes of action, it was necessary to turn to general principle to see if the claim could otherwise be sustained. Martin stated that the general requirement of negligence was well-established in connection with injury to the person and personal property, albeit with certain exceptions, and that he could see no reason why damage to real property should be gov-

[46] See, e.g., *Cambridge Water Co Ltd v Eastern Counties Leather plc* [1994] 2 *Appeal Cases* (AC) 264, 299 per Lord Goff.
[47] (1865) 3 H&C 774, 789.
[48] Ibid.
[49] (1865) 3 H&C 774, 790.
[50] Ibid.
[51] (1865) 3 H&C 774, 790–1.
[52] (1865) 3 H&C 774, 792.

erned by a different rule.[53] He also stated that, even if the defendants' could be held liable for the negligence of their contractors (which was by no means certain), the allegation of negligence failed for want of proof that the contractors knew or had notice of the underground passages which allowed the water to flow into the plaintiff's mine: "How can a man be said to be negligent when he is ignorant of the circumstance which requires the exercise of care?"[54]

Chief Baron Pollock, delivering the third, decisive judgment, considered that the plaintiff's right to be free from foreign water, if it was a right recognised by the law at all, applied only to surface-water and not to water coming otherwise onto his land. In the absence of relevant authority, "the safer course" was to find for the defendants.[55] Pollock concluded by stating that the plaintiff had shown neither that the defendants' contractors had been negligent, nor that (even if they had been) the defendants should be held responsible for that negligence.[56] 12

b) Exchequer Chamber (1866)

In a judgment delivered by Blackburn J, the six judges of the Exchequer Chamber preferred Bramwell's approach in the court below,[57] and stated the principle (set out above[58]) that has come to be known as "the rule in *Rylands v Fletcher*." On its face, it makes no mention of either trespass or nuisance, or any other specific cause of action, but Blackburn immediately went on to justify the principle in terms which suggest he viewed it as the crystallisation of a number of existing liabilities:[59] 13

> The person whose grass or corn is eaten down by the escaping cattle of his neighbour, or whose mine is flooded by the water from his neighbour's reservoir, or whose cellar is invaded by the filth of his neighbour's privy, or whose habitation is made unhealthy by the fumes and noisome vapours of his neighbour's alkali works, is damnified without any fault of his own; and it seems but reasonable and just that the neighbour, who has brought something on his own property which was not naturally there, harmless to others so long as it is confined to his own property, but which he knows to be mischievous if it gets on his neighbour's, should be obliged to make good the damage which ensues if he does not succeed in confining it to his own property. But for his act in bringing it there no mischief could have accrued, and it seems but just that he should at his peril keep it there so that no mischief may accrue, or answer for the natural and anticipated consequences. And upon authority, this we think is established to be the law whether the things so brought be beasts, or water, or filth, or stenches.

[53] (1865) 3 H&C 774, 793.
[54] (1865) 3 H&C 774, 794–5.
[55] (1865) 3 H&C 774, 798.
[56] Ibid.
[57] *Fletcher v Rylands* (1866) LR 1 Exch 265, 278.
[58] No. 7.
[59] *Fletcher v Rylands* (1866) LR 1 Exch 265, 280.

Of the specific causes of action mentioned here as illustrations of Blackburn's general proposition, and analogies to the case before him, the first is the long established but "highly special"[60] liability for cattle trespass, the second (invasion by filth) an example derived from the case of *Tenant v Goldwin*,[61] which Blackburn seems also to have considered to be trespass,[62] and the third (fumes and noisome vapours) is clearly nuisance. To these he apparently added another in a later passage of his judgment: the strict liability attaching to the keeper of an animal which he knows to have a vicious propensity (the *scienter* action).[63]

14 Having set out and justified his principle of strict liability, Blackburn then addressed its role relative to that of negligence. He admitted that there were many cases in which proof of negligence was indeed essential, but stated that they were distinguishable from the case before him:[64]

> Traffic on the highways, whether by land or sea, cannot be conducted without exposing those whose persons or property are near it to some inevitable risk; and that being so, those who go on the highway, or have their property adjacent to it, may well be held to do so subject to their taking upon themselves the risk of injury from that inevitable danger; and persons who by the licence of the owner pass near to warehouses where goods are being raised or lowered, certainly do so subject to the inevitable risk of accident. In neither case, therefore, can they recover without proof of want of care or skill occasioning the accident; and it is believed that all the cases in which inevitable accident has been held an excuse for what primâ facie was a trespass, can be explained on the same principle, viz., that the circumstances were such as to shew that the plaintiff had taken that risk upon himself.

It is evident, then, that Blackburn considered strict liability ("action at peril") to be the general principle, and liability for negligence the exception – justified by the plaintiff's voluntary assumption of the risk of non-negligent injury. He therefore reached the same conclusion as Bramwell as to the correct standard to apply in collision cases – but for different reasons. (Bramwell had relied upon the difficulty of causal attribution in the absence of a requirement of fault.) For both of them, however, strict liability was the default position.

[60] P.H. Winfield (supra fn. 2), 194.

[61] (1704) 2 *Lord Raymond's Reports* (Ld Raym) 1089, 1 *Salkeld's King's Bench Reports* 21, 360. In fact, Salkeld (unlike Raymond) reports Chief Justice Holt as deciding on the basis of trespass.

[62] See (1866) LR 1 Exch 265, 286 where he adopts the language of Salkeld's report of the decision, saying "he whose stuff it is must keep it that it may not trespass". The difficulty with this analysis is that the action was brought in case, not trespass. Cf. Lord Raymond's report, which does not employ the term "trespass". Most modern writers consider the case to be correctly regarded as one in private nuisance: see, e.g., R.F.V. Heuston/R.A. Buckley, *Salmond & Heuston on the Law of Torts* (21st edn. 1996), 53 and A. Dugdale (ed.), *Clerk & Lindsell on Torts* (18th edn. 2000), § 18-08. Cf. P.H. Winfield (supra fn. 2), 193 ("an innominate … [action] upon the case").

[63] (1866) LR 1 Exch 265, 280.

[64] (1866) LR 1 Exch 265, 286–7.

The Court's reasoning made it unnecessary to address the question of the defendants' liability for the negligence of their contractors.[65] 15

c) House of Lords (1868)

Only two members of the House of Lords are identified in the report: Lord Cairns, the Lord Chancellor (LC), and Lord Cranworth. (A third member of the House had to be present to ensure a quorum, and his identity has stimulated much discussion. He is now believed to have been the Archbishop of Armagh.[66]) Both Cairns and Cranworth expressly approved Blackburn's statement of the relevant law.[67] As has already been noted, Lord Cairns also expressed the principle in his own (rather long-winded) words, introducing the concept of "non-natural user". Having stated that the plaintiff could not have complained if the flooding had resulted from the defendants' "natural user" of the land (i.e. its use "for any purpose for which it might in the ordinary course of the enjoyment of land be used"), he continued:[68] 16

> On the other hand if the Defendants, not stopping at the natural use of their close, had desired to use it for any purpose which I may term a non-natural use, for the purpose of introducing into the close that which in its natural condition was not in or upon it, for the purpose of introducing water either above or below ground ..., – and if in consequence of their doing so ... the water came to escape and to pass off into the close of the Plaintiff, then it appears to me that that which the Defendants were doing they were doing at their own peril; and, if in the course of their doing it, the evil arose to which I have referred, the evil, namely, of the escape of the water and its passing away to the close of the Plaintiff and injuring the Plaintiff, then for the consequence of that, in my opinion, the Defendants would be liable.

Lord Cranworth, having endorsed Blackburn's statement of the rule, put the general principle in rather wider terms, without any mention of a "natural user" exception:[69] 17

> In considering whether a Defendant is liable to a Plaintiff for damage which the Plaintiff may have sustained, the question in general is not whether the Defendant has acted with due care and caution, but whether his acts have occasioned the damage ... [T]he doctrine is founded on good sense. For when one person, in managing his own affairs, causes, however innocently, damage to another, it is obviously only just that he should be the party to suffer. He is bound sic uti suo ut non lædat alienum.

[65] (1866) LR 1 Exch 265, 287.
[66] See R.F.V. Heuston, Who was the Third Lord in Rylands v Fletcher? (1970) 86 LQR 160.
[67] *Rylands v Fletcher* (1868) LR 3 HL 330, 340.
[68] (1868) LR 3 HL 330, 338.
[69] (1868) LR 3 HL 330, 338.

Like Bramwell and Blackburn, then, he considered strict liability to be the general rule, and liability for negligence the exception. The same cannot be said of Cairns who, in his formulation of the applicable principles, drew a distinction between natural and non-natural uses of land in such a way as to make the former appear the usual rule, and the latter (where strict liability applied) the exceptional case.

18 The question of the defendants' liability for their contractor's negligence was not at issue in the House of Lords.

3. Analysis

a) The Application or Extension of Pre-existing Principle?

19 The first question to address is whether liability under *Rylands v Fletcher* is an application of a pre-existing principle, even if by means of an extension of a recognised cause of action, or a new and independent liability. The former interpretation has been advanced by those who have been keen to minimize the case's impact. Five possible bases of liability may be considered.

(i) Trespass

20 Trespass was expressly relied upon by Baron Bramwell in the Court of Exchequer,[70] and parts of Blackburn's judgment in the Court of Exchequer Chamber provide a measure of support for the view that the liability was essentially one for trespass. Of the three illustrative cases he refers to in support of his rule, two may be considered trespass. However, both are problematic: cattle trespass has always been considered a case apart – "the law of torts has grown up historically in separate compartments and … beasts have travelled in a compartment of their own"[71] – while (as we have noted) it is far from certain that the case of the escaping filth, *Tenant v Goldwin*, is properly considered a case of trespass, rather than nuisance.[72] In fact, throughout his judgment, Blackburn seems to employ the term "trespass" rather more loosely than (say) Baron Martin in the Court of Exchequer. Later writers, however, have tended to side with Martin over both Bramwell and Blackburn on this point, finding the facts of the case to fall the wrong side of the direct/consequential borderline,[73] though Bohlen has noted how narrow the point at issue actually was:[74]

[70] Cf. *Nichols v Marsland* (1875) LR 10 Exch 255, 260 where he described *Rylands v Fletcher* as a case where "the defendant poured the water into the plaintiff's mine" without actually using the term "trespass". It appears that he preferred "pour" to "escape" because the latter misleadingly suggested that water was an active agent: *Carstairs v Taylor* (1871) LR 6 Exch 217, 221.

[71] *Read v J Lyons & Co Ltd* [1947] AC 156, 182 per Lord Simonds. The former common law liability has now been abolished and replaced with a statutory claim under Animals Act 1971, sec. 4.

[72] See no. 13 above.

[73] See, e.g., F.H. Bohlen (supra fn. 2), 311–3; J.G. Fleming, *The Law of Torts* (9th edn. 1998), 375. Cf. P. Keeton (supra fn. 2), 474 (not trespass because the invasion was unintentional). Most of the other leading texts do not even consider the possibility that trespass might be the basis of the cause of action.

[74] F.H. Bohlen (supra fn. 2), 311.

> Had the earth in the shaft given way as soon as the water was poured into the reservoir, instead of resisting the pressure for a few days, the injury would have been direct and the defendant admittedly liable in trespass.

Quite apart from these considerations, the structure of Blackburn's judgment as a whole shows that he cannot have treated trespass as the underlying basis of liability: the third illustration he gives of his general principle – pollution by fumes from an alkali works – is clearly a case of nuisance rather than trespass.

(ii) Nuisance

Conceding pollution by fumes to be nuisance, what of Blackburn's two other illustrations, that we have until now assumed to be cases of trespass? In fact, the case of invasion by filth, *Tenant v Goldwin*, is regarded by most commentators as in reality a case of nuisance, rather than trespass, and (at a stretch) cattle trespass could also be so considered, though its juristic roots are different.[75] Yet neither Blackburn nor the Law Lords at any point employed the term "nuisance". Nevertheless, the view that nuisance was the true basis of the liability in *Rylands v Fletcher* has been advanced by such distinguished commentators as Prosser[76] and Newark.[77] It has also received considerable judicial support, most notably in two recent decisions of the House of Lords, *Cambridge Water Co v Eastern Counties Leather Plc*[78] and *Transco plc v Stockport Metropolitan Borough Council*.[79] In the first of these decisions, Lord Goff expressly approved Newark's view that *Rylands v Fletcher* was "a simple case of nuisance", which merely affirmed that "negligence is not an element in the tort of nuisance", its only novelty lying in its application of the tort to a single, isolated escape from the defendant's land.[80] 21

However, if the liability under *Rylands v Fletcher* is indeed "a species of nuisance",[81] it is substantially distinct from nuisance as commonly understood, and the better view is that (private) nuisance and the liability under *Rylands v Fletcher* should be regarded as separate causes of action. Indeed in 1931 Winfield went so far as to identify nine differences between the two heads of claim,[82] and, even if not all remain convincing today, it is still possible to identify a number of incontrovertible points of distinction, notably the re- 22

[75] See no. 20 above.
[76] Supra fn. 2.
[77] The Boundaries of Nuisance (1949) 65 LQR 480.
[78] [1994] 2 AC 264.
[79] [2004] 2 AC 1.
[80] F.H. Newark (supra fn. 77), 487–8, cited approvingly by Lord Goff at [1994] 2 AC 264, 298. See also *Transco plc v Stockport Metropolitan Borough Council* [2004] 2 AC 1, 7 per Lord Bingham, and 15 and 17 per Lord Hoffmann. Dalton has disputed whether liability in nuisance for a single isolated escape really was novel: supra fn. 3, 148n.
[81] As F.H. Bohlen too was prepared to accept: supra fn. 2, 431.
[82] P.H. Winfield (supra fn. 2), 195–6. G.W. Paton, Liability for Nuisance (1942) 37 Ill L Rev 1, 3 and W.A. Seavey, Nuisance: Contributory Negligence and Other Mysteries (1952) 65 Harv L Rev 984, 985–6 also endeavour to distinguish the two liabilities.

quirement of escape under *Rylands v Fletcher*, which has no analogue in nuisance,[83] and the concept of non-natural use of land which, in nuisance, becomes the requirement of *unreasonable interference* with land. This shifts the focus from the defendant's use of land, considered in isolation, to the reasonableness of his interference with the claimant's land, which requires an evaluation of both his conduct and the extent of the interference.[84] Even more significantly, it introduces an evaluative element by substituting "unreasonable" for "non-natural", with the result that a nuisance can be considered a wrong which is prima facie to be prohibited by injunction,[85] whereas – under *Rylands v Fletcher* – the defendant's non-natural user was "a nuisance as it were held in suspense, not of itself unlawful, and so preventable by legal process, or actionable until harm actually results from it."[86] Given these differences, it is understandable that modern textbooks persist in treating the two liabilities in separate chapters,[87] and that recent contributions to the journal literature have argued for the "distinctiveness" of liability under *Rylands v Fletcher*.[88]

(iii) Sic utere tuo ut alienum non lædas

23 In the Court of Exchequer, one of the express bases of Baron Bramwell's judgment in favour of the plaintiff was the principle expressed by the Latin maxim,[89] and Lord Cranworth also expressly relied upon it in the House of Lords.[90] There is also later support for the view that this is the true principle of *Rylands v Fletcher*. In *Rickards v Lothian*, for example, Lord Moulton stated that the case was "nothing other than an application of the old maxim *Sic utere tuo ut alienum non lædas*",[91] and this was also accepted in several other decisions of the time.[92] However, Blackburn in the Exchequer Chamber at no

[83] Private nuisance normally involves something emanating from the defendant's land (*Hunter v Canary Wharf Ltd* [1997] 655, 685 per Lord Goff) but this is not a necessary element of the tort: see, e.g., *L.E. Jones (Insurance Brokers) Ltd v Portsmouth City Council* [2003] 1 *Weekly Law Reports* (WLR) 427.

[84] G. Williams/B. Hepple, *Foundations of the Law of Tort* (2nd edn. 1984), 123–7. Cf. J. Murphy (supra fn. 3), 644–56.

[85] *Pride of Derby and Derbyshire Angling Association Ltd v British Celanese Ltd* [1953] *Law Reports, Chancery Division, 3rd Series* (Ch) 149.

[86] F.H. Bohlen (supra fn. 2), 431. Cf. W.L. Prosser (supra fn. 2), who viewed the liability for "absolute nuisance" under Rylands v Fletcher (420) as distinguishable from intentional and negligent nuisances. W.A. Seavey (supra fn. 82), however, uses "absolute nuisance" to refer to the intentional creation of a dangerous condition (991).

[87] See, e.g., R.F.V. Heuston/R.A. Buckley (supra fn. 62); W.V.H. Rogers, *Winfield & Jolowicz on Tort* (16th edn. 2002); J. Murphy, *Street on Torts* (11th edn. 2003). In Australia, J.G. Fleming (supra fn. 73) kept a separate chapter for *Rylands v Fletcher* even after the High Court declared the principle to have been absorbed by the ordinary law of negligence (*Burnie Port Authority v General Jones Pty Ltd* (1994) 179 *Commonwealth Law Reports* (CLR) 520).

[88] J. Murphy (supra fn. 3), 669; D. Nolan (supra fn. 3).

[89] (1865) 3 H&C 774, 790.

[90] (1868) LR 3 HL 330, 338.

[91] [1913] AC 263, 275 per Lord Moulton.

[92] See, e.g, *Crowhurst v Amersham Burial Board* (1878) 4 *Exchequer Division* (Ex D) 5, 11 per Kelly CB; *Snow v Whitehead* (1882) 27 *Chancery Division, 2nd Series* (Ch D) 588, 591 per Kay J; *Musgrove v Pandelis* [1919] 2 *King's Bench* (KB) 43, 47 per Bankes LJ, 49 per Warrington LJ and 51 per Duke LJ.

point used the Latin phrase himself. Though the English version – "every one must so use his own as not to do damage to another" – appears twice in his judgment, both instances are in the same long quotation from Lord Raymond's report of Holt CJ's opinion in *Tenant v Goldwin*,[93] which Blackburn dealt with at length only to correct Martin's misrepresentation of the case in the court below.[94] Having done so, he was careful to formulate his own rule in narrower terms, limiting it to things the defendant brings and keeps on his land: "he who brings and keeps anything … on his premises, must at his peril prevent it from getting on his neighbour's, or make good all the damage which is the natural consequence of its doing so."[95]

Whether *sic utere* can meaningfully act as the underlying principle of strict liability may in any case be doubted. It provides no grounds for distinguishing those acts or "uses" that give rise to strict liability and those which do not, and it is "inaccurate" in so far as it suggests that *all* damage resulting from the defendant's use of his land is actionable.[96] (I take as read "the impossibility of general strict liability".[97]) In fact, it is not clear that *sic utere* necessarily embodies an absolute obligation at all, rather than one of reasonable care. Even if one assumes it expresses a strict liability, the difficulty still remains that it appears to express *the conclusion* that strict liability ought to be imposed, rather than the grounds on which the conclusion is reached.[98] 24

(iv) Liability for Contractors' Negligence

In his analysis of *Rylands v Fletcher* and "Liability without Fault", Thayer submitted that "[t]he true statement of the case is that the law charges the defendant with a non-delegable duty."[99] More recently, the majority of the High Court of Australia, in a collegiate judgment, has sought to assimilate liability under *Rylands v* Fletcher under the "ordinary" law of negligence on the basis of a non-delegable duty of care owed by those who store dangerous substances or allow dangerous activities on their premises.[100] Whether this reliance 25

[93] (1704) 2 Ld Raym 1089, 1092.
[94] (1866) LR 1 Exch 265, 283–5.
[95] Ibid., 285. Cf. Lord Cairns' distinction between natural and non-natural users: no. 16 above.
[96] *Sedleigh-Denfield v O'Callaghan* [1940] AC 880, 903 per Lord Wright, criticised by D.R. Coquillette, Mosses From an Old Manse: Another Look at Some Historic Property Cases About the Environment (1979) 64 *Cornell Law Review* (Cornell L Rev) 761, 781 who argues that *sic utere* only came into play once it had been established that the plaintiff had suffered actionable damage, and was simply designed to prevent the defendant excusing himself on grounds of social utility.
[97] S.R. Perry, The Impossibility of General Strict Liability (1988) 1 *Canadian Journal of Law & Jurisprudence* 147. See also P.H. Winfield, The Myth of Absolute Liability (1926) 42 LQR 37, 38. Cf. G. Calabresi (supra fn. 21), 64–7.
[98] D. Ibbetson, *A Historical Introduction to the Law of Obligations* (1999), 106. For further analysis, see C. Dalton (supra fn. 3), 169–72.
[99] E.R. Thayer (supra fn. 2), 808 and 809. See also F. Pollock (supra fn. 2), 55–56; F.H. Bohlen (supra fn. 2), 299n; P.H. Winfield (supra fn. 2), 193–4.
[100] *Burnie Port Authority v General Jones Pty Ltd* (1994) 179 CLR 520, §§ 35–42, per Mason CJ and Deane, Dawson, Toohey and Gaudron JJ.

upon a non-delegable duty is "ordinary" may perhaps be doubted. Still, it is quite clear that *Rylands v Fletcher* was *not* in fact decided on the basis of the defendants' responsibility for their contractors' negligence: Blackburn in the Exchequer Chamber stated expressly that it was unnecessary to consider the issue, given his finding for the plaintiff on other grounds,[101] and the matter was not even considered by the House of Lords.[102] It seems therefore unnecessary to pursue this interpretation of the decision any further.

(v) Personal Negligence

26 Even more transparently contrary to the evidence of the judgments themselves, it has been suggested that the case is best regarded as an example of liability for personal negligence, because non-natural and ultra-hazardous activites are inherently faulty, the fault being found "not in the manner of doing, but in the very doing itself."[103] However, whether or not there is any great difference between the two approaches in the practical result, which Thayer was inclined to doubt,[104] whether or not negligence might have been found on the facts of the case (*e.g.* under the doctrine of *res ipse loquitur*), as suggested by Jeremiah Smith,[105] and whether or not it would be advisable to reclassify the liability as one arising in negligence, as the High Court of Australia has quite recently done,[106] it is quite clear that both Blackburn and the House of Lord were imposing a liability *without fault*, hence their frequent use of the terminology of action at peril. It may perhaps be the case that, had the law of negligence been more developed than it was at the time, they would have seen no need to invoke a rule of strict liability,[107] but this only concedes that the liability was perceived by its authors as strict, not one for negligence. Though strict liability may indeed sometimes be imposed because fault is somehow present *in the background*,[108] it is my argument that *Rylands v Fletcher* was perceived as a true liability without fault, and not as an indirect way of bringing about the reparation of a wrong.

b) A New Tort

27 If the rule in *Rylands v Fletcher* cannot be fitted into any cause of action previously known to English law, it must be regarded as stating a new principle of liability – in fact, a new tort. That the majority of judges who decided the case thought that they were dealing with something new, not covered by existing caselaw, is indicated by a number of remarks in the judgments. In the Court of Exchequer, Bramwell stated that the issue arising was "singularly

[101] (1866) LR 1 Exch 265, 287.
[102] See no. 18 above.
[103] See, e.g., J.L. Coleman, *Risks and Wrongs* (1992), 368–9.
[104] E.R. Thayer (supra fn. 2), 807–8.
[105] J. Smith, Tort and Absolute Liability – Suggested Changes in Classification III (1917) 30 Harv L Rev 409, 410 and 414n.
[106] *Burnie Port Authority v General Jones Pty Ltd* (1994) 179 CLR 520.
[107] J. Smith (supra fn. 105), 414.
[108] See no. 68 below.

wanting in authority",[109] Pollock noted that it had "[a]pparently ... never before been the subject of litigation",[110] and Martin observed that none of the cases relied upon by the plaintiff was direct authority for the principle for which he contended.[111] It may be objected that these remarks are equally consistent with there being a lack of authority as to whether the case before the court was covered by an existing cause of action, but Blackburn's judgment in the Exchequer Chamber provides less equivocal support for the "new tort" thesis. It is, above all, the structure of his judgment that demonstrates that he viewed his rule as a rationalisation of several distinct causes of action, rather than an application or extension of any individual cause of action. As he derived his principle from a number of *different* liabilities – for straying cattle, overflowing filth (which *he* seems to have considered a trespass), and pollution by alkali fumes (nuisance) – it is quite clear that he did not view his rule as limited to any one amongst them. In any case, "[i]t would be wrong to dismiss it as a convenient summary of the principle underlying several specific torts which had existed long before 1866."[112] Its novelty lay precisely in its being a general principle in an area in which there had only previously been specific actions dealing with individual things (cattle, filth, fumes, etc.). Neither the *sic utere* doctrine nor the concept of action at peril were comparable, because in themselves they were too vague and too inclusive to provide a workable test of liability; they could only meaningfully be employed where it was established on other grounds that the plaintiff had suffered actionable damage (i.e. *injuria*, not merely *damnum*).[113]

Wigmore, in the closing years of the nineteenth century, provided a lyrical description of how the Exchequer Chamber's judgment brought together sundry 28
examples of liability for "action at peril" that had survived from the early law:[114]

> They wandered about, unhoused and unshepherded ... in the pathless fields of jurisprudence, until they were met ... by the master-mind of Mr Justice Blackburn, who guided them to the safe fold where they have since rested.

Blackburn, said Wigmore, was not the first to attempt "a co-ordination of these kindred instances", but:[115]

[109] *Fletcher v Rylands* (1875) 3 H&C 774, 788.
[110] Ibid., 797.
[111] Ibid., 792.
[112] P.H. Winfield (supra fn. 2), 193. See also E.R. Thayer, Judicial Legislation: Its Legitimate Function in the Development of the Common Law (1891) 5 Harv L Rev 172, 185.
[113] See no. 24 above, C. Dalton (supra fn. 3), 151–72 and Coquillette (supra fn. 96), 769–81. Dalton (156–7) argues that Bramwell's attempted innovation in the Court of Exchequer was to free the *sic utere* doctrine from specific and independently-recognised rights and duties, and to view such rights and duties as actually derived from the doctrine, not the other way around.
[114] J.H. Wigmore, Responsiblity for Tortious Acts: Its History – III (1894) 7 Harv L Rev 441, 454.
[115] Ibid., 455.

> What gave the exposition on this occasion its novelty and its permanent success was the broad scope of the principle announced, the strength of conviction of its expounder, and the clearness of his exposition, and perhaps, too, the fact that the time was ripe for its acceptance.

29 A number of factors may be advanced as reasons why "the time was ripe" for acceptance of Blackburn's doctrine. One, to which I shall return later, was the then-current debate as to how to reconcile private rights with competing public interests. Another was the upheaval that the legal system and legal procedures were experiencing as part of the transition from the old writ system – in which, in Maine's famous phrase, "substantive law has at first the look of being gradually secreted in the interstices of procedure"[116] – to the system of fact-pleading focused on substantive justice that was incrementally introduced by statute in the period 1832 to 1875.[117] Even before this time, the writ system had undergone extensive informal transformation as the once-rigid distinctions between forms of action were loosened,[118] and the first efforts were made to identify general grounds of liability (*e.g.* negligence).[119] But statute gave the transformation further impetus. A unified form of writ was introduced in 1832.[120] Subsequently, the Common Law Procedure Act of 1852 stipulated that it was no longer necessary to specify in the writ a particular cause of action, and allowed the joinder of different causes of action in the same proceedings; trespass could now be joined with case. By the time that *Rylands v Fletcher* came to be decided, therefore – as Baron Bramwell himself remarked in another case – the forms of action remained in name only, having been "practically abolished" with the intention of ensuring that, "as far as possible …, there should never be a question as to which was the form."[121] Substantive justice was the goal, not the application of accumulated procedural technicalities passed down from generation to generation: "all this useless, and worse than useless, learning should be disregarded, and the matter decided on its substance."[122]

30 *Rylands v Fletcher*, then, was "the product of a peculiarly open and transitional moment in the development of the common law … as the grip of the forms of action loosened, and the search for substantive principle intensified …"[123] For Pollock, writing in 1887, it was in the "classical period" of English law between the Common Law Procedure Act 1852 and the final abolition of the

[116] H. Maine, *Dissertations on Early Law and Custom* (1883), 389.
[117] See, e.g., J.H. Baker (supra fn. 6), 67–9.
[118] See, e.g., M.J. Prichard, Trespass, Case and the Rule in *Williams v. Holland* [1964] CLJ 234.
[119] See, e.g., P.H. Winfield, The History of Negligence in the Law of Torts (1926) 42 LQR 184, especially 194–9.
[120] Uniformity of Process Act 1832.
[121] *Bryant v Herbert* (1878) 3 *Common Pleas Division* (CPD) 389, 390.
[122] (1878) 3 CPD 389, 392 per Bramwell B.
[123] C. Dalton (supra fn. 3), 28–9. In contrast, G. Samuel's view that that the abolition of the forms of action left the common law "facing a genuine epistemological crisis" seems unduly alarmist: Classification of Obligations and the Impact of Constructivist Epistemologies (1997) 17 *Legal Studies* (LS) 448, 463.

forms of action in 1875 that "[t]he really scientific treatment of principles" began.[124] These years "were among the most illustrious in the course of English jurisprudence", as the law was "enriched" by the likes of Blackburn and Bramwell. "The old Court of Exchequer Chamber," Pollock asserted, "was never more brilliant than in the last ten years of its life."[125] This institutional context and intellectual climate – added to the evidence of the judgments – provides good reason for seeing in *Rylands v Fletcher* a self-conscious attempt to grapple with the most important substantive issue of nineteenth-century tort law: the respective roles of strict liability and fault.

C. *Rylands v Fletcher*, Strict Liability and the Rise of the Fault Principle

1. Initial Reactions: *Rylands v Fletcher* Under Attack

The English courts showed no initial reluctance to apply *Rylands v Fletcher*,[126] 31
suggesting they saw no incoherence in allowing a principle of strict liability to co-exist alongside other tortious liabilities for negligence. On the other side of the Atlantic, however, there was fierce criticism of the case. In two landmark decisions of 1873 – *Losee v Buchanan*[127] and *Brown v Collins*[128]– the Court of Appeals of New York and the Supreme Judicial Court of New Hampshire declined to follow the English precedent, which they affirmed was in direct conflict with the law as settled in the United States,[129] and attacked the decision as a throwback to "superficial, crude, and undigested notions" of responsibility for damage that were the product of an "immature" jurisprudence and not suited to "modern, progressive, industrial pursuits".[130] The demands of "civilized society" required individuals to give up many of their "natural rights", and to accept the risk of accidental injury from activities conducted by other persons without fault on their part.[131] In a particularly withering passage, Doe J of the New Hampshire court suggested that adoption of the rule in *Rylands v Fletcher* would represent a return to barbarism and an obstacle to progress:[132]

[124] F. Pollock, *The Law of Torts: A Treatise on the Principles of Obligations Arising from Civil Wrongs in the Common Law* (1887), vii (quoted by C. Dalton (supra fn. 3), 36).
[125] F. Pollock, The Law of England I-L Victoriae (1887) 3 LQR 343, 345. (It is, admittedly, unlikely that Pollock was thinking here specifically of *Rylands v Fletcher*.)
[126] See, e.g., *Crompton v Lea* (1874) LR 19 *Equity Cases* (Eq) 115, *Humphries v Cousins* (1877) 2 CPD 239 and *Powell v Fall* (1880) 5 *Queen's Bench Division* (QBD) 597. Even from the early days, however, a number of specific defences were recognised: see no. 67 below.
[127] (1873) 51 *New York Reports* (NY) 476, *American Reports* (10 Am Rep) 623.
[128] (1873) 53 *New Hampshire Reports* (NH) 442, 16 Am Rep 372.
[129] (1873) 51 NY 476, 486–7 per Earl C; *Brown v Collins* (1873) 53 NH 442, 450 per Doe J.
[130] *Brown v Collins*, 53 NH 442, 445 per Doe J.
[131] *Losee v Buchanan* (1873) 51 NY 476, 484 per Earl C.
[132] *Brown v Collins*, 53 NH 442, 448. For further analysis, see J.P. Reid, Experience or Reason: The Tort Theories of Holmes and Doe (1965) 18 Vand L Rev 405, 411–20 (1965).

> [I]t would … recognize the peculiar rights of savage life in a wilderness, ignore the rights growing out of a civilized state of society, and make a distinction not warranted by the enlightened spirit of the common law: it would impose a penalty upon efforts, made in a reasonable, skilful, and careful manner, to rise above a condition of barbarism. It is impossible that legal principle can throw so serious an obstacle in the way of progress and improvement.

32 Others have taken up the refrain of *Rylands v Fletcher* as the relic of a bygone age. There is certainly a whiff of it in the frequent, sniffy uses of the adjectives "primitive" and "crude" in various early discussions of the case,[133] and a hint of social Darwinism in analyses of "the process of evolution"[134] by which fault came to replace action at peril as the predominant standard of liability in English law. One recalls here Ames's famous encapsulation of the historical transformation: "The ethical standard of reasonable conduct has replaced the unmoral standard of acting at one's peril."[135] Most outspoken of all academic critics, Jeremiah Smith said of Lord Cairns' test of non-natural user, that it was "either hopelessly vague, or totally irreconcilable with the progress of civilization, or with anything save a return to savage life and primitive conditions."[136] And, for Thayer, another trenchant critic, "such a result as *Rylands v Fletcher* produces in our system is not tolerable, and those courts have done well who have flatly refused to have anything to do with it".[137] Usually, however, there was a begrudging acceptance that strict liability might, in spite of everything, be tolerated in rare cases for reasons of public policy,[138] though this was most often seen as a matter for the legislature rather than the courts.[139]

2. Holmes and Pollock

33 There was a more measured response from Oliver Wendell Holmes and Sir Frederick Pollock, who were the leading figures of the first generation of common law theorists coming after the decision.[140] Their closer proximity to it in point of time might be expected to have given them a fuller understanding of its legal context than that possessed by their successors. But we should be wary of treating them as impartial observers of events unfurling before them, for both had their own agendas to pursue. Dalton, in fact, has submitted that Holmes and Pollock shared a commitment to the fault principle as the unifying presence in modern tort law, and were therefore predisposed to find the strict liability of *Rylands v Fletcher* anomalous. Their response was to deliber-

[133] See, e.g., E.R. Thayer (supra fn. 2), 813; J. Smith (supra fn. 105), 413–4. See also J.B. Ames, Law and Morals (1908) 22 Harv L Rev 97, 97.
[134] *Read v J Lyons & Co* [1947] AC 156, 171 per Lord Macmillan.
[135] J.B. Ames, (supra fn. 133), 99.
[136] J. Smith, Liability of the Landowners to Children Entering without Permission – II (1898) 11 Harv L Rev 434, 443.
[137] E.R. Thayer (supra fn. 2), 814.
[138] See, e.g., J.B. Ames (supra fn. 132), 109.
[139] See, e.g., E.R. Thayer (supra fn. 2), 814–5.
[140] See, generally, C. Dalton (supra fn. 3), 28–29 and 43–58.

ately distance the decision from older liabilities for action at peril, and "to treat *Rylands* as a forward-looking policy exception to the rule" of general fault liability.[141]

Holmes's first published analysis of the case is in 1873, in his essay "The Theory of Torts".[142] At this time, he was prepared to accept that strict liability might be justified on grounds of public policy as a response to the risks inherent in certain non-negligent enterprises:[143] 34

> when, as in *Rylands v Fletcher*, modern courts hold a man liable for the escape of water from a reservoir which he has built upon his land, or for the escape of cattle, although he is not alleged to have been negligent, they do not proceed upon the ground that there is an element of culpability in making such a reservoir, or in keeping cattle ..., but on the principle that it is politic to make those who go into extra-hazardous employments take the risk on their own shoulders.

Holmes contrasted the "more or less thought-out views of public policy" in *Rylands v Fletcher* with the "conceptions of a much ruder sort" underlying the old examples of strict liability.[144] Payment of compensation was required not as the reparation of a wrong, but because the defendant had chosen to engage in an extra-hazardous activity and it was "politic" to make him shoulder the risk.

By 1880, in "Trespass and Nuisance",[145] Holmes has developed his analysis a little. He begins his discussion of the decision in much the same way as before, stressing that the liability is not imposed because "it is wrong to keep cattle or to have a reservoir of water."[146] Now, however, he expressly acknowledges that "[i]t may even be very much for the public good that the dangerous accumulation should be made."[147] If anything, this seems to move him closer to a theory of enterprise liability – which depends crucially on acceptance of the desirability of the defendant's risk-creating activity. But, as he moves towards enterprise liability in one sense, he seems to move away in another, as the only positive justification he offers for the imposition of strict liability is that proof of fault might be too difficult:[148] 35

> as there is a limit to the nicety of inquiry which is possible in a trial, it may be considered that the safest way to secure care is to throw the risk upon the person who decides what precautions shall be taken.

141 C. Dalton (supra fn. 3), 53.
142 O.W. Holmes, The Theory of Torts (1873) 7 *American Law Review* (Am L Rev) 652.
143 O.W. Holmes (supra fn. 142), 653.
144 Ibid., 652.
145 O.W. Holmes, Trespass and Negligence (1880) 14 Am L Rev 1, incorporated the next year in O.W. Holmes (supra fn. 2).
146 O.W. Holmes (supra fn. 145), 27.
147 Ibid., 28.
148 Ibid., 28.

He appears therefore to be impaled on the horns of a dilemma: is strict liability justified because the defendant's activity is *proper*, and properly conducted, but it is politic to make it pay its costs, or because it is *improper*, or improperly conducted, but it is difficult or impossible to prove its impropriety?

36 In fact, Holmes is notoriously difficult to pin down on the general question of strict liability versus fault, and often seems to contradict himself.[149] The dominant modern view, however, is that he endorsed a general fault principle and saw strict liability as marginal.[150] Recently, however, David Rosenberg[151] has offered a revisionist account in which Holmes appears as a champion of strict liability (limited by foreseeability): "his theory of torts is believed to be essentially the opposite of what it was in fact."[152] This is not the occasion to compare the competing claims by way of a full textual examination of Holmes' writings. Suffice it to say that I cannot see Holmes as a champion of strict common law liability as he was quite explicit that it was blameworthiness (in law) that was "the general foundation of legal liability", and that liability without blameworthiness required special justification.[153] Nevertheless, he was keen to ensure his theory was compatible with such pockets of strict liability as then existed. In an illuminating passage, written with typical Holmesian bravado, he argued:[154]

> the public generally profits by individual activity. As action cannot be avoided, and tends to the public good, there is obviously no policy in throwing the hazard of what is at once desirable and inevitable upon the actor … Unless my act is of a nature to threaten others, unless under the circumstances a prudent man would have foreseen the possibility of harm, to make me indemnify my neighbor against the consequences is no more justifiable than to make me do the same thing if I had fallen upon him in a fit, or to compel me to insure him against lightning.

This, contrary perhaps to first appearances, is not an argument against strict liability on grounds of its inhibiting effect upon industry. Whether a prudent man would have foreseen the possibility of harm is not the same as whether he would have taken adequate precautions against that possibility. And Holmes

[149] Consider, e.g., his apparent endorsement of the sentiment that "[n]o case or principle can be found, or if found can be maintained, subjecting an individual to liability for an act done without fault on his part" (supra fn. 2, 94–95).

[150] G.E. White, *Tort Law in America: An Intellectual History* (2nd edn. 2003), 12–19 and 293–6; R.W. Gordon, Book Review (1981) 94 Harv L Rev 903, 916; P.J. Kelley, A Critical Analysis of Holmes's Theory of Torts (1983) 61 *Washington University Law Quarterly* 681, 687–92; T.C. Grey, Accidental Torts (2001) 54 Vand L Rev 1225. E. Ursin, Judicial Creativity and Tort Law (1981) 49 *George Washington Law Review* 229, 271–6 argues that Holmes initially favoured fault liability, but came by the time of "The Path of the Law" in 1897 (supra fn. 34) to support particular innovations tending towards enterprise liability.

[151] D. Rosenberg, *The Hidden Holmes: His Theory of Torts in History* (1995), criticised by A.W.B. Simpson, The Elusive Truth About Holmes (1997) 95 Mich L Rev 2027.

[152] D. Rosenberg (supra fn. 151), 1.

[153] O.W. Holmes (supra fn. 2), 125 and 115–17.

[154] O.W. Holmes (supra fn. 145), 12. Incorporated in O.W. Holmes (supra fn. 2), 95–6.

subsequently confirmed that he intended the formulation to be wide enough to cover strict liability:[155]

> liability to an action does not necessarily import wrong-doing. And this may be admitted without at all impairing the force of the argument in the foregoing lecture, which only requires that people should not be made to pay for accidents which they could not have avoided.

The common justification for both strict liability and liability for fault, therefore, was the defendant's choice to impose foreseeable and avoidable risks on others. But this does not mean that he viewed the two liability standards with equal favour, and there is nothing here which requires us to dissent from the orthodox view that Holmes regarded fault as the general principle, and strict liability as the exception.

In England, Pollock shortly afterwards adopted an analysis of *Rylands v Fletcher* 37
that was very near that of his close friend, with a similar emphasis on the difficulties of proving fault in the conduct of extra-ordinarily dangerous activities:[156]

> the ground on which a rule of strict obligation has been maintained and consolidated by modern authorities is the magnitude of the danger, coupled with the difficulty of proving negligence as the specific cause, in the particular event, of the danger having ripened into actual harm … [T]he course adopted in England has been to preclude questions of detail [sc. as to fault] by making the duty absolute … The law takes notice that certain things are a source of extra-ordinary risk, and a man who exposes his neighbour to such risk is held, although his act is not of itself wrongful, to insure his neighbour against any consequent harm not due to some cause beyond human foresight and control.

The tone here is reluctant acquiescence, not positive enthusiasm. In Pollock's view, "[a] rule casting the responsibility of an insurer on innocent persons is a hard rule, though it may be a just one."[157] It needed, however, to be supported by very strong arguments, and it could be doubted whether *Rylands v Fletcher* had made out the case. Though he refrained from saying so unequivocally, it is clear that Pollock's preference would have been to deal with dangerous accumulations through the ordinary law of negligence, "requiring the defendant to insure diligence in proportion to the manifest risk."[158]

It seems that Pollock's initial analysis was constrained by the perceived needs 38
of deference to judicial authority. In the following decades, that deference slipped away and he admitted, first, to "not much liking" the rule in *Rylands v Fletcher*, which it was "far from certain … was a necessary or politic rule."[159] Subsequently, almost half a century after the decision, Pollock was prepared to

[155] O.W. Holmes (supra fn. 2), 149 referring to his lecture on "Trespass and Negligence" that formed the previous chapter of *The Common Law* (supra fn. 2), 77–129.
[156] F. Pollock (supra fn. 2), 52.
[157] Ibid., 55.
[158] Ibid., 56. In other words, Pollock was arguing for a non-delegable duty of care.
[159] F. Pollock, The Dog and the Potman: Or "Go it, Bob" (1909) 25 LQR 317, 321.

say unequivocally that he "regretted" it.[160] Interestingly, though, his grounds for doing so were not, he said, the alleged "dogma" of "no liability without fault" – of which he remarked: "[a]s an English lawyer, I can only say that we never heard of it here" – but the unnecessary complication it introduced into the law, which was already well-served by other principles having the same practical effect (especially *res ipse loquitur* and the general law of nuisance).[161]

39 In the case of both Holmes and Pollock, therefore, there is considerable substance in the claim that they were inclined to view strict liability under *Rylands v Fletcher* as an anomalous exception to the general rule of liability for fault. The latter was the standard applied in "the great mass of cases."[162] Though they felt obliged to find some justification for the decision, as their analyses were preeminently reasoned explanations of the existing law, they did so without great enthusiasm – and their lack of enthusiasm perhaps skewed their interpretations of the case, particularly in the view, which both Holmes and Pollock advanced, that the rule of strict liability was merely a means of ensuring the culpable were held legally responsible where proof of fault was difficult or impossible.

3. Strict Liability at the Time of *Rylands v Fletcher*

40 The view that liability for fault was at the time the general rule is diametrically opposed to that taken by Bramwell, Blackburn and Cranworth in *Rylands v Fletcher*. To them, action at peril appeared fundamental, and the rule restricting liability to cases of fault was exceptional and required special justification.[163] Who was right?

41 Judged by sheer weight of numbers, liability for fault – in particular, negligence – might well have come by then to appear the norm. Even in the days of horse-drawn conveyances, the highway could be a dangerous place, the more so as better roads lead to considerable increases in average speeds.[164] Though few road traffic claims came before the courts, this appears to have been because – as Chief Justice Cockburn explained in 1869 – "[s]treet accidents generally occur to poor persons who are satisfied with comparatively small compensation, which is readily given them."[165] No doubt the fault principle cast its shadow over such settlements. Meanwhile the advent of the railways produced what has been described as "the first wave of personal injury litigation in English legal history": "Mass transportation … [gave] rise to mass litigation."[166] It was chiefly railway passengers who benefited, however, as most claims by railway employees were barred by the "common employment" rule.[167] In the case of both road

[160] F. Pollock, "A Plea for Historical Interpretation" (1923) 39 LQR 163, 167.
[161] Ibid.
[162] O.W. Holmes (supra fn. 142), 653.
[163] See nos. 10, 14 and 17 above.
[164] W.R. Cornish/G.deN. Clark, *Law and Society in England 1750–1950* (1989), 484.
[165] *Fair v London & North Western Railway* (1869) 21 *Law Times Reports, New Series* 326, 327.
[166] R.W. Kostal, *Law and English Railway Capitalism 1825–1875* (1994), 290 and 255.
[167] Ibid., 257–79. The common employment rule was abolished by the Law Reform (Personal Injuries) Act 1948.

traffic accidents between strangers, and railway accidents pitting passenger against carrier, negligence came to be accepted as the correct standard of liability – as of course it did in several other contexts, too, where claims may have been less frequent. For highway collisions, this had been settled for most practical purposes in the case of *Williams v Holland* in 1833,[168] which ruled that the plaintiff might sue in case instead of trespass even though his injury was the immediate result of the defendant's act, provided the collision was unintentional. (The decision was of great practical importance because only case recognised the maxim *respondeat superior*, and the plaintiff was not necessarily to know at the outset of proceedings whether it was the master or the servant who had been at the reins – and would be non-suited if he chose the wrong action.) For the action on the case, negligence had been recognised as a requirement from the seventeenth century.[169] For railway passengers, authoritative adoption of the negligence standard was almost contemporaneous with the decision in *Rylands v Fletcher*.[170] Intriguingly, Blackburn was the only judge amongst the nine involved in the case who thought a strict liability standard should apply, but he was outvoted in the Court of Queens' Bench,[171] and the majority decision was upheld by a unanimous Exchequer Chamber, in which Baron Bramwell sat but did not deliver a judgment. Blackburn's views here sit rather uncomfortably with his analysis of highway accidents in *Rylands v Fletcher*, where he thought that a negligence test applied because road-users voluntarily assumed the risk of non-negligent injury.[172] In the railway passenger case, the Exchequer Chamber justified the application of the negligence standard by much the same argument. If nothing else, however, Blackburn's judgment confirmed that he considered the action at peril doctrine to have a wider application than simply to actions between neighbouring landowners. In fact, in *Rylands v Fletcher* itself, and in subsequent cases where he considered the scope of the rule, it is apparent that he assumed strict liability would apply not just to interference with interests in land, but also injury to the person and personal property.[173]

[168] (1833) 10 *Bingham's Common Pleas Reports* 112. See further M.J. Prichard (supra fn. 118).

[169] *Mitchil v Alestree* (1676) 1 *Ventris' King's Bench Reports* 295 (bystander); *Aston v Heaven* (1797) 2 *Espinasse's Nisi Prius Reports* 533 (passenger). In the case of the passenger, the same standard applied whether the claim was for breach of duty (tort) or assumpsit (contract).

[170] *Readhead v Midland Railway Co* (1869) LR 4 *Queen's Bench* (QB) 379.

[171] *Readhead v Midland Railway Co* (1867) LR 2 QB 412.

[172] See no. 14 above.

[173] See, e.g., *Fletcher v Rylands* (1866) LR 1 Exch 265, 280 (where Blackburn thought there was an analogy with the strict liability on the owner of an animal he knows to have "a vicious propensity to attack man") and 286 (where he talked of "drowning" as if this would be a mischief covered by the rule: but cf. fn. 238 below); *Jones v Festiniog Railway Co* (1868) LR 3 QB 733, where he applied the rule in a case of damage to a chattel (the plaintiff's haystack); and *Cattle v Stockton Waterworks Co* (1875) LR 10 QB 453, 457, where he suggested that workers in a flooded mine would be able to claim for damage to their clothes and tools. See further J. Murphy (supra fn. 3), 653–4. It may be noted that, though private nuisance is certainly now regarded as a tort to land, it still seems to allow for the award of damages for consequential loss of chattels: see *Hunter v Canary Wharf Ltd* [1997] AC 655, 706 per Lord Hoffmann, criticised by K. Oliphant, Un-blurring the Boundaries of Nuisance (1998) 6 *Tort Law Review* 21, 28.

42 At this time, there were also continuing questions as to whether liability under the writ of trespass was – at least formally[174] – strict or fault-based. Even in respect of highway collisions, where negligence had long governed actions in case, it was not until 1875 that the Court of Exchequer unequivocally ruled that wilful or negligent conduct was an element of liability for claims brought in trespass.[175] Amongst the judges that day was Bramwell, who in *Rylands v Fletcher* (it will be recalled) had stated that a fault requirement had to apply in collision cases, as there would otherwise be no reason to attribute the collision to one party rather than the other.[176] Giving the leading judgment in the new case, he declared:[177]

> For the convenience of mankind in carrying on the affairs of life, people as they go along roads must expect, or put up with, such mischief as reasonable care on the part of others cannot avoid.

The dictum provides some reason to believe that Bramwell considered highway collisions to be exceptional in requiring fault, and hence strict liability still to be the general rule.[178] This is supported to a degree by defence counsel's very substantial reliance in argument[179] upon Blackburn's dicta about accidents on the highway in *Rylands v Fletcher*.[180] It is also notable that the decision was subsequently understood as having a special significance for highway cases.[181] But, whether or not Bramwell thought his decision was limited to collisions on the highway, it is patent that the standard of liability in trespass generally was the subject of lively debate in the second half of the nineteenth century. And beyond: the matter was not authoritatively resolved by an appellate court until 1965.[182]

43 It is not possible to give detailed consideration here to Dalton's claim that there was, in the years running up to *Rylands v Fletcher*, a "system of [strict] activity-based liability that was ... at least as coherent and systematic ... as the inchoate elements of the fault system then existing, like activity-based liability, in the shadow of the forms of action."[183] Suffice it to note that the concept of action at peril had not by that time become a relic of the past, an anachro-

174 For an argument that the defence of "inevitable accident" made the liability substantially fault-based, see J.H. Baker (supra fn. 6), 404–5.

175 *Holmes v Mather* (1875) LR 10 Exch 261.

176 See no. 10 above.

177 (1875) LR 10 Exch 261, 267.

178 As is argued by C. Dalton (supra fn. 3), 101. She also observes (253) that Bramwell's analysis of the collision cases is now suggestive of Blackburn's approach in the Exchequer Chamber, based on the plaintiff's implied assumption of the risk of non-negligent injury, whereas previously, in Rylands v Fletcher, he had focused on the difficulties of causal attribution in the absence of a criterion of fault.

179 (1875) LR 10 Exch 261, 263.

180 See nos. 14 and 41 above.

181 *Fowler v Lanning*[1959] 1 QB 426, 439 per Diplock J.

182 *Letang v Cooper* [1965] 1 QB 232, building on the first-instance decisions in *Stanley v Powell* [1891] 1 QB 86 and *Fowler v Lanning* [1959] 1 QB 426.

183 C. Dalton (supra fn. 3), 279–80.

nistic survival of some primitive notion of responsibility. In fact, it was a living presence in English law, and its proper scope relative to liability for fault was intensely debated in the courts. In *Rylands v Fletcher*, Bramwell, Blackburn and Cranworth saw themselves as contributing to that debate.

D. *Rylands v Fletcher* and the Theory of Enterprise Liability

Proponents of enterprise liability have often identified *Rylands v Fletcher* as a precursor to enterprise liability in the modern law. For Keating, *Rylands v Fletcher* is (with vicarious liability) one of "[t]he two chief sources of modern enterprise liability".[184] For Clutterbuck, "the history of the development, academic acceptance and judicial implementation of enterprise liability theory ... begins with the classic English case of *Rylands v Fletcher*."[185] And for Robert Keeton, *Rylands v Fletcher* and the recognition of strict liability for ultra-hazardous activities represented "[t]he most important decisional development cited in support of conclusions concerning the influence of risk-spreading capacity."[186] So great has the decision's influence been in the United States that it has even been described as one of "[t]he great landmarks of *American* tort law".[187] Critics of modern enterprise liability, too, have found *Rylands v Fletcher* to have a played a crucial role in its historical development. As one of their number has put it, "enterprise liability as it exists today would be incomprehensible without the rejuvenation of strict liability doctrines" for which *Rylands v Fletcher* was largely responsible.[188] Not all have agreed, however: Rabin, for one, has written that the strict liability in *Rylands v Fletcher* "had nothing to do with the ideology of enterprise liability".[189] 44

In the United States, despite the initial hostility of the courts, and their continued reluctance to admit they were influenced by the English decision, strict liability for such hazardous activities as blasting and the storage of explosives came to receive judicial acceptance,[190] paving the way for the inclusion of 45

[184] G.C. Keating, The Idea of Fairness in Enterprise Liability (1997) 95 Mich L Rev 1266, 1367.
[185] J.B. Clutterbuck (supra fn. 29), 1132. See also G.K. Gardner, Insurance Against Tort Liability – An Approach to the Cosmology of Law (1950) 15 *Law & Contemporary Problems* 455, 462 (emphasising the role the case played in "living tort law" as the expression of commonly-held beliefs about enterprise responsibility).
[186] R.E. Keeton (supra fn. 7), 402.
[187] P. Schuck, Introduction, in P. Schuck (ed.), *Tort Law and the Public Interest* (1990), 17 (emphasis added).
[188] D. Abraham, Liberty and Property: Lord Bramwell and the Political Economy of Liberal Jurisprudence Individualism, Freedom, and Utility (1994) 38 *American Journal of Legal History* (Am J Leg Hist) 288, 299.
[189] R.L. Rabin (supra fn. 7), 1193.
[190] For overviews, see J. Smith, Liability for Substantial Physical Damage to Land by Blasting – The Rule of the Future (1920) 33 Harv L Rev 542 and 667; C.O. Gregory (supra fn. 7), 370–82; V.E. Nolan/E. Ursin, The Revitalization of Hazardous Activity Strict Liability (1987) 65 *North Carolina Law Review* 257; and W.K. Jones, Strict Liability for Hazardous Enterprises (1992) 92 Colum L Rev 1705.

strict liability for "ultrahazardous activities" in the first *Restatement of Torts*.[191] It was in fact the only general provision included in the first *Restatement* under the heading of "Absolute Liability", the rest of which dealt with the specific strict liabilities arising in respect of animals. Strict products liability was not included until the production of the second *Restatement* in 1965.[192] But the concentrated effort that was necessary to get recognition for strict products liability inevitably diverted attention away from liability for "abnormally dangerous activities", as they were renamed in the *Restatement (Second)*,[193] and lead to the liability being regarded as something of a sideshow.[194] Yet, at the same time, *Rylands v Fletcher* acquired an almost mythical status as the *fons et origo* and exemplar of modern strict liability.[195]

46 There was, however, an ambiguity in accounts according *Rylands v Fletcher* a significant role in the genealogy of modern enterprise liability: was the case merely an adventitious survival of the medieval principle of action at peril, happily but fortuitously suited to the modern industrial world, or was it actually a self-consciously forward-looking decision that reflected a thought-through (if undeveloped) theory of enterprise liability? This is the question to which I turn in the concluding section of my paper.

1. Private Rights and Public Interest in the Law of Nuisance

47 Though the analogies that Blackburn J drew on in his famous judgment in *Rylands v Fletcher* were old, the case can plausibly be seen to be addressing an issue of contemporary social policy that had attracted considerable legal attention: how to reconcile private rights with competing public interests.[196] This was a question that had recently been before the courts in a series of cases in the law of private nuisance, and it was in the course of that history that Baron

[191] Cf. American Law Institute, *Restatement of the Law of Torts*, vols. 1–4 (1934–1939), §§ 519–520. See further R.W. James, Absolute Liability for Ultrahazardous Activities: An Appraisal of the Restatement Doctrine (1949) 37 *California Law Review* (Cal L Rev) 269.

[192] American Law Institute, R*estatement of the Law (Second), Torts*, vols. 1–4 (1965–1979), § 402A.

[193] Ibid., §§ 519–520. Strict liability for abnormally dangerous activities is maintained in American Law Institute, *Restatement of the Law (Third), Torts: Liability for Physical Harm (Proposed Final Draft No. 1)* (2005), § 20. See further W.K. Jones (supra fn. 190), 1709–15 and K.N. Hylton (supra fn. 15), 1433–36. For an English lawyer's perspective, see K. Stanton (supra fn. 3), 88–95.

[194] See, e.g., G.T. Schwartz (supra fn. 3), 238 ("plays a rather subsidiary role in modern American tort law"). Cf. V.E. Nolan/E. Ursin (supra fn. 190) and J.G. Anderson, The Rylands v. Fletcher Doctrine in America: Abnormally Dangerous, Ultrahazardous or Absolute Nuisance? 1978 *Arizona State Law Journal* 99.

[195] See, e.g., W.E. Knepper, About Tomorrow's Tort Trends (1966) 18 *Syracuse Law Review* (Syracuse L Rev) 1, 4; M.S. Shapo, A Representational Theory of Consumer Protection: Doctrine Function and Legal Liability for Product Disappointment (1974) 60 Va L Rev 1109, 1281 and citations in no. 44 above.

[196] See A.W.B. Simpson, Victorian Judges and the Problem of Social Cost: *Tipping v St Helen's Smelting Company*, in: *Leading Cases in the Common Law* (1995); J.K. Brenner, Nuisance Law and the Industrial Revolution (1973) 3 J Leg Stud 403; J.P.S. McLaren, Nuisance Law and the Industrial Revolution – Some Lessons from Social History (1983) 3 OJLS 155.

Bramwell in particular began to set out a more or less explicit theory of enterprise liability.

Translated into legal terms, the question was whether the public interest in the 48
defendant's (typically) industrial activity was sufficient to make lawful what would otherwise have been an unlawful nuisance. A finding that the defendant was liable in damages meant that his use of land was unreasonable and that the claimant was prima facie entitled to an injunction to stop the interference or reduce it to acceptable levels. The matter had repeatedly been before the courts, and for some time there were two divergent streams of authority. One held that "no action lies for the use, the reasonable use, of a lawful trade in a convenient and proper place, even though some one may suffer annoyance from its being carried on,"[197] the other that the carrying on of a lawful trade in a proper place might still be a nuisance if it resulted in unreasonable interference with another's use or enjoyment of land. In 1682, just three years before *Rylands v Fletcher* reached the Court of Exchequer, the Exchequer Chamber opted for the latter view in *Bamford v Turnley*[198] (Pollock CB dissenting), where the plaintiff complained of the defendant's burning of bricks in kilns on his land. Bramwell was one of the judges, and in a remarkably modern judgment he advanced what appears as a theory of enterprise liability based on notions of cost-internalization. He began by rejecting public benefit as a defence to liability in nuisance:[199]

> it is said that … [the brick-burning] is lawful because it is for the public benefit. Now, in the first place, that law to my mind is a bad one which, for the public benefit, inflicts loss on an individual without compensation. But further, with great respect, I think this consideration misapplied … The public consists of all the individuals of it, and a thing is only for the public benefit when it is productive of good to all those individuals on the balance of loss and gain to all. So that if all the loss and gain were borne and received by one individual, he would on the whole be a gainer. But whenever this is the case – whenever a thing is for the public benefit – the loss to the individuals of the public who lose will bear compensating out of the gains of those who gain. It is for the public benefit that there should be railways; but it would not be unless the gain of having the railway was sufficient to compensate the loss occasioned by the use of the land required for the site; accordingly, no one thinks it would be right to take an individual's land without compensation to make a railway. It is for the public benefit that trains should be run, but not unless they pay their expenses.

Bramwell's concern here was to resist the argument that the public benefit re- 49
sulting from the defendant's activity should render him immune from liability in damages. On the contrary, thought Bramwell, if the activity was truly in the

[197] *Hole v Barlow* (1858) 27 *Law Journal Reports, Common Pleas* 207, 208 per Sir John Byles.
[198] (1862) 3 *Best and Smith Reports* (B&S) 62, 122 ER 25.
[199] (1862) 3 B&S 62, 84–5.

public interest, it would be able to pay compensation to those whom it injured, and still make a profit. There are foreshadowings here of the sort of cost-benefit analysis that underpins modern economic analysis of law,[200] but that is perhaps not surprising: this was, after all, the golden age of classical economics, and Bramwell was an enthusiastic supporter of the theories of Adam Smith.[201]

50 Before moving on to consider Bramwell's views in more detail, however, we should note that the conflicting case-law authorities were ultimately resolved before the House of Lords in 1885, in its decision in *Tipping v St Helen's Smelting Co*,[202] a case of pollution by fumes from the defendant's copper-smelting works. The House of Lords came down in favour of the line of authorities culminating in *Bamford v Turnley*, and ruled that it was no defence to an action in nuisance that the defendant was carrying out a lawful trade in a proper place with reasonable care. Even in such a case, liability would arise if the plaintiff suffered material or sensible damage in his use or enjoyment of land. The plaintiff's interests were not to be sacrificed for the promotion of the public good. This is certainly a consideration that underpins modern enterprise liability theory, yet we are still a distance away from enterprise liability proper. It will be recalled that a finding of nuisance entails not only a duty to compensate but also a prima facie liability to an injunction requiring the defendant to stop the nuisance and prevent its repetition or continuation.[203] The award of an injunction, it must be stressed, is totally inconsistent with the theory of enterprise liability, which sees the defendant's activity not as a wrong to be prohibited but as so highly desirable that it ought to be continued, notwithstanding the injuries it causes. In fact, Bramwell seems to have been aware of the difficulty relating to injunctions in *Bamford v Turnley* itself, as he adverted to the possible objection to his reasoning that "by injunction or by abatement of the nuisance a man who would not accept a pecuniary compensation might put a stop to works of great value, and much more than enough to compensate him."[204] In his view, there was a case for amending the law so as to "legalise" the defendant's activity on his payment of compensation[205] but no reason to allow the plaintiff's loss to go uncompensated.

[200] See, e.g., R.A. Epstein, For a Bramwell Revival (1994) 38 Am J Leg Hist 246, 277 ("here is the standard test of economic efficiency accurately stated … a half century before it made its way into standard economic theory").

[201] See R.A. Epstein (supra fn. 200); D. Abraham (supra fn. 188); and A. Ramasastry, The Parameters, Progressions, and Paradoxes of Baron Bramwell (1994) 38 Am J Leg Hist 322.

[202] (1865) 11 Clark & Finelly's House of Lords Reports (HLC) 642, 122 ER 588.

[203] For further consideration of the nineteenth-century impact of the rule, see W.R. Cornish/ G.deN. Clark (supra fn. 164), 154–7.

[204] (1862) 3 B&S 62, 85–6. Is this an indication that Bramwell failed to grasp that value is a function of individual preferences? For further comment, see P.S. Atiyah, Liability for Railway Nuisance in the English Common Law: A Historical Footnote (1980) 23 *Journal of Law and Economy* (J Law & Econ) 191, 194.

[205] In fact, Lord Cairns' Act of 1858 was later interpreted as giving the courts of equity the power to award damages for yet-to-be-sustained losses in lieu of an injunction, thereby effectively legalising the nuisance, but the Act was not so understood at this time, and the new jurisdiction was only authoritatively confirmed by the House of Lords in 1924 (*Leeds Industrial Co-op Society Ltd v Slack* [1924] AC 851). See further J.A. Jolowicz, Damages in Equity – A Study of Lord Cairn's Act [1975] CLJ 224, 224–8.

Readers of the House of Lords decision in *Tipping v St Helen's Smelting Co* could be excused if they were left afterwards with the wholly misleading impression that the case was solely concerned with damages, for that was the only remedy with which the Law Lords were concerned. But that was only because, in the days before the integration of the courts of common law and equity in 1875, the successful plaintiff was required to make a separate application in equity if he wanted an injunction. In fact, Tipping did just that, and was successful in the Court of Appeal in his chancery suit.[206] It appears that the defendants were obliged to close down their works and move their smelting operations some three miles further away from Tipping's estate.[207] 51

2. Baron Bramwell's Prototype Theory of Enterprise Liability[208]

Baron Bramwell's judgments in *Bamford v Turley* and elsewhere[209] have been identified as "envision[ing] new uses for strict liability in tort law"[210] and foreshadowing twentieth-century accounts of enterprise liability, especially in their sophisticated grasp of economic principles. It is reported that Sir Ronald Coase, the founding father of modern law and economics,[211] considered Bramwell to have had an instinctive understanding of economic principle, and quoted from his opinions (though not in his published work).[212] For Richard Epstein, Bramwell's treatment of "collective action, coordination, and public goods problems" revealed a "theoretical grasp of the issue … [that] was unrivalled for his time, not only for lawyers but economists as well."[213] In his judgment in *Bamford v Turnley*, he "anticipate[d] the next century's welfare economics."[214] For Robert Gordon, Bramwell was "the Richard Epstein of his day".[215] 52

In his judgments of the period, it can be said that Bramwell anticipated modern enterprise liability in his recognition of several fundamental points. First, public policy does not require the total elimination of accidents, but only their reduction to the level at which accident costs are exceeded by benefits. Secondly, the efficient level of accidents need not be stipulated by Parliament or 53

[206] (1865) 1 *Chancery Appeal Cases* 66.
[207] A.W.B. Simpson (supra fn. 196), 190–91.
[208] See further P.S. Atiyah (supra fn. 204) and A. Ramasastry (supra fn. 201), especially 356–363. In a breathtakingly wrong-headed article, David Abraham (supra fn. 188) credits Bramwell for the continuing and widespread perception that strict liability is "monstrous" (299), portrays his judgment in *Bamford v Turnley* (misspelled) as a demonstration that "public utility could not be served in a regime of strict liability" (297; Bramwell was in fact arguing the opposite), and heaps obloquy on *Rylands v Fletcher* without any mention at all of the fact that Bramwell had actually given judgment in the case for the plaintiff.
[209] Especially *Brand v Hammersmith and City Railway Co* (1867) LR 2 QB 223 and *Powell v Fall* (1880) 5 QBD 597.
[210] A. Ramasastry (supra fn. 201), 327.
[211] See especially R.H. Coase, The Problem of Social Cost (1960) 3 J Law & Econ 1.
[212] A.W.B. Simpson (supra fn. 196), 174.
[213] R.A. Epstein (supra fn. 200), 248–9.
[214] Ibid., 276.
[215] R.W. Gordon, Simpson's Leading Cases (1997) 95 Mich L Rev 2044, 2052.

the courts but can be left to economic incentives, including the incentive effect of tort law's liability rules. Thirdly, in the absence of liability rules, accident costs will be borne by third parties, and so distort the economic incentives on the entrepreneur. (Bramwell, in fact, was "one of the first to recognize the problem of externalities."[216]) Lastly, efficiency can nevertheless be achieved by internalising the costs of the activity to the party who derives the chief benefit from it, a familiar trope of the modern law and economics literature and central to the theory of enterprise liability. Inefficient activities will be "suppressed", as he writes in a later judgment,[217] if the entrepreneur's liability costs exceed his financial gains. This, at least in broad outline, is Calabresi's notion of "market" or "general deterrence".[218]

54 Bramwell's analysis was pre-eminently economic, but his theory went well beyond the naïve laissez-faire ideology that is sometimes attributed to him.[219] He does not appear to have had an absolute belief in the infallibility of markets, for his adoption of the cost-internalization approach amounted to a tacit admission that, for whatever reason, market methods cannot be relied upon to produce the efficient solution. Indeed, in his analysis in *Bamford v Turnley* of the hold-out who will not be bought off by the offer of compensation, and insists on exercising his right to injunctive relief, he raises the issues of strategic and irrational behaviour that have become an increasing focus for contemporary law and economics.[220] Bramwell, concludes Epstein, "better than anyone else, … explained why and how the just compensation principle becomes part of a legal system that can no longer make do exclusively with the principles of private property and freedom of contract."[221]

55 Bramwell also appears to have had some sympathy with the loss-distribution version of enterprise liability. He clearly understood that compensation costs could be regarded as an incidental business expense and factored into the pricing of goods and services. In a judgment of 1876 dealing with the liability of a railway company, he wrote:[222]

> It is to be remembered that that compensation comes from the public which gets the benefit. It comes from those who do the damage, but ultimately from the public in the fares they pay.

What is more, Bramwell clearly accepted that the case for liability was not exclusively economic: the injured person had a moral claim to compensation too. Even before embarking upon his economic analysis in *Bamford v Turnley*,

[216] A. Ramasastry (supra fn. 201), 326.
[217] *Powell v Fall* (1880) 5 QBD 597, 601.
[218] G. Calabresi (supra fn. 21), ch. 5.
[219] E.g. by P.S. Atiyah, *The Rise and Fall of Freedom of Contract* (1979), 377.
[220] See, e.g, I. Ayres/E. Tally, Solomonic Bargaining: Dividing a Legal Entitlement to Facilitate Coasean Trade (1995) 104 Yale LJ 1027; W. Farnsworth, Do Parties to Nuisance Cases Bargain after Judgment – A Glimpse Inside the Cathedral (1999) 66 U Chi L Rev 373.
[221] R.A. Epstein (supra fn. 200), 278.
[222] *Brand v Hammersmith and City Railway Co* (1867) LR 2 QB 223, 230.

he stated: "in the first place, that law to my mind is a bad one which, for the public benefit, inflicts loss on an individual without compensation."[223] Of course, this could be dressed up in economic terms as the preference for Pareto efficiency, where a transaction is only efficient if those who gain compensate the losers out of their winnings, over Kaldor-Hicks efficiency, where the winners must be hypothetically able to pay such compensation but need not in fact do so.[224] Ultimately, however, the choice between the two approaches is more moral than economic, and it is clear that Bramwell – who instinctively backed the individual against the collective – thought that the imposition of liability on the entrepreneur was not only efficient but also right.

3. Statutory Compensation Clauses

Bramwell's judgments show that ideas of enterprise liability had been intro- 56
duced into judicial discussions of common law compensation rights in the years before *Rylands v Fletcher*. That the same or similar ideas had entered into the political arena at roughly the same time is attested by the broadly contemporaneous enactment of statutory compensation clauses in respect of the confiscation of land and other interferences licensed by private Acts of Parliament.[225] Private legislation was typically necessary because some public project required the infringement of private rights, and, in those circumstances, Parliament was in a position to demand, as the price for its statutory authorization, that the undertaker accept a liability in damages for injury caused even by lawful activities conducted with due care. Such provisions fit very well with modern theories of enterprise liability. They have the same rationale, that accident costs should be regarded as a business expense, and the same method – cost-internalization. The express authority given to the activity in the Act attests to its public benefit, but at the same time renders the entrepreneur immune from normal common law and equitable remedies[226]. The in-

[223] (1862) 3 B&S 62, 84.

[224] For a summary and critique, see R.A. Posner, The Ethical and Political Basis of the Efficiency Norm in Common Law Adjudication (1980) 8 *Hofstra Law Review* (Hofstra L Rev) 487, and J.L. Coleman, Efficiency, Utility, and Wealth Maximization (1980) 8 Hofstra L Rev 509.

[225] See A.W.B. Simpson (supra fn. 3), 218–20.

[226] *Vaughan v Taff Vale Railway Co* (1860) 5 *Hurlstone and Norman* 679; *Hammersmith and City Railway Co v Brand* (1869) LR 4 HL 171. The defence of statutory authorisation does not apply if the defendant has acted negligently (ibid.). In the absence of an express immunity, however, the very existence of the defence may be considered questionable. Enterprise liability theory holds that the public interest in the activity is no reason to withhold the payment of compensation to the statistically inevitable victims of its pursuit. From this perspective, it appears that the courts went further than was necessary in treating the statutory permission to conduct the activity as impliedly substituting fault for strict liability. Why should they not allow the activity but require compensation at the same time? In fact, Bramwell was exceptional in arguing for the survival of strict common law liabilities in such cases: see *Brand v Hammersmith & City Rly Co* (1867) LR 2 QB 223, 234 (obiter); *Hammersmith and City Railway Co v Brand* (1869) LR 4 HL 171, 193. (Bramwell had also gone with the plaintiff in the Court of Exchequer in *Vaughan v Taff Vale Railway Co* (1859) 3 *Hurlstone & Norman's Exchequer Reports* (H&N) 743.) In both the leading cases, Blackburn was on the other side, acceding to the view that the plaintiff's common law rights had been effectively revoked: see (1860) 5 H&N 679, 688–89 and (1869) LR 4 HL 171, 197.

jured party cannot obtain injunctive relief, but benefits from what is effectively a liability rule: the compensation claim under the statute.

57 As Simpson has argued,[227] these statutory principles were very likely in the judges minds as they decided *Rylands v Fletcher*, even though the reservoir in that case was not built under a private Act of Parliament. He points out that, shortly before *Rylands v Fletcher*, there had been two major reservoir disasters in England.[228] In 1852, a badly-designed and ill-maintained dam at Holmfirth in Yorkshire collapsed catastrophically, releasing an enormous volume of water that swept down the valley, killing 78 people, and rendering homeless or destitute thousands more. In 1864, another catastrophic dam breach lead to the inundation of the city of Sheffield to a depth of three meters with water flowing from a reservoir belonging to the Sheffield Waterworks Company; at least 238 people died. In response to the first of these catastrophes, Parliament had been persuaded to give statutory authority for new reservoir construction only on condition that the undertaker accept a statutory responsibility to compensate the victims in the event of a breach. Such terms came to be known as "Holmfirth clauses", after the village where the disaster had occurred. Subsequently there were legislative proposals to consolidate the law governing reservoirs built under private Acts, including those already enacted/built, so as to ensure the inclusion of a compensation provision. The proposal was dropped in 1867 – after the Exchequer Chamber's decision in *Rylands v Fletcher*.[229] The result was a patchwork of different legal provisions governing the single issue of liability for bursting reservoirs, with statutory compensation clauses applying in some cases but not in others.[230]

58 The Rylands reservoir did not require statutory authorization as it was constructed on private land, and the courts were therefore confronted with the question whether the common law should offer the same protection for private rights as would have been available under the statutory Holmfirth causes, and the proposed – but never enacted – consolidation legislation. The decision in *Rylands v Fletcher* can be seen as affirming that it did. The outcome was entirely consistent with the prototype theory of enterprise liability Bramwell had enunciated in *Bamford v Turnley*.

4. *Rylands v Fletcher*, or the Dog that Didn't Bark

59 One might have thought that *Rylands v Fletcher* was the perfect testing ground for Bramwell's prototype enterprise liability theory. In *Bamford v Turnley*, he had come up against the harsh truth that his economic argument for strict liability, relying upon the cost-internalizing effect of legal liability rules, fell

[227] A.W.B. Simpson (supra fn. 3), a revised version of an earlier article: A.W.B. Simpson, Legal Liability for Bursting Reservoirs: The Historical Context of *Rylands v Fletcher* (1984) 13 J Leg Stud 209. For criticism, see Schwartz (supra fn. 3), 236–7.

[228] Ibid., 199–208.

[229] Ibid., 205–6.

[230] Ibid., 218.

down in the face of the successful plaintiff's prima facie entitlement to an injunction. This grant of the property entitlement to the plaintiff placed the onus on the defendant, according to classical economic analysis of law, to bargain for the right to interfere "efficiently" with the plaintiff's use of the land. In a Coasian world of rational actors and zero transactions costs, the designation of this property entitlement would make no difference to the ultimate allocation of resources. But Bramwell realised that imperfections in the bargaining process would often frustrate that outcome in the real world. (Consider his example of the hold-out.) His response at the time was to suggest legislative reform to allow damages to be awarded in lieu of an injunction as a once-and-for-all expropriation of the plaintiff's rights.[231]

This difficulty did not arise in *Rylands v Fletcher* where, because the con- 60
struction of the reservoir was not a wrong in itself, and because the escape of the water was an inevitable accident, there was no question of granting an injunction. If there was a nuisance, as Bramwell considered there was, it was "not in the reservoir, but in the water escaping".[232] "The digging a reservoir in a man's own land," stated Baron Martin, "is a lawful act."[233] Blackburn, in the course of argument before the Exchequer Chamber, interjected to make much the same point: "the difficulty here is in saying that what was rightful in the first doing, became wrongful in the continuance."[234] If its continuance was not wrongful, there was no case for an injunction.

Various external factors also came together to make the case an especially 61
propitious one for the imposition of strict liability on the entrepreneur. At the time *Rylands v Fletcher* came to the Court of Exchequer, there was widespread public concern about the risks inherent in industrial activities in general, and, following the Holmfirth and Sheffield dam-bursts, reservoir construction in particular. Considerable sympathy for the victims of human disasters, generally resulting in the organisation of a public charitable appeal for their benefit, was coupled with a feeling that the entrepreneur (even if providing a public service) should pay his way.[235] Additionally, the statutory compensation clauses (Holmfirth clauses) included in the private Acts of Parliament under which many reservoirs had been constructed, provided a ready example of the enterprise liability policy being put into effect – to say nothing of the proposed inclusion of a general strict liability clause in the consolidation legislation then under consideration.

[231] See no. 50 above.

[232] (1865) 3 H&C 774, 790. Bramwell's formulation is the reverse of the modern view that nuisance liability arises in respect of a single, isolated occurrence only if it results from a continuing state of affairs for which the defendant is responsible, the latter being the nuisance: see, e.g., Rogers (supra fn. 87), § 18.11; J. Murphy (supra fn. 87), 400.

[233] Ibid., 792.

[234] (1866) LR 1 Exch 265, 270.

[235] See, generally, A.W.B. Simpson (supra fn. 3), 202–08. He suggests (212) that *Rylands v Fletcher* may have be plucked from the comparative obscurity of informal arbitration precisely because, after the Sheffield disaster, it was seen as a potentially leading case.

62 The stage was therefore set for Bramwell and his judicial colleagues to apply his fledgling theory of enterprise liability to a set of facts that provided its best testing ground yet. Yet – if we may invoke Holmes again, but Sherlock this time, not Oliver W. – *Rylands v Fletcher* turned out to be a case of the dog that didn't bark. Bramwell's judgment in the Court of Exchequer was wholly devoid of any analysis reminiscent of that he had first advanced five years earlier in *Bamford v Turnley*. His approach was purely legal, based on case-law and established (though not immutable) principle, without any whiff at all of economics or loss distribution. Nor was there any in the judgments delivered by Blackburn, Cairns or Cranworth. As far as the latter are concerned, the likelihood is that they simply did not know, think of, sympathise with or understand Bramwell's economic musings. In Blackburn's case, his record in other judgments of the same period suggests that his intuitions were very far from being compatible with the ideas that underlie enterprise liability. When a railway operated under statutory authority caused damage and annoyance to the owner of adjacent premises, and the question was whether she was entitled to damages at common law, statutory compensation or neither, Blackburn was the only one of the judges whose advisory opinion was requested by the House of Lords who would have rejected both common law and statutory claims.[236] And subsequently, when considering a statutory provision imposing what appeared on its face as a strict liability, he effectively recognised a presumption that statutory liabilities were to turn on fault unless the contrary was expressly stated.[237]

63 Blackburn in *Rylands v Fletcher*, I have argued, was not simply applying or extending an existing cause of action, but was consciously developing a new principle of liability. Yet he did so by a backward-looking synthesis of assorted pockets of strict liability dating from medieval times, and not by radically re-conceptualising the nature, scope and purpose of strict liability. Though he was surely aware of the recent reservoir disasters, to which he may have inadvertently made passing reference in his remark that the characteristic risk of water was "drowning",[238] and the proposed legislative reforms in the area, there is no evidence that he would have approached the case any differently if those factors had not been present. He was no doubt satisfied that his ruling accorded with the perceived needs of society in the dam-burst scenario, but that is all. A more plausible external influence on his judgment was, as Dalton has persuasively argued,[239] the recent effective abolition of the forms of ac-

[236] *Hammersmith and City Railway Co v Brand* (1869) LR 4 HL 171, on appeal from *Brand v Hammersmith and City Railway Co* (1867) LR 2 QB 223.

[237] *River Wear Commissioners v Adamson* (1877) 2 AC 743. But cf. Blackburn's support for strict liability in *Readhead v Midland Railway Co* (1867) LR 2 QB 412 and text accompanying fns. 170–171 above. It is for their lack of consistency, above all, that his judgments on tort are notable.

[238] (1866) LR 1 Exch 265, 286. The argument is made by A.W.B. Simpson (supra fn. 3), 217. More likely, however, Blackburn was just using "drown" to mean "flood", which is how he later employed the term in *Cattle v Stockton Waterworks Co* (1875) LR 10 QB 453, 457 ("drowned mine").

[239] C. Dalton (supra fn. 3).

tion, which encouraged the courts to look beyond the often artificial limits of the old writs, and address the underlying issues of substance. For the judges in *Rylands v Fletcher*, that meant asking how (if at all) strict liability was to be combined in the modern law with liability for fault. Blackburn, like Bramwell and Cranworth, answered on the basis of the authorities, which they all took to reveal a traditional priority for strict liability over fault, the latter being the exception that required special justification.

Bramwell, of course, is the more interesting case. How could he have ignored the theory he himself had advanced five years earlier in *Bamford v Turnley*? A possible, if rather unexciting, explanation is that, in the earlier case, he had been confronted with an argument that an otherwise good claim in nuisance should be denied for reasons of public benefit, whereas his principle task now was to determine whether or not the was a cause of action that would avail the plaintiff on the facts. This was the focus of counsels' argument, and no one put to Bramwell the public benefit defence which caused him to reach for his economic theory in *Bamford v Turnley*. Still this is only speculation and, in truth, we simply do not know why he did not invoke the same considerations in *Rylands v Fletcher*. 64

The omission is even more striking because Bramwell seems subsequently to have come to see *Rylands v Fletcher* in the economic terms he had previously set out. In *Powell v Fall*,[240] he was a member of a Court of Appeal that applied the by now established rule to a case of fire damage caused by sparks from a steam locomotive traction engine operated on the public highway. The engine was constructed and conducted with all reasonable care and in conformity with the provisions of the applicable Locomotive Acts. Bramwell gave the leading judgment, in the course of which he returned to the theory of economic incentives he had elaborated in *Bamford v Turnley*:[241] 65

> It is just and reasonable that if a person uses a dangerous machine, he should pay for the damage which it occasions; if the reward which he gains for the use of the machine will not pay for the damage, it is mischievous to the public and ought to be suppressed, for the loss ought not to be borne by the community or the injured person. If the use of the machine is profitable, the owner ought to pay compensation for the damage.

Another notable aspect of the case was that Bramwell (like Blackburn) had in *Rylands v Fletcher* viewed negligence as the correct standard for highway cases, not strict liability.[242] It seems that the non-reciprocal nature of the risk that the traction engine posed to ordinary road users must have been crucial in persuading him to take a different approach in the later case.

[240] (1880) 5 QBD 597.
[241] (1880) 5 QBD 597, 601.
[242] See nos. 10 and 14 above.

E. Conclusion

66 Our examination of *Rylands v Fletcher* and the emergence of enterprise liability in the common law began with a close look at the case itself, with a view to determining whether or not, as some have alleged, it was of no more significance than a simple application, or marginal extension, of some existing cause of action. We concluded that that claim could not be sustained, and that the structure of Blackburn J's judgment in particular, presenting "the rule" as the principle underlying a number of disparate liabilities recognised in the earlier law, was only consistent with his conscious development of a new cause of action. We also noted that Blackburn, like Bramwell in the Court of Exchequer and Cranworth in the House of Lords, assumed that strict liability was the general principle of English law, and liability for fault the exception that required special justification. In the next section of the paper, we observed that, although the adoption of a strict liability standard in *Rylands v Fletcher* has been viewed as anachronistic by some, liability without fault had certainly not disappeared from the face of English law at the time in question. In fact, the procedural reforms that culminated in the abolition of the forms of action had stimulated debate into substantive issues of tort law that had been to some extent been obscured by the technicalities of the old writs, and *Rylands v Fletcher*, located in the middle of this transitional period, can usefully be regarded as a contribution to ongoing discussions about the respect roles of fault and strict liability. In the last section of the paper, we considered the decision in the context of emerging ideas of enterprise liability, partially developed by one of the judges in the case itself, Baron Bramwell, and also evident in various statutory compensation clauses which applied to a number of discrete activities effectively licensed by the State. *Rylands v Fletcher* has acquired a reputation as the source of the enterprise liability theory that was so influential in twentieth-century American tort law, but our examination of the judgments gave no reason to believe that ideas of loss-distribution, deterrence, etc., were in the minds of the judges who participated in the decision. Even Bramwell, already the author of a fledgling theory of enterprise liability, was silent on such matters.

67 So the question I posed at the outset – was *Rylands v Fletcher* the first example of enterprise liability in the common law? – must be answered in the negative. In fact, it may be argued that it is precisely the courts' failure to elaborate a convincing modern rationale for the imposition of strict liability that has lead in the Commonwealth – especially England and Australia – to the rule's protracted but seemingly inexorable demise. The supposedly strict liability was first of all infused with notions of fault as the concept of non-natural user was defined so as to exclude activities that were "for the general benefit of the community",[243] and the scope of the available defences was

[243] *Rickards v Lothian* [1913] AC 263, 280. But note the doubts expressed by Lord Goff in *Cambridge Water Co Ltd v Eastern Counties Leather plc* [1994] 2 AC 264, 308.

extended so that – where the agency of a third party or natural forces was involved – "the claim based on *Rylands v* Fletcher merges into the claim in negligence."[244] Then the analogy with private nuisance was taken to require the limitation of the liability to claims of damage to land which could only be brought by the holder of a proprietary interest in the land affected; claims for personal injury were excluded.[245] The analogy was also employed to justify the longstanding, but debilitating, requirement of an escape from the defendant's land.[246] The result of all these doctrinal limitations has been to render the rule in *Rylands v Fletcher* so irrelevant that, when the House of Lords was required in 2003 to consider its scope, not a single example of a successful claim under the rule could be found in the last 60 years.[247] In Australia, the High Court had already previously decided that enough was enough, and effectively abolished the liability as a separate head of claim, integrating it into the general law of negligence and non-delegable duties of care.[248] The House of Lords was encouraged to go down the same route, but declined, even though it was hard to find any rational justification for the rule and the exceptions to it.[249]

In the absence of any clear rationale for the imposition of liability without fault, *Rylands v Fletcher* has been pushed further and further into the sidelines. Unlike in the United States, common law (i.e. non-statutory) enterprise liability has never established itself in English law. On the contrary, such strict liabilities as do exist at common law may be regarded as reflecting different underlying theories, for example, the protection of property rights against expropriation (in the torts of trespass to land and conversion), and the balancing of competing rights in areas where there is a particular need for clear rules to guide future action (in the tort of defamation and those areas of private nuisance where liability is strict). Outside these cases, common law strict liability often reflects a view that fault is somehow present, if only in the background, as in cases of the breach of statutory duty. Despite the name, the liability in fact arises at common law and is conceptually distinct from liability in negligence.[250] It is characteristically a strict liability,[251] but it clearly reflects a different paradigm of strict liability than that presumed by enterprise liability theory, where the activity – far from being contrary to law – is deemed to be beneficial. The alternative paradigm may be seen as justifying strict liability only in cases of presumed or attenuated fault, rather as Holmes and Pollock 68

244 *Perry v Kendricks Transport Ltd* [1956] 1 WLR 85, 91 per Jenkins LJ.

245 *Transco plc v Stockport Metropolitan Borough Council* [2004] 2 AC 1, 10 per Lord Bingham, and 19 per Lord Hoffmann.

246 *Read v J Lyons & Co* [1947] AC 156. For criticism, see J. Murphy (supra fn. 3), 644–56.

247 *Transco plc v Stockport Metropolitan Borough Council* [2004] 2 AC 1, 19 per Lord Hoffmann.

248 *Burnie Port Authority v General Jones Pty Ltd* (1994) 179 CLR 520.

249 *Transco plc v Stockport Metropolitan Borough Council* [2004] 2 AC 1, 20 per Lord Hoffmann.

250 *London Passenger Transport Board v Upson* [1949] AC 155.

251 Ibid., 168 per Lord Wright. This is not always so, however, as the standard of liability depends upon the precise statutory language: K. Stanton et al., *Statutory Torts* (2003), § 8.001.

saw the rule in *Rylands v Fletcher* itself.[252] Lacking committed advocacy of its own in the decisive case, it is no surprise that the idea of strict liability as a licence fee levied on lawful enterprise, reflecting policies of loss distribution and accident prevention, never took hold in the English common law.

[252] See nos. 33–39 above.

VI. The Precautionary Principle *versus* a General Principle for Compensation of Victims of Dangerous Activities in Belgian Law

Geneviève Schamps

Insere, Daphni, piros: carpent tua poma nepotes

(Plant pear trees, Daphne: your grandsons will harvest the pears)
VIRGIL

A. INTRODUCTION

1. The Evolution of Civil Liability in Belgian Law

a) The Civil Code

1 Last year it was the two hundredth anniversary of the Belgian Civil Code! In fact the Napoleonic Code is still used in Belgium. Dangers unknown at the time of its adoption have progressively appeared since then. Although two centuries have gone by, the provisions of the Civil Code are still used for the compensation of damage linked to the occurrence of most risks.

2 The promoters of the Civil Code were well aware of the need to compensate victims for injuries caused by the dangerous behaviour of other people[1]. Thus they imposed an obligation to compensate for the damage caused by one's own fault (in artt. 1382 and 1383 C.C.). Furthermore they created types of vicarious liability: for instance, the principal (*le commettant*) is presumed to be liable for the fault committed by his appointee (*le préposé*) (art. 1384 al. 3 C.C.). A presumption of liability is also applied to parents for damage caused

[1] B. de Greuille, Rapport fait au tribunal dans la séance du 16 pluviôse an XII (6 février 1803), in: G. Locré (ed.), *Législation civile, commerciale et criminelle ou commentaire et complément des codes français* VI (1836), 282; Tarrible, Exposé des motifs dans la séance du corps législatif du 9 pluviôse an XII (30 janvier 1803) in: G. Locré (ed.), 280.

by their minor children, to teachers for their pupils and to craftsmen for their apprentices (art. 1384 al. 2 et al. 4 C.C.). There is also a presumption of liability *juris et de jure* to the owner of a collapsing building (art. 1386 C.C.) and to the owner or guardian of an animal (art. 1385 C.C.).

3 The regime of tort law based on fault – sometimes presumed – reflected the liberal and individualist principles which developed after the French Revolution. It was suitable for the needs of a rural society with a slow pace of life and a low density of population. However new risks appeared with the Industrial Revolution at the end of the nineteenth century. Some authors then suggested various mechanisms to make it easier for victims to obtain compensation.

4 For example, they tried to extend the presumption of liability for collapsing buildings to accidents caused by industrial machines. But the judges did not accept this idea. From the 1890s, others asserted that fault was not the fundamental basis of tort law. In their opinion, the employer could be held liable, even if he had not committed a fault, simply because his activity had caused damage and he had thus created a danger.

5 The idea of a "professional risk", an "industrial risk" or a "profit-risk" then gave rise to the well-known risk theory. This theory was not however accepted as a general basis for tort law. Nevertheless this theory probably inspired the Belgian legislator when it adopted a statute giving the employer a no-fault liability for work accidents in 1903[2]. This regime was then replaced by a social security system and a specific insurance scheme[3].

6 The risk theory was also partially an underlying consideration when judges created, at the end of the nineteenth century, a veritable general principle of no-fault liability for the behaviour of a thing. The presumption of liability was inscribed in art. 1384, first line, of the Belgian Civil Code. It can be applied nowadays to almost all accidental injuries caused by any thing, provided however that this thing has a defect. A few years ago, French law went even further than Belgian law when the *Cour de cassation* (Supreme Court) admitted, in 1991, that art. 1384, first line, of the Civil Code also contained a general principle of vicarious liability[4].

b) The Statutes Based on Strict Liability

7 Nevertheless, the systems proposed in the nineteenth and twentieth centuries did not go far enough to make it easy to compensate victims for dangerous risks in line with scientific and technological progress, even if the case law explains the Civil Code provisions in a very broad, victim-friendly way.

[2] Loi du 24 décembre 1903 sur la réparation des dommages résultant des accidents du travail.

[3] Loi du 19 avril 1971 sur les accidents du travail.

[4] Cass. fr., 29 March 1991, [1991] *Juris-classeur périodique (La Semaine Juridique)* (J.C.P.) II, 21673. This concept was refused by the Supreme Court of Belgium, Cass., 19 June 1997, [1997] *Journal des Tribunaux* (JT), 582.

The Belgian legislator then adopted several regimes of strict liability, either spontaneously or as a result of ratification of international agreements. For example, in the fields of aviation, atomic energy, oil pollution, exploitation of mines, transport of gas, gas storage, drilling and pumping of subterranean water, poisonous waste, fires in public places, spatial objects or road traffic accidents[5]. 8

Belgium has moreover transposed into national law the directive of 25 July 1985 concerning liability for defective products. Regarding the environment, Belgium will have to transpose the directive of 21 April 2004 on environmental liability with regard to the prevention and remedying of environmental damage. It is sometimes wondered whether the directive creates a real regime of tort law or whether it only goes half way between a regime of tort law and a public law regime[6]. Finally and more recently, the promoter of any experiments with human beings has become strictly liable. A statute was adopted into Belgian law on 7 May 2004, following the directive of 4 April 2001 relating to the clinical trials on medicinal products for human use. 9

This expansion of statutes on strict liability occurred in line with the evolution of the economic and social conditions of the last century. The development of social security has also contributed to the current expectation of a right to safety. The increase in private insurance has enabled a significant expansion to tort law and a tendency towards an abstraction of the concept of fault. In France, particularly, damage compensation has been aided by the creation in case law of obligations for safety. In addition to insurances and social security systems, the collectivization of risks also occurs through guaranteed funds. Specific statutes of strict liability can impose their creation for some dangerous situations. 10

2. The Emergence of the Precautionary Principle

Since the 1980s, the existence of serious and scientifically unknown risks have contributed to the emergence of a new concept: the precautionary principle. Various potential risks, not scientifically founded, to the environment, health, and safety in general, appeared some years ago. They are related for instance to new technologies, high-voltage lines, mobile telephone installations, ionising radiations or genetically modified organisms. Such potential risks may also arise through the use of instruments or products in industrial, chemical, medical, and pharmaceutical sectors or even in food, livestock, agriculture or energy production. This list is not exhaustive. 11

[5] For an analysis of foreign statutes based on strict liability, see e.g. G. Schamps, *La mise en danger: un concept fondateur d'un principe général de responsabilité. Analyse de droit compare* (1998), 107–118 (Italy); 234–249 (The Netherlands); 325–249 (Switzerland); 470–511 (England); 735–806 (Belgium and France).

[6] See e.g. X. Thunis, En guise de conclusion: le poids des responsabilités, [2004] *Aménagement-Environnement* (Amén.), special issue, 237 et seq.; P. Steichen, La directive 2004/35 sur la responsabilité environnementale en ce qui concerne la prévention et la réparation des dommages environnementaux – Un droit de compromis pour une responsabilité nouvelle, [2004] Amén., special issue, 109–127.

12 The emergence of these new potential risks has produced a climate of caution. Precaution is distinguished from prevention[7]. Prevention relates to the possible occurrence of risks that are known, whilst precaution concerns unknown risks. The concept of precaution underlines the awareness of a duty towards future generations, in a context of sustainable development[8]. However if many rules of soft law or international agreements make reference to it[9], this concept has not been given a single definition in the legal texts or by authors[10]. Sometimes the word precautionary "principle" is used, sometimes only the word precautionary "approach"[11]. The extent, the conditions for application and the guidelines for these concepts vary.

[7] Ph. Kourilsky, *Du bon usage du principe de précaution* (2002), 45; G. Viney/Ph. Kourilsky, *Le principe de précaution, Rapport au Premier ministre* (2000), 18; European Environment Agency, *Late lessons from early warnings: the precautionary principle 1896–2000* (2002), 1–13.

[8] About sustainable development, see e.g. O. Godard, Le développement durable, la recherche et les entreprises: les conditions d'une synergie, [2004] *Cahiers Laboratoire d'économétrie*, 2004-011, 1–7; F. Chaltiel, L'Union européenne et le développement durable, [2003] *Revue du Marché commun et de l'Union européenne*, 24 et seq.; E. Zaccaï, *Le développement durable. Dynamique et constitution d'un projet* (2002); M. Haïdarlis, Durabilité, développement durable et droit hellénique, [2002] *Revue juridique de l'environnement* (RJ•E) 3, 413 et seq.; G. Fievet, Réflexions sur le concept de développement durable: prétention économique, principes stratégiques et protection des droits fondamentaux, [2001] *Revue belge de droit international*, 1, 164 et seq.

[9] See e.g. the conventions cited by A. Trouwborst, *Evolution and Status of the Precautionary Principle in International Law* (2002), 33 et seq.; P.W. Birnie/A.E. Boyle, *International Law & the Environment* (2nd edn. 2002), 116 et seq.; J. Cameron, The Precautionary Principle in International Law, in: T. O'Riordan/J. Cameron/A. Jordan (eds.), *Reinterpreting the Precautionary Principle* (2001), 113–142; N. de Sadeleer, L'émergence du principe de précaution, [2001] JT, 395; A. Kiss/J.-P. Beurier, *Droit international de l'environnement* (2nd edn. 2000), 122, no. 265.

[10] About the Precautionary Principle, see e.g. the contributions to the book E. Vos/G. van Calster (eds.), *Risico en voorzorg in de rechtsmaatschappij* (2004); G. Schamps, Le principe de précaution justifie-t-il une nouvelle responsabilité en droit civil belge? D'autres alternatives existent …, in: A. Wijffels (ed.), *Le Code civil entre ius commune et droit privé européen* (2005), 517–542; G. Schamps, Le principe de précaution, dans un contexte de droit communautaire et de droit administratif: vers un nouveau fondement de la responsabilité civile?, in: *Mélanges offerts à Marcel Fontaine* (2003), 211–244; G. Schamps, Le relâchement des liens entre les responsabilités pénale et civile. La mise en danger, distincte du principe de précaution, in: *Liber Amicorum Jean du Jardin* (2001), 381–429; C. de Roany, Des principes de précaution. Analyse de critères communs et d'interprétation différenciée, [2004] RJ•E, 143–156; N. de Sadeleer, Le principe de précaution. Un nouveau principe général de droit, [2003] *Journal des Tribunaux – Droit européen* (J.T.dr. eur.), 129–134; N. de Sadeleer, *Environmental Principles. From Political Slogans to Legal Rules* (2002), 91 et seq.; H. Cousy, Le principe de précaution et ses relations avec le droit des assurances, in: *Mélanges offerts à Marcel Fontaine* (2003), 681 et seq; J.-L. Fagnart, La conception des produits pharmaceutiques. Précaution et responsabilité, in: *Mélanges offerts à Marcel Fontaine* (2003), 749 et seq.; M. Faure/E. Vos, *Juridische afbakening van het voorzorgsbeginsel: mogelijkheden en grenzen* (2003); O. Godard/C. Henry/P. Lagadec/E. Michel-Kerian, *Traité des nouveaux risques. Précaution, crise, assurance* (2002).

[11] See e.g. Principle 15 of the Declaration of Rio de Janeiro at the UN Conference on Environment and Development: "In order to protect the environment, the precautionary approach shall be widely applied by States according to their capabilities. Where there are threats of serious or irreversible damage, lack of full scientific certainty shall not be used as a reason for postponing cost-effective measures to prevent environmental degradation"; R. Cooney, *The Precautionary Principle in Biodiversity Conservation and Natural Resource Management: An issues paper for policy-makers, researchers and practitioners* (2004).

In France, the precautionary principle is inscribed in the Environmental Charter which has been given constitutional status[12]. According to art. 5 of this Charter, "If damage occurs, although it may be uncertain in the light of scientific knowledge, and it may affect the environment in a serious and irreversible way, the public authorities must ensure, by application of the precautionary principle and according to their powers, the implementation of procedures to evaluate the risks and the adoption of temporary and proportional measures to prevent damage occurring"[13]. 13

International institutions, such as the International Court of Justice and the World Trade Organisation, have some reservations regarding the acceptance of the precautionary principle as an international customary rule[14]. In the European Community, the Court of First Instance has decided that, although the precautionary principle is mentioned in the Treaty only in connection with environmental policy[15], it is broader in scope. It is intended to be applied in order to ensure a high level of protection of health, consumer safety and environment in all the Community's spheres of activity[16]. 14

[12] See Lois constitutionnelles n° 2005-204 du 1er mars 2005 modifiant le titre XV de la Constitution et n° 2005-205 du 1er mars 2005 relative à la Charte de l'environnement; see also Loi n° 95–101 du 2 février 1995 relative au renforcement de la protection de l'environnement (art. L. 200-1 al. 3 Code rural); Y. Jegouzo, Le principe de précaution ne s'appliquera qu'en cas de réelle incertitude scientifique, [2003] *Recueil Dalloz* (D) 1843–1845; O. Godard, Le principe de précaution doit-il être interdit de Charte de l'environnement?, [2004] *Cahiers Laboratoire d'économétrie* 2004–015, 1–12.

[13] Free translation.

[14] In favour of the acceptance of the precautionary principle as an international customary rule, see e.g. J. Cameron/J. Abouchar, The Status of the Precautionary Principle in International Law, in: D. Freestone/E. Hey (eds.), *The Precautionary Principle and International Law. The Challenge of Implementation* (1996), 52; A. Trouwborst (supra fn. 9), 284 and the authors cited. About this question, see e.g. M. Dias Varella, Différences d'interprétation sur un même sujet: le principe de précaution, la CIJ, l'OMC et la CJCE, [2004] *Revue européenne de droit de l'environnement*, 19–29; the contributions to the book C. Leben/J. Verhoeven (eds.), *Le principe de précaution. Aspects de droit international et communautaire* (2002); M. Arbour, Le principe de précaution dans le contexte du commerce international: une intégration difficile, in: *Le principe de précaution*, [2002] *Les Cahiers de Droit*, special issue, 36; N. Salmon, An European perspective on the precautionary principle, food safety and the free trade imperative of the WTO, [2002] *European Law Review*, 148 et seq.; J.-F. Neuray, *Droit de l'environnement* (2001), 78.

[15] Art. 174.2 Treaty EC.

[16] Court of first instance, T-392/02, 21 October 2003, *Solvay Pharmaceuticals* BV, § 121; Court of first instance, T-74/00, T-76/00, T-83/00 to T-85/00, T-132/00 and T-141/00, 26 November 2002, *Artegodan*, § 184; Court of first instance, T-147/00, 28 January 2003, *Les Laboratoires Servier*, § 53; see also Court of first instance, T-70/99, 11 September 2002, *Alpharma*; Court of first instance, T-13/99, 11 September 2002, *Pfizer Animal Health*, § 115. About these two last cases, see e.g. E. Vos, Antibiotics, the Precautionary Principle and the Court of First Instance, [2004] *Maastricht Journal of European and Comparative Law* (MJ) 2, 187–200; J.L. da Cruz Vilaça, The precautionary principle in EC Law, [2004] *European Public Law*, 369–405. See also Court of first instance, T-177/02, 10 March 2004, *Malagutti-Vezinhet S.A.*, § 54; Court, C-41/02, 2 December 2004, *Kingdom of the Netherlands*, §§ 44–46.

15 In Belgian law, a question arises: is the precautionary principle now a new basis for tort liability? Before examining this question, a brief outline of the way in which the precautionary principle appears in Belgium will be given (B). Its possible effect on tort law will then be examined (C). Finally a brief presentation will be made of the guidelines of the general principle that I suggest to improve the compensation of victims for risks which are already known at this moment in time (D).

B. The Existence of the Precautionary Principle in Belgian Law

1. The Belgian Statutory Rules

16 In Belgian law, statutes or decrees make reference to the precautionary principle, particularly with regard to the policy to be adopted on environment and water protection issues. Generally, they also refer to other principles, such as the polluter-pays, the principle of preventative action or the principle on sustainable management.

17 According to the decree of the Flemish Region of 5 April 1995 (art. 1.2.1. § 2), the environmental policy aims at a high level of protection on the basis of evaluation of the various social activities. This policy is based in particular on the precautionary principle. This principle also appears in the decree of the Flemish Region of 18 July 2003 (art. 6).

18 The precautionary principle is also inscribed in the federal statute of 29 January 1999 on the marine environment protection in Belgian territorial waters: users of territorial waters and public authorities must adopt measures of prevention "when there are reasonable causes to worry about marine pollution, even if there is not conclusive proof of a causal link between the introduction of substances, energy or material in the marine waters and their harmful effects". This statute also contains a regime of no-fault liability, against the perpetrator of any damage or environmental incident affecting marine waters following an accident or a violation of this statute.

19 The Walloon Region also adopted, on 27 May 2004, a decree relative to Book I of the Code of Environment[17]. According to this decree, the environmental policy of the Region is inspired in particular by the precautionary principle.

20 Moreover approval statutes to several international conventions referring to the precautionary principle were adopted[18]. Other regulations have imposed

[17] This decree has not yet come into force.

[18] See e.g. Loi du 15 mars 2004 portant assentiment au Protocole de Cartagena sur la prévention des risques biotechnologiques relatif à la Convention sur la diversité biologique, et aux

measures for protection and safety procedures concerning scientifically unknown risks, particularly in food safety, radiations, dangerous substances, electromagnetic waves or following the chicken contamination by dioxin or the spread of BSE, the "mad cow" disease[19].

2. The Jurisprudence in Public Law and in Tort Law

In public law, some people express reservations about an autonomous application of the precautionary principle. They believe however that this principle is implicit during the verification of the validity of the public decision under attack or during the examination of the compliance with procedures. The judge can decide that the risk evaluation procedures have not been respected or that the public decision to authorise or prohibit, taken for the environment or public health protection, was justified or not, given the scientific uncertainty of the risk. 21

The precautionary principle underlies the interpretation by the *Conseil d'Etat* (Public Law Juridiction) of e.g. the concept of "risk of serious and difficult to repair damage", which is linked to the immediate execution of the decision being attacked. Some decisions refer to the precautionary principle e.g. about permits on the installation of high voltage wires, mobile telephone masts or electrical substations[20]. 22

As yet in tort law, no judgment has based a fault-liability on the precautionary principle. The question whether the precautionary principle will have any special effect upon tort law has been a subject of some discussion, particularly in France. Some people say that this influence will be significant. Others say it will be non-existent. More nuanced, we may say that even if the reference to 23

Annexes, faits à Montréal le 29 janvier 2000; Loi du 13 mai 2003 portant assentiment au Protocole sur l'eau et la santé à la Convention de 1992 sur la protection et l'utilisation des cours d'eau transfrontières et des lacs internationaux, fait à Londres le 17 juin 1999; Loi du 29 septembre 2000 portant assentiment à la Convention sur la protection et l'utilisation des cours d'eau transfrontières et des lacs internationaux, et les annexes I, II, III et IV, faites à Helsinki le 17 mars 1992.

[19] See e.g. Arrêté royal du 22 février 2001 organisant les contrôles effectués par l'Agence fédérale pour la Sécurité de la Chaîne alimentaire et modifiant diverses dispositions légales; Arrêté royal du 29 avril 2001 fixant la norme pour les antennes émettant des ondes électromagnétiques entre 10 MHz et 10 GHz; Arrêté royal du 6 mai 2001 déclarant nuisibles certains produits d'origine animale présentant des risques au regard des encéphalopathies spongiformes transmissibles; Arrêté royal du 17 juillet 2002 modifiant l'arrêté royal du 24 mai 1982 réglementant la mise sur le marché de substances pouvant être dangereuses pour l'homme ou son environnement; Arrêté royal du 20 juillet 2001 portant règlement général de la protection de la population, des travailleurs et de l'environnement contre le danger des rayonnements ionisants. About the ALARA Principle ("As low as reasonably achievable") relating to inonising radiations, see S. Lierman, *Voorzorg, preventie en aansprakelijkheid. Gezondheidsrechtelijke analyse aan de hand van het gebruik van ioniserende straling in de geneeskunde* (2004), 110 et seq.

[20] M. Pâques, Le Conseil d'Etat et le principe de précaution. Chronique d'une naissance annoncée, [2004] JT, 169–179. See also *Conseil d'Etat*, 10 April 2003, no. 118.214; *Conseil d'Etat*, 13 May 2004, no. 131.426.

the precautionary principle may have an impact on the evaluation of some conditions for fault-based liability, the principle cannot be a basis for awarding compensation the way the Belgian law stands at the moment.

C. Is the Precautionary Principle a new Basis for Belgian Tort Law?

1. Functions of Tort Law

24 Tort law can fulfil several main functions: compensation, loss shifting and spreading, deterrence of undesirable behaviour, avoidance of economically inefficient behaviour. No one function can, in itself, fully explain tort law[21].

25 Those in favour of an economic analysis of law lay the emphasis on the function of deterrence and the efficiency of tort rules. In their opinion, these rules should provide incentives to avoid socially harmful behaviour, such as behaviour that does not lead to an optimal allocation of resources. In this approach, the need to reduce the costs of accidents and to take efficient precautions to avoid them is rightly emphasized[22].

26 In Belgian law however, compensation is generally viewed as the prime function of tort law. Some people say that in the fields where it appears – health, safety, environment – the precautionary principle may be taken into consideration in the context of fault-based liability to help it develop into having a more deterrent function.

27 However, fault-based liability is not really considered as the most satisfactory device to achieve the objective of deterrence where dangerous activities or situations are involved. It does not have a really dissuasive effect when the damage is due to unavoidable human errors or to the use of dangerous objects. The damage occurring as a result of dangerous activities is often attributable to chance or to technical imperfections or even to physical or psychological deficiencies inherent to the nature of the ordinary man[23]. Furthermore, when uncertain damage is only likely to happen over the long term, the person con-

[21] W. van Gerven/J. Lever/P. Larouche, *Tort Law* (2000), 18 et seq. About the functions of tort law, see also e.g. G. Viney/P. Jourdain, *Traité de droit civil. Les effets de la responsabilité* (2nd edn. 2001), 18 et seq.; T. Hartlief, De meerwaarde van het aansprakelijkheidsrecht, in: T. Hartlief/S. Klosse (eds.), *Einde van het aansprakelijkheidsrecht?* (2003), 9 et seq.; M. Faure, De meerwaarde van het aansprakelijkheidsrecht voor het milieu, in: T. Hartlief/S. Klosse (eds.), *Einde van het aansprakelijkheidsrecht?* (2003), 226 et seq.

[22] See the authors cited by W. van Gerven/J. Lever/P. Larouche (supra fn. 21), 27.

[23] W. van Gerven/J. Lever/P. Larouche (supra fn. 21), 26; J.-P. Leyens, Causalité, prévision et choix: un processus infiltré de théories naïves, in: Ch. Hennau-Hublet (ed.), *Le défaut de prévoyance à l'épreuve des faits et du droit. Droit belge et droit comparé*, [1994] *Revue de droit pénal et de criminologie* (RDPC), 273 et seq.

cerned may be indifferent to what might happen a long time after his death or after the company dissolution.

In Belgian law, the regime of tort law does not accept the awarding of punitive damages[24] to the perpetrator. Finally, the existence of a compulsory insurance or not can blunt the deterrent effect albeit its regime includes factors to encourage prevention – such as excess, recuperation procedure in case of a serious or intentional fault, premium increase, or safety measures likely to be imposed by the contract[25]. 28

2. The Precautionary Principle with Regard to the Conditions of Fault-based Liability

a) The Fault

In future, the reference to the precautionary principle may imply an extension to the concept of fault. In Belgian law, fault may consist in a violation of a written rule which imposes a specific obligation. The violation of this rule is considered to be unlawful *per se*. The fault may also consist in a violation of the general rule of careful behaviour. In this second eventuality, the behaviour of the person concerned is judged in comparison with that of a normally careful and reasonable person, faced with the same circumstances. 29

The precautionary principle may encourage the adoption, by statutes, of new rules which impose specific safety measures or procedures, in particular as regards environment or health. An obligation to inform and warn the public and an obligation to monitor closely the risk and to regularly update the data may also be required. The non-compliance with these rules would then be sufficient in itself to constitute a fault. 30

It is especially with regard to the general rule of careful behaviour that the precautionary principle may imply an extension to the concept of fault. This principle may cause the judge to be more severe when he has to examine whether leaders of industry, public authorities, private decision-makers or controllers have respected the general rule of careful behaviour. The level of care required might be analysed in relation to a less known amount of scientific knowledge. The existence of a defence, such as an insurmountable mistake or ignorance, would possibly be judged more severely. 31

In future, the public authorities may be judged to have committed a fault, on the basis of the precautionary principle, for example when they issue an authorization to exercise an activity which presents an uncertain risk or when 32

[24] S. Carval, *La responsabilité civile dans sa fonction de peine privée* (1995).

[25] About the precautionary principle and insurance, see H. Cousy, Le principe de précaution et ses relations avec le droit des assurances, in: *Mélanges offerts à Marcel Fontaine* (2003), 681 et seq.; L. Mayaux, Réflexions sur le principe de précaution et le droit des assurances, [2003] *Revue générale du droit des assurances* (RGDA), 269–286.

they do not take sufficient supervisory measures. It would however be appropriate to avoid a limitless application of the precautionary principle because it could encourage decision-makers to take excessive measures, without correct evaluation of the risks and true policy of management.

33 Be that as it may, even if the judge were to accept in future an extension to the concept of fault on the basis of the precautionary principle, the victim would still have to establish the existence of a causal link and a certain and foreseeable damage in Belgian law.

b) The Causal Link

34 When damage occurs in the remote future or when it appears during complicated processes, it might be difficult to establish the existence of a causal link between the dangerous behaviour and the actual damage. Besides the scientific uncertainties, the investigation of evidence and the identification of the potential responsible person would not be easy.

35 It is sometimes suggested to make the conditions for causal link more flexible, for the application of the precautionary principle[26], by accepting a legal presumption of causation or a solution derived from the Convention on civil liability for damage resulting from activities dangerous to the environment. In accordance with this Convention, the court must take due account of the increased danger of causing such damage inherent in the dangerous activity (art. 10).

36 In my opinion, this flexibility should be better applied under a regime of strict liability and not a fault-based liability. A liability for fault implies an evaluation of the behaviour of the person responsible. So the existence of a fault, damage and causal link has to be established for certain, in order that the person held liable feels the compensation to be justified. On the contrary, strict liability does not need such an evaluation. Such a regime has been created to make it easier to compensate for the damage, because the factors linked with the person deemed responsible are more flexible than with fault-based liability. A moderate approach towards the establishment of the causal link can then be applied more easily in a regime of strict liability. But then there is no need to refer to the precautionary principle because strict liability does not require a fault.

c) The Certain and Foreseeable Damage

37 Finally, if in future the concept of fault has to be widened and the proof of causal link be moderated by a judicial application of the precautionary principle, the last condition of the fault-based liability would still have to be met to justify an award for compensation of damage. This condition is the presence

[26] Against such concept, see e.g. J.-L. Fagnart, La conception des produits pharmaceutiques. Précaution et responsabilité, in: *Mélanges offerts à Marcel Fontaine* (2003), 769.

of a certain and foreseeable damage[27]. Therefore this requirement is difficult to reconcile with the precautionary principle.

In Belgian law, the acceptance of civil liability for infringement of a general obligation to take care implies that the damage resulting from the behaviour is foreseeable. 38

In addition, in a fault-based liability, the damage must be certain. This damage may happen in the future but its occurrence must be certain. The precautionary principle does not satisfy these conditions. In fact, this principle deals with uncertain risks. Sometimes it is suggested that the simple threat of damage or the creation of a serious or irreversible risk, not scientifically founded, should be accepted as compensable damage[28]. However this idea is closer to the dissuasive function under criminal law. But in criminal law in Belgium a fault and the foreseeable nature of the damage must be proven[29]. 39

Even if the loss of a chance theory is used, it is not possible, in the current state of Belgian law, to establish a fault-based liability on the precautionary principle. According to this theory, the loss of a chance to obtain a particular advantage or to avoid a specific damage can be compensated if this chance has been lost because of the fault of the person concerned. The victim has to supply proof of the loss of chance and this loss must be certain. Moreover, a decision of the Belgian *Cour de cassation* seems to indicate a setback for acceptance of the concept of "loss of chance"[30]. 40

3. A Deterrent Role of the Precautionary Principle in Public Law

Hence, the precautionary principle does not satisfy the requirements of current fault-liability, in Belgian law, as a basis for a compensation award. 41

Public law could provide a better deterrent role using the precautionary principle. A dissuasive effect could be achieved by the prior establishment of safety standards, procedures or suitable systems for evaluating the risks and for making decisions. The precautionary principle should, above all, encourage an active management of uncertain but sufficiently credible risks within the scientific community, in an ethical, social and economically acceptable vision. This should be also an incentive to draw up procedures to communicate with the citizens and to continually monitor such risks. 42

[27] R.O Dalcq/G. Schamps, Examen de jurisprudence (1987 à 1993). La responsabilité délictuelle et quasi délictuelle, [1995] *Revue critique de jurisprudence belge* (RCJB), 536–537.

[28] C. Radé, Le principe de précaution, une nouvelle éthique de la responsabilité, [1995] RJ•E, 84; contra O. Godard/C. Henry/P. Lagadec/E. Michel-Kerian (supra fn. 10), 176 et seq.

[29] Cass., 12 May 1987, [1988] RDPC, 711; G. Schamps, L'autonomie croissante de l'action civile par rapport à l'action publique. La loi du 10 juin 1998 modifiant le régime de la prescription de l'action civile. L'érosion de l'autorité de la chose jugée au pénal sur le civil, in: *Actualités de droit pénal et de procédure pénale* (2001), 115 et seq.

[30] Cass., 1 April 2004, no. C010211F; S. Lierman, Verlies van een kans bij medische ongevallen, [2005] *Nieuw juridisch weekblad* (NJW), 641 et seq.

43 It is suggested to avoid any policy of exaggerated measures out of all proportion to the likely threat and which would not take account of the potential benefits that a particular activity could offer. Nor should we go towards a zero risk option. However, the protection of public health, the environment and safety should take priority over economic considerations. Decisions could be taken after calm and thoughtful discussions between public authorities, private decision-makers and citizens' associations, taking particular account of soft law provisions.

D. The Advantage of Creating a General Principle Based on a Specific Danger

1. To Improve Compensation for Damage Linked with Risks which are Already Known

44 Instead of distorting the requirements of civil liability by means of the precautionary principle, it would be better to find a solution to make it easier for the victims to obtain compensation for damage linked to current risks which are already certain and which, when they happen, can have dramatic consequences on the life and health of victims. For instance, asbestos, use of particularly poisonous or dangerous substances or devices, foodstuffs contaminated by dioxin, as happened in Belgium a few years ago with chicken, contaminated blood, etc.

45 At the moment, Belgian civil liability based on fault or presumption of fault is not able to offer a suitable way of compensating victims for damage caused by such risks or to avoid discrimination between them. Belgian statutes on strict liability have the disadvantage of being limited in number and of being adopted one by one, often when catastrophes have already happened or under pressure from public opinion. They are not the result of any global consideration regarding the dangerous nature of activities or situations covered by the statutes. Moreover they do not apply to all similar risks.

46 To improve prevention and compensation for damage linked to specific activities or situations, it is possible to conceive the concept of "endangering someone" (*mise en danger*) which could justify a general principle. This principle could imply a regime of strict liability or a no-fault compensation scheme[31] for victims when they have suffered damage because of the realisation of the known danger.

47 Such a general principle could fill the current gaps and be applied to those risks that will be known in future. Specific statutes to govern the compensa-

[31] About No-fault Compensation in the Health Care Sector, see e.g. the contributions to the book J. Dute/M.G. Faure/H. Koziol (eds.), *No-fault Compensation in the Health Care Sector* (2004).

tion for risks should no longer have to be adopted on an *ad hoc* basis. However the intention is not to eliminate all risks to society. Many risks have scientific, economic or private benefits. They are tolerated because of their social usefulness but this tolerance must also take account of the potential victims' interest.

2. The Guidelines for a General Principle Based on a Specific Danger

a) The Two Pillars of the General Principle

For the design of this general principle I suggest[32], I took particular inspiration 48
from provisions of Italian[33], Dutch[34], Swiss[35], English law[36] and from the *First*[37] and *Second*[38] *Restatements of Torts*. My intention is not to propose here the actual wording for a general principle but merely to give guidelines[39].

[32] See G. Schamps, *La mise en danger: un concept fondateur d'un principe général de responsabilité. Analyse de droit comparé* (1998), 1140; for a summary, see La mise en danger: un concept fondateur d'un principe général de responsabilité. Les grandes lignes de la thèse et ses répercussions, Quinquennial Prize of the Revue Critique de Jurisprudence Belge, [2001] RCJB, 13412/1 et seq.

[33] See in particular art. 2050 *Codice civile* (Italian Civil Code): Chiunque cagiona danno ad altri nell svolgimento di un'attività pericolosa, per sua natura o per la natura dei mezzi adoperati, è tenuto al risarcimento, se non prova di avere adottato tutte le misure idonee a evitare il danno. See G. Schamps (supra fn. 32), 17–133.

[34] See particularly art. 6:175 *Burgerlijk Wetboek* (BW, Dutch Civil Code): Degene die in de uitoefening van zijn beroep of bedrijf een stof gebruikt of onder zich heeft, terwijl van deze stof bekend is dat zij zodanige eigenschappen heeft, dat zij een bijzonder gevaar van ernstige aard voor personen of zaken oplevert, is aansprakelijk, wanneer dit gevaar zich verwezenlijkt. Onder degene die een bedrijf uitoefent, wordt mede begrepen elke rechtspersoon die de stof in de uitoefening van zijn taak gebruikt of onder zich heeft. Als bijzonder gevaar van ernstige aard geldt in elk geval dat de stof ontplofbaar, oxyderend, ontvlambaar, licht ontvlambaar of zeer licht ontvlambaar, dan wel vergiftig of zeer vergiftig is volgens de criteria en methoden, vastgesteld krachtens artikel 34, derde lid, Wet milieugevaarlijke stoffen. See G. Schamps (supra fn. 32), 134–256.

[35] P. Widmer/P. Wessner, *Révision et unification du droit de la responsabilité civile. Avant-projet de loi fédérale*, 1–411. See G. Schamps (supra fn. 32), 257–407.

[36] See particularly *Rylands v. Fletcher*, [1866] *Law Reports* (LR), 1 279–280: "We think that the true rule of law is, that the person who for his own purposes brings on his lands and collects and keeps there anything likely to do mischief if it escapes, must keep it in at his peril, and, if he does not do so, is prima facie answerable for all the damage which is the natural consequence of its escape". See also The Law Commission, *Civil Liability for Dangerous Things and Activities, Laid before Parliament by the Lord High Chancellor pursuant to section 3(2) of the Law Commissions Act 1965* (1972); Royal Commission on Civil Liability and Compensation for Personal Injury, *Report presented to Parliament by Command of Her Majesty* I (1978). See G. Schamps (supra fn. 32), 408–535.

[37] American Law Institute, *Restatement of the Law, Torts*, vol. 3, Divisions 3–9, (1938), 41 et seq., §§ 519 and 520.

[38] American Law Institute, *Restatement of The Law Second. Torts 2d*, vol. 3, § 504–707A, (1977), 34 et seq., §§ 519 and 520. According to § 519: "(1) One who carries on an abnormally dangerous activity is subject to liability for harm to the person, land or chattels of another resulting from the activity, although he has exercised the utmost care to prevent the harm. (2) This strict liability is limited to the kind of harm, the possibility of which makes the activity abnormally dangerous". See G. Schamps (supra fn. 32), 535–593.

[39] Fore more details, see G. Schamps (supra fn. 32), 843–995.

49 For some people, the reference to danger cannot be a valid foundation for a compensation system for victims. This concept would be vague and would vary according to circumstances. Danger would be summarised as any potential capacity to cause damage. I think that it is, however, possible to separate some degree of danger according to the risks involved. When this degree of danger is exceeded, it may be a basis for a regime other than a fault-based liability. In fact, it is not appropriate to treat in the same way, for example, a hydroelectric dam, an inflammable gas tank, a misplaced vase of flowers or an unsteady ladder.

50 The dangerousness covered by the general principle would be supported by two pillars: a "characterized risk" on the one hand and a specific activity or situation on the other hand. The person who carries out such an activity has to compensate for the damage that may be linked to the occurrence of the characterized risk that this activity – or the situation arising after it stops – entails, even if this activity is legally tolerated.

(i) A Characterized Risk

– A First Level of Dangerousness – A High Likelihood of Great Severity of Injury

51 The characterized risk could be determined according to exceeding a first level of dangerousness as well as objective criteria, as a high likelihood of a great severity of injury.

52 The first level of dangerousness would be the unavoidable nature of the risks in spite of reasonable precautionary measures. This threshold can mark a demarcation between the risks suitable for inclusion under a strict liability compensation system and those which must continue to be governed by the current legal system. If there were any reasonable measures to avoid the danger and these had not been adopted, this should be considered as fault. On the other hand, the human failing to avoid the danger emphasizes a greater dangerousness than that which may be eliminated by due care and attention. The risk from a vase of flowers or from an unsteady ladder is not therefore covered by the general principle.

53 Besides the criteria for exceeding a first level of dangerousness, the characterized risk under the general principle should include a high degree of likelihood of generating serious damage. These objective criteria also appear in the foreign rules examined and they are approved by the scientific experts in the risks sciences, in French "*les cindyniques*"[40].

[40] See e.g. G.-Y. Kervern/P. Rubise, *L'archipel du danger. Introduction aux cindyniques* (1991), 63 et seq.

– Objective Indications

However, an exact grading of theses criteria is not really achievable as a general rule and *a priori*, particularly given the large number of risks. The difficulty in grading the objective criteria for dangerousness in a general and abstract manner may thus be compensated by the elaboration of objective indications, which are not exhaustive. 54

These indications may, for example, be measures adopted by the legislator to govern those activities which it considers particularly dangerous, such as safety and accident prevention measures or the issue of permits to carry out an activity. The vulnerability of potential victims faced with the danger, statistical data and the higher rating of insurance premiums could be previous signs of dangerousness. It is the same for the obligation to contribute to guarantee funds or to take out an insurance. This last indication was also proposed by the Law Commission[41] and the Pearson Commission in English law[42]. 55

There are already some indications of dangerousness in specific statutes on strict liability. The judge could also take these into account for risks which are similar but which are not covered by the statutes. Besides these indications, the judge would also be able to refer to scientific studies on danger or to reports of human failures in the organisation and management of any activity. 56

The judge's task could be facilitated by consulting non-exhaustive lists mentioning dangerous activities that, automatically or possibly, correspond to the characterised risk. It is obvious that the elaboration of these lists would probably give rise to bitter negotiations among the representatives from the sectors in question. Such a system has the advantage of informing the chief operator (*l'exploitant*) that his/her activity can generate a specific compensation scheme. This person would then have the possibility to improve, in full awareness of the facts, the prevention of danger, for instance by changing his operating methods. Nevertheless, the method used by the Dutch legislator (Art. 6:175 B.W.) should not be followed. Indeed, the definition of the risk in this article implies tiresome research in a legislative labyrinth which largely decreases the interest of a rule with general scope. 57

The judge must not examine whether the person liable could have realized that a damage of great severity may or may not occur. The reference, at this stage, to the subjectively foreseeable nature of the danger would constitute a disguised return to fault liability. It is indeed advisable to avoid the discussions relating to the kind of scheme which appeared in Italian law (Art. 2050 *Codice Civile*) and following the case *Cambridge Water Co Ltd.* relating to the rule *Rylands v. Fletcher* in English law[43]. 58

[41] Law Commission (supra fn. 36), 11.

[42] Royal Commission on Civil Liability and Compensation for Personal Injury (supra fn. 36), 344, nos. 1649–1651.

[43] *Cambridge Water Co Ltd. v. Eastern Counties Leather plc*, [1994] *The All England Law Reports* (All E.R.) 1, 53.

59 The reference to the common perception of risks must not be retained, just as the concept of reasonable expectation, as in the directive of 25 July 1985 concerning liability for defective products. Indeed, these concepts imply a reasonable foreseeable nature of the damage. They may implicitly refer to the concept of fault. However the fault can only be taken into account during the examination of the first level of dangerousness.

(ii) A Specific Dangerous Activity

60 Besides the characterized risk, the second key-element of the general principle is the fact of carrying on a specifically dangerous activity. We should not however adopt the approach, according to which the public interest nature of the activity would prevent the application of the general principle. Furthermore, such an activity is only tolerated because of its utility in spite of its dangerous nature. The *Learned-Hand formula* and the *Risk-Utility test*, existing in the United States, are not applied.

61 The suggested general principle concerns human interventions or situations that arise after their cessation. The specifically dangerous aspect of the activity results from its nature, that of the means employed or their interaction. The proposed definition is close to that formulated by the Italian Supreme Court[44]. The activity would entail a combination of phases, processes, coordinated or otherwise, involving a minimum of continuity and organisation. It does not mean any one single operation. The possible omission of precautionary measures is not taken into account at this stage since it has been considered during the examination of the first level of dangerousness.

62 In addition to the material and the technical risk, the "endangering of someone" (*mise en danger*) also concerns the organisational risk. This appears particularly in modern companies, in particular because of the complexity of their structures. This dangerousness can be related to automatic equipment, standardised procedures, specializations, productions and services which are increasingly more extended. They imply very ramified organisation of work and distributions of responsibilities. It also appears with important gatherings of people, such as during sporting competitions. The catastrophes of Heysel, in Belgium, or of Bastia, in France, which occurred a few years ago, are such examples. The introduction of a general liability for the risk's organization has also been defended in Switzerland[45].

63 The means submitted to the general principle are in particular substances, instruments, installations or energy sources. Their utilisation offers man extra power which he is not always able to master completely.

[44] Cass., 24 February 1983, no. 1425, [1983] *Responsabilità civile e previdenza* (Resp. civ. prev.), 774.

[45] P. Jäggi, Intervention lors du Congrès de Neuchâtel, [1967] *Revue de droit social* (R.D.S.) II, 754 et seq.; P. Widmer, Responsabilité du fait des produits et responsabilité du fait de l'organisation, in: *Mélanges en l'honneur de Jacques-Michel Grossen* (1992), 352 et seq.

The concept of a defective thing, as in art. 1384, first line, of the Belgian Civil Code, is not used to define the specific dangerous activity. In fact, this concept does not really emphasize the danger and does not refer to the activity. It is more often the interaction between an action and the means employed that increase the dangerousness. Furthermore, the requirement for a thing to be defective is a source of discussion. In addition, the definition of the defect does not relate to dangerousness in particular and there is no close relationship between danger and the existence of a defect. 64

The condition of "common usage", in the meaning of the *Restatement of Tort*, is not retained in the general principle I propose. Indeed, it is not because a dangerous activity is usually carried on that it has lost its dangerousness. The requirement of the escape of a thing, as in the *Rylands v. Fletcher* rule in English law, is too restrictive and introduces discrimination between victims, since only those who are outside the ground may have the possibility to introduce an action based on this rule. 65

Unlike the Dutch law relating to the use or the possession of a dangerous substance (Art. 6:175 B.W.), the activity has not to be carried on within the framework of an enterprise or a profession. In Italian law, the attempt to limit art. 2050 of the Civil Code to the activities of a company did not succeed. Indeed, the dangerousness can increase when the activity is carried on by a private individual who does not have the structure and the equipment of a company. 66

b) Possible Schemes for the General Principle

The scheme of such a general principle could be a strict liability regime or a no-fault system. It would be useful to take account of the advice of the proponents of an economic analysis of law for the choice of the scheme. Moreover, the effectiveness of different kinds of compensatory systems and their ability to spread losses over groups of potential persons, through private insurance, social security or pricing mechanisms, should be the object of a global analysis[46]. 67

Strict liability has the advantage of not taking into account the behaviour of the person held responsible. Furthermore, it can easily adapt to any adjustment to, or suppression of, the proof of a causal link. 68

In the general principle I suggest, when the victim has proved the likelihood of a connection between the damage and the characterized risk of the specific dangerous activity, it would be presumed that the damage lies within the scope of this risk. It would then be up to the chief operator (*l'exploitant*) to show that the connection does not really exist. The theories of the *conditio sine qua non* or the adequate causality are not retained. The general principle is more an application of the theory of the aquilian relativity. The damage can 69

[46] W. van Gerven/J. Lever/P. Larouche (supra fn. 21), 32.

only be compensated if it can be connected with the characterized risk of the specific dangerous activity.

70 If a strict liability regime were to be adopted, the liability could be, at first sight, directed towards the chief operator. This can be an individual or legal entity with responsibility for the management and supervision of the specific dangerous activity generating the profit. As the individual or legal entity have the technical know-how and the operational resources for this activity, they are best equipped to reduce the characterized risk and to set the cost of damage against, for instance, the cost of insurance premiums or by setting the appropriate price for the goods and services offered.

71 As stress is placed upon protection and compensation for victims, the exonerating factors should only be accepted with great reservation. Moreover, the matter of limitation of liability to a maximum amount of compensation should be analysed. The majority of Swiss statutes on strict liability do not have a liability ceiling. The unlimited nature of liability does not prevent a limitation on insurance cover. The possibility of an order to pay a higher compensation than that provided for under the insurance cover also plays a part in the prevention.

72 An obligation to take out insurance or to arrange a financial guarantee could be imposed upon the chief operator. It could also affect the granting of an authorization or a licence to carry out an activity. If the public interest justifies the activity, in spite of the possible future insolvency of the person who carries it out, the compensation for the victims must then be guaranteed by other means. Besides the contributions to a guaranteed fund, it could be possible to impose an intervention by the public authorities.

E. Conclusion

73 The precautionary principle appears particularly in the fields of environmental, health and consumer protection. Its extent, conditions for application and guidelines vary however. A question arises in Belgian law: Is the precautionary principle a new basis for a fault-based liability?

74 The answer is negative: This principle does not satisfy the requirements of this liability. Even if judges were to accept in future an extension to the concept of fault, on the basis of the precautionary principle, the victim would still have to establish the existence of a causal link and a certain and foreseeable damage.

75 The reference to the precautionary principle on the other hand is a matter of interest, at national or international level, before the occurrence of any damage. It should be an incentive to establish safety standards, procedures or suitable systems for evaluating the risks and for making decisions. Public law could have a better deterrent role using the precautionary principle.

At the European Community level, the Court of First Instance has decided that, although the precautionary principle is mentioned in the Treaty only in connection with environmental policy, it is broader in scope. It is intended to be applied in order to ensure a high level of protection of health, consumer safety and environment in all the Community's spheres of activity. 76

Instead of distorting the requirements of civil liability by means of the precautionary principle, it would be better to find a solution to make it easier for victims to obtain compensation for damage linked to risks which are already known and which, when they happen, can have dramatic consequences on the life and health of victims. 77

To improve the prevention and compensation for damage linked to specific dangerous activities or situations, it is possible to conceive the concept of "endangering someone" (*mise en danger*) which could justify a general principle. This contribution has briefly presented the guidelines of such principle. It could imply a regime of strict liability or a no-fault compensation scheme for victims when they have suffered damage linked to the known danger. 78

This general principle could fill the current gaps and be applied to those risks that will be known in future. Specific statutes to govern the compensation for risks should no longer have to be adopted on an *ad hoc* basis. However the intention is not to eliminate all risks to society as many risks have scientific, economic or private benefits. They are tolerated because of their social usefulness but this tolerance must also take account of the potential victims' interest. The above quotation of Virgil is still topical … 79

Reports

I. Austria

Barbara C. Steininger*

A. Legislation

1. *Bundesgesetz, mit dem das Kraftfahrzeug-Haftpflichtversicherungsgesetz 1994, das Eisenbahn- und Kraftfahrzeughaftpflichtgesetz, das Reichshaftpflichtgesetz, das Rohrleitungsgesetz und das Gaswirtschaftsgesetz geändert werden* (Act changing the act on obligatory liability insurance for motor vehicles as well as several strict liability statutes)[1]

1 This Act almost triples the present minimum insurance sums for motor vehicles.[2] For cars the new minimum insurance sum amounts to € 3 million. In comparison with other European countries the sums foreseen in Austria were rather low and, according to the legislator, the former minimum sums were not able to secure insurance coverage in case of momentous accidents.[3] At the same time, the caps foreseen in the *Eisenbahn- und Kraftfahrzeughaftpflichtgesetz* (Railway and Motor Vehicle Liability Act, EKHG) were raised to the same extent[4] in order to ameliorate the level of protection for this strict liability regime.[5] As the caps foreseen in several other strict liability statutes (for

* I would like to thank Donna Stockenhuber for proof-reading the text.

[1] *Bundesgesetzblatt* (Federal Law Gazette, BGBl) I 115/2004, 10 August 2004. Available at http://www.ris.bka.gv.at/bgbl-pdf. Austrian legislation is available at http://www.ris.bka.gv.at/bundesrecht.

[2] The present Act also allows motor vehicle liability insurers to raise premiums in relation to the consumer price index.

[3] *Regierungsvorlage* (government bill, RV), 556 *Beilagen zu den stenographischen Protokollen des Nationalrates* (BlgNR) 22. *Gesetzgebungsperiode* (legislative period, GP) 1 et seq.

[4] According to § 15 EKHG, strict liability for personal injury and death is now limited to a maximum of € 800,000 (or instead to an annual rent of € 48,000) per person injured and to a total amount of € 2,400,000 per keeper of a motor vehicle and accident if more than one person was injured. Special caps apply for busses, lorries and vehicles transporting dangerous goods. The new cap for damage to property amounts to a total of € 400,000 (applicable even if more than one object was damaged).

[5] RV 556 BlgNR 22. GP 3.

mains, pipelines and gas mains) were linked to the caps of the EKHG, the caps foreseen in those statutes were raised accordingly.

To raise caps seems to be a step in the right direction, especially when taking into account that some newer strict liability statutes[6] do not foresee caps. The same is true for the general rules of the draft revision of Austrian tort law to be published in 2005. 2

Finally, the present Act revokes the so-called "hitchhiker-provision", according to which the EKHG was not applicable in relation to persons conveyed by a motor vehicle in their own interest and without payment to the keeper of the car. The legislator justifies the abolition of this exemption from strict liability arguing that damage in such cases could be covered by mandatory liability insurance anyway.[7] 3

The changes provided for in the present Act entered into force on 1 October 2004. 4

B. Cases[8]

1. *Oberster Gerichtshof* (Austrian Supreme Court, OGH) 13 January 2004, 5 Ob 242/03d[9]: Medical Malpractice; Adjustment of Damages due to Benefits Received in Case of Compensation of Non-Pecuniary Loss (*Vorteilsausgleich*)

a) Brief Summary of the Facts

When opening a coffee cream lid, the plaintiff's thumb flexor tendon was torn. The plaintiff went to hospital but, notwithstanding clear indications, the injury was not diagnosed correctly. Had the injury of her thumb flexor tendon been detected immediately, an operation preserving at least a certain flexibility of the plaintiff's thumb would have been possible. When the torn thumb flexor tendon was finally diagnosed, it was too late for an operation. The plaintiff's thumb will remain permanently stiff. Because of this, the plaintiff is no longer able to crochet, her favourite hobby, which she used to practise for several hours a day before the accident. The plaintiff claims damages for non-pecuniary loss amounting to € 5,000. The defendant argues that the operation would also have been painful. Therefore, in the view of the defendant, this 5

[6] Like the *Atomhaftungsgesetz* (Nuclear liability Act, AtomHG), the *Forstgesetz* (Forestry Act, ForstG), the *Mineralrohstoffgesetz* (Mineral Resources Act, MinroG) and the *Produkthaftungsgesetz* (Product Liability Act, PHG).

[7] RV 556 BlgNR 22. GP 5.

[8] Cases are available at http://www.ris.bka.gv.at/jus.

[9] [2004] ecolex, 444 with cmt. by E. Helmich = [2005] *Zeitschrift für Verkehrsrecht* (ZVR), no. 28.

spared pain will – in accordance with the rules on adjustment of damages due to benefits received (the so-called *Vorteilsausgleich*) – have to be taken into account when assessing the amount of damages for non-pecuniary loss.

b) Judgment of the Supreme Court

6 According to the OGH, the question whether there should be an adjustment of damages for non-pecuniary loss by non-pecuniary benefits received or a consideration of spared pain need not be decided in the present case: The OGH argues such an adjustment would presuppose that the same damaging event caused both, damage and a benefit for the person harmed. According to the OGH, a consideration of spared pain would require that, despite the medical malpractice, the person harmed is in a similar physical condition as she would have been had she received the correct treatment. The Court, therefore, postulates similar "final conditions" (e.g. a stiff thumb with or without the operation). Only if the final conditions are similar, does the OGH consider it possible to check whether, through this "final condition" caused by the damaging event, also allowable benefits emerged. In the case at hand, the OGH comes to the conclusion that the "final conditions" – either a stiff thumb or a flexible thumb – are not comparable and that, therefore, taking into account the "final condition" of her stiff thumb, the plaintiff did not spare herself anything.

c) Commentary

7 The OGH's argument that an adjustment of damages requires similar final conditions is not convincing: Different "final conditions" are typical for cases of adjustment of damages due to benefits received.[10] The same is true for the present case: Here similar final conditions would either mean a stiff thumb with or without the operation or a flexible thumb in both scenarios. In the former case, there would be no causal link between the medical malpractice and the damage and in the latter case, there would be no damage.[11] The question left open by the OGH whether an "adjustment of damages by non-pecuniary benefits received" should be possible, will, in my view, have to be answered in the positive. Under certain circumstances such an adjustment might even be necessary: Damages for pain and suffering are awarded in order to compensate the non-pecuniary loss suffered. If spared pain and suffering were not taken into account, the compensation would be higher than the non-pecuniary loss actually suffered.

8 Notwithstanding these objections to the OGH's reasoning, the result of the court's decision seems correct: an amount of € 5,000 is adequate in the present case. It has to be taken into account that the plaintiff not only suffered physical pain but also suffers non-pecuniary loss because of the fact that her thumb will remain stiff for the rest of her life. To reduce the damages awarded to € 2,000 as demanded by the defendant would neglect this fact.

[10] E. Helmich in her cmt. to the present decision, [2004] ecolex, 445.

[11] E. Helmich (supra fn. 10).

In all it can be held that an "adjustment of damages by non-pecuniary benefits received" has to be employed carefully and will only be admissible if the person injured really derived an objective advantage.[12] 9

2. OGH 16 April 2004, 1 Ob 38/04a[13]: Public Liability, Injunctions

a) Brief Summary of the Facts

The first and second defendant wanted to attend a performance of "La Bohème" at the Vienna state opera, but when they entered the auditorium shortly after the opera had started, their seats were already taken. Consequently, they were asked by the usher to follow her to the foyer where heated discussions arose between the two defendants and employees of the claimant, the Vienna state opera company (*Wiener Staatsopern GmbH*). The sole shareholder of the claimant company is the *Bundestheater-Holding GmbH*, whose sole shareholder is the Republic of Austria. 10

Some time after the incident, the first and second defendant took part in a television broadcast together with the third defendant, who is one of Austria's three ombudsmen. This TV broadcast is regularly used as a forum by the Austrian Ombudsman Board. There, the first and second defendant claimed that they had been in the auditorium on time, that their seats had already been taken and that the usher had refused to help them and escorted them out of the auditorium. Moreover, they held that in the foyer employees of the state opera snatched the tickets from the first defendant's hands and insulted both defendants. The third defendant supported the first and second defendant in this broadcast and invited the audience to report similar cases to the Ombudsman Board. 11

According to the findings of the court of first instance, the allegations were not true. First of all the first and second defendant only entered the auditorium after the opera had started and moreover, the tickets were neither snatched out of the first defendant's hands nor were the first and second defendant insulted by state opera employees. The state opera company claimed a preliminary injunction in relation to these allegations. 12

b) Judgment of the Supreme Court

The interesting part of the decision deals with the question whether such a claim is admissible in relation to the third defendant, who, being an ombudsman, is a state organ. According to Art. 148a subs. 2 of the Austrian Constitution (*Bundesverfassungsgesetz*, B-VG), the Ombudsman Board is entitled to inspect *ex officio* assumed grievances in the Federation's administration, in- 13

[12] Compare K. Schäfer in: *J. von Staudinger's Kommentar zum Bürgerlichen Gesetzbuch mit Einführungsgesetzen und Nebengesetzen* (12th edn. 1986), § 847 no. 76; E. Karner, *Der Ersatz ideeller Schäden bei Körperverletzung* (1999), 122.

[13] [2004] *Medien und Recht* (MR), 188 = [2004] *Österreichisches Recht der Wirtschaft* (RdW), 661 = [2004] *Österreichische Richterzeitung* (RZ), 258.

cluding acts of the Federation as subject under private law (*Privatwirtschaftsverwaltung*). However, according to the Constitutional Court,[14] this presupposes that the Federation acts as a legal entity in its own right under private law. Therefore, the Ombudsman Board is not competent to control legal entities different from the Federation like the state opera company in the present case.

14 According to the OGH, there are no indications that the third defendant actually wanted to control the State Secretary for the Arts and Media. Moreover, the third defendant would not have been competent to control the State Secretary for the Arts and Media as, according to the allocation of duties, the latter falls within the field of responsibility of another of the three ombudsmen. Consequently, the third defendant was, according to the OGH, not competent in relation to the claimant.

15 However, the OGH stresses that acts of the Ombudsman Board are part of sovereign public administration (*Hoheitsverwaltung*). If a task has to be considered as sovereign public administration, the same will, according to prevailing practice, apply for all acts connected with its completion – even if an organ acts in excess of its competences. According to the OGH, the statement of the third defendant in the TV broadcast is – notwithstanding his lack of competence – in such a close relationship to the third defendant's sovereign tasks that the statement has to be considered as a sovereign act. This qualification has important consequences as, according to § 1 subs. 1 and § 9 subs. 5 Austrian Official Liability Act (*Amtshaftungsgesetz*, AHG), no claim will be admissible against an organ acting in a sovereign way.

c) Commentary

16 If someone, by divulging untrue facts, endangers the credit, income or promotional opportunities of someone else, the person endangered will, according to § 1330 subs. 2 ABGB, have an action for injunction and a claim for revocation and publication of this revocation. However, if an organ acted in a sovereign way, this is, according to prevailing opinion, not the case, as § 1 subs. 1 and § 9 subs. 5 AHG exclude a direct claim against the organ. The problem is that, while the AHG provides a claim for compensation in money against the public legal entity, it does not provide for an action for injunction. This means that the person endangered will, on the one hand, have no claim against the organ (*in casu* the third defendant) and, on the other hand, can only claim compensation in money but no injunction in relation to the public legal entity (*in casu* the Ombudsman Board). This leads to a gap in legal protection.[15]

17 Arguing that the notion of sovereign public administration has been interpreted in a very wide sense in official liability cases, it has been suggested to close

[14] *Sammlung der Erkenntnisse und Beschlüsse des Verfassungsgerichtshofes* (VfSlg), 13.323.

[15] See R. Reischauer, in: P. Rummel, *Kommentar zum ABGB* II/2b (3rd edn. 2004), § 1330 no. 34; W. Schragel, *Kommentar zum Amtshaftungsgesetz* (3rd edn. 2003), § 1 no. 171.

this gap in legal protection by granting the person endangered a claim against the organ in cases not falling within the core area of sovereign public administration. To do so, the AHG is interpreted in such a way that it does not cover actions for injunctions (which would be compatible with the wording of the said Act).[16] This solution has, however, been criticised arguing that injunctions against the organ by a court decision might violate the separation of powers.[17] Moreover, it has been put forward that, according to the clear sense of the AHG, there should be no direct claim against organs acting in execution of the law.[18] Although those arguments must not necessarily exclude the suggested solution, as the latter does not intend to cover core areas of sovereign public administration, it might bring about very difficult questions of delimitation.

3. OGH 5 May 2004, 9 Ob 67/03y[19]: Liability of a Court Expert

a) Brief Summary of the Facts

In a criminal trial in which the defendant had served as court expert, the plaintiff had been convicted for negligent bankruptcy by a final judgment but acquitted for other offences. In the criminal trial, the defendant had submitted an expertise in three parts which was based on the dynamic notion of insolvency. Later the court asked the defendant to supplement his expertise by answering the relevant questions on the basis of the static notion of insolvency. The defendant's fees were determined by a court order. 18

The plaintiff was ordered by the criminal court to pay the costs of the criminal proceeding, the most important part of which consisted of the fees for the court expert. The plaintiff, in a civil claim, now argues that the first three parts of the defendant's expertise were incorrectly based on the dynamic notion of insolvency and claims € 35,000 as well as a declaratory judgment establishing the defendant's liability for all consequences of the incorrect first three parts of the expertise. The plaintiff holds that he had to pay for private expert opinions in order to disprove the relevant parts of the defendant's expertise and claims extra costs for his defending counsel. 19

b) Judgment of the Supreme Court

The OGH first holds that a court expert submitting an incorrect expertise in a criminal procedure will be liable towards the defendant of this criminal trial. However, the OGH also stresses that the person convicted on the basis of an expertise may not claim compensation from the expert on the basis of the incorrectness of the expertise as long as the conviction is extant. The OGH then argues that the plaintiff, in the present case, in principle accepts the binding 20

[16] A. Kletečka, [1993] ecolex, 441 et seq.; compare also id., [1990] ecolex, 608 and [1996] ecolex, 597 et seq.

[17] W. Schragel (supra fn. 15), § 1 no. 171.

[18] W. Schragel (supra fn. 15), § 1 no. 171.

[19] [2004] *Der Sachverständige* (SV), 152, with cmt. by H. Krammer; [2005] RdW, 30.

force of the final convicting judgment and does not claim to have suffered damage on the basis of the expertise itself but sees his damage in the court expert fees he has to pay for as well as in his costs for private expert opinions and his legal counsel when disproving the (first three parts) of the expert opinion.

21 The OGH then holds that the duty to pay for the costs of the criminal trial is an automatic consequence of the conviction. Therefore, according to the OGH, the defendant's conduct was not causal for the plaintiff's damage. That the criminal court did not have to examine the correctness of the expertise in its proceedings to determine the fees does, according to the OGH, not lead to a deficiency in legal protection as a court expert will have a right to fees even if his expertise was incorrect. Only in special cases might the expert's claim be reduced or cancelled, but *in casu* there was no such special situation.

22 The OGH states that it is bound by the assessment of fees by final court order of the criminal court. It concludes that, as the expert would have had a right to fees even if the expertise had been incorrect, the plaintiff's damage does not fall within the protective purpose of the norm. According to the OGH, this is not only true for the defendant's fees but also in relation to the costs for the private expert opinions and the legal counsel.

c) Commentary

23 The result of the present decision in relation to the costs of the criminal trial is in line with the OGH's practice on the binding force of criminal court decisions.[20] The expert fees were determined by the criminal court by final court order and cannot be reassessed in a civil trial for compensation against the court expert. The OGH's arguments that the defendant's conduct was not causal and that the claimant's damage does not fall within the protective purpose of the norm do, however, seem to be problematic in relation to the claimant's costs for private expert opinions and for his counsel. Had the defendant used the static notion of insolvency in the first parts of his expertise, the claimant would not have had to spend money for private expert opinions or extra fees for his counsel. A causal link is therefore clearly given. Although it is not clear whether the defendant violated a duty of care, the plaintiff's extra costs would probably fall within the protective purpose of such a duty of care.

24 In the present case, the criminal court had decided that the defendant was instructed by the court to use the dynamic notion of insolvency for his expertise. The justification for the OGH's result could, therefore, be seen in the fact that awarding the plaintiff a compensation claim for costs for private expert opinions and for his counsel would interfere with the final order of the criminal court.

[20] Compare OGH in *Entscheidungen des Österreichischen Obersten Gerichtshofes in Zivil- und Justizverwaltungssachen* (SZ), 68/195.

4. OGH 1 July 2004, 2 Ob 141/04f[21]: Damages for Non-Pecuniary Loss for Close Relatives; Bereavement

During the past few years, the OGH has developed a court practice on compensation for non-pecuniary loss of close relatives of the primary victim.[22] The OGH distinguishes two different groups of cases: the so-called shock-damage cases in which the relative suffered an injury to health on the one hand and compensation for the close relative's bereavement (in these cases there is no injury to health) on the other hand. In the former case the relative will be eligible for compensation even if the tortfeasor only acted with slight negligence, whereas compensation for bereavement will only be awarded in cases of gross negligence or intent on the part of the tortfeasor.[23] In 2004 the OGH advanced this practice and clarified open points.[24] 25

a) Brief Summary of the Facts

The plaintiff's 61 year old mother was killed in a car accident. Although the plaintiff, who was born in 1963, no longer shared the same household as his mother, they had an excellent and very close relationship. Their houses were opposite each other and they had daily contact. The plaintiff's mother helped in her son's business and looked after his children. She was in the best of health. As a consequence of his mother's death in the car accident, the plaintiff suffered severely. There was, however, no injury to his health. The plaintiff claims bereavement damages amounting to € 22,000. 26

The defendant argued that there should be no compensation for bereavement in the present case as the plaintiff was grown up and did not live in the same household as his mother. In such a case the loss of a parent is, according to the defendant, part of the normal risk of life. 27

b) Judgment of the Supreme Court

The OGH holds that children (independent of their age) mourning a parent form the nuclear family typically meriting protection and stresses that the age of the deceased person and termination of a common household cannot exclude a child's claim for bereavement damages from the outset. In the view of the OGH, the decisive factor for awarding bereavement damages is the intensive emotional relationship between close relatives. 28

[21] [2004] *Juristische Blätter* (JBl), 792 = [2004] ZVR, no. 86 = [2005] ecolex, 39.

[22] See E. Karner/H. Koziol, *Der Ersatz ideellen Schadens im österreichischen Recht und seine Reform*, 15. ÖJT vol. II/1 (2003), 74 et seq.

[23] Compare OGH in [2001] JBl, 660 = [2001] ecolex, 668 with cmt. by E. Helmich = [2001] ZVR, no. 73 with cmt. by E. Karner = [2001] *Arbeits- und Sozialrechtskartei* (AsoK), 323 with cmt. by L. Stärker = [2002] RdW, 215. Compare also B.C. Steininger, Austria, in: H. Koziol/B.C. Steininger (eds.), *European Tort Law 2001* (2002), nos. 69 et seq. (case 14).

[24] In addition to the present decision there was a second case on this topic. See infra, nos. 51 et seq. (case 8).

29 The tortfeasor will, however, have the possibility to prove that, notwithstanding the formal affiliation, no such intensive emotional relationship exists. The OGH mentions the example of hostile spouses in the course of divorce proceedings. However, the OGH also refers to an earlier shock-damage case,[25] considering a temporary disturbance of the emotional relationship to be insufficient to destroy this relationship, the continuity of which was in that case proven by the shock the plaintiff suffered.

30 Concerning the amount to be awarded, the OGH considers the intensity of the relationship as a determining factor. Next to the age of the accident victim and the relative claiming compensation, the question whether the plaintiff and victim lived in the same household will be of importance. The OGH argues that setting up a separate household and family will usually loosen the relationship between parents and children. In the case at hand, the OGH considers bereavement damages amounting to € 13,000 to be adequate.

31 As an award of compensation for bereavement presupposes gross negligence or intent on the part of the tortfeasor and there were no findings in relation to this question in the decision of the court of first instance, the case was referred back to the latter.

c) Commentary

32 The decision can be approved of and brings about a consistent advancement of the OGH's practice on compensation for non-pecuniary loss of close relatives. First, the decision specifies the circle of persons eligible for bereavement damages. While in shock-damage cases the occurrence of the shock forms an objective indication for the existence of a close emotional relationship, such an objective indication does not exist in bereavement cases, where the close relative does not suffer an injury to health. This means that the formal family relationship will be of higher importance.[26] In the present decision the OGH clarifies that children will be eligible for compensation irrespective of both their age and the existence of a common household, arguing convincingly that only the existence of a close emotional relationship can be decisive. Taking this decisive factor into account, not only children but also parents, spouses and cohabitants must be part of the circle of persons entitled to bereavement damages.[27] Second, the decision provides information about the factors to be taken into account when determining the amount of compensation. The OGH holds that the intensity of the emotional relationship is decisive and convincingly resorts to objectively detectable factors such as the age of the persons in-

[25] OGH in [2001] JBl, 659 = [2001] RdW, 531 = [2001] ZVR, no. 52 with cmt. by E. Karner. Compare also B.C. Steininger (supra fn. 23), no. 51 (case 10).

[26] E. Karner, cmt. on OGH 29 August 2002, 8 Ob 127/02p in [2002] ZVR, 393; E. Karner/H. Koziol (supra fn. 22), 84.

[27] See also E. Karner (supra fn. 26); E. Karner/H. Koziol (supra fn. 22), 83 et seq.

volved and the existence of a common household.[28] Of course the degree of kinship will also be an important factor in this respect.[29]

5. OGH 12 August 2004, 1 Ob 231/03g[30]: Public Liability

a) Brief Summary of the Facts

The plaintiff is a Polish national who has been living in Austria for several years. After her right to unemployment benefits was exhausted, she applied for emergency assistance. Her application was rejected by an administrative decree (*Bescheid*) of the competent authority on the basis of § 34 subs. 1 *Arbeitslosenversicherungsgesetz* (Unemployment Insurance Act, AlVG). This provision, amongst others, sets out the condition that the applicant was born in Austria or lived there for half of his life. The plaintiff did not fulfil these prerequisites. The negative administrative decree included a caution (*Rechtsmittelbelehrung*) that appeal was possible within two weeks. The plaintiff then talked to one of the authority's employees on the phone and asked her what she could do. She was told that an appeal would be useless as she did not fulfil the conditions set out by the relevant provision. Hence, the plaintiff did not appeal. 33

Subsequently, § 34 AlVG was annulled by a decision of the Constitutional Court.[31] However, for cases prior to this decision, § 34 AlVG remained applicable, except for the so-called prompting cases (*Anlassfälle*). In order to be qualified as prompting case, the plaintiff would have had to appeal the decision of the authority and, consequently, to bring a judicial review procedure in respect to the constitutionality of the act (*Gesetzesprüfungsverfahren*) before the Constitutional Court. 34

The plaintiff now sues the Republic of Austria for her loss with the following arguments: 1. Although the competent authority knew that proceedings were pending before the Constitutional Court, the caution did not include the information that the decree has to be appealed to be able to bring a judicial review procedure before the Constitutional Court to enjoy the advantages of prompting cases. 2. When the relevant version of § 34 subs 1 AlVG was introduced,[32] the then federal minister was informed by her experts that the draft was unconstitutional. Therefore, the minister, against her better judgement brought an unconstitutional draft before the parliament. 3. Finally, the plaintiff bases 35

[28] Thereby avoiding the unpleasant result of having to pick the relation of the plaintiff and his deceased relative into pieces during the trial.

[29] E. Karner/H. Koziol (supra fn. 22), 87 et seq.

[30] [2005] JBl, 184 = [2005] *Evidenzblatt der Rechtsmittelentscheidungen* in: *Österreichische Juristen-Zeitung* (EvBl), no. 65.

[31] VfSlg 15.506.

[32] This provision's predecessor, geared to Austrian nationality, had been declared to violate the European Convention on Human Rights by the the European Court of Human Rights (16.9.1996; 39/1995/545/631; *Gaygusuz vs Austria*) and had subsequently been annulled by the Austrian Constitutional Court (VfSlg 15.129).

her claim on Art. 50 European Convention on Human Rights (ECHR) arguing that the rules on prompting cases violate human rights and deprive persons who did not file their complaint with the Constitutional Court before the latter opens oral proceedings in a judicial review procedure of their right to an effective remedy before a national authority according to Art. 13 ECHR.

b) Judgment of the Supreme Court

36 In relation to the plaintiff's third argument, the OGH stresses that the fact of Constitutional Court decisions having no retroactive effect except for prompting cases does not infringe Art. 13 ECHR as the plaintiff could have appealed the decree and consequently could have brought a judicial review procedure before the Constitutional Court. Moreover, the Court points out that Art. 50 only allows the European Court of Human Rights to afford satisfaction to an injured party in its decision if a decision by a national authority violates the Convention and internal law only allows partial reparation. Therefore, this article can, according to the OGH, not form a basis for awarding compensation for legislation infringing the Convention outside proceedings before the European Court of Human Rights itself.

37 Concerning the second argument put forward by the plaintiff, the OGH argues as follows: As the plaintiff is Polish and therefore was not an EU citizen during the relevant time period, the rules on EC state liability for legislative wrong are not applicable in this case. Outside of Community law there is, according to the OGH, no legal basis for compensation in case of legislative wrong.[33] The OGH then examines whether the plaintiff's claim can be based on the AHG with regard to the minister's acts preparing legislation, which presupposes that those acts are qualified as executive acts.[34] Contrary to its earlier practice,[35] the OGH comes to the conclusion that such acts preparing legislation cannot be considered as executive acts but form part of legislation: The OGH refers to arguments put forward in doctrine[36] and stresses that in the preparation of legislation an administrative act with an effect on the outside world is not performed, which would normally be the case with executive acts. According to the OGH, the result of the act of preparing legislation depends on relative political strength. This result is, therefore, not foreseeable and has to be attributed to the solely responsible parliament. Moreover, the OGH refers to systematic arguments: the Constitution deals with legislative

[33] § 1 of the Austrian Official Liability Act (*Amtshaftungsgesetz*, AHG) foresees liability of the state only for wrongful executive acts whereas there is no liability for legislative wrong.

[34] According to § 2 subs. 2 AHG, an official liability claim is excluded if the person harmed could have avoided the damage by appealing against the relevant decision. However, in the present case this does, according to the OGH, not hinder the plaintiff's claim: As she was informed that an appeal would make no sense, the fact that she did not appeal cannot be considered as faulty behaviour.

[35] In its decision 30 June 1998, 1 Ob 116/97h, the OGH had, in relation to an alleged omission of introducing a government bill in time, taken the position that only formal acts of legislation are excluded from official liability.

[36] W. Schragel (supra fn. 15), nos. 56 et seq.

proposals under the heading of "legislation of the federation", while the executive is addressed in the next chapter called "executive of the federation". Acts preparing legislation will, therefore, entirely have to be considered as part of legislation.[37] In addition the OGH holds that individuals do not have a legal claim to the enactment of a certain law.

Finally, the OGH deals with the plaintiff's first argument and comes to the conclusion that a duty to include such an extensive caution as claimed by the plaintiff would overstretch the authority's duty of care, especially when taking into account that generally a caution only has to provide information about procedural questions but need not include instructions as to the merits of the claim. 38

c) Commentary

The decision is based on detailed reasoning and the result can be agreed with. 39
Its most interesting part is of course the OGH's change in practice concerning the applicability of the AHG to acts preparing legislation. The former court practice was questionable as it circumvented the exception of legislation from official liability predetermined by the Constitution and neglected parliament's responsibility. After all, parliament may well decide to pass an unconstitutional norm in the rank of a constitutional provision.

Even if acts preparing legislation were considered as executive acts, it would 40
still be debatable whether the plaintiff would have a compensation claim. As the OGH stresses correctly, individuals do not have a legal claim to the enactment of a certain law. Therefore, it is questionable whether, in this case of mere psychological causation, the potentially violated duties of the minister (e.g. a duty to inform parliament about the assumed unconstitutionality of the draft) have the purpose of protecting individuals from harm caused by unconstitutional legislation. Such a presumption might equally disregard parliament's responsibility.

6. OGH 26 August 2004, 6 Ob 83/04f[38]: Defamation

a) Brief Summary of the Facts

The plaintiff is the vice president of the Carinthian school authority (*Landes-* 41
schulrat), while the defendant is a member of the second chamber of the Austrian parliament as well as a school supervisor in Carinthia (*Landesschulinspektorin*). The plaintiff had heavily criticised the defendant's nomination as school supervisor as politically motivated, non-transparent and not justifiable from the point of view of the defendant's qualifications. In a letter to the editor of a local newspaper, the defendant – in reaction to this criticism – held that the plaintiff had passed on incorrect information to the media "as in other

[37] The OGH also stresses that the same is true for omissions of legislative initiatives.
[38] [2004] MR, 325.

comparable cases in which the vice president has been convicted for breach of official secrecy". The defendant had been convicted for breach of official secrecy in one trial concerning the data of two persons. In a second trial he was acquitted, but the prosecutor had appealed this decision. The Carinthian media had reported on these cases. The defendant was seeking an injunction in relation to these allegations, arguing that the latter were not true as he had only been convicted once. Moreover, he bases his claim on § 113 *Strafgesetzbuch* (Criminal Code, StGB) that prohibits accusing somebody of a criminal act for which the penalty has already been executed. The plaintiff had already paid the pecuniary penalty imposed on him.

b) Judgment of the Supreme Court

42 If damage to someone's reputation is at the same time a violation of a person's honour as in the case at hand, the defendant will, according to the OGH, have to prove the correctness of the alleged facts as well as the lack of wrongfulness. In the view of the OGH, a statement is untrue if its core part does not correspond to reality. The OGH argues that the core part of the defendant's allegation was true as the plaintiff had indeed handed over data concerning two individuals and that the defendant had never claimed that the plaintiff had been convicted more than once. Moreover, the OGH holds that, even from the perspective of the readers of the newspaper in question, the defendant's statement was not understood in that way because the newspaper had reported on the plaintiff's conviction extensively, so that the readers knew that there had only been one conviction. Therefore, the OGH denies the plaintiff's claim for injunction based on § 1330 subs. 1 and 2 ABGB. Moreover, the OGH argues that the plaintiff's claim for injunction cannot be justified on the basis of § 113 StGB either: According to the OGH, in a political debate as in the case at hand, the (true) allegation that the plaintiff had been convicted for abuse of authority because of a breach of official secrecy is justified by Art. 10 of the European Convention on Human Rights, even if the penalty has already been executed.

c) Commentary

43 In accordance with the practice of the European Court of Human Rights, the OGH has, in several decisions, drawn the limits for tolerable criticism of politicians wider than in relation to private persons. The freedom of opinion is interpreted in a wide sense here so that even insults to a politician might be justified in political discussion, especially if the politician himself made provocative statements in this discussion.[39] Therefore, the conclusion reached by the OGH in the present case, according to which the defendant's mention of the conviction in the course of the concrete political discussion was justified even though the penalty had already been executed, can be agreed with.

[39] Compare R. Reischauer in: P. Rummel (supra fn. 15), § 1330 nos. 42 et seq., 46.

7. OGH 26 August 2004, 6 Ob 40/04g[40]: Defamation

a) Brief Summary of the Facts

The plaintiff holds a doctorate in medicine and theology, is head of a gynaecological department in Vienna's General Hospital, president of the Austrian bioethics-commission and president of the Austrian society for family planning. He also operates a surgery for gynaecology and obstetrics. The defendant, an Austrian bishop, had claimed in a provoking letter to the editor that the plaintiff performs abortions. The plaintiff brought an action for injunction in relation to this allegation as well as its revocation. Moreover, he claims compensation amounting to € 500 arguing that he has already lost patients as a consequence of the allegation and asks the court to declare the defendant liable for all future loss caused by the allegation. 44

Decisive for the present case is the notion of abortion. According to Catholic ethics, human life starts with conception, i.e. before nidation of the fecundated human ovum in the endometrium. This means that every destruction of human life even before nidation is considered as abortion. As the morning-after pill prevents nidation, it is qualified as abortion according to the concept of Catholic ethics. The legal and general term of abortion presupposes nidation, as pregnancy only starts with nidation of the fecundated human ovum in the endometrium. The plaintiff had never performed abortions in the latter sense, but he accepts the morning-after pill as an emergency contraceptive. 45

Moreover, the plaintiff was mentioned as co-author of a medical study on a question in relation to abortions that had been published in the internet. However, the plaintiff had – in accordance with existing usage – only been mentioned without having taken part in drafting the article as his department had done research on nitrogen oxide that was of importance for this study. 46

b) Judgment of the Supreme Court

The OGH first holds that an action for injunction according to § 1330 ABGB presupposes that the defendant divulged untrue facts. According to prevailing practice, a statement is untrue if its core part does not correspond to reality. Moreover, the OGH stresses the necessity of a weighing of interests in relation to the defendant's freedom of opinion and refers to the practice of the European Court of Human Rights on this question. The OGH points out that even the public interest in information cannot justify incorrect statements infringing interests worth protection of the person affected by the statement. 47

According to the OGH, the letter to the editor in no way clarified that the allegation of having performed abortions only meant that the plaintiff used methods of contraception preventing nidation. Especially on account of the fact that the letter referred to "the dismemberment of a child in its mother's 48

[40] [2004] MR, 327.

womb" and mentioned that abortions are only exempt from punishment but still illegal in Austrian law. Therefore, the OGH considered the core part of the allegation to be untrue. Although the allegation was made in the course of a public discussion of a topic of important public interest, it can, according to the OGH, not be qualified as a mere value judgment. The OGH holds the allegation to violate both the plaintiff's honour and credit and therefore declares the plaintiff's action for injunction to be justified.

49 While an action for injunction can be granted irrespective of any fault on the part of the defendant, the OGH states that the plaintiff's other claims presuppose fault. As the defendant neither contacted the plaintiff before publication nor verified in any other way why the plaintiff's name was mentioned in the relevant survey or whether the plaintiff indeed performed abortions, he did – in the view of the OGH – act negligently.

c) Commentary

50 When stating that § 1330 presupposes the dissemination of untrue facts, the OGH does not draw a clear distinction between subs. 1 and 2 of § 1330. While subs. 2 is applicable to the dissemination of untrue facts endangering credit, income or promotional opportunities of a third person, subs. 1 only requires a violation of a person's honour without focusing on truth or untruth, which means that even the dissemination of true facts might violate a person's honour.[41] Notwithstanding the aforesaid unclarity, the OGH's result can be approved of:[42] The decision stresses the importance of a weighing of interests in relation to the defendant's freedom of opinion and – in my view – rightly comes to the conclusion that the freedom of opinion cannot justify untrue allegations.[43]

8. OGH 23 September 2004, 2 Ob 178/04x[44]: Damages for Non-Pecuniary Loss for Close Relatives; Contributory Negligence

a) Brief Summary of the Facts

51 The intoxicated defendant caused a car accident in the course of which his likewise drunken passenger, the plaintiff's husband, was killed. The defendant was condemned in the criminal trial. The plaintiff suffered psychiatric damage[45] to be qualified as injury to health and claims compensation for her non-pecuniary loss. The defendant argues that the contributory negligence of the plaintiff's husband has to be taken into account.

41 See R. Reischauer in: P. Rummel (supra fn. 15), § 1330 no. 1.

42 In the present case, the defendant's allegation falls under both subsections as it violates both the plaintiff's honour and his credit by the dissemination of untrue facts.

43 Compare R. Reischauer in: P. Rummel (supra fn. 15), § 1330 no. 47 with further references.

44 [2004] ZVR, no. 105 with cmt. by K.-H. Danzl; [2005] ecolex, 112.

45 Referred to as *Schockschaden*, i.e. shock-damage in Austrian law.

b) Judgment of the Supreme Court

The OGH refers to its practice on contributory negligence of an intoxicated driver's likewise drunken passenger: if a passenger gets drunk before departure and thereby disables himself to realize whether the driver is fit to drive, this will lead to contributory negligence on his part, except for those cases in which the passenger cannot be blamed for getting drunk. This will amongst others be the case if, when getting drunk, the passenger did not have to anticipate being given a lift by an unfit driver. In the case at hand, the OGH holds that the findings of the court of first instance are not sufficient for deciding this question. 52

In the most interesting part of the decision, the OGH deals with the question whether contributory negligence of the first victim has to be taken into account when adjudicating damages for non-pecuniary loss of close relatives of this first victim. Referring to Karner[46] the OGH comes to the conclusion that in both psychiatric injury and bereavement cases, the first victim's contributory negligence has to be taken into account: if the first victim contributorily causes his own damage, the event comes close to a stroke of fate to be borne by the close relative himself. Moreover, the OGH argues that, although the secondary victim as a directly harmed person has an own claim, this claim only exists because the secondary victim is a close relative. Therefore, this kinship will, according to the OGH, also have to be taken into account when determining the extent of the tortfeasor's liability. In the view of the OGH it would "contradict the legal sense of equilibrium" to take a certain factor into account as incriminating but not as exonerating. Finally, the OGH also stresses that this result corresponds to the solutions for this problem by German, Swiss and French courts. 53

c) Commentary

The decision can be fully approved of. The OGH follows the convincing arguments put forward by Karner[47] and reaches a consistent further development of its practice on compensation for close relatives of the first victim for their non-pecuniary loss. As Karner rightly stresses, a different solution will be appropriate if the quality of being closely related is not the decisive factor for justifying liability: a person suffering the psychiatric injury who is not a close relative will have a claim for compensation if she was involved in the accident, which will particularly be the case if the shock-damage victim was seriously endangered in this accident. In these cases the contributory negligence of the first victim cannot be taken into account. In such situations of personal involvement the same must be true for close relatives as here the kinship is not decisive for the tortfeasor's liability.[48] 54

[46] [2001] ZVR, 288 et seq.

[47] E. Karner, [2001] ZVR, 288 et seq.; see also K.-H. Danzl, in: K.-H. Danzl/K.Gutiérrez-Lobos/O.F. Müller, *Das Schmerzengeld in medizinischer und juristischer Sicht* (8th edn. 2003), 72 et seq.; E. Karner/H. Koziol (supra fn. 22), 85 et seq.

[48] E. Karner, [2001] ZVR, 289; E. Karner/H. Koziol (supra fn. 22), 86.

9. OGH 20 October 2004, 7 Ob 220/04k[49]: Proof of Causation; Alternative Lawful Behaviour

a) Brief Summary of the Facts

55 The plaintiff had inherited shares and did not want to sell them. In order to hedge against a slump in prices, the plaintiff, upon the advice and procurement of her bank, the defendant, bought put-options. The defendant granted the plaintiff credit for the purchase price of these put-options. The plaintiff suffered a loss of about € 279,000 and claimed compensation for this loss from the defendant, arguing that the latter had not adequately warned and informed her about the risk of this transaction.

56 According to the findings of the court of first instance, the defendant bank had indeed violated a duty of information, but the court also held that it could not be ascertained whether the plaintiff, had she been informed adequately, would not have bought these put-options.

b) Judgment of the Supreme Court

57 The OGH first refers to its practice on the burden of proof for the causality of violations of information duties. It stresses that it only departed from the principle that the person harmed has to prove causation in cases of medical malpractice. Because of the special difficulties of patients to prove causation in such cases, only the attending physician will, in the view of the OGH, have the necessary means and knowledge for this proof. Therefore, the OGH argues, "prima-facie causation" has to be assumed. In other cases of violations of duties of information and enquiry, this is, according to the OGH, not the case. The person harmed will, therefore, have to prove the causality of the defendant's conduct.

58 For the present case the OGH comes to the conclusion that the plaintiff can rather be burdened with the proof of causation than the defendant: As the question is how the plaintiff would have decided had she been adequately informed, she is, according to the OGH, "closer to proof" than the defendant.

c) Commentary

59 The problem at the root of the present decision is the question on whom the burden of proof for violations of information duties will be imposed in cases of omissions. Concerning positive acts, a distinction can be drawn between natural causation of damage on the one hand and alternative lawful behaviour, i.e. the question whether the damage would also have occurred had the wrongdoer not violated any duty of care, on the other hand. The burden of proof for the former will fall on the plaintiff, while the defendant will have to prove alternative lawful behaviour. However, such a distinction between causation and alternative lawful behaviour is not possible in cases of omissions: would

[49] [2005] ÖBA, with cmt. by B.C. Steininger (in preparation).

the damage also have occurred had the defendant carried out the positive act due, the omission cannot be considered causal. Therefore, the burden of proof cannot be split between plaintiff and defendant either.

The OGH's result in the present case is not convincing. First of all, violations of information duties will typically and not only in medical liability cases lead to special difficulties concerning proof. After all, the hardly ever feasible proof of a hypothetical decision is at stake. However, the OGH's result for medical liability cases can be justified by the fact that medical interventions are considered as bodily injury, unless they are justified by the patient's valid consent.[50] Here causation of the bodily injury is clear, the only open question is whether the physician's acts were justified. In reality we are confronted with damage caused by a positive act and not by an omission, which means that the burden of proof for causation can be split between plaintiff and defendant according to the general rule, i.e. the physician will have to prove that the patient would also have decided to undergo the medical intervention had he been adequately informed. However, this does not bring a solution for the present omission case. 60

According to the OGH, the plaintiff is "closer to proof" than the defendant. When taking into account the purpose of the information duty, however, this solution cannot convince. Information duties are to give the person harmed the possibility to decide whether they want to take the risk that finally materialized or not. The breach of duty by the wrongdoer deprives the person harmed of this possibility to decide and brings about important difficulties in relation to proof. As it was the wrongdoer who caused these difficulties by his breach of duty of care, he should be the one who bears the risk that the hypothetical decision cannot be clarified.[51] Therefore, the defendant is – in my view – "closer to proof" than the plaintiff. 61

10. OGH 23 November 2004, 1 Ob 226/04y[52]: Medical Malpractice; Limitation

a) Brief Summary of the Facts

The plaintiff went to see the defendant, her gynaecologist, for a medical check up in October 1996. The defendant took a cervical smear but could not find anything noticeable. In May 1997 the plaintiff consulted another doctor who, in preparation of a planned sterilisation took a cervical smear and consequent- 62

[50] E.A. Kramer, Die Kausalität im Haftpflichtrecht: Neue Tendenzen in Theorie und Praxis, [1987] *Zeitschrift des Bernischen Juristenvereins* (ZBJV), 297 et seq.; E. Karner, *Der Ersatz ideeller Schäden bei Körperverletzung* (1999), 108 et seq.; H. Koziol, Der Beweis des natürlichen Kausalzusammenhanges, in: A. Koller (ed.), *Haftpflicht- und Versicherungsrechtstagung 1999* (1999), 88.

[51] H. Koziol (supra fn. 50), 89 et seq. with further references. Compare also G. Schiemann in: *J. von Staudinger's Kommentar zum Bürgerlichen Gesetzbuch mit Einführungsgesetzen und Nebengesetzen* (13th edn. 1998), § 249 no. 11.

[52] [2005] *Recht der Medizin* (RdM), 57.

ly diagnosed cancer. The doctor informed the plaintiff that this disease may develop very quickly. After a case of medical malpractice of another gynaecologist was reported on in the media, the plaintiff contacted the patients' attorney. A medical expertise attested medical malpractice on the part of the defendant. The small galls strips on which the cervical smear was kept had been lost during the termination of the defendant's surgery. The plaintiff claims damages amounting to € 123,550, amongst others for pain and suffering, loss of earnings and hospital costs. The defendant argues that the claim was time-barred.

b) Judgment of the Supreme Court

63 According to the OGH, the three year limitation period will, in medical malpractice cases, not start as long as the person harmed does not know that there was medical malpractice – even if the damage and the person of the (potential) wrongdoer are known in principle. If the person harmed is a layperson, and if knowledge of the factors establishing fault presupposes expertise, the limitation period will – in the view of the OGH – regularly only start, when the person harmed is informed by an expert opinion, while mere speculations about the basis of the claim are not sufficient. In the present case, the plaintiff had been informed that the disease may develop very quickly. Notwithstanding this information the plaintiff might, according to the OGH, have suspected that the defendant could have detected her disease in the course of the relevant check up. However, in the view of the OGH, she did not even have reasonably reliable indications that this potential suspicion might be legitimate. Therefore, the plaintiff did not have to obtain a (costly) expert opinion to clarify whether there had been medical malpractice on the part of the defendant.

64 According to the OGH, it is quite comprehensible that the plaintiff assumed medical malpractice of the defendant in the course of the check up only when she read about the medical malpractice of another gynaecologist. Only from that moment on was she – in the view of the OGH – obliged to make enquiries in order to avoid limitation of her claim.

c) Commentary

65 This decision is in line with the OGH's practice on the beginning of the limitation period in medical malpractice cases. The court of first instance had considered the claim to be time-barred, arguing that it is a matter of common knowledge that cervical smears serve to diagnose cancer as early as possible and that it was, therefore, clear that the cancer had either developed very quickly or that there had been medical malpractice on the part of the defendant. In the view of the court of first instance, the plaintiff, therefore, should have started enquiries. Contrary to this decision both, the court of appeal and the OGH, denied a duty of the plaintiff to start such enquiries right away, the latter with the argument that the duty to start such enquiries may not be stretched too far. The main reason for the – in my view rather patient friendly – decision in the present case seems to have been the fact that the plaintiff was informed by her doctor that the cancer might develop very quickly.

C. Literature

1. M. Karollus/M. Lukas, Dritthaftung der Bank aus einer unrichtigen Bankbestätigung? [2004] *Juristische Blätter* (JBl), 686

In the course of the formation of a joint stock company (*Aktiengesellschaft*, AG) or a limited liability company (*Gesellschaft mit beschränkter Haftung*, GmbH) by cash subscription, proof of payment of the cash subscription by a bank confirmation is a prerequisite for registration in the company register. The same is true for an increase of capital by cash deposit for such companies. The relevant Acts only provide for liability of the bank in relation to the correctness of such a confirmation towards the company. In the present article the authors examine in detail whether there will moreover be a liability of the bank towards third persons and they come to the conclusion that this is not the case: They argue that the legislator deliberately opted for a liability only towards the company. This result may, according to the authors, not be circumvented by falling back on general rules of tort law. A parallel to auditors' liability towards third persons is, in the view of the authors, not admissible, as the reasons for departing from the law's principle of a liability only towards the company in the last-mentioned case are not – or only to a much lesser extent – applicable in relation to bank confirmations on cash deposits. The authors therefore deny a liability towards third persons of the bank issuing the confirmation, be it based on a qualification of the norms on liability towards the company as norms with protective purpose towards third persons, on an assumption of a contract with protective purpose towards third persons or objective legal duties of care or on § 1300 ABGB (liability for incorrect information). Even § 1295 subs. 2 ABGB on malicious violation of *bonos mores* will, according to the authors, rarely justify liability as this would require a specific intent of the bank in relation to the damage of the third person. The authors conclude that a liability will only be possible in case of participation of the bank in a criminal offence under the condition that this criminal rule also aims to protect third persons. This will, according to Karollus and Lukas, only be the case for § 122 of the Act on limited liability companies (*GmbH Gesetz*, GmbHG). 66

2. H. Koziol, Schadenersatz für reine Vermögensschäden, [2004] JBl, 273

In the present article Koziol examines under which conditions pure economic loss is currently compensated under Austrian law and develops basic criteria for compensation of such loss. The author first deals with arguments against awarding compensation for pure economic loss: the floodgates argument and the limits a general duty to compensate pure economic loss would impose on the liberty of action of all individuals, the fact that pure economic interests are neither manifest nor clearly delimited and the comparatively low rank of these interests. He then examines in which cases protection of pure economic interests is admitted (e.g. contract, intentional infliction of harm, mere relocation 67 of harm etc.) and, on the basis of this consideration, formulates ten basic rules on compensation of pure economic loss: such compensation will, according to Koziol, be justified the more, 1. the lower the danger of an unlimited number of persons harmed; 2. the less the protection of pure economic interests would lead to additional duties of care; 3. the closer the relationsship between the persons involved; 4. the higher the probability of other persons being swayed by the incorrect information; 5. the harder it is for the person potentially harmed to protect herself; 6. when the torfeasor knows about the third person's financial interests or if those were at least manifest; 7. the clearer the economic interests are delimited; 8. when the tortfeasor acted intentionally; 9. the more important the financial interests will typically be for the person harmed and 10. the more the tortfeasor is acting on behalf of his own economic interests. According to Koziol, all these factors should be applied in terms of a flexible system weighing the number and importance of the factors involved. Finally, Koziol applies these rules to cable cases, pure economic loss as a consequence of traffic jams (and denies liability in both cases) as well as to liability of auditors towards third persons (where he reaches a differentiated solution).

3. M. Leitner, Zum Ersatz von Raucherschäden nach österreichischem Recht, [2004] *Österreichische Juristen-Zeitung* (ÖJZ), 93

68 In his article the author deals with so-called smoking or tobacco damage, i.e. damage to health caused by tobacco products in relation to active smokers. While previous argumentation in doctrine was reluctant to assume fault liability for such damage, Leitner holds that a fault-based liability for such damage might be justified on the basis of the advertising for tobacco products. According to the author, the ABGB also protects frivolous or lightheaded persons from abuse of their irrationality by others. In the view of Leitner this speaks for qualifiying advertising for cigarettes, which he considers as inducing others to harm themselves in one's own financial interest, as wrongful. In case of smokers who are minors this is, according to Leitner, even clearer. Moreover, Leitner qualifies the restriction on advertising for tobacco products in the *Tabakgesetz* (Tobacco Act) as norms with a protective purpose. In relation to the causal link between advertising and smoking, Leitner holds that the burden of proof will fall on the tobacco producer. Concerning the causal link between smoking and the plaintiff's damage to health, the latter can, in the view of the author, benefit from *prima facie* evidence. Finally, Leitner briefly deals with the question whether liability can be based on the *Produkthaftungsgesetz* (Product Liability Act, PHG)[53] and comes to the conclusion that, though cigarettes will normally not be defective in the sense of the PHG, as one cannot expect cigarettes to be unperilous, such defectiveness might nevertheless have to be assumed in case of light-cigarettes and addiction advancing additives, as here safety expectations of consumers might not be met.

[53] See also the contributions on this topic mentioned infra, no. 85.

Leitner's arguments for qualifiying advertising for tabacco products as generally wrongful in relation to active smokers cannot convince. In cases of mere psychological causation the law is very reluctant to accept duties of care. Generally qualifiying the advertising of tobacco products as wrongful would neglect this and, moreover, would not sufficiently take into account the smoker's self-responsibility. Even if wrongfulness is clearly given, e.g. in case of violations of the restrictions on advertising for tobacco products foreseen in the Tobacco Act, it remains doubtful whether the tobacco producer will be liable, as the reversal of the burden of proof for psychological causation Leitner assumes is also questionable: According to Leitner, the law accepts potential causation as far as joint tortfeasors are concerned if they act jointly and intentionally and he holds that this idea can be generalized to be applicable to cases in which a person intentionally tries to reach a certain conduct by influencing someone else psychologically. However, in my view, such a generalization is not possible. The difference between those cases is that, in case of multiple tortfeasors, it is clear that there is an intentional joint act of the tortfeasors, whereas in cases of psychological causation by advertising such a joint decision to act does not exist. In cases of multiple tortfeasors it is clear that there has been a joint action though it might remain open whether this joint action actually caused the damage while, in relation to advertising for smoking, it is not clear whether there has been a joint action at all (here between the producer advertising the tobacco product and the potential victim). 69

4. O. Riss, Hypothetische Kausalität, objektive Berechnung bloßer Vermögensschäden und Ersatz verlorener Prozesschancen, [2004] JBl, 423

Starting point for this article is a case of lawyer's liability, in which the plaintiff sues his lawyer from an earlier trial. In that trial on a time-barred claim there had been no negligence of the lawyer in relation to the prescription – i.e. that the court qualified the claim as time-barred was part of the normal litigation risk. However, during the trial there was a negligent omission on the part of the lawyer on the basis of which the plaintiff's claim, had it not been time barred before the claim was brought before the court, would at any rate have been time-barred at the end of oral proceedings. On the basis of this case and variants of it, the author examines a wide range of questions in detail. The article in particular covers hypothetical causation, objective calculation of pure economic loss and compensation for loss of chance of successful lititgation. Riss clearly shows that, depending on the definition of damage and the method of calculating damage chosen, solutions for a question of liability may be found on different levels (as e.g. damage, causation, protective purpose of the norm, etc.). For his starting case Riss comes to the conclusion that the lawyer will in principle be liable for the damage through litigation costs if he acts negligently when asserting a claim in trial even though *ex post* the claim turns out to have been non-existent. Thereby, the extent of the claim will, according to the author, depend on the method of calculation of damage chosen as well as on the prospect of success the claim has *ex ante*. 70

5. T. Schoditsch, Schädigermehrheit und gesetzliches Haftungsprivileg, [2004] JBl, 557

71 The present article focuses on questions arising in case of concurrence of a plurality of wrongdoers on the one hand and liability privileges on the other hand. The author deals with both, cases of contract and tort and examines the effect of a liability privilege on the part of one of a plurality of persons liable on the liability of the other liable person(s). The author distinguishes three possible solutions: 1. a solution to the detriment of the non-privileged wrongdoer, who has to cover the whole loss; 2. a solution with limited external effect where the non-privileged wrongdoer is liable in full towards the person harmed, but is granted a right of recourse against the privileged wrongdoer and 3. a solution with absolute external effect, where the claim of the person harmed towards the non-privileged wrongdoer is reduced to the extent for which the privileged wrongdoer is responsible. Schoditsch discusses questions of contractual and delictual capacity, the liability privilege of § 3 EKHG, the family privilege according to § 67 *Versicherungsvertragsgesetz* (Insurance Contract Act, VersVG) and the employer's privilege and examines which of the above-mentioned solutions is applicable to those cases.

6. C. Fischer-Czermak et al. (eds.), *Festschrift für Rudolf Welser* (Manz, Vienna 2004)

72 The present liber amicorum *inter alia* contains several contributions on questions of delictual and also contractual liability. Amongst others, attorneys' liability and prescription, liability of notaries, public liability for university organs as well as questions of depreciation of damaged cars, even though the cars have been repaired completely, are dealt with.

7. Further Selected Literature

73 **ABGB**: P. Rummel, *Kommentar zum Allgemeinen bürgerlichen Gesetzbuch* II/2b (3rd edn. 2004). This is the first of the third edition's two volumes on the ABGB provisions on contractual and delictual liability commented on by R. Reischauer. This volume covers §§ 1313 to 1341 ABGB. The second volume covering §§ 1295 to 1312 ABGB is due in 2005.

74 **Abstract annuity**: A. Wittwer, Zum Comeback einer Rechtsfigur – die abstrakte Rente lebt weiter! [2004] *Zeitschrift für Verkehrsrecht* (ZVR), 51.[54]

75 **Air traffic**: P. Csoklich, Neuerungen im Internationalen Lufttransportrecht, [2004] *Österreichisches Recht der Wirtschaft* (RdW), 648.

76 **Employers' liability**: P. Apathy, Risikohaftung des Arbeitgebers für Personenschäden? [2004] JBl, 746; A. Vonkilch, Haftpflicht für Kfz-Schäden von

[54] Cf. also B.C. Steininger, Austria, in: H. Koziol/B.C. Steininger (eds.), *European Tort Law 2003* (2004), nos. 56 et seq.

Dienstnehmern, Arbeitgeberprivileg und Haftpflichtversicherung nach der 48. ASVG Novelle, [2004] ZVR, 40.

Internet: D. Altenburger, *Hyperlinks. Haftung für fremde Inhalte* (2004). 77

Nuclear liability: M. Hinteregger/S. Kissich, *Atomhaftungsgesetz 1999* (2004). 78

Privacy: M. Lukas, Schadenersatz bei Verletzung der Privatsphäre, [2004] *Österreichische Richterzeitung* (RZ), 33[55]; G. Wilhelm, Carolines Privatsphäre – Zur Drittwirkung europäischer Grundrechte, [2004] ecolex, 671. 79

Product liability: H. Fitz/A. Grau/P. Reindl, *Produkthaftungsgesetz* (2nd edn. 2004); R. Welser/Ch. Rabl, *Produkthaftungsgesetz* (2nd edn. 2004); R. Welser, Das Österreichische Produkthaftungsgesetz in der Rechtsprechung, in: *Festschrift für Ernst A. Kramer* (2004). 80

Product monitoring: F. Linder, Produktbeobachtung, Rückruf und Versicherungsschutz, [2004] *Wirtschaftsrechtliche Blätter* (wbl), 449. 81

Professional liability: Ch. Winternitz/L. Aigner, *Die Haftung des Anlageberaters für fehlerhafte Beratung* (2004). 82

Public liability: R. Rebhahn, Amtshaftung für „Bankprüfer" – Wohltat oder Irrweg? [2004] *Österreichisches Bank-Archiv* (ÖBA), 267.[56] 83

Schools: G. Walchshofer, Probleme des Aufenthalts von Schülern im Schulgebäude vor Beginn der gesetzlichen Aufsichtsphase, [2004] ÖJZ, 375. 84

Smoking: K. Davani, *Die Haftung der Tabakindustrie für Gesundheitsschäden von Rauchern* (2004); id., Der Konstruktionsfehler der Zigarette nach dem PHG in Österreich, [2004] ecolex, 437. 85

Sports: K. Markowetz, Haftungsrechtliche Ansprüche im Zusammenhang mit Doping, [2004] ÖJZ, 401; M. Stefula, Haftungsfragen bei Luftsportvereinen, [2004] ZVR, 148. 86

Unlawful benefits: H. Krejci/W. Brandstetter, Verlust verbotener Vorteile als Schaden? [2004] ecolex, 520; M. Schauer, Geheimnisbruch und Steuerschaden, [2004] RdW, 324. 87

[55] Cf. also B.C. Steininger (supra fn. 54), nos. 1 et seq.
[56] Cf. also B.C. Steininger (supra fn. 54), nos. 27 et seq.

II. Belgium

Isabelle C. Durant[1]

A. Legislation

1. Act of 7 May 2004 Concerning Human Experiments[2]

1 On the occasion of complying with the European Directive on clinical trials on medicinal products for human use,[3] the Belgian legislator has adopted an Act which gives a legal frame to experiments on human beings. The scope of this Act is therefore larger than the scope of the European Directive. It concerns not only the clinical trials on medicinal products, but, more generally, experiments on human beings.

2 The basic idea of the Act is that experiments are necessary, but subjects, individuals who participate in them, have not to become instruments: they have to be protected. Therefore, any clinical experiment may not be conducted on human beings without their previous written informed consent.[4] Such as in the European Directive, special provisions have been adopted concerning experiments on minors and on incapacitated adults who are not able to give informed legal consent.[5] Although the informed consent of the parents or legal representative must be obtained, the minor is implied in the decision taking into account his/her age and his/her maturity.[6] Concerning adults incapable of giving informed legal consent, the informed consent of their legal representative must be ob-

[1] At the time of writing this report, the author was employed by the Austrian Academy of Sciences. She would like to express her most sincere thanks towards the *Österreichische Akademie der Wissenschaften* as well as towards Prof. Dr. H. Koziol. For the writing of this report, she has also benefited from a special scholarship (*bourse post-doctorale FSR*) granted by the Université catholique de Louvain (Louvain-la-Neuve, Belgium) for which the author is sincerely grateful.

[2] *Loi du 7 mai 2004 relative aux expérimentations sur la personne humaine/Wet dd. 7 mei 2004 inzake experimenten op de menselijke persoon*, Belgian official journal of 18 May 2004, 2nd edn. (*Moniteur belge/Belgisch Staatsblad*).

[3] Directive 2001/20/EC of the European Parliament and of the Council of 4 April 2001 on the approximation of the laws, regulations and administrative provisions of the Member States relating to the implementation of good clinical practice in the conduct of clinical trials on medicinal products for human use, OJ L 121, 1.5.2001, 34–44.

[4] Art. 6.

[5] Artt. 7 and 8.

[6] Art. 7.

tained, but the explicit wish of the subject to refuse to participate in the experiment must be taken into consideration in certain circumstances.[7] Individuals who cannot consent due to emergency are also protected.[8]

With the aim of protecting the subjects, a second rule has been adopted: the experiment may not start as long as the sponsor[9] and the investigator[10] are not in possession of a favourable opinion issued by an Ethic Committee.[11] Moreover, according to the European Directive, when the experiment consists in a trial on a medicinal product, the trial may only start inasmuch as the Ministry of Public Health has not given any grounds for non-acceptance.[12] 3

Chapter XVII of the Act of 7 May 2004 concerns liability (art. 29, sec. 1) and insurance (art. 29, sec. 2 and 3). 4

According to art. 29, sec. 1, the sponsor is strictly liable for the damage the experiment caused directly or indirectly to subjects participating in the experiment and/or to their successors. According to the parliamentary documents, the sponsor must face up to responsibilities connected with the experiment, considering that subjects have to be protected as best as possible. Nevertheless, art. 29 does not prevent the sponsor from taking recourse against the one who acted with fault.[13] 5

According to art. 29, sec. 2 and 3, the sponsor has to take out a liability insurance covering the liability of all participants in the experiment before the experiment starts, and the sponsor or a legal representative of the sponsor must be established in the European Community. Moreover, the subjects or their successors are allowed to take legal action directly against the insurer before a Belgian court. 6

2. Act of 16 July 2004 Introducing a Code of International Private Law[14]

Until recently, Belgium did not have any Code of International Private Law. The gap is now filled: since 1 October 2004, the Belgian Code of International Private Law has been in force.[15] 7

[7] Art. 8.
[8] Art. 9.
[9] Sponsor: an individual, company, institution or organisation which takes responsibility for the initiation, management and/or financing of an experiment (art. 2, 21).
[10] Investigator: a doctor or a person who practises a profession described in the Royal Decree no. 78 of 10 November 1967 concerning the exercise of professions in the field of medical care, who are qualified to carry out an experiment (art. 2, 17).
[11] Art. 10, sec. 1.
[12] Art. 10, sec. 2.
[13] Cf. Parliamentary documents (*Chambre des Représentants, Exposé des motifs du 10 février 2004/Kamer van Volksvertegenwoordigers, Memorie van toelichting dd. 10 februari 2004*, doc. 51-0798/001, 26).
[14] *Loi du 16 juillet 2004 portant le Code de droit international privé/Wet dd. 16 juli 2004 houdende het Wetboek van internationaal privaatrecht*, Belgian official journal of 27 July 2004 (*Moniteur belge/Belgisch Staatsblad*).
[15] Art. 140 of the Act of 16 July 2004.

8 This Code concerns, in international situations, the jurisdiction of Belgian courts, the determination of applicable law and the recognition and enforcement in Belgium of foreign judgments and authentic instruments. The Act shall (obviously) be applied without prejudice to international treaties, law of the European Union and provisions contained in specific acts.[16]

9 Chapter IX of the Act of 16 July 2004 concerns (contractual and non-contractual) obligations. This chapter is divided into two sections: international jurisdiction (sec. 1) and applicable law (sec. 2).

10 Concerning jurisdiction, according to the general provision, Belgian courts are competent if the defendant is domiciled or habitually resident in Belgium at the moment of bringing procedure.[17] In matters relating to tort, Belgian courts are also competent: (a) if the harmful event occurred or may occur totally or partially in Belgium; (b) if and insofar as the damage occurred or may occur in Belgium.[18] The section relating to jurisdiction is probably of minor importance due to the existence of international conventions,[19] especially the Council Regulation (EC) no. 44/2001 of 22 December 2000 on jurisdiction and the recognition and enforcement of judgments in civil and commercial matters.[20]

11 Concerning applicable law, the new Code is probably of greater importance in matters of tort, except, however, in cases of traffic accidents which are indeed generally governed by the Hague Convention of 4 May 1971.[21] Without any doubt, the European Council Regulation project has inspired the authors of the new Belgian Code.[22]

12 Art. 99 of the new Code concerns law applicable to obligations resulting from a harmful event. Sec. 1 contains the general rule and sec. 2 concerns specific torts. With this provision, the new Code breaks old rules, follows the evolution of comparative law and aims to assure the foreseeability of solutions.[23]

[16] Art. 2 of the Act of 16 July 2004.

[17] Art. 5 of the Act of 16 July 2004.

[18] Art. 96 of the Act of 16 July 2004.

[19] Parliamentary documents (*Sénat de Belgique, session de 2003–2004, 20 avril 2004, Rapport fait au nom de la commission de la justice/Belgische Senaat, zitting 2003–2004, 20 april 2004, Verslag namens de commissie voor de justitie*, doc. 3-27/7, 169).

[20] According to this Regulation, persons domiciled in a Member State shall be sued in the courts of that Member State (art. 2, general provision). Nevertheless, in matters relating to tort, they may be sued in the courts for the place where the harmful event occurred or may occur (art. 5, special jurisdiction).

[21] According to art. 3 of the Hague Convention on the Law Applicable to Traffic Accidents, the applicable law is the internal law of the State where the accident occurred. Exceptions are made to this provision in the subsequent articles of the Convention.

[22] Parliamentary documents (*Chambre des Représentants, Rapport fait au nom de la commission de la justice du 23 juin 2004/Kamer van Volksvertegenwoordigers, Verslag namens de commissie voor de justitie*, doc. 51-1078/005, 13)

[23] Parliamentary documents (*Sénat de Belgique, session extraordinaire de 2003, 7 juillet 2003/ Belgische Senaat, buitengewone zitting 2003, 7 juli 2003*, doc. 3-27/1, 20). According to the old rule, in matters of tort, the applicable law was governed by the law of the State where the harmful event occurred.

The general rule, contained in art. 99, sec. 1, is divided into three points and provides a chain of connecting factors: first of all, non-contractual liability will be governed by the law of the State where the tortfeasor and the victim are habitually resident at the moment the harmful event occurred; secondly, in the absence of habitual residence in the same State, liability will be governed by the law of the State where the harmful event and the damage totally occurred or may occur; finally, in other cases, liability will be governed by the law of the State with which the obligation resulting from tort is the most closely connected. 13

Sec. 2 of art. 99 concerns five specific tortious situations. Obligations resulting from a harmful event will be governed: (1) in case of defamation, attack on privacy or personality rights: by the law of the Sate where the harmful event or the damage occurred or may occur, as chosen by the victim, except if the tortfeasor shows that he could not have foreseen that the damage could have occurred in this State; (2) in case of unfair competition or commercial practices: by the law of the State where the damage occurred or may occur; (3) in case of property damage or personal damage resulting from threats to environment: by the law of the State where the damage occurred or may occur; (4) in case of liability of the producer, importer or supplier of a good: by the law of the State where the victim is habitually resident at the moment the damage occurred; (5) in case of a traffic accident, by the law applicable under the terms of the Hague Convention of 4 May 1971 on the Law Applicable to Traffic Accidents. Moreover, parties may choose the applicable law after the occurrence of the dispute, without prejudice to the above mentioned Hague Convention and without prejudice to the rights of third parties.[24] Whatever the applicable law, rules concerning security and behaviour, applicable at the moment the harmful event occurred, will be taken into account.[25] 14

Art. 103 concerns the scope of the applicable law. The applicable law shall determine, in particular: 1) the conditions and extent of liability; 2) liability for persons, property or animals; 3) the grounds for exemption from liability, any limitation of liability, and any division of liability; 4) the existence and kinds of damage which may have to be compensated; 5) the measures which may be ruled by the judge to ensure prevention or cessation of damage; 6) the mode and extent of repair; 7) the persons who may claim compensation for the damage they have personally suffered; 8) the extent to which the right to damages may be exercised by the successors; 9) the rules of prescription and forfeiture based on the expiry of a period, including rules relating to the commencement, the interruption and the suspension of this period; 10) the burden of proof and presumptions of law. 15

[24] Art. 101 of the Act of 16 July 2004.

[25] Art. 102 of the Act of 16 July 2004. For example, Highway Code, regulations concerning the composition of products, environmental rules, etc.

16 The law applicable to the direct legal action of the victim against the insurer is mainly governed by the law applicable according to the above mentioned rules and the law applicable to the legal subrogation is governed by the law applicable to the obligation of the third party who indemnified the victim.[26]

B. Cases[27]

1. *Cour de cassation/Hof van Cassatie*, 16 October 2003, C.01.0580.N: Impact of Early Retirement Pension on Damage

a) Brief Summary of the Facts

17 On 4 August 1982 a traffic accident occurred, causing damage to a worker on his way to his workplace. From October 1986 the worker received early retirement pension. The injuries were healed on 30 October 1990. The industrial accident insurer of the employer paid damages to the worker not only for medical costs, transport costs, prosthesis costs and aid of third persons, but also for compensation of temporary and permanent work incapacity.[28]

18 Afterwards, the industrial accident insurer sued the motor vehicle insurer of the driver who had caused the traffic accident for obtaining the reimbursement of the amounts paid to the victim. The industrial accident insurer is indeed subrogated in the rights of the victim against the one who is liable for the accident. The court of appeal gave no satisfaction to the industrial accident insurer as far as its demand concerned the compensation of temporary and permanent work incapacity allowed for the period following the date of early retirement. The court of appeal was of the opinion that after that moment (in this case it means after 27 October 1986), the worker did not suffer any more loss of income. Therefore, according to the court, the motor vehicle insurer did not have to compensate any work incapacity from the moment of early retirement.

19 The industrial accident insurer did not agree with this decision. It was of the opinion that the early retirement pension did not have the same base and the same purpose as the paid damages. According to the industrial accident insurer, first of all, the early retirement pension is based on the labour contract existing between the victim and his employer and on the law concerning retirement and, secondly, the early retirement pension did not aim to compensate the damage caused by the accident. Consequently, for the assessment of the damage incurred by the victim (and to the insurer which is subrogated in the rights of the victim), the early retirement pension has not to be taken into consideration.

[26] Art. 106 and art. 107 of the Act of 16 July 2004.

[27] All the commented decisions are to be founded on the official website of the Belgian judicial power: www.juridat.be.

[28] One is reminded that each employer must take out an industrial accidents insurance policy with a private recognised insurer.

b) Judgment of the Supreme Court

The Supreme Court quashed the decision of the court of appeal. According to the Supreme Court, the benefit from an early retirement pension does not necessarily imply that the victim lost totally his/her economic value. In other words, the victim may still have an economic value. Therefore, it was not legal to say that there was no more damage for the loss of the possibility to obtain work income after the early retirement. 20

c) Commentary

By this decision, the Supreme Court gave some indication concerning the evaluation of the damage suffered by an employee when this employee takes early retirement before the day of the healing of the injuries. The Supreme Court is of the opinion that the one who receives an early retirement pension can nevertheless still have an economic value which must be compensated if this value is lost following an accident. Such reasoning was already adopted by the Supreme Court more than ten years ago in a (different but similar) case wherein the victim was unemployed and received unemployment benefits.[29] According to the Supreme Court, the base of these benefits is not the same as the base of the damages. The unemployment benefits do not aim to repair the damage resulting from a faulty conduct. Therefore, they do not have to be taken into consideration at the moment of the evaluation of the damage. According to the here commented case (of 16 October 2003), one has to conclude that the early retirement pension does not necessarily remove from the victim his/her economic value which has to be compensated according to the rules of tort law (if lost due to tort). 21

2. *Cour de cassation/Hof van Cassatie*, 19 November 2003, P.03.0890.F: Reduction of Retirement Pension as Part of the Damage

a) Brief Summary of the Facts

After an accident, the victim's mother lost her job and sued the one who was liable for the accident of her son with the aim of obtaining compensation for the financial consequences of this loss. The existence of a causal link between the accident and the loss of the job was not contested before the court which awarded the mother damages to compensate various costs, moral damage, loss of income and loss of a chance to find a new job. Concerning the loss of income, the court of appeal awarded the mother damages covering a period of 32 months, namely from the moment her labour contract was terminated (which is the end of the notice she received from her employer) until the moment her son went back to home (after hospitalization), considering that from that moment the aid of a third person was already compensated (through the damages awarded to the son). 22

[29] Cass., 28 April 1992, 5230; [1993–1994] *Rechtskundig Weekblad* (RW) 38, 1361, comment A. Van Oevelen, De weerslag van de werkloosheid van het slachtoffer van een onrechtmatige daad op diens vordering tot vergoeding van inkomstenschade.

23 Nevertheless, the mother did not totally agree with the decision of the court of appeal because the court had refused to compensate the effect of the loss of her job on her (future) retirement pension. According to the mother, due to the (actual) loss of income, her (future) retirement pension would be reduced and this reduction also had to be compensated by the one who is liable for the accident that caused the loss of job (and income). The court of appeal gave no satisfaction to the mother considering that compensation for the loss of income and compensation for the reduction of the later retirement pension would have covered the same damage.[30] The mother appealed to the Supreme Court.

b) Judgment of the Supreme Court

24 At the outset, the Supreme Court stated that the entire loss has to be compensated. Then, the Supreme Court noted that the loss of professional income caused by an accident and the reduction of the (later) retirement pension do not constitute the same damage. Consequently, the court of appeal could not refuse to compensate the reduction of the (later) pension by saying that the victim could not draw compensation of this reduction and compensation of the loss of income, as far as the same damage is concerned. Therefore, the decision of the court of appeal was quashed.

c) Commentary

25 At first sight, the commented decision seems to be in contradiction with other decisions of the Supreme Court.[31] Indeed, in two old decisions, the Supreme Court stated that the reduction of the pension did not have to be compensated. Nevertheless, the apparent contradiction is not a real one due to the fact that the periods for which the allowance of damages is subject to discussion are not the same in the different cases.

26 In the two previous cases, the pension was paid prematurely either because the victim died (in this case, the pension was paid to the widow), or because the victim retired prematurely due to the accident. This pension was less important than a normal pension due to the fact that it was paid prematurely. For the period between the accident and the normal age of retirement of the victim, the difference between the received pension and the normal (hypothetical) pension did not have to be compensated, because the victim already received compensation for loss of professional income.

27 In the commented case, the mother asked for damages to compensate the reduction of the pension but for the period *after* her retirement. Therefore, this damage had not already been compensated for by the award of damages to

[30] The court of appeal referred to two past decisions of the Supreme Court: Cass., 29 May 1974, [1974] *Pasicrisie* (Pas), I, 1000; Cass., 13 May 1970, [1970] Pas, I, 804. Nevertheless, the mother was of the opinion that these two decisions had not to be used as a precedent. The Supreme Court agreed with her.

[31] The decisions mentioned in the preceding footnote.

compensate the loss of income for the period before the retirement (the awarded 32 months).

3. *Cour de cassation/Hof van Cassatie*, 21 November 2003, C.02.0619.F: Notion of Defective Property

a) Brief Summary of the Facts

A traffic accident occurred on a damaged road. Shortly before the scene of the accident, there was a board warning the drivers of the presence of potholes. 28

Considering that the road was a defective thing due to the presence of potholes, the victim sued the guardian of this thing, namely the Walloon Region, but not successfully. Indeed, the first instance judges were of the opinion that the road was not defective due to the presence of the board: the driver was warned and had to be twice as attentive. The driver did not agree with this decision and appealed to the Supreme Court. 29

b) Judgment of the Supreme Court

The Supreme Court quashed the decision of the first instance judges. According to the Supreme Court, one can say that a thing is defective as soon as it presents an abnormal feature that is deemed to cause damage in certain circumstances. Then the Supreme Court added that the first instance judges could not deduce the absence of a defect from the fact that the victim knew or had to know the damaged state of the road. 30

c) Commentary

The guardian of a defective thing is liable for the damage caused by the defect of the thing on the basis of art. 1384, sec. 1 of the Civil Code.[32] Generally, it is said that three conditions have to be fulfilled to conclude the existence of a defective thing: the so-called defective thing must show a departure from the normal thing (the model), the departure has to be abnormal and the abnormal feature has to be deemed to cause damage in certain circumstances.[33] According to the Supreme Court, the first instance judges may not deduce the non-existence of the defect from the knowledge of the abnormal feature by the victim. This decision can be compared with the case law according to which public authorities are obliged to take the necessary measures to prevent abnormal dangers of the roads and streets, even if these dangers are visible.[34] 31

[32] "A person is liable not only for the damage he causes by his own act, but also for that which is caused by the acts of persons for whom he is responsible, or by things which are in his custody."

[33] F. Baudoncq/M. Debaene, De aansprakelijkheid voor zaken in het licht van artikel 1384, lid 1 B.W., in: B. Tilleman/I. Claeys (eds.), *Buitencontractuele aansprakelijkheid* (2004), 100, no. 21.

[34] Cass., 12 March 1999, C.98.0147.N.

32 Nevertheless, it is important to note that the faulty conduct of the victim may perhaps be analysed as a contributory negligence. In this case, the strictly liable party will not escape liability but he will not have to compensate the entire damage suffered by the victim.[35]

4. *Cour de cassation/Hof van Cassatie*, 12 January 2004, C.03.0327.F: Liability of Parents towards their own Children

a) Brief Summary of the Facts

33 On 5 July 1992, the driver of a car lost the control of his vehicle. The accident caused damage to one of the passengers, namely the very young daughter of the driver. The father was held liable for the accident. The baby received various medical treatment for which the mutual insurance company reimbursed the parents or which were directly paid by the mutual insurer. Afterwards, the mutual insurance company sued the civil liability insurer of the father with the aim of obtaining the reimbursement of the paid amounts.

34 The first instance judges gave satisfaction to the mutual insurance company. According to these judges, the one who benefited from the payments made by the mutual insurer was the baby. Therefore, this insurer was subrogated in the rights of the baby and might successfully sue the (liability insurer of the) father for obtaining the reimbursement of the payments.

35 The civil liability insurer of the father did not agree with this decision of the first instance judges and appealed before the Supreme Court. According to the civil liability insurer, although the mutual insurer was subrogated in the rights of the baby, it could not sue the father (or the liability insurer of the father) due to the fact, according to the insurer, that the baby herself could not have sued her father with the aim of obtaining the reimbursement of the amounts paid to doctors and pharmacists. The civil liability insurer was of the opinion that the baby had no legal action against her father for the reimbursement of these costs because, when the father paid the doctor or the pharmacist, he did not pay on behalf of his child but he carried out his own duty. Indeed, according to the Civil Code, parents have the duty to take care of their children.[36] According to the civil liability insurer, the asset of the child was therefore not reduced by the payments made by her father and the baby had no legal action against him for obtaining the reimbursement of these payments and, consequently, the mutual insurance, subrogated in the rights of the baby, has not got any either.

[35] H. Cousy/D. Droshout, Belgium, in: B.A. Koch/H. Koziol (eds.), *Unification of Tort Law: Strict Liability* (2002), 67; H. Cousy/D. Droshout, Contributory Negligence under Belgian Law, in: U. Magnus/M. Martín-Casals (eds.), *Unification of Tort Law: Contributory Negligence* (2004), 34; F. Baudoncq/M. Debaene, De aansprakelijkheid voor zaken in het licht van artikel 1384, lid 1 B.W., in: B. Tilleman/I. Claeys (supra fn. 33), 111, no. 40.

[36] Art. 203 of the Civil Code: "The father and the mother are obliged to assume in proportion to his or her means the accommodation, the support, the supervision, the education and the training of their children".

b) Judgment of the Supreme Court

At the outset, the Supreme Court stated that, according to law, the mutual insurance company has normally nothing to pay when the damage is compensated under tort law and that the holder of social rights may be held liable on the basis of tort law for the damage he caused.[37] 36

Then the Supreme Court noted that the parents may be held liable for the damage they caused to their children, regardless of the existence of a legal duty to take care of one's children. Consequently, the child who is the victim of damage may sue his/her parents on the basis of tort law if his/her parents caused him/her damage. 37

Finally, the Supreme Court noted that the mutual insurance company is subrogated in the rights of the beneficiary of its payments and may sue the one who is liable, on the basis of tort law, for damage caused to the beneficiary (or his civil liability insurer), even if this person is the holder of the social rights and even if this person is the father of the beneficiary. Therefore, the decision of the court of appeal was legally justified and did not have to be quashed by the Supreme Court. 38

c) Commentary

The main lesson of this decision of the Supreme Court is that parents may be held liable towards their children on the basis of common tort law and that the existence of a general duty to take care of one's children does not cancel the action of these children that would be based on tort law. 39

According to the public prosecutor, when the father or mother exercises his/her general duty in favour of his/her child, he/she makes an *advance* on the repair of the injuries which has finally to be supported by the one who is liable for the accident. The second reason to maintain the existence of a legal action against the parents is that it could be possible that the child paid the medical costs from his/her own assets. In this case, he/she must have the legal opportunity to obtain the reimbursement of his/her payments from the liable party. In this way, art. 24.1 of the International Covenant on Civil and Political Rights of 16 December 1966 is respected.[38] 40

[37] At the time of the decision, the subrogation was provided by art. 76 *quater*, sec. 2 of the Act of 9 August 1963 and by art. 241, sec. 1 of the Royal Decree of 4 November 1963 concerning compulsory health insurance (cf. currently art. 136 of the Act of 14 July 1994). In the present case, the father was the holder of the social rights (*le titulaire/de gerechtigde*) and the child was the beneficiary (*le bénéficiaire/de rechthebbende*).

[38] "Every child shall have, without any discrimination as to race, colour, sex, language, religion, national or social origin, property or birth, the right to such measures of protection as are required by his status as a minor, on the part of his family, society and the state".

5. *Cour de cassation/Hof van Cassatie*, 25 February 2004, P.03.1317.F: Impact of Contributory Negligence on Damage Suffered by Repercussion

a) Brief Summary of the Facts

41 A traffic accident occurred, following which the victim died. Considering the contributory negligence of the victim, she had to bear a third of her own damage. For his part, the master of the servant who was liable for the accident had to bear the other two thirds of the damage.[39]

42 The daughter and the granddaughter of the victim sued the master with the aim of obtaining compensation of two kinds of damage they had personally suffered: moral damage resulting from the death of their mother and grandmother and damage suffered by having seen her suffering. The first instance judges allowed compensation for the entire moral damage suffered by the daughter and granddaughter.

43 The master did not agree with this decision. According to him, he should not be held liable for the entire moral damage suffered by the relatives of the direct victim considering her contributory negligence.

b) Judgment of the Supreme Court

44 The Supreme Court agreed with the master and quashed the decision of the first instance judges. According to the Supreme Court, moral damage for which the daughter and granddaughter were asking compensation was personally suffered by them but "by repercussion": their personal damage found its source in the family and affectionate relationship between them and the primary (deceased) victim. Due to this relationship, which founded the right to obtain compensation, this right has to be limited considering the contributory negligence of the primary victim. The compensation of the damage suffered by the relatives has to be reduced in proportion to the contributory negligence.

c) Commentary

45 The damage suffered "by repercussion" is damage of the relatives and not damage suffered by the (first) victim. Nevertheless, this damage is due to the existence of the relationship with the (first) victim. Consequently, according to the Supreme Court, the compensation of damage by repercussion is affected by the contributory negligence of the primary victim. This point of view has been reflected in case law for many years.[40]

[39] According to art. 1384, sec. 3 of the Civil Code, the masters are liable for the damage caused by a fault of their servants committed in the course of their occupation.

[40] Cass., 1 February 1994, P.93.0037.N, [1994] Pas, I, 133; Cass., 5 October 1995, C.93.0305.N, [1995] Pas, I, 873. W. Van Gerven (ed.), *Cases, Materials and Text on National, Supranational and International Tort Law. Scope of Protection* (1999), 147.

6. *Cour de cassation/Hof van Cassatie*, 22 March 2004, C.03.0109.F: Notion of Guardian of Defective Property

a) Brief Summary of the Facts

A gas explosion occurred in a building causing damage. The explosion was attributable to a defective valve. Due to the defect of the valve, important quantities of gas could spread in the building. The valve was located inside the building, in the cellar, the company in charge of the gas distribution was the owner of the valve, of the connection and of all the equipment of the gas distribution network. 46

The owner of the building sued the company in charge of the gas network with the aim of obtaining damages. He founded his legal action on art. 1384, sec. 1 of the Civil Code, according to which the guardian of a defective property is strictly liable for the damage caused by a defect of that property. Nevertheless, he was not successful in his legal action. According to the court of appeal, although the company was the owner of the defective valve, it was not the guardian of it and could not be held liable for the damage. The owner of the building, who, consequently, had to bear the whole damage, did not agree with this decision and appealed to the Supreme Court. According to him, the company was the guardian of the defective valve because it had the power to control it intellectually. 47

b) Judgment of the Supreme Court

At the outset, the Supreme Court stated that, within the framework of art. 1384, sec. 1 of the Civil Code, the guardian of a property is the one who uses it for his own account, who enjoys or keeps it with powers of supervision, direction and control. 48

The Supreme Court then stated that it is the task of the first instance judges (and of the court of appeal) to decide who is the guardian of the defective thing. In this case, the court of appeal was of the opinion that the owner of the building was the guardian of the defective valve considering that the company in charge of the gas network was not allowed to go inside the private building without access authorization from the owner, that therefore the latter had the power to direct and supervise the valve and was the sole individual who could make a decision concerning the valve (for example, by asking the company to switch it off in case of problem). According to the Supreme Court, this reasoning was legally justified. Therefore, it did not quash the decision of the court of appeal. 49

c) Commentary

Although the guardian is generally the owner of the defective property, one can see that custody and property do not always coincide. This can be explained by the fact that custody implies a factual control of the defective 50 thing.[41] One can see in case law that the criterion of (in)accessibility is sometimes used to conclude that the legal owner is not the guardian of the thing. Such decisions were for example taken concerning gas meters.[42] In some cases, the tenant can also be considered as the guardian of the rented thing.[43]

7. *Cour de cassation/Hof van Cassatie*, 1 April 2004, C.01.0211.F-C.01.0217.F: Future of the Loss of Chance

a) Brief Summary of the Facts

51 The facts of this case are really horrifying. A young woman, Moroccan by birth and staying in Belgium for a few months to study, was the victim of an acid attack during the night of 21 February 1980. The man who threw vitriol was her ex-boyfriend, who was left by the victim due to his violence and who did not accept the break-up. He was sentenced to hard labour in perpetuity. The victim, who was seriously injured, and her parents sued the City of Liège and the Belgian State for damages. They reproached the local police[44] and the public prosecutor's office for faulty omissions.[45]

52 The local police and the public prosecutor's office had not actually carried out any investigation and had not taken any safety measures, although several warnings concerning the dangerousness of the man against the victim reached them during the weeks before the accident. They received warnings from a social worker and from the director working in the hostel for homeless where the victim had found refuge, and also from a professor of the university where she was studying. The victim herself had said many times that her ex-boyfriend had bought a vitriol can. In the circumstances of the case, one could say that the local police and the public prosecutor's office were negligent.

53 However, after having considered that the defendant's conduct had been faulty, the court of appeal of Brussels noted that it was impossible to maintain that the measures which should have been taken with the aim of preventing the aggression would have been effective. According to the court, when someone is determined to harm somebody else, he can show great imagination in evading obstacles. Consequently, the court of appeal said that it was not possible to maintain that the safety measures would have stopped the criminal acting.

[41] F. Baudoncq/M. Debaene, De aansprakelijkheid voor zaken in het licht van artikel 1384, lid 1 B.W., in: B. Tilleman/I. Claeys (supra fn. 33), 90, no. 9; H. Bocken, Tort Law, in: H. Bocken/W. de Bondt (eds.), *Introduction to Belgian Law* (2000), 262.

[42] Examples: Antwerp Court of First Instance, 2 December 1997, [1999] *Iuvis*, 982; Mechelen Court of First Instance, 2 December 1997, [1997–1998] RW 36, 1293.

[43] Example: Court of appeal of Mons, 9 April 1992, [1995] *Revue Générale des Assurances et des Responsabilités* (RGAR), 12537.

[44] For the acts of which the City is liable.

[45] For the acts of which the State is liable.

Nevertheless, concerning the application of the but-for test, the court of appeal said that it was *certain* that the victim would have had a chance to escape from her aggressor if measures had been taken. The court deducted from this consideration that the damage, which was in causal link with the omissions, consisted in the loss of the chance to have avoided the risk arising. 54

Then the court of appeal evaluated the lost chance to 80% (that means that, according to the court, if safety measures had been taken, in eight cases out of ten, the damage would not have occurred). 55

Finally, with the aim of determining the damage resulting from the loss of the chance to have avoided the occurring of the risk, the court used the method described by the French author J. Boré[46] and applied the above mentioned percentage of 80% to the damage caused by the occurrence of the risk (which means the damage that really happened). The complete damage incurred by the victim was provisionally evaluated at approx. € 100,000; therefore, the victim obtained an amount of approx. € 80,000.[47] 56

Neither the City of Liège nor the Belgian State agreed with this decision. Therefore, they appealed to the Supreme Court. The main criticism advanced by them concerned the causal link. They drew the attention of the Supreme Court to the fact that fundamentally the victim and her parents claimed compensation for a damage that really happened. Consequently, the damage for which compensation was claimed was not the fact of having lost a chance of avoiding the aggression but the real fact consisting in the aggression and its consequences. From the moment the court of appeal had decided that there was no certain causal link between the negligent omissions and the accident,[48] it could not conclude liability. 57

b) Judgment of the Supreme Court

The Supreme Court quashed the decision of the court of appeal. At the outset, the Supreme Court stated that the one who claims damages has to prove the existence of a causal link between the faulty conduct and the damage, that this causal link implies that without the faulty conduct the damage would not have occurred such as it occurred *in concreto* and that the judge may not allow a claim for damages if he decides that uncertainty remains concerning causation. 58

Then the Supreme Court adjudicated upon the criticism advanced by the City and by the Belgian State. First, the Supreme Court noted that the claim made by the victim aimed at the repair of the damage resulting from the aggression. 59

[46] J. Boré, L'indemnisation pour les chances perdues, une forme d'appréciation quantitative de la causalité d'un fait dommageable, [1974] *Semaine juridique Doctrine*, 2620 (especially no. 7).

[47] Court of appeal of Brussels, 4 January 2001, [2001] *Journal des Procès* 410, 22–31.

[48] The court of appeal said that it was impossible to assert that the omitted measures would have stopped the intention of the criminal.

Secondly, the Supreme Court noted that, according to the court of appeal, there was no certainty between *this* damage and the faulty behaviour. Thirdly, the Supreme Court considered that the decision of the court of appeal was not legally justified because it did not say that without the faulty omissions the damage alleged by the victim and her parents would not have occurred as it occurred *in concreto*.

c) Commentary

60 Before briefly analysing the decision of the Supreme Court, one has to mention that it is the second decision of this Court in the same case – a fact which is extremely rare and highlights the perplexity which the loss of chance implies.

61 In 1998, the Supreme Court quashed a decision pronounced by the court of appeal of Liège. Applying the but-for test, the court of appeal of Liège had said that if safety and dissuasion measures had been taken (in other words, without the faulty behaviour), these measures would have provided the victim with the opportunity to escape the terrible consequences of the events, because all the events are partially determined by the definite moment at which they are committed.[49] The court of appeal had, therefore, come to the conclusion that without each of the faulty omissions, the damage would *maybe* not have occurred as it did, in such a way that the victim, due to these faulty omissions, lost a chance to avoid it. By restraining the criminal wish or by delaying the execution of this wish (which means by taking positive measures in place of doing nothing), the policemen and the prosecutor would have given to the victim a chance to avoid the severe consequences. The court of appeal evaluated the lost chance to 50%.[50] The City of Liège and the Belgian State appealed to the Supreme Court, the decision of which was the same as the decision pronounced in 2004 and here commented.[51]

62 Since the Supreme Court pronounced these decisions (and especially the second one), the question has arisen whether the Court still admits the concept of the loss of a chance, at least when this concept is used in cases of causal uncertainty towards a definitely occurred damage. One author is of the opinion that this question must be answered negatively: the use of the concept would no longer be admitted, with the aim of masking or avoiding causal uncertainty.[52] Should the real occurred damage not certainly be caused by the faulty conduct of the defendant, then the victim should not obtain any compensation.

[49] According to the judges, by keeping the criminal from acting at the place, in circumstances and at the time he acted, the policemen and the prosecutor would perhaps have avoided the occurrence of the damage.

[50] Court of appeal of Liège, 27 November 1996, [1997] *Journal des Procès* 318, 22–28.

[51] Cass., 19 June 1998, C.97.0142.F-C.97.0152.F.

[52] I. Boone, Het "verlies van een kans" bij onzeker causaal verband, [2004–2005] RW 3, 92–97 (especially no. 9). Nearly convinced that the case law has been modified by the Supreme Court: N. Estienne, L'arrêt de la Cour de cassation du 1er avril 2004: une chance perdue pour les victimes de fautes médicales, [2005] *Journal des Tribunaux* (JT) 6182, 359–361 (especially no. 5).

Nevertheless, at this present time, it is perhaps not yet absolutely certain that the concept of the lost chance is definitely dead (when used in cases of causal uncertainty and concerning an occurred damage).[53] One word used by the Supreme Court in the commented decision can perhaps cast a doubt on this death: according to the Supreme Court, it was not proven that without the faulty omissions the *alleged* damage would have happened. The Supreme Court noticed that the claim aimed at the repair of the damage resulting from the aggression. Therefore, it is not absolutely certain that the decision of the Supreme Court would have been the same if the claim had been otherwise expressed, aiming to repair the lost chance. However, if one reads again the pleas of the public prosecutor, it is without a doubt that his intention was to condemn definitely the reasoning consisting in changing the description of the damage (from the real occurred damage to a lost chance), with the aim of obtaining a partial repair of the really occurred one.[54] 63

8. *Cour de cassation/Hof van Cassatie*, 22 April 2004, C.01.0484.N: Causal Uncertainty

a) Brief Summary of the Facts

Two children set fire to the warehouse of a company in which flax was stored. A judicial action was raised against the parents (and their insurer) by the company, who was successful in its claim. During the legal proceedings the question arose whether the company should also be held liable for the fire and its consequences. The problem was that a small door had not been closed. So it was easy (or easier?) for the children to go inside the warehouse. According to the court of appeal, to some extent, the open door was an invitation to go inside the shed, but not an invitation to play with fire. Consequently, the court of appeal considered that there was no causal link between the fact that the door was left open and the fire. Only the parents were held liable and not the company. The parents, who did not agree with this decision of the court of appeal, appealed to the Supreme Court. 64

b) Judgment of the Supreme Court

More clearly than ever, the Belgian Supreme Court expressed its causal idea: the existence of a causal link, which is necessary to be proven to hold someone liable, requires that, but for the fault, the damage would not have hap- 65

[53] In a similar sense, cf. C. Eyben, La théorie de la perte d'une chance défigurée ou revisitée?, [2005] *Revue Générale de Droit Civil* (RGDC) 6, 307–321 (especially no. 27).

[54] For many years, lawyers and judges have used a kind of "subterfuge" in case of causal uncertainty for helping the victims: they say that the faulty conduct caused certainly a damage consisting in the loss of a chance to avoid the damage. By such reasoning, to some extent, lawyers change the damage for which they claim compensation. They do not claim damages any more to compensate the real occurred damage but they claim damages to compensate the lost chance of having avoided it. They have imagined or created a new kind of damage, a special kind of damage: *the lost chance*. But they do not brush aside the but-for test. They still continue to apply it by saying that without the faulty conduct, the victim would not have lost its chance. We will see whether the judges still accept this reasoning despite the commented decision.

pened such as it happened *in concreto*. Moreover the Court added that the pursuer will not be successful if the judge notices that the causal link is *uncertain*.

66 In the present case, the court of appeal had noticed that if the door had been closed, it would have been less easy for the children to go inside the shed. But the court of appeal did not say that but for the faulty conduct of the owner of the shed (having left the door open), the children would not have gone inside the warehouse. Consequently, the Supreme Court considered that the court of appeal did not decide that without the faulty behaviour of the owner, the damage would not have happened. So the Supreme Court considered that the court of appeal correctly denied the existence of a causal link between the company's behaviour and the fire. The decision of the court of appeal was not quashed by the Supreme Court.

c) Commentary

67 It results from the commented decision that some justifications given by the lower judges for considering that there is no causal link between the faulty conduct and the damage are not accepted by the Supreme Court. It is notably the case when the judge considers that the faulty conduct was the *occasion* of the damage without having noticed that but for it the damage would also have happened.[55] In the present case, the court of appeal had simply said that without the faulty conduct ("if the door had been closed"), it would have been less easy for the children to go inside the shed and then had decided that there was no causal link between this faulty conduct and the fire. The Supreme Court concluded that the court of appeal did not exclude the possibility that without the faulty conduct, the damage would also have occurred, and considered therefore that the decision of the court of appeal was legally justified.

68 By comparing this decision dated 22 April 2004 with a decision of 30 April 2003,[56] one has *probably*[57] to conclude that, according to the Supreme Court, when the judges are not convinced that without the faulty conduct the damage would also have happened they have to deny the existence of the causal relationship; nevertheless, they have apparently to word their decision by saying that there is uncertainty rather than by saying that the faulty conduct was only an occasion and not a cause.

69 This decision is the occasion to note that, under Belgian tort law, the causal link must be *certain* to lead to compensation. For obtaining compensation, it is not sufficient to say that but for the faulty conduct the damage would *maybe* not have occurred.[58] But once the causal link is considered by the judges to be

[55] Cass., 30 April 2003, P.03.0168.F.

[56] Ibid.

[57] As observed by B. Weyts, the wording used by the court of appeal and by the Supreme Court is unusual. Cf. B. Weyts, Blijft het Hof van Cassatie trouw aan de equivalentieleer bij een samenloop van fouten?, [2004–2005] RW 21, 828–830.

[58] Cass., 4 March 1966, [1966] Pas, I, 864; Cass., 17 February 1992, [1992] Pas, I, 534; Cass., 19 June 1998, [1998] Pas, I, 763.

certain and therefore established, the victim will receive full compensation of his/her damage. Belgian tort law has adopted an all-or-nothing approach.

However, the certainty which is required is not a scientific certainty but a legal one. It means that the claimant has to convince the judges that, in the present case, the damage would not have occurred without the faulty behaviour of the defendant. Concerning the appreciation of the elements which are produced by the claimant to influence the judge's decision, there are no legal criteria (like proof beyond reasonable doubt or proof on the balance of probabilities).[59] The claimant has to demonstrate the existence of the causal link in such a way that there remains no serious doubt any more. The lower judges decide whether the causal link is established with certainty. Nevertheless, it seems that the Supreme Court is not favourable to a relaxing of the proof rules and that it requires such a high level of certainty that it should be (nearly) absolute.[60] 70

9. *Cour de cassation/Hof van Cassatie*, 2 September 2004, C.01.0186.F: Professional Fees of Attorneys and Technical Counsel

a) Brief Summary of the Facts

A couple wanted to build a new house. After construction works had been executed, several serious problems appeared, notably cracks in the new building. The owners sued the architect and the building contractor. The judicial proceedings took a very long time and the owners needed not only the help of a lawyer but also the help of a technical (private) counsel with the aim of defending their own interests. 71

At the moment the owners evaluated the amount of the damage that had to be compensated, they considered the fees paid to their lawyer and technical counsel as a part of it. The court of appeal admitted they were right, to some extent, considering that, according to general rules of tort law, the entire damage resulting from a faulty conduct has to be compensated. 72

Concerning the fees of the lawyer, the court of appeal was of the opinion that without the construction problems the owners would not have had to appeal to a lawyer for help. The court added that the help of a lawyer was necessary due to the complexity of the procedure (the judicial expert had to be replaced; discussions had to be conducted with the judges on site; papers had to be written for the judicial expert; etc.). Therefore, the court admitted the *principle* of reimbursement of the fees by the architect and by the building contractor (but not yet the evaluation of these fees). 73

Concerning the fees of the technical counsel, the court of appeal was of the opinion that a part of these fees had to be reimbursed by the building contrac- 74

[59] H. Bocken, Toerekening van aansprakelijkheid op grond van de equivalentieleer, in: B. Tilleman/I. Claeys (supra fn. 33), 221, no. 18.

[60] Cass., 23 September 1974, [1975] Pas, I, 87; Cass., 17 September 1981, [1982] Pas, I, 90.

tor, namely the part corresponding to the work of the (private) technical counsel which was supplementary and useful, even indispensable, to the judicial expert. In this case, it was noteworthy that the (private) technical counsel really helped the judicial expert to find the technical cause of the cracks. The judicial expert had thought of two possible causes and the technical counsel suggested a third one which was finally the real one (faulty creation of foundations of the building which provoked a sinking phenomenon). Consequently, due to the *useful* intervention of the technical counsel, the court of appeal could say that, without the faulty conduct of the constructors, the couple should not have paid the fees of a technical counsel. On the contrary, the court of appeal refused to consider the *useless* technical fees as being a part of the final damage of the owner.

75 In short, the architect and the building contractor were held liable *in solidum* for the reimbursement of the legal fees and the sole architect was held liable for the reimbursement of a part of the technical fees.

76 The architect and the building contractor did not agree with the decision of the court of appeal. They were of the opinion that the fees of legal and technical counsels were not a part of the damage suffered by the victims but were fees incurred with the aim of helping them in the defence of their interests. Therefore, according to the architect and the building constructor, the assistance of the victim might not lead to any (additional) damages.

b) Judgment of the Supreme Court

77 At the outset, the Supreme Court mentioned two basic principles which are laid down in the Civil Code: in case of breach of a contract, the debtor has to compensate the actual loss (*damnum emergens*) and the lost gain (*lucrum cessans*);[61] secondly, damages may only cover immediate and direct results of the non-performance of the contract.[62]

78 Then the Supreme Court noted that the fees of legal and technical counsel incurred by the victim of a faulty breach of contract may constitute a part of his/her damage as far as these costs present a necessary feature.[63] From the moment the court of appeal had considered that the fees were a part of the damage caused and rendered necessary by the faulty breach of contract, its decision was legally justified. Therefore, the Supreme Court did not quash it.

c) Commentary

79 This decision of the Supreme Court was given on the basis of articles of the Civil Code concerning breach of contract (especially art. 1149 and art. 1151), and not on the basis of those articles concerning tort law (artt. 1382 et seq.).

[61] Art. 1149 of the Civil Code.

[62] Art. 1151 of the Civil Code. The third important rule is expressed in art. 1150: the debtor is only liable for foreseeable damage.

[63] On the meaning of the word "necessary", cf. the commentary.

Nevertheless, the first commentators are of the opinion that this (revolutionary) decision can easily be transposed in tort law. This can be explained by the fact that, according to the Supreme Court, the immediate and direct consequences of the non-performance of the contract for which the creditor may claim damages (art. 1151)[64] are the necessary consequences of the non-performance and that the necessary consequences are those consequences which would not have happened without the faulty breach of contract.[65] Consequently, one can say that the rules governing contractual and non-contractual liability are very similar.

In this case, concerning the professional fees of the lawyer and the fees of the (private) technical counsel, the court of appeal applied at once the but-for test. 80
The court came to the conclusion that, without the construction problems, the couple would not have had to pay such fees. This first part of the reasoning is not surprising. Nevertheless, as mentioned above, the court of appeal *added* in a second time that in this case, the intervention of a lawyer was *necessary* and that the intervention of the technical counsel was *useful* due to the complexity of the problems. Seeing that the court of appeal probably used the adjectives "necessary" and "useful" to mean "required" or "indispensable", its additional observation seems to have been useless: in Belgium the but-for test is the sole test for causation to be established. Although this additional observation should have been seen as useless, it has become of a certain importance considering the decision of the Supreme Court (which refers to the costs rendered necessary by the breach of contract).

The decision of the Supreme Court is disturbing because it used the word "ne- 81
cessity" *perhaps* with two different meanings. First of all, when the Supreme Court spoke about the *necessary* feature of the costs, one can think that it used its traditional wording which refers to the but-for test. Indeed, it refers to the necessity just after having mentioned the principle laid down in art. 1151 of the Civil Code and referring to this principle. But afterwards, the Supreme Court added that the decision of the court of appeal was legally justified because the fees were rendered *necessary* by the contractual non-performance. As mentioned above, when the court of appeal spoke of fees rendered necessary by the non-performance, it probably meant "useful" or "indispensable" costs.

Consequently, the question arises whether the reimbursement of the fees 82
would depend on two different and cumulative criteria: first, the but-for test and then the test of "usefulness". Some commentators of the decision are actu-

[64] "Even in the case where the non-performance of the agreement is due to the debtor's intentional breach, damages may include, with respect to the loss suffered by the creditor and the profit which he has been deprived of, only what is an immediate and direct consequence of the non-performance of the agreement" (translated by Georges Rouhette, Professor of Law, with the assistance of Anne Berton, Research Assistant in English, http://www.legifrance.gouv.fr/html/codes_traduits/code_civil_textA.htm).

[65] Cass., 24 June 1977, [1977] Pas, I, 1087.

ally of the opinion that the Supreme Court fixed a limitation for obtaining the reimbursement of the fees from the tortfeasor (debtor): the fees would be refundable as far as they were necessary in the sense of "indispensable" or "not exaggerated".[66] Nevertheless, one has here to mention that, for all kinds of damage, the first instance judges decide on the extent of the damage.[67]

83 In short, the decision of the Supreme Court is revolutionary. By recognizing that the professional fees of the lawyer and of (private) technical counsel can be a kind of damage, the Supreme Court broke its traditional case law. Indeed, since 1956, the Supreme Court has been of the opinion that these fees could not be a part of the damage considering that they were precisely incurred to recover damages resulting from a tort or from a breach of contract.[68] Nevertheless, and it is the second lesson of the commented decision, the Supreme Court seems to want the reimbursement of the fees restricted to reasonable (not exaggerated) fees. A guideline is thus given to the first instance judges.

10. *Cour de cassation/Hof van Cassatie*, 7 September 2004, P.04.0315.N: The Fate of the Survivor's Pension

a) Brief Summary of the Facts

84 After an accident had occurred, a survivor's pension was paid. The one who was liable for the accident was of the opinion that the judges had to take the amount of this pension into consideration at the moment of evaluating the damage. The first instance judges agreed with the liable party, but the relatives of the victim did not agree with this decision and appealed before the Supreme Court.

b) Judgment of the Supreme Court

85 At the outset, the Supreme Court stated that to compensate the damage im-

[66] B. De Coninck, Répétibilité et responsabilité civile: un arrêt de principe, [2004] JT 6148, 684; D. Philippe, Les honoraires d'avocat et les frais d'expert constituent un élément du dommage, [2004] *Jurisprudence de Liège, Mons et Bruxelles* (JLMB) 30, 1324–1331; D. Sterckx, Des frais et honoraires d'avocat et de conseil technique comme élément du dommage, [2004] *Revue du Notariat belge* (Rev not b) 2979, 472–474. Concerning the decision of 2 September 2004, cf. also V. Callewaert/B. De Coninck, La répétibilité des frais et honoraires d'avocat après l'arrêt de la Cour de cassation du 2 septembre 2004: responsabilité et assurances, [2005] RGAR, 13944; G. Closset-Marchal/J.-Fr. Van Drooghenbroeck, La répétibilité des honoraires d'avocat à l'aune du droit judiciaire, [2005] RGAR, 13945.

[67] Cass., 8 December 1999, P.99.0998.F; Cass., 5 December 2001, P.01.1115.F.

[68] Concerning the fees of the lawyer: Cass., 11 April 1956, [1956] Pas, I, 841; Cass., 11 June 1956, [1956] Pas, I, 1098; Cass., 18 June 1964, [1964] Pas, I, 1121. Concerning the fees of the technical counsel: Cass., 7 June 1956, [1956] Pas, I, 1073; Cass., 30 April 1959, [1959] Pas, I, 885; Cass., 14 June 1990, [1990] Pas, I, 1159; Cass., 20 October 1994, C.93.0506.F; Cass., 5 May 1999, P.98.1309.F. Nevertheless, concerning the fees of technical counsel the Supreme Court had already admitted the idea of a possible reimbursement under certain circumstances in a decision of 28 February 2002 (C.99.0193.N). This last decision is commented in D. Droshout, Belgium in: H. Koziol/B.C. Steininger (eds.), *European Tort Law 2002* (2003), 108.

plies that the victim has to be placed in the situation where he/she would have been without the faulty conduct.

The Supreme Court then noted that the amounts paid to the victim or to his/ 86
her successors (after the faulty event) by a third party may only be taken into account to evaluate the amount of compensation if the paid amount aimed to repair the same damage as the damage caused by the faulty conduct of the tortfeasor.

Applying the principle in the present case, the Supreme Court came to the 87
conclusion that the survivor's pension is due according to the social legislation, that this pension has no compensation feature and, therefore, does not aim to compensate the damage resulting from the tort. Consequently, the pension might not be taken into account to evaluate the amount of compensation. The decision of the first instance judges was quashed.

c) Commentary

One of the principles governing the allowance of damages is that the victim 88
may obtain damages based on tort law and damages based on other legal provisions (for example, social security provisions) if the latter do not aim to compensate the damage resulting from the tort. Most of the time, in case of benefits allowed by a social security organ, which can take recourse against the one who is liable for the damage on the basis of tort law, one can say that the social benefits aim to compensate the damage.[69]

Concerning the survivor's pension, the Supreme Court came to the conclusion 89
that it does not aim to compensate the damage even if it is paid after the occurrence of a tort. This point of view has constituted the case law for several years.[70]

11. *Cour de cassation/Hof van Cassatie*, 13 October 2004, P.04.0896.F: Theft and Receiving

a) Brief Summary of the Facts

A buyer bought a stolen car in good faith. The salesman was the boyfriend of 90
the buyer's hairdresser. Having heard from her client that she was looking for a second-hand car, the hairdresser had proposed to her client to meet her boyfriend. After the sale, the car was found again but due to the fact that the buyer bought the car in good faith, it was impossible to give the car back to his owner and the owner's insurer had to pay indemnities to the owner.

[69] D. Simoens, Recente ontwikkelingen inzake schade en schadeloosstelling, in: B. Tilleman/I. Claeys (supra fn. 33), 300, no. 48.

[70] Cass., 26 June 1990, 3335; Cass., 21 January 1998, C.95.0467.N.

91 Afterwards, the insurer sued the hairdresser before the criminal court. The hairdresser was recognized by the criminal court to be a receiver, because she acted as an intermediate knowing about the illegal activities of her boyfriend, she cooperated in the sale of the car to a sincere buyer and she contributed to make the restitution of the car to the owner impossible.[71] The court held both the thief and the hairdresser liable for the whole damage suffered by the owner of the car (and consequently by his insurer).

92 The hairdresser did not agree with this decision. According to her, the damage suffered by the owner of the car was entirely caused by the thief and not by her: she was "only" a receiver. Therefore, she appealed to the Supreme Court.

b) Judgment of the Supreme Court

93 The Supreme Court did not quash the decision of the criminal court. According to the Supreme Court, the receiver may be held liable for the whole damage suffered by the owner of the stolen good when one can say that, without the faulty conduct of the receiver, the damage would not have happened as it did concretely.

94 In this case, according to the Supreme Court, the criminal court might decide that there was a causal link between the faulty conduct of the receiver and the damage suffered by the owner of the car because the hairdresser acted as an intermediate, cooperated in the sale and contributed to make the restitution of the car impossible.

c) Commentary

95 Concerning the consequences of theft and receiving, it seems that the Supreme Court makes a difference between two situations.

96 If one can say that both the thief and the receiver committed a "common fault" (*faute commune/gemeenschappelijke fout*), then the receiver may be held liable for the whole damage suffered by the owner of the stolen good.[72] In this case, the receiver may be held liable if one can say that, without his faulty conduct, the damage would not have happened as it did *in concreto*. However, if the judge considers that there is no common fault, then it is no longer possible to say that without the faulty conduct of the receiver there would not have been any damage: the good would have been stolen anyway. In that case, the receiver may be held liable only for the damage resulting from the receiving and not for the damage resulting from the theft.[73] The notion of "common

[71] The restitution of the car was no longer possible because the buyer acted in good faith.

[72] Cass., 14 October 2003, P.03.0518.N. Cf. also Cass., 18 November 1987, [1988–1989] RW 10, 333–334.

[73] Court of appeal of Antwerp, 20 May 2003, [2004] *Tijdschrift voor Strafrecht* (T Strafr) 5, 295–299, comment G. Stessens, Is de heler mede burgerrechtelijk aansprakelijk voor de schade veroorzaakt door de steler? Cf. also P. Helsen, Heling: is een veroordeling op burgerlijk gebied mogelijk?, [2000–2001] *Algemeen Juridisch Tijdschrift* (AJT), 149–151; L. Delbrouck, Over diefstal, heling en gemeenschappelijke fout, [2004] *Rechtspraak Antwerpen Brussel Gent* (RABG) 6, 379–382.

fault" is thus central. In order to say that multiple tortfeasors committed a "common fault", a joint intentional element is required.[74] They must have co-operated knowingly and willingly.[75]

12. *Cour de cassation/Hof van Cassatie*, 25 October 2004, S.03.0072.F: Faulty Conduct and Violation of a Specific Rule

a) Brief Summary of the Facts

The National Office for Social Security (*Office national de sécurité sociale/ Rijksdienst*) is a public organisation that manages the financing of the social security for employees. This Office may decide that there is a labour contract or that there is no labour contract between two parties and therefore may decide that the one who does not meet the legal conditions may not benefit from the social security for employees. 97

In this case, on 16 July 1985, after an inquiry, the Office considered that there was no labour contract binding a worker and a so-called employer. Consequently, according to the Office, the worker might not benefit from the social security system for employees (especially in this case this part of the system concerning the unemployment benefits and concerning rights to retirement pension). The worker did not agree with this decision and brought the Office before the courts which gave him satisfaction on 18 February 1994, considering that he was actually bound by a labour contract to his employer. 98

After having obtained satisfaction concerning the existence of a labour contract, the employee sued the Office for having refused him the application of the social security system for employees. This refusal caused him damage. On 9 May 2003, the labour court of appeal considered that the Office had acted with fault by refusing the application of the social security system for employees considering that there was no labour contract. According to the labour court of appeal, the decision of the Office violated the Act of 27 June 1969 concerning social security and constituted a faulty conduct regarding art. 1382 of the Civil Code. One is reminded that this article still remains the statutory basis of tort law in Belgium. The Office did not agree with this decision and appealed before the Supreme Court. 99

According to the Office, its conduct had not been faulty. First of all, the Office stated that in tort law the fault consists either in the breach of a regulatory provision which imposes a well-defined conduct or in the violation of the general rule of careful behaviour. Secondly, the Office said that in this case it did not violate any specific provision which would have foreseen that the worker was an employee. Thirdly, the Office observed that the breach of the general duty of care is a departure from the conduct of the good and reasonable man, the 100

[74] Cass., 3 May 1996, C.95.0016.F.

[75] H. Cousy/D. Droshout, Multiple Tortfeasors under Belgian Law, in: W.V.H. Rogers (ed.), *Unification of Tort Law: Multiple Tortfeasors* (2004), 32.

so-called *bonus pater familias*. According to the Office, in this case, the judges should have compared its conduct with the conduct of a good and reasonable public organisation placed in the same circumstances. Considering that the judges did not make this comparison, they could not say that the Office acted with fault and, consequently, their decision was not legally justified.

b) Judgment of the Supreme Court

101 At the outset, the Supreme Court mentioned that the conduct of a public authority is faulty either when it violated the general duty of care (in comparison with the behaviour of a good and reasonable authority placed in the same circumstances), or when it violated a regulatory provision which imposes on this authority a duty to abstain from doing something or, on the contrary, to act in a certain way.

102 Then, the Supreme Court applied this rule in the present case. First of all, the Supreme Court noted that there was not any regulatory provision which imposed on the Office a duty to abstain from doing something or to act in a certain way, when it has to qualify a contractual relation between two parties. To say merely that the Office violated the Act of 27 June 1969 without any other details was not sufficient. Secondly, the Supreme Court observed that the labour court of appeal did not notice any conduct which would have been a departure from the conduct of the good and reasonable public authority. Consequently, the decision of the labour court of appeal was not legally justified and had to be quashed: the judges observed neither the violation of a specific provision imposing a defined conduct nor the violation of the general duty of care.

c) Commentary

103 According to the Supreme Court, faulty conduct[76] consists in the violation of a specific rule or in the violation of the general rule of careful behaviour. One has to add that in the former case (violation of a specific rule), the regulation must describe a well defined behaviour in order that its violation may constitute a faulty conduct.[77]

104 Although this case law is persistent,[78] the commented decision of 25 October 2004 is interesting because it shows the difficulty in establishing the violation of a specific rule in certain situations. In this case, the public prosecutor was of the opinion that the Office had violated artt. 1 to 4 of the Act of 27 June 1969 concerning the social security for workers. These provisions define the scope of application of the Act. The general rule is that the law is applicable to those people who are bound by a labour contract. Some other workers also

[76] It would be more accurate to speak about the objective element of the fault or about the unlawfulness. Cf. H. Cousy, Belgium. Wrongfulness in Belgian Tort Law, in: H. Koziol (ed.), *Unification of Tort Law: Wrongfulness* (1998), 31.

[77] L. Cornelis, *Principes du droit belge de la responsabilité extra-contractuelle. L'acte illicite* (1991), 67.

[78] Ibid.

benefit from the protection of the Act. The public prosecutor analysed the provisions as imposing on the Office a duty to act or not to act in a certain way. According to the Office, to act would mean in this context, to bring the employee into the social security system for employees if the legal conditions are met; to abstain from acting would mean not to bring the employee into this system. The Supreme Court did not follow the opinion of the public prosecutor. According to the Court, on the contrary, the above mentioned provisions do not contain any regulation which would impose on the Office a well defined conduct. Consequently, these provisions may not be used to conclude that a specific rule was violated.

C. Literature

1. B. Dubuisson/P. Henry (eds), *Droit de la responsabilité. Morceaux choisis* (coll. Commission Université-Palais, Larcier, Brussels 2004), 328 pp.

This book contains five reports on various topics in tort law. First of all the undersigned handles general features of causation under Belgian tort law, including some comments about the loss of a chance[79] and the break of the causal chain. Then Prof. Dr. B. Dubuisson gives an overview of the civil immunities and comments extensively on the Act of 10 February 2003 relating to liability of and for Personnel of Public Legal Bodies[80]. The third subject concerns the liability for defective products (P. Henry and J.-Th. Debry). The liability of the organisers or sellers of package holidays is then analysed (P. Fauconnier). Finally some attention is given to the question whether attorneys' fees could be regarded as recoverable damage (R. Bindels and L. Misson).[81] 105

2. B. Tilleman/I. Claeys (eds.), *Buitencontractuele aansprakelijkheid* (coll. Recht en Onderneming n° 11, Die Keure, Brugge 2004), 361 pp.

This book, published 200 years after the adoption of the (French) Civil Code, is the occasion to take stock on tort law at the beginning of the 21st century. The book contains nine chapters. The first is principally devoted to the grounds of justification, such as necessity and lawful authority, and their relationship with *force majeure* (Dr. I. Claeys), the second concerns the civil immunities and comments on the Act of 10 February 2003 relating to liability of and for Personnel of Public Legal Bodies[82] (Prof. Dr. B. Dubuisson), the third 106

[79] Cf. also the important decision of the Supreme Court of 1 April 2004, commented above. This decision was pronounced after the writing of the report.

[80] For a comment of this Act, D. Droshout, Belgium, in: H. Koziol/B.C. Steininger (eds.), *European Tort Law 2003* (2004), 59.

[81] Cf. also the important decision of the Supreme Court of 2 September 2004, commented above. This decision was pronounced after the writing of the report.

[82] For a comment of this Act, D. Droshout, Belgium, in: H. Koziol/B.C. Steininger (supra fn. 80), 59.

analyses the liability of the guardian for defective things (F. Baudoncq and M. Debaene), the fourth concerns the liability of the guardian of animals (Prof. Dr. B. Tilleman) and the fifth vicarious liability (Prof. Dr. J.-L. Fagnart). The three following chapters examine (some aspects of) two fundamental notions of tort law and the relationship between them: causation (chapter 6, Prof. Dr. H. Bocken), damage and damages (chapter 8, Prof. Dr. D. Simoens) and the relationship between causation and damage (chapter 7, Prof. Dr. L. Cornelis). Finally, the last chapter contains an overview of private international law in the context of tort law (chapter 9, J. Decoker).

3. H. Bocken (ed.), *De nieuwe wet op de aansprakelijkheid van en voor ambtenaren. De wet van 10 februari 2003* (coll. Gandaius. Ontmoetingen met recht n° 5, Kluwer, Mechelen 2004), 193 pp.

107 Several authors examine in great detail the new rules concerning liability of and for personnel of public legal bodies. As developed in the last Yearbook, "the Act brought the rules governing the liability of statutorily appointed personnel of public legal bodies ("civil servants") in line with the rules governing the liability of employees".[83]

4. H. Vandenberghe (ed.), *De professionele aansprakelijkheid* (Die Keure, Brugge 2004), 286 pp.

108 This book contains several reports concerning liability of holders of liberal professions. Four important professions are analysed: liability of doctors (Prof. Dr. H. Vandenberghe), of attorneys (P. Depuydt), of notaries (Prof. Dr. H. Casman)[84] and of architects (Prof. Dr. A. Verbeke and C. Meert).

5. W. Peeters/M. Van den Bossche (eds.), *De behandeling van lichamelijke schadedossiers en tien jaar Indicatieve Tabel/Le traitement de sinistres avec dommage corporel et dix ans de Tableau Indicatif* (Larcier, Brussels 2004), 396 pp.

109 Within the scope of traffic accidents, the National Unions of Belgian first instance judges have elaborated a working instrument to promote the standardization of case law. The suggestion they made is to use this instrument, called

[83] D. Droshout, Belgium, in: H. Koziol/B.C. Steininger (supra fn. 80), 59. Cf. also the reports of B. Dubuisson in the first two presented books. About this Act of 10 February 2003, one can also mention the following articles: H. Bocken, De aansprakelijkheid van en voor het overheidspersoneel. Een nieuwe regeling, [2003] *Nieuw Juridisch Weekblad* (NjW) 25, 330–335; S. Covemaeker, De nieuwe wet van 10 februari 2003 betreffende de aansprakelijkheid van en voor personeelsleden in dienst van openbare rechtspersonen, [2003] RGDC 7, 477–487; B. Dubuisson, La loi du 10 février 2003 relative à la responsabilité civile des personnes publiques et de leurs agents, [2003] JT 6102, 507–512; L. Kerzmann, La loi du 10 février 2003 relative à la responsabilité des agents des services publics, [2004] RGAR 6, 13877; A. Van Oevelen, De nieuwe wettelijke regeling betreffende de aansprakelijkheid van en voor personeelsleden in dienst van openbare rechtspersonen, [2003–2004] RW 5, 161–179.

[84] Cf. also H. Casman, Quelques réflexions en matière de responsabilité professionnelle du notaire, [2004] Rev not b 2979, 450–465.

tableau indicatif/indicatieve tabel when the existence of the damage is certain but when this damage may not be evaluated *in concreto* because exact criteria to evaluate it are missing. The tariff proposes lump sums. The first version of it dates from 1994 and the last from May 2004.[85] On the occasion of the tenth anniversary of the tariff, a conference was organised and the book presents the reports of the speakers. Some reports concern the tariff itself. Others concern more generally various aspects of compensation in cases of accidents involving bodily damage (questions relating to tax law, medical expert assessment, protection of the legally incompetent victims).

6. Th. Vansweevelt, *Jurisprudentiebundel. Buitencontractueel aansprakelijkheidsrecht* (3rd edn., Maklu, Antwerp 2004), 467 pp.

This third edition of the compendium provides a selection of the most important decisions of the Belgian Supreme Court in the field of tort law. Concerning certain topics, some decisions of first instance judges and some foreign decisions are also published. One also finds in the book the main legal texts on tort law and the indicative tariff (*tableau indicatif/indicatieve tabel*).[86] 110

7. E. Montero/H. Jacquemin, La responsabilité civile des médias, in: J.-L. Fagnart (ed.), *Responsabilités. Traité théorique et pratique* (Kluwer, Brussels 2003), vol. 1 and vol. 2, 50 + 47 pp.

Each year, this treaty on tort law grows with new books. The one written by Prof. Dr. E. Montero and H. Jacquemin concerns tort law and mass media. The authors examine the Belgian and European legal texts, especially art. 10 of the European Convention for the Protection of Human Rights on the right to freedom of expression. They also analyse case law relating to duties and liability of mass media. 111

8. B. Weyts, De aansprakelijkheid van de ouders en van de toezichthouders van de minderjarige, in: Centrum voor Beroepsvervolmaking in de Rechten, *Jongeren en Recht* (Intersentia, Antwerp 2003), 413 pp.

This report is to be found within a book concerning young people and law. It analyses the liability of parents, teachers, educators and establishments for youth, etc. 112

[85] On this new version: A. Boyen, Indicatieve tabellen van de magistraten, [2004] *Consilio Manuque. Revue belge du dommage corporel et de la médecine légale* (Con M) 1–3, 57–65; Th. Papart, Le barème indicatif des magistrats, [2004] Con M 1–3, 67–103; W. Peeters/J. Desmecht, Tableau indicatif, [2004] *Circulation, Responsabilité, Assurances* (CRA) 3, 176–187; M. Van den Bossche, De indicatieve tabel – Een situering, [2004] NjW 72, 614–621.

[86] Concerning this tariff, cf. supra no. 109. The last version of it, the fourth one, dates from May 2004. It is freely available on the website of the review *Nieuw Juridisch Weekblad*: http://www.njw.be.

9. E. De Kezel, Wrongful birth en wrongful life. Een stand van zaken, [2004] *Nieuw Juridisch Weekblad* (NjW) 70, 546–551

113 On the occasion of the publication of a decision of the court of appeal of Antwerp of 8 September 2003, the author gives an overview of the case law on wrongful birth and wrongful life. First, she explains the meaning of these expressions. Then she indicates the questions to which such legal actions can lead in the context of tort law. She analyses the notion of faulty conduct, causation and damage.

10. E. De Kezel, Problematiek van verborgen letselschade en verjaring: reflectie over een speciale vergoedingsregeling n.a.v. zgn. "asbestschadevorderingen", [2004] *Tijdschrift voor Privaatrecht* (TPR) 1, 107–143

114 This report examines the risks related to exposure to asbestos. Various problems can notably result from the fact that quite a long time can separate the exposure (or the period of exposure) from the moment the damage occurs. Special attention is drawn to the rules concerning prescription (termination) of the legal actions under Belgian and Dutch law.

11. D. Simoens, Plicht tot schadeloosstelling en plicht tot schadebeperking: twee facetten van eenzelfde wetsvoorschrift, [2004] *Revue Générale de Droit Civil* (RGDC) 8, 425–428

115 This article concerns the duty to mitigate arising from art. 1382 of the Civil Code and the principle of entire compensation. The legal grounds of the duty are sought, the costs incurred with the aim of mitigating the damage are examined and the consequences of the breach of the duty are analysed. Case law is also analysed.

12. A. Van Oevelen, Een vergelijking tussen de rechtspraak van het Belgische Hof van Cassatie en die van het Europese Hof van Justitie inzake de aansprakelijkheid van de Staat voor ambtsfouten van magistraten, [2004] TPR 1, 903–943

116 This paper analyses the decisions of the Belgian Supreme Court concerning liability of the State in case of faulty conduct of judges. The author then pays some attention to the judgment of the Court of Justice of the European Communities of 30 September 2003 (*G. Köbler v. Republik Österreich*)[87] and makes a comparison between Belgian and European case law.

[87] Case C-224/01, Gerhard Köbler, [2003] ECR, I-10239.

III. Czech Republic

Jiří Hrádek

A. Legislation

1. *Zákon č. 47/2004 Sb., kterým se mění zákon o pojištění odpovědnosti z provozu vozidla (*Act No. 47/2004 Coll., which changes the Act on liability insurance against damage caused by the operation of motor vehicles and the Civil Code)[1]

The amendment to Act No. 168/1999 Coll. (hereinafter the Motor Vehicle Liability Insurance Act) shall approximate the area of liability insurance against damage caused by the operation of motor vehicles, especially with the relevant provisions of EC law,[2] in order for Czech insurance legislation to reach full compatibility. At the same time it changes the present law so that the wording takes into consideration all experience with the application of the Motor Vehicle Liability Insurance Act. 1

The most important issues of the amendment in respect to tort law are the determination of the applicable laws for rendering damages, and the obligation of the insurance company to appoint a claim representative for dealing with an application for compensation asserted in a country other than the country in which the insurance policy was taken out. 2

If damage is caused in the area of any Member State, the law of the Member State where the damage was sustained shall govern any compensation for the damage. However, if the scope of the insurance based on the insurance contract is more favourable for the injured party, this law shall prevail. 3

[1] Zákon č. 47/2004 Sb., kterým se mění zákon č. 168/1999 Sb., o pojištění odpovědnosti za škodu způsobenou provozem vozidla a o změně některých souvisejících zákonů (zákon o pojištění odpovědnosti z provozu vozidla), ve znění pozdějších předpisů, zákon č. 586/1992 Sb., o daních z příjmů, ve znění pozdějších předpisů, zákon č. 200/1990 Sb., o přestupcích, ve znění pozdějších předpisů, a zákon č. 40/1964 Sb., občanský zákoník.

[2] Directives 72/166/EEC; 84/5/EEC; 87/344/EEC; 90/232/EEC; 2000/26/EC etc.

4 The insurer is obliged to appoint the claim representative in all Member States of the EU. The state in which the insurer's damage liability insurance license was issued presents an exception from this duty. However, a few insurers may appoint one claim representative. The representative acts on behalf and at the expense of the insurer when dealing with events in which damage has occurred, including final disposal of applications for damages. The main purpose of the position is to collect all necessary information regarding the compensation for damage caused by the operation of motor vehicles and to take the necessary measures to negotiate the settlement of the claims on behalf and at the expense of the insurance companies, including disbursement of the insurance policy coverage. Due to these functions, it is set forth that the claim representative should be sufficiently authorized to represent the insurance company towards the injured.

5 Pursuant to Sec. 6 of the Motor Vehicle Liability Insurance Act, which implements Art. 3 of Directive No. 2000/26/EC,[3] the insured is entitled to receive from the insurer compensation, in accordance with the special provisions to the full extent and amount, for his claimed and proved compensation claims for (i) damage to health or homicide, (ii) damage sustained through the damage, destruction or loss of an object, as well as damage caused by the theft of property if the natural person has lost the ability to take care of it, (iii) loss of earnings and (iv) reasonably expended costs combined with legal representation for the assessment of the claim pursuant to (i) – (iii) if the event establishing the damage and attributable to the insured party occurred during the term of the damage insurance liability.

6 As interference with personality rights pursuant to Sec. 11 et seq. of the Act No. 40/1964 Coll. (hereinafter the Civil Code) might not fulfil the precondition for making a direct claim by the injured against the insurer[4] (even though this opinion may be disputable), together with the amendment to the provisions of the Motor Vehicle Liability Insurance Act, an absolutely fundamental amendment to the Civil Code was approved, reflecting both the existing judicature on the compensation for non-material harm and the European law.

7 Currently there are two rulings of the courts in the Czech Republic which reflect this issue: a decision of the Regional Court Ostrava[5] and of the Higher Court[6] in Prague.[7] Both cases use such an interpretation of Sec. 11 of the Civil Code, which states that a breach of the right to life of a certain person could

[3] Directive No. 2000/26/EC on the approximation of the laws of the Member States relating to insurance against civil liability in respect of the use of motor vehicles and amending Council Directives 73/239/EEC and 88/357/EEC (Fourth motor insurance Directive); M. Cilínková/D. Kuboň, Odškodnění při usmrcení osoby blízké, [2004] *Bulletin Advokacie* 10/2004, 30 et seq.

[4] M. Cilínková/D. Kuboň, Odškodnění při usmrcení osoby blízké, [2004] *Bulletin Advokacie* 10/2004, 33; judgment No. 36 C 16/2004.

[5] 23 C 52/96.

[6] 2 Co 96/99.

[7] J. Švestka, *Občanský zákoník – komentář* (2004), § 11.

interfere with the private sphere of another person. A similar consideration assumes that between people there are various social, moral and cultural relations based on their private and family life, and the breach of a person's right to life damages private relations and the private sphere. The Czech Constitutional Court also considered this issue in decision II US 517/99 concerning Sec. 8 ECHR when it alleged that the family relationship creates a part of a person's private life and this relation consists not only of moral or social relations, but also of the material interests of a person.

Based on the above mentioned, there are two new provisions of the Civil 8
Code, namely Sec. 444 para. 3 and Sec. 449a, which read as follows:

Sec. 444 para. 3

"(3) A lump sum compensation belongs to the survivor for damage suffered by homicide, in particular to the:

a) wife or husband CZK 240,000 (i.e. € 8,000);
b) each child CZK 240,000;
c) each parent CZK 240,000;
d) each parent in case he/she loses an unborn child CZK 85,000 (€ 3,000);
e) each sibling CZK 175,000 (€ 6,000);
f) any other close person living with the homicide victim in a common household at the time of the occurrence of the event, being the cause of the damage to health with fatal consequences, CZK 240,000."

§ 449a

"Future claims pursuant to Sec. 445 can be compensated by a lump sum based on a written contract between the injured and the obliged person, concerning their full and final settlement. The same shall be applied to the future claims pursuant to Sec. 446–449."

The adoption of the provision allowing the compensation claims of the injured 9
party under Sec. 445–449 based on lump sum compensation presents a fundamental and radical change compared to the present regulation of tort law which restricts the private autonomy of persons for the benefits of the power of courts, i.e. state regulation. It will be mentioned below (see the comments to the Insurance Contract Act, infra nos. 11 et seq.) that the possibility to compensate the injured party has also been taken into consideration in the provisions on reimbursement of the insurance policy coverage.

However, this amendment left an important issue unchanged. Sec. 579 of the 10
Civil Code states that "an obligation shall be discharged upon the death of the creditor if performance (fulfilment) was limited to him personally; at the same time his right to receive compensation for pain suffered and aggravated social position shall also be terminated". As the provisions of the new Sec. 444 para. 3 of the Civil Code are taken in under this kind of compensation, which is subject to the provisions of Sec. 579 of the Civil Code, the disputable provision

must be applied hereto. Due to the fact that many relatives cannot be compensated even though they are affected by the damage or harm caused, we wish this provision to be changed in the future.

2. *Zákon o pojistné smlouvě* (Act No. 37/2004 Coll., on the insurance contract)[8]

11 The new regulation of the insurance contract shall, in addition to the Motor Vehicle Liability Insurance Act, approximate the Czech insurance legislation to the EC law[9] and the area of private insurance law shall conform to the acknowledged standards of the free market and conditions of the internal market. Before Act No. 37/2004 Coll. (hereinafter the Insurance Contract Act), the regulation of the insurance contract was based on provisions of the Civil Code, in particular set forth in Chapter XV., even though (until 1964) it was historically always a subject of a special act. The new regulation replaces the present one and deletes the relevant part of the Civil Code. However, the Insurance Contract Act shall remain subsidiary in relation to the Civil Code.

12 The purpose of the Insurance Contract Act is to regulate the mutual relationships of the participants of private insurance, i.e. contractual insurance. The participants are contractual parties, i.e. the insurer who undertakes through the insurance contract to provide insurance policy coverage if an insurable event arises, and the policyholder, who has entered into the contract with the insurer and who is obliged to pay the set insurance premium. Another participant is the insured, who need not be identical to the policyholder. Apart from these main participants, another person may also be involved in the insurance policy, especially persons having a claim for insurance policy coverage. The Insurance Contract Act, as opposed to the present regulation, tries to define all participants and to determine their rights and duties.

13 The Insurance Contract Act includes, besides the provisions regarding the content of the insurance contract and the conclusion of the insurance agreement, a new regulation of the limitation period, which is presently subject to Sec. 104 of the Civil Code.

14 The right to insurance coverage shall become subject to limitation within three years, and in the case of life insurance, within 10 years. The termination period commences one year after the occurrence of the insurable event. This applies also to cases in which the injured party has a direct claim for payment against the insurer or when the insured requests reimbursement for the amount which he/she provided to the injured in order to compensate him for damage.

Damage Liability Insurance

15 The Insurance Contract Act regulates, apart from other kinds of insurance policies, damage liability insurance. Based on this insurance, the insured is enti-

[8] *Zákon č. 37/2004 o pojistné smlouvě (zákon o pojistné smlouvě).*
[9] For example: Directives 88/357/EEC; 2002/65/EC; 87/344/EEC; 92/96/EEC; 2002/87/EC etc.

tled to ask the insurer to compensate under the conditions of the insurance contract the damage which he/she caused to another and which he/she is held liable for, either based on law or on a contract. If not limited, the insurer has to provide full coverage to the amount of the actual damage which the insured is held liable for.

When the insured compensates the injured party directly, he/she acquires the right against the insurer to ask for reimbursement for the payment that the insurer would otherwise have paid pursuant to the insurance contract. The insured is obliged to inform the insurer that the injured party has raised a claim for compensation against him, to express his/her view on the matter and disclose any further information relating to the event in which the damage occurred. At the time of the notification of the event, the insured has authorized the insurer to open the case. 16

As long as the damage was caused by the insured under a condition which he/she caused to himself through his/her own fault and it resulted in the diminished ability to judge the consequences of his/her conduct, the insurer has a right of recourse against the insured. 17

An insurer which reimburses claims based on the damage liability insurance of the obliged person may offer to pay the entitled party lump sum compensation for future claims for compensation for loss of earnings after the end of the inability to work, maintenance of survivors, or other claims which will repeatedly arise in the future. If an agreement concerning the form of the compensation between the entitled party and the insurer is concluded, all existing and future claims are settled through a lump sum payment. 18

Apart from the Insurance Contract Act and the Motor Vehicle Liability Insurance Act there were two further laws approved in 2004 concerning the insurance issue. They may not have a direct impact on the area of tort law, but they are significant to the proper functioning of the entire system of compensation for damage suffered. 19

They are Act No. 38/2004 Coll., concerning the insurance agent and independent insurance adjustor for insurable events[10] and Act No. 39/2004 Coll., which amends Act No. 363/1999 Coll., Insurance Act[11]. 20

The basic purpose of the amendment of Act No. 363/1999 Coll. (hereinafter the Insurance Act) is the approximation of the public regulation of the private insurance system to EC law, especially in respect to the third generation of EC 21

[10] Zákon č. 38/2004 Sb., o pojišťovacích zprostředkovatelích a samostatných likvidátorech pojistných událostí a o změně živnostenského zákona (zákon o pojišťovacích zprostředkovatelích a likvidátorech pojistných událostí).

[11] Zákon č. 39/2004 Sb., kterým se mění zákon č. 363/1999 Sb. ČR, o pojišťovnictví a o změně některých souvisejících zákonů (zákon o pojišťovnictví), ve znění pozdějších předpisů, a některé další zákony.

Directives concerning life and non-life insurance. The Insurance Act introduces to the Czech insurance legislation the system of a "single European passport" and relative issues hereto. This system is based on the fact that a license issued in one Member State remains valid in all other Member States of the EU, and the insurance company does not need to ask for further licenses for providing an insurance policy when it intends to widen its scope of business into other territories. Based on these provisions, only a notification obligation must be fulfilled to establish an insurance business in the Czech Republic.

22 The basic condition for setting up and working as an insurance agent or insurance adjustor is the registration of such a person who works in the relevant business with the register maintained by the Supervisory Authority. The conditions for the registration and for the activity of natural and legal persons as agents or insurance adjustors are set forth in a comprehensive manner by Act No. 38/2004 Coll. (hereinafter the Insurance Agent Act) and they aim to increase consumer protection against incompetent persons engaging in this business.

23 The existence of agents and adjustors relies on their contract with a certain insurance company, which is held fully liable for their activities. The insurance companies have to check the background and qualifications of the person, and they shall be liable for the agent's professional competence and on-going professional training. Some agents are required to take out liability insurance against damage caused by their activities.

3. *Zákon o některých službách informační společnosti* (Act No. 480/2004 Coll., concerning certain services of the information society and an amendment to some Acts)[12]

24 Act No. 480/2004 Coll. (hereinafter the E-Commerce Act) implements the Directive of the European Parliament and Council No. 2000/31/EC of 8 June 2000 on certain legal aspects of information society services into Czech legislation, in particular electronic commerce, in the internal market (Directive on electronic commerce), which had to be implemented on the day of the Czech accession into the EU on 1 May 2004. Some parts of the Directive had already been implemented; however, especially the provisions on Internet providers' liability and on electronic contracts remained unchanged.

25 The main purpose of the regulation of providers' liability for information society services is the need to establish limits for their responsibility, and to lay down clear conditions in respect hereto. It was especially necessary to set forth conditions for the content of transferred, cached or hosted information and for commercial communication (spam). The provisions regarding the providers' liability are subject to Sec. 3–6 of the E-Commerce Act.

[12] Zákon č. 480/2004 Sb., o některých službách informační společnosti a o změně některých zákonů (zákon o některých službách informační společnosti).

The provision of Sec. 3 of the E-Commerce Act determines cases when the provider can be held liable for the content of the information transferred, regardless of whether the consumer/user is connected to the network by a dial-up or LAN connection. As the provider only transfers some information, it is not possible to request that it supervise the content and possibly be liable for it. Therefore, the provider shall be held liable only in the case that it initiates the transmission, selects the receiver of the transmission or selects or modifies the information contained in the transmission. 26

Sec. 4 of the E-Commerce Act regulates liability, or determines its limits, in the case of caching. The provider uses caching as protection from the excessive use of its servers, and therefore caching must be understood as a technically based procedure. Therefore, the provider shall be held liable for the content of cached information if it adopts such a measure that it is reasonable to hold him liable for the content, e.g. when it modifies the information, does not comply with conditions on access to the information, does not comply with rules regarding the updating of the information widely recognized and used by the industry or interferes with the lawful use of technology widely recognized and used by the industry in order to obtain data on the use of the information and used by industry, or blocks access to such information. 27

When the provider allows users to store their information on the provider's servers it happens due to a private law contract on the hosting of information or data. In accordance with the law, in particular Sec. 5 of the Information Society Services Act, only the users are liable for the content of such hosted information, and the providers have no obligation to supervise the content of the materials hosted. However, if a certain provider has actual knowledge of illegal activity or information and, as regards claims for damages, is aware of facts or circumstances from which the illegal activity or information is apparent, and upon obtaining such knowledge or awareness does not act expeditiously to remove or to disable access to the information, it becomes liable for the hosted content. 28

B. Cases

1. *Nejvyšší soud České republiky* (Supreme Court of the Czech Republic) 29 April 2004, 25 Cdo 1307/2003: Nature of damage suffered by a person with fishing rights

a) Brief Summary of the Facts

The District Court in Český Krumlov, in its decision dated 26 March 2001 ruled on the defendant's obligation to pay the plaintiff damages. It decided on compensation for damage caused to the plaintiff's fish in various fishing districts by otters, an animal whose number cannot be reduced. 29

30 As Act No. 115/2000 Coll., concerning compensation for damage caused by certain protected animals (hereinafter the Damage Compensation Act) cannot be applied to this case because the plaintiff's damage arose before it became effective, i.e. 10 May 2000, the court of first instance determined the amount of damage according to an expert's opinion, based on findings beyond doubt that the otter is a species of animal that has spread rapidly in the region. The expert appraised the amount and the value of the fish consumed by otters in the given period in a sum amounting to CZK 94,500 (€ 3,150).

31 The Regional Court in České Budějovice, in its decision dated 4 February 2003 upheld the decision of the court of first instance (after the Supreme Court decided on the case in a judgment dated 29 October 2002)[13]. Bound by the legal opinion of the Supreme Court, it concluded that the strict liability of the state to compensate the damage exists pursuant to the provisions of the Hunting Act No. 23/1962 Coll. (hereinafter the Hunting Act), even though no law regulating details of compensation for the period for which the plaintiff claimed damages was issued by the authorized state body. In such a case, it is necessary to apply the general provisions of the Civil Code (Sec. 442 et seq. of the Civil Code) concerning damages.

32 The defendant stated in its application for appellate review of the decision that the owner of freely living animals (fish and other water animals living in rivers) can only be the state, as it is the owner of rivers in the Czech Republic. The plaintiff can only be entitled to appropriate for himself the fish that he has already caught. In the defendant's opinion, there is no damage to property on the plaintiff's side, i.e. the loss of its property as a consequence of an event in which damage occurred, because the plaintiff is not the owner of freely living fish, and therefore the provision of the Hunting Act[14] cannot be applied to the present case. The plaintiff acquires the ownership right to fish pursuant to Sec. 6 of Act No. 102/1963 Coll., on fishery (hereinafter the Fishery Act) only after he catches them.

b) Judgment of the Court

33 Pursuant to Sec. 8 of the Fishery Act, the Ministry of Agriculture shall transfer for free the fishery right in fishing areas especially to branches of the Czech Fishery Association and other business enterprises. Based on this regulation, it is apparent that the fishing right belongs to the state, which is entitled to enable the performance of such a right to third parties for free. However, neither the Fishery Act nor any other acts expressly deal with the ownership right to freely living fish.

34 The Fishery Act determines only that the entitled subject of the fishing right acquires fish into his or her property by catching them, i.e. by the original ac-

[13] J. Hrádek, in: H. Koziol/B.C. Steininger (eds.), *European Tort Law 2003* (2004), 91.

[14] Sec. 34 para. 3 of the Hunting Act regulating the framework for compensation.

quisition of a property ownership right, based on the legal provisions of the Fishery Act.

The legal theory concludes that, as opposed to fish living in ponds and seas, an ownership right to fish in a river is not possible and the uncaught fish in rivers must be considered as having no owner.[15] 35

In the case of state liability for damage caused before 10 May 2000, i.e. before the Damage Compensation Act came into effect, the kind and extent of the compensation must be subject to the general provisions of the Civil Code concerning damages. It is necessary to apply the provision of Sec. 442 of the Civil Code, stating that compensation for actual damage and loss of profit shall be provided. Pursuant to paragraph 2 of this section, the damage shall be compensated in money or, if the injured party so demands and if it is possible and expedient, by restitution in kind. 36

The actual damage is harm, which means the loss of property owned by the injured party in comparison with the proprietary situation before the event in which the damage occurred, and it presents the values necessary for restoring or replacing the destroyed or damaged property to the previous condition. A loss of profit means basically any loss of the proprietary benefit and consists of an unrealised increase in the property value of the injured party, an increase that may be reasonably expected in respect to regular development. 37

Therefore, it is apparent that the loss of uncaught fish living in rivers due to the fact that they were consumed by otters does not qualify as a loss in the property of the plaintiff (the entitled subject to the fishing right) which had no ownership right at the moment the loss occurred (their value did not constitute the plaintiff's owned property), because he had not acquired the fish by catching them and they were therefore not his property. The court of second instance determined correctly the actual damage from the loss of earnings if it had concluded that the plaintiff had suffered damage in a loss of earnings due to the fact that he was not able to catch and sell the fish consumed by the otters and, as a consequence, was unable to increase the value of his property. 38

The amount of lost profit must be determined in such a manner as to enumerate the value of the presumed gains after reducing it to costs which would have been expended under normal circumstances, i.e. if the fish had not been consumed by otters. 39

[15] M. Kindl, K jednomu regálu (Co může a co nemůže být předmětem výhradního vlastnictví státu na příkladu rybářského práva), [1996] *Právník*, 735 et seq.; M. Tomsa, Právní problematika náhrady škody rybářským organizacím vypouštěním závadných odpadů, [1984] *Hospodářské právo*, 766 et seq.

c) Commentary

40 The Supreme Court ruled twice in this case. In the first case it concluded that damages, based on the strict liability of the state imposed under the provisions of the Hunting Act, must be awarded, even though the authorized state body has not issued any law regulating the details of such compensation. In the second case the Supreme Court decided in the matter of the nature of the damage suffered by the entitled Fishery Association, consisting of the loss of fish, e.g. consumed by a protected animal.

41 The Supreme Court reached the conclusion that such damage cannot be qualified as actual damage, but a loss of earnings, because the harm suffered by the Fishery Association does not constitute a loss of its property, as it has no ownership right to the fish at the moment in which the damage occurred, but only the right to catch the fish (and acquire the ownership right).

2. *Nejvyšší soud České republiky* 29 April 2004, 25 Cdo 1915/2002: Liability of a person operating a campground

a) Brief Summary of the Facts

42 The plaintiff claimed compensation for damage, amounting to CZK 23,750 (€ 791) plus default interest starting from 1 September 1996 until payment, which was caused when an unknown perpetrator stole his two bikes from a campground operated by the defendant. The plaintiff and his friends stayed at the campground in question from 30 August 1996 to 1 September 1996. The plaintiff had leaned his two bikes, in accordance with the instructions of the receptionist, against a tree and locked them with special padlocks.

43 The District Court in Mladá Boleslav rejected the claim in a judgment dated 27 April 1998 and concluded that the defendant is not an operator providing accommodation services pursuant to Sec. 433 para. 1 of the Civil Code, because its scope of business, pursuant to its trade licenses, is the operation of a campground for setting up tents and it is not the operator of an activity which usually involves storing objects pursuant to Sec. 433 para. 2 of the Civil Code.

44 The Regional Court in Prague reversed the judgment of the court of first instance in its resolution dated 3 November 1999. The Regional Court discovered that the plaintiff had placed the bikes in a place that was determined by an employee of the defendant, and it dealt further with the issue of whether the plaintiff claimed his right in a proper manner. As the law does not set forth any requirements for the form of the claim for damages, it is sufficient for the assessment of the claim that the aggravated party undertakes such a unilateral oral act, from which it is apparent who, when, how and to what amount damage occurred, including the requirement for compensation. As the plaintiff had asserted such a claim properly with the employee at the reception of the campground that morning, in the Court's opinion the claim could not have lapsed.

The defendant stated in its application for appellate review on the decision that the conclusion on the liability pursuant to Sec. 433 para. 2 of the Civil Code contradicts substantive law, because it is not a provider of an activity which is connected with storing bikes. It is apparent from the rules of the public campground that it is not a watched or otherwise guarded structure. The defendant offered only a place for the placement of tents and other conditions were set in the rules of the public campground. 45

b) Judgment of the Court

The Supreme Court upheld the decision of the Regional Court. Pursuant to Sec. 433 para. 2 of the Civil Code "if the operation of any activity is usually connected with storing objects, the person providing such an activity shall be held liable to a natural person for damage to the object put in a place designated for that purpose or in a place where such things are customarily put, unless the damage would have occurred in any event." Pursuant to para. 3 of this provision "nobody may exonerate himself from liability through a unilateral declaration or an agreement." 46

The subject of the liability for damage pursuant to this provision is determined by the fact that it operates an activity which is usually connected with storing things. This includes such activities in which the customer is forced to halt supervision of his/her things for a certain period of time and set them aside. "Things" in the meaning of this provision are those things whose storage is connected with the use of a certain service. From that point of view, a bike is not excluded from becoming a thing in the meaning of the provision of Sec. 433 para. 2 of the Civil Code; however, it is fundamental that it must be stored in connection with the activity whose operation requests that the bike be stored. 47

It is logical that visitors bring into a campground, apart from those things necessary for accommodation, various personal items which are to be used during the stay in the camp (e.g. bikes etc.). In order to make use of the service provided by the operator of the campground, i.e. to camp in a specific place, it is necessary to store things which are to be used in connection with the camping within the area of the campground. Such things are usually not put in a tent or a van. The operation of the campground, i.e. the offer of a place for camping within a certain area, is therefore an activity which is connected with storing things, because the use of a certain place requires that the customer is unable to constantly supervise his/her things. 48

c) Commentary

The judgment of the Supreme Court deals with the practical issue of the liability of the campground operator for damage to things stored within the campground. The Supreme Court reached the conclusion that the operator of any activity usually connected with storing things must become a subject of liability for such things, provided that the use of the service requires that supervision over one's things is interrupted. 49

50 The Supreme Court has ruled in a similar matter many times in the past; however, in the present case it expressly acknowledged the legal position of a campground as an establishment whose operator is subject to strict liability.

3. *Nejvyšší soud České republiky* 24 May 2001, 25 Cdo 1946/2000: Loss of profit; 20 February 2004, 25 Cdo 1702/2002: Compensation for loss of profit acquired in conflict with good morals

a) Brief Summary of the Facts

51 The plaintiff was travelling for a business meeting with company E to which it was to deliver, as an agent under an agreement concluded with R, the binding orders of a purchase agreement for deliveries to third parties. The personal involvement of the plaintiff in this meeting was necessary, because it was the last possible date for the conclusion of agreements with diesel oil suppliers. However, on the way the plaintiff's vehicle was damaged in a road accident caused by the defendant. As a result of this, the plaintiff was unable to participate in the mentioned meeting and due to the plaintiff's absence the orders and purchase agreements could not be accepted. It is obvious from an expert's opinion that if the customers had purchased the ordered volume of oil, the plaintiff would have been entitled to a certain commission.

52 The court of first instance granted the claim for payment of this amount, because it concluded that the preconditions of liability for damage pursuant to Sec. 420 of the Civil Code were fulfilled, as the defendant had breached his legal duty and caused a road accident. As a result of the breach of legal duty the plaintiff suffered damage (property loss) in the form of the loss of profit pursuant to Sec. 442 of the Civil Code.

53 The Regional Court rejected the action and reversed the judgment, because it reached the conclusion that there was no causal connection between the unlawful act of the defendant and the damage incurred by the plaintiff. It concluded, especially in respect to the previous judgment of the Czechoslovak Supreme Court published under R 7/79, that the loss of the provision is not a direct result of the road accident.

b) Judgment of the Court – 25 Cdo 1946/2000

54 The Supreme Court reached the conclusion in its judgment 25 Cdo 1946/2000 dated 25 May 2001, that the immediate cause of the lost profit was the circumstance that agreements, based on which the plaintiff was to gain a certain benefit, failed to be concluded. The damage of the plaintiff's vehicle, as a result of which the plaintiff was not able to attend the mentioned meeting, is not a new and isolated circumstance to such an extent that it would enter the mechanism of causes and effects independent of the defendant's action.

55 A distinction needs to be made between an effect consisting of physical damage to an object and an effect manifested by the fact that the object was put out

of operation and could not serve the purpose for which the plaintiff was using it at the time or possibly intended to use in the foreseeable future. This effect of the damage caused to the object, resulting in the non-functionality of the object, is the reason why the injured plaintiff lost the benefit which he would otherwise, under normal circumstances, have achieved.

Taking into account the specific factual findings in the assessed matter, it therefore needs to be inferred that even the circumstance that the defendant is responsible for the damage to the plaintiff's vehicle does not exclude the causal connection between the breach of duty resulting in the damage and the damage which the plaintiff incurred in the form of lost profit. 56

c) Other Facts

The plaintiff should have procured at the business meeting an oil purchase from company E for companies A, S and R and received a provision amounting to CZK 0.35 per litre. However, the plaintiff was at the same time the interest holder and the managing director of the company R. 57

The statutes of company R, in the version valid on the day of the execution of the agency agreement, did not contain any regulation for the competition clause concerning managing directors and interest holders different from the provision of Sec. 136 para. 1 letter a) and b) of the Act No. 513/1991 Coll., Commercial Code (hereinafter the Commercial Code). Based on this fact, it must be concluded that if the plaintiff procured for the benefit of company E a business transaction with his company R in which he was the managing director and the interest holder, he acted in contradiction to the provision of Sec. 136 of the Commercial Code. 58

Pursuant to Sec. 136 of the Commercial Code, unless the memorandum of association or the statutes imply further restrictions, a managing director may not: a) conclude in his own name and at his own expenses commercial transactions which are connected with the business activity of the company, b) act as a broker (negotiator, agent) for other parties in the company's business transactions etc. 59

Based on these findings the Supreme Court decided in the matter whether the defendant should compensate the plaintiff when the damage incurred was based on an activity in contradiction to good morals, or whether such circumstances are irrelevant. 60

d) Judgment of the Supreme Court – 25 Cdo 1702/2002

The Supreme Court concluded that the breach of the competition clause is not irrelevant to the relationship between the plaintiff who suffered damage in the form of a loss of profit and a person who impeded him through a breach of a legal duty. 61

62 It was revealed in the present case that the plaintiff would have acquired a part of the lost profit, which establishes the subject of the proceedings, based on a trade which was in conflict with the competition clause pursuant to Sec. 136 of the Commercial Code, namely by accepting the provision for trade conducted with company R. The plaintiff was acting as an agent of company R. However, at the same time he was the managing director of the company. The assumed profit of such a transaction was therefore based on an activity which qualifies as being unlawful in relation to both the plaintiff and the company and which in relation to company R may deflect from the principles of fair business transactions.

63 Regardless of the particular sanctions connected by law with the relationships between business subjects and whether these sanctions were applied, it would be in conflict with good moral judgment if the defendant who obstructed the plaintiff from obtaining such a profit were to be obliged to compensate for the lost profit within the framework of liability for damage.

e) Commentary

64 Both decisions of the Supreme Court are disputable. It is widely acknowledged[16] that in its first decision, the Supreme Court wanted to change a 20-year-old decision of the Supreme Court of the Czech Republic, published under R 7/1979. The Supreme Court originally concluded that causality between the activity of a wrongdoer and damage occurred cannot be concluded from a fact which is a result for which the wrongdoer can be held liable for another reason. This is the case if somebody suffers a mental shock after realizing that another person has suffered a fatal injury caused by a wrongdoer. This decision had a far-reaching impact on the theory of causality and in many cases it was impossible to award damages.

65 In case 25 Cdo 1946/2000, the Supreme Court suddenly changed its opinion concerning the causality and decided that even the circumstance that the defendant is responsible for the damage of the plaintiff's vehicle does not exclude the causal connection between the breach of duty resulting in the damage and the damage which the plaintiff incurred in the form of lost profit. The Supreme Court argued in its reasoning that in the present case the logical chain of causes and results was not interrupted because the direct cause of the establishment of the lost profit was a fact that was a direct result of the damaging of the car caused by the wrongdoer. No new fact had therefore entered into the chain of causes and results but only a fact which had already been foreseeable for the wrongdoer before he caused the damage in question. The chronological point of view for the establishment of damage is not conclusive because it cannot be required that harm must arise immediately after the wrongdoer's action.

[16] B. Petr, Ušlý zisk, vývoj právní úpravy a aktuální problémy spojené s hledáním mezí v rozhodovací činnosti soudů, [2004] *Právní rozhledy*, 573 et seq.

With its arguments concerning relevant cause, the Supreme Court weakened the concept of the direct and indirect result, even though not dramatically. In particular, it must be acknowledged that cases of direct and indirect result should not be differentiated from the point of view of compensation, as the practise currently is, because the indirect damage does not always need to be unforeseeable for the wrongdoer. However, with the latter decision, the Supreme Court restricts its previous decision, which could have been understood by some people as too courageous and helpful. Using the argument of good morals, the Supreme Court rejected the damages in the present case even though, and it must be emphasized, it does not explicitly contest the previous conclusion. 66

4. *Nejvyšší soud České republiky* 25 February 2004, 25 Cdo 863/2003: Claim for damages for harm to a vehicle asserted by a person not being its owner[17]

a) Brief Summary of the Facts

On 30 October 1995 plaintiff B and the defendant entered into an agreement on the leasing of a parking space in a garage for an unlimited period of time for the purpose of parking a car, which was the property of plaintiff A. On 13 August 1996 plaintiff B realized that the car, which was parked by him on 2 August 1996, had been damaged. He notified this fact immediately to the owner of the parking space and the police, and on the next day to the insurance agency which is the insurer of plaintiff A. After the insurance agency rejected reimbursement for the damage, plaintiff A asked the defendant once again in a letter dated 14 August 1996 for compensation. 67

The District Court in Prague 4 in its judgment rejected the claim of both plaintiffs for payment amounting to CZK 120,000 (€ 4,000). The Court concluded in the case that when the car was parked by plaintiff B, who is not the owner of the car, in the garage, it was not evident from his conduct that he was acting on behalf of plaintiff A, who is the injured party. Further the Supreme Court concluded that the fifteen-day time limit pursuant to Sec. 436 of the Civil Code had expired. The Municipal Court in Prague confirmed the previous judgment of the court of first instance in respect to the defendant's duty to pay the claimed compensation. 68

The plaintiffs allege in their application for appellate review on the decision that the claim was asserted within the time limit pursuant to Sec. 436 of the Civil Code, because in their opinion it is not necessary that the claim be made to the obliged party directly by the entitled party. They refer to the wording of Sec. 436 of the Civil Code which does not define in any more detail the person who has to undertake the relevant notification. 69

[17] [2004] *Právní rozhledy*, 443.

b) Judgment of the Court

70 The provision of Sec. 435 of the Civil Code defines the person liable (the operators of garages and similar enterprises) and the thing to which the relationship of responsibility relates. The liability of the owners of garages and similar enterprises pursuant to Sec. 435 of the Civil Code is based on a contractual relationship which is mostly concluded by the parties by implication, e.g. by the fact that the car is parked in the watched parking space with the consent of the supervisor.

71 The provision of Sec. 435 of the Civil Code relates to such parking spaces and enterprises where the cars are parked based on such contracts. This provision neither limits the liability to such means of transport which were put there by specific persons nor defines the category of persons to which the operator is liable. Whilst in the case of accommodation services (and other services which are usually connected with storing objects – see above Case 2 (25 Cdo 1915/2002, supra nos. 42 et seq.)) the contractual relationship is bound to the person who was accommodated, in the case of parking and keeping a car in a garage the content of the contractual relationship relates to the certain means of transport.

72 If everybody has the right, based on the parking contract, to park the particular means of transport for which the parking space was contracted, the strict liability of the operator shall, consequently, relate to this particular means of transport regardless of who has put the car in the garage.

73 In accordance with Sec. 436 of the Civil Code, "the claim for the right to compensation for damage must be made to the operator without undue delay. The right expires if the injured party does not make a claim within 15 days of discovering the damage." The first sentence of this provision sets forth the manner in which the claim shall be asserted by the operator (unilateral act), however without stating the condition that only the injured party shall do so. Therefore, the entitled party to the claim against the operator of the garage may also be without a doubt the person who entered into the contract on the parking of a car and parked it there, even if not the owner of the car.

74 If the claim for compensation for damage caused to the particular car parked in the garage was asserted by the operator of the garage within the mentioned time period (Sec. 436 of the Civil Code) and this car was the object of the service provided, it is of no importance whether the owner suffering the damage or a person who entered into the contract on the lease of parking space and parked the car there asserted the claim.

c) Commentary

75 In this case the Supreme Court decided on a matter which had never been subject to judgment by the Supreme Court. The issue was who may claim compensation for damage in a case in which different persons enter into a contract on the lease of a parking space and suffer damage to a car parked there?

The Supreme Court concluded that, in the case of parking, the content of the contractual relationship relates to a certain means of transport. Therefore, the individual entitled to the claim may also be the person who entered into a mutual contract with the operator of the garage and parked a car there, even if he/she is not the owner of the car. His/her right to assert a claim is based on the mutual contract with the operator. 76

5. *Nejvyšší soud České republiky* 19 February 2004, 25 Cdo 1923/2002: Qualification of hazardous operation in respect to the starting stage of a racing competition

a) Brief Summary of the Facts

The plaintiff made a claim for compensation for damage he sustained by compensation of his employee for a work accident. The employee was hit and injured while recording an interview at the start of a racing competition organized by the defendant. 77

The court of first instance reached the conclusion that the defendant shall be held liable for such damage as the operator of a hazardous operation pursuant to Sec. 432 of the Civil Code. A hazardous operation is usually understood as a human activity which is connected with the high probability of causing damage. Therefore, this definition includes not only the racing competition itself, but also the time close to the start, as at this moment many people are still assembled at the starting position and the cars are already rolling by. 78

The court of second instance reversed the judgment and concluded that only the racing competition must be understood as a hazardous operation and not the organizational preparation before its commencement. Based on this opinion, it rejected the liability of the defendant pursuant to Sec. 432 of the Civil Code and decided to consider the possible liability of the defendant in accordance with the general provisions of the Civil Code concerning damages. 79

b) Judgment of the Court

The Civil Code does not contain any definition for hazardous operation since this term is relative, and it must be interpreted in respect to the particular circumstances of each case. A hazardous operation is mostly an activity using technical means and natural energy sources and for which it is typical that, despite exercising due care and using the latest knowledge, objective control over every process arising from the activity is not always possible. Taking this fact into account, such processes are a source of direct danger to the surroundings. The source of danger can be an object whose purpose is usually without consequences to the surroundings, i.e. a car or train. However, the activity of this object can, under certain circumstances, have additional effects causing a higher degree of probability for damage. On the other hand, the liability pursuant to Sec. 432 of the Civil Code is given only in the event that the damage caused is in causality with such an effect of the operation, which is naturally a qualified hazard. 80

81 In the present case it was revealed that the damage to the employee's health arose as a result of the collision with a racing car driving at a speed of 5–10km/h when he stepped into the road and suffered a leg injury. It happened within the starting area at the time when the cars were being driven to their starting positions. The movement of the racing cars at such a moment cannot be qualified as an activity during which the used technical means would be able to be controlled only to a limited extent, and as a result no direct danger of serious damage exists.

82 The operation of the racing competition at this phase, which is demonstrated by a minimal use of the engine potential of the racing cars, does not fulfil the preconditions for liability pursuant to Sec. 432 of the Civil Code, because the nature of the operation in that stage of the competition, operated by the defendant, does not qualify as being hazardous.

c) Commentary

83 The Supreme Court ruled in the matter of whether the organizational preparation of a racing competition could be qualified as a hazardous operation which is subject to strict liability in accordance with the Czech Civil Code. In such a case the operator could be exonerated from liability only if he/she proves that the damage could not have been prevented, even by making every effort which could be demanded in this respect.

84 As there is no definition for hazardous operation within the Civil Code because this concept is relative, and it must be interpreted in respect to the particular circumstances of each case, it is important that the Supreme Court considers particular cases and creates "precedents" showing what the limits of this concept are.

85 In the present case the Supreme Court rejected the qualification of the starting phase of a racing competition as a hazardous operation because the used technical means can be put under complete control and any uncontrolled danger is under threat.

6. *Nejvyšší soud České republiky* 17 December 2003, 25 Cdo 552/2003: Damage suffered by the owner of land due to soil pollution

a) Brief Summary of the Facts

86 The plaintiff claimed compensation for damage amounting to CZK 60 million (€ 2,000,000) against the state with the reasoning that he suffered damage through the devaluation of his property by soil pollution caused by contaminated water coming from the neighbouring land. This land belonged to the former state enterprise K, which was charged with a duty imposed on 27 March 1997 by the Czech Environmental Inspection. The duty consists of adopting measures to eliminate water and soil pollution; the decontamination, however, was not undertaken.

The court of first instance concluded that the claim cannot be successful because the plaintiff alleges that it suffered damage caused by the pollution of the soil on his land, whereas the amount of the damage is equal to the price of decontamination works which company K should have provided. In the court's opinion, as these measures had not been undertaken, the plaintiff did not suffer any damage, because the relevant damage arises only at the moment when the works are provided and the actual expenses are known. 87

The Municipal Court affirmed the judgment in its decision dated 18 October 2002. The court stated that the basic precondition for liability is the existence of damage; if the plaintiff states that the damage to the property arose through the loss of the land's value due to the soil pollution and it would have been possible to determine the damage before the performance of the decontamination work, such an allegation presents, in the court's opinion, an inadmissible novelty pursuant to Sec. 205a para. 1 of the Civil Procedure Code and must be rejected. 88

In his application for appellate review to the decision, the plaintiff argues that the damages claimed consist of the loss of the market value of the land due to the soil pollution and that the amount only corresponds to the costs for decontamination work. The diminishing of the value of the land had already occurred and he does not agree with the opinion that the damage will not occur until the decontamination work is performed. 89

b) Judgment of the Court

The legal opinion of the court of second instance that the damage to the property of the plaintiff did not occur and the plaintiff is, consequently, not entitled to claim damages (it is not the holder of the alleged right), incorrectly identifies the plaintiff's allegation of facts concerning what the damage consists of (the devaluation of its land) with the plaintiff's reasoning of the amount claimed for compensation (the cost of decontamination work which should have been undertaken by K). 90

The certain amount of the damage does not present the precondition of liability and the court will come to the determination hereof only if the claim is given, i.e. when all preconditions for the liability for damage are met. The particular amount of damages results, then, from the circumstance which was the cause of the damage; however, the court is not bound to its decision to the scope of compensation in the manner of determination suggested by the plaintiff. 91

If the damage consists of the devaluation of the land due to pollution coming from the neighbour's land, it is evident that – if proved and correct – the value of the land and the property owned by the land's owner diminishes, regardless of whether he has already expended some costs for limiting or restraining the source of the contamination or for restoring the land to its previous condition. 92

c) **Commentary**

93 In this case the Supreme Court had to change the opinions of the lower courts regarding the assessment of damage. The plaintiff claimed that he suffered damage through the loss of the market value of the land due to the soil pollution coming from the neighbour's land and he determined the damage as equal to the expenses requested for the decontamination of his land.

94 The Supreme Court accepted this opinion and decided that the owner of the land suffered damage already through the actual loss of value caused by the soil pollution, regardless of the fact whether he, as the owner, has already expended some costs. Since the preconditions of the liability are already met when the injured suffered damage which is in causality with the fact for which the defendant shall be held liable, the conclusion of the Supreme Court that the fulfilment of no other preconditions of liability can be demanded is correct and damages must be awarded.

C. Literature

1. R. Ondruš, *Přehled judikatury, odpovědnost státu za nesprávný výkon veřejné moci* (ASPI Publishing s.r.o., Prague 2004)[18]

95 This book is a collection of the Supreme Court's judicature concerning the liability for damage caused by maladministration and illegal decision-making.

96 Currently, this liability is subject to Act No. 82/1998 Coll., concerning the liability for damage caused by maladministration or illegal decision-making (State Liability Act), a successor of the related Act No. 58/1969 Coll. The author introduces the relevant judicature to both acts, as well as some older judicature relating to the Austrian Civil Code (ABGB), valid until 1950 in the area of the former Czechoslovakia.

2. J. Handlar, Několik poznámek ke koncepci odpovědnosti jako sekundárního právního vztahu, [2004] *Právník*, 169 et seq.[19]

97 In this article the author deals with the issue of legal liability as a secondary legal relationship, especially as introduced by Prof. J. Bejček into the Czech law. The author further mentions the opinion of A. Brejcha who published his opinions in his monograph Liability in Private and Public Law[20], and who also understands liability as a secondary legal relationship.

98 Handlar concludes that liability in law cannot be understood as either a secondary or any other legal relationship. The legal relationship can be character-

[18] Overview of judicature, state liability for wrongful performance of public authority.
[19] Some notes on the concept of liability as a secondary legal relationship.
[20] A. Brejcha, *Odpovědnost v soukromém a veřejném právu* (2000).

ized only by rights and duties which are the content of the relationship. A secondary legal relationship itself cannot thus in any way encumber the liable entity, this can be caused only by its content, i.e. a newly established duty.

In Handlar's opinion, the theory under which the legal liability is a secondary legal relationship is therefore wrong and also presents a wrong attitude towards the concept of liability. 99

3. J. Handlar, Právní odpovědnost – netradiční zamyšlení nad tradičním pojmem, [2004] *Právník*, 1041 et seq.[21]

This article deals with the term "legal relationship" from the point of view of private law, i.e. civil law liability. In the first part of the article the author presents the particular theories concerning liability in the area of the former Czechoslovakia, especially the theories of V. Knapp, Š. Luby and M. Knappová, J. Macur, J. Švestka and J. Eliáš and finally critically analyses the particular theories. 100

Handlar reaches the conclusion that the concept of liability cannot be understood as a legal concept, but only a common concept, i.e. having no specific legal content and being used in the law under its common meaning. In this case, liability must be understood as the attribution of something to somebody, and only particular legal terms, for instance liability for damage or liability for defective products, would be understood through legal concepts. 101

4. M. Cilínková/D. Kuboň, Odškodnění při usmrcení osoby blízké, [2004] *Bulletin Advokacie* 10/2004, 30 et seq.[22]

The authors deal with the issue of compensation for killing the next of kin and for immaterial harm suffered in Czech law. They examine the relevant provisions of European law, especially Directive 2000/26/EC on the approximation of the laws of the Member States relating to insurance against civil liability in respect of the use of motor vehicles. Finally they deal with the new amendment to the Civil Code concerning compensation for homicide and the lump sum compensation issue, and in that direction present some comparative notes. 102

5. M. Holub, Jednorázové odškodnění při usmrcení podle novely občanského zákoníku (zák. č. 47/2004 Sb.), [2004] *Bulletin Advokacie* 6/2004, 46 et seq.[23]

Holub examines the latest amendment to the Civil Code, especially Sec. 444 constituting a regulation granting certain amounts to close persons of a homicide victim. The author analyses the concept of compensation for homicide, especially in the direction of whether it shall be understood as compensation 103

[21] Legal liability – untraditional consideration of a traditional concept.
[22] Compensation for the killing of the next of kin.
[23] Lump sum compensation for homicide under the amendment to the Civil Code.

for damage or compensation for immaterial harm, whereas he concludes the latter. Further, he deals with the terminology used and with the issue concerning the relation of the new provision to parallel Labour Code regulations.

6. B. Petr, Ušlý zisk, vývoj právní úpravy a aktuální problémy spojené shledáním mezí vrozhodovací činnosti soudů, [2004] *Právní rozhledy*, 573 et seq.[24]

104 In this article Petr responds to discussions caused by his last commentary on the Supreme Court's judgment concerning compensation for loss of profit due to a road accident (see supra nos. 51 et seq.). In the first part of his article Petr introduces an overview of the development of judicature relating to loss of profit, from the interpretation of Sec. 1293 of the ABGB to the present Sec. 442 of the Civil Code. He is of the opinion that the rule for proper interpretation of the loss of profit must be Sec. 379 of the Commercial Code. In the second part he critically deals with decision No. 25 Cdo 1946/2000, especially with the issue of causality.

7. P. Valečková, Odpovědnost státu za škodu způsobenou jednotlivci porušením práva ES, [2004] *Bulletin Advokacie* 9/2004, 29 et seq.[25]

105 A completely new concept of liability, in particular the liability of the state for damage caused to an individual by a breach of the EC law, was introduced to Czech law as of 1 May 2004. The article deals with the scope of liability in relation to the similar concept of Czech law, which is substantially narrower than European-based law. The author provides a detailed overview of this legal concept.

8. J. Salač, K otázce předpokladů odpovědnosti za škodu, [2004] *Právní rozhledy*, 680 et seq.[26]

106 The author examines the interpretation of the Supreme Court's judgment No. 20 Cdo 1499/2000 with the following recital of the law: "The existence of a wrongful act as a precondition for liability for damage is also given when the wrongdoer has breached his/her duty resulting from an agreement concluded between him and a person other than the injured, when the obligation which is the subject of the breach had an impact on the sphere of the injured party." In the present case, the object was an agreement on controlling the use of financial means concluded between company A and the bank B, which aimed to protect the rights of third parties depositing money in the account.

107 The author critically evaluates especially the interpretation of the phrase "impact on the sphere of the injured party," because such a statement is very vague and does not provide sufficient protection from the possible liability of

[24] Loss of profit, development of the legal regulation and actual problems of finding the limits of the court's decision-making.
[25] The liability of the state for damage caused to an individual by the breach of the EC law.
[26] On the issue concerning conditions of liability for damage.

third parties. The author anticipates that the Supreme Court could have introduced a certain general duty of contractual provision, which could collide, as a consequence, with the general duty to prevention pursuant to Sec. 415 of the Civil Code.

9. T. Těmín, Odpovědnost za výrobek, [2004] *Právní rádce*, 18 et seq.,[27] Odpovědnost za škodu způsobenou vadou výrobku, [2004] *Právní rádce* 10/2004[28]

In both articles the author introduces the issue of product liability in Czech law. Both articles are of a very informative nature, pointing out practical issues. This is, however, to be expected in this kind of journal, entitled, *The Legal Advisor*. 108

10. J. Prchalová, Právní úprava odpovědnosti za škodu na životním prostředí – současnost a výhled do budoucna, [2004] *Právo a podnikání* 1/2004, 11, 12[29]

In a short overview the author presents the issue of environmental damage, in particular in respect to Czech contemporary legislation and the proposal of a European directive on environmental liability with regard to the prevention and remedying of environmental damage. 109

11. T. Tichá, Deliktní odpovědnost v ochraně přírody a krajiny, [2004] *Právo a podnikání* 12/2004, 7 et seq.[30]

The author deals with delict liability concerning the protection of nature and landscape in Czech environmental legislation, i.e. with the liability based on provisions of administrative and criminal law. 110

[27] Product Liability.
[28] Liability for damage caused by a defective product.
[29] Legal regulation of environmental liability – the present and future prospect.
[30] Delict liability in the protection of nature and landscape.

IV. Denmark

Vibe Ulfbeck

A. LEGISLATION

1 No new tort law legislation was introduced in 2004.

B. CASES

1. *Højesteret* (Danish Supreme Court, H) 27 May 2004, *Ugeskrift for Retsvæsen* (Weekly Law Report, U) U 2004. 3040/2 H (*Højesteret*, Supreme Court): Industrial injury

a) Brief Summary of the Facts

2 A, who was a bricklayer with 43 years of experience, was working for E. In connection with the erection of a building, A and his gang were to construct some window seats on the first floor. During the course of this work, A and another bricklayer carried 200–300 litres of cement up to the first floor over 1–2 days. A was carrying two buckets of cement when he suddenly felt a sharp pain in his back. The injury was later diagnosed as a slipped disc. A demanded damages from E for the loss of his ability to work. He claimed that the general organization of the work and the arrangement of the workplace did not comply with the general safety standards. Thus, no hoist had been available so A and the other bricklayer had been forced to carry the cement by themselves. Furthermore, there had been no instruction or supervision as to the amount of cement carried in the buckets.

b) Judgment of the Court

3 The court found that E had not been acting negligently by organizing the work in such a way that the cement had to be carried by the bricklayers. The court reached this conclusion by considering the nature and amount of work that had been performed. In the opinion of the court, there was no proof that the amount of cement carried in each bucket exceeded the maximum amount in the general safety regulations. Nor could it be considered negligent that the

employer had left it in the hands of an experienced bricklayer to perform simple and ordinary work of the kind in question without specific instruction or inspection. Consequently, E was acquitted.

c) Commentary

Under Danish law, it is the general rule that the liability of employers for industrial injuries is based on the negligence rule. Sometimes, however, the rule is applied in such a way that the liability of the employer in fact comes close to being a strict liability.[1] However, this case shows that the negligence rule is still viable in this area of the law. The case shows that, in relation to the duty of the employer to instruct the employee, not only the type of work in question but also the individual background of the employee can play a role. Thus, there is no doubt that it was decisive for the court not only that the work carried out was simple and ordinary work but also that A was a very experienced bricklayer. 4

2. *Højesteret*, 22 April 2004, U 2004.1866 H: Damages for loss of the ability to work

a) Brief Summary of the Facts

A, who was an accountant, started his own practice in 1990, but went bankrupt in 1992. In 1993 A had to undergo an operation which caused a brain infection. Consequently, A's intellectual capacity was reduced. Nevertheless, by the end of 1993, A started an accountant practice again and earned an amount in 1994 which exceeded the earnings of the years 1990–91. However, by the end of 1994, A was forced to permanently stop his practice because of the injury. It was later concluded that A had permanently lost his ability to work because of the brain infection. A claimed damages for this loss. The question was how to asses the loss, i.e. the value of A's ability to work at the time of the injury. According to § 7, sec. 1 of the Danish Liability Act[2], the loss is normally to be assessed by using the income of the year prior to the accident. However, according to § 7, sec. 2, "special circumstances" can justify an assessment at the discretion of the court. The parties agreed that in this case § 7, sec. 2 was to apply. However, there was disagreement as to whether the income figures of 1990–91 or of 1994 were relevant. A argued that the income figures of 1990–91 were irrelevant since A had only started his practice at that time whereas the income figure of 1994 had to be taken into account. The defendant held the opposite view, claiming that the income figure of 1994 was irrelevant. 5

b) Judgment of the Court

The court held that the income figure of 1990 was close to irrelevant since A had only started his practice this year. The income figure of 1991 had to be 6

[1] B.von Eyben/H. Isager, *Lærebog i erstatningsret* (5th edn. 2003), 148 et seq.
[2] Act No. 750 of 4 September 2002.

taken into consideration but only with some caution since the injury did not happen until 1993. Finally, the court held that the income figure of 1994 was relevant although it concerned the time after the injury. The reason given for this was that there was hardly any other information available that could serve as a proper basis for the assessment. Consequently, A was awarded damages calculated on the assumption of a yearly income for A of DDK 340,000 (approx. € 49,000).

c) Commentary

7 The reasoning behind the Supreme Court's decision seems to be an overall evaluation of the different annual earnings compared with the different reasons for these results. In particular it is worth noticing that the income of 1994 is regarded relevant as part of the basis of the assessment although the injury happened before this year. The fact that it is the general starting point under § 7, sec. 1 that it is the income of the year *prior* to the injury that is relevant does not prohibit an income from a later year from being taken into consideration under sec. 2.

3. *Højesteret*, 24 September, U 2004.2389 H: Construction work causing electrical cables to break

a) Brief Summary of the Facts

8 A constructor T had contracted with the owner, a consultant firm, B, to erect a building that could serve as a new office for B. The new building was to be located on the adjoining plot to B's current place of business. A subcontractor U was hired by T to tear down the old buildings. During the demolition two high tension lines belonging to NESA (supplier of electricity) were destroyed. This happened because U used an excavator to tear down the concrete foundation of the house although it had been pointed out that there was a risk that the cables were inside the concrete which turned out to be the case. The cut cable caused a power cut in several buildings in the area including the one belonging to B. Six days later a low tension line also belonging to NESA was cut by one of T's employees who used an excavator although he had been instructed to proceed by hand digging in the cable area. As a consequence of the cable cuts B's entire firm was without power twice. B claimed damages for loss of profits from T and U for the first power cut, and from T for the second one. T and U argued that since B was only indirectly injured he was not entitled to damages unless T and U had acted grossly negligently or to a considerable extent negligently.

b) Judgment of the Court

9 The court started out by stating that, according to general tort law rules, it is only the person who is directly injured who can claim damages. However, as regards the first incident, the court stated that, by using an excavator to remove the concrete with the high tension line attached to it, U's act had created "an obvious danger" of a power cut which could lead to a loss of profit for the

surrounding companies. Under these circumstances U and T were liable for B's loss. As regards the second power cut, the court found that the employees of T had acted "to a considerable extent negligently". The court also emphasised that it had been clear to T that a cut of this cable connecting B's firm with the electricity net would result in lost profits for B. Consequently both U and T were held liable.

c) Commentary

In Danish law it is the general rule that only the directly injured person can claim damages. The court starts out by referring to this rule and it is therefore clear that it is not the intention to give up the rule in general. In accordance with this, the court also clarifies the special circumstances of the case. In relation to U, it is decisive for the court that U, by his act, created "an obvious danger" of causing loss to enterprises located nearby. The court hereby uses the expression which has been applied in a number of other decisions[3] as a criterion for an act that is categorised as grossly negligent. Consequently, it must be assumed that, in the eyes of the court, U has acted with gross negligence. In relation to T it is specified that he acted negligently "to a considerable extent". Presumably hereby is meant that, although the act of T cannot be categorised as an act of gross negligence, it is still an act that reflects more than ordinary negligence. It is also emphasised that B's loss had been foreseeable to T. In other words, both defendants acted with qualified negligence and this is part of the reason why a claim is permitted. The other part of the reason is the fact that the injured party geographically was placed close to the place where the lines were cut. Thus, the decision only allows for damages to indirectly injured parties in a cable case under special circumstances. The criteria laid down by the court seem to be the degree of negligence and the geographical proximity of the place where the cable was damaged and the place where the loss was suffered. It is not clear to what extent these criteria will be applicable in other cases concerning indirectly injured persons. 10

4. *Højesteret*, 24 September, 2004, U 2004.1294 H: No liability for not taking an offer under EU-tender

a) Brief Summary of the Facts

The Danish mail service (*Post Danmark* (P)) sent out an invitation to submit tenders on delivering uniforms in accordance with EU Directive 93/96/EØF, stating that the order would go to "the economically most favourable" offer. A and B, along with several others, tendered for the delivery of the uniforms. P chose the bid from B and A submitted a complaint to the complaints board for tenders. The complaints board reached the conclusion that P had violated the rules for tenders. Consequently, A filed a lawsuit against P claiming damages 11

[3] Notably U 1995.737 H. See B. von Eyben/H. Isager (supra fn. 1), 351–354 and J. Nørgaard U 1996B.191.

for lost profit or alternatively for the expenses he had incurred by making the offer.

b) Judgment of the Court

12 The court started out by pointing to the fact that the formulation of the conditions according to which the order would go to "the economically most favourable bid" left P with a wide discretion as regards the selection of one of the offers. There was no basis for setting aside P's own estimate as to which offer was financially most attractive to P. Consequently, it was only in the event that A could prove that he would have got the contract had it not been for the violation of the (formal) tender rules that A could claim damages for lost profits. The court did not find sufficient proof that this would have been the case. As to A's alternative claim, the court found that there was no reason to believe that A would have refrained from giving an offer even if no mistake as to the formal tender rules had been made by P. Consequently P was acquitted.

c) Commentary

13 Under Danish law it has not been quite clear whether it is possible to achieve compensation for lost profits on the basis of a violation of tender rules.[4] The uncertainty has existed because it could be argued that it is not the purpose of the public law rules in this area (the tender rules) to protect private interests. The purpose is to achieve cost efficient contracts. This case is in line with other recent cases[5] assuming that private interests are in principle protected. Thus, although P is acquitted, this happens only because A is not able to prove that he would have got the contract had it not been for the mistakes made by P.

5. *Vestre Landsret* (Danish Court of Appeal, West), U. 2004.889 V: Inn responsible for food poisoning of guest

a) Brief Summary of the Facts

14 On 18 August 1997, A and his colleague B dined at an inn, K. They both had a beefsteak and they both became sick with diarrhoea the day after. B recovered within two days but A was hospitalized on 6 September with signs indicating food poisoning. Later on it was established that A had in fact been food poisoned by salmonella bacteria and also had been suffering from an infection in his joints which – according to medical experts – most likely had been caused by the salmonella infection. Due to A's special tissue type he was predisposed to develop this kind of infection following a salmonella infection. A sued K claiming damages based on the Danish Product Liability Act.[6] The question was whether there was sufficient proof that the beefsteaks had contained salmonella bacteria and that these bacteria had caused A's illness. Med-

[4] Orla Friis, in: Jens Gade et al., *Forvaltningsret, Almene emner* (4th edn. 2004), 582–583.
[5] See for example U 1999.11 H.
[6] Act No. 371 of 7 June 1989.

ical experts explained that in this case the most likely source of the type of salmonella infection in question was beef. A and B explained that the beefsteaks had been served "rare" whereas K maintained that the inn always served beef "well done". There was no technical evidence to establish whether or not the beef steaks served had in fact contained salmonella.

b) Judgment of the Court

The court started out by stating that, according to the Danish Product Liability Act, it was up to the plaintiff to prove that the meal had in fact contained salmonella bacteria and that these bacteria had caused the illness. The court found that the fact that both A and B became ill the day after the dinner at K together with the fact that beef according to the experts was the most likely source of the salmonella infection was sufficient to establish proof that the beef steak had contained salmonella bacteria. Secondly, the court also found that the fact that – according to the medical experts – it was most likely that the infection in the joints was caused by the salmonella infection was sufficient to establish proof of causation. Consequently, A was awarded damages. 15

c) Commentary

The case shows that although the burden of proof of the existence of a defect and of causation is on the plaintiff, the courts do not necessarily require technical evidence to regard the burden of proof as lifted by the plaintiff. An interesting issue which was not brought up in the case was the question of the significance of A's predisposition. Thus, it could have been argued by K that the infection in the joints suffered by A was an unforeseeable injury for which he should not be liable. However, under Danish law it is the general rule that "the tortfeasor must take the victim as he finds him". Therefore, it is not likely that K would have succeeded with this argument. 16

6. *Østre Landsret* (Danish Court of Appeal, East), U 2004.1439. Ø: Liability of real estate agents for incorrect estimation of the value of a house

a) Brief Summary of the Facts

A married couple, H and W, wanted a divorce. They therefore had two real estate agents (A1 and A2) estimate the value of their house. This task was difficult since the house was a unique house (*liebhaverejendom*) – not a standard type house. In September 2000 A1 estimated the value of the house to be DDK 5,950,000 (approx. € 850,000), whereas A2 estimated the value of the house to be DDK 6,250,000 (approx. € 893,000). When the couple was divorced in January 2001, H took over the house at an agreed (average) price of DKK 6,100,000 (approx. € 871,000). However, already in September 2001 H succeeded in selling the house at a price of DKK 10 million (approx. € 1,428,000). W now sued A1 and A2 claiming damages on the basis that A1 and A2 were liable under the general rule of negligence in Danish law because they had committed an error in estimating the value of the house. Alternative- 17 ly, W argued that A1 and A2 were liable under the Real Estate Act (the Act on the Sale and Acquisition of Real Estate)[7], § 24, sec. 2. According to this rule, the seller can claim compensation if the real estate agent has estimated the value of the house to a large extent incorrectly. An expert called by the court estimated that the value of the house in September 2000 would have been DKK 7,250,000 (approx. € 1,035,714).

b) Decision of the Court

18 The court started out by stating that it had not been proven that A1 and A2 in estimating the value of the house had committed any mistakes that could lead to liability under the ordinary negligence rule. The court then turned to § 24, sec. 2 in the Real Estate Act. The court found that, in judging whether the estimates of A1 and A2 had been to a large extent incorrect, it was relevant to compare these estimates with the estimate of the expert called by the court. Although there was quite a big difference between the results reached by A1 and A2 on the one hand and the expert called by the court on the other hand it also had to be taken into account that this was a unique house, the price of which could vary to a considerable extent dependent on which buyers were on the market. Considering these factors, the court found no basis for saying that A1 and A2 had estimated the value of the house to a large extent incorrectly. Consequently, A1 and A2 were acquitted.

c) Commentary

19 The case illustrates some of the difficulties in handling the rule in § 24, sec. 2 in the Real Estate Act. The difficulties consist in finding out when an estimate is "to a large extent" incorrect. In a previous case[8] concerning the interpretation of this paragraph, the court of appeal (west) held that an estimate which was 15–16% wrong was not "to a large extent incorrect". The above case hardly throws any light on where to draw the line. The real problem in this case was the fact that it concerned a unique house. This makes it even more difficult than in other cases to estimate the value of the house. It is however puzzling and open to critique that the court, without any real argument, just states the estimate of the expert witness and not the actual price achieved by selling the house in September 2001 which must form the basis of the comparison with the estimates made by A1 and A2.

[7] Act No. 453 of 30 June 1993 with later amendments.
[8] U 2002.1075 V.

C. Literature

1. V. Ulfbeck, *Erstatningsretlige grænseområder. Professionsansvar og produktansvar* (Copenhagen, 2004)

The aim of this book, "Borderline areas between contract and tort", is to present some borderline areas between contract and tort and to show that in these areas of the law problems are often solved independently of the distinction between contract and tort. The book is divided into two parts dealing with professional liability and product liability respectively. As regards professional liability, the book contains a description of the liability of different professional actors, notably the liability of lawyers, accountants, real estate agents, and banks but also construction and transport liability is dealt with. Throughout this part of the book the focus is on the extent to which it is possible for the professional actor to limit his liability towards his client by means of contract and to what extent there are extra-contractual requirements to the professional service provider that are immune to contractual regulations. The liability towards third parties is also dealt with. As regards product liability, the book starts out by generally introducing the growing impact of EU law on national product liability. It then focuses on four different topics comprising 1) the distinction between the liability for non-conforming products and product liability; 2) product liability disclaimers; 3) the development risk defence and 4) international product liability (product liability under CISG and product liability in relation to conflicts of laws). Throughout the part dealing with product liability contractual and tort law aspects of product liability are pointed out. 20

2. J. Rostock-Jensen/A. Kvist-Kristensen, *Produktansvar. Produktansvarsloven med kommentarer* (Copenhagen, 2004)

The book is mainly a commentary on the Danish Product Liability Act,[9] 1989 implementing the EU Directive on product liability but also contains an overview of the judge-made product liability law applicable as a supplement to the Act. The commentary gives a good and clear picture of the interpretation of the rules laid down in the Act and also contains numerous references to court decisions published as well as unpublished. In addition, several foreign decisions are referred to signalizing the EU background of the Act. 21

3. B. Gomard, Offentlige myndigheders erstatningsansvar (Liability of public bodies), [2004] *Ugeskrift for Retsvæsen, sektion B* (Weekly Law Report, section B), UfR2004B.383

In this article on the liability of public bodies, Gomard briefly outlines the development of the law in this area since 1946 and concludes that today it is assumed to be the general rule that public bodies are liable according to the 22

[9] Act No. 371 of 7 June 1989.

same principles as private persons, i.e. the rule that employers are liable for the negligent acts carried out by their employees in the course of their work. The article then goes on to describe how the liability of public bodies is often close to being a strict liability due to the application of a very objectified negligence standard. However, this is not always the case. In some areas of the law, notably in cases concerning the liability of public bodies exercising public authority, the liability seems to be mild. Liability is only imposed in case of clear mistakes. According to the author, this can be explained by the fact that the imposition of liability on public bodies exercising public authority does not serve a preventive purpose.

V. England and Wales

Ken Oliphant

A. Legislation and Official Reports

1. Civil Partnership Act 2004

The main purpose of the Act is to establish a regime of registered civil partnerships for same-sex couples, but it has important knock-on effects for fatal accident cases in tort. Three changes may be highlighted. First, the class of "dependants" entitled to damages for loss of dependency resulting from another person's wrongful death has been extended to include the deceased's civil partner or former civil partner, and any person *living as* the deceased's civil partner, in the same household, for at least two years up to the deceased's date of death.[1] Secondly, a person whom the deceased treated as a child of the family by virtue of a civil partnership also becomes a "dependant".[2] Lastly, the special statutory claim for bereavement damages (currently fixed at £10,000/€ 15,000)[3] now benefits civil partners as well as husbands and wives.[4] Unlike the claim for loss of dependency, this claim does not extend to merely cohabiting partners, whether same- or mixed-sex, no matter how long they have been together. The reforms are consistent with the Law Commission's view that there should be equality of treatment in this area as between same-sex and heterosexual relationships,[5] though the Commission's proposals for further extending the right to damages for loss of dependency[6] and bereavement[7] are still to be enacted. 1

[1] Sec. 83(2)–(3), amending Fatal Accidents Act 1976, sec. 1(3).
[2] Sec. 83(4), amending Fatal Accidents Act 1976, sec. 1(3).
[3] I have employed throughout a pound:euro exchange rate of 1:1.5.
[4] Sec. 83(7), amending Fatal Accidents Act 1976, sec. 1A(2).
[5] Law Commission, *Claims for Wrongful Death*, Consultation Paper 148 (1997), §§ 3.18–19 and 3.153; Law Commission, *Claims for Wrongful Death*, LAW COM No. 263 (1999), § 6.25.
[6] LAW COM No 263, § 3.46.
[7] Ibid., § 6.31.

2. Better Regulation Task Force, *Better Routes to Redress* (Cabinet Office Publications, London 2004)

2 A man driving his new Winnebago motor home set it on cruise control, then went into the back to make himself a cup of coffee; the vehicle left the highway, crashed and overturned – and the man successfully sued the manufacturers for failing to advise him not to leave the driving seat! More evidence of the excesses of our compensation culture? Well, no: just one of the myths, often perpetuated by an uncritical news media, that have grown up about the tort system, and are exposed in this new report by the Better Regulation Task Force, an independent advisory group supported by the Cabinet Office whose task is to advise the Government on matters related to regulation and its enforcement. The reality, the report claims, is that the number of accident claims has fallen: from over 600,000 in 2002/03, to around 550,000 in 2003/04 (p. 12). It must be said that this is a rather selective use of statistics, for accident claims had in fact risen in three of the four years to 2003/04 and – if disease claims are added to the equation – the total number of personal injury claims had risen for two successive years.[8] Nevertheless, the statistics do not provide any clear evidence of a litigation "explosion", despite the general perception to the contrary, and estimated tort costs as a percentage of gross domestic product are lower in the United Kingdom (0.6%) than in most other developed countries, including France (0.8%), Germany (1.3%), Italy (1.7%) and the United States (1.9%).[9] It is the perception of a compensation culture, however, that the Task Force highlights as the real issue to be addressed, though its analysis of the problems resulting from that perception is rather cursory, amounting to little more than an assertion that it encourages people to pursue misconstrued or trivial claims, and leads to over-cautious practice by potential defendants. The report suggests that the tide may now be turning as a result of the recent House of Lords' decision in *Tomlinson v Congleton Borough Council*,[10] which emphasised that people should be responsible for their own actions and anticipate risks. Nevertheless, the report makes a number of recommendations for Government intervention, including the official supervision and (if necessary) regulation of claims management companies, some of whom are alleged to have been guilty of unethical conduct in the past (e.g. by encouraging frivolous litigation). The report also recommends that the Government consider raising from £1,000/€ 1,500 to £5,000/€ 7,500 the financial threshold under which personal injury cases are presumptively to be tried by the informal small-claims process, in which – significantly (though the report does not note this) – successful claimants have no right to recover their legal costs from the other side. The hidden agenda here seems to be to remove the financial incentive for lawyers to foment trivial claims in the hope of nui-

[8] According to unpublished statistics from the Compensation Recovery Unit, whose figures were relied upon by the Task Force.

[9] Pg. 15, citing Tillinghast-Towers Perrin, *US Tort Costs 2000: Trends and Findings on the Costs of the US Tort System* (2002).

[10] [2003] *United Kingdom House of Lords* (UKHL) 47, [2004] 1 *Appeal Cases* (AC) 46, noted in H. Koziol/B.C. Steininger (eds.), *European Tort Law 2003* (2004), 132–5.

sance-value settlements, though the report mentions only the advantages to claimants of the less expensive and less stressful procedures.

3. Law Commission, *Pre-Judgment Interest on Debts and Damages*, Law Com No. 287 (The Stationery Office, London 2004)[11]

In a full review of pre-judgment interest, the Law Commission sought "to introduce a system ... that provides fair compensation to claimants without unduly penalising defendants and which encourages faith in the civil justice system by meeting the legitimate expectations of litigants" (§ 1.9). Its two main recommendations were that (1) there should be a specified interest rate set annually at 1% above the Bank of England base rate – to reflect the assumed cost of commercial borrowing – rather than the fixed rate of 8% routinely applied in practice, though courts would have a discretion to vary the rate in individual cases, and (2) the courts should have the power to award compound (rather than simple) interest in appropriate cases, for example, where large sums of money (£15,000/€ 22,500 or more) were involved. The Commission considered that compound interest better compensated claimants for being kept out of their money, whether it resulted in the incurring of commercial borrowing costs or the loss of investment income, as this was the measure of interest employed in the real world. However, the extra cost of calculating compound interest might not be justified in all cases, and the Commission considered that there should be no discretion to award compound interest in respect of personal injury damages for non-pecuniary loss (where a fixed rate of 2% applies): it was futile to look for precision in respect of losses which had no exact monetary equivalent, while compounding a rate as low as 2% would make little difference to the interest recovered – too little to justify the extra calculation costs. Personal injury damages for past pecuniary loss were to be subject to the general regime recommended by the Commission, which recognised that – where compound interest was awarded – this would necessitate a departure from the normal "half rate" approach to loss of earnings and other continuing losses spread evenly over the pre-judgment period (because simple interest increases linearly but compound interest increases exponentially). As interest is routinely calculated in practice with the aid of computer programmes, it should prove possible to do the appropriate calculations without any increase in costs. 3

[11] Available electronically at http://www.lawcom.gov.uk/files/lc287.pdf (accessed 1 May 2005).

B. Cases

1. *Chester v Afshar* [2004] *United Kingdom House of Lords* (UKHL) 41, [2005] 1 *Appeal Cases* (AC) 134, [2004] 4 *All England Law Reports* (All ER) 587: Negligent Failure to Warn of Treatment Risks; Causation[12]

a) Brief Summary of the Facts

4 The claimant was referred to the defendant neurosurgeon in connection with her severe, recurrent lower back pain. The defendant recommended the surgical removal of three intravertebral discs but did not, as the trial judge subsequently found, adequately inform her of the small risk – in the order of 1–2% – of serious neurological damage. The claimant agreed to undergo surgery, which the defendant performed three days later, but the risk of neurological damage materialised and the claimant suffered permanent partial paralysis. She sued for damages. At trial, the judge found that, although the defendant had conducted the operation with due care and skill, he had negligently breached his duty to inform the claimant of the risks involved in the proposed surgery, and had thereby caused her injury because she would not have consented to surgery at that time but would have discussed the matter with others and explored different options. The judge did not make any finding that she would not have undergone the surgery at a later date. The Court of Appeal affirmed the judge's decision.[13] The defendant appealed to the House of Lords.

b) Judgment of the House of Lords

5 The House of Lords dismissed the appeal by a majority of 3-2 (Lord Bingham and Lord Hoffmann dissenting). Lord Steyn, Lord Hope and Lord Walker started from the proposition that the claimant satisfied the "but for" test in that she would not have consented to surgery at the time the defendant had actually operated upon her if he had complied with his duty to inform her of the risk of serious neurological damage; even if she would in any case have consented to the operation at some later date, the chance of her suffering the same injury in *that* operation was still only 1–2%. However, her claim did not satisfy the "conventional" requirements of causation because the risk to which the defendant's breach of duty exposed her was no greater than that to which she would very likely have been exposed anyway. The breach of duty was a *causa sine qua non* of her injury but not the *causa causans*. Nevertheless, it was appropriate to depart from the conventional rules of causation for reasons of justice and public policy. If the claimant in such a case were to have no remedy, the doctor's duty to warn of treatment risks would be "a hollow one, stripped of

[12] Noted by Foster (2004) 154 *New Law Journal* (NLJ) 1644, Perry (2004) 154 NLJ 1711, and Stevens (2004) 121 *Law Quarterly Review* (LQR) 189.

[13] [2002] *England and Wales Court of Appeal (Civil Division)* (EWCA Civ) 724, [2003] *Queen's Bench* (QB) 356. Noted in H. Koziol/B.C. Steininger (eds.), *European Tort Law 2002* (2003), 152–4.

all practical force and devoid of all content."[14] Their Lordships noted that this was the outcome reached by the High Court of Australia on similar facts in *Chappel v Hart*,[15] a decision that had met with a large measure of academic approval.[16] They also derived support from the House of Lords' own recent decision in *Fairchild v Glenhaven Funeral Services Ltd*,[17] which showed that a modification of causation principles was permissible where justice and policy demanded.[18]

Lord Bingham and Lord Hoffmann, dissenting, argued that the but-for test was not in fact satisfied. The claimant had failed to show that, but for the defendant's negligent failure to warn, she would not have undergone surgery – only that she would not have undergone surgery on the given date – and the timing of the operation was irrelevant to the injury she suffered because it would have been as liable to occur whenever and by whosoever the operation was performed.[19] It was immaterial that the claimant, if properly warned, might have "changed the scenario in some irrelevant detail."[20] There was no justification for a special rule that departed from established principles of causation and effectively made doctors insurers against the materialisation of risks of which they had negligently failed to warn. 6

c) Commentary

Five aspects of this decision call for comment, the first relating to causation. The majority of the House of Lords thought that the but-for test was satisfied, but that the application of "conventional" principles of causation would nevertheless have precluded liability. It is not entirely clear what those principles are. Only Lord Hope offers any elaboration, observing that "to expose someone to a risk to which that person is exposed anyhow is not to cause anything."[21] But that is not so. Consider how the criminal law treats cases of pre-empted causation: is it a defence to murder for D1 to say that, if he had not pulled the trigger, D2 would certainly have done so? The question is who *actually* pulled the trigger, not who might have done so if things had worked out differently. Similarly, on the present facts, the question is whether the defendant's breach of duty caused her to undergo the actual operation in which she was injured, not whether she might have been exposed to the same risk in some hypothetical operation at some future point of time. That consideration is clearly relevant to the assessment of damages, but it does not negate (factu- 7

[14] § 87 per Lord Hope. See also §§ 24–25 per Lord Steyn and § 101 per Lord Walker.

[15] (1998) 195 *Commonwealth Law Reports* (CLR) 232. It is notable, however, that the High Court considered that the hypothetical future operation would probably have involved *less* risk to the plaintiff in that case.

[16] See, e.g., T. Honoré, Medical non-disclosure, causation and risk: *Chappel v Hart* (1999) 7 *Torts Law Journal* (Torts LJ) 32,

[17] [2003] 1 AC 32, noted in H. Koziol/B.C. Steininger (supra fn. 13), 144–50.

[18] § 23 per Lord Steyn. See also § 101 per Lord Walker.

[19] § 8, per Lord Bingham.

[20] § 31, per Lord Hoffmann. Cf. §§ 97–98, per Lord Walker.

[21] § 81.

al) causation. It is clear, for example, that the claimant would have been entitled to damages for the period between the actual and hypothetical operations if, by causing her to have the operation sooner than was necessary, the defendant had increased the duration of her loss.

8 Secondly, if they were not principles of causation, what were the "conventional" principles which – if applied – would have precluded liability? The House of Lords was clearly influenced by the consideration that the defendant's negligence had not increased the risks inherent in the surgical procedure that the claimant would inevitably, at some time, have undergone. But there is certainly no "conventional" way of reflecting that consideration in doctrinal terms, as is perhaps indicated by their Lordships' failure to cite any clear caselaw authority for what they had in mind at all. One possible approach would be to refer to the scope of the defendant's duty of care: the surgeon's duty was to inform the claimant of the known risks of the proposed treatment, and to take reasonable care in performing it, but he had no duty to safeguard the claimant from unavoidable risks associated with a procedure which the claimant was bound to undergo at some stage.[22] Alternatively, one might refer to the purpose of an award of damages: the aim of tort compensation is to put the claimant in the position she would have occupied if the defendant had complied with his duty. If the claimant cannot recover damages for an injury which she would have suffered anyway,[23] she should not be entitled to damages for being exposed to the risk of injury to which she would have been exposed anyway. There is some sleight of hand here, however, as the compensatory goal is normally expressed by reference to the position the claimant would have been in if she had not suffered *the injury*[24] or *the accident*.[25] To support the conclusion that the House of Lords assumed to be correct in principle, the formulation has to refer not to the injury or the accident – as the present claimant suffered an accidental injury she would otherwise have been very unlikely to suffer – but to the defendant's breach of duty.[26] That may well be a sustainable analysis, but the matter is far from being as obvious as their Lordships apparently believed.

9 Thirdly, the House of Lords majority relied upon an analogy with *Fairchild v Glenhaven Funeral Services Ltd* to justify their modification of conventional

[22] Cf. *Banque Bruxelles Lambert SA v Eagle Star Insurance Co Ltd* [1997] AC 191, where the House of Lords ruled that property valuers had a duty only to provide accurate information to their clients, and could not be held liable for losses attributable to fluctuations in the property market which they would have suffered even if the valuations had been correct.

[23] *Jobling v Associated Dairies Ltd* [1982] AC 794.

[24] See, e.g., *Jobling v Associated Dairies Ltd* [1982] AC 794, 820 per Lord Bridge.

[25] See, e.g., *Jobling v Associated Dairies Ltd* [1982] AC 794, 814 per Lord Keith, *Hodgson v Trapp* [1989] AC 807, 826 per Lord Oliver, *Lagden v O'Connor* [2004] 1 AC 1067, 1078 per Lord Hope.

[26] The classic formulation of Lord Blackburn in *Livingstone v Rawyards Coal Co* (1880) 5 *Appeal Cases* (App. Cas.) 25, 39 is ambiguous on this point as it refers to the defendant's *wrong*. (Does this refer to the defendant's breach of duty *per se* or to the breach of duty *and* the consequent injury?).

principles on grounds of policy, but the analogy is not entirely convincing. In *Fairchild*, there was no (but-for) causation but the defendant's breach of duty increased the risk of injury. In *Chester*, there was causation but no increased risk. A better analogy would be with *Baker v Willoughby*,[27] which is properly understood as a policy-motivated exception to the compensatory principle discussed above. The House of Lords there ruled that the victim of two successive (and independent) torts is entitled to full damages from the first tortfeasor even though the second tort would on its own have brought about the same loss. The aggregate of the two damages awards would otherwise fall short of the claimant's total loss.[28]

Fourthly, the policy consideration that weighed most heavily with the majority was that the doctor's duty to inform of treatment risks would otherwise be devoid of content. But once one accepts that, in principle, the patient has a good claim in respect of the notional intervening period between actual and hypothetical operations, this "hollow duty" argument rather loses its force. Furthermore, from the doctor's *ex ante* point of view, the duty clearly does have practical force as he is without doubt liable for his failure to inform if it is subsequently found that the patient would not have gone ahead with the treatment if made aware of the risks. 10

Lastly, the injury that is really attributable to the doctor's failure to warn in such cases is the patient's loss of autonomy and dignity, as the majority Law Lords seem to have accepted.[29] If that is the case, then why not compensate for it directly? In the House of Lords, it was only Lord Hoffmann who adverted to this possibility. He accepted that there might be case for "a modest solatium" for the affront to the patient's personality and subsequent feelings of grievance, but he was on balance opposed to the idea because there would be difficulty in fixing a suitable figure and the amounts in question would in any case be too small to justify the costs of litigation.[30] Others might not find these practical concerns so convincing, but there are major doctrinal impediments to such awards: liability in negligence cannot be established on the basis of mere injury to autonomy or dignity, while a failure to inform of treatment risks does not vitiate the patient's consent to what would otherwise be a battery (where such losses *are* compensated).[31] Having said that, however, if (as the House of Lords majority found) there was scope for a policy-motivated departure from conventional principles on the facts, maybe modification of one of *these* principles would have produced an outcome that better reflects the patient's true injury, and more consistently sanctions the doctor's failure to warn. As it is, the patient who would have gone ahead with the original treatment even if adequately informed of the risks has no claim at all, though his loss of autonomy 11

[27] [1970] AC 467.
[28] *Jobling v Associated Dairies Ltd* [1982] AC 794, 815 per Lord Keith.
[29] § 24 per Lord Steyn, § 77 per Lord Hope, and § 92 per Lord Walker.
[30] § 34.
[31] *Chatterton v Gerson* [1981] QB 432.

and dignity is the same, and the doctor's duty to inform is (in such cases) truly devoid of content.

2. *Gorringe v Calderdale Metropolitan Borough Council* [2004] UKHL 15, [2004] 1 *Weekly Law Reports* (WLR) 1057, [2004] 2 All ER 326: Liability of Highway Authority[32]

a) Brief Summary of the Facts

12 The claimant was driving too fast for safety on an undulating country road. When she reached the crest of a rise, it appears that she saw a bus coming towards her in the opposite direction and, perhaps thinking that it was on her side of the road, braked sharply causing her wheels to lock and her car to skid head-on into the bus's path. She suffered very serious injuries and was never able subsequently to give an account of the accident. She brought an action for damages against the defendant council, the relevant highway authority, alleging that it ought to have painted the word 'SLOW' on the road surface on the rise towards the crest. She contended that this duty arose either under the Highways Act 1980, sec. 41 (duty to maintain the highway), or at common law. In fact, the road had previously been marked with a 'SLOW' warning but that had disappeared, probably when the road was repaired seven or eight years prior to the accident. The claimant was successful at trial but the defendant council appealed successfully to the Court of Appeal,[33] which (by a majority) found that the council was not in breach of any duty to the claimant. The claimant appealed to the House of Lords.

b) Judgment of the House of Lords

13 The House of Lords unanimously dismissed the claimant's appeal. The defendant's statutory duty to 'maintain' the highway did not extend to the painting of warning markings on it, and related only to the physical condition of the road as such, as their Lordships had previously determined in the case of *Goodes v East Sussex County Council*.[34] The defendant's other statutory obligations in relation to road safety were neither enforceable by a private individual in an action for breach of statutory duty nor sufficient to give rise to a duty of care at common law. It was difficult, perhaps impossible,[35] to conceive of a case where a statutory duty which was not actionable in itself gave rise to a common law duty that would not otherwise have come into being. Lord Woolf, delivering the judgment of the Court of Appeal in *Larner v Solihull*

[32] Noted by Howarth [2005] *Cambridge Law Journal* (CLJ) 546 and Morgan (2005) 121 LQR 43.

[33] [2002] EWCA Civ 595, [2002] *Road Traffic Reports* (RTR) 446.

[34] [2000] 1 WLR 1356 (duty did not extend to gritting or salting the road to prevent the accumulation of ice or to the removal of snow). The decision was reversed by statute: Railways and Transport Safety Act 2003, sec. 111 adds to the duties owed under Highways Act, sec. 41 the duty "to ensure, so far as reasonably practicable, that safe passage along a highway is not endangered by snow or ice".

[35] In this, Lord Scott appears to have gone further than his fellow Law Lords: see § 71.

Metropolitan Borough Council,[36] had been wrong to say that common law liability might exceptionally arise "if an authority acted wholly unreasonably."[37] Recognition of a common law duty would be contrary not only to principle but also to policy because it would expose highway authorities to expensive and lengthy legal proceedings and the risk was that litigation costs would consume much of the road safety budget.[38] In fact, the policy arguments went the other way: as Lord Roger observed, "[b]y insisting that drivers always look out for dangers themselves and not rely on others, the law supports the overall policy of promoting road safety."[39]

c) Commentary

This decision continues the judicial fight-back against the perceived rise of a 'compensation culture', which so concerned the House of Lords last year in *Tomlinson v Congleton Borough Council*.[40] As in the earlier case, their Lordships clearly considered that the accident was essentially the claimant's own fault and that she should not be allowed to look to the defendant to protect her from her own wrong.[41] 14

The present decision reasserts the restrictive approach to the superimposition of common law duties on a statutory framework that was evident in *Stovin v Wise*,[42] where the leading majority speech was delivered by Lord Hoffmann, who also sat here. In the intervening years, a number of House of Lords decisions (notably *Barrett v Enfield London Borough Council*,[43] *Phelps v Hillingdon London Borough Council*,[44] and *W v Essex County Council*[45]) gave some reason to believe that a more expansive approach was coming to prevail. But these, we are now told, are to be regarded as turning upon the existence of factors that would give rise to a duty of care independently of the statutory context, for example, an assumption of responsibility for the claimant's welfare, or the creation of a source of danger. The House of Lords did not consider that, in the present case, the failure to paint a "SLOW" marking on the road amounted to the creation of a danger, though it accepted that there might be other, comparable cases where the contrary conclusion was warranted, Lord Brown giving the examples of a "crass mistake" in the painting of road markings indicating it was safe to overtake, and the signalling of a one-way street with no "No Entry" signs at the other end; such mistakes might "induce … a perfectly careful motorist into the path of danger."[46] However, their Lordships were notably unen- 15

36 [2001] RTR 469.
37 [2001] RTR 469, 475.
38 § 33, per Lord Hoffmann, and § 74, per Lord Scott.
39 § 82. Note also Lord Brown's cautionary words about the dangers of "warning overload" (§ 103).
40 [2003] UKHL 47, [2004] 1 AC 46.
41 See, e.g., § 8, per Lord Hoffmann, and § 100, per Lord Brown.
42 [1996] AC 923.
43 [2001] 2 AC 550.
44 [2001] 2 AC 619.
45 [2001] 2 AC 592.
46 § 102.

thusiastic about the Court of Appeal's decision in favour of the claimant in *Bird v Pearce*,[47] where it considered that the local highway authority had negligently created a hazard by removing and failing to repaint give-way markings at a junction of roads. Quite why this decision so troubled the House of Lords is hard to fathom: surely a clear indication of who has priority at a road junction is one of the most basic expectations of modern road-users, and the absence of such markings an obvious source of danger even to careful drivers. *Bird* seems a far stronger case for liability than Lord Brown's example of a crass mistake in the painting of overtaking markings: all drivers know that, whether overtaking is permitted or not, they should only overtake if they have a clear view of the road ahead and sufficient time and space to do so.

16 The present decision confirms the tendency of the House of Lords, when seeking to rein in the scope of liability in negligence, to fall back on the "no duty" argument. This was also their Lordships' approach in the *Tomlinson* case last year. In my commentary to that decision in *Yearbook 2003*, I argued against the "no duty" approach as "an unnecessary complication which pre-empts the truly important questions: whether the defendant acted reasonably and whether and to what extent the accident can be attributed to the claimant's own conduct."[48] These comments are equally applicable to the present decision. Their Lordships might doubtless have reached the same conclusion by other means, for example, by ruling that there was insufficient evidence of fault on the defendant's part, or that the claimant had, by her driving, voluntarily assumed the risk of the accident (*volenti non fit iniuria*). Indeed, the *volenti* doctrine offers a far more transparent mechanism for upholding notions of personal responsibility in the law, which the House of Lords saw as a crucially important task. The "no duty" argument acknowledges these notions only implicitly, not expressly, and reinforces the claimant's responsibility for the accident only by denying or diluting the defendant's. In addition, it is a rather blunt tool, which (as noted above) threatens to absolve local highway authorities of responsibility for matters of basic road safety even in circumstances where their neglect would expose quite careful drivers to unreasonable danger.

17 What is more, relying on the "no duty" response in claims against public authorities is somewhat akin to shutting the stable door after the horses have bolted. By sec. 6 of the Human Rights Act 1998, public authorities have a duty to act compatibly (or "not incompatibly") with the Convention rights[49] of others, and – at least in the jurisprudence of the European Court of Human Rights – it is well settled that the effective protection of those rights may require positive action on the part of a public authority. There is no mention of this at all in *Gorringe*, which in one sense is unsurprising as the claimant's accident occurred before the Act came into effect. But might one not have ex-

[47] [1979] RTR 369.

[48] H. Koziol/B.C. Steininger (supra fn. 10), 134.

[49] I.e. those rights under the European Convention for the Protection of Human Rights and Fundamental Freedoms that are specified in Schedule 2 of the Act. In effect, the term covers all the substantive rights under the Convention.

pected some acknowledgement that their Lordships' decision reflected a broader legal context that no longer exists today, and that it may shortly have to be re-evaluated in the light of the changed circumstances?

3. *Fytche v Wincanton Logistics plc* [2004] UKHL 31, [2004] 4 All ER 221: Strict Liability; Statutory Interpretation

a) Brief Summary of the Facts

The claimant was employed by the defendant company as the driver of a milk tanker. During a spell of exceptionally wintry weather in the South of England, his tanker got stuck on an icy country road. The company's standard instructions in such circumstances were to telephone for assistance and wait in the cab, but the claimant decided to dig himself out of the snow. With the assistance of the cowman of the farm from which he was collecting, he worked for three hours in sub-zero temperatures before finally succeeding in freeing the tanker. Unfortunately there was a tiny hole in one of the boots that the defendants had supplied to him as personal protective equipment (PPE). His foot got wet and he suffered frostbite in his right little toe. He was consequently off-work for a number of months and his toe became permanently sensitive to cold. He claimed damages on the basis of his employer's breach of duty both at common law and under various statutory regulations, but his claim failed at every stage below the House of Lords. In the House of Lords, he relied exclusively on the employer's obligation under reg. 7(1) of the Personal Protective Equipment at Work Regulations 1992, which read (insofar as is relevant) as follows: 18

> Every employer shall ensure that any personal protective equipment provided to his employees is maintained (including replaced or cleaned as appropriate) in an efficient state, in efficient working order and in good repair.

The claimant's boots, which incorporated steel toe caps, were supplied so as to protect him in case a milk churn or some other heavy object should fall on his toes, not to keep his feet dry in the wet or to protect against extreme weather conditions.

b) Judgment of the House of Lords

Dismissing the claimant's appeal by a majority of 3-2, the House of Lords ruled that the obligation under reg. 7(1) was impliedly limited by its context. The words "in good repair" had to be construed by reference to the risk or risks in respect of which the employer was required (by reg. 4) to supply PPE. The regulation did not impose an absolute obligation on the employer to effect repairs which had nothing to do with the equipment's protective function. As the toe caps were to protect against the risk of impact injuries, and the claimant was not expected to do work which required him to have waterproof boots, the existence of a hole did not constitute a breach of the obligation to keep the boots in good repair. 19

20 Dissenting, Lord Hope and Baroness Hale considered that the absence of limiting words in reg. 7 indicated that the phrase "in good repair" was not intended to be subject to qualification. In fact, this was supported by consideration of the statutory context, for the regulations elsewhere spoke of the employer's duty to take account of "any risks which the equipment itself may create" in assessing its suitability (reg. 6(2)b)). The obligation to keep the equipment in good repair therefore required the employer to keep it free of defects which affected its ability to protect the employee not only from the risks which triggered the duty to supply PPE, but also from those risks that the equipment created itself. The risk of water penetration through the hole in the claimant's boot was such a risk. Policy considerations also supported such a conclusion. Strict liability ensured compensation for workers if health and safety legislation failed in its primary purpose of protecting against injury, and its value would be reduced if the employee had the burden of proving that the risk that eventuated was one the equipment should have guarded against. Additionally, the regulations left all the choices about the provision, use and maintenance of PPE to the employer, and required the employee to use the equipment provided in the manner the employer prescribed. In the circumstances, it was the employer, not the employee, who should bear the risk that PPE supplied for one reason should turn out to have an incidental defect which caused the employee an injury at work.

c) Commentary

21 The majority reasoning is consistent with the generally restrictive approach of English law to strict liability. It was common ground that the employer would have been liable irrespective of fault if the toecap had failed to provide the necessary protection against impact injuries. But the scope of the employer's absolute duty was to be construed narrowly, and limited to defects which prevented the equipment performing its protective function; the liability did not extent to incidental defects. For Lord Hoffmann, the contrary result would have been "very strange and arbitrary".[50] As he noted, the question of liability would not have arisen if there had been no risk from heavy objects and the claimant had accordingly been supplied with ordinary boots without steel toe caps: the boots would not then have been PPE. Against that, there was the argument raised by Lord Hope that, once the boots were classified as PPE, the employee had no option but to use them in the manner prescribed: the whole matter was predetermined for him by the regulations and the employer's assessment of the risks.[51] Lord Hoffmann considered that this did not distinguish the claimant from employees who are contractually obliged to use their employers' non-PPE equipment,[52] but – as Lord Hope responded – they are at least free to bargain with the employer about the equipment's terms of use, which is not an option where the duty is laid down by statute.[53]

[50] § 7.
[51] § 42.
[52] § 20.
[53] § 42.

Lord Hoffmann also considered that the claimant's argument would produce absurd results in other cases. He posited this example: in a noisy workshop, the employer provides earmuffs which guard against hearing loss, and fits them with radios so that employees who so wish can listen to music while they work.[54] If the radios break down and the employer fails to repair them, does he commit an offence under the regulations? That to Lord Hoffmann would be "absurd". It was quite different from the case in which the equipment had created its own risk, for example, where the radio's volume control was defective and exposed employees to ear-splitting surges in sound. This is certainly a challenging example, which supports the reading of the phrase "in good repair" as subject to some implied qualification, and the dissenting opinions do not contain any convincing response to it. One possible answer is that the radio was separate equipment incorporated in the earmuffs, to which they were an unnecessary add-on, whereas Mr Fytche's toecaps had necessarily to be incorporated in the rest of the boot which therefore formed an indivisible whole. Alternatively, "good repair" in the regulation could be taken to refer to freedom only from dangerous (as opposed to merely qualitative) defects. 22

The effect of the majority's reasoning is that, where PPE suffers from an incidental defect, the employer will be strictly liable under the regulations if the defect itself creates a risk of injury which materialises (e.g. where a safety helmet has a chinstrap that causes dermatitis), but not if it merely fails to guard against an external risk, as in the present case. One can well understand that an employee such as Mr Fytche might well have difficulty appreciating the point of the distinction and its fairness. But the truth is that English law does not recognise a general strict liability for employment-related injuries and such strict liabilities as do exist form part of no rational scheme. Until such a scheme is developed, anomalous distinctions are inevitable, and removing one will simply result in its replacement with another, as Lord Hoffmann convincingly illustrated with his comparison of employees injured respectively by PPE and non-PPE equipment. 23

4. *Campbell v MGN Ltd* [2004] UKHL 22, [2004] 2 AC 457, [2004] 2 All ER 995: Privacy[55]

a) Brief Summary of the Facts

The defendant's newspaper, the Daily Mirror, published a front-page story about the internationally-known fashion model, Naomi Campbell, under the headline, "Naomi: I am a drug addict". Additional pages were given to the story inside. In generally sympathetic and supportive tones, the newspaper recounted how the model was attending regular Narcotics Anonymous (NA) meetings in an effort to overcome her addiction. The story was accompanied by photographs of the model in the street on her exit from the meeting place. 24

[54] § 19.
[55] Noted by Morgan (2004) 120 LQR 563.

The pictures were taken by a freelance photographer employed by the newspaper for that very purpose. In at least one of the pictures, the building in which the meeting had taken place was clearly identifiable, though the article itself did not name the venue. The source of the newspaper's information was never confirmed. On the same day the articles were published, Campbell commenced proceedings against the defendant, claiming damages for breach of confidence and compensation under the Data Protection Act 1998. (It was later accepted that the latter claim stood or fell with the former.) The newspaper's response was to publish more stories and photographs, this time highly critical of the model. Prior to these events, the claimant had made repeated public denials that she had used illegal drugs.

25 At first instance, Morland J found for the claimant on both heads of her claim and awarded her £2500/€ 3750 in compensatory damages, plus £1000/€ 1500 in aggravated damages in respect of the newspaper's coverage of her after she had commenced proceedings.[56] The defendant appealed successfully to the Court of Appeal.[57] The claimant then appealed to the House of Lords.

b) Judgment of the House of Lords

26 The House of Lords allowed the appeal by a majority of 3-2 and restored the decision of Morland J. The newspaper was entitled, as the claimant conceded, to put the record straight about her addiction to drugs and to reveal the fact that she was receiving treatment for it. But its printing of details about the therapy, including NA's role in its provision, and its use of photographs of the claimant leaving the NA meeting place, went beyond what was proper to correct the claimant's false statements and lend its correction credibility, and amounted to a breach of confidence. This additional information was private and imported an obligation of confidence.[58] Contrary to the view of the Court of Appeal,[59] it concerned what was – or was tantamount to – medical treatment.[60] The next question was whether the revelation of that private information was justified by the right to freedom of expression. Their Lordships adopted the approach inherent in artt. 8 and 10 of the European Convention for the Protection of Human Rights and Fundamental Freedoms, which treated the right to privacy and the right to freedom of expression as of equal value, with neither afforded primacy, and allowed interference with the one to protect the other only to the extent that was necessary. Ultimately, the question was one of proportionality. The majority accepted that newspapers should be allowed a proper degree of journalistic margin, but on the facts this consideration was outweighed by the distressing nature of the intrusion into the claimant's private life in circumstances in which she needed privacy in order to successfully address her addiction. Recovering addicts could easily lose their

[56] [2004] *England and Wales High Court* (EWHC) 499.
[57] [2002] EWCA Civ 1373, [2003] QB 633.
[58] § 95 per Lord Hope, § 147 per Baroness Hale, and § 165 per Lord Carswell.
[59] [2003] QB 633, 659.
[60] §§ 97–99 per Lord Hope.

resolve and relapse,[61] and the revelation of details about the claimant's treatment threatened to set back seriously her recovery.[62] She would be deterred from going back to the meeting place identifiable from the photographs, and would no longer view NA as a safe haven.[63] (For Lord Hope, it was the photographs that tipped the balance.[64])

27 The minority Law Lords (Lord Nicholls and Lord Hoffmann) adopted the same general approach but considered that the additional information to whose publication the claimant objected was not private because it was so "unremarkable and consequential" upon what she accepted could lawfully be put into the public domain that it could not reasonably be distinguished from it. Even if the information did retain a private character, the claimant's privacy was outweighed by considerations of free speech: the invasion of her privacy was comparatively minor, and allowed the newspaper to add colour and conviction to a legitimate and sympathetic story.

c) Commentary

28 This is the first occasion on which the House of Lords has explicitly protected a claimant's right to privacy by way of the remedy for breach of confidence. The development was widely-anticipated,[65] and all members of the House accepted that the remedy could be employed to protect private information even when it had not been acquired in the course of a confidential relationship. (Lord Goff in *Attorney General v Guardian Newspapers Ltd (No 2)*[66] had previously argued for exactly that.) The only wonder is that the development was so long in coming: it was the English law on breach of confidence, and in particular the leading case of *Albert v Strange*,[67] that Warren and Brandeis famously argued in 1890 provided the basis for a new tort of invasion of privacy,[68] with a decisive influence on the subsequent development of American tort law.

29 The defendant's stories were published after the Human Rights Act 1998 had come into effect, but that does not seem to have had any material effect upon the outcome of their Lordships' deliberations. With the exception of Baroness Hale,[69] no member of the House relied upon the court's duty under the Act as a public authority to act compatibly with the claimant's Convention right to

[61] § 144, per Baroness Hale.
[62] § 157 per Baroness Hale, and § 169 per Lord Carswell.
[63] §§ 153 and 155 per Baroness Hale.
[64] § 121. Lord Carswell explicitly declined to isolate which aspect of the publication tipped the balance: § 170.
[65] See, e.g., Phillipson, Transforming Breach of Confidence? Towards a Common Law Right of Privacy under the Human Rights Act, (2003) 66 *Modern Law Review* (MLR) 726.
[66] [1990] 1 AC 109, 281.
[67] (1849) 2 *De Gex & Smale's Chancery Reports* 652, (1849) 64 *English Reports* 293.
[68] The Right of Privacy, (1890) 4 *Harvard Law Review* 193.
[69] § 132.

privacy.[70] Furthermore, although by sec. 12 of the Act the House was obliged to "have particular regard to the importance of the Convention right to freedom of expression", it did not consider that this gave the right under art. 10 of the Convention priority over that under art. 8. The two rights were of equal weight and qualified each other, and the court's task was to strike a balance between them. To Lord Nicholls, the nomenclature "breach of confidence" was "misleading", and "[t]he essence of the tort is better encapsulated now as misuse of private information."[71] In his opinion, the competing considerations should be addressed explicitly by an approach reflecting the structure of art. 8, rather than by application of the traditional requirements of the English cause of action, namely, that (i) the information was confidential, (ii) the defendant owed an obligation of confidence, and (iii) he made unauthorised use of it. Under art. 8, one asked first whether the published information was within the sphere of the claimant's private or family life, before proceeding to consider whether interference with the claimant's private or family life was justified by (amongst other things) the need to protect freedom of expression. His Lordship's analysis here is wholly persuasive, and – though some vestiges of the traditional terminology are apparent[72] – his fellow Law Lords in fact approached the case on broadly the same basis.

5. *Barber v Somerset County Council* [2004] UKHL 13, [2004] 1 WLR 1089, [2004] 2 All ER 385: Liability for Work-Related Stress[73]

30 This case warrants a brief note, being a successful appeal to the House of Lords from one of the four cases before the Court of Appeal in *Hatton v Sutherland*,[74] on which I reported in *Yearbook 2002*.[75] The claim was one for psychiatric illness attributable to employment-related stress. Having taken on new responsibilities in his employment with the defendant council, the claimant complained of overwork and took time off on grounds of stress. On his return, he met with the senior management team to discuss his workload and health, though nothing material was done to remedy the situation. Some months later, the claimant had a mental breakdown which resulted in his taking early retirement. He brought an action for damages and succeeded at trial, but the Court of Appeal concluded that the judge had been wrong to find the defendant employer in breach of its duty of care. The House of Lords (Lord Scott dissenting) allowed the claimant's appeal on the basis that the trial judge had been

[70] Lord Hoffmann stated that the Act provides "a guarantee of privacy only against public authorities" (§ 49) and wholly failed even to acknowledge the by now well-established argument that the Act, by treating the courts as public authorities, requires them to develop existing causes of action so as to protect Convention rights. Lord Nicholls touched on the issue but observed that it was unnecessary to decide whether the court's duty extended to questions of substantive law as distinct from questions of practice and procedure (§ 18).

[71] § 13, 14.

[72] See, e.g., §§ 88–89 per Lord Hope (asking "was the information confidential?" and concluding that there was "an obligation of confidence").

[73] Noted by Brodie (2004) 33 *Industrial Law Journal* 261 and Njoya (2005) 121 LQR 33.

[74] [2002] EWCA Civ 76, [2002] 2 All ER 1.

[75] H. Koziol/B.C. Steininger (supra fn. 13), 155–7.

entitled to form the view that the defendant's senior management team had breached its duty of care. Though it was not a clear case of a flagrant breach of duty, neither was it an obviously hopeless claim, and there was insufficient reason for the Court of Appeal to set aside the judge's finding. The House of Lords emphasised that it was the judge who had seen and heard the witnesses. The decision turned entirely on questions of fact, and the law was assumed throughout to have been as stated by the Court of Appeal. No further comment is necessary.

C. Literature

In addition to the items highlighted below, readers should note several significant additions to the journal literature on tort in 2004. These included articles on the theoretical foundations of liability for negligently-inflicted harm,[76] as well as work on more particular issues in the law of negligence such as liability for psychiatric damage,[77] wrongful conception,[78] and negligent misstatement.[79] There was also renewed consideration of the thorny question of English negligence law's compatibility with the European Convention of Human Rights.[80] Other notable contributions to the journal literature dealt with governmental liability,[81] breach of statutory duty,[82] inducing breach of contract,[83] strict liability,[84] vicarious liability,[85] tort law and insurance,[86] and feminist tort theory.[87] 31

Amongst the new editions of existing books that appeared last year,[88] it is necessary to highlight the 10th edition of Tony Weir's *Casebook on Tort*,[89] which 32

[76] N. Jansen, Duties and Rights in Negligence: A Comparative and Historical Perspective on the European Law of Extracontractual Liability, (2004) 24 *Oxford Journal of Legal Studies* (OJLS) 443; N.J. McBride, Duties of Care – Do They Really Exist?, (2004) 24 OJLS 417.

[77] D. Nolan, Psychiatric Injury at the Crossroads, [2004] *Journal of Personal Injury Law* 1; P. Case, Secondary Iatrogenic Harm: Claims for Psychiatric Damage Following a Death Caused by Medical Error, (2004) 67 MLR 561.

[78] B. Golder, From *McFarlane* to *Melchior* and beyond: Love, sex, money and commodification in the Anglo-Australian law of torts, (2004) 12 Torts LJ.

[79] S. Middlemiss, The Truth and Nothing but the Truth? The Legal Liability of Employers for Employee References, (2004) 33 ILJ 59.

[80] T. Hickman, The 'Uncertain Shadow': Throwing Light on the Right to a Court under Article 6(1) ECHR, [2004] *Public Law* 122.

[81] D. Nolan, Suing the State: Governmental Liability in Comparative Perspective, (2004) 67 MLR 844.

[82] K.M. Stanton, New Forms of the Tort of Breach of Statutory Duty (2004) 120 LQR 324.

[83] A.P. Simester/W. Chan, Inducing Breach of Contract: One Tort or Two?, [2004] CLJ 132.

[84] J. Murphy, The Merits of *Rylands v Fletcher*, (2004) 24 OJLS 643.

[85] R. Weekes, Vicarious Liability for Violent Employees, [2004] CLJ 53.

[86] J. Morgan, Tort, Insurance and Incoherence, (2004) 67 MLR 384.

[87] J. Richardson, Feminist perspectives on the law of tort and the technology of risk, (2004) 33 *Economy and Society* 98.

[88] See also P. Giliker/S. Beckwith, *Tort* (2004).

[89] T. Weir, *A Casebook on Tort* (10th edn. 2004).

the author has announced will be the last. This has been a hugely stimulating if rather idiosyncratic resource since its first appearance in 1967, and its dry, acerbic wit has enlivened the subject for generations of students – and their teachers. In his final preface, however, the tone is one of frustration and grim foreboding, as Weir gloomily predicts that the United Kingdom's accession to the European Community will prove to be the crucial influence on its tort law in the coming years. He comments (p. vii):

> the transfer of supreme legislative and judicial power to bodies theretofore foreign involves the abandonment of the worldwide unity of the English-speaking common law ... There will be no more editions of this Casebook: predictable developments might well be too painful to relate.

Not all readers of this *Yearbook* will agree with these sentiments, but I am sure that they will join with me in hoping that Weir will find alternative outlets for the expression of his trenchant and provocative views in the future.

1. Gert Brüggemeier, *Common Principles of Tort Law: A Pre-Statement of Law* (British Institute of International and Comparative Law, London 2004)

33 This is a revised and updated version of a book previously published in German.[90] By means of a comparative account of German and US tort law, the author seeks to lay the foundations for the identification of principles of *transnational* tort law. His vision goes beyond a common *European* tort law, for "[t]he internationalization of legal communication cannot stop at the external borders of the EU" (p. 36). Hence the choice of the US, rather than (say) England, as the common law comparator – a choice one may say that is abundantly justified by the greater range of doctrinal solutions that is to be found in a country with 50 separate state jurisdictions, to say nothing of the extensive and wide-ranging scholarly literature. After an introductory essay, Brüggemeier considers in Part One of his book the foundations of tortious liability (protected interests, fault *versus* strict liability, causation, etc.), before turning in Part Two to various "complementary rules", including what common lawyers would call the law of damages, contributory negligence and other defences, civil procedure, and insurance. The book's analytical framework is based upon German legal categories, but this does not generally get in the way of its accessibility to common lawyers as the relevant principles are clearly explained with pertinent comparative comments. Throughout, the author displays a formidable grasp of American as well as German materials (and others too!). All in all, this is a very welcome addition to the English-language literature on comparative tort law.

[90] *Prinzipien des Haftungsrechts. Eine systematische Darstellung auf rechtsvergleichender Grundlage* (1999).

2. Carol Harlow, *State Liability: Tort Law and Beyond*, Clarendon Law Lectures (Oxford University Press, Oxford 2004)

As a leading authority on public law who has also written widely on the law of tort,[91] the author is ideally-positioned to write about State liability, which was in fact the subject of her doctoral dissertation and first published monograph.[92] This 149-page volume presents the revised text of a series of lectures delivered at Oxford University in October 2003, and – as befits such origins – the pace is fast and the style informal, with rhetorical impact sometimes taking precedence over academic rigour. Harlow issues a powerful warning against extensions of the State's tortious liabilities, for which there is an ever-increasing demand in what she, adopting the popular terminology, calls our "compensation culture". As she explains, this demand is stimulated by the "cascade effect of globalization", in which developments in one legal system come to trigger change in others. Here, Harlow fingers the "forum shopping" that is frequently a part of litigation over mass torts as a particular source of pressure – and also the growing influence of transnational courts and tribunals (notably the European Court of Justice and the European Court of Human Rights) which compete with each other to develop new and more powerful remedies. The result, she claims, has been to impinge on the resources that are available to the State for the satisfaction of collective needs. Her prescription is for government and the legislature to take more responsibility for the specification of compensation entitlements, so as to facilitate a move *beyond* tort law to the provision of (limited) compensation via statutory and administrative schemes. Whether or not one agrees with Harlow's conclusions, there is certainly much here to inform, interest and provoke. 34

3. Pat O'Malley, *Risk, Uncertainty and Government* (Glasshouse Press, London 2004)

In the last 20 years or so, there has been an explosion in the sociological literature on risk, exemplified by Beck's analysis of "risk society" and Ewald's of *l'état-providence*. O'Malley is a leading member of the second generation of risk theorists, and this important book gathers together a number of his published articles, some considerably revised. There are also four new chapters, including a very helpful introduction which provides an excellent, and accessible, overview of the existing literature. In this, law is just another technique for dealing with risk and uncertainty – to be considered alongside (for example) insurance – but tort law in particular provides fertile ground for the application of risk theory, and O'Malley's second chapter ("From Independence to Social Security") contains suggestive analyses of the standard of reasonable foresight, the introduction of strict product liability ("a risk-based technique for distributing the cost of harms socially"), and the general international trend to displace tort in favour of social insurance in respect of workplace ac- 35

[91] The third edition of her introductory text, *Understanding Tort Law*, was published in January 2005.

[92] C. Harlow, *Compensation and Government Torts* (1982).

cidents. Other chapters deal illuminatingly with contract law, insurance and criminal justice. Throughout the author highlights how different configurations of risk and uncertainty lend themselves to varying political conceptions of the responsible individual. On occasion, his legal analysis may strike some lawyers as a little thin, and over-reliant on a narrow range of sources, and a few minor errors have crept in, but O'Malley must ultimately take great credit for pointing his legal readers towards new ways of understanding such fundamental institutions as tort and insurance.

4. Jenny Steele, *Risks and Legal Theory*, Legal Theory Today (Hart Publishing, Oxford 2004)

36 This timely and impressive volume is the first to treat themes in modern "liberal" legal theory with systematic reference to the recent sociological literature on risk, to which O'Malley (see review, above) is one of the most influential contributors. In Part I of the book, Steele summarises the "four perspectives on risk" that will inform her later analysis. In Part II, the most substantial, she considers a number of contributions to tort law scholarship in which notions of risk have played a crucial role, with special focus on the work of Priest, Honoré and Ripstein, before turning to Dworkin's analysis of hypothetical insurance markets in his recent work on equality and distributive justice. Part III is concerned with environmental law, which – as the author notes – has become a particular testing ground for risk analyses. From a tort lawyer's viewpoint, it is disappointing that the focus here is almost exclusively on regulatory approaches to environmental risk, with little or nothing on responsibility for those risks that materialise. Still, Steele has plenty of interesting and perceptive things to say about the tort theories she discusses in the second part of her book, and argues persuasively that the differences between them often reflect different perspectives on risk, which is identified by some as a phenomenon to be controlled by insurance-derived techniques, and by others as the underlying basis for the imposition of tortious liability. The former approach has a considerable amount in common with sociological analyses which view risk in the aggregate, concern themselves with statistical regularities, and seek to manage it prospectively. The latter, by contrast, looks backwards to particular decisions taken by free individuals, and is concerned with responsibility and remedy rather than regulation and control. It is ultimately this approach to risk, Steele argues, that has greater relevance for liberal legal theory, though existing analyses of responsibility for outcomes have tended to assume – erroneously – that it precludes consideration of distributive issues.

5. Christian Witting, *Liability for Negligent Misstatements* (Oxford University Press, Oxford 2004)

37 This appears in the OUP list of practitioners' titles but it clearly also aspires to being viewed as an academic monograph. It offers an in-depth, comparative survey of tortious liability for negligent misstatements in the common law,

dealing in turn with misstatements causing physical damage ("directly" and "indirectly"), and misstatements causing pure economic loss. Witting's starting point in discussing the latter is the great case of *Hedley Byrne & Co Ltd v Heller & Partners Ltd*,[93] but he rightly emphasises that the House of Lords' reasoning suffers from a number of analytical inadequacies when seen in retrospect. In his view, the defendant's conscious assumption of responsibility towards the claimant is one, but only one, of the factors that determine whether the necessary relationship of proximity exists between the parties; liability can arise even in the absence of a conscious assumption of responsibility and the phrase 'assumption of responsibility' is potentially misleading if employed in circumstances where the court *attributes* responsibility to the defendant on other grounds. The book deals accurately and informatively with the law in England and Wales, Canada, Australia and New Zealand, and contains much very helpful analysis, but it may be regretted that the comparative analysis does not extend to the civil law world – especially given the author's involvement in this Centre's own work in the past.[94] Nevertheless, this new volume deserves to become a reference point for some considerable time to come for those interested in tortious liability for negligent misstatements under the law of England and Wales and the other treated jurisdictions.

[93] [1964] AC 465.
[94] W. van Boom/H. Koziol/C. Witting, *Pure Economic Loss* (2004).

VI. Estonia

Irene Kull[1]

A. LEGISLATION

1. Introduction

1 The present system of Estonian private law consists of various acts that were enacted into law over different periods of time. Despite the fact that the many separate areas of private law have not all been enacted by passage of a single legal act – such as a comprehensive civil code – the Estonian civil law is a codified system, based on the pandectic model of the civil code. The civil law was reformed step by step, gradually proceeding to a legal system based on current developments in modern European private law. In 1993, the Law of Property Act[2] entered into force as the first new source of civil law, followed by the General Part of the Civil Code Act[3] and Family Law Act[4] in 1994. The Commercial Code, which primarily deals with commercial enterprises and business organisations, was passed in 1995, to be followed by the Law of Succession Act in 1996. The last part of the codified civil law was the Law of Obligations Act (*Võlaõigusseadus*, LOA) which entered into force in 2002 together with the new General Part of the Civil Code Act. The Law of Obligations Act aims at creating as homogeneous a regulation as possible in the whole area of the law of obligations, including, *inter alia*, provisions for special contracts and extra-contractual obligations, including provisions of tort liability. The Law of Obligations Act is the most important act regulating compensation of damage in cases provided in LOA and in other legal acts unless otherwise provided by these acts. In addition to the LOA, there are a number of independent statutes containing special provisions dealing with rather narrowly defined tortious situations.

[1] I would like to thank Dr. Heikki Leesment for correcting the text.

[2] Law of Property Act, 9 June 1993, [1993] *Riigi Teataja* (RT, State Gazette) I, 39, 590; consolidated text [1999] RT I, 44, 509, entered into force on 1 December 1993. Available in English: http://www.legaltext.ee/et/andmebaas/ava.asp?m=022.

[3] General Part of the Civil Code Act, 27 March 2002, [2002] RT I, 35, 216.

[4] Family Law Act, 12 October 1994, [1994] RT I, 75, 1326. Available in English: http://www.legaltext.ee/et/andmebaas/ava.asp?m=022.

2. Law of Obligations Act[5] of 26 September 2001, [2001] *Riigi Teataja* (RT)[6] I, 81, 487; [2002] RT, 53, 336; [2003] RT, 78, 523; [2004] RT, 13, 86

The LOA consists of a general part dealing with problems common to all obligations, which is followed by parts addressing various types of contracts, the law of torts, unjustified enrichment, actions taken without authority and public promises to pay. Provisions regarding liability for unlawful infliction of loss or injury are drafted generally on the model of the German BGB. Chapter 53 of LOA, which regulates the unlawful causing of damage, consists of general provisions (§§ 1043–1055), liability for risks created independent of fault (§§ 1056–1060) and liability for defective products (§§ 1061–1067). The LOA system of tort liability is a system of fault-based liability with a rebuttable presumption of fault. The general basis for contractual liability provided by LOA is similar to the approach taken in Art. 8:108 Principles of European Contract Law (PECL) and Art. 79 UN Convention on the International Sale of Goods (CISG), which is based on so-called control liability. According to this rule (§ 103 LOA), a party's non-performance is excused if the party proves that the failure is due to an impediment beyond its control and that it could not reasonably have been expected to take the impediment into account at the time of the execution of the contract, or to have avoided or overcome the impediment or its consequences. The employer's liability for his or her employees does not allow exculpation as in the German BGB. 2

Provisions of tort liability are not independent and self-sufficient provisions of the LOA but must often be read in conjunction with the General Part of the LOA. Some important illustrations may be pertinent at this point. The general rules concerning compensation of damage are regulated in the general part of LOA (§§ 127–140), such as the definition of fault (§ 104); the question of contributory negligence of the victim which makes the obligation to compensate the negligent plaintiff depend on what proportion of the injury has been caused predominantly by the one or the other party (§ 139); the manner of compensation for damage (§ 136) which allows monetary compensation for injury to body or health, for the deprivation of liberty, in cases provided by law or by contract and in other cases where money damages are reasonable under the circumstances; limits on compensation for damage (§ 140) which allows the court to reduce the amount of compensation if compensation in full would be grossly unfair with regard to the obligated person or not reasonably acceptable for any other reason; compensation for non-pecuniary damage (§ 134) for damage arising from deprivation of liberty or violation of a personal right, in particular by defamation, the wrongful death of a person or infliction of serious bodily injury or damage to one's health, or property destruction or loss. It must be pointed out that the general right to claim 3

[5] In force from 1 July 2002. Available in English: http://www.legaltext.ee. The most important Estonian legislative acts are available in English at: http://www.legaltext.ee.

[6] RT (State Gazette).

monetary compensation for non-pecuniary damage is still disputable in cases not directly provided by law.

4 Similar to the French *Code Civil*, the regulation of torts in Estonia as an extra-contractual obligation is based on the general provision requiring compensation for damage, supplemented with provisions concerning specific types of liability. According to § 1043 LOA, a person (tortfeasor) who unlawfully causes damage to another person (victim) shall compensate for the damage sustained if the tortfeasor is guilty of causing the damage or is liable for causing the damage pursuant to law. Interests protected by law (§ 1045 LOA) are similar to those enumerated by § 823 I BGB but unlike the German law the list of interests is merely illustrative[7]. The infliction of damage is unlawful if, above all, it results in death, bodily injury, or damage to the health of the victim, deprives the victim of liberty, violates a personal right, such as right of ownership or a similar right or right of possession of the victim, interferes with the economic or professional activities of a person, violates a duty arising from law or is intentional behaviour contrary to good morals. For an action based on torts the following requirements must be satisfied – there must be a violation of rights or interests which is both unlawful and culpable (intentional or negligent) and a causal link between the defendant's conduct (which can be an act or omission) and the plaintiff's resulting harm as defined in law. Sec. 104 of LOA consists of the definitions of carelessness, gross negligence and intentional conduct. Pursuant to § 104 LOA, carelessness is the failure to exercise necessary care and gross negligence is a material and substantial failure to exercise the necessary care. Thus, the general definition of negligence stresses an objective standard of care. Definitions of carelessness and gross negligence are based on the same objective theory of fault contained in the German BGB (§ 276). For liability in tort the LOA enacts the concept of subjective fault taking into account the situation, age, education, knowledge, abilities and other personal characteristics of a person (§ 1050 (2) LOA).

5 Compensation for damage arising from the violation of contractual obligations cannot be claimed on the basis of tort law provisions (chapter 53 LOA), unless otherwise provided by law. Damages claims for violation of contractual obligations may be filed on the basis of provisions in chapter 53 LOA if the objective of the violated contractual obligation was not intended to prevent the damage for which compensation is claimed. If the death, bodily injury or damage to the health of a person is caused as a result of the violation of a contractual obligation, the tortfeasor shall be liable for such damage on the basis of tort liability provisions.

6 If damage is caused as a result of a danger characteristic to a thing constituting a major source of danger or from an extremely dangerous activity, the person who manages the source of danger shall be liable for causing damage regardless of the person's fault. A person who manages a major source of danger

[7] This opinion is still disputable.

shall be liable for causing the death of, bodily injury to or damage to the health of a victim, and for damaging property of the victim in all events. Special provisions of LOA also provide liability for those in possession of motor vehicles, owners of dangerous structures or things, owners of land under a structure or persons who have rights in real property on the basis of which the structure is created, and keepers of animals.

Provisions regulating liability for defective products (§§ 1061–1067 LOA) 7
have their origin in the European Directive on general safety of products (2001/93/EC) and the Directive on the Harmonization of laws on liability for defective products (Directive 1999/34/EC of the European Parliament and of the Council of May 1999 amending Council Directive 85/374/EEC on the Approximation of the Laws, Regulations and Administrative Provisions of the Member States Concerning Liability for Defective Products).

3. State Liability Act[8] of 2 May 2001, [2001] RT I, 47, 260

On 1 January 2002 a new law entered into force governing the bases of and 8
procedure for the protection and restoration of rights violated upon the exercise of powers of public authority and performance of other public duties, and compensation for damage caused (State Liability Act). In addition to the State Liability Act, the provisions concerning compensation for damage also apply to claims for compensation caused by the exercise of public authority, unless otherwise provided by law and if it is not in conflict with the nature of public law relationships.

The liability of the state for damage caused upon the exercise of powers of au- 9
thority is construed under principles of strict liability except in the case of compensation for loss of income. A loss defined under this Act is defined as direct proprietary damage and loss of income. Apart from compensation for proprietary damage, the injured party has the right to claim non-proprietary injury upon wrongful degradation of dignity, damage to health, deprivation of liberty, violation of the sanctity of home, private life or confidentiality of communications, or defamation of honour or good name of the person. Loss of income is not compensated if the person liable to compensate for the lost income proves that he or she is not at fault in causing the damage. A person whose rights are violated by the unlawful activities of a public authority may claim compensation for damage caused to the person if damage could not be prevented and cannot be eliminated by the protection or restoration of rights in some other manner provided in law. In addition to the injured person, third persons are entitled to claim compensation for related expenses incurred, such as loss of support and non-proprietary damage upon the causing of death or a bodily injury or damage to health on the bases provided by private law.

[8] State Liability Act is available in English: http://www.legaltext.ee/et/andmebaas/ava.asp?m=022.

10 Proprietary damage shall be compensated in money. Compensation shall create the financial situation in which the injured party would have been, had his or her rights not been violated. If the injured party suffers a bodily injury or impaired health, he or she may claim compensation also for expenses caused thereby.

11 The right to be compensated for damage covers, first of all, unlawful decisions made by a government authority, breach of a duty to act and make a decision within a statutory time limit, inactivity, undue delays in the proceedings and other unlawful violation of the rights and interests of natural and legal persons protected by law. The Act also includes special cases of state liability, such as damage caused by legislation of general application, proprietary damage caused by a lawful administrative act or measure which in an extraordinary manner restricts the fundamental rights or freedoms of the person, damage caused in the course of judicial proceedings and extrajudicial hearing of matters concerning administrative offences.

12 Both the actions of public authority which cause damage as well as the failures to act or refusal to take measures in due course entitle injured persons to compensation for the resulting damage. Any damage caused directly by a natural person performing the functions of a public authority, regardless of whether the functions are performed on the basis of a service relationship, contract, single order or on another basis, is deemed to be damage caused by the public authority.

4. Public Service Act of 25 January 1995, [1995] RT, I, 1995, 16, 228; consolidated text State Gazette I, 1999, 7, 112

13 The Public Service Act regulates the liability of a public official as a result of a breach of duties for damage wrongfully caused to the state or local government in whose agency the official was employed at the time the damage was caused. The Act provides that compensation paid by the state or local government for damage caused to a third party as a result of a breach of duties is deemed to be damage caused to the state or local government by the official. If damage is caused by several officials jointly, each official shall be liable to the extent corresponding to his or her fault. The amount of compensation is determined on the basis of the economic situation of the official, the extent of damage as compared to the salary of the official, the assessment of the risk of causing damage arising from the nature of duties, lack of experience objectively arising from the length of service, the service-related orders and instructions issued to the official, and other circumstances which would render compensation for damage by the official in full unfair. Liability of the official is restricted in case of non-intentional cause of damage to six times the amount of the total salary and additional remuneration.

5. The Compensation for Damage Caused by the State to Persons by Unjust Deprivation of Liberty Act[9] of 11 June 1997, [1997] RT I, 48, 775; [2001], 47, 260; [2002], 56, 350; 61, 375

Another important legislative act *lexis specialis* is the Act extending liability to the state for unjust deprivation of liberty of persons who were held in custody with the permission of a court and criminal proceedings which were terminated at the stage of pre-trial investigation or in a preliminary hearing, or persons with regard to whom a judgment of acquittal has entered into force; persons who were detained on suspicion of a criminal offence or released when the suspicion ceased to exist; persons who were held in prison and whose judgment of conviction has been annulled and criminal proceedings in whose matters were terminated or persons with regard to whom a judgment of acquittal has been entered; persons whose period of imprisonment has exceeded the term of the punishment imposed; persons with regard to whom unfounded coercive psychiatric treatment has been ordered by a court in connection with the commission of an unlawful act provided for in the Penal Code and the court ruling has been subsequently annulled; persons who served detention and the judgment ordering detention has been annulled; and persons who were unjustly deprived of liberty by a decision of an official authorised to deprive persons of liberty without conducting disciplinary proceedings, misdemeanour proceedings or criminal proceedings if such proceedings were compulsory. State liability for unjust deprivation of liberty is based on strict liability which means that damage could be compensated regardless of the guilt of an official. 14

The injured person has the right to compensation for each twenty-four hour period during which the person was unjustly deprived of liberty. The amount of compensation must be calculated on the basis of daily rates as specified in the Act (§ 5). If an application for compensation is denied or is not reviewed, the person may file an action with an administrative court to compel the payment of compensation under the conditions provided by law. 15

In the case of unlawful decisions of public authorities, unlawful arrests or other forms of deprivation of personal liberty, in addition to compensation for time unlawfully restrained, the injured party is also entitled to compensation for proprietary damage caused by the unjust deprivation of liberty. Loss of profit and other non-pecuniary damage caused thereby are deemed to be compensated by payment of compensation provided for in the Act. The amount of compensation for direct pecuniary damage is determined in accordance with the provisions of the State Liability Act. 16

[9] Available in English: http://www.legaltext.ee/et/andmebaas/ava.asp?m=022.

B. Cases

1. *Riigikohus* (State Court), 10 December 2003, No. 3-2-1-125-03, RT III, 06.01.2004, 1, 9: Legal Malpractice, Pecuniary Damages

a) Brief Summary of the Facts

17 In August 1997 a sales contract for purchase of real estate was duly notarised by a notary. Following notarisation, the appropriate register entry was made into the Land Register and the buyer became the lawful owner. At the closing of the sale, the seller was not present, being instead represented by a person purporting to be the legal representative of the seller under power of attorney. The alleged legal representative of the seller was also the buyer. In 2001, the previous owner of the real estate sued the notary, claiming that she had never authorised anyone to sell her real estate on her behalf and that the power of attorney submitted to the notary was false and fraudulent. The prior owner claimed that the notary failed to establish the authenticity of the power of attorney presented by the buyer, and thereby violated her official duties as required by law. The previous owner claimed damages of EEK 1,000,000 (€ 64,102), the market value of the real estate as compensation for the loss of ownership.

b) Judgment of the Court

18 The State Court of Estonia decided that Art. 20 (1) of the Notaries Act[10] which was in force at the time of these events and until February 2002 (the liability of the notary is broader and more expansive under Art. 14 (1) of the New Notary Act[11] in force from 1 February 2002) provides that a notary is answerable for direct pecuniary damage resulting from wrongful acts performed by the notary either intentionally or through gross negligence. For the notary to be liable, the actions of the notary must be wrongful and performed either intentionally or with gross negligence, and result in injury to another. There must also be a direct causal link between the wrongful act and the resulting loss. The Supreme Court found that the act of the notary – notarising the transaction without establishing the validity of the power of attorney purportedly validated by a foreign official – was grossly negligent. The Court also stated that the causal link between the wrongful act and the resulting injury must not always be direct, but could also appear as the causal chain of events initiated by the tortfeasor's wrongful act. The plaintiff must prove that without the wrongful act of a notary, the consequences of the causal chain could have been avoided. Since the Notary Act provides for liability of notaries for wrongful acts performed intentionally or due to gross negligence, the counterclaim of the notary to reduce the amount of damages was dismissed.

[10] Notaries Act, 17 June 1993, [1993] RT I, 45, 640.
[11] Notaries Act, 6 December 2000, [2000] RT I, 104, 684.

c) Commentary

The decision of the Supreme Court was one of the more controversial ones at that time. It demonstrated to the public the general proposition that professionals who fail to perform their duties with proper care are liable for the consequences of their acts. The professional duties of notaries were set forth in detail in the Notary Act of 1993, which is applicable to the present case. This Act provided that notaries shall confirm and consummate the transactions of parties only after the submission of all necessary documents and the payment of all prescribed sums of money. Prior to notarial certification of a transaction, a notary shall assess the passive and active legal competence and the capacity to exercise the will of the persons who are parties to the transaction. If a transaction is made through a representative, a notary shall assess the legal authority of the representative. A notary shall refuse to perform a notarial act if documents submitted for performance of the notarial act do not meet these requirements. The Notary Act in force in 2002 contained only general provisions regarding liability. The obligations of a notary concerning powers of attorney and other authorisations of representation are regulated in greater detail in the new Notarisation Act[12] (2003). The current Act provides that a notary shall refuse to perform a notarial act if the notary is not satisfied of the legality and genuineness of a submitted power of attorney. A document submitted in order to prove the right of representation for one of the principals shall be appended to a notarial deed as an original or as a copy thereof. If a notary cannot establish or doubts the lawfulness of the purported representation, and certification of the transaction is requested regardless of that fact, the notary shall indicate such fact in the notarial deed. In the commented case, the power of attorney submitted to the notary was executed abroad and was not legalised by Estonian officials. The mere certification by an official of a foreign state and attachment of an apostil is not sufficient if notarial certification is required by Estonian law and international agreement or treaty does not prescribe otherwise. The decision of the Supreme Court of Estonia in this case is part of the ongoing development of the law towards expanding the scope of the duty to compensate parties for losses caused by the providers of legal services. At present, all law professionals (except judges and prosecutors) are obligated to carry compulsory civil liability insurance in order to provide legal services to the public. 19

2. *Riigikohus*, 11 February 2004, No. 3-2-1-11-04, RT III, 03.03.2004, 6, 66: Defamation; Non-Pecuniary Loss

a) Brief Summary of the Facts

The plaintiff was a chairwoman of the condominium association whose activities were criticised in articles anonymously published in a local newspaper in 2002, under the title "The Hard Life of Some Condominium Association 20

[12] Notarisation Act, 14 November 2001, [2001] RT I, 93, 564. Available in English: http://www.legaltext.ee/et/andmebaas/ava.asp?m=022.

Chairmen or an Answer to Letter of Roza Romanko" ("Mõningate korteriühistu esimeeste raskest elust ehk vastus Roza Romanko kirjale") and "Gaping Hole in Estonian Laws" ("EV seadustest vaba tsoon"). She claimed that her honour, dignity, reputation and good name were besmirched by these articles and therefore sued the publisher for non-pecuniary damages (€ 1282). The plaintiff also demanded the publication of a retraction at the defendant's expense. The trial court held that there was no violation of personal rights and that the plaintiff failed to prove her claim for damages. The circuit court awards the plaintiff damages in the amount of € 641. The Supreme Court dismissed the case entirely.

b) Judgment of the Court

21 The judgment of the Supreme Court was based on the old General Part of the Civil Code Act which was in force in 2002 (enacted in 1994) which provides that in cases of defamation a person has the right to demand, through the courts, termination of the defamation, retraction of defamatory materials, and compensation for moral and pecuniary damage caused by the defamation, unless the defamer proves the accuracy of the published information. The Supreme Court analysed prior precedents in defamation cases and stated that there are two kinds of defamation – by inaccurate information and/or defamation by way of value decisions. If there is a text which provides information about facts, these facts could be examined and the plaintiff could prove that these facts are incorrect. If the information reported by the defendant about the plaintiff is untrue, the court can order that the inaccurate information be retracted in the same way and with the same prominence with which the defamatory report was published. If the opinion of the defendant was given as a value decision which deprecates the plaintiff's personality and has negative meaning in the Estonian culture, there is no claim for retraction of the wrongful information. Deprecation of the personality of the plaintiff could be considered to be defamation if there is no basis in fact for that kind of negative evaluation. The Court pointed out that for deprecation to constitute defamation, it must be directed to one certain person and not be directed to people generally and that insignificant defamation does not deserve compensation in money. Defamation also depends on the circumstances of the publication and requires the careful weighing of competing societal values.

22 In addition, the Court considered it necessary to note that in order for the plaintiff to be entitled to monetary damages for non-pecuniary injury to her honour and dignity, the plaintiff must nevertheless prove the injury and show how that injury manifested itself. For the Court to award monetary damages, it is not enough to simply allege that the defendant violated the rights of the plaintiff. In each such case the Court must concretely establish whether any such injury has in fact been inflicted which requires compensation by monetary means. In matters alleging the violation of personal rights, non-pecuniary injury to the plaintiff may be presumed, but every insult does not provide cause for awarding monetary damages since the fact that the Court has considered the given matter

and issued a final decision on the merits of the case may be sufficient to redress the injury suffered by the plaintiff. Such injury may be reflected in substantial inconvenience or discomfort, adverse impact upon the plaintiff's personal life or her interpersonal relationships, or significant damage to her reputation in the community. Monetary damages cannot be awarded simply for mental anguish, embarrassment and temporary loss of self-esteem caused by the defamation. However, when the publication entails release into the mass media of egregiously offensive or outrageous materials, there is reason to presume that the reputation and standing of the plaintiff has been substantially injured.

c) Commentary

This decision is important in the development of Estonian law regarding defamation since it provides essential guidance for both courts and the legal community in matters involving demands for monetary compensation of non-pecuniary injuries. The Supreme Court has also clarified the burden of proof of the parties in dispute over compensation of non-pecuniary damage. It is possible to summarise the principal points made by the Court regarding legal redress for injury to one's honour and reputation. First of all, the plaintiff must convincingly prove that prior to the insulting publication at issue, she enjoyed good standing and had a good reputation in the community. Second, the plaintiff must prove that the publication has, in fact, caused damage and injury to her standing. It is not simply to be assumed that the plaintiff enjoyed a position of respect and good standing in the community. The Court has distinguished and differentiated the two types of value judgments to be made regarding non-pecuniary injury: personal and societal. Considering injury from the personal perspective, injuries are to be presumed in all cases of violation of personal rights since the emotional state of the plaintiff has been adversely impacted. To prove such injury, the Court considers it sufficient that the plaintiff prove the utterance of the statements at issue and provide some basis for why it should be considered insulting or degrading. In such cases, the injury can usually be adequately redressed without resort to monetary damages by ordering the defendant to terminate the defamation and/or compel the publication of a suitable retraction. In order to justify the award of monetary damages, the plaintiff bears the burden of proving particular facts and circumstances flowing from the defamation, which would allow the court to consider whether the award of monetary damages as compensation for non-pecuniary injuries can be justified in the given case. In cases of defamation, among the relevant matters for the courts to consider are the manner in which the defamatory publication took place, its reach and scope, the nature of the material, and many other such material considerations. If the court concludes, from its review of the evidence presented that cessation of the defamatory actions, retraction and/or apology are insufficient to compensate the plaintiff for the injury sustained, it should determine the appropriate amount of monetary damages to fully compensate the injured party. The award of monetary damages is an expression of the community's denunciation of the unlawful acts of the defendant and placates the sense of injustice to the injured party. 23

3. *Riigikohus*, 23 December 2003, No. 3-2-1-152-03, [2004] RT III, 3, 35: Non-Pecuniary Damages

a) Brief Summary of the Facts

24 Two well-known Estonian architects were winners of a competition to design a new community centre for one of Estonia's many small islands. Following selection of the winning design, a contract was concluded with another architectural firm for completion of technical and structural drawings. Thereafter, another competition was announced for the selection of contractors and preparation of detailed plans and specifications for construction. The architects who won the design competition did not participate in this last competition, since they assumed that construction plans and specifications would certainly be ordered from them. The job of preparing detailed construction plans and specifications was instead given to the builder. It later became apparent that the detailed construction plans and specifications deviated substantially from the original design submitted by the winners. The disappointed architects brought legal action against the local governing body of the small island, claiming non-pecuniary damages on the basis of § 12 subs. 1 par. 3 and 4; § 13 subs. 1 par. 10 and § 14 Copyright Act[13] in the amount of € 12,820 (EKR 200,000).

b) Judgment of the Court

25 The trial court determined that there was no basis for an award for non-pecuniary damages. The plaintiffs contended that the community centre as built deviated so substantially from their submitted design that they did not want their names associated with the project. They were, however, unable to specify to the satisfaction of the court exactly what rights of theirs had been violated by the hall being built as constructed and the precise nature of the deviations from their design. The circuit court agreed with the trial judge and affirmed the decision of the lower court. The Supreme Court was not, however, in agreement with the circuit court, reversed the decision and remanded the matter to the circuit court for a new hearing. The Supreme Court included in its decision guidance regarding the legal issues to be considered in retrial. At the retrial, the circuit court concluded that the personal non-pecuniary rights of the design architects had been violated since the revisions made during construction materially altered the concept and architectural integrity of the original design. The circuit court entered an award of damages on behalf of the plaintiffs and dismissed the counterclaim of the local governing body seeking for reduction in the amount of damages. The Supreme Court again overturned the decision of the circuit court and remanded the case for a second retrial. The Supreme Court considered that the circuit court had failed to consider the scope and character of the injury claimed by the architects in addressing the issue of non-pecuniary damages, as well as the level of culpability of the alleged tortfeasor. The amount of monetary damages must be ascertained from

[13] Copyright Act, 11 November 1992, [1992] RT I, 49, 615; consolidated text [2000] RT I, 16, 109. Available in English: http://www.legaltext.ee/et/andmebaas/ava.asp?m=022.

the particulars of the violation, its extent and scope, and the conduct of the parties. Since the plaintiffs decided not to be engaged with the client and building contractor in the construction plan completion phase, deviations and departures from their original design concepts were unavoidable. The actions of the plaintiffs contributed to the outcome. In light of these considerations, the Court concluded that the demands of the plaintiffs for monetary damages to vindicate their asserted violation of rights in the design of the building are reasonably resolved by an award of € 3,205 to be shared by both (EEK 50,000).

c) Commentary

This case is important primarily for its development of legal standards applicable to compensation for non-pecuniary injury. The judgment of the Supreme Court recognizes that even small changes in the design can be violations of the creator's personal rights. During the trial, the issue of whether the submitted design was an appropriate architectural solution responsive to the situation of the building on a small island and the needs of the community was argued on several occasions. The Court concluded, however, that the architect, as the author of the creative design, comes within the reach and protection of laws regarding creative and artist works. Were he not to come within the umbrage of these laws, the creative achievement of the architect would not receive the public recognition it deserves. Likewise, the unauthorized distortion and alteration of the architect's design invites public disrespect of the architect and his body of work. 26

See, in this respect, § 12 Copyright Act, which sets forth the interests that must be considered in matters of rights of authorship. In contrast to violations of other types of personal rights, in matters such as the present case, courts have to consider the impact of their decisions on professional standing and the public repute of all classes of artisans involved in the creative process. Loss of respect and standing manifests itself in several ways, including condemnation by colleagues, clients and critics, doubts about the artist's honesty, etc. In Estonian court cases we find a growing body of case law involving claims for damages for violations of rights of authorship. At the same time, comparing the experience of Estonia with that of many other countries in issues of compensation for non-pecuniary injury, we can safely say that Estonia prefers to compensate non-pecuniary injury to a greater extent than our neighbours – whereas other countries have widely endorsed the concept of restitution-in-kind, Estonian courts have primarily resorted to the award of single payment money damages. Our court cases reveal, however, that there is no one and universally applied standard for determining the amount of money damages. The court decisions under review will most certainly influence future court cases in their calculation of money damages. 27

C. Literature

1. I. Kull/M. Käerdi/V. Kõve, *Võlaõigus I. Üldosa* (Law of Obligations I. General Part) (Juura, Tallinn 2004)

28 This is a first textbook written in Estonian and based on the Estonian Law of Obligations Act (2002), court practice and legal doctrine. The textbook consists of general principles of the law of obligations, performance of obligations, remedies, general principles of compensation for damage, securities, termination of obligations, transfer of claims and obligations and plurality of persons in obligations. The authors comment on the Law of Obligations Act and corresponding theoretical analyses based on comparative research and illustrate with examples from Estonian court practice and court practice from other European countries.

2. J. Lahe, The Concept of General Duties of Care in the Law of Delict, [2004] *Juridica International* 1, 108–115

29 The author explains and analyses the main problems relating to general duties of care. The first part of the article focuses on why the concept of general duties of care should be recognised at all – what its meaning is in the law of delict. The second part discusses the nature and substance of general duties of care. In the third part of the paper, the author tries to answer the question of how the derivation of unlawfulness from a violation of general duties of care affects the general structure and relationship of elements of delict. The author considers the distinction between violation of general duties of care and neglect in the form of failure to exercise the care required in ordinary social intercourse, tackled in the last part of the article, to be the most intriguing issue discussed in this article. As a violation of general duties of care results in unlawful behaviour, the question of a distinction between carelessness and the violation of general duties of care can also be regarded as one of distinction between fault and unlawfulness.

3. J. Lahe, Lepingueelsete kohustuste ning eellepingu rikkumisest tulenev tsiviilõiguslik vastutus (Civil Law Liability Pursuant to the Infringement of Pre-contractual Obligations and Preliminary Contracts), [2004] *Juridica* 10, 681–687

30 With the entering into force of the Law of Obligations Act on 1 July 2002, a regulation on pre-contractual obligations and preliminary contracts was introduced into Estonian positive law. There is still no clarity, however, as to whether to apply the general rules for breach of obligations or delict law as the basis for a compensation claim for damages pursuant to the infringement of pre-contractual obligations or of preliminary contracts. In analysing the relevant provisions of the Law of Obligations Act, the author adopts the position that liability following the infringement of pre-contractual obligations is delictual liability.

4. M. Kingisepp, Scope of Claim for Consequential Damage in Delict Law, [2003] *Juridica International* 1, 203–210

The purpose of the article is to analyse the question of the scope of claims for compensation of damage in delict law from the position of the persons whose damage consists of consequential damage only. The author therefore first tries to explain which damage may be treated as consequential damage and to point out the differences between consequential damage and direct damage. The analysis that follows mainly focuses on the circumstances and conditions under which the payment of or refusal to pay compensation is justified in the case of consequential damage. The discussion is structured mainly according to the modern legal principles generally accepted in Europe, the regulation of the Estonian Law of Obligations Act, as well as the traditions common to current judicial practice. 31

5. T. Tampuu, Riskivastutus ja tootja vastutus võlaõigusseaduses (Strict liability and producer's liability in the Law of Obligations Act), [2003] *Juridica* 3, 161–168

The author explores the nature of strict liability and its specific features in comparison with liability based on fault as well as the content, extent and purposes of strict liability. Also, the author analyses the definition of source of major danger, examines the circumstances precluding strict liability and matters related to the entitled and obligated subjects of strict liability. The author's comments are illustrated with numerous examples. In addition, an overview is given of the provisions of Chapter 53 Division 3 of the Law of Obligations Act regarding the liability of a producer, which is a mixture of fault-based liability and strict liability and is based on the Council Directive 85/374/EEC. 32

6. T. Tampuu, Deliktiõiguslik vastutus teise isiku tekitatud kahju eest (Delict law liability for damage caused by another person), [2003] *Juridica* 7, 464–474

The author introduces and comments on delict law liability for damage caused by another person (vicarious liability). He analyses problems which have been encountered in the court practice or may arise from the ambiguity of some of the provisions of the Law of Obligations Act and the General Part of the Civil Code Act in force as of 1 July 2002. The four types of delict law liability are examined: liability of a user of a service for the damage caused by the provider of the service, liability for damage caused by persons under 14 years of age and by persons between 14 and 18 years of age, and liability of a curator for damage caused by a mentally disabled person incapable of a delict. In addition, the liability of an obligatory liability insurer for delicts of the policyholder and the liability of a legal person for delicts of a member of its body under the General Part of the Civil Code Act. The author's aim is to draw attention to the problems rather than solve them and comment on the court practice. 33

7. T. Tampuu, Deliktiõigus võlaõigusseaduses. Üldprobleemid ja delikti üldkoosseisul põhinev vastutus (Tort law in the Law of Obligations Act: general problems of delictual liability), [2003] *Juridica* 2, 71–82

34 T. Tampuu focuses on the general features of tort law, the preconditions for tort liability, the objectives of tort law, matters concerning the moment of creation of the obligation to compensate for loss, the competition between contractual and tort claims, and the principles of determining the amount of damages. The aim of the article is to give an overview of the main theories of delictual liability in German law and compare these with Estonian regulations. The author analyses the major amendments regarding the extent of claims and grounds for tort liability: violation of rights or interests which is both unlawful and culpable and a causal link between the defendant's conduct and the plaintiff's resulting harm as defined in law.

8. T. Uusen-Nacke, Kolmandat isikut kaitsev leping. Asjatundja vastutus kolmandate isikute ees (Contract with protective effect for a third party: liability of an expert to a third party), [2003] *Juridica* 8, 536–542

35 The author analyses whether this principle also applies under the Law of Obligations Act, i.e. whether the protection of the rights of persons not participating in the execution of a contract is also justified in both Estonian contract law and tort law. The contractual protection cannot extend to any person affected by the failure to perform a contract as required and, therefore, preconditions for claims to compensate for damage caused to third parties are outlined in the article. In addition, the author analyses whether a contract with a protective effect for a third party is in line with the constitutional principle of private autonomy. The author examines in detail the liability of an expert to a third party and explains the possibilities prescribed by the Law of Obligations Act for compensation for damage caused to a person due to the failure to perform as required by a contract executed between an expert and client.

9. M. Kingisepp, Kausaalõpetused ja võlaõigus (Causal theories and the law of obligations), [2003] *Juridica* 3, 154–160

36 The author looks at the causal theories from the point of view that in civil law, it is not sufficient to rely only on philosophical generalisations. Specific characteristics of individual cases should also be taken into account. The article deals with generalisation theories and individualisation theories of causality. The author also criticises the Soviet theory of law negating the application of the *conditio sine qua non* theory and the adequacy theory.

10. J. Lahe, Kannatanu süü kahju tekkimisel kahjuhüvitise vähendamise alusena (Fault of the injured party as a ground for reducing compensation), [2002] *Juridica* 1, 30–36

The author mainly analyses the questions of presumption of the fault of a person who has caused loss and its justification from a comparative point of view. For this purpose, the article focuses on the applicability of the principle of fault in the case of penal liability and civil liability on the other hand. He also stresses practical points of civil procedure like burden of proof and legal presumptions in the case of delictual liability. For that purpose the author analyses the process of proving fault in criminal proceedings, and examines the reasons for application of presumption of innocence in criminal procedure and why presumption of innocence cannot be an absolute legal principle applicable to civil liability. Finally, the author analyses why the presumption of fault in the case of civil liability is justified. 37

11. J. Lahe, Deliktivõimetus süülist vastutust välistava asjaoluna (Incapacity to commit a criminal offence as a circumstance precluding fault liability), [2002] *Juridica* 6, 391–400

J. Lahe looks at the concept of such incapacity in different legal systems and examines to what extent incapacity to commit a criminal offence is regarded as a circumstance precluding liability, what is the maximum extent of such incapacity and how it is possible to justify the no-fault liability of a person without the capacity to commit a criminal offence. The author examines the corresponding provisions of the Law of Obligations Act taking into account the incapacity to commit a criminal offence arising from age and that arising from a disability. The author examines conditions under which the no-fault liability can be considered justified and whether a person without the capacity to commit a criminal offence can be held liable under the risk liability provisions. 38

VII. Finland

Suvianna Hakalehto-Wainio[1]

A. Legislation

1. Tort Liability Act/Personal Injury

1 The most significant Finnish statute applying to liability in damages is the Tort Liability Act (412/1974; *vahingonkorvauslaki*). The Tort Liability Act applies both to tort liability and the quantum of damages. In contrast, it does not apply to contractual liability or damages, nor to liability provided in another act, unless otherwise provided.

2 A bill (509/2004) was finally passed in 2004 introducing changes to the provisions on compensation for personal injury, loss of maintenance and suffering. The changes are described in Yearbooks 2001 and 2002. The bill will come into force on 1 January 2006.

2. Act on Compensation for Crime Damage

3 The Act on Compensation for Crime Damage (935/1973; *rikosvahinkolaki*) governs the payment of compensation from State funds for injury or loss caused through a criminal offence. The State, then, recovers the amount of the compensation from the offender. In international comparison, the compensation regime according to the Finnish Act is exceptionally comprehensive. Nevertheless, it has been deemed necessary to reform the Act for reasons relating to the general improvement of the situation of crime victims and to the recently enacted amendment to the Tort Liability Act.

4 In February 2004, the Minister of Justice appointed a working group to look into the types of injury or loss that, as a matter of legal policy, should be compensated for under the Act on Compensation for Crime Damage, how to delimit the sphere of entitled beneficiaries and what is the appropriate standard of compensation especially as regards pure economic loss. The working group was also to look into the rationalisation of the procedures for awarding com-

[1] English translation by Mr Sami Sarvilinna.

pensation and the promotion of awareness of the compensation system among crime victims.

The Working Group for Crime Damage Legislation issued its report in December 2004. The report recommends the repeal of the current Act and its replacement with a new enactment with the same title. It is proposed in the report that the right of crime victims to compensation be expanded and that the provisions on compensation be clarified. The Working Group proposes also that the provisions on compensation for personal injury be revised so that they are in concord with the new provisions in the Tort Liability Act. The situation of victims of serious violent crime is to be improved by entitling the victims of attempted homicide, aggravated assault and simple assault to compensation also for suffering. It is proposed that the compensation for suffering under the Act on Compensation for Crime Damage be capped at € 8,000 in the case of sex offences and at € 3,000 in the case of other violent crime and offences against personal liberty. The minimum amount of compensation is proposed to be raised from € 34 to € 170. The Working Group also proposes certain measures for the promotion of crime victims' awareness of the compensation system. 5

In addition, the Working Group proposes the clarification and revision of the provisions relating to the compensation payable to those individuals close to the crime victim. A person close to the victim could be compensated for expenses and loss of income incurred by taking care of the victim, as well as for the other costs arising from the injury. The enactment of the new Act on Compensation for Crime Damage will also entail the implementation of the EU Council Directive relating to compensation to crime victims. The objective is to have the new legislation enter into force at the same time as the amendment to the Tort Liability Act, on 1 January 2006. 6

3. Equality Act

The Equality Act (21/2004: *yhdenvertaisuuslaki*) entered into force on 1 February 2004. It prohibits discrimination on the basis of age, ethnic or national origin, citizenship, religion, personal belief, opinion, state of health, handicap or sexual orientation. 7

The Equality Act is applicable both in public and private activity, when the matter relates to the preconditions of the pursuit of a profession or business, business subsidies, taking into employment, working conditions, terms of employment, personnel training, career advancement, training or career advice, or membership in a union or employers' federation. Moreover, the Act is applicable to ethnic discrimination, when the matter relates to social welfare and health services, social support, subsidies or benefits, the performance of military national service, women's voluntary military service or civilian national service, or the supply or availability of housing, movable or real property or services to the public otherwise than in relationships between private individuals. 8

9 According to the Equality Act, the victim of the violation may demand reparation from the violator in a court of law. The award of reparation does not turn on whether the violation of the prohibition of discrimination has been intentional or negligent. The purpose of the reparation is to make good the anguish that the victim can be deemed to have experienced owing to this violation of his or her person. No proof of anguish need be supplied, as an award of reparation can be based on the nature of the violation alone.

10 Depending on the nature of the violation, the amount of the reparation varies, up to a maximum of € 15,000. When the quantum of the reparation is being assessed, the seriousness of the anguish caused by the violation must be taken into account. Circumstances to be considered in the assessment are the nature and extent of the discrimination, its duration, the attitude of the violator to his or her act, the possible reconciliation of the parties, the restoration of an equitable state of affairs, the financial situation and other personal circumstances of the violator, as well as the other monetary sanctions imposed for the same violation of another person. The award of reparation can be waived if the violation of the Equality Act is of minor significance and if a waiver of sanctions is reasonable in view of the nature of the violation and the status of the parties. For special reasons, the maximum amount of reparation may be exceeded, where justified in view of the duration and seriousness of the violation and the other circumstances. The award of reparation does not preclude the victim from demanding compensation for economic loss under the Tort Liability Act or some other act.

B. Cases

11 The main task of the Supreme Court (*Korkein oikeus*, KKO) is to hand down precedents on points of law that are important for the whole legal system and in this way to give guidance for the application of the law. In 2004, the Supreme Court handed down 137 precedents, 25 of which dealt with tort law matters. All the precedents have been published in *Korkeimman oikeuden ratkaisuja – Avgöranden av högsta domstolen 2004 I* (2004) and *II* (2005). They have been reissued with commentaries in P. Timonen (ed.) *KKO:n ratkaisut kommentein I* (2004) and *II* (2005).

1. Supreme Court, 15 January 2004, KKO 2004:3: Right of a murdered parent's infant child to compensation for anguish

a) Brief Summary of the Facts

12 A had killed B, who left a five-month-old baby. The District Court convicted A of manslaughter and sentenced him to imprisonment. The District Court also rendered A liable in damages to the baby for the anguish caused by the untimely death of the parent. The Court of Appeal upheld the judgment. In his appeal to the Supreme Court, A requested that the liability ruling be overturned or that the quantum of the damages in any event be decreased.

b) Judgment of the Court

The basic premise of the Tort Liability Act is that liability for personal injury normally covers only the injury sustained by a person directly as a result of the tortious event. Chapter 5, sec. 4a, of the Tort Liability Act contains a provision on the compensation for anguish payable for the close ones of a person who has been killed. Under paragraph 1 of the said section, the parents, children, spouse and other comparable persons close to the deceased are entitled to compensation for the anguish resulting from the death if the death has been caused deliberately or through gross negligence, and if the award of compensation is deemed reasonable in view of the closeness of the deceased and the person claiming compensation, the nature of the tortious act and the other circumstances. 13

The Supreme Court referred to the preparatory works relating to this provision, where it is stated that the compensation forms a reparation for the anguish for the sudden loss of a close one, comparable mostly to grief and a feeling of deprivation. The main purposes of the compensation is to promote the processing of one's grief and to help the grieving person to adjust to an unexpected change arising from the sudden loss of a close one. The Supreme Court noted that the purpose of the provision thus is to enable the reparation of the anguish arising from the loss of an especially close person at or around the time of the death. 14

In the present case, the Supreme Court pondered whether a five-month-old child can experience the kind of anguish referred to in chapter 5, sec. 4a, of the Tort Liability Act. The Supreme Court noted that an infant is not only physically, but also emotionally and intellectually dependent on the care and maintenance received from a parent or other custodian. The severance of this relationship is no doubt conducive to impairing the development and the emotional well-being of a little child. In Finnish law, it has not been considered that the loss of a parent would be a compensable injury *per se*. The child is certainly entitled to compensation for the material loss arising from the death of a parent, that is, the loss of maintenance. In contrast, the damage to the emotional or mental development of the child is not compensable as such under any statute. 15

The Supreme Court held that compensation under chapter 5, sec. 4a, of the Tort Liability Act was subject to certain special criteria, based on the dependence of the anguish of the act from which the death has ensued. The Supreme Court noted that the very first year of a baby's life and the interaction between the baby and the caregiver are very important for the development and the security of the baby, and that there is evidence of even a babe-in-arms reacting to mourning in the family. Nonetheless, held the Supreme Court, it is evident that a five-month-old child cannot comprehend the reasons for the absence of a parent. Hence, the negative consequences of the absence of the parent cannot be considered to depend on the manner of the parent's death or the act by 16 which it was caused. The Supreme Court held that where a child of this age experiences the loss of a parent, the adverse consequences of the same are by their nature different from the anguish meant in chapter 5, sec. 4a, of the Tort Liability Act.

17 Accordingly, the Supreme Court held that the possible negative consequences to a five-month-old child from the death of a parent do not constitute compensable anguish under chapter 5, sec. 4a, of the Tort Liability Act. In view of the wording and objective of the provision, and in contrast to the rulings of the lower courts, any liability in damages cannot be based on the future anguish of the child once he or she learns of the manner of the parent's death, either. On this basis, A was released from liability as regards the compensation for anguish payable to the child.

c) Commentary

18 On the same date, the Supreme Court handed down another ruling in a similar case, KKO 2004:2. In that case, an eighteen-month-old lost one parent to violent crime. In earlier case-law, the Supreme Court has awarded compensation to four- and five-year-old children in a like case (KKO 2002:83), where the basis for compensation was not considered problematic at all. The main focus of the Supreme Court has been on the type of incorporeal interest that chapter 5, sec. 4a, of the Tort Liability Act is intended to protect. With the compensable anguish being linked to the time of death, the possible later anguish experienced by a little child cannot be compensated under this section. The ruling of the Supreme Court makes it clear that the award of compensation to a child requires an immediate experience of anguish arising from the death. Moreover, it is clear that the stage of development of the child is of essential importance when the possibility of anguish is being assessed. This ruling, in parallel with the ruling in KKO 2004:2, makes it clear that the little children of a person who has been killed cannot receive compensation under chapter 5, sec. 4a, of the Tort Liability Act on the basis that the knowledge of the manner of the parent's death would cause him or her anguish at a later stage of life, when his or her understanding is more developed.

19 This interpretative rule of the Supreme Court can also be applied to anguish experienced not only by little children but also by others if this anguish occurs clearly later than the tortious event and the immediate mental anguish ensuing from the same.

2. Supreme Court, 28 May 2004, KKO 2004:50: Liability of the owner of real estate for personal injury sustained by a tenant entrepreneur

a) Brief Summary of the Facts

20 A kept a café as a tenant in business premises owned by a corporation. The café had a doorway into a second-floor hallway, which led also to other business premises. The hallway also led to an outdoor terrace, which again led to

two residential apartments and a service elevator. The businesses used the elevator for the transport of goods, and it was also accessible to customers. A was on his way out through the doorway, when the glass of the door shattered and fell on A, resulting in injury. The cause for the shattering of the glass could not be ascertained. The doorway had been in regular use by at least thirteen persons over the period 1997–2000. A claimed damages from the owner of the property for the hand injuries he had sustained.

b) Judgment of the Court

It has been consistently held in the case-law that the owner of business premises is responsible for the condition of the generally accessed areas of the property and building, so that they are safe to use. If the owner of the business premises cannot prove that the defective condition of the premises has arisen from circumstances beyond the responsibility of the owner, the owner is rendered liable for the injury sustained by customers or others visiting the premises. The cases relating to the liability of keepers of public premises have normally concerned injuries sustained by customers. The principle has been that the keeper of the premises has quite extensive responsibility for maintaining the safety of the premises. For instance, in its ruling KKO 1989:114, the Supreme Court noted that the operator of an airport was responsible for the design and construction of the airport so that it was safe also for persons who moved in an irregular manner owing to illness, injury, state of mind or other reason. In KKO 2001:1 it was held that the owner of a shopping mall was responsible for the structures of the building not causing a danger to the safety of the persons visiting the mall. 21

When the injured party is in fact a tenant in the premises, it is possible that he has been more aware of at least some of the safety issues on the premises than a random visitor would be. The Supreme Court noted that an entrepreneur who is a tenant in business premises is under no obligation to monitor the condition in the generally accessed areas of the building, unless such an obligation appears in the lease or can otherwise be inferred. Hence, a tenant entrepreneur must not merely because of the tenancy relationship be held to a different standard than customers or other persons who visit the premises, when the matter is of compensation for injury arising from defects in the condition of the premises. 22

The Supreme Court rendered the corporation liable to A for the injuries sustained because of the shattering of the glass door. The Supreme Court justified this ruling by noting that the cause for the shattering remained unknown and that the corporation had not proven that it had been caused by a circumstance beyond the sphere of responsibility of the corporation as the owner of the premises. This same rule for the allocation of the burden of proof was applied in KKO 2001:1, where a customer had been injured by a shattered glass pane that had fallen on him, again due to an unknown cause. The keeper of the premises was held liable owing to the reversed burden of proof. When the owner 23 had not proven that the shattering of the glass had been caused by a circumstance beyond its sphere of responsibility, the keeper of the premises would be liable.

c) Commentary

24 This ruling reinforces the earlier case-law of the Supreme Court as regards the burden of proof placed on the keeper of generally accessed premises. If a customer sustains an injury while on the premises, it is for the keeper to prove that the cause for the injury was outside of his or her sphere of responsibility. Failing this, liability will arise, also in the event that the real cause of the injury cannot be discovered. The ruling also adds to the case-law, in that the tort law protection of a tenant entrepreneur in such premises is generally the same as that of a customer visiting the premises.

3. Supreme Court, 23 June 2004, KKO 2004:65: Liability of a public corporation for loss arising from the exhaustion of a fisheries quota

a) Brief Summary of the Facts

25 The Ministry of Agriculture and Forestry and the Government of the autonomous Åland Islands had agreed on the division between mainland fishermen and Åland fishermen of Finland's 1997 salmon-catch quota under the EU fisheries regime. On the basis of this agreement, the Government of Åland had allocated its share of the quota to individual fishing boats operating from Åland. In this allocation, fisherman A had first received a quota of 3,415 salmon, which had in September 1997 been revised upwards to 5,821 salmon.

26 However, Finland's quota for 1997 had been exhausted before the end of the year, at which time the Ministry of Agriculture and Forestry had decided on the suspension of salmon fishing. Based on this suspension, the Government of Åland prohibited salmon fishing on 30 October 1997 for the remainder of the year. A had not used all of the quota allocated to him and, after the prohibition, could not use the rest at all. Consequently, A sued the Government of Åland for damages for the economic loss thus incurred. A considered that the Government had acted negligently, when it had not in its decision mentioned that salmon fishing might be prohibited later for reason of quota exhaustion before the end of the year.

27 A had already been reimbursed with € 43,800 for the unused quota from funds made available by the Åland Parliament for the promotion of the fishing industry. However, A averred that his total loss amounted to € 48,900 and hence demanded compensation for the remainder, that is € 5,100.

b) Judgment of the Court

28 Under chapter 3, sec. 2, a public corporation is vicariously liable in damages for injury or loss caused through an error or negligence in the exercise of public authority. This provision diverges somewhat from the regular provision on

liability on grounds of negligence. However, the liability of the public corporation arises only if the performance of the activity or task, in view of its nature and purpose, has not met the reasonable requirements set for it.

The Supreme Court noted the European law aspects of the fishing quota rules. 29
The applicable norm was Council Regulation (EEC) No 2847/93 of 12 October 1993 establishing a control system applicable to the common fisheries policy. Under Art. 21 of the Regulation, all catches of fish subject to quota made by fishing vessels were to be charged against the quota applicable to the flag Member State. Once the quota was suspended, the Member State was to suspend the fishing. Thereafter the Commission was to confirm that the quota was indeed exhausted, resulting in a halt of fishing for the rest of the quota period. Hence, the fishing of salmon had become prohibited in the autumn of 1997 already by virtue of the Regulation. Thus the decision of the Government of Åland had not been discretionary and, accordingly, it had not impacted A negatively. In consequence, the possible liability of the Government of Åland could not be justified by reference to the decision to suspend fishing.

The plaintiff argued in support of his demand that the Government of Åland 30
had not made reservations as to the continuous validity of the quotas when it had allocated them. The Government had also not alerted the plaintiff to the possibility that he might lose the quota allocated to him in case the total quota of Åland or Finland were to be exhausted. It was necessary for the Supreme Court to assess the extent to which A himself was responsible for his error, as well as the obligation of a public corporation to provide information on the prevailing legal circumstances. In earlier case-law, the obligation of a public corporation to provide information was discussed in KKO 1989:50, where a State employment adviser had given erroneous advice to a returning expatriate regarding the content of the norms affecting his situation. The customer's own responsibility to procure information and to stay up-to-date was omitted from the liability consideration and the State was rendered liable to the customer for the loss arising from the erroneous advice.

The allocation of a fishing quota to A was an administrative decision. In its 31
reasoning, the majority of the Supreme Court emphasised the right to rely on the assumption that an administrative decision with legal effects on an individual does not contain essential restrictions that are not evident on the face of the decision or the information supplied with it. This right having been violated, the Government of Åland was rendered liable in tort for the loss sustained by the plaintiff.

However, the majority of the Supreme Court held that an individual fisherman 32
could not be sure that he would succeed to catch fish up to his allocated quota before the exhaustion of the national quota. Even though the fisherman would probably have been able to make a bigger catch than that he eventually made had he pushed forward with the fishing effort, he would not have had a justified reason to believe that he would exhaust the whole of his allocated quota.

As the damages claimed by the plaintiff were relatively insignificant in proportion to the amount already paid to him in compensation, the majority considered that there was no reason to assess the loss higher than the amount of compensation already paid, and dismissed the claim.

33 Also the minority of the Supreme Court deemed that there was no proof of loss. The minority noted that if all fishermen were to be informed of the possible exhaustion of the fishing quota, all fishermen, not only A, would have had an incentive to catch up to their quota as early as possible. Under such circumstances, it would have been extremely unlikely that A would have used up all of his quota.

c) Commentary

34 The ruling of the Supreme Court reinforces the protection of the legitimate expectations of the addressee of an administrative decision. The addressee has the right to rely on the assumption that the decision does not contain such essential conditions or restrictions that do not appear on the face of the decision or the information supplied with it. The issue of an administrative decision may also include the duty to supply information on subsequent events warranted by legislation if these may restrict the enjoyment of the benefit linked to the administrative decision.

C. Literature

1. Vilja Hahto, *Uhrin myötävaikutus ja rikoksentekijän vastuu* (Contributory conduct by a crime victim and the liability of the offender) (Edita, Helsinki 2004)

35 The doctoral dissertation of Vilja Hahto is a criminal law and tort law study of the victim's conduct prior to the criminal offences against his or her physical integrity. The objective is to determine how the conduct of the injured party may affect the criminal liability and tort liability of the offender. Dr. Hahto aimed to combine a criminal law and a tort law point of view, so as to determine holistically the consequences of criminal behaviour to the offender. The emphasis of the dissertation is on the criminal law evaluation of contributory conduct. One quarter of the page count is allocated to tort law issues.

36 Vilja Hahto examines the objectives of tort law and compares them to the objectives of criminal law. The dissertation looks into the compatibility of the objectives of tort law to the consideration of the contributory conduct of the victim. A point of focus is chapter 6, sec. 1, of the Tort Liability Act where it is stated that contributory negligence by the injured party either rules out liability or is reason for a reduction of damages. Dr. Hahto proposes that the wording of the provision be amended so that the adjustment of damages on grounds of reasonableness and the reduction of damages on grounds of contributory negligence can be better distinguished from one another.

2. Marko Mononen, *Yritysten välinen tuotevastuu* (Business-to-business product liability) (Talentum, Helsinki 2004)

Dr. Mononen, who serves as a docent of civil and commercial law at the University of Helsinki, has written a monograph on the legal issues of product liability in business-to-business relationships. This theme has not been much discussed in Finnish legal scholarship so far, which in the product liability context has concentrated almost solely on issues relating to the liability of businesses to consumers. However, business-to-business product liability is a more significant legal phenomenon both in terms of number of cases and their economic weight. 37

In Finland, product liability is regulated mainly by contractual practice, case-law and certain general principles. The work provides an overall view of the legal norms relating to product liability in business-to-business relationships. The chapters cover the product liability regime, the concept of product defect, the preconditions for product liability, the quantum of damages and, briefly, the management of product liability risks. The focal point of the volume is the chapter on the cause for liability, where the cause is discussed both in terms of non-contractual and contractual liability. Dr. Mononen covers many of the basic problems of tort law in this chapter, which makes his work very interesting also from the viewpoint of general tort law. 38

VIII. France

Michel Cannarsa, Fabien Lafay, Olivier Moréteau
and Caroline Pellerin-Rugliano

A. Legislation

1. Law no. 2004-575 of 21 June 2004, known as the *Loi pour la confiance dans l'économie numérique*, *Journal Officiel* of 22 June 2004, 11168 et seq., dealing with the confidence in the digital economy

1 The Internet has become an essential tool in business and commerce, with more and more transactions taking place "on line". The sale and exchange of information are, of course, dependent on the reliability of the system and also on the trustworthiness of those using it. While several countries have been noticeably reluctant to interfere in this largely unrestricted and open medium, it would be hard to imagine French legislators allowing the web to continue developing without any legal framework. Even so, the law introduced on 21 June 2004[1] is not a sign of *dirigiste* or protectionist interventionism. Instead, its aim is to increase the confidence of current and potential users of the Internet so that they are not put off by the risks inherent in frequenting this open, frontierless medium, over which the state can have only limited influence. It represents a delicate approach, one that modifies existing laws only slightly, particularly with regard to questions of civil liability. The Act, which is principally intended to implement the European Directive of 8 June 2000[2] entitled "Electronic commerce", has made few changes to the previous treatment of questions of liability. Rather, its effect is simply to confirm or reinforce certain developments in case law, without diverging significantly from the courts' traditional practice.

2 The law of 21 June 2004, then, aims to define a legal framework that will give comfort to those buying and selling over the Internet and is intended to reassure future Internet users in terms of clarifying more precisely the degree to

[1] Law no. 2004–575 of 21 June 2004, *Loi pour la confiance dans l'économie numérique*, *Journal Officiel* of 22 June 2004, 11168 et seq.

[2] L. Marino, La non responsabilité des prestataires d'Internet, [2004] *Responsabilité Civile et Assurances* (RCA), September 2004, 4.

which each party is liable, while respecting the guidelines laid down by the Directive.

The Act is divided into six sections, dealing with the following issues: free- 3
dom of communication over the Internet, e-commerce, security in the digital economy, satellite systems, the development of the information and communication technologies and, finally, some concluding provisions. Only the first three sections, which deal specifically with the topic of liability, will be considered here. The first section is a declaration of principles on freedom of communication in an electronic medium. Its wording suggests that French legislators have not forgotten the 1789 Declaration of the Rights of Man. As Art. 1 of the Act states: "*Communication to the public by electronic means shall be free. The exercise of this freedom may be limited only to the extent required, firstly, by respect for other people's humanity, liberty and property, for the pluralist nature of the expression of thoughts and opinions, and secondly, by the need to safeguard public order, by the requirements of national defence, by the demands of public service, by the technical constraints inherent in the means of communication, and by the need, in the case of audiovisual media, to develop audiovisual production.*" Art. 3 then stipulates that the state, local municipalities, public authorities and those deemed to be charged with a public service task must take steps to enable their employees to access and use the new information technologies. Overall, it appears that there is a right to access the Internet and an emphasis on freedom of communication but not, in our opinion, on freedom of expression, which is somehow restricted, as we will see below[3].

These declarations of principle are followed by more technical provisions, of 4
which those dealing with liability on the part of web hosting providers are covered in Art. 6.

Here, both criminal and civil liability is based on a common principle: that of 5
"non-liability". In other words, according to the new law, the providers of such services "*may only be held liable if* …"[4]. They can be held liable only if they were aware of the illegal nature of the information provided and if they did not take action to prevent it being transmitted or stored[5]. The question of their being held criminally liable is decided in a similar way[6].

[3] If we now add the various criminal provisions, created for humanitarian reasons, that outlaw the mention of certain discussion topics, and the setting up of bodies charged with ensuring that these laws are respected, it becomes more accurate to say that freedom of expression is, in fact, restricted in a number of ways. The intentions behind such laws are easy to understand, but if such a level of vigilance in these areas is indispensable, then surely the very principle of imposing a uniform attitude to discussion (*une pensée unique*) – albeit in areas where there is little room for disagreement – makes freedom of expression on such issues impossible in reality.

[4] As D. Mazeaud notes, it appears that greater protection is being given to those providing Internet services than to the users of those services. (D. Mazeaud, Responsabilité civile: panorama 2004, [2005] *Dalloz* (D.), 185–194, especially 193).

[5] Art. 6-I-2.

[6] Art. 6-I-3.

6 The Act specifies that web hosting services and providers of Internet access are not subject to a general duty to monitor the information passing through their service "*without prejudice to any temporary targeted monitoring activity requested by the judicial authorities*"[7]. They must, however, take steps to prevent the transmission or accumulation of data in relation to specific areas, such as the defence of crimes against humanity, incitement to racial hatred, and child pornography (Art. 6-I-7). §4 states that: "*To this end, they* [the web hosting services and Internet service providers] *must provide a readily accessible and visible tool that allows all persons to bring this type of data to their attention. They are also required firstly to inform without delay the competent public authorities of any illegal activity of the type mentioned in the previous paragraph that has been notified to them and that the recipients of their services may be conducting and secondly to make public the methods that they will utilise in the fight against such illegal activities.*"

7 A parallel is then drawn with the provisions flowing from the law on the press (*la loi sur la presse*)[8], as web hosts are subject to a duty of professional secrecy and are required to allow a right of response where necessary[9]. As well as the reference to the law on the press expressly stated in the new Act, web hosting services are also required to store and if necessary pass to the judicial authorities any information that might allow the authors of the banned forms of communication to be identified. A failure to adhere to this requirement is deemed to constitute a criminal offence.

8 Next, Section II of the new law deals with the topic of e-commerce. It begins with a definition of this activity. In the words of Art. 14 (1): "*Electronic commerce is the economic activity by which a person remotely and by electronic means proposes or facilitates the supply of goods or services.*" §2 details the following provisions: "*The field of electronic commerce also includes services such as those involving the provision of information on line, commercial communications, and tools for researching, accessing and retrieving data, and for accessing a communication network or information hosting network, even when such services are not paid for by those receiving them.*"

9 Art. 15, relating to the liability of persons engaged in e-commerce, merely reiterates the standard approaches derived from general contract law: "*Any natural or legal person carrying on the activity defined in the Article 14 (1) is* de jure *liable towards the purchaser for the correct performance of the duties arising from the contract, whether these duties are to be performed by itself or by other service providers, without prejudice to its right to bring proceedings against the latter. Nevertheless, it may be released from all or part of its liability if it provides proof that the non-performance or defective performance of*

[7] Art. 6-I-7 Paragraphs 1 and 2.

[8] Ibid. Law of 29 July 1881.

[9] It goes without saying, of course, that the majority of those involved in website hosting are not professional journalists.

the contract was caused either by the purchaser or by the unforeseeable and unpreventable action of a third party unconnected with the supply of the services governed by the contract, or by an instance of force majeure."

There are, then, no new developments here. Those drafting the law merely wished to emphasise that e-commerce is still subject to the jurisdiction of the French courts whenever the person engaging in such an activity is established in France. In this respect, the following provision is outlined in Art.14 (3): "*A person is considered to be established in France for the purposes of this section when it has settled there in a stable and durable manner in order to perform effectively its activity, wherever, in the case of a legal person, its registered address is situated.*" 10

As a result of this, however, there is a danger that a contract concluded between a French consumer and a business established outside France might fall outside the jurisdiction of the French courts – a fact that does not inspire confidence in the digital economy. Though how could it be otherwise, one might well ask. And how many Internet users are likely to bother researching exactly where the other party is located before concluding a contract on line? One of the authors of this paper has conducted investigations on some sites that are well-known internationally and operate under a ".fr" address, though with little success, however. It proved extremely difficult to locate the physical address of the organisation with which the user is meant to be concluding a contract. Would it not therefore have been preferable – in order to facilitate the settlement of cases and to avoid conflicts of law and jurisdiction – to state clearly in the new Act that any site with a ".fr" web address is deemed to have a base in France? This would surely have increased consumer confidence. Furthermore, this solution actually corresponds to reality if the charter of the organisation responsible for governing the allocation of ".fr" domain names is to be believed (AFNIC or the *Association française pour le nommage Internet en coopération*). 11

The next section of the Act deals with electronic advertising. Here, the first provision once again makes reference to a declaration of principle: "*All advertising, of whatever form, that can be accessed by a public online communication service should be clearly identifiable as such. It should make the natural or legal person on whose behalf it is being provided clearly identifiable.*" The subsequent provisions of the Act also accord with traditional practice in this area. 12

Section III covers encryption and the difficulties associated with this technical requirement, a little-discussed topic, which has, however, been touched upon in civil law. Some recent legislation has had to tackle this area[10], while a 1998 13

[10] Decree no. 2001–272 of 30 March 2001, dealing with implementation of Art. 1316-4 of the Civil Code in respect of electronic signatures.

décret also provided guidelines on how encryption could be used[11]. Encryption, of course, is a technical procedure that allows information transferred or stored to be kept confidential by converting the data involved using special electronic methods. Since this is an area of technology in which confidentiality and security are paramount, criminal provisions have been built into the law in order to maintain users' confidence in the system. In the opinion of the present authors, this is a point of fundamental importance in a statute dealing with trust in the digital economy, since the exchange of names, addresses and personal data can only be considered secure if these details are guaranteed to remain confidential. Art. 32 of the new Act indicates a strongly protective attitude in this regard: "*Except for the purposes of demonstrating that they have not committed an intentional fault or a fault of negligence, any persons providing encryption services for reasons of confidentiality are by virtue of providing these services and notwithstanding any contrary contractual stipulation liable for the loss, damage or injury caused to persons entrusting them with the management of their confidential agreements in the event of an attack on the integrity, confidentiality or availability of the data converted in support of these agreements*." It is, however, difficult to provide evidence that no intentional fault or fault of negligence was committed in this field, where technology is evolving on a daily basis. This recalls, perhaps, the fact that in French civil law doctors are required to keep themselves informed of the "*latest advances in science*".

14 It is worth pointing out that the liability described here is different from the liability specified for "*the providers of electronic certification services*" who are liable "*for the loss, damage or injury caused to persons who reasonably relied on the certificates described by* [the providers] *as being qualified*[12] *in each of the following cases: (1) The information contained in the certificate, on the date of its delivery, was inexact; (2) The data required for the certificate to be regarded as qualified was incomplete; (3) The delivery of the certificate did not lead to the verification that the signatory was in possession of the private agreement corresponding to the public agreement of that certificate; (4) The service providers did not, where required, take steps to ensure that the withdrawal of the certificate was registered and did not keep this information available for third parties.*

15 *The service providers are not liable for the damage, loss or injury caused by use of the certificate over and above the limits specified for its use or for the*

[11] Decree no. 98–101 of 24 February 1998, *Journal Officiel* of 25 February 1998. This specified the circumstances in which declarations may be signed and authorisation given in respect of encryption methods and services.

[12] According to the EU Electronic Signature Directive 1999/93/EC, a "qualified certificate" may be defined as "a digital attestation which attributes a public key or a similar device to an individual person and verifies the identity of the person, by requiring its physical appearance before an (accredited) certification service provider, or through appropriate other measures" and which contains a specified set of other details (http://www.chiark.greenend.org.uk/pipermail/ukcrypto/1998-April/040663.html).

value of the transactions for which it may be used, provided that these limits are featured in the certificate and are accessible by the users.

They [the service providers] *must show that they have an adequate financial security, specially provided for the payment of any amounts that they might owe to any persons who reasonably relied on the qualified certificates that they deliver, or* [have] *an insurance policy that will cover the monetary consequences of their professional liability in civil law*." 16

We might well conclude that all this represents an increase in the duties incumbent on those providing encryption services and at the same time a limitation of the liability of the Internet service providers. The concepts of "intentional fault" and "fault of negligence" are common to both groups and, indeed, are already strongly evident in French law generally. Let us remember that the assessment of intentional fault has been considered a point of fact to be decided by judges in the lower courts since a ruling of the First Civil Chamber of the *Cour de Cassation* in 2000[13]. This decision was also recently reinforced by the Second Civil Chamber, which also accepted that the decision of the lower courts was final on the matter[14]. 17

Several provisions in criminal law further entrench the shortfalls in all of this. In the eyes of the law, it therefore appears to be more "dangerous" to offer encryption services than to host a website! This is all the more true since – in view of the skill of today's pirates and hackers – it is impossible to offer an absolutely infallible encryption system. 18

In conclusion, we can say that while the new statute is not precise or coherent in all of its provisions, it does have the merit of setting down a framework of liability in an environment where none existed before. It remains to be seen how its provisions will be interpreted in practice and by the courts. Rest assured, however, that the present authors will be monitoring events closely. (F.L./O.M.) 19

2. Law no. 2004-1343 of 9 December 2004 concerning simplification of the law: Art. 29 amending Art. 1386 *Code civil* (French Civil Code, C. civ.)

Liability of the supplier: The French implementation of Directive 85/374/EEC on liability for defective products stated that the seller, the person hiring out such products or any other professional supplier would be responsible in the same way as the producer for damage or injury caused by the product's lack of safety. This decision was in line with previous rulings of the French courts on professional sellers, who were already subject to strict liability arising from their contractual duty to deliver goods free of latent defects (*action* 20

[13] C. cass. 1st civ., 4 July 2000, *Bulletin des arrêts des chambres civiles de la Cour de cassation* (Bull. Civ.) I, no. 203.
[14] C. cass. 2nd civ., 18 March 2004, Bull. Civ. II, no. 130.

en garantie). This is because claims for liability in contract are ordinary claims directed first and foremost against the supplier.[15] The situation in respect of suppliers is governed by Art. 1386-7 *Code civil* (Civil Code, C. civ.), the first paragraph of which deals with their liability, while the second outlines their right to take action against the producer: "*A seller, a hirer, with the exception of a finance lessor or of a hirer similar to a finance lessor, or any other professional supplier is liable for the lack of safety of a product in the same conditions as a producer.*" The rule contained within the French law appeared more straightforward than the method of identifying the producer stipulated by the Directive, which limits the liability of the supplier to circumstances in which it has failed to make known the identity of the producer within a reasonable timescale. Under the French system, the supplier is automatically liable, unless he brings proceedings against the producer. This is because the claimant is in most instances more familiar with the seller or hirer than with the producer of the product concerned.

21 In the opinion of the European Court of Justice (ECJ), however, this constituted incorrect implementation of the Directive by France[16] since the Directive stipulates that the supplier is only secondarily liable[17]. In French law, however, the seller (or other professional supplier) was placed in the same position as the producer. The ECJ holds that the question of which party may be held liable and the circumstances under which this may occur are a matter exclusively for European law.

22 The French government, for its part, did not contest the fact that Art. 1386-7 C. civ. deviated from Art. 3 (3) of the Directive. It believed, however, that Art. 1386-7 C. civ. still led to the result foreseen by the Directive, since the supplier identified by the victim could still bring third-party proceedings against the producer[18]. Nevertheless, in the view of the ECJ, the French solution risked leading to an unnecessarily large number of claims against the supplier, a situation that would be avoided if claims were directed, as intended, against the producer. In Art. 2 (d) of the Directive 92/59/EEC, we read, however, that the term "producer" refers not only to the manufacturer of the product and to any other person presenting himself as the manufacturer of the product but also to "*other professionals in the supply chain, insofar as their*

[15] Consider a recent ruling of the Toulouse *Cour d'appel*, given on the basis of Artt. 1386-1 et seq. of the Civil Code, particularly Art. 1386-7. Here, the judges stated that a supplier of contaminated horsemeat is liable since one could not claim that the state of scientific knowledge did not allow the existence of the defect to be detected. *Cour d'appel de Toulouse*, 22 February 2000, [2000] D., *Informations rapides*, 269, [2000] *La semaine juridique* (JCP), II, 10429, note Ph. Le Tourneau, [2000] RCA, 369, note L. Grynbaum, [2001] *Contrats Concurrence Consommation* (Contrats Conc. Consom.), no. 52, obs. G. Raymond.

[16] ECJ 25 April 2002 – C-52/00, [2002] ECR I-03827; P. Oudot, L'obligation de sécurité et la responsabilité du distributeur, [2003] Contrats Conc. Consom., July, Chron. no. 8, 7.

[17] Art. 3 (3) of Council Directive 85/374/EEC of 25 July 1985 on the approximation of the laws, regulations and administrative provisions of the Member States concerning liability for defective products, OJ L 210, 7.81985, 29.

[18] Paragraph 37 of ECJ 25 April 2002 – C-52/00, [2002] ECR I-03827.

activities may affect the safety properties of a product placed on the market". As a result of a recent case heard by the ECJ, Art. 29 (2) of the law relating to simplification of the law (adopted on 9 December 2004)[19] states that the first paragraph of Art. 1386-7 C. civ. has now been revised with the following wording: "*A seller, a hirer, with the exception of a finance lessor or of a hirer similar to a finance lessor, or any other professional supplier is liable for the lack of safety of a product under the same conditions as a producer only where the identity of the producer is not known.*" Commenting on this change in the law, M.B. Saugey described this amendment together with the suspension of Art. 1386-12 § 2 C. civ. as an essentially technical matter. In reality, however, the consequences for the claimants in such cases are far from merely technical, particularly in instances where the actual producer has no funds available to meet the cost of claims brought against it.

For its part, the EU Council responded to the ECJ's ruling by giving its own view on the liability of the supplier, in the following terms.[20] "*This legal situation gives rise to concern, since as pointed out in paragraph 3 the Directive does not, apart from Article 3(3), contain provisions concerning the liability of the supplier. The possibility to lay down rules on liability of suppliers, including rules on strict liability, could involve benefits to the consumers, regardless of whether these rules are laid down at national or Community level. In relevant cases the consumer would then be able to raise his claim against the producer, subsequent suppliers, including the seller of the product, or them all. This could improve consumers' possibility of actually obtaining compensation. The Council also recalls that one of the general objectives of the Community is to promote consumer interests and ensure a high level of consumer protection, cf. Articles 95 and 153 of the Treaty.*" The Council believes "*that against this background there is a need to assess whether Directive 85/374/EEC, as amended by Directive 1999/34/EC, should be modified in such a way as to allow for national rules on liability of suppliers based on the same ground as the liability system in the Directive concerning liability of producers.*" 23

There is, then, some disagreement between the Council and the Commission on this matter. In its report dated 31 January 2001[21] on the implementation of the Directive the Commission stated its view that holding the supplier liable in 24

[19] Law no. 2004-1343 of 9 December 2004, *Journal Officiel* of 10 December 2004, 287.

[20] Council Resolution of 19 December 2002 on the modification of the Directive on liability for defective products, OJ C 6/2 of 4 February 2003. The Council recalled that at the time the Directive was adopted, "*With regard to the interpretation of Articles 3 and 12, the Council and the Commission are in agreement that there is nothing to prevent individual Member States from laying down in their national legislation rules regarding liability for intermediaries, since intermediary liability is not covered by the Directive. There is further agreement that under the Directive the Member States may determine rules on the final mutual apportionment of liability among several liable producers (see Article 3) and intermediaries.*"

[21] COM (2000) 893 final.

situations other than those provided for by Art. 3 (3) of the Directive is not justified.

25 **The *obligation de suivi* (obligation to monitor the effects of products):** Previously, Art. 1386-12 (2) C. civ. included a duty to monitor the effects of products (an *obligation de suivi*) that limited the scope for release from liability, an obligation absent from the Directive itself. The ECJ, however, interpreted Directive 85/374/EEC fairly narrowly in respect of the duties incumbent on the producer once a product has been released to the market. It stated that while the Directive does allow Member States to withdraw from the provisions on exemption from liability set down in Art. 7 (c) it does not entitle them to modify the terms under which such exemptions might apply or to ignore the terms of exemption set down in Art. 7 (d) (i.e. exemption from liability in cases where the defect is due to the compliance of the product with mandatory regulations issued by the public authorities). Art. 29 (3) of 9 December 2004 Law on simplification of the law therefore provided for the suspension of the offending second paragraph of Art. 1386-12 C. civ.[22]. (M.C.)

B. Cases

1. C. cass. 2nd civ., 21 October 2004, Bull. civ. II, 202: Liability for the Acts of Others: the Requirement for Proof of Negligence in a Sport-related Case

a) Brief Summary of the Facts

26 A rugby player who was a member of a sporting club was taking part in a training session with his team mates. As he tried to make a tackle, he fell and suffered an injury to his spine because the player he was trying to tackle managed to evade him. He therefore sought to assign liability to the sporting club and its insurance company.

b) Judgment of the Court

27 The Pau *Cour d'appel* agreed that the sporting club was liable on the grounds that the claimant's injury had been caused by one of the club's members during a training session, such training being "[a] *necessary aid and part of the preparation*" for every competition in which the club participates as a club affiliated to the French Rugby Federation (the *Fédération française de Rugby*).

28 In response to a subsequent appeal brought by the club, the *Cour de cassation* ruled that the club was not liable and reversed the decision of the *Cour d'appel*. The judges stated that Art. 1384 (1) C. civ. does not allow the club to be held liable for the actions of one of its members if no "established fault" (in French, a *faute caractérisée*) has been committed by one of these members:

[22] Law no. 2004-1343 of 9 December 2004, *Journal Officiel* of 10 December 2004, 287.

"[...] *on the basis of this text* [Art. 1384 (1) C. civ.], [....] *sporting clubs, having the role of organising, guiding and monitoring the activity of their members, are liable for the injuries that* [their members] *cause on such occasions* [only] *on the grounds that an established fault taking the form of a breach of the rules of the game can be attributed to one of the club's members, even* [if the particular member concerned was] *not identified.*"

c) Commentary

Here, the *Cour de cassation* was simply echoing decisions reached by the courts over several years in relation to sporting activities. These decisions had indeed accepted the principle that a club may be held liable for the actions of its members.[23] In these past cases, however, the courts also ruled that a club could be held liable for its members' actions only if one of these members committed an "established fault"[24]. In those instances where the courts appeared to show more indulgence towards the claimant, damages were being awarded on the basis of fault even if the person responsible for the fault could not be identified.[25] Even then, however, a fault was still required[26]. In the case discussed no such fault could be established since the avoiding action taken by the alleged negligent party "*was perfectly normal*", a fact stated by the representative of the club and not contested by the claimant. 29

These past decisions confirm that the simple fact of being a member of a sporting club does not entitle a person to sue the club or its insurers each time he injures himself while taking part in an activity organised by the club. The person has no grounds for a claim if his injury results from his own actions. This treatment of claimants could be said to be particularly well justified when it comes to sports such as rugby, which are inherently risky activities. Furthermore, the courts require the existence of an "established fault" (*faute caractérisée*) in such instances. Accordingly, a *faute caractérisée* in a sporting 30

[23] C. cass. 2nd civ., 22 May 1995 (1st case), Bull. civ. II, no. 155 (dealing with the liability of a rugby club arising from injuries caused during a match by an unidentified member of its team to a player on the opposing team), [1995] *Rapport annuel de la Cour de cassation* (R.), 319; [1995] JCP, II, 22550, note J. Mouly; [1995] JCP, I, 3893, no. 5, obs. G. Viney, [1995] *Revue Trimestrielle de Droit Civil* (RTD Civ.), 899, obs. P. Jourdain, [1995] RCA, Chron., 36, H. Groutel; C. cass. 2nd civ., 22 May 1995 (2nd case), [1996] *Gazette du Palais* (Gaz. Pal.), 1, 16, note F. Chabas, [1996] D., Somm. 29, obs. F. Alaphilippe, [1996] *Répertoire du notariat Defrénois* (Defrénois.), 357, obs. D. Mazeaud; C. cass. 2nd civ., 3 February 2000, Bull. civ. II, no 26, [2000] R., 399, [2000] D., 862, note S. Denoix de Saint Marc, [2000] D., Somm. 465, obs. P. Jourdain, [2000] JCP, II, 10316, note J. Mouly, [2000] JCP, I, 241, no 15, obs. G. Viney, [2000] Defrénois, 724, obs. D. Mazeaud, [2002] Gaz. Pal., 724, note Peltier, [2000] RCA, 110, note H. Groutel (similar decisions).

[24] Civ. 2nd, 20 November 2003: Bull. civ. II, no 356; R, 451; [2004] D., 300, note G. Bouché; [2004] JCP, II. 10017, note J. Mouly; [2004] *Revue trimestrielle de droit civil* (RTD Civ), 106, obs. P. Jourdain.

[25] Same case.

[26] It has now become clear that the fault must involve an action that runs counter to the normal progress of the game and is "in breach of the rules of the game", as stated earlier this year by the Second Civil Chamber of the *Cour de cassation* in a similar context: Civ. 2nd, 13 January 2005, still to appear in the bulletin, appeal number: 03-18617.

context might be understood as an action that represents a deliberate infringement of the normal rules of the game[27]. Certain commentators have interpreted this decision as constituting a reintroduction of the need for a fault on the part of the defendant if damages are to be awarded[28]. The present authors, however, view the ruling as evidence of greater consistency in the courts' treatment of cases involving risky activities, with a stricter interpretation of the involvement (*implication*) of the alleged tortfeasor and his guarantor in the activity in question.

31 However, one eminent theorist has noted that the decision does nothing to increase "*the coherence of our laws on civil liability for the actions of others*"[29]. It is indeed true that the court's treatment of such cases differs from their handling of parental liability for the actions of one's children (Art. 1384 (4)), where there is no requirement for the child to have committed a fault. In the Blieck case of 1991[30], the *Cour de cassation* seemed to be extending this rule to cover all cases of liability for the actions of others on the basis of Art. 1384 (1) C. civ., the application of which was requested in the case under discussion. The Blieck case, however, involved assigning liability to an association whose job was to care for mentally ill individuals who were unaware of the consequences of their actions (or lacked *discernement* in French law) and whose actions could not therefore be reasonably described as negligent (*fautif*). The case under discussion in this paper, in contrast, involved responsible adults voluntarily undertaking leisure activities.

32 It is pleasing to see the *Cour de cassation* once again taking a more logical approach by demanding evidence of fault on the part of "*persons for whom one is responsible*", where the action brought by the claimant is not based on one of the special cases set down in the special provisions of Art. 1384 C. civ. While the guiding principle of providing protection for victims may justify holding parents liable in instances where their child has caused damage or injury without, however, committing a fault, it is difficult to see why liability for the actions of others should in all other cases be divorced from any fault on the part of the person for whom one is considered responsible. When it comes to liability for the actions of one's employee, then fault on the part of the employee is considered a prerequisite (Art. 1384 (5) C. civ.)[31].

33 Since the case under discussion involves an inherently risky activity, we can only welcome the fact that the courts are demanding evidence of an "established fault". Pleasingly, this brings more consistency in the many judgments based on the brief provisions in the Code relating to liability for others. The different treatments available for cases involving liability in such cases are

[27] Ibid.

[28] Jean-Baptiste Laydu, Responsabilité du fait d'autrui: l'embarrassant retour de la faute confirmée, [2005] D., 2005, jur., 40–43.

[29] D. Mazeaud, Responsabilité civile: panorama 2004, ibid., 188, [2005] *Dalloz* (D.), 185, at 188.

[30] Cass. Ass. Plén., 29 March, [1991] D., 324, note C. Larroumet.

[31] See also Art. 6:102(1) in the Principles of European Tort Law.

dictated by the wide variety in the types of actions brought. It has become impossible in French law to establish a coherent and all-encompassing system for dealing with liability for the actions of others within a single article, without then seeing a virtually infinite growth in the number of paragraphs in this article. The courts' decisions are therefore a vital source of law in this field, an area in which the legal codes themselves can give only a general orientation. (F.L.)

2. C. cass. 2nd civ., 18 March 2004, *juris-data* no. 2004-022856; [2004] JCP, jur., 1429–1431, note S. Moisdon-Châtaignier: Civil Claim Brought by Parents against Grandparents for Failure to Supervise the Child

a) Brief Summary of the Facts

A man and woman left their 10-year old son to be looked after by his grandparents while they were away on holiday. The child, driven by a sudden urge and in the company of a group of other children, set fire to a canister of petrol (gasoline) in a shed. The child suffered burns and his parents sued the grandparents for damages. 34

b) Judgment of the Court

The Poitiers *cour d'appel* did not accept that the grandparents were liable. The child's parents appealed on the grounds that the grandparents had committed a *faute de surveillance* ("fault" or "lack" of supervision) in respect of the child, since the fuel was located in an unlocked shed. The *Cour de cassation* dismissed the appeal on the basis that the child, being 10 years old, was capable of discerning the consequences of his actions, had been staying with his grandparents for more than three weeks and no longer needed constant supervision, and that he was neither undisciplined, boisterous nor particularly reckless in comparison with other children and was not therefore owed a special duty of supervision (*obligation de surveillance*). 35

c) Commentary

The judges' decision was based on Art. 1382 of the Civil Code, which deals with personal liability (*responsabilité du fait personnel*), rather than on the primary liability of parents for damage or injury caused by their child (*responsabilité de principe des parents pour les dommages provoqués par leur enfant*), as set down in Art. 1384 (4). Now is not the time, however, for us to revisit the thorny question (in French law) of parental liability for a child's actions, since this is not the issue raised by this case. Instead, the judgment focuses on the grandparents' liability resulting from their alleged lack of supervision. 36

The *Cour de cassation* took account of the child's character and attitude when considering whether the grandparents had committed a *faute de surveillance*. As Ms Moisdon-Châtaignier noted in her comments on this decision, it ap- 37 pears that the courts do not view it necessary in such cases to consider the child's attitude in exactly the same way as they do when assessing whether parents should be held liable for faults committed by their child. There is both a legal and practical explanation for these differences in treatment.

38 In law, the grounds for liability are different: the grandparents are covered by Art. 1382, with any possible liability being dependent on fault on their part, while parents, in contrast, are subject to strict liability under Art. 1384 of the Civil Code[32]. From a practical point of view, since the grandparents do not live permanently with the child, the obligations incumbent upon them should be assessed in light of the fact they are not in a position to be as familiar with the child's behaviour as his parents might be.

39 Nevertheless, we might ask whether the courts would have accepted a claim in contract instead of in tort in this case. It would certainly have been interesting to see parents bring proceedings against members of their own family on the basis of a contract they had concluded, under which the principal obligation was the responsibility of supervising the child. Would the courts have considered the obligation of the grandparents in terms of the way in which they had supervised the child (an *obligation de moyen*) or in terms of the situation resulting from their supervision (an *obligation de résultat*)? In such a case, what criteria would be considered? We can be sure that the courts would have taken account of the child's personality and they would probably also have considered the circumstances in which the damage and injury occurred. Would the contractual obligations involved be held to be identical to the duties under tort law?

40 It is worth noting that if the court had accepted the existence of an implied contractual obligation to perform childcare duties[33], it might also have inferred from this a requirement to do so in a safe way (an *obligation de sécurité de moyen*)[34]. We should recall that, unlike an *obligation de résultat*, where the simple act of failing to perform a duty renders the party involved contractually liable without there being any need to prove the existence of a fault, an *obligation de moyen* requires the person who has suffered the harm to prove that the other party behaved negligently – a condition that is very similar to that imposed in cases of fault-based tortious liability. In such circumstances, the grandparents could be criticised for not having taken enough care to protect the child from danger in that they had left the shed unlocked. Furthermore, they might even face criticism for failing in their duty of supervision (*obliga-*

[32] Art. 1384 does not apply to grandparents: Civ. 2nd, 18 September 1996: Bull. civ. II, no 217; [1998] D., 118, note M. Rebourg; [1997] D., Chron. 327, by G. Blanc; [1997] *Droit de la famille* (Dr. fam), no. 83.

[33] Jean-Marc Lhuillier, La responsabilité de la *baby-sitter*, ou la 'nuit juridique', *Drôles de droits*, Mélanges en l'honneur de François Terré (1999), 377 et seq.

[34] Civ. 1st, 18 November 1997: with regard to Art. 1147: "a person, whether remunerated or not, who is entrusted with the care of young children, is subject only to a duty to perform his or her duties in a safe way [an *obligation de moyen*] in respect of the children's health."

tion de surveillance), which the courts often impose on top of an obligation to perform one's duties in a safe way (*obligation de sécurité de moyen*)[35]. Let us remember, though, that the *Cour de cassation* refuses to subject grandparents to a duty of supervision (*obligation de surveillance*). It is therefore highly unlikely that the court would accept in this case the existence of an implied contract in respect of caring for the child. The court might well have reached a quite different decision if those taking care of the child had not been the child's grandparents but a babysitter, a registered childminder, or an organisation. (F.L.)

3. C. cass. 2nd civ., 19 February 2004 (the "Liebrand 2" case), Bull. Civ. II, 75: Liability for Things in one's Care: the "Active Role" Played by Immobile Glass Panels

a) Brief Summary of the Facts

The claimant had re-entered a shopping mall he had left a short time before. As he walked into the entrance area, he bumped into a glass panel with full force. The glass panel shattered as a result of the impact and injured him. 41

b) Judgment of the Court

The injured party sued the shopping mall for damages on the basis of Art. 1384 C. civ. dealing with *responsabilité du fait des choses* (liability for things in one's care). His claim was rejected by the Chambéry *Cour d'appel* (on 29 June 1998) on the grounds that he had provided no evidence of any abnormality or failure to maintain the glass panel and that he had not, therefore, demonstrated that the glass panel was the cause of his injury. Unhappy with this decision, the claimant lodged an appeal. 42

The *Cour de cassation* (C. cass. 2nd civ., 15 June 2000) reversed the lower court's decision, stating that "*the involvement of the glass panel in causing the injury to occur [had already been] established as a point of fact by the* cour d'appel" and could not, therefore, be challenged. Accordingly, it sent the case back to the Grenoble *Cour d'appel* (30 April 2002), where the shopping mall and its insurance company were found liable for the claimant's injury, albeit with damages reduced by one-third. The claimant lodged a second appeal on the basis, principally, that his own negligence in terms of not paying adequate attention (his *faute d'inattention*) was not sufficiently "established" (or *caractérisée*) for him to have been held partly liable. 43

[35] See Civ. 2nd, 16 May 1988, Bull. no. 117: "Required to consider a claim for damages in respect of the harm suffered by a party as a result of a fire caused by two minors who had been entrusted to that party's care fnr the duration of the summer holidays, the *Cour d'appel* – which held that children aged between 10 and 12 with no intellectual or other shortcomings did not require special supervision `t all times, and that the claimant could not be criticised for having failed to supervise the children's games more closely – felt able to conclude that the claimant had not committed a faute de surveillance."

44 The Second Civil Chamber of the *Cour de cassation*, however, dismissed this new appeal, reiterating the views of the Grenoble *Cour d'appel*: the claimant, the judges stated, was familiar with the premises, having just left them, and had therefore committed a *faute d'inattention* that had contributed to his suffering an injury. The previous ruling that had found that the shopping mall was at least partly liable for the injury was thus implicitly confirmed.

c) Commentary

45 Having developed the general concept of *responsabilité du fait des choses* (liability for things in one's care) at the end of the 19th century[36], the French courts have gradually refined the terms under which this can be applied. The first requirement is that the object concerned was in the care of someone, and the second is that the object was the direct cause of the injury or damage. Accordingly, the object needs to have played an active role, something which will be assumed by the courts if the object was in motion. If the object was immobile, on the other hand, the claimant must prove that it played an active role. For this to be the case with regard to a glass panel, it would be necessary to demonstrate that the glass was excessively fragile or that insufficient indication was given of its presence[37], or else that it was situated in an abnormal position. The object's custodian (its *gardien*) will therefore be found liable unless it can demonstrate that there was a *faute d'inattention* on the victim's part; in that case, liability will be shared between the parties. These rules, in fact, were established some time ago now by the Second Civil Chamber of the *Cour de cassation*[38].

46 Nevertheless, recently the courts have begun to interpret these rules in respect of immobile objects more flexibly, both on a general basis and with particular regard to glass panels. This case therefore provides us with a good opportunity to recall and to comment on the recent changes in the law on liability for immobile things in one's care.

47 A rapid survey of cases heard over the last ten years basically shows that there have been two types of judgments: those in line with traditional practice (where proof is required of the active role played by the object concerned), and those tending rather to overturn the traditional rules for the sake of compensating the claimant.

48 This trend towards granting compensation more generously was first seen in 1980[39] and then again in 1990[40] in two isolated rulings, even though the *Cour*

[36] Civ., 16 June 1896, Teffaine case, [1897] S., 1, 17 and Chbres réun. (joint session of the Chambers), 13 February 1930, Jand'heur case, *Grands arrêts*, vol. 2, no. 193.

[37] For details of the first cases in which the principle was applied, see: Civ. 2nd, 16 November 1978, Bull. civ. II, no. 240, and Civ. 2nd, 7 March 1979, Bull. civ. II, no. 75.

[38] For a fairly recent case in which these rules were applied, see Civ. 2nd, 2 April 1997, [1997] RCA, no. 255.

[39] C. cass. 2nd, 2 May 1980, Bull. civ. II, no. 113; [1980] D., IR 414, obs. C. Larroumet; [1981] RTD Civ., 161, obs. G. Durry.

[40] C. cass. 2nd, 4 July 1990, Bull. civ. II, no. 165; [1990] RCA, comm. 359.

de cassation has continued to restate its preference for making a distinction between immobile objects and those in motion[41]. Even so, this tendency is becoming more pronounced, with an increased number of judgments being reached where an immobile object is deemed to have played an active role even when no abnormal circumstances were demonstrated[42].

In view of the uncertainty in this area, when the *Cour de cassation* was called to hear a second appeal by the claimant in 2004 one might reasonably have expected that the court would sit in plenary session (*Assemblée plénière*) – its highest form, which meets when a delicate issue needs to be considered or when there is an indication that the views of the court's different constituent chambers need to be harmonised. While it is true that the focus of this second appeal lay more on the reality of the claimant's *faute d'inattention* than on the active role of the glass panel since the fundamental question being considered was really one of causality, the court did have a good opportunity here to clarify its position on these matters. Unfortunately, however, this was not to be, and the *Cour de cassation* restricted its role to confirming the decision of the *Cour d'appel* on the pretext that the point was one of fact and not of law. 49

It is difficult to draw any general conclusions from this case, which could well be termed an *arrêt d'espèce*. What's more, the implicit confirmation of the decision given at the first appeal, combined with the fact that the *Cour de cassation* refrained from calling a plenary session, implies that the court is appearing to respect a rule that has already been confirmed. In reality, though, we are no closer to seeing a clear and firm criterion established for assessing the liability of immobile objects. 50

First of all, because the active role of an immobile object depends on whether or not it is classed as "abnormal", certain commentators have suggested that the very fact that a pane of glass shatters indicates that there is a clear abnormality (*anormalité*) involved[43], an opinion reaffirmed repeatedly in 2002 by the courts in cases where an object was classed as dangerous[44] or defective[45]. This analysis, though highly attractive, actually runs counter to several judgments where the judges held that the object was the cause of the damage or in- 51

[41] C. cass. 2nd, 11 January 1995, Bull. civ. II, no. 18;. [1995] RCA, comm. 86.

[42] See, for example: C. cass. 2nd, 29 April 1998, Bull. civ., no. 142; [1998] RTD Civ., 913, for details of a case involving a glass door pushed by a young boy; C. cass. 2nd, 23 March 2000, Bull. civ. II, no. 51 and C. cass. 2nd, 15 June 2000, for a case where glass panels had injured people who had bumped into them; C. cass. 2nd, 18 September 2003, [2003] JCP, II, 10013, and Bull. civ. II, no. 287, for a case involving a concrete post in the street that was used to demarcate a pedestrian route. With regard to this last case, see N. Damas, Responsabilité du fait des choses: vers la disparition de la distinction entre chose en mouvement et chose immobile?, [2004] D. jur., 25, and S. Godechot, Mise au point sur l'exigence d'anormalité dans la responsabilité du fait des choses, [2004] D., jur., 2181 et seq.

[43] S. Godechot, [2004] D., *Jurisprudence*, 2181 et seq.

[44] Civ. 2nd, 7 May 2002, Bull. civ. II, no. 92 (concerning an old stone staircase).

[45] Civ. 2nd, 11 July 2002, Bull. civ. II, no. 175 (concerning a flight of stairs).

jury even though no abnormality was said to be present[46]. Let us then set aside this rather circular view of events.

52 The second possible explanation assumes that the courts see in the breaking of a pane of glass a sort of movement, as follows: Although the glass remains fundamentally inert, on shattering it does – as a result of the action of an outside agent – become mobile, and so the courts would infer from this movement an active role, as they might with a galloping horse. While tempting, however, this interpretation of the courts' behaviour is not really satisfactory. Firstly, the simple fact that an immobile object may be brought into motion by the action of an individual is not sufficient for the courts to ascribe an active role to it, since the *Cour de cassation* has not accepted that a trampoline can play an active role in causing injury[47]. Secondly, an inanimate object that remains immobile following impact may, in contrast, be considered as the cause of the damage, as the court ruled in relation to the concrete post[48].

53 Another explanation would be to infer that an "active" role was played by the contact between the object and the claimant. In all of the cases considered, those awarded damages came into contact with the object concerned. Two comments might be made on this notion of "contact", however, relating first to the issue of causality and second to the actual nature of the contact.

54 First of all, those commentators proposing this explanation[49] are making a clear choice in favour of "adequate causality" (*causalité adequate*), or in other words the idea that, among the events that could have led to the injury, the courts will only focus on the one that brought with it an inherent probability that the injury might occur. Is it reasonable, though, to suggest that a pane of glass has an inherent potential for causing injury, and an unavoidable potential at that? The answer must surely be no[50], since as far as immobile objects are concerned, the likelihood of injury depends primarily on the injured party's lack of attention (in situations where the glass panel is not badly situated or defective). In such cases, it is the very "abnormality" that holds the potential for causing injury – a fact that brings us back to the traditional understanding of damage or injury caused by immobile objects, according to which liability may only stem from the abnormal state of the object concerned. In other words, the *Cour de cassation*, in reaching the decisions we have seen in such cases, is effectively saying that the glass panel is indeed the direct cause of the injury, though its custodian (*gardien*) may still be released from liability for reasons of *force majeure*. But herein lies the problem: this would mean that the claimant's negligence (his *faute*) – where it can be characterised as *force majeure* – would constitute grounds for release from liability, a path that in reality the courts ap-

[46] Civ. 2nd, 25 October 2001, Bull. civ. II, no. 162 (regarding a letterbox sited in a normal position) or Civ. 2nd, 18 September 2003, ibid. (regarding concrete post in the street).
[47] C. cass. 2nd, 8 June 1994, [1995] RTD Civ., 121.
[48] Civ. 2nd, 18 September 2003, ibid.
[49] See P. Jourdain on the "Liebrand 1" case, [2000] RTD Civ. 849.
[50] For more on the same point, see S. Godechot (supra fn. 42), 2181 et seq.

pear reluctant to take. All in all, then, the court's attitude here indicates that the causes involved are being confused, since it is the contact with the glass, rather than the glass itself, that is the direct cause of the injury. We therefore need to ask what caused the contact in the first place – a question that brings us back, once again, to the abnormal or immobile state of the object.

This focus on "contact" as an essential factor runs up against problems in the aforementioned case involving the trampoline, where it was, of course, only intermittent. Accordingly, for causality to be inferred for the claimant's benefit, it seems that there has to have been a single contact (even a brief one) with the inanimate object. This therefore excludes non-continuous or multiple contacts. While this analysis works in the case of the trampoline and for items that people bump into, it raises difficulties with regard to slippery floors (which *per se* remain immobile). On the grounds that a person places one foot in front of the other, he will remain in constant contact with the ground; in our analysis, then, damages should be paid to a claimant who constantly kept one foot on the ground but not to one who was hopping along – a quite ridiculous solution, of course. However, we know that in the case of an injury involving a slippery floor of which no warning is given, the custodian of the floor will not be held liable on the grounds of the action of the thing (the *fait de la chose*)[51], whereas, if due warning is given[52] then liability is shared between the custodian and the claimant. Here, of course, contact with the ground was the same in both cases. This is simply nonsensical, and this notion of continuous contact as a criterion should therefore also be abandoned. 55

This leaves us with the analysis under which there is no longer a requirement for the inanimate object to play an active role; instead, the simple fact that it was physically involved in the injury is deemed sufficient for the custodian to be held liable. Accordingly, contact no longer becomes a prerequisite for the object to play an active role in the injury (an issue of relevance when it comes to the burden of proof) but instead simply a criterion for implicating the object. In this way, liability – as outlined in Art. 1384 of the Civil Code – will simply be based on the involvement of the object in the accident. This brings us back, then, to the theory in French law of the *équivalence des conditions*, according to which every event that played a part in the injury or damage can be deemed by the courts to have played an equivalent role in the injury. Two thoughts spring to mind here. 56

Firstly, if it is the physical involvement of the object that is held as grounds for awarding damages, then this becomes a necessary or even irreducible condition in such instances, making it impossible for the defendant to be released from liability for reasons of *force majeure*[53]. This is more than a little severe 57

[51] Civ. 1st, 29 May 1996, Bull. civ. I, no. 227; [1996] JCP G, 1996, IV, 1633. Interestingly, this judgment was issued by the First Civil Chamber of the *Cour de cassation* and not the Second.
[52] Civ. 2nd, 11 December 2003, Bull. civ. II, no. 386.
[53] S. Godechot (supra fn. 42), 2181 et seq.

on the custodian (*gardien*) of, say, a glass panel, who may have respected safety standards and applied basic common sense when he installed the glass. Secondly, the involvement (*intervention*) of the object does not necessarily equate to physical contact, so that the concept of the action of the object (the *fait de la chose*) could also be applied to an immobile object where no collision occurred. One might therefore ask whether this could even occur with a pane of glass in which someone sees a frightening reflection: if that person is injured when running away, maybe the custodian of the glass could be held liable!

58 But although we seem to be getting no further with these attempts at explaining the courts' decisions, these seemingly disparate cases may in fact reveal a single underlying principle: since the mere involvement of an object seems to represent sufficient grounds for awarding damages[54], there is a danger that the courts are treating the *fait des choses* in the same way that they deal with road traffic accidents[55]. In these, nothing more than the involvement (*implication*) of a vehicle is sufficient to guarantee an award of damages against the driver.

59 It is worth remembering here that this rather special situation came about with the single goal of enhancing the compensation available to claimants, irrespective of any negligence (*faute*) or abnormality. Ultimately, this may well be the only way of explaining the Liebrand cases and the others that will follow in their wake. (C.P.)

4. Versailles *Cour d'appel*, 3rd Chamber, 30 April 2004, 2 cases, [2004] RCA, October 2004, 12, note C. Radé: Liability of a Pharmaceutical Company

a) Brief Summary of the Facts

60 1st case: A woman sought compensation for the harm she had suffered in contracting clear-cell adenocarcinoma. This was caused, it was claimed, by her exposure *in utero* in 1968 to Distilbène[56], a type of oestrogen produced and marketed in France by the UCB Pharma group. The claim was based on the alleged defectiveness of the product.

61 2nd case: In a comparable claim, another woman was seeking damages from UCB Pharma in connection with a similar condition. The difference in this second claim lay in the date of the claimant's exposure to the drug – 1973.

[54] Certain commentators have suggested that the courts are assuming the existence of a *fait causal* (causative action) in such cases, as they do in cases involving liability for the actions of one's children. The treatment of both types of cases is therefore becoming increasingly convergent. For more on this, see S. Godechot (supra fn. 42), 2181 et seq.

[55] S. Godechot (supra fn. 42), 2181 et seq.

[56] The generic name of this oestrogen is diethylstilbestrol or DES (the name most frequently used in the United States).

b) Judgment of the Court

1st case: Here, the *Cour d'appel* agreed with every point of the decision in favour of the claimant reached by the Nanterre *Tribunal de grande instance* (district court) on 24 May 2002. As a result, UCB Pharma was required to pay damages to be based on an expert assessment of the victim's injury. The judges based their decision on Artt. 1382 and 1383 of the Civil Code, without giving effect to the provisions of Art. 1147 of the Civil Code (on contractual liability) and of Art. L. 221-1 of the Consumer Code (on the obligation for professionals to carry out their duties safely), the principal and subsidiary arguments made in support of the claim. The manufacturer was therefore found liable in tort on the basis that it had committed a *faute caractérisée*, or what might be termed here as an "established fault". The existence of a causal link between exposure to the product and the victim's condition was deemed to be "highly probable" by the court[57]. In addition the court accepted that the product, which had been recognised by the World Health Organisation as a carcinogen since 1974, was defective. This fact, however, was deemed of secondary importance insofar as the claimant was exposed to the product in 1968. At that time the defectiveness of the product – while strongly suspected – had not yet been clearly established. The pharmaceutical company had "failed in its duty of supervision and committed a series of faults" by neglecting to "monitor the effectiveness of the product in question", in spite of the existence of medical and scientific studies (particularly those published in 1939 and 1962–63) that drew attention to the risks associated with diethylstilbestrol. 62

2nd case: The court considered 1971 to be a key date: in the previous case, it was stated that "even if, from 1971 onwards, certain doctors were still recommending Distilbène for the prevention of miscarriages, others considered it to be dangerous." Furthermore, the US *Food and Drug Administration* had in 1971 withdrawn its approval for the product concerned. In view of this, the court found that the continued distribution of the product after 1971 by the company constituted a fault on its part. The absorption of the product by the claimant's mother represented a "major factor" in the development of the claimant's condition, "while the prescription of such a drug could not, in 1973, be counted as one of the preferred preventative treatments for women at risk of miscarriage." A causal link was therefore established. 63

c) Commentary

Distilbène ("DES" in the United States) also featured in two further court cases. This product was a form of oestrogen that was widely prescribed to pregnant women between the 1950s and 1970s to prevent miscarriage. While the babies born subsequently were apparently totally healthy, a large number of female children born to mothers who had been prescribed the drug came to 64

[57] The absorption of the product constituted, in the court's view, the "major risk factor" behind the appearance of the claimant's condition.

develop uterine cancer some 20 years later[58]. In a judgment given on 24 May 2002, the Nanterre *Tribunal de grande instance* stated that evidence of a causal relationship between the claimant's exposure to Distilbène *in utero* and her development of a malignant tumour was borne out by serious, precise presumption of facts that were sufficiently coherent[59]. In the view of the Nanterre court, the pharmaceutical company should, on the basis of Art. 221-1 of the Consumer Code, be held strictly liable for the defectiveness of its product, Distilbène, as demonstrated by its effect on the claimant's health, irrespective of the principal object of its use. This was because Art. L 221-1 imposed an obligation of safety on manufacturers, an obligation that could be considered a results-based contractual obligation (in other words, a duty to ensure that a product achieves its results safely, or an *obligation de sécurité-résultat*).

65 The Versailles *Cour d'appel* dismissed this last argument and also ruled that there were grounds for a claim based on contractual liability. In respect of the article cited from the Consumer Code, the court found that while this does refer to a duty of prevention, a failure to fulfil this duty does not in itself render the pharmaceutical company liable. As for liability in contract, no contractual relationship could be said to exist between the claimants on the one hand and the manufacturer of the product on the other and similarly, the claimants could not, in the court's view, benefit from the contractual relationship that existed between their mothers and the manufacturer. Nevertheless, the court found that on the basis of Artt. 1165, 1382 and 1383 of the Civil Code "those not party to a contract are justified in invoking any failure by the defaulting party to the contract when that failure has caused them loss, damage or injury, and they are not required to produce further evidence." Accordingly, the pharmaceutical company's failure to fulfil its contractual obligations under the terms of its contract with the claimants' mothers constituted negligence in tort (a *faute délictuelle*) to the detriment of the claimants[60].

66 Evidence of the defective nature of the product was not an issue here, as this had been acknowledged since the 1970s. The existence of a causal relationship was, in fact, also affirmed by the court, even though the judges accepted that the product was not the sole cause of the injury. In respect of injuries caused by pharmaceutical products, it can be extremely tricky to prove causality. The *Cour de cassation* (the final court of appeal), most notably in the context of cases relating to blood transfusions, showed its eagerness to assist claimants in such cases as evidenced by the following statement: "*When a*

[58] The first batch of cases was the subject of a decision reached by the Nanterre *Tribunal de grande instance* on 24 May 2002, Bobet/UCB Pharma, [2002] D., IR, 1185.

[59] Nanterre *Tribunal de grande instance*, 24 May 2002, ibid.

[60] In: Distilbène ®: le laboratoire jugé responsable et coupable!, [2004] RCA, October, 12–13, C. Radé outlines previous cases relating to the overturning of the need for a contractual relationship to exist: C. cass. 1st civ., 18 July 2000, [2000] RCA, 372; [2000] JCP, II, 10415, conclusions P. Sargos; [2001] RTD Civ., 146, obs. P. Jourdain; C. cass. 2nd civ., 13 February 2001, [2002] JCP, II, 10099, note C. Lisanti-Kalczynski; [2001] RTD Civ., 367, obs. P. Jourdain; C. cass. com., 1 July 2003, [2003] RCA, 251.

person demonstrates firstly that the viral contamination by which he has been affected occurred after a blood transfusion and secondly that he presents no [other] mode of contamination specific to himself, then it is up to the blood transfusion centre being sued to prove that the blood products it supplied were free of any defect."[61]

The *Cour de cassation*, however, dismissed this argument in a case where the claimant was diagnosed with multiple sclerosis after being vaccinated against hepatitis B[62]. Yet, the judges at the lower *Cour d'appel* had emphasised the co-occurrence of the vaccination and the presentation of the condition, and also the absence of any other cause that might have set off the illness. On the basis of these factors, they had concluded that the vaccination had played a "*role in precipitating or triggering off the case of multiple sclerosis*"[63]. It therefore appeared that there was a "*lack of [the] safety that a user could legitimately expect, [a fact] indicating the defectiveness of the product*"[64]. This 67

[61] C. cass. 1st civ., 9 May 2001, [2001] D, 2149, report P. Sargos; [2002] JCP, I, 124, obs. G. Viney; see also C. cass. 1st civ., 10 July 2002, [2002] JCP, IV, 2530.

[62] C. cass. 1st civ., 23 September 2003, Bull. civ. I, no. 188; G. Mémeteau, Vaccination préventive de l'hépatite B et sclérose en plaques: être médecin ou être juriste?, *Les Petites Affiches* (PA), 22 April 2004, no. 81, 9; P. Mistretta/T. Faict, Conditions de la responsabilité d'un fabricant de vaccin à raison d'une sclérose en plaques faisant suite à des injections d'un vaccin contre l'hépatite B, [2003] JCP E, 1749; P. Mistretta, L'indemnisation des victimes du vaccin contre l'hépatite B: conditions de la responsabilité du fabricant, [2003] JCP, II, 10166; N. Joncquet/A.-C. Maillols/D. Mainguy/E. Terrier, Conditions de la responsabilité d'un fabricant de vaccin à raison d'une sclérose en plaques faisant suite à des injections d'un vaccin contre l'hépatite B, [2003] JCP 2003, II, 10179; C. Radé, Vaccination anti-hépatite B et sclérose en plaques: la Cour de cassation envahie par le doute, [2003] RCA, November, 4; Y.-M. Serinet/R. Mislawski, Vaccination contre l'hépatite B: les conditions de la responsabilité du fait des produits défectueux, [2004] D., 898; C. cass. 2nd civ., 20 November 2003, Bull. civ. II, no. 355; [2003] D., 2909, concl. Kessous, note L. Grynbaum; [2003] JCP, II, 10004, note B. Daille-Duclos.

[63] N. Joncquet/A.-C. Maillols/D. Mainguy/E. Terrier, [2003] JCP 2003, II, 10179. The authors emphasise that by using the argument related to blood-borne contamination, the *Cour d'appel* was in this instance assuming that there was at least a risk that the condition might be triggered by the vaccination and was not suggesting that this had definitely occurred, as would be the case with illnesses contracted from contaminated blood. They propose a method that might relieve the claimants in such cases from the burden of proof, which would involve confirming that there exists a "medically plausible risk and that as a result it is scientifically impossible to provide evidence of a causal relationship between the treatment that the patient underwent and the injury he or she suffered".

[64] The claimant was in perfect health before being injected with the first dose of the vaccine. The *Cour d'appel* had drawn attention to the co-occurrence of the vaccination and the appearance of the condition, something also noted in other patients. Furthermore no other factors were present that might have triggered off the illness in the patient (see P. Mistretta/T. Faict, [2003] JCP E, 1749). The authors point out that "the case law that has grown up around the obligation of safety to which manufacturers are subject indicates that judges are sometimes happy to conclude that a product is, to all intents and purposes, defective merely on the grounds that an injury has occurred in connection with the consumption of that product". In the opinion of Professor C. Radé, "It is precisely because the defectiveness of the vaccine has never been established with certainty that the Cour de cassation reversed the decision of the Versailles Cour d'appel." In the professor's view, however, an analysis "based on the requirements drawn from the principle of precaution should have led the judges to reject the appeal" in view of the "troubling circumstances" surrounding the appearance of the illness ([2003] RCA, November, 4).

stream of cases, the like of which had not been seen before in France – together with litigation relating to the damage to health caused by smoking – attest to the potential difficulties arising from the need for claimants to prove both the existence of a defect and a causal link between that defect and their injury.

68 In situations where it is difficult to establish causality, the American courts have used the well-known theory of "*market share liability*", first introduced in *Sindell v. Abbott Laboratories*[65]. In this case, the claimant, who was suffering from a condition allegedly caused by DES (Distilbène), claimed that the defendants should be held liable even though she was unable to establish the identity of the manufacturer that had produced the drug taken by her mother. There were approximately two hundred companies that could potentially have manufactured the product involved. The California Supreme Court ruled that liability should be divided between all of the manufacturers *pro rata* on the basis of their market share[66].

69 In the two decisions reached by the Versailles *Cour d'appel*, the judges focused on the manufacturer's duty of supervision (*obligation de vigilance*). For the period prior to 1971 – the year by which, in the opinion of the judges, the defectiveness of the product had been conclusively established – there was evidence of negligence (a *faute*) on the part of the pharmaceutical company, since the studies that cast light on the potential risks of the product should have suggested to the manufacturer that action was called for, ranging from the carrying out of experiments to the full withdrawal of the product in the event of a significant potential risk[67]. As far as the period subsequent to 1971 is concerned, the company's liability is even more marked in view of the unequivocal defectiveness of the product. It is worth noting that these two decisions illustrate several aspects of manufacturer's liability: for defects in design, for a failure to provide adequate information, and for a failure in the duty to monitor the effects of a product (the manufacturer's *obligation de suivi*). The French law that implemented Directive 85/374/EEC, by referring to all of the grounds by which producers could be exempted from liability, made the two following grounds for exemption – the "development risk" defence, and the fact that the product was in compliance with mandatory regulations issued by the public authorities – conditional on the manufacturer taking measures designed to prevent the potential harmful consequences when the defect becomes apparent during the ten years following the release of the product on the market[68]. This obligation to monitor the effects of a product (*obligation de suivi*) corresponds to the French understanding of liability, and

[65] 607 P.2d 924 (Cal. 1980).

[66] In the words of Justice Mosk (at 925): "Each defendant is responsible for the proportion of the judgment represented by its share of that market unless it proves that it could not have made the product that caused the plaintiff's harm."

[67] In C. Radé's opinion, this constitutes a recognition on the part of the Versailles *Cour d'appel* of the principal of precaution in respect of the period before 1971 (ibid.).

[68] Art. 1386-12 al. 2 *Code civil*.

particularly to the principle of "prudence and precaution" recognised in French law[69].

The European Court of Justice stated[70] that while the Directive does allow Member States to withdraw from the provisions on exemption from liability set down in Art. 7 (c) it does not entitle them to modify the terms under which such exemptions might apply or to ignore the terms of exemption set down in Art. 7 (d) (i.e. exemption from liability in cases where the defect is due to the compliance of the product with mandatory regulations issued by the public authorities). The French government claimed that it would be logical if the exclusion provided for under Art. 15 of the Directive could be made subject to a condition such as the obligation to monitor products. This could be justified under the obligations incumbent on Member States under Council Directive 92/59/EEC of 29 June 1992 regarding General Product Safety (an obligation taken up again in the new Directive 2011/95). In point 47 of its ruling, the ECJ stated simply that Art. 15 allows governments to withdraw from the provisions of Art. 7 (e) of the Directive but does not allow them to modify the conditions under which these might apply. Similarly, Art. 15 does not permit governments to ignore or to modify the rules for exemption set down under Art. 7 (d) (compliance of the product with mandatory rules set by public bodies). Moreover, Directive 92/59/EEC, which does not deal with manufacturer liability, cannot be held to justify any modification to the rules set down in Directive 85/374/EEC. 70

French legislators – eager to avoid the threat of further condemnation – recently brought French law into line with EU law by means of Art. 29.3 of the *loi de simplification du droit* ("Simplification of the Law Act") dated 9 December 2004. This article, which has been commented on above, provides for the repeal of Art. 1386-12 (2).[71] (M.C.) 71

5. Aix-en-Provence *Cour d'appel*, 8 June 2004, [2004] D., Jur., 2678, Note M. Boutonnet, [2005] D., 186, obs. D. Mazeaud: The Precaution Principle in the French Lower Courts

a) Brief Summary of the Facts

A mast supporting a mobile phone antenna was erected at a short distance from a school, just some 36 metres away from a classroom. The fear of possible damage by radiation caused the parents to register their children in other schools. The municipality, owner of the school building, sued the mobile phone company for nuisance, requesting an order to have the antenna removed. 72

69 G. Viney, L'introduction en droit français de la directive européenne du 25 juillet 1985 relative à la responsabilité du fait des produits défectueux, [1998] D., 291, and especially 297.
70 See the decision dated 25 April 2002, Aff. C-52/00.
71 Law no. 2004-1343 of 9 December 2004, *Journal Officiel* of 10 December 2004, 287.

b) Judgment of the Court

73 The lower court ordered the removal of the antenna, arguing that the precaution principle (*principe de précaution*) is part of French tort law and justifies preventive steps to avoid the possible occurrence of a damage, though uncertain[72]. The Aix-en-Provence Court of Appeal affirmed the judgment, yet without mentioning the precaution principle, pointing out that the municipality could no longer guarantee the users of the school the absence of a health risk due to the proximity of the antenna. They were therefore victim of a nuisance (*trouble de voisinage*) exceeding the normal inconvenience linked to vicinity and were therefore entitled to the removal of the antenna.

c) Commentary

74 In this case, there was no scientific evidence that the proximity of the antenna could cause the children a possible damage. It is however admitted that children are more sensitive to electromagnetic radiation. A scientific report, submitted in 2000 to the French Ministry of Health and cited in the judgment, recommends a moderate use of mobile phones, particularly by children, as well as protecting sensitive buildings such as schools or hospitals from direct exposure to electromagnetic waves where the antenna is located within 100 metres from possibly exposed areas. This is based on the precaution principle[73], enshrined in Art. 5 of the new Environment Charter, recently appended to the French Constitution[74].

75 It is to be noted that Art. 5 of the Environment Charter only creates obligations for the State authorities to implement procedures of risk evaluation as well as proportionate measures to prevent harm, wherever such harm, though uncertain according to present scientific knowledge, may affect the environment in a serious and irreparable manner. This might justify government authorities regulating the position of mobile phone antennas in sensitive areas. However, it has no direct impact on the law of tort. It is by way of case-law only that such an effect may be envisaged. Allowing the use of tort law for the prevention of uncertain damage would be a drastic change since so far, the only aim of tort law remains the compensation of existing harm. This is a cornerstone of tort law, recognised as well in the Principles of European Tort Law at Art. 2:101. Despite its limited constitutional recognition, the precaution principle remains very controversial and should not be stretched too far.

[72] Grasse *Tribunal de Grande Instance*, 17 June 2003, [2003] RCA, November 2003, 6, obs. S. Kowouvih.

[73] See *inter alia*, M. Boutonnet, *Le principe de précaution en droit de la responsabilité civile* (2003) (not published); P. Jourdain, Principe de précaution et responsabilité civile, [2000] PA 239, 51; G. Martin, Précaution et évolution du droit, [1995] D., Chron., 299; C. Thibierge, Libres propos sur l'évolution du droit de la responsabilité, [1999] RTD Civ., 561; D. Mazeaud, Responsabilité civile et précaution, [2001] RCA, June 2001, 72.

[74] Constitutional Law No. 2005-205 of 1 March 2005.

Some French lower courts appear to be ready to make the big step, openly in the case of the first court, more covertly in the Court of Appeal case. It is hoped that the *Cour de cassation* will not engage in such a venture, which may be a minefield for innovation: such a lack of judicial precaution may indeed have serious adverse consequences in a vast number of fields, hindering the development of promising and socially beneficial technologies. May we indeed prohibit activities wherever the actor is unable to prove that the activity in question is free from any defect which may cause some uncertain harm? (O.M.) 76

IX. Germany

Jörg Fedtke

A. Legislation

1. Product Liability: *Geräte- und Produktsicherheitsgesetz*

1 On 6 January 2004, new legislation concerning the safety of machines and technical products passed Parliament.[1] The so-called *Geräte- und Produktsicherheitsgesetz* (GPSG), which came into force on 1 May 2004, thereby combines the content of two older statutes – the *Gerätesicherheitsgesetz* (GSG)[2] and the more recent *Produktsicherheitsgesetz* (ProdSG).[3] The GSG, on the one hand, contained technical safety standards and was initially only aimed at the protection of professionals using machines in the worksphere. Its scope was, however, increasingly expanded over the years to include consumer products such as household technology, sports articles, or children's toys. The ProdSG, on the other hand, was concerned with the protection of consumers using technical products at home.[4]

2 The GPSG is supposed to simplify the old dual regime by eliminating doubts regarding the application of the GSG and the ProdSG, and contains a few new elements made necessary by European legislation. In line with Directive 2001/95/EC, the definition of a "product" thus now includes machines which are designed for professional use but are increasingly also used by private consumers (so-called "product migration").[5] The statute also contains a number of legal definitions and examples specifying the obligations of producers, importers and retailers, including the duty to provide adequate information about the identity of the producer and instructions concerning the correct use of the product (*Informationspflicht*),[6] to inform the competent authorities about

[1] *Gesetz zur Neuordnung der Sicherheit von technischen Arbeitsmitteln und Verbraucherprodukten*, [2004] *Bundesgesetzblatt* (Federal Gazette, BGBl) Vol. I, 2 and 219.
[2] Of 1968.
[3] Of 1997.
[4] See § 1 no. 1 ProdSG.
[5] § 1(1) GPSG.
[6] §§ 4, 5(1) no. 1 GPSG.

the launch of new consumer products (*Unterrichtungspflicht*),[7] and to monitor products once they have been made available to the public on the market (*Produktbeobachtungspflicht*).[8] Finally, the GPSG increases the competences of public authorities to intervene both under "regular" circumstances and in case danger arises from a certain product.[9]

The GPSG deals primarily with the "technical" side of product liability and thus exerts most of its influence on the process of the production, the distribution, and the monitoring of products falling within its scope of application by the competent public authorities. The various duties of producers, importers and retailers identified by the statute also provide the necessary standards of care and thus impacts on litigation if harm is caused by defective products.[10] 3

2. Air Traffic: Liability for Damage Caused to Passengers

As reported on the same occasion last year,[11] legislative steps were taken in 2003 to ratify the Montreal Agreement of May 1999 concerning liability for damage caused to passengers, baggage, and cargo in commercial air traffic.[12] This legislation passed Parliament in February and May 2004.[13] At the same time, the national system of liability for damage caused to passengers *not* covered either by EU law or the Montreal Agreement was brought in line with the standards of the latter.[14] Both pieces of legislation, which increase the amount of compensation for victims and introduce a comprehensive regime of compulsory insurance for carriers,[15] entered into force on 28 June 2004.[16] 4

3. Privacy: Criminal Sanctions for Unauthorised Photos

A new § 201a of the Criminal Code (*Strafgesetzbuch*, StGB) now reinforces the protection of the private sphere against infringements by unauthorised filming and photography.[17] So-called *paparazzi* who shoot photos of or film 5

[7] § 5(1) no. 1 GPSG.

[8] In accordance with the principles developed by the courts, § 5(1) no. 2 GPSG.

[9] § 8 GPSG.

[10] For a more detailed analysis see T. Klindt, Das neue Geräte- und Produktsicherheitsgesetz, [2004] *Neue Juristische Wochenschrift* (NJW), 465 et seq.

[11] J. Fedtke, Germany, in: H. Koziol/B.C. Steininger (eds.), *European Tort Law 2003* (2004), 182.

[12] *Entwurf eines Gesetzes zu dem Übereinkommen vom 28. Mai 1999 zur Vereinheitlichung bestimmter Vorschriften über die Beförderung im Internationalen Luftverkehr (Montrealer Übereinkommen), Bundestags-Drucksache* (printed matter of the *Bundestag*, BT-Dr) 15/2285 of 22 December 2003. The Montreal Agreement entered into force in November 2003.

[13] [2004] BGBl I, 458 et seq.

[14] *Gesetz zur Harmonisierung des Haftungsrechts im Luftverkehr*, [2004] BGBl I, 550 et seq.

[15] For recent summaries of this legislation see M.T. Fisher, Versicherungspflicht von Passagierhaftungsschäden bei Luftbeförderungen, [2004] *Versicherungsrecht* (VersR), 1372 et seq.; H.-G. Bollweg, Luftverkehrshaftung im Umbruch, [2004] *Zeitschrift für das gesamte Schuldrecht* (ZGS), 1.

[16] [2004] BGBl I, 1027.

[17] *36. Strafrechtsänderungsgesetz* of 30 July 2004, [2004] BGBl I, 2012. See J. Fedtke (supra fn. 11), 182–183.

persons with the help of hidden long-range cameras, "SpyCams" or mobile phones in their private homes or in other especially protected areas and thereby violate the intimate sphere of their victims (the so-called *höchstpersönlicher Lebensbereich*) as well as anyone who makes use of illicit audio-visual material or manipulates authorised images can now be fined or faces imprisonment of up to one year.[18] The images thereby need not be of a sexual nature; the so-called *Intimsphäre* protected by § 201a StGB also covers, *inter alia*, confrontations of the individual with death and illness, and scenes involving highly personal areas such as toilets, dressing rooms, the medical consulting rooms of doctors, and health facilities (e.g., solariums and saunas). Even a particularly secluded garden can qualify as an area protected by the provision,[19] which was endorsed by all political parties and came into force on 6 August 2004.[20] As a so-called "protective statute" (*Schutzgesetz*) within the meaning of § 823(2) of the Civil Code (*Bürgerliches Gesetzbuch*, BGB), § 201a StGB will also provide a basis for *Schmerzensgeld*. Professional organisations such as the German Press Council (*Deutscher Presserat*), though acknowledging the trend towards ever blatant infringements of the *allgemeines Persönlichkeitsrecht*, criticised the use of criminal law against journalists.[21] It remains to be seen how German public prosecuters will actually seek to enforce the new sanction in practice.

4. Anti-discrimination: *Antidiskriminierungsgesetz*

6 By the end of 2004 the ruling Social Democratic/Green majority in Parliament finalised draft legislation aimed at combatting discrimination in the private sphere. The so-called *Antidiskriminierungsgesetz* (ADG)[22] is designed to meet European requirements contained in EU Directives 2000/43/EC,[23] 2000/78/EC[24] and 2002/73/EC.[25] The draft, however, reaches far beyond the ambit of Community law, which is aimed mainly at the creation of equal opportunities in employment relationships. The ADG thus seeks to enforce the equal treatment of individuals with regard to gender, disabilities, religious and ideological views, sexual orientation, and age (§ 1 ADG) in wide areas of private law.[26] This broad approach is the reason why a substantial portion of the new rules was initially envisaged to form

[18] The original draft as proposed by the States of Baden-Württemberg even proposed a maximum imprisonment of two years.

[19] *Entwurf eines 36. Strafrechtsänderungsgesetzes*, BT-Dr 15/2466 of 10 February 2004, 5.

[20] Previous legislative initiatives include proposals by the liberal F.D.P. (BT-Dr 15/361) and the conservative CDU/CSU (BT-Dr 15/533).

[21] See, e.g., a statement of the *Deutscher Presserat* concerning the initiative of Baden-Württemberg at http://www.djv.de/downloads/stellungnahme_presserat.pdf.

[22] *Entwurf eines Gesetzes zur Umsetzung europäischer Antidiskriminierungsrichtlinien*, BT-Dr 15/4538 of 16 December 2004. For the full text of the draft see also [2005] NJW, XXXV–XLIV.

[23] Of 29 June 2000, see *Official Journal* (OJ) L 180, 22 et seq. Deadline for the transformation of this Directive was 19 July 2003.

[24] Of 27 November 2002; see OJ L 303, 16 et seq. Deadline for the transformation of this Directive was 2 December 2003.

[25] Of 23 September 2002, see OJ L 269, 15 et seq.

[26] See § 2(1) nos. 5–8 ADG.

part of the BGB;[27] under these plans, two additional statutes were to specifically address discrimination in the working sphere[28] and provide for an "Office for the Protection against Discrimination" located at the Federal Ministry for Family, Seniors, Women and Youth (the so-called *Antidiskriminierungsstelle*).[29] The draft ADG now combines these various elements in one statute.

Heavily criticised by the conservative and liberal opposition in Parliament as an interference with the freedom of contract (*Vertragsfreiheit*),[30] the ADG aims to protect individuals against unequal treatment not only in the sphere of work (§§ 6 to 19 ADG) but also in the formation, execution and termination of legal relationships (*Schuldverhältnisse*) which usually involve standardised conditions and are entered into by one party in large numbers without special regard to the personal characteristics of the other party involved.[31] As § 2(1) no. 8 ADG makes clear, this includes transactions of everyday life (such as access to goods and services, including accommodation). Private insurance contracts are covered specifically by § 20(1) no. 2 ADG. As pointed out in the legislative explanation, these rules will in most cases affect commercial entities rather than private individuals.[32] By virtue of § 20(5) ADG, relationships which involve an element of proximity or personal trust are excluded from the application of the statute. This exception can apply, e.g., to lease agreements where tenant and landlord live together in close quarters. 7

If one party provides circumstantial evidence indicating that it may have been treated unequally on the basis of one of the personal characteristics identified by § 1 ADG, the other party bears the burden of proof for the absence of an unlawful discrimination.[33] A number of grounds for an unequal treatment with regard to religious or ideological views, disabilities, age, sexual orientation, or gender are thereby mentioned in § 21 ADG. § 22 ADG identifies possible claims of the affected party. Unlawful discrimination must be stopped, and the affected party may ask for an injunction in case there is a danger of continued discrimination. Conclusion of a contract can only be claimed if the contractual relationship would have been established between these parties under normal circumstances. The discriminating party must compensate any loss suffered by the other side, which includes equitable compensation in money for pain and suffering.[34] The restriction of *Schmerzensgeld* to *severe* impairments not made good in other form, contained in previous versions of the draft,[35] was 8

[27] Bundesministerium für Familie, Senioren, Frauen und Jugend, Projektgruppe EuRi, *Entwurf eines Gesetzes zum Schutz vor Diskriminierungen* (of 6 May 2004), 18 et seq.

[28] So-called *Arbeitsrechtliches Antidiskriminierungsgesetz* (AADG).

[29] So-called *Antidiskriminierungsstellengesetz* (ADSG).

[30] See *Frankfurter Allgemeine Zeitung* (FAZ) of 22 January 2005, 1–2: *Streit im Bundestag über die Behandlung von Minderheiten.*

[31] So-called *Massengeschäfte*, § 20(1) no. 1 ADG.

[32] BT-Dr 15/4538, 39.

[33] § 23 ADG.

[34] § 22(3) ADG.

[35] Bundesministerium für Familie, Senioren, Frauen und Jugend, Projektgruppe EuRi (supra fn. 27), draft § 319 et seq. *Bürgerliches Gesetzbuch* (German Civil Code, BGB).

dropped from the ADG. Instead, the legislative explanation refers to the case law concerning the compensation for infringements of the *allgemeines Persönlichkeitsrecht* based on artt. 1 and 2 of the German *Grundgesetz* (Basic Law, BL). The same principles should be applied by judges in discrimination cases.[36]

9 The Federal Government justified this controversial legislative initiative with the need to enforce existing constitutional values in private relationships. Due to a variety of reasons which include, *inter alia*, the limited effect of human rights in the private sphere (*mittelbare Drittwirkung*), the difficulties in providing the necessary evidence victims of discrimination frequently encounter in civil litigation, and the personal embarrassment caused especially by cases involving unequal treatment due to gender or sexual orientation, legislative intervention is regarded necessary.[37] Experience had shown that the general clauses of private law (§§ 138, 242 and 826 BGB) did not provide adequate protection.[38] The initiative is also seen as a response to international developments, especially in France, the United Kingdom, and the Netherlands. The political opposition and members of the legal community criticised the draft as an unnecessarily harsh limitation of private autonomy; EU law, aimed only at preventing discrimination in the work sphere, did not require the state to mother citizens in each and every corner of everyday life.[39] Finally, the wording of the text is regarded as too open-ended, creating legal uncertainty. Critics of the *Antidiskriminierungsgesetz* also expect a flood of litigation.[40]

10 The ADG was introduced and saw a first reading in Parliament on 21 January 2005. Assent of the *Bundesrat*, the second federal legislative body representing the German States (currently dominated by the conservative CDU/CSU), is not required.

B. Cases

1. European Court on Human Rights, 24 June 2004, [2004] *Juristenzeitung* (JZ), 1015 et seq.: Privacy[41]

a) Brief Summary of the Facts

11 The plaintiff, Princess Caroline of Hannover, has, over the past years, tried to prevent the publication of unauthorised photographic material covering her private life by the yellow press in various European countries. The photos in

36 BT-Dr 15/4538, 44–45.
37 Ibid., 17–18.
38 Ibid., 37.
39 J.-H. Bauer, Antidiskriminierung ja – aber bitte nicht nach US-Vorbild!, [2004] NJW, III; [2005] NJW, VI.
40 [2005] NJW, XVI; [2005] NJW XVIII.
41 = [2004] NJW, 2647 et seq.

question here were published in Germany between 1993 and 1997 by *Freizeit Revue*, *Bunte* and *Neue Post*. The plaintiff's attempts to gain compensation in German courts for intrusions of her private sphere were only partially successful, though the German Federal Constitutional Court (*Bundesverfassungsgericht*, FCC) did identify an infringement of artt. 2(1), 1(1) and 6 BL due to the unauthorised publication of three photos showing the plaintiff together with her children.[42] The publication of a number of other photos was, however, accepted by the FCC because the plaintiff was regarded as a so-called "absolute person of contemporary interest" (*absolute Person der Zeitgeschichte*) and was, as such, subject to a lower level of legal protection under German law. The plaintiff subsequently applied to the European Court on Human Rights, invoking an infringement of her private and family life as protected under art. 8 of the European Convention on Human Rights (ECHR).

b) Judgment of the Court

The unanimous decision of the Court held that art. 8 ECHR was indeed in- 12
fringed by the decision of the FCC to deny full compensation because of the plaintiff's position as an "absolute person of contemporary interest" under German law. Drawing on its own jurisprudence, the Court had no difficulty in qualifying the disputed photos as pertaining to the plaintiff's private life. The judgment then focused on the decision of the FCC and analysed how the German judges had balanced press freedom and the right to privacy in this particular case. Acknowledging that the FCC had accorded the plaintiff a right to privacy but effectively limited her protection to especially "secluded" zones because of the importance of press freedom and the interest of the public to be informed about the life of "absolute persons of contemporary interest" even if the information was not linked to any of their public activities, the Court then balanced the protection of private life with the freedom of expression under the European Convention on Human Rights. The judgment thereby identified the following criteria: (1) the (private or public) nature of the images; (2) the contribution the published material could possibly make to a discussion of general public interest; and (3) the amount of time that had passed between an event and its publication by the press. Applying these criteria to the case, the Court also emphasised the difference between "official" occasions (e.g., in the lives of politicians) and purely private activities of celebrities, pointing out that the disputed photos of the plaintiff clearly belonged to the latter category and that their publication by the press was based on purely sensationalist motives. Furthermore, the Court attached some importance to the fact that the press had obtained the material secretly and without the knowledge or consent of the plaintiff. In the light of the particular importance of privacy (which is, in the view of the Court, not restricted to "intimate" situations or family life but also features a social dimension, i.e. the visit of a beach club with limited access to members of the press), the Court rejected the application of a lower level of protection to the plaintiff, who exercises no public function or office

[42] Decision of 15 December 1999, [2000] NJW, 1021.

either in Monaco (her father is Rainier Romain III of Monaco) or Germany. German courts had failed to develop criteria which could adequately protect individuals in the position of the plaintiff. Despite the discretion accorded to the signatories of the European Convention in striking a balance between the conflicting rights of the individual and the interests of the press, the plaintiff was thus infringed in her right to privacy.

13 The Court chose to postpone any decision on the claim for pain and suffering and the compensation of legal costs raised by the plaintiff until these points had been discussed between her and the Federal Republic of Germany. The German Government decided not to appeal the decision.[43]

c) Commentary

14 The decision of the European Court on Human Rights was heavily criticised by the German press, which felt that the Court had not adequately taken into account the public importance of monitoring the activities of celebrities even if these were not politicians but rather football players, musicians, or film stars. According to this view, the poor performance of a national football team, the use of drugs by a top sports star, or the fashion preferences of film directors are of public interest and the subject of wider debates even if these issues were regarded as less "serious" in nature. Former and current members of the *Bundesverfassungsgericht* participated in the discussions surrounding the judgment, voicing, in one instance, serious doubts concerning the level of protection given to press activity.[44]

15 Despite this criticism, however, the main aspects of the judgment are to be welcomed as necessary adjustments to the protection of the right to privacy in relation to a number of doubtful practices increasingly endorsed by parts of the German press. In balancing the competing constitutional interests found in artt. 2(1) and 1(1) BL (*allgemeines Persönlichkeitsrecht*) on the one hand and art. 5(1) BL (freedom of expression and freedom of the press) on the other, German courts have, over the past decades, shown much sympathy for the latter. The European Court on Human Rights shares the concerns of the FCC in regard to the importance of a free press in a democratic society but displayed, at the same time, a reluctance to accept lower standards of protection for individuals who do not perform a particular public function or could be seen as collaborating with the press for their own personal advantages. This does not render German law obsolete. More importance will, however, have to be accorded to (1) the nature of the public interest in the information (in this case, the Court failed to see *any* serious issue in the photos, which were published only for entertainment and sensation of the public); (2) the higher intensity of visual material (photos) as opposed to texts, which merely describe certain aspects of everyday life; and (3) a finer distinction between prominent individuals based on

[43] Press release of 1 September 2004; [2004] *Juristische Schulung* (JuS), XVI.

[44] Former Justice Dieter Grimm in the FAZ of 14 July 2004, 34. More balanced (current) Justice Wolfgang Hoffmann-Riem in FAZ of 13 October 2004, 16.

their public function (both in general and in the concrete circumstances of the case). The last aspect is of particular relevance for the development of a more coherent concept of *Personen der Zeitgeschichte* and may call for higher protection of individuals such as the plaintiff in this case.

It must, however, also be emphasised that the European Court on Human Rights failed to give much attention to the fact that even celebrities who do *not* perform public functions could be left with a lower level of protection if they deliberately surrender sections of their private lives to public scrutiny. The current German approach may thereby again seem too harsh. Individuals who invite the press for their own profit (this can be publicity or money) thus have enormous difficulty in drawing red lines when paparazzi "follow the scent." This all or nothing approach of German courts will, again, need some qualification in the light of the principles developed by the European Court on Human Rights, and criteria will have to be found in order to distinguish spheres of life which have been consciously opened to the press, and others which remain beyond public scrutiny. 16

Two final points should be made. First, this judgment will force German courts to reconsider the balance between the protection of the private sphere and press freedom.[45] A fruitful judicial dialogue between the FCC and the European Court on Human Rights will hopefully develop, not least because of indications that the German legislator is equally concerned about the current state of affairs when it comes to intrusions of the private sphere by members of the press.[46] The second concluding remark concerns the time factor. It took around twelve years for the plaintiff to successfully challenge the first set of photos, which were published in 1993. That is certainly a span of time which would have exhausted most "normal" plaintiffs. 17

2. BGH,[47] 28 September 2004, [2004] NJW, 56 et seq.: Privacy[48]

a) Brief Summary of the Facts

The plaintiff, a daughter of Princess Caroline of Hannover, participated in an international riding tournament in Paris. Photos were taken on this occasion, one of which was later published in the German weekly newspaper *Welt am Sonntag*. Neither the text explaining the details of the image nor the article itself contained relevant information about the event but were rather concerned with the love of the plaintiff for horses and competitive horseback riding as well as her apparently still dormant interest in boys. The plaintiff was still under age at the time of publication, and the photo appeared without the consent of her parents. The plaintiff, who seeks to prevent any future use of the image by the publisher of *Welt am Sonntag*, was successful in the lower courts. 18

[45] There are indications of this already happening – see the discussion of Case 2, below.
[46] See no. 5 above.
[47] *Bundesgerichtshof* (Federal Supreme Court).
[48] = [2005] VersR, 83 et seq.

b) Judgment of the Court

19 The BGH confirmed the judgments of the lower courts, emphasising that the plaintiff had in all likelihood consented implicitly to the publication of photos taken at the event in connection with reports dealing with the tournament *as such*. Any permission must, however, be construed narrowly so as to exclude the use of images outside this limited context. Balancing the interest of the general public in the information provided by the article in *Welt am Sonntag* on the one hand with the *allgemeines Persönlichkeitsrecht* of the plaintiff on the other, the BGH found that the use of the photo was not justified on public interest grounds either. Referring to the recent judgment of the European Court on Human Rights of 24 June 2004,[49] the Court pointed out (1) that the plaintiff does not hold any public office or other social position which could justify the publication of her image without consent; and (2) that any prior permission to report on *other* aspects of her private life could not impact negatively on her right to privacy in the present case. Any future publication of the photo in question would, furthermore, lack the necessary topicality provided by the riding tournament.

c) Commentary

20 This judgment by the BGH, delivered only months after the decision of the European Court on Human Rights mentioned above, draws first consequences from this judgment for German law. There is, of course, a difference in age between the 17-year-old daughter and her mother, Caroline of Hannover. Apart from that, the two plaintiffs are, however, practically identical. Neither of the two holds any public office or performs social functions which could be regarded as particularly relevant for the public interest. Despite the fact that they are – or, in the case of the daughter, soon likely to become – part of the international "jet-set" should not deprive them of the protection provided by the Basic Law when it comes to purely private matters.

3. OLG[50] Celle, 23 January 2004, [2005] VersR, 91 et seq.: Pain and suffering under strict liability[51]

a) Brief Summary of the Facts

21 The applicant in this procedure concerning legal aid (*Prozesskostenhilfe*) was a passenger in the truck of the first respondent and sustained personal injuries in an accident possibly caused by the driver, an employee of the respondent, on 17 August 2002. It is not clear at this stage whether he had used the seatbelt of the vehicle. The *Landgericht* estimated any compensation for pain and suffering based on the Road Traffic Act[52] (which establishes strict liability for damage caused in motorised traffic) not to exceed a maximum of € 3,420.

[49] See nos. 11–17, above.
[50] *Oberlandesgericht* (Higher Regional Court).
[51] Case 14 W 51/03.
[52] *Straßenverkehrsgesetz* (StVG).

This estimate was based on the assumption that a claim for *Schmerzensgeld* based on a strict liability statute should be lower than a claim based on the fault regime of the BGB.

b) Judgment of the Court

22 The OLG Celle did not adopt the distinction between claims for pain and suffering brought under strict liability statutes and claims raised on the basis of (simple) fault as drawn, in principle, by the *Landgericht*. In the light of comparable cases reported by the various *Schmerzensgeldtabellen*[53] and the recommendations recently made by the Annual Meeting on Road Traffic Law (*Verkehrsgerichtstag*), the Court estimated the likely maximum to be in the range of € 6,000 in this case. Acknowledging the dual function of awards for pain and suffering (which is, first, to compensate the victim for non-pecuniary loss[54] and, second, to take into account the fact that the victim should also be given some degree of satisfaction because of the injury caused by the other party[55]), the OLG argued that the first element – compensation – is usually dominant in traffic accident cases; the level of *Schmerzensgeld* awarded to victims under §§ 7(1), 11 StVG should thus be determined by applying the standards used in cases of simple negligence (*einfach fahrlässiges Verhalten*). The judgment pointed out that this was also the approach courts had taken when awarding compensation for pain and suffering in the (limited) areas of strict liability in which *Schmerzensgeld* could be claimed prior to the recent reform of tort law (which introduced a general claim for pain and suffering on 1 August 2002, immediately before this accident took place). This was true, e.g., for § 833 sent. 1 BGB (liability for damage caused by luxury animals) and § 53(1) *Luftverkehrsgesetz* (liability for damage caused by military aircraft). Finally, different levels of compensation would jeopardise, in the view of the OLG Celle, one of the central aims of the 2002 reform, which was to provide for a simple and objective allocation of risks in certain areas of life and, consequently, a reduction in the amount of litigation.[56] If the courts were to apply a lower standard in the determination of *Schmerzensgeld* on the basis of strict liability, many victims would in all likelihood try to seek higher awards on the basis of the (fault-based) general rules of tort law.

c) Commentary

23 The introduction of a general claim for *Schmerzensgeld*[57] was a crucial aspect of the 2002 reform of German tort law.[58] Various justifications were brought

[53] Publications which seek to compile cases according to the injuries sustained by victims and the amount of *Schmerzensgeld* awarded by courts on an annual basis.

[54] So-called *Ausgleichsfunktion*.

[55] So-called *Genugtuungsfunktion*.

[56] See the legislative explanation to the 2002 reform: *Begründung des Regierungsentwurfs des Zweiten Gesetzes zur Änderung schadensersatzrechtlicher Vorschriften*, BT-Dr 14/7752, 15.

[57] See § 253(2) BGB.

[58] See J. Fedtke, Germany, in: H. Koziol/B.C. Steininger (eds.), *European Tort Law 2001* (2002), 229 et seq.; J. Fedtke, Germany, in: H. Koziol/B.C. Steininger (eds.), *European Tort Law 2002* (2003), 206 et seq.

forward for the change, and this decision of the OLG Celle correctly identifies the simplification or, if possible, avoidance of litigation as one of the most important considerations of the legislator. Strict liability did not, in practice, reduce the workload of the courts as victims were in many cases forced to prove fault anyway because compensation for pain and suffering was not made available under the old rules. This restrictive approach of German law, the result of a traditional suspicion towards *Schmerzensgeld* in general, was rightly regarded as outdated and should not be substituted by yet another – more subtle – distinction when it comes to the level of compensation.

24 This seems particularly true for road traffic accidents. The OLG is right to emphasise that most injuries caused by motorists will not require a special "sanction" in the form of a higher payment aimed at providing satisfaction (*Genugtuung*); many victims will be content to receive – quickly and without legal dispute – mere *compensation* of pain and suffering. There are, of course, a number of cases in which drivers cause accidents through reckless driving, under the influence of drugs or alcohol, or through otherwise extremely negligent behaviour (e.g., by using a mobile phone and driving at the same time). Here, satisfaction can indeed be a valid interest of the injured party. In line with this judgment, the approach of courts in dealing with the level of *Schmerzensgeld* under strict liability should, however, use simple negligence (on average the most frequent form of fault in this area of the law) as a standard, and leave it to the relatively small number of victims injured by more serious violations of traffic rules to seek higher damages by proving fault. Satisfaction will, in these cases, also be provided by criminal sanctions.

4. OLG Braunschweig, 22 April 2004, [2004] VersR, 924 et seq.: Compensation for pain and suffering[59]

a) Brief Summary of the Facts

25 The plaintiff, who is twelve years old, suffered severe impairments of both his physical and mental capacities due to medical malpractice of doctors employed by the defendant, the operator of a children's clinic. He was treated in the clinic following complications at birth. The mistakes of the doctors were established by an independent expert and are not in dispute between the parties. The defendant paid compensation of € 204,516.75 for pain and suffering. The plaintiff, whose condition is highly unlikely to improve in the future, claimed further payment of € 150,000. The defendant argued that the whole claim was time barred and, in any case, already satisfied by the payment made. The court of first instance awarded further damages of € 65,483.25.

b) Judgment of the Court

26 The OLG Braunschweig increased the compensation for pain and suffering to a total of € 350,000. After clarification of procedural issues concerning the ad-

[59] Case 1 U 55/03.

missibility of the appeal as such, the Court identified two elements which determine the amount of *Schmerzensgeld* appropriate in cases of this kind: (1) the exercise of equitable discretion by the judge, who must consider both functions of *Schmerzensgeld* (compensation and satisfaction), the nature and degree of the harm caused to the victim, the long-term effects of the injury, and – crucial to the evaluation in this case – comparable decisions of other courts; and (2) the fact that the claim of the plaintiff is not precluded by the nearly complete destruction of his personality or his inability to feel pain and sorrow due to the adverse effects of his injuries.[60] Applying these criteria to the case, the OLG focused on a series of decisions which have, over the past years, increased the level of *Schmerzensgeld* for victims of severe injuries.[61] The total amount of compensation awarded by the *Landgericht* in this case was, by comparison, regarded as too low.

c) Commentary

The level of compensation for the pain and suffering of severely injured victims has indeed been increased through a series of fairly recent court judgments. This development started in 2001 and led to a maximum of € 500,000 awarded separately to two children who were heavily impaired at birth.[62] The OLG Braunschweig stays clear of these two latter decisions, voicing concern over the extreme amounts awarded by the OLG Hamm, but correctly endorses the general trend towards a higher compensation in cases of this kind. More importantly, this decision clearly calls for a dialogue among judges who are confronted with similar cases. It emphasises the important function performed by so-called *Schmerzensgeldtabellen* (tables which systematically report the amount of compensation awarded for pain and suffering on an annual basis). 27

5. BGH, 30 November 2004, [2005] NJW, 354 et seq. : Liability of children in motorised traffic[63]

a) Brief Summary of the Facts

These cases jointly handed down by the BGH on 30 November 2004 involved two 9-year-old children who had each damaged correctly parked vehicles and were subsequently held liable by the owners on the basis of § 823(1) BGB. One child was engaged in a kickboard race while the other tried to manoeuvre its bicycle between parked cars and lost its balance. Both defendants invoked § 828(2) BGB, introduced in 2002,[64] which provides that children above sev- 28

[60] See BGH, [1993] VersR, 327 et seq.

[61] The Court discusses the following cases: *Landgericht* (Regional Court, LG) Gießen of 7 May 2001 (Case 4 O 563/00); OLG Naumburg of 28 November 2001, [2002] VersR, 1295 et seq.; OLG München of 20 June 2002 (Case 1 U 3930/96); and LG München I of 20 March 2003 (Case 9 O 6490/96).

[62] See OLG Hamm of 16 January 2002, [2002] VersR, 1163 = [2002] *Neue Juristische Wochenschrift – Rechtsprechungs-Report* (NJW-RR), 1604 and OLG Hamm of 21 May 2003, [2004] VersR, 386.

[63] Cases VI ZR 335/03 and VI ZR 365/03.

[64] The provision is applicable for accidents which occurred after 31 July 2002.

en but below ten years of age are not responsible for the harm which they cause to others by negligence in motorised traffic. The lower courts had rejected this defence, which was, in their view, introduced to take into account only difficulties young children encounter when confronted with *moving* vehicles.

b) Judgment of the Court

29 The BGH confirmed the reasoning of the lower courts and argued that the new wording of § 828(2) BGB indeed intends to provide a privilege for young children only if they are confronted with traffic situations typically requiring a certain degree of physical and mental development as well as experience with the rules and complexities of motorised traffic. These criteria do not apply to cases in which children damage parked vehicles due to negligence.

c) Commentary

30 This judgment of the BGH is in line with a number of recent court decisions in which owners of parked vehicles suffered damage by children between seven and ten years of age, usually when driving bicycles, using skateboards, or in the course of play.[65] The defendants were regularly denied the privilege of the new § 828(2) BGB, which provides a defence for negligently caused damage in traffic accidents. The wording of this provision is ambiguous and does not distinguish between moving and parked vehicles.[66] The legislative explanation accompanying the 2002 reform of the BGB does, however, lend support to the restrictive interpretation adopted by the BGH. Indeed, there seems to be no good reason why a child of this age group cycling on a pavement should not have to compensate the owner of a parked vehicle if it negligently swerves to the left and breaks the windscreen of the car, while it will be liable – subject to § 828(3) BGB[67] – if it swerves to the right and causes damage to the front window of a shop or a nearby pedestrian. There is hardly any difference between a parked car and a motionless shop window (though collisions with pedestrians, who walk or run at a certain speed and require some manoeuvring by the child, could resemble the situation envisaged by the legislator). The idea behind § 828(2) BGB is clearly the special kind of knowledge and experience required by a participation in *motorised* traffic.[68] The provision creates an immunity for weaker parties in dangerous traffic situations and is thus motivated by similar considerations as rules establishing strict liability for motorists.[69] *Motionless* vehicles, however, included in the interpretation of "traffic"

[65] See, e.g., AG Sinsheim, [2004] NJW, 453 et seq. and LG Koblenz, [2004] NJW, 858 et seq.

[66] This point is made by J. Jaklin/M. Middendorf, Haftungsprivileg nach § 828(2) BGB auch im ruhenden Verkehr?, [2004] VersR, 1104–1105.

[67] § 828(3) BGB declares that a person who has not yet completed his eighteenth year is, subject to the privileges established by paragraphs 1 or 2, not responsible for harm which he inflicts on another if, in causing this harm, he does not have the necessary insight to realise his responsibility.

[68] See, e.g., LG Heilbronn, [2004] NJW, 2391 where a 7-year-old child ran onto a road from behind an object. The impact caused damage to an approaching vehicle, which the driver could not stop in time. The child was not liable due to the privilege established by § 828(2) BGB.

[69] See, e.g., the French *loi Badinter* of 1985.

under § 7(1) StVG, will only rarely be the cause of this type of danger. Finally, it is worth noting a distinction drawn in the press statement of the BGH when announcing the two decisions. The text emphasised that both vehicles were parked "in accordance" with traffic regulations, which raises some doubts as to how § 828(2) BGB should be interpreted if vehicles are parked *illegally*. Considering the logic behind the privilege, this will, in most cases, again not make a difference. The evaluation could, however, change if the illegal position of the parked vehicle is, *in itself*, the reason for the mistake of the child (e.g., if an illegally parked car reduces the amount of space available on a bicycle lane or diverts the attention of the child by inhibiting its field of vision). While § 828(2) BGB might offer a solution for some of these cases, the claim of the owner could perhaps be reduced more flexibly under § 254 BGB depending on the degree of his contributory negligence.

6. BGH, 20 April 2004, [2004] NJW, 1943 et seq.: Compensation of value-added tax[70]

a) Brief Summary of the Facts

In August 2002, the vehicle of the plaintiff was severely damaged in an accident caused by a client of the defendant (an insurance company). A repair of the car would not have been economically viable (so-called *wirtschaftlicher Totalschaden*). The defendant accepted full liability and paid € 6,814 to the plaintiff, who neither repaired the damaged vehicle nor bought a new one. This amounts to the net costs of a comparable substitute car as determined by an independent expert (€ 9,913.79) less the gross rest value of the damaged vehicle (€ 3,100). The plaintiff demanded payment of an additional € 1,586. This amounts to the value-added tax which would have resulted from buying an adequate new car on the market. He based this claim on § 251 BGB, which allows for compensation in money if restoration in kind is possible only with disproportionate expenditure. The court of first instance awarded an additional € 427.38, which is the difference between the net costs of a comparable substitute car less the rest net value of the damaged vehicle and the first payment of the defendant. The *Landgericht* Osnabrück dismissed the appeal of the plaintiff. 31

b) Judgment of the Court

The BGH, in applying § 249(2) sent. 2 BGB rather than § 251 BGB, confirmed the decision of the *Landgericht*, emphasising that the latter provision only provides compensation in money (*including* VAT) for damaged objects if restoration is not possible at all or requires exceptionally high expenditure. In the case of heavily damaged vehicles, however, adequate substitute cars are usually available on the market without much difficulty. This is, according to the Court, compensation in kind[71] as envisaged by § 249 BGB. Following the 32

[70] = [2004] VersR, 876 et seq.; [2004] *Monatsschrift für Deutsches Recht* (MDR), 934 et seq.; Case VI ZR 109/03.

[71] So-called *Naturalrestitution*.

reform of this provision in August 2002, victims can thus claim VAT only if they actually incur tax by buying a new car or repairing the damaged vehicle. The Court stressed that this interpretation reflected the legislative intent as expressed in the explanatory section of the 2002 Act.[72]

c) Commentary

33 This decision of the BGH comes as no surprise.[73] The Court extended the scope of § 249(2) sent. 1 BGB by applying the new provision to cases in which the damage caused to a vehicle results in a complete financial loss. This confirms the distinction between §§ 249 and 251 BGB consistently drawn by the courts over the past years, and supports the intention of the legislator to reduce the extent of so-called "fictitious" damages by excluding VAT if tax is not paid by the victim in the aftermath of an accident. The solution addresses the risk of over-compensating victims. In practice, it was not unusual for plaintiffs to demand the full costs of a replacement or professional repair of the damaged vehicle (*including* VAT) while the car was not replaced or repaired at all – or repaired at a lower cost (either privately by self-repair or, in many cases, by recruiting illicit work *without* incurring VAT). The BGH thereby responded to the main argument of the plaintiff, who claimed that he might want to replace the damaged car at a later stage and would then have to bear the burden of paying VAT if tax were not included in the compensation, by pointing out that the *initial* payment of the insurance company (in this case € 6,814) would not preclude *further* compensation of VAT if and when tax was actually incurred by the plaintiff in dealing with the consequences of the accident. Until the full claim is time barred, this is indeed possible. In practice, the solution proposed by the BGH will, however, be difficult to operate. Insurance companies have much interest in closing their files as soon as possible, and further complications may arise through changes in tax law that can take place between the damaging event and a final settlement between the parties. The decision of the BGH may thus, at first blush, seem to be a success for the insurance sector; further analysis will be necessary, however, in order to fully determine its practical effects. Finally, it should be pointed out that rare vehicles (such as oldtimers) could still fall under § 251 BGB.

7. BGH, 23 October 2003, [2004] VersR, 332 et seq.: State liability[74]

a) Brief Summary of the Facts

34 The second plaintiff and his wife were owners of a farm, also home to the first plaintiff, their son. Between 7 January 1992 and 20 November 1995 the area experienced a series of fires, which affected five farms, including, on three oc-

[72] *Entwurf eines Zweiten Gesetzes zur Änderung schadensersatzrechtlicher Vorschriften*, BT-Dr 14/7752, 23–24.

[73] Previous cases already indicated a preference of the courts. See OLG Köln, [2004] ZGS, 38 et seq. (of 5 December 2003) and OLG Düsseldorf, [2004] ZGS, 395 et seq. (of 1 March 2004).

[74] = [2004] *Juristenzeitung* (JZ), 454 et seq.; Case III ZR 9/03.

casions, the farm of the second plaintiff. These fires caused serious damage and were suspected by the police to have resulted from arson. Clear proof could not, however, be found. Following further investigations after the last of these incidents, which included the use of telephone tapping equipment, the son was arrested in November 1997. The file presented to the judge prior to the arrest did not, however, contain vital information provided by a firefighter involved in combating one of the fires on the second plaintiff's farm. This exonerating evidence was revealed on appeal of the son against his detention. He was released in December 1997. The telephone tapping was found illegal. The son claimed compensation for pain and suffering caused by his detention and compensation of his legal costs; both plaintiffs claimed compensation for the mental distress caused by the illegal telephone tapping. The *Landgericht* and OLG confirmed these claims.

b) Judgment of the Court

The BGH dismissed the appeal in law brought by the defendant State (*Land*), arguing that the public prosecutor had failed to bring to the attention of the judge issuing the arrest warrant for the son and the telephone tapping permit for the premises all the facts necessary for a comprehensive legal evaluation. This amounted, in the view of the Court, to a negligent breach of an official duty owed to the plaintiffs.[75] The judgment emphasised that measures taken by law enforcement agencies should not, in the context of subsequent state liability claims, be reviewed with regard to their *legality*; taking into account, *inter alia*, the importance of a functionable system of law enforcement, acts of this kind need only be *justifiable* from an ex ante point of view. This, the Court decided, was not the case here. The evidence submitted by the firefighter raised serious doubts as to the chain of events and a possible involvement of the second plaintiff in that particular incident. State liability, however, does not result from the (flawed) evaluation underlying the decision of the public prosecutor to seek the arrest warrant, itself, but rather from the fact that the evidence given by the witness was not included in the application at all. The Court indicated that public prosecutors may thereby have some discretion in choosing the material which they present to the judge; a comprehensive picture of the alleged crime must, however, emerge. Finally, the privilege for court judgments contained in § 839(2) sent. 1 BGB – a provision which excludes state liability unless judges commit criminal acts[76] – cannot, according to the BGH, be invoked as far as the authorisation of technical surveillance is concerned. The decision to actually make use of such a permit as well as the responsibility to act in accordance with the law rests with the police authority. 35

[75] § 839(1) BGB declares: "If an official wilfully or negligently commits a breach of official duty incumbent upon him towards the third party, he shall compensate the third party for any damage arising therefrom. If only negligence is imputable to the official, he may be held liable only if the injured party is unable to obtain compensation otherwise".

[76] § 839(2) sent. 1 declares: "If an official violates his official duty by a decision in a legal issue, he is only responsible for the harm arising from this if the violation of duty consists of a criminal act".

c) Commentary

36 Following a number of court decisions[77] dealing with the legal requirements and the practical value of technical surveillance conducted by the police, this issue has recently received much attention in the public and legal debate.[78] The judgment of the BGH thereby clarifies a number of crucial points.

37 First, responsibility for the (continued) legality of technical surveillance remains with the public authority actually conducting the criminal investigation and is not shifted to the judiciary because of the need for an authorisation by a judge (so-called *Richtervorbehalt*). This is true not only for the initial application but also for any extension applied for by the public prosecutor.

38 Second, compensation for the breach of official duties by law enforcement authorities is not excluded by § 839(2) sent. 1 BGB. This seems correct for two reasons: (1) civil liability on the basis of the BGB should correspond to the legal responsibilities as defined by the Criminal Procedure Act,[79] and law enforcement authorities should not be allowed to hide behind a constitutional requirement (the involvement of a judge)[80] designed to protect the liberty of the citizen; and (2) the involvement of the judge both in the decision to issue an arrest warrant and the authorisation to conduct technical surveillance is not comparable to the "normal" court judgment as envisaged by § 839(2) BGB because both decisions are often made under time pressure and, more importantly, without the involvement of the suspect. The judge is thus highly reliant on the information provided by the public prosecutor, which must therefore present a full account of both incriminating and exonerating evidence.

39 Two final remarks should be made. This judgment is a good example of how important questions of administrative or criminal law are decided by *civil* courts in the context of state liability.[81] This much criticised[82] feature of German law, which runs contrary to the specialised court system of the country and places additional burdens on plaintiffs (time and costs), did not affect the quality of the decision or the coherence of the law in this particular case. The allocation of state liability cases to the ordinary courts on the basis of art. 34 BL should, however, be made subject to serious reform considerations in the future. The judgment also emphasises the increasing importance of state liability when it comes to the protection of the citizen. To be sure, law enforce-

[77] BVerfGE (*Entscheidungssammlung des Bundesverfassungsgerichts*; official collection of *Bundesverfassungsgericht* decisions) 96, 27 et seq.; BVerfGE 100, 313 et seq.; BVerfGE 103, 142 et seq.

[78] See, e.g., (H.-J. Albrecht/Cl. Dorsch/Chr. Krupe, *Rechtswirklichkeit und Effizienz der Überwachung der Telekommunikation nach den §§ 100a, 100b StPO und anderer verdeckter Ermittlungsmaßnahmen* (2003); O. Backes/Chr. Gusy, *Wer kontrolliert die Telefonüberwachung?* (2003).

[79] *Strafprozeßordnung* (StPO).

[80] See art. 104 of the German Constitution (Basic Law, BL) of 1949.

[81] For an example from the area of administrative law see J. Fedtke (supra fn. 11), 197–199.

[82] See, e.g., the critical remarks in B. Tremml/M. Karger, *Der Amtshaftungsprozess* (2nd edn. 2004), 6; S. Pfab, *Staatshaftung in Deutschland* (1997), 153–154.

ment in particular will only work if public officials can act without the danger of being held personally liable unless they breach their official duties with intent or gross negligence. In a similar vein, high financial risks for public budgets can inhibit necessary and timely state intervention. Compensation for miscarriages of justice, infringements of official duties, and mistakes made by public authorities are, however, a necessary consequence of the rule of law.[83] Individual justice can thereby come into conflict with considerations of public policy. By focusing on *legally justified* (rather than *legal*) decisions of public prosecutors, the BGH has shown much sensitivity in dealing with this tension.[84]

8. BGH, 30 March 2004, [2004] VersR, 789 et seq.: Social security (privileged tortfeasor)[85]

a) Brief Summary of the Facts

The parties are minors attending the same school. On 12 January 2000, they spent a recess between lessons in the yard together with other schoolmates. The defendant, who was thirteen years old at the time, lit a firecracker and threw it in the general direction of a group of children. The device exploded close to the plaintiff, who required medical treatment because her hearing was impaired by the detonation. She maintained that the defendant had acted with the intent of causing her physical harm at least in form of *dolus eventualis* when he threw the device in her direction. The defendant denied having aimed at the plaintiff and explained that he had wanted to scare a different group of schoolgirls standing nearby. The lower courts dismissed the plaintiff's claim for compensation based on § 823(1) BGB, arguing that the defendant was covered by the privilege contained in §§ 105, 106 of the Social Security Act (Book VII).[86] 40

b) Judgment of the Court

Confirming the decision of the lower courts, the BGH distinguished between injuries caused "in the context" of school activities and injuries caused only "on occasion" of a school visit. Since the plaintiff had accepted that the tortfeasor had not acted with intent of causing her physical injury when throwing the firecracker, this distinction became crucial for the decision of the case. Schoolchildren are protected from tortious liability by §§ 104 et seq. SGB VII if they cause damage to others "in the context" of school activities by negligence, but will be liable for both intent *and* negligence under the general rules of tort law if they cause harm only "on occasion" of their school attendance. Here, the Court identified a sufficiently close connection between the accident 41

[83] Art. 20(3) BL.

[84] For thoughts on the approaches of English and French judges in dealing with considerations of public policy in the context of state liability see B. Markesinis, *Comparative Law in the Courtroom and Classroom* (2003), 183 et seq.

[85] Case VI ZR 163/03.

[86] *Sozialgesetzbuch VII* (SGB VII).

and regular school activities. The incident had thus taken place in between classes and had involved careless behaviour of the kind which is typical in a school environment where children naturally tend to play, tease, tussle, fight or try to impress one another in various and often dangerous ways. The social law privilege was designed to maintain peace in school by excluding legal disputes among students and staff unless harm was caused intentionally, and the BGH stressed the importance of a wide interpretation of §§ 104 et seq. SGB VII in this particular context.

c) Commentary

42 This case illustrates the strong influence of German social security law on tort law. The privileges established by §§ 104 et seq. SGB VII cover a wide range of tortfeasors including, e.g., schoolchildren, students, family members, and co-workers. The main justification for these privileges, which exclude liability for harm caused by negligence, is the preservation of peace and harmony in certain spheres of life where individuals will usually know each other very well, are part of a closely knit community, and may even have to rely on one another despite the tensions which negligently caused accidents can create. The mechanism has advantages for victims, who will receive compensation through the social security system without having to prove the preconditions of a claim in tort. Lengthy, expensive, and often stressful litigation is avoided. They will, however, not be able to "target" the tortfeasor personally (which can be a similar problem in the area of state liability) and, more importantly, do not receive compensation for pain and suffering. Both restrictions lead to cases in which plaintiffs seek to pierce the protective veil of social security law, and the amount of litigation surrounding §§ 104 et seq. SGB VII is quite substantial. This casts some doubts on the peace keeping function of social security law, which might also come under increasing financial pressures. A number of victims, such as the plaintiff in this case, receive compensation without contributing to the system. Low public budgets and a struggling economy may, in future, make it more difficult to sustain this "social" regime.

9. BGH, 3 February 2004, [2004] NJW, 1449 et seq.: *Verkehrssicherungspflicht*[87]

a) Brief Summary of the Facts

43 The plantiff, who was 9 years old at the time, visited a public swimming pool operated by the defendant. Part of this facility was a 46m long water slide, which featured a completely closed sliding tunnel. From its entrance, users of the slide were not able to oversee either the tunnel itself or the lower end of the slide. Access was regulated by a sensor-driven light indicating whether the tunnel was free and thus safe for use. Two clearly visible signs gave safety instructions. Both the entrance to the slide and the end of the tunnel were monitored by CCTV. Staff could also access the slide directly or communicate with

[87] = [2004] VersR, 657 et seq.; Case VI ZR 95/03.

guests via a loudspeaker system. The plaintiff claims to have entered the slide while the light was showing green. He lost two of his front teeth in a collision with an elderly lady who was still in the tunnel at the time. The court of first instance awarded € 7,500 for pain and suffering and compensation for any further pecuniary and non-pecuniary loss resulting from the accident. The claim was dismissed on appeal.

b) Judgment of the Court

The BGH stressed the duty of the defendant to protect the users of the slide from any reasonably foreseeable dangers resulting from the facility. In addition to any contractual obligations, this delictual responsibility (in the form of a *Verkehrssicherungspflicht*) includes in particular a duty to prevent harm caused by dangers which are not clearly visible for guests and which involve a higher level of risk than can usually be expected in facilities of this kind. The operator must thereby take special precautions if children are allowed access. Applying these standards to the case, the BGH came to the conclusion that the defendant had exercised all possible care at the time of the accident. CCTV observation, the light mechanism, and the two signs with both graphic and textual safety instructions were sufficient. Operators of swimming facilities could not be asked to deploy staff to permanently monitor each and every possible source of danger (which includes malfunctions of the sensors in the slide due to violations of the safety instructions by guests). The appeal of the plaintiff was thus dismissed. 44

c) Commentary

Each year, numerous court decisions deal with *Verkehrssicherungspflichten*, duties of care designed to protect individuals from dangers created by access to certain facilities (e.g., roads, waterways, buildings, amusement parks or, as in this case, swimming pools). Based on § 823(1) BGB, the increasingly dense web of such duties has thereby led to a stricter liability regime and thus expanded the "grey area" between fault and strict liability in Germany. The approach of the courts is, however, flexible and judges will, for instance, take into account the feasibility of safety measures in the concrete circumstances of the case. Here, the BGH thus seems to draw a sensible distinction between precautions which can reasonably be expected in a swimming facility on the one hand and, on the other, an excessive degree of safety, which could make the operation of such facilities financially impossible. 45

10. BGH, 27 April 2004, [2004] VersR, 909 et seq.: Medical malpractice; reversal of the burden of proof[88]

a) Brief Summary of the Facts

The plaintiff suffered a motorcycle accident and was treated in the hospital operated by the first defendant. While a number of injuries were diagnosed 46

[88] Case VI ZR 34/03.

and treated, the doctors (the third, fourth and fifth defendants in the case) failed to identify a fracture of the pelvis. The plaintiff was mobilised four weeks after the accident. This was done without the help of crutches. On the second day she reported that walking was causing her considerable pain. This was not, however, followed up by the doctors. The plaintiff was released from the hospital a week later, again without crutches. The pain caused by walking did not subside, and a subsequent examination conducted by an independent doctor revealed the fracture. It is undisputed that X-rays would have shown the fractured pelvis at an earlier stage and that the plaintiff would have been advised to use crutches in order to reduce the pressure if this had been done. The fracture healed in a slightly unaligned position. The plaintiff, who has suffered considerable pain ever since, claimed compensation for pain and suffering (not less than € 20,451.68) and reimbursement of the costs of treatment in the hospital of the first defendant subject to possible *cessio legis* in favour of the health insurer or third parties. The *Landgericht* dismissed the claim in full. On appeal, the OLG Braunschweig awarded *Schmerzensgeld* of € 3,000 for pain and suffering.

b) Judgment of the Court

47 The BGH confirms the view of the OLG Braunschweig that the failure to examine the cause of the pain reported by the plaintiff amounted to medical malpractice. The fracture of the pelvis could have been identified without much difficulty, and prescription of crutches would have been the obvious and adequate medical response to relieve the pain suffered by the plaintiff.

48 The OLG, however, held that this would in all likelihood *not* have improved the healing process or prevented the negative long-term effects caused by the unaligned pelvis. This view was based on expert evidence, which estimated with a probability of up to 90% that the outcome would have been the same even if the plaintiff had used crutches from the outset. Any remaining uncertainty concerning the effects of the incorrect treatment was not sufficient, in the view of the OLG, to shift the burden of proof to the defendants. Apart from compensation for pain and suffering caused by the delayed prescription of crutches (€ 3,000) the claim of the plaintiff was thus thought unfounded.

49 This reasoning is rejected by the BGH. The Court thereby clarifies its position concerning the burden of proof in cases of severe medical malpractice. If the patient suffers harm which is a typical result of the mistakes made by the doctor in the case at hand, the burden of proof is thus shifted from the patient to the doctor *unless* (1) the likelihood of *any* causal link between the harm suffered by the patient and the wrong treatment is *extremely* low; (2) the specific risk which a correct treatment is designed to address did not materialise in the case; or (3) the chain of events leading to the damage sustained by the patient is unclear not only because of the doctor's mistake but also due to substantial intervention of the patient *himself*. These exceptions did not, in the view of the BGH, apply to the case at hand. The "simple" mistake of not establishing the

cause of the plaintiff's pain (so-called *Befunderhebungsfehler*) thereby amounted to a severe case of medical malpractice because the omission is highly likely to have been the cause of the failure to prescribe crutches, which was, in turn, highly negligent under the given circumstances.

c) Commentary

This decision of the BGH confirms the all or nothing approach of the Court when it comes to the burden of proof in cases of medical malpractice. Unless the exceptions mentioned above apply, doctors will thus have to show that their mistakes did not lead to the harmful consequences suffered by patients. This solution may seem harsh in the present case; the likelihood of a better outcome for the plaintiff if her fractured pelvis had been diagnosed and treated accordingly was, after all, very low. The problems of such a patient in proving the causal link between the (established) medical mistake and the damage sustained are, however, not less difficult than in all other cases of this kind. The Court is thus right in focusing on the requirement of severe medical malpractice and shifting the burden of proof in *all* cases unless one of the (limited) exceptions applies. As the BGH correctly points out in this judgment, judicial discretion in the law of evidence would indeed run contrary to legal certainty and make it even more difficult for victims of medical malpractice to predict the possible outcome of litigation. 50

C. Literature

1. B. Tremml/M. Karger, *Der Amtshaftungsprozess* (Verlag Vahlen, 2nd edn. 2004)

This book provides a comprehensive introduction into the German system of state liability. The first two chapters contain basic information concerning the increasing practical relevance of claims against state authorities in Germany, the importance of case law, as well as a number of recent developments and reform considerations. Chapters 3 and 4 then analyse in great depth the main types of action, correctly placing much emphasis on claims based on § 839 BGB and art. 34 BL. A number of topics which are of particular relevance for legal practice are then discussed in the third part of the book titled *Sonderfragen der Amtshaftung*. These include activities of public authorities in the areas of building and planning, trade regulation, the licensing of restaurants, duties of care with respect to roads, pavements, waterways and harbours, public warnings concerning defective products, and activities of the armed forces. Part 4 of the book provides some insight into the procedural aspects of claims against the state, while the final sections focus on the liability of public notaries (*Notarhaftung*) and the emerging area of state liability for infringements of Community law. The book is authored by two practitioners, which is certainly an advantage given the fact that this area of the law is, to a large extent, made by judges. It is characterised by its focus on practically relevant issues, though academics and students will find it equally helpful. 51

2. H. J. Kullmann, *Produkthaftungsgesetz* (Erich Schmidt Verlag, 4th edn. 2004)

52 The German Product Liability Act (*Produkthaftungsgesetz*) was introduced in 1989 as a reaction to Community Directive 85/347 EEC. The law has not been frequently invoked by plaintiffs; its practical impact on court decisions is thus still surprisingly low. This commentary, now in its fourth revised edition, analyses the less than twenty provisions of the Act by drawing on case law and academic writing. Extensive references, presented both in the context of the single provisions and in a separate section at the beginning of the book, provide a comprehensive picture of important German and European cases as well as academic contributions to the subject. Comparative reflections on the state of the law outside the European Union make this publication a valuable resource for both academics and practitioners.

3. G. Mäsch, *Chance als Schaden* (Mohr Siebeck, 2004)

53 This *Habilitationsschrift* by Gerhard Mäsch analyses the liability of providers of services (so-called *Dienstleister*) if the causal link between professional mistakes and the damage suffered by clients remains in doubt. These cases arise most frequently in the area of medical and legal malpractice and involve both substantive rules of tort law and procedural rules dealing with the burden of proof. The study compares the approaches taken by courts and academics in Germany with the solutions found in various European and Common law systems including Austria, France, Belgium, England, the US, Canada, and Australia. The national approaches identified by Mäsch thereby vary to a considerable extent; sometimes (as in Germany) an overall solution has not yet even emerged, and cases are solved differently according to the subject matter at hand. A new theory, liability for the loss of a chance, might thereby provide a more coherent basis for the solution of the problem. According to this approach, the contractual or statutory duty of the provider is only to do his best in order to achieve a result which is (as both parties acknowledge) not entirely under his control. Liability is thus not linked to the harm eventually suffered by the client but rather to the loss of a chance to prevent such harm. The author is confident that this theory may, eventually, lead to a more harmonised approach both in Germany and on the European level.

4. M. Fuchs, *Deliktsrecht* (Springer, 5th edn. 2004)

54 This is one of the few textbooks on tort law published in 2004. Now in its fifth edition, the book is again completely revised and discusses, in particular, judicial reactions to the *Schadensersatzrechtsreform* of 2002 and the impact of Community law in the area of state liability. A distinct feature of this publication, which covers all major claims of the BGB as well as a number of strict liability statutes, is the frequent use of citations from court decisions. This makes the book attractive for readers without easy access to German legal journals or the official collection of the BGH. It must be noted, however, that this work by Fuchs can only be a first point of reference for anyone with a deeper interest in German tort law.

5. H. Lange/G. Schiemann, *Schadensersatz* (Mohr Siebeck, 3rd edn. 2003)

This treatise by Hermann Lange and Gottfried Schiemann, published in 2003, deals with the compensation of damage (*Schadensersatz*) in all its aspects. Following an extensive introduction which explains the scope of the law of compensation, its basic structures and principles, as well as the most recent developments and reform considerations, the authors present their material in eleven dense chapters. These cover, *inter alia*, the definition of damage, its various forms, causation, hypothetical chains of events and the relevance of a legally correct alternative behaviour (so-called *rechtmäßiges Alternativverhalten*), the different forms of compensation, pecuniary and non-pecuniary loss, as well as contributory negligence and recourse. The book, which already takes into account the substantial changes of the law introduced in 2002, is warmly recommended for students, academics and practitioners. 55

6. R. Martis/M. Winkhart, *Arzthaftungsrecht aktuell* (Verlag Dr. Otto Schmidt, 2003)

This noteworthy commentary on medical malpractice was already published in 2003. Designed to provide quick and comprehensive information for the legal practitioner, this book presents the most important issues of medical law in alphabetical order. The topics covered include information of patients, abortion, protective measures for suicidal patients, contributory negligence, various cases of seriously incorrect treatment (so-called *grobe Behandlungsfehler*), as well as procedural issues such as time limitation, burden of proof, access to patient files, and expert evidence. The two authors are experts in their field of work, and provide an abundance of references mainly to the case law of the BGH and the *Oberlandesgerichte*. 56

7. Bibliography of Selected Books and Articles

General: N. Jansen, *Die Struktur des Haftungsrechts* (Mohr Siebeck, 2003); G. Schlegelmilch et al, *Geigel. Der Haftpflichtprozeß* (C.H. Beck, 24th edn. 2004); *Münchner Kommentar zum Bürgerlichen Gesetzbuch*, Band 5, Schuldrecht – Besonderer Teil III, §§ 705–853, (C.H. Beck, 4th edn. 2004). 57

Air traffic: M.T. Fischer, Versicherungspflicht von Passagierhaftungsschäden bei Luftbeförderungen, [2004] VersR, 1372 et seq.; W. Müller-Rostin, Art. 50 Montrealer Übereinkommen – eine unscheinbare, aber bedeutungsvolle Vorschrift zur Pflichtversicherung für Luftfrachtführer, [2004] VersR, 832 et seq.; A. Staudiger/R. Schmidt-Bendun, Neuregelung für Ausgleichs- und Unterstützungsleistungen für Fluggäste, [2004] NJW, 1897 et seq. 58

Attorneys: B. Borgmann, Die Rechtsprechung des BGH zum Anwaltshaftungsrecht in der Zeit von Mitte 2002 bis Mitte 2004, [2005] NJW, 22 et seq.; A. Walter, *Spezialisierung und Sorgfaltsstandard im Arzt- und Anwaltshaftungsrecht* (Gieseking Verlag, 2004). 59

60 **Computer viruses**: R. Koch, Haftung für die Weiterverbreitung von Viren durch E-Mails?, [2004] NJW, 801 et seq.

61 **Contract**: S. Grundmann, Der Schadensersatzanspruch aus Vertrag, [2004] *Archiv für die civilistische Praxis* (AcP), 569 et seq.

62 **Defamation and media law**: A. Beater, Deliktischer Äußerungsschutz als Rechts- und Erkenntnisquelle des Medienrechts, [2004] JZ, 889 et seq.

63 **Experts (§ 839a BGB)**: M. Finn, Zur Haftung des Sachverständigen für fehlerhafte Wertgutachten gegenüber Dritten, [2004] NJW, 3752 et seq.; M. Kilian, Zweifelsfragen der deliktischen Sachverständigenhaftung nach § 839a BGB, [2004] ZGS, 220 et seq.

64 **Fictitious costs of repair**: J. Luckey, Fiktive Schadensberechnung bei wirtschaftlichem Totalschaden, [2004] VersR, 1525 et seq.

65 **First aid**: F. Ehmann, Anwendung von Amtshaftungsgrundsätzen für die rettungsdienstliche Tätigkeit, [2004] NJW, 2944 et seq.; H.-D. Lippert, Die Haftung des Notarztes für Fehlbehandlungen – oder die liebe Not mit dem Staatshaftungsrecht, [2004] VersR, 839 et seq.

66 **Genetical engineering**: H. Fenger, Genmedizin und Haftungsrecht – Die Situation in Deutschland, [2004] VersR, 307 et seq.

67 **Housewives (compensation for loss of working capacity)**: R. Heß/M. Burmann, Der Haushaltsführungsschaden bei verletzten Personen, [2004] NJW-Spezial, 351 et seq.

68 **Medical liability**: E. Deutsch, Deregulierung und Patientenschutz im Arzneimittelrecht, [2004] VersR, 937 et seq.; M. Gehrlein, Neuere Rechtsprechung zur Arzt-Berufshaftung, [2004] VersR, 1488 et seq.; K. Hofmann, Auswirkungen der §§ 218, 218a StGB auf das Haftungsrecht nach der Rechtsprechung des BGH, [2004] NJW, 984 et seq.; L. Jaeger, Arzthaftung – Schmerzensgeld bei unerwünschter Schwangerschaft, [2004] MDR, 1280 et seq.; H.-D. Lippert, Die klinische Prüfung von Arzneimitteln nach der 12. Novelle zum AMG – eine erste Bestandsaufnahme, [2005] VersR, 48 et seq.; M. Rehborn, Aktuelle Entwicklungen im Arzthaftungsrecht, [2004] MDR, 371 et seq.; A. Spickhoff, Die Entwicklung des Arztrechts 2003/2004, [2004] NJW, 1710 et seq.; A. Spickhoff, Grober Behandlungsfehler und Beweislastumkehr, [2004] NJW, 2345 et seq.; G. Spindler, Neue Versorgungsformen in der gesetzlichen Krankenversicherung und zivilrechtliche Folgen im (Arzt-)Haftungsrecht, [2005] VersR, 4 et seq.; P. Weidinger, Die Auswirkungen der Schuldrechts-, Schadensersatzrechts- und ZPO-Reform auf die Haftpflicht von Ärzten und Krankenhäusern, [2004] VersR, 35 et seq.

Mining: M. Terwiesche, Die Entschädigung für irreparable Bergschäden an Gebäuden, [2004] MDR, 486 et seq. 69

Minors: R. Heß/M. Burmann, Das Kind und der ruhende Verkehr, [2005] NJW-Spezial, 63/64; J. Jaklin/M. Middendorf, Haftungsprivileg nach § 828 Abs. 2 BGB auch im ruhenden Verkehr?, [2004] VersR, 1104 et seq.; T. Simon, „Grundrechtstotalitarismus" oder „Selbstbehauptung des Zivilrechts"?, [2004] AcP, 264 et seq. 70

Pain and suffering: H. Becker-Toussaint, Schmerzensgeldansprüche Beschuldigter bei Medieninformationen der Staatsanwaltschaften, [2004] NJW, 414 et seq.; G. Bischoff, Schmerzensgeld für Angehörige von Verbrechensopfern, [2004] MDR, 557 et seq.; S. Hacks/A. Ring/P. Böhm, *Schmerzensgeld-Beträge* (ADAC/DeutscherAnwaltVerlag, 23rd edn. 2005); R. Heß, Das (Teil-)Schmerzensgeld, [2004] NJW-Spezial, 63 et seq.; W. Pauker, Die Berücksichtigung des Verschuldens bei der Bemessung des „Schmerzensgeldes", [2004] VersR, 1391 et seq.; M. Terbille, Die Schmerzensgeldteilklage – anwaltliche Pflicht oder risikobehaftet?, [2005] VersR, 37 et seq.; G. Wagner, Ersatz immaterieller Schäden: Bestandsaufnahme und europäische Perspektiven, [2004] JZ, 319 et seq. 71

Persönlichkeitsrecht: K. Friedrich, *Internationaler Persönlichkeitsrechtsschutz bei unerlaubter Vermarktung* (C.H. Beck, 2003). 72

Privacy: A. Heldrich, Persönlichkeitsschutz und Pressefreiheit nach der Europäischen Menschenrechtskonvention, [2004] NJW, 2634 et seq.; K.-H. Ladeur, Die Anpassung des privaten Medienrechts an die „Unterhaltungsöffentlichkeit", [2004] NJW, 393 et seq.; R. Mann, Auswirkungen der Caroline-Entscheidung des EGMR auf die forensische Praxis, [2004] NJW, 3220 et seq.; G. Müller, Produkthaftung im Schatten der ZPO-Reform, [2004] VersR, 1073 et seq.; O. Sosnitza, Die Zwangsvollstreckung in Persönlichkeitsrechte – Plädoyer für eine Neuorientierung, [2004] JZ, 992 et seq.; P.J. Tettinger, Steine aus dem Glashaus, [2004] JZ, 1144 et seq. 73

Product liability: D. Gesmann-Nuissl/Chr. Wenzel, Produzenten- und Produkthaftung infolge abfallrechtlicher Produktverantwortung, [2004] NJW, 117 et seq.; T. Klindt, Das neue Geräte- und Produktsicherheitsgesetz, [2004] NJW, 465 et seq.; T. Lenz, Das neue Geräte- und Produktsicherheitsgesetz, [2004] MDR, 918 et seq.; G. Spindler, IT-Sicherheit und Produkthaftung – Sicherheitslücken, Pflichten der Hersteller und der Softwarenutzer, [2004] NJW, 3145 et seq. 74

Property: B. Gsell, *Substanzverletzung und Herstellung* (Mohr Siebeck, 2003). 75

Protective statutes (§ 823 subs. 2 BGB): E. Deutsch, Schutzgesetze aus dem Strafrecht in § 823 Abs. 2 BGB, [2004] VersR, 137 et seq. 76

77 **Sexual abuse of children**: E. Beduhn, *Schadensersatz wegen sexuellen Kindesmissbrauchs* (Nomos Verlagsgesellschaft, 2004).

78 **Psychiatric injury**: R. Heß/M. Burmann, Die Ersatzfähigkeit psychischer Folgeschäden nach einem Verkehrsunfall, [2004] NJW-Spezial, 15 et seq.

79 **Smoking**: M. Adams/A. Bornhäuser/M. Pötschke-Langer/B. Grunewald, Die Haftung der Zigarettenhersteller für durch Rauchen verursachte Gesundheitsschäden, [2004] NJW, 3657 et seq.; M. Molitoris, Tabakprozesse in den USA, Deutschland und anderen europäischen Ländern, [2004] NJW, 3662 et seq.

80 **Social security**: K. Hofmann, Zahlungsklage auf künftige Schadensersatzrente bei Forderungsübergang auf den Sozialversicherungsträger, [2004] MDR, 1391 et seq.; K. Stöhr, Haftungsprivileg bei einer gemeinsamen Betriebsstätte und bei Verkehrsunfällen, [2004] VersR, 809 et seq.; R. Waltermann, Haftungsfreistellung bei Personenschäden – Grenzfälle und neue Rechtsprechung, [2004] NJW, 901 et seq.

81 **Sports**: J. Fritzweiler, Rechtsprechung zum Sportrecht in den Jahren 2002 und 2003, [2004] NJW, 989 et seq.

82 **State liability**: C. Kremer, Staatshaftung für Verstöße gegen Gemeinschaftsrecht durch letztinstanzliche Gerichte, [2004] NJW, 480 et seq.; H. Meyer-Mews, Zivilrechtliche Entschädigungsansprüche des Beschuldigten im Strafverfahren, [2004] MDR, 1218 et seq.; B. Rohlfing, Amtshaftungsprozess – Die Nachprüfbarkeit verwaltungsgerichtlicher Eilbeschlüsse, [2004] MDR, 1089 et seq.; U. Stelkens, Amtshaftung und Regress bei Schädigungen durch Verwaltungshelfer, [2004] JZ, 656 et seq.

83 **Strict liability**: L. Jaeger, Bemessung des Schmerzensgeldes bei der Haftung aus Gefährdungshaftungstatbeständen, [2004] ZGS, 217 et seq.

84 **Value-added tax**: T. Heinrich, Die Erstattung der Mehrwertsteuer bei wirtschaftlichem Totalschaden, [2004] NJW, 1916 et seq.; C. Peetz, Kfz-Totalschaden und Umsatzsteuer, [2004] ZGS, 370 et seq.

85 **Verkehrssicherungspflicht**: R. Bittner, Winterdienst zugunsten von Fahrradfahrern, [2004] VersR, 440 et seq.; H.-J. Hötzel, Verkehrssicherungspflicht für Bäume – Zehn Jahre Rechtsprechung zum Visual Tree Assessment, [2004] VersR, 1234 et seq.

86 **Weiterfressender Mangel**: Deliktsrechtlicher Eigentumsschutz bei „weiterfressendem" Mangel, [2004] NJW, 1913 et seq.

87 **Whiplash syndrome**: R. Heß/M. Burmann, Das – ewige – HWS-Trauma, [2004] NJW-Spezial, 303 et seq.

X. Greece

Eugenia Dacoronia

A. Legislation

Art. 11 of law 3242/2004 regulating the organization and operation of the Government, the administrative procedure and the local administration (in Greek O.T.A.)[1] provides that public servants not complying with final court decisions are subject not only to disciplinary punishment under art. 5 of law 3068/2002[2] but to civil liability as well according to the provisions of art. 105, 106 of the Introductory Law of the Greek Civil Code; the said civil liability of public servants presupposes the imposition of the disciplinary punishment according to the provisions of §§ 1 and 2 of art. 5 of the law 3068/2002. 1

According to the legislator, with the said provision, the Administration's obligation to comply with final court decisions, as required by the Greek Constitution, is completed. Establishing civil liability for public servants, provided that their non-compliance with court decisions has been disciplinarily judged, aims mainly at entrenching an increased sense of responsibility regarding the observance of the principle of legality of public administration. 2

B. Cases

1. *Areios Pagos* 895/2004[3]: Concurrence of Contractual and Delictual Liability

a) Brief Summary of the Facts

The plaintiff, who had formed with the defendants the limited partnership "S.G.5", aimed at guarding and protecting people, shops, houses, money transportations, dissolved this partnership setting forth as an important reason for the dissolution the fact that the defendants violated their contractual obli- 3

[1] Official Gazette A'/102.
[2] Official Gazette A'/274.
[3] [2004] *Chronika Idiotikou Dikaiou* (ChrID) D', 1009.

gations by forming another limited partnership with the same name and purpose, to which they transferred the entire property and the customers of the first company. The plaintiff alleged that, due to the dissolution of the company, he sustained pecuniary and non-pecuniary damage and demanded compensation, invoking the contractual liability of the defendants and, in addition, tortious liability as the legal basis for his claim.

b) Judgment of the Court

4 The Court emphasized that the partner is provided with the claim for reparation according to art. 914 Greek Civil Code (GCC) only when the culpable prejudicial act or omission with which the contractual obligations are violated, would in itself, i.e. without the contractual relation, be unlawful as contrary to the general duty of "not culpably damaging another", which is imposed by law (*Areios Pagos* 967/1973 sitting in full bench). In the present case the Court held that unlawfulness is constituted solely because of the contractual non-performance; without the contractual relation, no unlawful behaviour on the part of the defendants can be perceived.

c) Commentary

5 Given that the violation of contractual obligations is governed by specific rules (artt. 330, 335 et seq., 362 et seq., 382 et seq. of the GCC), it may be argued that the said provisions, as special provisions, prevail over those regarding tortious liability and they do not concur with them (principle of *non cumul*). The Greek jurisprudence, on the contrary, adopts the principle of "free concurrence of claims"; according to this principle, when the act or omission which constitutes the contractual non-performance is simultaneously and in itself unlawful, the two liabilities, delictual and contractual, concur[4].

6 No such concurrence exists when the contractual non-performance is not in itself unlawful, that is it is not contrary to the general duty of "not culpably damaging another", which is imposed by law. In such a case only the provisions regarding the violation of contractual obligations apply[5].

7 When the two liabilities, delictual and contractual, concur, the majority of Greek scholars consider that it is more correct dogmatically to accept that not two independent claims are born (*Anspruchskonkurrenz*) but only one, founded on two different legal bases (*Anspruchsnormenkonkurrenz*)[6]. There are no important practical reasons, however, that dictate this choice[7].

[4] See relatively P. Kornilakis, *Law of Obligations, Special Part* I (2002), § 79 4, 461 et seq. M. Stathopoulos, *Law of Obligations, General Part* (2004), § 15, no. 10.

[5] See M. Stathopoulos (supra fn. 4), no. 11.

[6] For the advantages of the said view, mainly expressed by Ap. Georgiades, *Die Anspruchskonkurrenz im Zivilrecht und Zivilprozeßrecht* (1968), see, from the most recent bibliography, P. Kornilakis (supra fn. 4), 465, 466. M. Stathopoulos (supra fn. 4), no. 12.

[7] M. Stathopoulos (supra fn. 4), nos. 12, 13.

2. *Areios Pagos* 220/2004[8]: Abusive Exercise of Rights as Unlawful Behaviour

a) Brief Summary of the Facts

The defendant knew about the dissolution of the general partnership "L. o K. General Partnership", aiming at operating a private educational institution, which took place on 3 July 1996. She was also aware of the agreement between all of the partners apart from D for the re-establishment of the partnership with M and of the fact that such an agreement would be void because of D's disagreement. However, she concluded an agreement with the partners, except for D, which was partially a preliminary agreement on the exit of the partners from the partnership and her entering, and partially a contract by which she undertook the company's debts and the direction of the company. The said agreement was concluded even though the defendant knew it was void because of D's disagreement. The defendant fully and exclusively administered the affairs and transactions of the company and she determined the fate and development of the company according to her personal abilities from the beginning of June 1997 until mid-August 1997, when she announced to her contracting parties that she would cease to concern herself with and take an interest in the company because she discovered the illegality of its continuation. The plaintiffs alleged that the aforementioned culpable behaviour of the defendant flagrantly exceeded the limits of her right not to perform her contractual obligations because of the agreement being null and void, causing them pecuniary and non-pecuniary damage. 8

b) Judgment of the Court

The Court acknowledged that, according to artt. 914 and 919 GCC combined with art. 281 GCC, if someone causes damage to another by a culpable unlawful act which consists of the exercise of his rights in a way flagrantly exceeding the limits dictated by *bona fides* (i.e. the straightforwardness and fairness in transactions) and the social-economic purpose for which the right was granted or if he causes damage by a willful act contrary to *bonos mores* (i.e. the ideas of a right and prudently thinking member of society at the time), he is bound to make reparation to the other for the damage thus caused. However, the Court refused to accept that the above-mentioned behaviour of the defendant was unlawful, for the exercise of her right was not abusive, i.e. according to the Court, it neither exceeded the limits dictated by *bona fides* and its social-economic purpose nor contravened *bonos mores.* 9

c) Commentary

In the commentary by G. Iatrou following the above decision, it is mentioned that it is generally accepted that when, apart from the conditions laid down in art. 281 GCC, those in art. 914 GCC are also met, the abusive exercise of the right gives rise to a claim for compensation. In the above case, the Court of 10

[8] [2004] ChrID D', 602.

Cassation held that unlawfulness as a condition of tortious liability laid down in art. 914 is always met when a right is abusively exercised, for the abuse of a right is an act contravening art. 281 and therefore always illegal. It must be noted though that it has been argued by scholars[9] that the violation of art. 281 alone cannot be considered unlawful in the meaning of art. 914 GCC; only when a certain right or legal interest of the person who sustained the damage is violated by the abusive exercise of the tortfeasor's right, can the abuse of a right give rise to tortious liability provided for in art. 914 GCC. This last point of view appears to be more consistent with the prevailing view on art. 914 GCC, which requires not merely the violation of any kind of rule of law, but the violation of a provision which either establishes a right or protects a legal interest of the person suffering damage for establishing unlawfulness.

3. *Areios Pagos* 289/2004[10]: Injury at Work – Violation of Safety Terms as Unlawful Behaviour

a) Brief Summary of the Facts

11 The plaintiff, who was an engineer on a ship, claimed compensation from the ship-owner based on artt. 297, 298 and 914 GCC for the severe injuries he sustained caused by an accident which took place on the ship while working. He alleged the accident was caused due to the chief engineer's omission to take proper measures for the maintenance and function of the ship's engine.

b) Judgment of the Court

12 According to art. 16 of law 551/1915 and art. 66 of law 3816/1958 "on the ratification of the Code of Private Maritime Law", in case of injury at work, the person suffering disablement or, in case of his death, his relatives are entitled to claim compensation according to artt. 297, 298 and 914 GCC only when the accident can be attributed to malice on the part of either the employer or of his auxiliaries or when provisions on the safety of the employees are violated. The Court emphasized that special provision is required; not complying with safety terms as stipulated by common knowledge and the general duties of providence and care required in everyday business life does not suffice. The accident must have been the result of non-compliance with safety regulations imposed by provisions which specially define the necessary safety terms and mention specific measures, ways and means for attaining the safety for the employees.

[9] Ap. Georgiades, *General Principles of Civil Law* (in Greek) (3rd edn. 2002), § 23, no. 31, fn. 49.

[10] [2004] *Ephimeris Ellinon Nomikon* (EEN), 565.

c) Commentary

Under the influence of the Greek literature[11], there is a clear tendency in the jurisprudence[12] of broadening the meaning of the term "illegally" in art. 914, so as to include therein not only the violation of a prohibitory provision of the law, but also the violation of the general duty of providence and care dictated by the principle of good faith; so, whoever does not take the appropriate measures in order to avoid the risk of provoking a detriment to the goods of other persons may be liable to pay damages for the damage caused. 13

Especially in relation to car accidents, the Supreme Court has repeatedly pointed out that abiding with the minimum prerequisites imposed by the Highway Code on the drivers of vehicles when they drive does not free such drivers from the obligation to go even beyond what is dictated by the said Code when this is necessary in order to avoid a detriment or in order to diminish the detrimental consequences of an act[13]. 14

In the cases of injuries at work, however, the Supreme Court holds that not complying with safety terms as stipulated by common knowledge and the general duties of providence and care required in everyday business life does not suffice in order that the person suffering disablement or, in case of his death, his relatives, can claim compensation according to artt. 297, 298 and 914 GCC. The accident must have been the result of non-compliance with safety regulations imposed by special provisions. 15

4. *Areios Pagos* 513/2004[14], 1094/2004[15], 430/2004[16]: Concurrent Fault

a) Brief Summary of the Facts

Areios Pagos 513/2004: The negligent driving of X caused the death of his wife and mother of their children. The children of the deceased asked that the company which had insured the car compensate them for pain and suffering. 16

[11] Ap. Georgiades, *Law of Obligations – General Part* (1999), art. 914, no. 30. P. Kornilakis (supra fn. 4), § 84 IV, 492–494; M. Stathopoulos (supra fn. 4), § 15, nos. 39 et seq.

[12] AP 1145/2003 (not published); 1500/2002 (not published); 50/2002 [2002] *Nomiko Vima* (NoV) 50, 1701, 1702. For a brief summary of the facts and the judgment of the Court (in English) in the said cases see E. Dacoronia, Greece, in: H. Koziol/B.C. Steininger (eds.), *European Tort Law 2003* (2004), 217, 218, nos. 18, 19 and *European Tort Law 2002* (2003), 234, nos. 10–15; AP 447/2000 [2001] NoV 49, 836 et seq., followed by a very interesting note of Ph. Doris, 839, 840. For a brief summary of the facts and the judgment of the Court (in English) in the said case see also E. Dacoronia, Greece, in: H. Koziol/B.C. Steininger (eds.), *European Tort Law 2001* (2002), 271, nos. 8, 9; AP 812/1998 [1998] *Elliniki Dikaiosini* (EllDni) 39, 1549; 678/1998 [1999] NoV 47, 1416; 1891/1984 [1985] EEN 52, 754. Athens Court of Appeal (EfAth) 3919/1999 [1999] EllDni 40, 1108; 9671/1998 [2000] EllDni 41, 535; 5356/1996 [1997] *Armenopoulos* (Arm) 51, 337; EfAth 9778/1991 [1992] Arm 46, 221. For more jurisprudence see P. Kornilakis (supra fn. 4), § 84 IV, 494, note 36.

[13] AP 1500/2002 (supra fn. 12); 447/2000 (supra fn. 12).

[14] [2004] ChrID D', 619.

[15] Not published.

[16] [2004] ChrID D', 719.

17 *Areios Pagos* 1094/2004: Due to a collision between a car driven by A and a tractor driven by B, B's wife, who was also a passenger in the tractor, passed away. The accident was caused by the negligent driving of both A and B. The said accident was due, according to the Court of Appeal, to the concurrent fault of B at a percentage of 70%. No concurrent fault has been proved on the part of the deceased. The family of the deceased demanded compensation for pain and suffering.

18 *Areios Pagos* 430/2004: A was riding his motorcycle, without plates and without insurance coverage, on a 6.70 metre wide road with no lights turned on, though it was already 6:30 p.m. and there were no lights at the side of the road, while another motorcycle driven by B, a minor, was moving in the opposite direction. A, without exhibiting the care and attention required by the average driver, tried to overtake a tractor, without having ascertained that he could do so without hindering or causing danger to road traffic. As a result he entered the opposite lane and crashed into the motorcycle driven by B, who was driving carelessly close to the dividing line of the road. B also did not have insurance coverage. According to the Court of Appeal, the collision of the motorcycles, which resulted in both drivers' death, was caused by the negligent violation of the Highway Code by both A and B, the latter's behaviour having caused the accident at a percentage of 40%.

b) Judgment of the Court

19 *Areios Pagos* 513/2004: According to the ruling of the Court, in case of prejudice caused by negligence, the existence of family relations between the tortfeasor and the aggrieved person does not primarily bar the claim for moral harm or pain and suffering; however, it is taken into consideration and can lead to a reduction of the amount of money adjudicated.

20 *Areios Pagos* 1094/2004: The Court, when exercising its discretion to determine the extent of non-pecuniary damages (art. 932 GCC), takes into consideration factors such as the fault of the tortfeasor, the concurrent fault of the beneficiary, the social and economic status of the parties. In case of a car collision, however, the concurrent fault of one of the drivers is not imputed to the deceased passenger of the car, unless the conditions of art. 300 § 2 GCC are met. Accordingly, such a concurrent fault must not be taken into consideration when adjudicating compensation for pain and suffering to the family of the deceased, otherwise art. 932 GCC would be violated. Moreover, by the combination of art. 926 and art. 927 GCC, it derives that, in case of multiple tortfeasors, joint and several liability is established and the person who suffered the damage may demand compensation from either one of them, without them being entitled to invoke such a concurrent fault as a basis for the reduction of damages (same as AP 13/2002 sitting in full bench).

21 *Areios Pagos* 430/2004: The Court held that, from the provisions of art. 10 of law 3950/1911 on liability of car drivers and artt. 297, 300, 330 and 914 GCC, it derives that, in case of car accidents, culpability of the driver who provoked

the accident and a causal relation between the driver's act or omission and the collision are required as necessary conditions for establishing liability. The existence of the tortfeasor's culpability is not in principle excluded by the fact that the injured party has contributed by his own conduct to the car accident, as long as the causal relationship is not interrupted. The violations of the provisions of the Highway Code by the driver who provoked the accident alone does not annul the existence of the injured party's concurrent fault, because the said violation does not in itself constitute the basis for culpability in case of a car accident. However, it is an element to be taken into consideration by the Court together with the existence of a causal relationship between the particular violation and the result caused. As to the present case, the Supreme Court noted that the decision of the Court of Appeal lacked sufficient justifications as to the establishment of B's culpability.

c) Commentary

Areios Pagos 513/2004 and 1094/2004 deal with the interesting issue of whether the existence of family relations between the tortfeasor and the victim precludes or diminishes the compensation of the family of the victim for pain and suffering in case of the victim's death. According to the first decision, such a factor does not preclude claims for pain and suffering but it leads to a reduction of the amount of money adjudicated, though in the second one, which follows the decision 13/2002 (in its full bench), it is stated that such a factor, i.e. the existence of family relations, must not be taken into consideration when adjudicating compensation for pain and suffering, unless the conditions of art. 300 § 2 GCC are met. According to the Court, if there is no field for application of the said article, the only factors to be taken into consideration are the fault of the tortfeasor, the concurrent fault of the victim and the social and economic status of the parties. 22

According to the decision 430/2004, in case of car accidents, the concurrent fault of the injured party does not exclude the tortfeasor's culpability as long as the causal relationship is not interrupted and the violations of the provisions of the Highway Code as such by the driver who provoked the accident do not annul the existence of the injured party's concurrent fault; said violations are, however, co-estimated together with the existence of the causal relationship between the particular violation and the result caused. 23

5. *Areios Pagos* 18/2004 (full bench)[17]: Issue of a Cheque without Provision; Payment by a Previous Legal Bearer and Endorser of the Cheque

a) Brief Summary of the Facts

The defendant issued a cheque to the order of the plaintiff, who endorsed it to bank A. The latter presented the cheque to the paying bank B in due time, but 24

[17] [2004] EllDni 45, 1322.

no payment was made because there were no available funds in the defendant's account. As a result the plaintiff – being the previous legal bearer and endorser of the cheque – paid the amount of the cheque to bank A after a relevant recourse. The plaintiff filed an action against the defendant claiming damages.

b) Judgment of the Court

25 The Greek *Areios Pagos*, sitting in its full bench, held that the legal bearer of a cheque has a claim for damages, according to art. 914 GCC, against the person who issues the cheque if the cheque is not honoured when presented for payment. On the contrary, a previous legal bearer and endorser of the cheque, who paid the amount of the cheque to the legal bearer after a relevant recourse does not have such a claim, as the damage he sustained from the payment of the cheque is not causally linked to the issue of the cheque, which was not honoured when presented for payment; his damage is causally linked to his liability as a legal bearer and endorser of the cheque to pay the cheque after a relevant recourse. This liability is especially provided by law.

26 According to the view of two members of the Court, however, the person who issues the cheque is liable against all the endorsers for damages, according to art. 914 GCC, as their damage is causally linked to the lack of capital at the paying bank, when the cheque is presented for payment.

c) Commentary

27 On the controversial issue of whether the previous legal bearer and endorser of a cheque, who paid the amount of the cheque to the last legal bearer after a relative recourse, has a claim for damages according to art. 914 of the GCC against the person who issued the cheque[18], the Court of Cassation (sitting in its full bench) confirms once again its position expressed in its decision no. 30/2003, according to which the previous legal bearer and endorser of a cheque has no claim for damages according to art. 914 of the GCC against the person who issued the cheque if the cheque is not honoured when presented for payment and the previous legal bearer is obliged to pay it. According to the Court, only the last legal bearer has such a claim against the person who issued the cheque.

28 A minority of two members of the Court, however, follow the contrary view, which was, indirectly but clearly, accepted by the Penal Division of *Areios Pagos* in the decisions 320/2001 and 691/2002.

[18] For this issue (in English) see also under AP 280/2003 in E. Dacoronia, Greece, in: H. Koziol/B.C. Steininger (eds.), *European Tort Law 2003* (2004), 226, 227.

6. *Areios Pagos* 22/2004[19], 959/2004[20]: Vicarious Liability

a) Brief Summary of the Facts

Areios Pagos 22/2004: Corporation A was the owner of a supermarket. In December 1992 A concluded an agreement with the general partnership B, according to which A appointed B to operate the butcher's section of the supermarket. According to the terms of the said agreement, B undertook to provide – on a monthly basis – A with a share in the profits stemming from the operation of the butcher's section and to comply with A's instructions as to its operation and function. C, who was B's employee in charge of the butcher's section, hired D as a saleswoman and he assigned to her the use of a special meat-cutting machine without giving her instructions on how to use it, although he was aware that she lacked experience and that she did not know how to operate it. As a result, while trying to use the machine, D's arm was amputated. 29

Areios Pagos 959/2004: A, who was hired as a manager by the co-operative organization B, issued – without being authorized by the organization's statutes – in the name of the co-operative organization a post-dated cheque for the sum of 79,891,773 drachmas (€ 234,458.61) to the order of the private limited company C which endorsed it to corporation D. When D pursued to collect the money from the paying bank, no payment was made because there were no funds in the bank. The Court of Appeal noted that D ought to have known that A was not authorized to issue cheques in B's name, given that the statutes of the co-operative organizations are kept in the district courts and held that B was not liable under art. 922 GCC for the tort committed by its manager, because A's action, even though exceeding his powers, was not causally connected with his service. D appealed against this judgment to the Supreme Court. 30

b) Judgment of the Court

Areios Pagos 22/2004: According to the judgment of the Court it derives from art. 922 of the GCC that the person who appoints another to perform a function (the *principal*) is strictly liable to make reparations to a third party for the harm caused by an unlawful and culpable act or omission committed by the other (the *auxiliary performer*) in the execution of his task. Moreover, if, in conformity with the will of the principal, the auxiliary performer had the potential to use third parties (sub-performers) in the execution of the task of the principal, the latter is also strictly liable for the harm caused by such sub-performers. For such liability, it is not additionally required that the principal exercises control or gives instructions to such sub-performers. 31

Areios Pagos 959/2004: The Court held that from art. 922 GCC, which dictates that a person, either physical or legal, who receives services from another 32

[19] Not published.
[20] Not published.

(the principal) is vicariously liable for the culpable and illegal acts of such other person when the latter offers his services with the will of the principal in order to bring a business to an end and, in general, in order to serve his interests under the guidance and orders of the principal on how he must fulfil his duties, it derives that the principal is vicariously liable even if the servant or the person assigned has acted in abuse of his service. Such an abuse exists when the illegal act has taken place in excess of the limits of the servant's duties and contrary to the guidance and orders of the principal, provided that between the illegal act and the business to be brought to an end there exists an internal relationship, which means that the illegal act would not have been committed had the principal not asked for the services of the servant, and the third party who sustained the damage was neither aware of the abuse nor was obliged to be aware. However, in the particular case, such an internal relationship had not been established, according to the Supreme Court, and the decision of the Court of Appeal was confirmed.

c) Commentary

33 One of the presuppositions for the vicarious liability of the principal is that the auxiliary performer who caused the prejudice serves the principal's interests under the latter's guidance and orders on how he must fulfil his duties[21]. If, however, in conformity with the will of the principal, the auxiliary performer had the potential to use third parties (sub-performers) in the execution of the task of the principal, it is accepted by the Court that the latter is also strictly liable for the harm caused by such sub-performers, without the need to examine, for the establishment of his liability, whether he exercised a control or guidance over the sub-performers as well.

34 On the issue whether the abuse on the part of the auxiliary performer precludes the vicarious liability of the principal, the prevailing view in the jurisprudence[22] dictates that the principal is vicariously liable even if the servant or the person assigned has acted in abuse of his service. It has been argued, however, that the principal is not liable if the prejudiced person knew (or ought to have known) that the servant or the person assigned has acted in abuse of his service; and this either on the ground of lack of causal link between the act and the service or on the ground that the prejudiced person accepted the act and he no longer relies on the "guarantee" that the person of the principal offers[23].

[21] See relatively M. Stathopoulos (supra fn. 4), § 7, no. 46.
[22] For the relative decisions see M. Stathopoulos (supra fn. 4), § 7, no. 47, fn. 54.
[23] See relatively M. Stathopoulos (supra fn. 4), § 7, no. 47.

7. *Areios Pagos* 3/2004 (full bench)[24]: Compensation for Deprivation of Alimony

a) Brief Summary of the Facts

An Albanian citizen was mortally wounded in a car accident. His wife and daughters asked for compensation for the deprivation of alimony that the deceased would have provided them with from his labour as a builder and gardener, for which he did not possess the necessary work permit in Greece. 35

b) Judgment of the Court

The Court held that from artt. 1389, 1390, 1485 and 1489 § 2 GCC it derives that the wife and children of a foreigner, who is not a citizen of a Member State of the European Union and who has continuously worked without a work permit in Greece, are entitled to alimony from him calculated on the basis of the income from his work, even though his employment contract is null and void according to art. 23 §1 of the law 1975/1991 combined with artt. 3, 174 and 180 GCC. Furthermore, according to art. 928 sent. b' GCC, in case of infliction of death of the said foreign worker, the person liable for his death is obliged to pay damages to his wife and children, given that, according to the usual course of things, the deceased would have continued to work had the death not occurred. Greek law applies according to artt. 14 § 2 and 18 § 2 GCC. 36

According to the view of the minority of the Court (1 member), however, the wife and children of the deceased foreign worker cannot ask to be compensated for the income the latter would have received from work that is forbidden by law. 37

c) Commentary

The Court of Cassation sitting in its full bench, with the above decision, overruled its decision 375/2003[25]. The said decision 375/2003 had followed the prevailing view in Greek jurisprudence and theory, according to which: a) compensation for loss of profit is not granted if such loss of profit originates from an activity that is contrary to the law or to *bonos mores* and b) a claim for loss of profit from the procurement of labour, without the permit required by law, is illegal, and had ruled that, from artt. 298, 914, 928 sent. b' and 929 of the GCC, it derives that the heirs of a foreigner who worked without a work permit in Greece cannot ask to be compensated for the income the foreigner would have received from work forbidden by the law (view followed also by the minority of the present decision). 38

[24] [2004] EllDni 45, 385 = [2004] ChrID D', 214. See also AP 375/2003 (contra), (supra fn. 18), 223.

[25] For the different views expressed in the decision 375/2003 of the Supreme Court and the commentary thereon by E. Kastrisios see (in English) E. Dacoronia (supra fn. 18), 223, 224.

8. *Areios Pagos* 197/2004[26]: The Function of the Independent Claim of Art. 931 of the GCC (Additional Compensation for Disfiguration)

a) Brief Summary of the Facts

39 The plaintiff alleged that, because of the defendant's culpable act, she suffered severe injuries in her left leg which medically led to a permanent partial disablement, influencing her professional, economic and social future, for it renders the practice of her profession as a cleaner problematic. In particular, she will no longer be able to meet the demands of her weary and fatiguing profession as a cleaner, which calls for steady movements, dexterity, muscular strength, etc. and she will be forced to seek a job less demanding and less profitable. The plaintiff claimed 20,000,000 drachmas (€ 58,694.05) as additional compensation for the unfavourable influence of the tort on her professional, economic and social development.

b) Judgment of the Court

40 The Court reiterated that the provision of art. 931 GCC introduces an independent claim for the compensation of a future pecuniary damage not covered by artt. 929 or 932 GCC[27]. From art. 931 GCC combined with artt. 298, 299, 914, 929 and 932 GCC, it derives that the disablement or disfiguration caused to the victim, irrespective of sex, besides the effect it can have on the claims based on artt. 929 and 932 GCC, can also establish an independent claim for compensation if it affects the victim's future. For the establishment of the independent claim of art. 931 GCC particular incidents, other than those required for the establishment of the claims based on artt. 929 and 932 GCC, are required. These particular incidents have to determine how the disablement or disfiguration of the victim affects his future, that the damages asked for are the specific result of the disablement and not only of the inability to work and gain income – given that art. 929 GCC provides for the reparation of such damage – and how this specific result would affect the professional, economic and social future of the victim.

c) Commentary

41 Though the legal doctrine firmly supports the view that art. 931 of the GCC does not introduce an independent claim for the compensation of a future pecuniary damage as, when applying art. 929 or 932 of the GCC, full damages must be granted, the Supreme Court, in a string of decisions, continues to consider that art. 931 GCC introduces an independent claim for the compensation of a future pecuniary damage, for the establishment of which particular incidents, other than those required for the establishment of the claims based on artt. 929 and 932 GCC, are required[28]. These particular incidents have to de-

[26] [2004] ChrID D', 517 = [2004] EllDni 45, 1349.

[27] Similarly AP 289/2004, [2004] EEN 2004, 566.

[28] For the relevant doctrine and jurisprudence see (in English) E. Dacoronia, Greece in: H. Koziol/B.C. Steininger (eds.), *European Tort Law 2001* (2002), 279, 280 and in: *European Tort Law 2002* (2003), 240–242.

termine how the disablement or disfiguration of the victim affects his future, that the damages asked for are the specific result of the disablement and how this specific result would affect the professional, economic and social future of the victim.

9. *Areios Pagos* 1051/2004[29]: Non-Pecuniary Damage – Burden of Proof in Case of a Consumer's Action

a) Brief Summary of the Facts

The plaintiff bought a standardized product (a cheese-pie) manufactured at the defendant's factory. While cutting a piece, she discovered a pin in it, which caused her great and justified anxiety, for she had already tasted the cheese-pie and feared she might have already swallowed a pin. She rushed to hospital and, after being examined, it was ascertained that no pin had been swallowed. Given that this ordeal had caused her grave fear and intense anxiety, she filed an action demanding compensation for non-pecuniary damage. The Court of First Instance adjudicated 300,000 drachmas (€ 880.41), while the Court of Appeal raised the amount adjudicated to 1,000,000 drachmas (€ 2,934.70). The case was brought before the Supreme Court by the defendant, who alleged that the plaintiff's action was not legally founded, for it did not deal with the requisite of fault as stipulated by artt. 914, 932 GCC and the law 2251/1994 for the protection of consumers. 42

b) Judgment of the Court

Areios Pagos held that from the combination of artt. 1 § 4a, 6 § 1 and art. 7 of law 2251/1994 for the protection of consumers, it derives that the said law does not offer a legal basis for claims on moral harm or pain and suffering; compensation for moral harm suffered by the consumer because of the defectiveness of the product is governed by the provisions on torts. Therefore, in such a case, the claim for non-pecuniary damages is based on artt. 914 and 932 GCC, provided that the conditions laid down in those articles are met. Moreover, according to the general provision of art. 338 § 1 GCCP, which provides for the burden of proof in case of an action for moral harm caused by tort, it is the plaintiff who must invoke and prove all of the elements of art. 914. However, the Court emphasized that particularly in case of a consumer's action against the producer of a defective product – as the consumer is not familiar with the production line and, therefore, he would be unable to prove the cause of the defect which falls within the producer's liability sphere – art. 925 GCC applies by analogy and the consumer is burdened with invoking and proving only the defect of the product, the damage caused by the latter and the causal connection between them, without being required to also prove the producer's fault. On the contrary it is the producer who must prove the absence of fault on his part, and, in particular, that the product's defectiveness is not owed to improper manufacture or maintenance at the factory or that the 43

[29] Not published.

improper manufacture or maintenance is not attributed to either his fault or the fault of the persons for whom he is held liable throughout the stages of the production. Accordingly, the Court concluded that the requisite of fault is not an element of the legal basis of the consumer's action against the producer according to the provisions of law 2251/1994 in combination with artt. 914 and 932 GCC.

c) Commentary

44 Art. 925 GCC deals with the liability of the owner or possessor of a building or structure in case of damage caused by their total or partial collapse. The said persons are presumed to be liable, unless they prove that the collapse is not due to a defective construction or to a faulty maintenance of the building or the structure. The liability is still based on the fault of the owner or possessor, but the burden of proof is reversed; the said persons are held liable, unless they prove the contrary.

45 For almost already thirty years the Greek courts have applied by analogy the said article to producer's liability and hold the producer liable for the defect and the damage caused to the consumer, unless he proves that he is not responsible for the defectiveness of the product[30] and this because the consumer is not familiar with the production line and cannot throw light on the facts that have led to his damage. Such facts are found in the area of risks of the producer, who has, as the above mentioned persons (owners or possessors of buildings or structures), a general duty of care and providence arising from the requirement of good faith taking into consideration business usages (artt. 200, 281 and 288 GCC); in order to avoid liability, he has to prove the absence of fault on his part ("principle of the origin of risks" or "principle of the fields of influence").

10. *Areios Pagos* 795/2004[31]: Notion of the Term "Family of the Victim" in Art. 932 GCC

a) Brief Summary of the Facts

46 For the death of I.S., his spouse asked compensation for pain and suffering for her 16-year old daughter from a previous marriage. According to the plaintiff, her daughter suffered from the death of I.S., whom she had loved as her father and with whom she had cohabited.

b) Judgment of the Court

47 The Court acknowledged that the term "family of the victim" is not specifically defined in art. 932 GCC. Taking into consideration, however, that the provision aims at the relief of the moral pain of the persons who were closely

[30] Leading decision was the decision 1259/1977 of the Court of Appeal of Thessaloniki, [1978] Arm 32, 121.

[31] [2004] ChrID D', 897.

connected with the deceased and suffered from his loss, regardless of whether they cohabited with him or not, the Court held that the persons entitled to compensation for pain and suffering are the parents of the deceased, his spouse, his children, his (half) brothers and (half) sisters, his relatives by marriage of first degree, i.e. fathers and mothers-in-law, sons and daughters-in-law as well as the children of his spouse born of a previous marriage.

c) Commentary

Who belongs to the family of the victim so as to be entitled to compensation for pain and suffering according to art. 932 GCC, is an issue that has been brought to the Supreme Court many times[32]. Taking into consideration that the provision aims at the relief of the moral pain of the persons who were closely connected with the deceased and suffered from his loss, regardless of whether they cohabited with him or not, the Court of Cassation has come to the conclusion that members of the family are: the parents of the deceased, his spouse, his children, his (half) brothers and (half) sisters, his relatives by marriage of first degree, i.e. fathers and mothers-in-law, as well as sons and daughters-in-law, provided, of course that said persons were closely connected with the deceased and suffered from his loss. The present decision adds to the already long list also the children of the spouse of the deceased, who were born of a previous marriage. 48

11. *Areios Pagos* 57/2004[33], Court of First Instance of Rhodopi 18/2004[34]: Prescription

a) Brief Summary of the Facts

Areios Pagos 57/2004: On 27 September 1991 a motorcycle driven by the plaintiff collided with the car of the first defendant. As a result the plaintiff suffered head and leg injuries, for which he received medical treatment. The accident was 80% due to the negligent conduct of the plaintiff and 20% to the concurrent fault of the defendant (no use of helmet). During the first years after the accident, the plaintiff did not face particular health problems; however, since 3 August 1994 he has suffered from recurring seizures which came about as a result of his head traumas as well as from psychoneurotic depression with behaviour disorders and self-destructive tendencies. As a result he became incapable of work. The sudden health deterioration could not have been medically predicted at the time the accident had taken place. On 21 December 1998 the plaintiff filed an action against the owner of the car and the company which had insured it claiming damages. 49

Court of First Instance of Rhodopi 18/2004: The plaintiff owned a company in Greece since 1990. At the beginning of 1995 he founded a new company in Bulgaria where he transferred all of his technical equipment. The plaintiff was 50

[32] See relatively (in English) E. Dacoronia (supra fn. 28), 280–282 and 245, 246 respectively.
[33] Not published.
[34] [2004] NoV 52, 1604.

obliged to spend much time abroad due to his professional engagements. He had entrusted the keys of his company in Greece to the first defendant, who was a former business associate of his, and had allowed him to issue invoices in case of sale of the merchandise which had remained in the no longer operative factory in Greece. On 31 October 1995 the defendant, taking advantage of the plaintiff's absence abroad, issued an invoice for 8,593,704 drachmas (€ 25,219.96) plus V.A.T. for 1,310,904 drachmas (€ 3,847.11) concerning services provided by the plaintiff's company, which, in reality, were never provided. The said invoice was issued with neither the plaintiff's knowledge nor consent; the first defendant, acting in collaboration with his spouse, the second defendant, who worked as an accountant at the plaintiff's company, forged the plaintiff's signature. The plaintiff filed an action against both his former business associate and his spouse based on art. 914 GCC in August 2002. The defendants invoked art. 937 GCC and maintained that the plaintiff's claim had been prescribed because the latter had acquired knowledge of the damage and of the identity of the tortfeasors in May 1996 and argued that, accordingly, the action should have been filed by May 2001.

b) Judgment of the Court

51 *Areios Pagos* 57/2004: The Court held that the claim of the injured third party against the insurer is subject to the short two-year prescription period provided for in art. 10 §§ 1 and 2 of the law 489/1976. This period starts to run the day after the accident, according to art. 241 GCC, and not from the time the injured party has acquired knowledge of the injury and of the identity of the person bound to make reparations, according to art. 937 GCC. The provision of art. 937 GCC is not applicable in this case because the claim of the injured third party against the insurer is not a claim deriving from an unlawful act, but from the law. Thus, the above mentioned provision of art. 10 § 2 of the law 489/1976 prevails over the general provision of art. 937 GCC. The aforementioned two-year prescription period, however, starts to run the day after the accident only in the case of foreseeable, from the beginning, damage of the victim, and not in the case of unforeseeable damage. The damage is unforeseeable in case of unpredictable, according to the medical data, deterioration of the victim's health. If the injured party anticipates, however, the plea of prescription by the insurer, he must either exercise the rights of the insured against the insurer (art. 72 GCCP) or found his claim on the assumption of the driver's debt by the insurer (art. 477 GCC); according to art. 43 of law 2094/1992, from the deposition of the certificate of the insurance at the police station by the insurer derives that the insurance company has assumed the driver's debt in parallel to him. The injured party cannot, however, invoke these bases for his claim in his written pleadings or his appeal for the first time; this would consist of either a non-acceptable modification of the basis of the claim or an inadmissible addition of a new basis for the claim. In the present case, the plaintiff had not invoked the assumption of the driver's debt as a legal basis for his claim against the insurance company already when filing his action, but later in his written pleadings and in his appeal; this has been considered by

the Court as constituting an impermissible modification of the legal basis of the action, which was initially based – as regards the insurance company – only on art. 10 § 1 of law 489/1976 and not on the assumption of debt.

Court of First Instance of Rhodopi 18/2004: According to art. 937 GCC, claims based on torts are prescribed five years after the injured party gained knowledge of the damage and of the identity of the tortfeasor. In the present case, the Court clarified that the condition of knowing the tortfeasor's identity laid down in art. 937 GCC is met when the injured party gains knowledge of as many facts as to be able to file an action successfully against a certain person. Mere suspicions, presumptions or ignorance because of negligence do not suffice. If the tortfeasor's name and address can be ascertained, the injured party is regarded as having knowledge of the identity of the tortfeasor at the time he – after inquiring – could have been informed of it[35]. In the present case, the Court was convinced by the evidence brought forward by the defendants that the plaintiff's claim had indeed been barred by prescription. 52

c) Commentary

Areios Pagos 57/2004: A short prescription period can be imposed by law for different reasons, such as in the interest of everyday transactions, which requires a rapid termination of conflicts. If the provision that provides for such a prescription is a special one, it prevails over the general longer provision. Also in case of cumulative claims, however, such a shorter prescription period provided for one of the claims prevails over the longer provision provided for the other claim, with which there is concurrence; otherwise the aim of the provision, e.g. the rapid termination of conflicts, which imposes the shorter prescription, could not be realized. If, however, no specific reason for a shorter prescription exists and there is a concurrence of claims, it is suggested that the longer prescription should apply to both claims[36]. 53

12. *Areios Pagos* 84/2004[37]: Defrauding of Creditors and Tort

a) Brief Summary of the Facts

On 23 October 1996 a public compulsory auction of the hotel of corporation A took place. The hotel was auctioned at the price of the first offer (600,007,000 drachmas, € 1,760,842.25), whilst its real market value was no less than 2,000,000,000 drachmas (€ 5,869,405.72), to the sole bidder, company B, whose shareholders were all close relatives of the president of corporation A. They were all aware of A's debts and they jointly organized the sale of the hotel to B at the particular auction where they were the only bidders, instead of postponing it so that more bidders could appear. Their aim was to avoid the payment of the debts of corporation A, which lacked other property and thus became insolvent towards its creditors. Among the said creditors belonged the 54

[35] AP 374/2001, [2002] EllDni 43, 157.

[36] See relatively Ap. Georgiades (supra fn. 9), § 21II 4, no. 19.

[37] [2004] ChrID D', 405.

plaintiff who had a claim of 14,477,380 drachmas (€ 42,486.80) against A and who, when trying to confiscate the hotel on 15 September 1998 found out about the auction and that A had no other property that he could confiscate in order to satisfy his claim. The Court of Appeal held that the plaintiff was entitled to damages as the act of defrauding the creditors constitutes an unlawful act in the meaning of art. 914 GCC.

b) Judgment of the Court

55 The Supreme Court quashed the decision of the Court of Appeal. It ruled that the act of defrauding the creditors, especially regulated in artt. 939 et seq. GCC, does not constitute an unlawful act in the meaning of art. 914 GCC. And this because, though the act by which the debtor disposes of his property so that he becomes insolvent towards his creditors constitutes an illegal behaviour since it is forbidden, its consequence, according to the law, is not the payment of damages but the cancellation of the disposing act. Even when the defrauding of creditors constitutes the offence provided for by art. 397 of the Greek Penal Code (GPC), it does not have as a consequence the payment of damages but the cancellation. Only when the debtor commits the offence of art. 397 GPC in one of the ways described therein, other than the disposing act, so that the case of cancellation does not come up, can a question of damages possibly arise.

c) Commentary

56 E. Nezeriti, in a commentary following the decision, points out that the act of defrauding creditors is similar to torts, given that it comprises of a culpable illegal behaviour resulting in the prejudice of the creditor. However, it differs in that the consequence dictated by law is not the payment of damages but the rescission of the contract[38]. It is questioned whether the two claims (one deriving from the tort and the other from the act of defrauding the creditors) may concur. According to one view[39], it is possible – under certain circumstances – that the act of defrauding the creditors meets the conditions stipulated by art. 919 GCC; in such a case, the creditor is entitled to demand compensation not only from his debtor but from the third party as well. According to another view[40], however, the provisions of artt. 939 et seq. GCC introduce specific rules and therefore the application of the tort provisions is excluded.

[38] See, however, P. Zepos, Defrauding the creditors as a *sui generis* civil wrong, [1954] EEN 21, 1201 et seq.

[39] Banakas, in Áp. Georgiades/Ì. Stathopoulos (eds.), *Civil Code*, art. 939, no 13. Ap. Georgiades (supra fn. 11), § 67, no. 11. P. Kornilakis (supra fn. 4), § 116 1 II 4, 718. AP 1344/1997, [1998] *Epitheorisi Emporikou Dikaiou* (EEmpD), 284.

[40] P. Filios, *Law of Obligations, Special Part* Vol. II/2, (4th edn. 1998), 208. P. Kargados, in: *Interpretation of the Civil Code*, (*Ermineia Astikou Kodikos*, ErmAK), Introduction to artt. 939–946, no. 95.

13. *Areios Pagos* 821/2004[41]: Civil Liability of Banks

a) Brief Summary of the Facts

The defendant – a bank – and the plaintiff – a client of the bank – concluded six successive contracts, by virtue of which the bank undertook to debit the plaintiff's accounts with certain sums of money and to credit the sums to company X, so that the latter acquired liquidity in cash enabling it to face the needs of its commercial trade. X sold a lot of clothes to the Libyan state organization V, the purchase price of which X would collect through the defendant bank. After a relevant agreement with X, the plaintiff asked the bank and the latter accepted to credit his accounts with the purchase price so that X's debt towards him would be paid off. However, not only did the bank fail to respond to the plaintiff's demand, but also pledged X's claim on the purchase price so as to enable X to get extra credit. As a result, X's debt towards the plaintiff was not paid-off and the latter sustained positive damage as well as loss of profit amounting to 730,000 US dollars. The plaintiff claimed reparations, invoking as a legal basis for his claim not only the contract he had concluded with the bank, but also the provisions on torts. He argued that the tortious behaviour of the bank was well established, given that by willfully acting against *bonos mores* not only did the bank omit to inform him that it would not be possible to draw money from X's accounts without its consent, which would render the pay-off of his claim impossible, but itself also granted credit in favour of X by pledging its claim without informing him and so he continued to finance X, adding to his damage. 57

b) Judgment of the Court

The Court held that behaviour – being a requisite of tortious liability for which art. 914 GCC provides – can be either a positive act or an omission. An omission gives rise to an obligation to pay damages when it is illegal, i.e. when the tortfeasor omitted to act even though he was obliged to by law, by contract, by good faith according to the prevailing social understanding, by his previous behaviour or by the general spirit of law. Furthermore the Court reiterated that the principle of good faith – encountered in artt. 200, 281, 288 GCC – entails the straightforwardness in transactions displayed by an upright and prudent person. In that sense, good faith constitutes a criterion of behaviour and consequently a rule of law, according to which there is an obligation on the part of the bank to protect its clients' interests by accurately notifying them of the limits up to which its management can be extended and by explicitly declining the execution of orders it cannot carry out. The Court concluded that the bank's aforementioned omission to inform its clients constitutes an omission of an act required by the principle of good faith, i.e. an act which – when the rest of the terms laid down in art. 914 GCC are met – gives rise to an obligation to pay damages. 58

[41] [2004] ChrID D', 985.

c) Commentary

59 According to the Court, the bank's omission to protect its clients' interests by accurately notifying them of the limits up to which its management can be extended and by explicitly declining the execution of orders it cannot carry out is contrary to the principle of good faith and, therefore, illegal, giving rise to an obligation for damages, when the rest of the terms laid down in art. 914 GCC are met. A recourse to art. 919 is not necessary in order to establish the liability of the bank.

C. Books and Articles

Books

1. M. Stathopoulos, *Law of Obligations (General Part)* (2004)

60 In this extensive edition (1543 pages) of the General Part of the Law of Obligations, a paragraph (§ 15, 75 pages) is dedicated to the recent developments in theory and the latest jurisprudence related to "Torts".

Articles

1. S. Paterakis, Problems on Compensating Moral Harm and Contemporary Development of Science and Technology, [2004] EllDni 45, 1 et seq.

61 The rapid development of contemporary technology has multiplied the violations of fundamental human rights, among which the right to personality and the right of privacy. The author looks into the various ways of gross infringement of the said rights: through mass media, Internet, biogenetics, globalization and international terrorism. At first he deals with the conflict between the right to personality and the right of the freedom of the press, both of which are protected by the Greek Constitution, and puzzles over the permissibility of the presence of mass media during court proceedings, which entails danger regarding the rightful administration of justice. He notes that in countries where substantial amounts of money are adjudicated as non-pecuniary damage, the violations of the right to personality by mass media have decreased. Moreover, he presents the dangers to personality posed by digital technology, in particular by the electronic processing of personal data and by the outburst of criminal activity in cyberspace, acknowledging the inherent difficulties in compensating moral harm in such cases. In regard to the problems of compensating moral harm caused by the applications of biogenetics, special reference is made to matters of cloning, artificial insemination, wrongful birth and wrongful life. Finally, the author presents the dangers to personality emerging from international terrorism and nuclear weapons, as well as from the projection of violence on television, noting that in such cases globalization hinders the compensation of moral harm.

2. G.N. Vasilakakis, Moral Harm and Media. Contemporary Questions and Tendencies of the Civil Courts' Jurisprudence, [2004] *Episkopisi Emporikou Dikaiou* (EpiskED) 2004/B, 275 et seq.

The author notes that during the last years there has been a significant increase in civil court decisions dealing with offences occurring through the press, the legal basis of which is founded on the provisions of the Greek Civil Code on the right to personality and torts. This, according to the author, has to do with the fact that the legislator has fixed the minimum amount adjudicated as moral harm in cases of offences through the press, which is, if compared with the amounts of money usually adjudicated in cases e.g. of car accidents or accidents at work, significantly large: art. 4 of law 2328/1995 states that the amount adjudicated according to art. 932 GCC for illegal acts by the media cannot be less than 100,000,000 drachmas (€ 293,470.28) for television stations with national range, 30,000,000 drachmas (€ 88,041) for television stations with local range, 50,000,000 drachmas (€ 146,735.14) for radio stations broadcasting in many prefectures and 20,000,000 (€ 58,694.05) for the remainder. It has been argued that fixing minimum limits is unconstitutional. The Greek Supreme Court, although it clearly stated that art. 4 of law 2328/1995 is not contrary to the Greek Constitution, held that when judging a case it needs to be *in concreto* examined whether the adjudication of the aforementioned minimum amounts violates the principle of proportionality between the means used and the purpose aimed at[42]. First Instance Courts as well as Courts of Appeals, complying with the constitutional principle of proportionality, adjudicate amounts lower than the limits fixed by the legislator, taking into consideration the economic status of the plaintiff[43]. The author approves of the application of the principle of proportionality, given that in many cases brought before the courts the offence is so insignificant that adjudicating the minimum amounts prescribed by the law would not be justifiable. 62

3. K.G. Karagiannis, The Operation of an Entity Rendering Medical Services without License as Illegal Behaviour and as Behaviour against *Bonos Mores* and the Claim for its Cessation and Omission in the Future, [2004] NoV 52, 922 et seq.

The decision 925/2003 of the First Instance Court of Rethymno[44] drove the writer to contemplate on the establishment of unlawfulness or opposition to *bonos mores* as preconditions of tortious liability in case of rendering medical services without license and generally in cases where the rules imposed for the exercise 63

[42] AP 1043/2001 [2001] ChrID A', 819. See also (in English), E. Dacoronia, in: H. Koziol/B.C. Steininger (eds.), *European Tort Law 2001* (2002), 288, 289.

[43] Thessaloniki Court of Appeal 2863/2003, Thessaloniki Court of First Instance 5966, 5967, 28775/2003, unpublished.

[44] [2004] NoV 52, 1018. The case was brought before the Court by doctors and providers of medical services legitimately exercising their profession in Rethymno, who suffered losses from the operation of an entity which rendered medical services in the same area without having been granted a permit to do so. They demanded that the operation of the entity cease and not recur in the future.

of a professional activity are either violated or not complied with. The writer advocates that in such cases unlawfulness is clearly established and argues that the rules which require minimum conditions and the issue of a permit for the exercise of medical professions protect not only the public interest but private interests as well, among which are included both the interests of fellow doctors and the interests of patients. The author also notes that the unlawful or *contra bonos mores* violation of either a right or legally protected interest according to artt. 914 and 919 GCC may give rise not only to a claim for damages but also – even though not explicitly provided for in artt. 914 and 919 GCC – to a claim for the cessation of the offence and the non-recurrence thereof in the future. This claim, according to the author, is of major importance in case unlawfulness does not stem from the violation of an absolute right, because the law explicitly provides for this claim in such cases (e.g. artt. 57and 1108 GCC), but when unlawfulness stems from a violation of a legally protected interest or violation of property, especially when the illegal behaviour continues. Finally, the author looks into the relation between artt. 914 and 919 GCC, noting their differences, acknowledging the possibility of them being concurred, drawing his attention to the practical significance of art. 919 GCC, especially when the conditions laid down in art. 914 are not met, by referring to cases which fall into it.

4. A.-O. Mitsou, Chances of the Claim for Damages of the Legal Bearer of a Cheque without Cover in Case of Bankruptcy of the Person who Issued it, [2004] *Dikaio Epicheiriseon kai Etaireion* (DEE) 10, 407 et seq.

64 With the occasion of the decision 213/2003 of *Areios Pagos*[45], which held that non-payment of a post-dated cheque presented for payment after the declaration of bankruptcy of its issuer and not honoured cannot establish the element of fault and, accordingly, cannot give rise to a claim for damages according to art. 914 GCC, the author puzzles over the issuer's criminal and civil liability. The relevant legal framework consists of art. 914 GCC and art. 79 of law 5960/1933. Art. 79 provides for the criminal offence of non-payment of a cheque due to lack of capital either at the time of the issue of the cheque or at the time of its payment. Even though the writer approves of the Supreme Court's decision, which considered that there is no fault regarding the non-payment of the cheque after the bankruptcy given that the debtor's capitals are blocked in favour of the group of his creditors, she deems it necessary to note that the Court omitted to examine the existence of fault on the part of the issuer at the time he issued the post-dated cheque. According to her opinion, in case of fault at the time the cheque is issued, the criminal offence of art. 79 of law 5960/1933 is constituted; however, tortious liability is not established, for bankruptcy interrupts the causal relation between the issue of the cheque without cover and the legal bearer's damage from its non-payment, given that the cheque would not be honoured even if the capitals were sufficient because, as a result of the bankruptcy, they would be blocked in favour of the group of the issuer's creditors.

[45] [2003] DEE 9, 971 = [2003] ChrID C', 253 with comments by I. Markou.

XI. Hungary

Attila Menyhárd

A. Legislation

There was no relevant legislation to be reported in 2004. 1

B. Cases

1. *Legfelsőbb Bíróság* (Supreme Court) Legf. Bír. Pf. III. 26.339/2001. sz. EBH 2003 no. 941 and BH 2004 no. 143: No Compensation for Wrongful Birth

a) Brief Summary of the Facts

The plaintiff reported for permitted abortion at the defendant's clinic. The permission had been given to her taking regard of her young age and her bad living and social conditions. The doctor, as employee of the defendant, performed the abortion but, after the operation, a special and obligatory routine control examination was neglected. Twelve weeks after the operation at a gynaecological examination it was discovered that the plaintiff was still pregnant. The defendant's doctor offered to perform the abortion again but the plaintiff refused considering the risks of the abortion at this advanced stage of her pregnancy. The plaintiff gave birth to a healthy child and sued the defendant claiming non-pecuniary damages because of the failed abortion. 2

b) Judgment of the Court

The Court declared that the plaintiff should have proven the infringement of her personality rights to be entitled to non-pecuniary damages. The plaintiff does not have any personality rights recognized by the law, which could have been infringed by giving birth to a child even if it was against the will of the plaintiff. The Court accepted that the birth of the child would bring significant changes into the life of the plaintiff but these changes cannot be considered as the worsening of the quality of the plaintiff's life. Her right to self-determination had also not been infringed, since she had the possibility to decide to have 3 an abortion in the twentieth week of her pregnancy, even with a higher degree of risks. According to the judgment, the plaintiff could not show that her personality rights had been infringed and the Court, on that ground, rejected the claim for non-pecuniary damages.

c) Commentary

4 This is the first reported Supreme Court decision regarding wrongful birth and has some remarkable implications for problems of non-pecuniary damages. The Court avoided establishing the decision upon moral assessment and arguments about the concept of damages or the moral value of birth and life. The Court's reasoning focuses on the concept of non-pecuniary damages instead. The drafters of the Hungarian Civil Code in 1959 did not accept the possibility of non-pecuniary damages. Later, an amendment of the Civil Code provided that non-pecuniary damages shall be awarded if the plaintiff's life or the plaintiff's position in society became significantly worse as the result of the defendant's conduct. The Constitutional Court deleted this precondition. They found that it is unconstitutional to restrict the right of persons to non-pecuniary damages. Since that time it is unclear where the boundaries of non-pecuniary damages should be set and this induces uncertainty in court practice. The theory, which prevails today is that non-pecuniary damages can be awarded only as a special consequence of an infringement of personality rights. In the court practice one can also find cases where the court does not explain the decision with infringement of personality rights or they interpret it in a very wide sense.[1] The Hungarian Civil Code protects personality rights with a general clause, which is open to wide interpretation. The Court establishes the decision here with the lack of accepted personality rights of the plaintiff and it is hard to decide whether it is the reinforcing of the principle that non-pecuniary damages is the special sanction of infringement of personality rights or the Court only tries to find a reason for its decision based on the maxim that life cannot be treated as a harm.

2. *Legfelsőbb Bíróság* Legf. Bír. Gf. I. 31.192/2002. sz. EBH 2003 no. 954: Liability of the Stock Exchange for Failing to Put a Basis Price into the Exchange System

a) Brief Summary of the Facts

5 The plaintiff's employee, a professional broker, put an offer into the electronic exchange system of the Budapest Stock Exchange. While typing in the data of

[1] In a decision from 1998 the Supreme Court awarded non-pecuniary damages on the ground that the travel agency failed to inform the plaintiff about the hard conditions of approaching the rented resort house lying upon a hill, far from the village. The Court found that, since the plaintiff could not spend his holiday in a quiet place as he contracted for with the travel agency, he lost his possibility for recreation and lost the holiday experiences as well as the entertainment and relaxation of a holiday abroad. The Court had not established its decision on the infringement of personality rights; the "right to have the holiday" or "recreation" surely cannot be treated as such. See Legf. Bír. Pfv. VIII. 23.243/1996. sz. BH 1998. No. 278 Supreme Court.

the offer he made a mistake: he changed the price and the quantity and he made an offer to sell 7,350 OTP shares at a price of HUF 50/share instead of 50 shares at a price of HUF 7350/share. The 7,350 shares were bought for the erroneously disclosed price through the electronic exchange system. The defendant, the Budapest Stock Exchange, on that day had not fixed the daily basis price in the morning as it usually did. The plaintiff argued that the purchase according to the mistyped terms could have occurred only because the defendant on that day failed to fix the daily basis price in the electronic exchange system.

b) Judgment of the Court

The Court rejected the claim. The Court found that even if the fixing of the daily basis price usually serves as a block in the system because the system refuses the offers which deviate more than a certain degree from the basis price, the aim of fixing the basis price is to prevent brokers from infringing the Stock Exchange Regulation and not to protect them from their own mistake. The obligation of the Budapest Stock Exchange covered only the disclosing of the daily basis price but not to fix it in the system, even if it was a daily practice to do so in order to prevent brokers from too great deviances. The Stock Exchange had not failed to disclose the daily price on that day but did so through a special information channel of the intranet system. The method of informing brokers must also have meant for them that they could not rely on the electronic system to filter their erroneously indicated offers on that day. 6

c) Commentary

According to the judgment, the brokers must have known that they cannot rely on the electronic system to correct their offers if they make a mistake and because of this, the Stock Exchange cannot be liable (regardless of the fact that the defendant was not obliged to fix the basis price in the system). It is not clear from the decision whether the Court rejected the claim on the ground of lack of causation or because of the contributory negligence of the plaintiff. 7

3. *Legfelsőbb Bíróság* Legf. Bír Pfv. III. 20.845/2000. sz. BH 2004 no. 11: Employer Shall be Liable for the Damage Caused by its Employee under Vicarious Liability only if the Damage was Caused in Connection with the Employment Relationship

a) Brief Summary of the Facts

A police officer, during his leisure time kept his loaded weapon on a bookshelf at one of his relatives. The first defendant took the weapon from the bookshelf with the permission of the officer and pointed it at the child of the plaintiffs. He shot the plaintiffs' child dead. The plaintiffs sued the first and the second defendant, the district police station as employer of the officer, and claimed for pecuniary and non-pecuniary damages. 8

b) Judgment of the Court

9 The Court decided in favour of the plaintiff in relation to the first defendant but rejected the claim against the second defendant. The Court established that the damage was caused outside of the employment relationship between the two defendants and, because of this, the second defendant cannot be liable under the rules relating to vicarious liability.[2]

c) Commentary

10 § 348 of the Hungarian Civil Code requires that the employee has to act in connection with his employment to establish the vicarious liability of the employer. This formulation is relatively wide since it also embraces the cases where the employee acts not – in the strict sense of the word – in the sphere of activity or is working outside of the control of his employer.[3] On the other hand, if the activity of the employee falls outside his employment relationship, especially if the act occurs outwith working hours, the court practice rejects the claims against the employer. If e.g. a doctor is acting during his holiday outside the territory of his practice without remuneration, his employer is not vicariously liable because his activity is not in connection with his employment.[4] The Court's opinion is in line with the general practice. Court practice also applies this approach. If, for example, the employee exceeds his authorization and acts as false procurator without the right to do so in the name of his employer and orders goods with false documents, committing a crime, the employer shall be vicariously liable towards the other party with whom the contract could not be concluded, but who acted as it would have been so, knowing nothing about the false representation.[5]

4. *Legfelsőbb Bíróság* Leg. Bír. Pfv. VIII. 22.088/2000. sz. BH 2004 no. 17: Consequences of Non-Disclosure in Insurance

a) Brief Summary of the Facts

11 The plaintiff signed an insurance contract with the defendant insurance company to insure the house where he lived with his family. On the underground floor of the house there was a garage. Four years after concluding the insurance contract the plaintiff equipped the garage in order to carry out a car body welding business. The plaintiff began pursuing his welding business with the permission of the local authority. The plaintiff failed to inform the defendant

[2] The Hungarian Civil Code, under the title "Damages Caused by Employees, Members of Cooperatives, Representatives, and Agents", deals with three special forms: the liability of employers for employees, the liability of principals for agents, and the liability of the state for public officers. According to § 348 (1) of the Civil Code if an employee causes damage to a third person in connection with his employment, unless otherwise provided by law, the employer shall bear liability towards the injured person. This provision shall also be applied in the instance of a member of a cooperative who causes damages to a third person in connection with his membership.

[3] G. Eörsi, *Kötelmi jog, általános rész* (Law of Obligations General Part) (1981), 298.

[4] Legf. Bír Pfv. V. 20.063/1995. sz. BH 1996/89 Supreme Court.

[5] Legf. Bír. Gf. I. 31.500/1993. sz. BH 1994/96 Supreme Court.

about the change of the function of this room in the house. One day, as the plaintiff was working on a car, the sparks bursting out from the grinding machine caused a fire and the house was damaged. The defendant refused to compensate the plaintiff. The defendant argued that the plaintiff had failed to inform the insurer of the house about the change of function of the underground premises, which had increased the risk of accidents significantly. The plaintiff argued that the insurance contract did not impose on him any special duty to inform the defendant about the changes in the functions of the rooms in the house. The plaintiff sued the defendant for compensation of the damage resulting from the fire according to the insurance contract.

b) Judgment of the Court

The Court rejected the claim of the plaintiff. The Court declared that even if 12
there was not any special obligation in the insurance contract to inform the defendant about changes in the function of the rooms in the house, the general requirement of contract law to inform the other party about every important circumstances of the contract[6] is applicable also in this situation. Since the change of the function and the activity pursued in the house increased the risks covered by the insurance, the plaintiff should have conveyed this to the defendant. The plaintiff failed to fulfil this duty.

c) Commentary

In this case the Court applied the general duty to cooperate and disclose rele- 13
vant information in an insurance contract and established the duty to inform the defendant even in the lack of explicit contractual obligations to do so.

5. *Legfelsőbb Bíróság* Leg. Bír. Pfv. IV. 20.289/2002. sz. BH 2004 no. 104: Protection of Good Reputation of Public Persons

a) Brief Summary of the Facts

The defendant published an article written by a group of candidates to the lo- 14
cal election. The article informed the public that all of the other candidates were trying to be local representatives of the ethnic minority only for speculative purposes. The plaintiff, who belonged to that circle of candidates which was accused in this article as taking part in the elections only for speculative purposes, sued the defendant and asked the court to declare that his personality rights have been infringed through publishing the article, since the article interfered with his personality rights violating his reputation. He also claimed non-pecuniary damages.

[6] According to § 277 (2) and (3) of the Hungarian Civil Code, the parties shall be under an obligation to co-operate in the performance of a contract. The obligor shall act to perform the contract in the manner that can generally be expected in the given situation, while the obligee shall promote performance in the same manner. The parties shall be under an obligation to inform each other of any important circumstances affecting performance of the contract.

b) Judgment of the Court

15 The Court rejected the claim and declared that unfavourable comments and expressing poor opinion in itself cannot be a ground for declaring infringement of personality rights if they relate to public persons, even if the comments show exaggerated, unbounded emotions. People who take part in public life must expect that their political enemies (especially in the pre-election period) will strongly criticize their activity and will also inform the public about this. People who take part in public life must bear the expressing of opinion and criticism which gives a negative evaluation of their activity and puts their conduct in an unfavourable light.

c) Commentary

16 The Court strengthened in this decision the principle[7] that public persons shall have to bear criticism even if it violates their reputation and that the threshold of legal response by them is much higher than is the case with average citizens.

6. *Legfelsőbb Bíróság* Legf. Bír. Pfv. VIII. 22.188/2001. sz. BH 2004 no. 109: Liability of an Insurance Company for its Agent in Case of Breach of Duty to Inform and Cooperate

a) Brief Summary of the Facts

17 The plaintiff bought a used car and insured it with the defendant. The insurance contract had been concluded before delivery of the car. In the insurance offer that the plaintiff addressed to the defendant insurance company it was agreed that with the car two original keys shall be given to the plaintiff as buyer. When the buyer took possession of the car, the agent of the defendant was present. On delivery of the car, three keys had been passed to the plaintiff instead of the two and no one checked whether they were the original keys or not. The car had been stolen and it turned out that from the three keys only one was original, another had been manufactured afterwards and the third one was a simple copy. The defendant refused to compensate the plaintiff. The defendant referred to the insurance contract concluded on the basis of the plaintiff's offer, which stated that two original keys shall be provided. In fact, the plaintiff had only one of the original keys. The plaintiff asked the Court to put the defendant under the obligation to fulfil the insurance contract and to pay him the compensation for the stolen car.

[7] Also declared in former decision in Legf. Bír. Pfv. IV. 22.904/1999. sz. BH 2001 no. 522 (Supreme Court) where the Court decided that if a public person expresses his unfavourable opinion about another public person, this cannot establish infringement of personality rights even if it is exaggerated and in Legf. Bír. Pfv. IV. 23.955/1998. sz. BH 2000 no. 293 (Supreme Court) where the Court stated that a caricature about a public person mixed with her photo cannot infringe this pubic person's rights to her image.

b) Judgment of the Court

The Court decided in favour of the plaintiff and declared that the agent of the defendant, who was present at the delivery of the car and who must have realized that three keys had been passed to the plaintiff, should have warned the plaintiff of the importance of the keys and should have brought to the plaintiff's notice the importance of the number of the keys and the potential risk which could arise if the two original keys were not presented to him. 18

c) Commentary

The decision has been established on the general duty to cooperate and to inform according to § 277 of the Civil Code (see supra fn. 6) and on vicarious liability. The defendant was held liable for breach of contract based on the infringement of the general duty to co-operate and the liability of the defendant as employer for the acts of the employed agent. 19

7. *Legfelsőbb Bíróság* Legf. Bír. Pfv. III. 21.290/2001. sz. BH 2004 no. 145: Thief and Receiver of the Stolen Goods are Multiple Tortfeasors

a) Brief Summary of the Facts

Eight defendants stole different kinds of packaged weed-killers from the store of the plaintiff and two other persons received and retailed the stolen goods. The plaintiff claimed for damages for the value of the stolen goods from the eight thieves and the two receivers. The plaintiff asked the Court to declare that the ten defendants as multiple tortfeasors are jointly and severally liable. The two receivers as defendants pleaded that they did not cause the harm of the plaintiff, because the theft and not the retailing of the stolen goods caused the harm. 20

b) Judgment of the Court

The Court decided in favour of the plaintiff, awarded damages and declared that the receivers with the thieves are jointly and severally liable defendants,[8] because the common causation of the harm can be established even if the tortfeasors' conduct constitutes separate consecutive acts, but they contributed within the same causation link to the occurrence of damage. The receiver contributed to the damage by completing that chain of conduct which caused the harm of the plaintiff. 21

[8] According to § 344 of the Civil Code, if two or more persons cause the damage jointly, their liability shall be joint and several towards the aggrieved person, while their liability towards one another shall be divided in proportion to their respective degree of responsibility. Liability for damage shall be divided in equal proportions among the responsible persons if the degree of their responsibility cannot be established. The Court shall be entitled to put aside a declaration of joint and several liability and condemn the persons having caused the damage in proportion to their respective contributions, if a) doing so does not jeopardize or considerably delay compensation for damage, or b) the aggrieved person has himself contributed to the occurrence of the damage or has procrastinated in enforcing his claim without any excusable reason.

c) Commentary

22 The argument of the Court and the decision are in line with theory and practice,[9] which accept that the multiplicity of the tortfeasors can be established also by successive events. The multiplicity of the tortfeasors shall be established even if they did not act together but their activity can be brought within the same causal link.

8. *Legfelsőbb Bíróság* Legf. Bír. Pf. IX. 26.426/2001. sz. BH 2004 no. 235: Non-Pecuniary Damages for Misrepresentation Regarding Educational Services

a) Brief Summary of the Facts

23 The defendant established an institution for higher education and promised the students that, on graduating, they would receive a higher education degree. The plaintiffs enrolled in the defendant's school trusting in receiving the promised degree on graduation. After the school was opened, the Ministry of Culture and Education informed the defendant that the school would not be entitled to provide a degree of higher education due to its failure to fulfil certain statutory preconditions. The plaintiffs continued studying for a year at the defendant's school and when they realized that they could not obtain the promised degree there they decided to leave the school and sued the defendant claiming damages.

b) Judgment of the Court

24 The Court decided in favour of the plaintiffs and awarded non-pecuniary damages between HUF 50,000 and HUF 100,000 to each of the plaintiffs (approx. between € 200 and € 400). The Court found that the defendant infringed the plaintiff's personality rights (their right to education and their general personality rights) because it induced the plaintiffs to make efforts at the cost of their family life and spare time superfluously for a year. While performing their obligations to fulfil the requirements of the school – first of all the passing of the exams – their family life and working life suffered. Finally, they became disappointed and lost their ambition to attain a higher education degree.

c) Commentary

25 Here the interpretation of non-pecuniary damage and personality rights seems to be wider and looser than in other cases, especially in case 1 above. In a strict sense one cannot say that the plaintiffs' right to education has been infringed since no one prevented them from studying and from choosing the school for their higher education. They might have been misled but this cannot be interpreted as preventing them from studying. Neither is more convincing the Court's reference to the general personality rights. The uncertainties mentioned in the comments to case 1 are only reinforced here. It is hard to say

[9] Gyula Eörsi, *A polgári jogi kártérítési felelősség kézikönyve* (The Handbook of the Liability for Damages) (1966), 263.

whether in the case of wrongful birth the infringement of personality rights as a precondition of non-pecuniary damages was interpreted on the basis of moral values but the Court avoided referring to them clearly, or whether here the Court went further in favour of the plaintiffs than it should have interpreting personality rights and non-pecuniary damage too wide.

9. *Legfelsőbb Bíróság* Legf. Bír. Pfv. VIII. 22.799/2001. sz. BH 2004 no. 361: Consequences of the Failure to Disclose Relevant Information before Concluding an Insurance Contract by the Contracting Party

a) Brief Summary of the Facts

The plaintiff bought a used car. The seller of the car informed the plaintiff that the car had already had an accident in which it was seriously damaged. The plaintiff had the car repaired and insured it with the defendant. The plaintiff did not inform the defendant before concluding the insurance contract about the former serious damage of the car and gave false information in this respect in the defendant's pre-contractual questionnaire. One year after concluding the insurance, the plaintiff was involved in a car accident, in which the car was badly damaged and written off. The defendant, who realized the indications of the former accident in the course of the inspection of the car after the second accident, refused to compensate the plaintiff for the damage he suffered. The defendant, referring to § 210 (4) of the Hungarian Civil Code, declared the contract void on the basis of the plaintiff's misrepresentation. The plaintiff sued the defendant and asked the Court to order the defendant to fulfil the obligations of the insurance contract and to pay compensation for the damage he suffered because of the destruction of the car. 26

b) Judgment of the Court

The Court rejected the plaintiff's claim. The Court declared that the plaintiff misled the defendant by concealing the former accident of the car and the plaintiff's misrepresentation makes the insurance contract invalid, because the former serious damage that the car suffered was significant information. If the defendant had known about the former serious damage of the car, it would not have concluded the insurance contract or would have done so only according to special terms and conditions. 27

c) Commentary

According to § 210 (1) of the Civil Code, if someone acts at the time of conclusion of the contract under a mistake in any essential contractual circumstance, he shall be entitled to avoid his contract if his mistake had been caused or could have been recognized by the other party (mistake). § 210 (4) provides that if a person has been persuaded to conclude a contract by misrepresentation he shall be entitled to declare the contract void (misrepresentation). This is a clear case where both the tests for mistake and for the misrepresentation are fulfilled and lead to the contract being declared void. 28

10. *Legfelsőbb Bíróság* Legf. Bír. Pfv. VIII. 20.120/2002. sz. BH 2004 no. 409: Contracting Party's Breach of Duty to Inform the Insurance Company Leads to the Relief of the Insurance Company only if it is in Causal Link with the Insured Occurrence

a) Brief Summary of the Facts

29 The plaintiff's husband concluded a life insurance policy with the defendant. The beneficiary of the insurance was the plaintiff. The plaintiff's husband died three years after the conclusion of the insurance contract. The cause of the death was heart disease. It turned out that, before concluding the insurance contract, the plaintiff's husband had suffered from stomach complaints and had undergone medical examinations, where doctors advised him to take tranquillisers and vitamins. In spite of this fact he stated in the defendant's questionnaire that he was not suffering from any kind of disease of the digestive system. The defendant refused to indemnify the plaintiff as the beneficiary on the ground that the plaintiff's husband had given false information regarding his health condition and argued that the misrepresentation of the plaintiff's husband relieves the defendant of his duty to perform the insurance contract.

b) Judgment of the Court

30 The Court decided in favour of the plaintiff and declared the defendant's duty to perform the payment according to the insurance contract. The Court established that the failure of the plaintiff's husband to provide a correct answer to the defendant's question about the disease of the digestive system was not in causal link with the death of the plaintiff's husband from heart disease and as such did not influence the defendant's obligation to pay.

c) Commentary

31 See comments to case 11 (infra no. 34).

11. *Legfelsőbb Bíróság* Legf. Bír. Pfv. VIII. 20.276/2002. sz. BH 2004 no. 414: Information About Former Health Condition Relates to Significant Facts and Circumstances from the Point of View of the Insurer's Risk in Case of Life Insurance

a) Brief Summary of the Facts

32 In 1999 the plaintiff undersigned a life insurance contract with the defendant. To the question whether she had attempted suicide in the last five years, she gave negative answer in spite of the fact that she had attempted to commit suicide in 1996 by deliberately taking an overdose of tablets. In 2000 the plaintiff was declared as 100% disabled, which was an event that would have led to the insurer's obligation to perform payment to the plaintiff. The defendant refused to perform his obligation referring to the false answer that the defendant provided before concluding the insurance contract regarding former suicide attempts.

b) Judgment of the Court

The Court rejected the claim of the plaintiff. The Court declared that the plaintiff gave a false response to the defendant's question relating to an important circumstance of the insurance contract and this exempted[10] the defendant from the obligation it undertook as insurer in the insurance contract. The Court stated that even if the insurance event of declaring the plaintiff disabled was not in direct causal link with the former and undisclosed suicide attempt, the declaration of full disability was based on psychological reasons where also the former suicide attempt was assessed and taken into account. 33

c) Commentary

Both this case and case 9 (supra nos. 26 et seq.) deal with the consequences of breach of the contractual party's duty to disclose material facts before concluding an insurance contract. The obligation to disclose material facts is an important factor in correcting the information asymmetry, which could prevent the insurer from assessing the level of risk taken under the insurance. The breach of this duty in itself can only relieve the insurer if it is in causation with the occurrence of the insured event. In case 10 (supra nos. 26 et seq.) the relevance of the breach of this duty was already established by a relatively remote connection, since the undisclosed fact was only one factor leading to the occurrence of the insured event. 34

12. *Fővárosi Ítélőtábla* (Budapest Court of Appeal) Fővárosi Ítélőtábla 9. Pf. 20.002/2003/2. sz. ÍH 2004 June no. 55: Awarding Non-Pecuniary Damages because Issuing Arrest Warrant Constitutes Omission of the Court

a) Brief Summary of the Facts

Two arrest warrants were issued against the plaintiff who had been taken to the court for hearing on both occasions, in 1998 and in 2000. On the second occasion he was arrested and was taken into custody for more than two months. In 1997, as a criminal procedure had started against him (as the result of this he had been found guilty and sentenced to a pecuniary penalty), the plaintiff informed the police about his address from where he could be summoned. On both occasions, in 1998 and 2000, the arrest warrants were issued because the police had tried to summon him from the address registered earlier and completely ignored the fact that, during the trial, he had declared his 35

[10] According to § 540 (1) of the Civil Code, for the purpose of an insurance contract, the insured must disclose all of the circumstances of which he was or must have been aware of that are important in terms of providing insurance coverage. The party shall satisfy his disclosure obligation by truthfully filling out the questionnaire furnished by the insurer. Leaving the questions unanswered shall not in itself constitute a violation of the disclosure obligation. § 540 (3) provides that, in case of a breach of the duty to disclose and report changes, the obligation of the insurer shall not take effect, unless it is proved that the insurer was aware of the concealed or undisclosed circumstance at the time the contract was concluded or that such circumstance had no influence on the occurrence of the insurance event.

current address where he could have been found. He was in custody for more than two months because he was declared as someone who would attempt to hide from the public authorities. The plaintiff claimed non-pecuniary damages because of the violation of his personality rights as a result of an omission of the authorities.

b) Judgment of the Court

36 The Court stated that the authorities failed to register the address, which had been given by the plaintiff, and this has led to his arrest and a period of custody of more than two months. The Court awarded non-pecuniary damages to the plaintiff. The amount of the awarded damages was HUF 500,000 (approx. € 2,000).

c) Commentary

37 The case here was decided as a case for vicarious liability of the state for judgment failures. As the plaintiff had informed the authorities about his actual place of living from where he could be found and disclosed it, the Court should not declare that there is a danger of hiding and hindering the criminal procedure. The period of custody, which was longer than two months, was an infringement of the personality rights of the plaintiff and non-pecuniary damages were awarded on the ground of infringement of personality rights.

C. Literature

1. Ágnes Dósa, *Az orvos kártérítési felelőssége* (The liability of doctors) (HVG-ORAC, Budapest 2004)

38 The author is an assistant at the Institute for State and Legal Sciences of the Hungarian Scientific Academy, teaches law in different institutions and also assists in legislative processes. The book is based on an extensive research study and analysis of Court practice. The author studied more than one thousand cases, among them unpublished decisions. The author deals with each of the topics discussed in the book from a comparative perspective, then analyses the Hungarian Court practice. The discussion of the different topics in the book is divided into three main parts, which are connected in the analysis of medical malpractice cases. The book presents the changes of the function of non-pecuniary damages in relief, and there is a clear tendency for non-pecuniary damages to play an increasingly greater role of indemnity than compensation. One of the highlighted problems is the question of limitation of liability, which is a very important issue considering the limited cover for claims in the budget. In other words, the question is raised whether the limits of the system and the state budget can determine the boundaries of the claim. The consideration of the tendencies of court practice in medical malpractice cases raises the question, whether the principle is tenable that private law has only a reparative function while the aim of public law is redistribution. The question,

whether the relationship between the doctor (hospital) and the client is a contractual one, and if yes, how one can qualify the contract, is often discussed in Hungarian literature. The author takes the view that the role of qualifying the contract and ranking it under one of the heads of specific contracts is decreasing and the content of the contract becomes decisive. One of the important conclusions of the author is that the doctor/client relationship is loosing its fiduciary character but is yet treated in the court practice and literature as an obligation of reasonable care. It is a question what the fiduciary character shall mean in those circumstances where the patient cannot freely choose a doctor for himself. After analysing each of the elements of liability the author discusses – crossing the borders of the narrower theme of the book and going beyond them – the basic problems of tort law and liability, such as wrongfulness, causation and damages. As far as unlawfulness is concerned she emphasises that the duty to inform and the requirement of informed consent are statutory obligations and the court practice does not explicitly reverse the burden of proof of informed consent imposing it on the hospital but is only easing it, even if it leads to a similar result. The question remains, whether this relief is tenable in cases of omission. It seems that this is not the case. One of the peculiarities of the problem of causation is that this shall be approached not by starting from the cause but the fact of damage, assuming that from the unlawfulness of damage follows that the cause itself shall also be unlawful. The notion of damage raises kinds of questions which are new in the Hungarian legal theory and practice and are partly yet open, such as whether the death of a relative or the birth of a child can be treated as damage or not, how the liability of experts shall be assessed and how the doctor/patient relationship shall be qualified, which seems to be in fact a relationship based on authority rather than of equal parties. The modern tort law developments raise the necessity of reconsidering inherent principles of Hungarian tort law such as that causing harm is always unlawful if the law does not provide otherwise. The standpoint of the constant refusal of punitive damages also shall be reconsidered.

2. Péter Bárdos, Az új Ptk. kárfelelősségi fejezete (The Tort Law Chapter of the new Hungarian Civil Code), [2004] *Polgári Jogi Kodifikáció* 1, 3–6

The author is a practising lawyer and has written extensively in the field of tort law. The subject of the article is the tort law regulation of the new Hungarian Civil Code. The article is a contribution to the professional discussions about the new Civil Code. The author argues that the requirements of the modern society call for a tort law regulation, which has, as its main function, compensation even without fault and this would – according to the author's opinion – also be in line with the tendencies of the recent developments of European tort laws. He suggests that the tort law regulation of the new Hungarian Civil Code should be based on a no-fault liability system with the possibility only of a narrow and strictly formulated exculpation. He provides a suggested text with comments to the basic rules of a tort law regulation. 39

3. Györgyi Fülöp, Az állam kártérítési felelőssége a közösségi jog megsértése esetén (The Liability of the State for Infringement of EU Law), [2003] *Polgári Jogi Kodifikáció* 6, 18–23

40 The author is a judge to the County High Court of Budapest. The article assesses the problem of state liability from the perspective of the liability of the state for failing to enforce the human rights of the parties to access to justice and to a fair trial. The author provides an analysis of theory and court practice and formulates suggestions for the new Hungarian Civil Code. She suggests inserting into the Civil Code a special provision for the liability of the state for infringement of obligations derived from an international convention.

4. László Kecskés, Európa-jogi tapasztalatok az állam jogszabályalkotással okozott károkért való felelősségének megalapozásához (European Law Experiences in Establishing State Liability for Damage Caused by Legislation), [2003] *Polgári Jogi Kodifikáció* 4, 3–19

41 The author, who is Professor of Civil Law at the Law Faculty of the University of Pécs, in this article presents the development of the European Court of Justice case law regarding the liability of the Member States for failing to implement EU legislation. The article accepts the possibility – as it has already been raised in Hungarian legal literature – of a new form of liability established by the ECJ practice and is of the opinion that the tort liability of the state for legislation and the state liability for failure of implementing EU legislation shall be assessed together and shall be brought under the same theoretical explanation.

5. Gábor Jobbágyi, Az ember, mint kár? (The Human Being as Harm), [January 2004] *Jogtudományi Közlöny*, 1–9

42 The author is a university lecturer in civil law and his main research field is bioethics. The article focuses on the practice of the Constitutional Court and the Constitutional Court's arguments in its decisions about the regulation of abortion. He criticizes the practice of the Hungarian Supreme Court, which is tending to award damages to children who are born disabled as the result of medical malpractice. He is of the opinion, on moral grounds, that the birth of a child never can be harm.

XII. Ireland

Eoin Quill

A. Legislation

1. Personal Injuries Assessment Board (PIAB); www.piab.ie/

The Personal Injuries Assessment Board Act, 2003, which was noted in last year's report,[1] has been brought into effect in stages during 2004. The PIAB was officially established on the 13 April 2004.[2] Initially only the procedural aspects of the legislation were initiated and the appropriate rules governing the application procedure, various necessary notifications and authorisations and the setting of appropriate fees were put in place before the provisions governing the actual hearing of claims were activated.[3] From 1 June 2004 claims in respect of workplace injuries came under the jurisdiction of the PIAB.[4] All other personal injuries claims, except medical negligence claims and other claims excluded from the scope of the Act, came under the jurisdiction of the PIAB from 22 July 2004.[5] 1

[1] E. Quill, Ireland, in: H. Koziol/B.C. Steininger (eds.), *European Tort Law 2003* (2004), at §3. A more detailed analysis of the legislation can be found in P. Quigley/W. Binchy, *Personal Injuries Assessment Board Act 2003: Implications for the Legal Practice* (2004). See also R. Byrne/W. Binchy, *Annual Review of Irish Law, 2003* (2004), at 608–631; D. Nolan, The Personal Injuries Assessment Board Act 2003: A Critical Analysis, [2004] *Bar Review* (Bar Rev) 9, 7; C. O'Dwyer, New Procedures for Personal Injuries Claims, [2004] Bar Rev 9, 199.

[2] Statutory Instrument (SI) 156/04 Personal Injuries Assessment Board Act 2003 (Establishment Day) Order 2004.

[3] SI 155/04 Personal Injuries Assessment Board Act 2003 (Commencement) Order 2004 activated the procedural sections of the Act; SI 219/04 Personal Injuries Assessment Board Rules 2004 set out the administrative rules governing the applications process and the forms for notifications and authorisations required under the Act; SI 251/04 Personal Injuries Assessment Board (Fees) Regulations 2004 set out the various fees payable to the Board – the claimant pays € 50; each respondent pays € 850; additional charges for exceptional expenses may also be charged and the definition of exceptional is relative to expenses typically incurred, with medical expenses expressly stated to be exceptional. The Rules of Court have also been amended to accommodate the introduction of the Board; SI 526/04 amends the District Court Rules, SI 542/04 amends the Circuit Court Rules and SI 517/04 amends the Superior Court Rules.

[4] SI 252/04 Personal Injuries Assessment Board Act 2003 (Commencement) (No.2) Order 2004.

[5] SI 438/04 Personal Injuries Assessment Board Act 2003 (Commencement) (No.3) Order 2004. Certain categories of claim are excluded by sec. 4(1) of the 2003 Act; principally these are claims by police officers injured in the line of duty and claims for breach of constitutional rights or claims under sec. 3 of the European Convention on Human Rights Act, 2003.

The procedure adopted by the PIAB of dealing directly with claimants, rather than through the claimant's appointed solicitor was recently challenged in the courts and the Law Society of Ireland was granted leave to make submissions to the court.[6] The High Court (HC) found the procedure to be *ultra vires*.[7]

2 On the 2 June 2004 the PIAB published a Book of Quantum, which sets out guidance for general damages for pain and suffering for a range of injuries. It classifies injuries in accordance with version 9 of the World Health Organisation's International Classification of Diseases. It identifies injuries according to four main body regions – head injuries, arm injuries, neck back and trunk injuries and leg injuries. It then provides a list of particular body parts and particular types of injury to those parts and gives a financial range for compensation for each injury type, though it is far less comprehensive than the leading Irish practitioner's guide to quantum.[8] While it is useful to have a Book of Quantum, it is subject to a number of shortcomings. This is understandable, given the short time frame in which it had to be produced. It is to be hoped that over time the content will be revised to provide clearer guidance on quantum. The first point of note is that general damages awarded by a court cover pain, suffering and loss of amenity;[9] the Book does not specifically refer to loss of amenity. It is likely that this is merely an oversight in nomenclature; otherwise the entire process would proceed on an incorrect basis. More significantly, a claimant with no legal knowledge may not appreciate the distinction between general and special damages and so might not be able to fully appreciate the full value of their claim. Most misunderstandings can be easily remedied in the assessment process by the PIAB, which does specifically alert claimants for the need to include receipts for expenses and an employer's statement in respect of lost income, but if a claimant settles directly with the tortfeasor and does not proceed to assessment, then significant errors are possible. There may be some cases where even the PIAB process cannot resolve the problems in relation to income loss; in exceptional circumstances where future income loss is difficult to predict (such as a permanent injury to a child) it is accounted for in the assessment of general damages, rather than as an item of special damages. This would bring the amount of general damages required to adequately compensate the plaintiff outside the range provided for in the Book of Quantum.[10] A second diffi-

[6] *O'Brien v PIAB*, Irish Times, 5 October 2004 (noting the initiation of proceedings); Irish Times, 2 December 2004 (on the granting of leave to the Law Society); Irish Times, 15 December 2004 (commencement of the hearing before the HC).

[7] Judgment of McMenamin J, 25 January 2005, noted in the Irish Times, 26 January 2005.

[8] R. Pierse, *Quantum of Damages for Personal Injuries 1999* (1999). This includes special damages in addition to general damages and provides a more detailed indication of quantum. The leading English book on quantum is also far more detailed; Judicial Studies Board, *Guidelines for the Assessment of General Damages in Personal Injury Case* (7th edn. 2004).

[9] See *Reddy v Bates* [1983] *Irish Reports* (IR) 141, at 151 per McCarthy J, Supreme Court (SC); *Sinnott v Quinnsworth* [1984] *Irish Law Reports Monthly* (ILRM) 523, at 531 per O'Higgins CJ (SC).

[10] See, for example, *O'Sullivan (A Minor) v Kiernan & Anor* unrep. HC, 2 April 2004 http://www.bailii.org/ie/cases/IEHC/2004/78.html. The plaintiff was awarded € 250,000 in respect of

culty with the Book of Quantum is the wide gap between the minimum and maximum amount for some categories of injury; there is little indication of what criteria are to be used by assessors to determine the appropriate point on the scale in particular cases. Byrne and Binchy argue that the detailed figures may mislead claimants into a false belief that there is an objective, scientific basis to the calculation process.[11] A significant omission from the Book of Quantum arises in respect of psychiatric injuries or psychological effects of physical injuries; no figures are provided for these. While pure psychiatric injury claims are relatively rare, psychological consequences are a common feature of personal injury claims; in some cases the psychological effects can lead to a greater award than the physical injury.[12] Another omission is injury to reproductive organs; such organs do not appear on the list of internal injuries. One final point of note is that the maximum amounts listed in respect of some categories of harm may not be an accurate reflection of judicial practice. The highest amount available under the Book of Quantum is € 300,000 and this only applies to quadriplegia and paraplegia; even in cases of such injuries the amount awarded may vary, depending on a variety of factors, so the maximum may not be awarded in all cases.[13] By contrast, judicial practice has been to make the maximum amount available in all cases of 'catastrophic permanent disablement', except where the plaintiff lacks mental awareness of their plight.[14] Furthermore, there is considerable judicial authority that € 300,000 may not be the appropriate maximum

Erbs Palsy, a major dysfunction of the arm and shoulder, caused at birth during delivery. The damages included damage to career prospects, due to a reduction in the range of careers open to the plaintiff. The highest amount provided for in respect of shoulder injuries in the Book of Quantum is € 74,500; the most available for an arm injury is € 197,000 for amputation of both arms. Clearly the damages awarded by O'Neill J in the above case would be unlikely to be awarded under the PIAB guidelines.

11 R. Byrne/W. Binchy (supra fn. 1), at 629–30.

12 Take, for example, *Ledwith v Dublin Bus* unreported SC, 24 June 2003, noted in R. Byrne/W. Binchy (supra fn. 1), at 631; the plaintiff was assaulted, suffering a minor laceration on his lip and post-traumatic stress disorder; the SC upheld an award of € 90,000. The facial injuries included in the Book of Quantum are confined to broken facial bones, soft tissue injuries or dislocation of the jaw and loss of teeth. Loss of a tooth is measured at € 5,300–€ 12,800 and a claimant with a cut lip could easily believe that their injury was less serious than this and consequently worth less. R. Pierse (supra fn. 8) includes a broad range of cases on lip injuries with varying physical and psychological effects. The absence of such awards from the Book of Quantum was also criticised in an article in the Irish Times on 4 August 2004.

13 The specified factors are the level of movement, the level of pain and suffering, depression and the level of achievable rehabilitation, age and life expectancy.

14 *Connolly v Bus Éireann* [Irish Bus Company] unrep HC 29 January 1996; some support for confining the maximum tariff to quadriplegia can be found in *McEneany v Monaghan County Council*, unrep HC, 26 July 2001, noted by E. Quill, Ireland, in: H. Koziol/B.C. Steininger (eds.), *European Tort Law 2001* (2002), at §§51–53; this decision is out of line with the general jurisprudence of the Irish courts on catastrophic injuries. The deduction for lack of mental awareness is based on the SC decision in *Cooke v Walsh* [1984] ILRM 208. The Book of Quantum provides a maximum of € 129,000 for serious and permanent head injuries; it is arguable that a court would award more than this in some cases and that the maximum amount should be available for the most severe cases, provided the victim is conscious of his or her plight.

amount for general damages.[15] Finally, Byrne and Binchy have highlighted other areas where the level of award specified in the Book of Quantum may be lower than the amount actually considered appropriate by the courts.[16] To give just one example, the Book provides a range from € 62,800 to € 85,900 for serious and permanent back conditions, yet the SC recently upheld an award of € 80,000 for a case that was far from the most serious injury of this type.[17] All of these shortcomings in the current Book of Quantum could be particularly important in light of the fact that courts are now required to take cognisance of the book when assessing general damages for personal injuries.[18]

2. Civil Liability and Courts Act 2004 (Number 31 of 2004)

3 Part 2 of this Act provides for extensive reform of court procedures for the handling of personal injuries claims, mainly aimed at speeding up the administration of claims in order to reduce the cost of administering the tort system for personal injuries litigation.[19] The most noteworthy changes are a reduction in the time limit for the initiation of claims, the introduction of an early notification requirement to alert the defendant to the possibility of a claim and modifications to pleading rules.

4 The general limitation period for personal injuries actions is reduced from 3 to 2 years, with effect from 31 March 2005.[20] The time period will run from ei-

[15] The original tariff was set in *Sinnott v Quinnsworth* [1984] ILRM 523; it has been revised in a number of cases to keep pace with changing monetary values; the most detailed revision was by O'Sullivan J in *McEneany v Monaghan County Council*, unrep HC, 26 July 2001, suggesting a figure of approximately € 380,000. Subsequent cases have tended to use € 317,500 (£250,000), but the SC has stated that this tariff should apply in cases where the award for special damages is very high; a higher figure for general damages may be appropriate if special damages are not particularly high – *Gough v Neary & Cronin* [2004] 1 ILRM 35. For further consideration of the upper tariff see E. Quill, *Torts in Ireland* (2nd edn. 2004), at 536–7; B.M.E. McMahon/W. Binchy, *Law of Torts* (3rd edn. 2000), at §§44.146-44, 171.

[16] R. Byrne/W. Binchy (supra fn. 1), at 630–31.

[17] *Breen v Fagan & the Motor Insurers Bureau of Ireland* unrep. SC, 14 May 2004. In this case the plaintiff had been able to return to work. See also *Lydon v McBreen* unrep HC, 30 July 2004 (O'Donovan J) € 100,000 awarded for a moderate neck and back injury, with some psychological consequences.

[18] Sec. 22 of the Civil Liability and Courts Act 2004; the courts may also have regard to other factors and so, are not confined to making awards within the parameters established by the book.

[19] This is part of an ongoing reform process designed to reduce insurance costs in Ireland. The PIAB also forms part of this process; for further aspects see The Houses of the Oireachtas Joint Committee on Enterprise and Small Business, First Report on Reforms to the Irish Insurance Market, July 2003. The procedural reforms were influenced by the 29th Report of the Committee on Court Practice and Procedure, submitted to the Minister for Justice in June 2004 (following a request from the Minister to the Committee to conduct an investigation into reform of civil procedure in 2002). The Report is noted by E. Hall, Reforming Practice & Procedure, [2004] *Law Society Gazette* (Gazette) 98 (6), 20. The 2004 Act is noted by D. Nolan, [2004] Bar Rev 9, 181.

[20] Sec. 7 of the 2004 Act; the operative date for the provision is provided for in the Civil Liability and Courts Act 2004 (Commencement) Order 2004 (SI 544/2004). There is a transitional provision in sec. 7 (d), which provides that for actions where the date of accrual or knowledge precedes the coming into force of sec. 7 then the shorter of the following periods shall apply – the original 3 year period under the 1991 Act or 2 years from the commencement of sec. 7.

ther the date of accrual of the cause of action, or the date of discoverability of key elements of the cause of action as provided for in the Statute of Limitations (Amendment) Act 1991. A new requirement, effective from 20 September 2004, is that plaintiffs must provide defendants with a written notice of the nature of the alleged wrong within 2 months of the date of accrual, or date of knowledge (if later).[21] Failure to do so, without reasonable cause, will permit the court to draw adverse inferences and to make an appropriate deduction from any costs payable to the plaintiff (including a complete refusal of plaintiff's costs). Secs. 10–14 of the Act provide for a more streamlined pleading process, intended to reduce the time lag between initiating claims and actually proceeding with the trial, or settling the case.[22] The courts will retain a degree of discretion with respect to time limits and amendments to pleadings, so it remains to be seen how much difference the provisions will actually have. The legislative intent clearly shows a preference for a speedier process, and places emphasis on drawing adverse inferences and reduction or refusal of costs for parties failing to comply with procedural requirements in a timely fashion.

B. Cases

1. *Cooper-Flynn v RTÉ, Bird and Howard* Supreme Court, 28 April 2004; [2004] 2 IR 72:[23] Libel, Defence of Partial Justification

a) Brief Summary of the Facts

The first defendant, a national television company, broadcast a series of re- 5
ports that the plaintiff, a member of the Irish parliament and former bank employee, had advised the third defendant to invest in an offshore investment scheme to evade tax. The second defendant was the reporter that interviewed the third defendant and reported the story in the broadcasts. The plaintiff sued for libel and the jury in the HC found that the allegation that the plaintiff advised the third defendant to evade tax was untrue, but that the plaintiff had advised others to do so and in light of those matters the untruthful allegation had caused no harm to the plaintiff's reputation. All three defendants' costs were awarded against the plaintiff. The plaintiff appealed, seeking a new trial, on a number of procedural grounds relating to the admission of evidence and the judge's instructions to the jury. She also appealed on a substantive aspect of

[21] Sec. 8 of the 2004 Act and SI 544/2004 (supra fn. 20).

[22] For current practice in respect of the pleading process see M. Buckley, *Civil Procedure and Practice: An Introduction* (2004), at chapters 2 & 3; H. Delany/D. McGrath, *Civil Procedure in the Superior Courts* (2001), at chapters 2–5; H. Delany, The Obligation on the Courts to Deal with Cases Within a 'Reasonable Time', [2004] *Irish Law Times* (ILT) 22, 249. See also SI 63/04 and the recent decisions in *Gilroy v Flynn* unrep SC, 3 December 2004; http://www.bailii.org/ie/cases/IESC/2004/98.html and *Butler v Regan* unrep HC, 01 July 2004; http://www.bailii.org/ie/cases/IEHC/2004/326.html.

[23] http://www.bailii.org/ie/cases/IESC/2004/28.html; http://www.courts.ie/judgments.nsf/09859e7a3f34669680256ef3004a27de/db88b0274820068b80256e97003b2e3a?OpenDocument.

the finding in favour of the third defendant, claiming that he should not have been permitted to benefit from the evidence in relation to the other persons to whom she gave improper advice.

b) Judgment of the Court

6 The SC rejected all of the plaintiff's grounds of appeal. On the substantive ground of appeal, the Court found that although the third defendant could not rely on the statutory defence applicable to partial justification, he could benefit from a defence that the plaintiff had no reputation worth protecting in light of the information available to the jury about the plaintiff's advice to other persons.

c) Commentary

7 Partial justification can provide a full defence to a defendant who has made multiple allegations against the plaintiff, but cannot prove all of them. The circumstances in which this can arise are set out in sec. 21 of the Defamation Act 1961:

> In an action for libel or slander in respect of words containing two or more distinct charges against the plaintiff, a defence of justification shall not fail by reason only that the truth of every charge is not proved, if the words not proved to be true do not materially injure the plaintiff's reputation having regard to the truth of the remaining charges.

8 The trial judge had ruled that the third defendant could not avail of this provision, as he was only making an allegation in respect of the advice he himself claimed to have received. The first and second defendants could avail of this defence, as they made additional allegations against the plaintiff. The question for the SC on appeal was whether the third defendant could benefit from evidence put before the jury by the first and second defendants. A defendant can normally only introduce general evidence of bad character on the plaintiff's part, though evidence of specific instances of misconduct is admissible where the plaintiff has been convicted of a criminal offence.[24] Neither of those provisions would have permitted the third defendant to raise the issue of the plaintiff's advice to other persons, if the trial was one solely between the plaintiff and the third defendant. However, the plaintiff had chosen to sue all of the defendants together and the evidence was introduced by the first and second defendants in support of allegations they had made in their broadcasts. Once the evidence was legitimately before the jury it was fair to allow them to take that evidence into account in assessing the value of the plaintiff's character when considering the case against the third defendant. Evidence of bad character is

[24] The rule stems from *Scott v Samson* [1882] *Law Reports, Queens Bench Division* (QBD) 8, 491 and was further considered in *Plato Films Ltd. v Speidel* [1961] 1 *Law Reports, Appeal Cases* (AC) 1090. It has been considered in Ireland in *Browne v Tribune* [2001] 2 ILRM 424 and *Hill v Cork Examiner Publications Ltd.* unrep. SC, 14 November 2001, noted by E. Quill (supra fn. 14), at §§12–14.

offered in mitigation of damages, but in this instance the jury found that the plaintiff's reputation was sufficiently tarnished by the other instances of improper advice to be entirely worthless and the SC accepted that this was a fair conclusion in the circumstances and so the refusal to award any damages was upheld.[25]

2. *Griffin v Patton* SC, 27 July 2004:[26] Medical Negligence; Standard of Care

a) Brief Summary of the Facts

The plaintiff's foetus died, without fault on anyone's part, during the seventeenth week of pregnancy. Drugs to induce delivery of the foetus failed and the defendant then carried out surgery to remove it. A piece of bone of 5.5 centimetres length was left in the plaintiff, resulting in personal injury to her in having to undergo a second surgery for the removal of the piece of bone and post-traumatic stress disorder. The HC found that the defendant was not negligent in choosing the surgical option, but was negligent in not properly visually checking that all major bony structures were removed and in not carrying out an ultrasound scan to ensure that the foetus was fully removed.[27] The plaintiff was awarded € 100,000 damages and the defendant appealed against the finding of negligence. 9

b) Judgment of the Court

The SC dismissed the appeal, finding that there was evidence to support the finding of negligence in respect of not properly visually checking that all major bony structures were removed. The court found that the failure to carry out an ultrasound scan was not negligent. In coming to its decision the court relied on the principles set out by Chief Justice (CJ) Finlay in *Dunne v The National Maternity Hospital*,[28] governing the standard of care for medical practitioners. In respect of the ultra sound scan, the evidence from the trial was that it was not established practice to carry one out unless the doctor had some doubts as to the removal of all the parts of the foetus. The plaintiff had not pleaded or argued that this practice was defective. Consequently the SC applied the principle from *Dunne* that a medical practitioner following a general and approved practice is not negligent unless that practice is subject to inherent defects that would be apparent to a person giving the matter proper consideration. As there was evidence that the doctor had failed to properly check visually that all ma- 10

[25] Relying on *Grobbelaar v News Group Newspapers Ltd.* [2001] 2 *All England Reports* (All ER) 437; for analysis of this case see R. Mullender, (2001) *Cambridge Law Journal* (CLJ) 460.

[26] http://www.bailii.org/ie/cases/IESC/2004/48.html; http://www.courts.ie/judgments.nsf/f69fbd31c73dda2580256cd400020877/01d253fe1aa0fb8480256edf004861a5?OpenDocument.

[27] Unrep HC, 21 March 2003 (O'Donovan J).

[28] [1989] IR 91. For further consideration of the principles governing the standard of care for medical practitioners see J.P.M. White, *Medical Negligence Actions* (1996); S. Mills, *Clinical Practice and the Law* (2002), at chapter 7; E. Quill (supra fn. 15), at 108 et seq.; B.M.E. McMahon/W. Binchy (supra fn. 15), at §14.09 et seq.

jor bony structures had been removed, the court found that this supported a conclusion that she had not properly carried out the approved procedure and was therefore negligent.

c) Commentary

11 The decision is consistent with established practice in this field and with the approach to appellate decision making. The evidence in relation to the visual check was a finding of primary fact and, consequently, not capable of being overturned on appeal once it was supported by credible evidence. The secondary fact – the inference of negligence – was a necessary corollary to the primary fact and so also incapable of being overturned.[29] The SC did clarify one particular error by the HC on the question of whether the gynaecologist was negligent in failing to remove all the bony structures; the expert witnesses on each side disagreed as to whether the defendant had fallen below the requisite standard of care, but the trial judge found that the witnesses for the defence were operating on the basis of a misunderstanding of the underlying facts. The judge indicated that if there has been no such misapprehension and there was a genuine difference of opinion then he would be bound to find no negligence on the basis of the principle in *Dunne*, that where there is an honest difference of opinion between doctors on which is the better of two alternative courses of treatment, a doctor following one of those two courses is not negligent. The SC rightly took the view that this principle only applies to establishing whether the type of treatment decided upon was acceptable and has no application where the expert witnesses disagree on the evaluation of the doctor's behaviour as to whether it was negligent. The determination of whether the conduct falls below the acceptable legal standard is for the courts to make and cannot be left to the assessment of the profession under scrutiny.

3. *McGarth v Independent Newspapers* HC, 21 April 2004:[30] Libel; Defamatory Effect

a) Brief Summary of the Facts

12 The plaintiff worked as a fitter for the state rail company and in September 2001 the defendant published a photograph of the plaintiff alongside a story about a meeting of investors in Eircom (the principal telephone company in Ireland); the caption indicated that the plaintiff had invested £50,000 in Eircom shares and stood to lose a considerable amount of this. The plaintiff contacted the defendant, seeking an apology and correction, as he had no personal wealth and had borrowed money to buy the £9,600 worth of shares that he actually held. Without further consultation with the plaintiff, the defendant published a photograph of the plaintiff and a correction of the factual details of the plaintiff's investment, but without any apology. The plaintiff then instituted li-

[29] On the role of appellate courts see *Wolfe v St. James' Hospital & Buckley* unrep. SC 20 February 2002; noted in E. Quill, Ireland, in H. Koziol/B.C. Steininger (eds.), *European Tort Law 2002* (2003), at §§5–8; see also E. Quill (supra fn. 15), at 449–451.

[30] http://www.bailii.org/ie/cases/IEHC/2004/67.html.

bel proceedings relating to both publications. In respect of the original publication he alleged various issues by way of innuendo, mainly relating to inferences of dishonest concealment of wealth and misrepresentations of commitment to trade unionism. In respect of the second publication, the complaint was that the photograph and correction were published adjacent to an article concerning links between big business and terrorism and that the natural effect of this was to infer a link between the plaintiff and terrorism. The case came before the HC to determine two preliminary questions; first, did the correction serve as an accord and satisfaction of the cause of action arising out of the first publication? Secondly, could the juxtaposition of the second photograph and the story on links between terrorism and business carry the meaning alleged?

b) Judgment of the Court

Gilligan J ruled in favour of the plaintiff on the first issue and in favour of the defendant on the second issue. The photograph and correction could not operate as an accord and satisfaction, since the plaintiff had sought an apology in addition to the correction and the defendant had not felt that an apology was required; consequently the parties had not reached a sufficiently complete and certain agreement. 13

In relation to the meaning of the second publication, Gilligan J stated: 14

> I take the view that the headline, the article, the accompanying photograph, and the caption underneath the photograph have to be considered in totality as published and that further the correct criterion to be applied is the meaning which the title, the article, the accompanying photograph, and the caption underneath would convey to the mind of the ordinary reasonable fair minded reader.

Since the article related to multinational companies, which Eircom is not, and it did not suggest any criminal or terrorist involvement by the companies or their officers or associates, the effect of the totality of the publication was not capable of supporting the defamatory meanings alleged by the plaintiff.

c) Commentary

The decision with respect to the first publication is plainly correct. If the defendant is to show that the plaintiff agreed to forego proceedings in exchange for a suitable apology and correction, then the defendant must show that an agreement was reached and that the defendant has complied with it. Given the differing importance that the two sides placed on the issue of apology, no completed agreement could be properly said to have been reached. 15

The ruling on the meaning of the second publication follows the House of Lords decision in *Charleston & Another v Newsgroup Newspapers Limited & Another*,[31] where it was held that a publication can have only one meaning and 16

[31] [1995] 2 AC 65; noted by Prescott [1995] *Modern Law Review* (MLR) 58, 752.

this required consideration of the entirety of the publication. In that case the plaintiffs unsuccessfully argued that some readers would only look at the picture and headline and could draw defamatory inferences, while others would read the entire article in which the defamatory inference was negated by the provision of further and more accurate detail. This will certainly assist defendants, though its benefit to the public is questionable, as it promotes the use of sensationalist headlines, pictures and captions, which can then be offset by the substance of the accompanying article.

4. *Hayes v Minister for Finance* HC, 17 February 2004: Standard of Care, Police Pursuit of Traffic Offender

a) Brief Summary of the Facts

17 The plaintiff was a pillion passenger on a motorbike and was injured in a collision with a car. At the time of the accident the driver of the motorbike was fleeing from a police car, which was pursuing him in respect of a speeding offence; during the pursuit, the driver lost control of the motorbike and crashed into a car. The plaintiff suffered extensive injuries, including the loss of the foetus she was carrying and several broken bones. As a result of the continuing effects of her injuries, a later pregnancy was much more difficult that it would otherwise have been and delivery of her baby had to be by caesarean section. Furthermore, any future children she might have would also have to be delivered by caesarean section. The plaintiff sued the defendant as employer of the police officers that conducted the chase, alleging that they were concurrent wrongdoers along with the driver of the motorbike in respect of the injuries she suffered.[32] The driver was not a party to the proceedings.

b) Judgment of the Court

18 Finlay Geoghegan J upheld the plaintiff's claim and awarded her € 243,829.95 in damages, of which € 230,000 was by way of general damages for pain, suffering and loss of amenity. She found that once it became apparent to the police officers that that driver was speeding up to evade them, combined with the fact that the officers had heard no reports of any other crimes with which the driver might be connected, their continued pursuit was a breach of the duty owed to other road users, including the plaintiff, a passenger on the vehicle being pursued. The evidence showed that the driver was travelling at 80 mph when the police began the pursuit, but shortly after the police found themselves driving at 100 mph to keep up with the motorbike. Further, Finlay Geoghegan J found that the manner in which the pursuit continued through a small town, involving the motorbike and the police car driving on the hard

[32] Sec. 11 of the Civil Liability Act 1961 provides that two or more persons are concurrent wrongdoers where they cause the same damage to a third person, irrespective of whether the wrongdoers are acting independently or in concert. Sec. 12 of the Act provides that each concurrent wrongdoer is liable for the full extent of the damage, subject to the constraint that the plaintiff may only recover once for his or her loss.

shoulder on the wrong side of the road at one point, also involved a failure by the police to meet the appropriate standard of care.

c) Commentary

It is highly questionable whether the state should be paying out compensation in circumstances such as these and the decision surely sends out the wrong signal to traffic offenders and unduly constrains the police in responding to risks generated by offenders. While there are few written judgments specifically addressing the obligations of emergency vehicles, it is clear that such vehicles do owe a duty of reasonable care to other road users and that the behaviour required to meet the standard imposed does take account of the public benefit derived from the particular service in the particular circumstances. Thus, while some latitude is afforded to drivers of emergency vehicles in determining reasonable driving, it does not give them free reign to do as they please.[33] Clearly in the case of police officers pursuing an offender, the level of risk has to be balanced against the potential seriousness of the criminal activity. The judge does take this balance into account, being influenced by the speed of the initial pursuit and the fact that the only known offence was a traffic offence. However, if one considers the issue from another perspective a very different view emerges; most drivers do not attempt a dangerous evasion of the police for a relatively minor offence, so the flight of the offender should alert the police to the possibility that the driver is engaged in other criminal activity. The police are surely required to engage in a vigorous pursuit if they have serious suspicions about the fleeing driver. The behaviour faulted by the judge – driving at 100 mph on a main national route and driving on the wrong side of the road in a built up area, while another police vehicle held back oncoming traffic[34] – do not appear disproportionate, if one takes account of the fact that the police had no way of knowing at this point that the traffic offence was the only one committed by the driver. The judge's focus on whether other crimes had been notified to the police officers over the radio is surely an unduly constrained approach to determining the potential seriousness of the criminal activity. 19

The judgment also sends out the wrong message to offenders, in that it suggests that if someone flees at high speed, then the police should not pursue them. Consequently flight is rewarded instead of punished, as there will clearly be cases where the police will either not be able to trace the offender, or not be able to prove the offence. One final point of note is that there is no information provided on why the fleeing driver was not a party to the case, although 20

[33] See *Strick v Treacy* unrep HC 10 June 1993 involving a collision between a fire tender and a car, as the fire tender proceeded through a junction against the lights; both drivers were found to be culpable, as was the driver of an accompanying police vehicle, who had not taken sufficient precautions to control the junction. *O'Keeffee v Ladola and Dublin Corporation* unrep CC 12 January 2000, where a bus and an ambulance collided at an intersection; the bus driver was found to be 80% responsible, as he had failed to look properly to see if the road was clear; the ambulance was travelling at approximately 40 mph in a 30 mph zone.

[34] There must also necessarily have been some weaving through town traffic, but this is not emphasised in the judgment.

he was a witness. Clearly his wrongdoing was the principal cause of the incident and his conduct was far more blameworthy than that of the pursuing police driver. Surely the proper target for the plaintiff's compensation should be the insurer of the motorbike or, absent valid insurance coverage, the Motor Insurer's Bureau of Ireland (MIBI).[35]

5. *Philp v Ryan & Bon Secours Hospital* HC 11 March 2004:[36] Medical Negligence, Misdiagnosis, Reasonable Belief of Reduced Life Expectancy

a) Brief Summary of the Facts

21 In June 2001 the plaintiff was admitted to the Bon Secours Hospital under the care of Mr. Ryan. He was diagnosed with acute prostatitis and discharged in early July, with a follow up meeting shortly afterwards. During a subsequent follow up visit in December a test was carried out and prostate cancer was discovered. The plaintiff had left the country to return to work in Saudi Arabia before the test results were available. The results of the test were posted in January 2002 to the plaintiff in Saudi Arabia, but did not reach him until March 2002. Shortly after receiving the results, he underwent surgery in Saudi Arabia; while the surgery was beneficial, the plaintiff was nonetheless terminally ill. The plaintiff sued the defendants on the basis that his cancer should have been diagnosed in July 2001 and that earlier treatment could have prolonged his life expectancy.

b) Judgment of the Court

22 Peart J found that the first defendant was negligent in not diagnosing the plaintiff's condition earlier, as the evidence showed that a significant amount of the information available to him was inconsistent with acute prostatitis.[37] At the very least further tests in respect of the possibility of prostate cancer should have been carried out shortly after the meeting of the doctor and patient on 12 July 2001. The doctor was also held to be negligent in failing to make more vigorous efforts to contact the plaintiff when he got the test results. There was a difference of opinion among the medical expert witnesses and the literature cited before the court on whether early treatment or delayed treatment was best in respect of prostate cancer. Consequently, even if a correct diagnosis had been made the plaintiff might not have been treated earlier, as the first defendant may have opted to wait before embarking on the relevant treatment and could not be held to be negligent in doing so.[38] Therefore Peart J

[35] For details of the MIBI agreement for compensating victims of uninsured or untraceable drivers see D. Richardson, MIBI – A New Approach to Processing Claims, [2004] Bar Rev. 9, 163.

[36] http://www.bailii.org/ie/cases/IEHC/2004/77.html.

[37] Even the expert witness for the defence said he would not have made that diagnosis, though he said it was reasonable for the defendant to do so.

[38] Based on the principle in *Dunne v The National Maternity Hospital* [1989] IR 91; where there are two or more schools of thought within the profession and each has the support of a respectable body of professional support, a doctor who follows one of those approaches cannot be held negligent, even if it transpires that the alternative approach would have produced a better outcome for the patient.

could not reach a definitive view that life expectancy was actually shortened. He did find that the failure to diagnose and the failure to inform the patient of his condition did deprive him of the opportunity of being involved in the process of selecting the appropriate course of action.

Peart J found that, as a matter of probability, the specifics of the plaintiff's condition were such that he had a reasonable belief that he would have benefited from early treatment and would have had a resulting longer life expectancy. The defence argument that not knowing of his condition saved the plaintiff some months of distress was rejected; it was held that the patient has a right to know of terminal illness at the earliest possible time, unless he has clearly waived that right in advance; he also has a right to plan his future in light of that knowledge. The plaintiff's reasonable belief that his life was shortened by between 8 months and 2 years as a result of the doctor's negligence, which deprived him of a chance for earlier treatment, led to mental distress over and above that of having a terminal illness. The plaintiff was awarded € 45,000 plus costs. 23

c) Commentary

While the award of damages to the plaintiff is just in the circumstances, the decision lacks any clear support from prior authorities and actually runs counter to recent SC authorities on negligently inflicted psychiatric harm. It has previously been held that where a person suffers no physical injury, but suffers mentally as a result of negligent behaviour, one of the prerequisites to recovery of damages is that they must have suffered a medically recognised psychiatric illness. This decision gives no indication that this threshold has been met and refers only to mental distress suffered by the plaintiff.[39] Given that the judge was unable to conclude that an actual shortening of life expectancy occurred, there is no physical injury present. If physical injury had been present, this would allow for an award in respect of related distress without having to meet the threshold.[40] However, the court did find that there was a loss of a chance of treatment, which might have proved beneficial and it seems appropriate that where medical mis-diagnosis has deprived a person of this opportunity, there should be some compensation available for the consequences.[41] 24

[39] The two leading SC decisions are *Kelly v Hennessy* [1995] 3 IR 253 and *Fletcher v Commissioners of Public Works* [2003] 2 ILRM 94; noted in last year's report, E. Quill (supra fn. 1). Neither decision is mentioned in Peart J's judgment.

[40] Awards for mental distress, falling short of a medically recognised illness, are routinely made in cases where there is some physical harm to the plaintiff. Such an award may even be made in cases of property damage or economic loss, provided the associated mental suffering is a foreseeable consequence of the initial harm.

[41] Liability based on loss of a chance was permitted in *Carroll v Lynch*, unrep. HC, 16 May 2002, but the decision was overruled on procedural grounds unrelated to the loss of chance issue by the SC, 15 May 2003.

6. *Redmond v The Minister for the Environment, Ireland & the Attorney General (AG)* HC, 13 February 2004:[42] Breach of Constitutional Right, Loss of a Chance

a) Brief Summary of the Facts

25 The plaintiff was precluded from standing in National and European elections because his financial circumstances prevented him from being able to raise the deposit required by the applicable legislation.[43] The deposit system was found to be unconstitutional in an earlier HC hearing.[44] The current hearing was to determine whether any damages were due to the plaintiff for the infringement of his constitutional rights.

b) Judgment of the Court

26 Herbert J found that the plaintiff had no real prospect of success, as he had not made any real campaign plans, so there was no actual damage suffered by him. He accepted that loss of chances like winning the election, making a profit or material gain, or an opportunity of an acting or sporting career could form the basis of an award, but not the loss of a chance merely to put one's political opinion before the public. He also found that the violation of constitutional rights which did occur was not wilful and conscious and in knowing disregard of the plaintiff's rights; it was an honest but misguided attempt to prevent abuse of the electoral system, therefore no exemplary damages were awarded.[45] The plaintiff was awarded nominal damages of € 130.[46]

c) Commentary

27 The award of nominal damages is appropriate in the circumstances. There was an infringement of constitutional rights, but no ensuing harm. The court was correct in holding that the opportunity to put one's views before the electorate, as opposed to having an organised campaign with some prospect of success, is too vague a right to measure in monetary terms. The award indicates that the plaintiff had a legitimate grievance, worthy of the courts attention and costs can be expected to be recovered. This is sufficient to vindicate the right infringed.

[42] http://www.bailii.org/ie/cases/IEHC/2004/24.html.

[43] Sec. 47 of the Electoral Act 1992, governing elections to Dáil Éireann (Irish national parliament); sec. 13 European Parliament Election Act 1997.

[44] Unrep. HC, 31 July 2001 (Herbert J); the deposit system has been replaced by a nomination system under Electoral (Amendment) Act 2002; one requires the support of 30 registered electors to stand for the national parliament; the support of 60 registered electors is required in respect of the European parliament. The constitutional validity of the new system was upheld in *King v The Min for the Environment, Ireland & the AG* unrep., HC 19 December 2003.

[45] The criterion of wilful and conscious disregard of constitutional rights as a basis for an award of exemplary damages was set out in *Conway v The Irish National Teachers Organisation* [1991] 2 IR 305; for further consideration of exemplary damages in Irish law see E. Quill (supra fn. 15), at 519 et seq.; B.M.E. McMahon/W. Binchy (supra fn. 15), at §44.09 et seq.

[46] In accordance with the principles set out in *Kearney v The Minister for Justice* [1986] IR 116 and *The Mediana* [1900] AC 113, 116 per Lord Halsbury LC.

7. *McGrath v Trintech Ltd.* HC 29 October 2004:[47] Occupational Stress, Negligently Inflicted Psychiatric Harm, Statutory Duty

a) Brief Summary of the Facts

The plaintiff worked for the defendant company and was temporarily posted overseas in Uruguay for a period of over five months to take charge of a transition of control from the Montevideo office to the Dublin head office of the company. Due to the stress arising out of his work there, he suffered psychologically. On returning to Ireland he remained on sick leave until being made redundant approximately three months later. He sued for breach of contract in respect of the termination of his employment and he also sought damages for breach of common law and statutory duties by his employer, leading to his psychological ill health. The breach of duty related to an alleged lack of sufficient support when industrial relations problems emerged during his time in charge in Uruguay. 28

b) Judgment of the Court

Laffoy J held that the principles governing an employer's duty of care at common law in respect of physical injuries could be assimilated into cases involving psychiatric injury. On the facts she found that the plaintiff did suffer a medically recognised psychiatric injury as a result of his work, but that his susceptibility to such illness was not foreseeable by the defendant. It was aware of physical health problems suffered by the plaintiff as a result of prior work overseas for the company and the plaintiff was medically examined to establish his fitness for the position before being sent. Both parties were aware in advance that the work was going to be difficult and both the plaintiff and senior management in the defendant felt that he was up to the challenge, having worked in the industry for many years. Furthermore, while the actual crises which occurred during the plaintiff's time in Uruguay made the job more demanding than had been anticipated, these crises were unpredictable and the plaintiff's level of pressure was no different from that of other senior personnel involved in their resolution. The plaintiff had not given the defendant any notice of his psychological history and had not made any complaints either during or after his time in Uruguay. 29

In relation to breach of statutory duty, the plaintiff argued that the provisions of the Safety, Health and Welfare at Work Act 1989 and the Safety, Health and Welfare at Work (General Application) Regulations imposed virtually absolute liability on employers once the injury was caused by the employee's work. Laffoy J held that, while stress was caused by the plaintiff's work, he had not shown that a stress induced injury had been caused by a breach of duty; she held that even if the employer had taken the measures suggested by the plaintiff, it was not clear as a matter of probability that the injury would have 30

[47] http://www.bailii.org/ie/cases/IEHC/2004/342.html.

been avoided. She added, *obiter*, that the level of obligation argued for by the plaintiff would impose a wholly unrealistic burden on employers.

c) Commentary

31 While the decision on the facts may well be correct, a number of problems arise out of the manner in which the legal principles were stated. The application of the established principles of employers' liability in respect of physical injury to workers to cases of psychiatric injury is to be welcomed and is consistent with the tenor of earlier Irish authorities.[48] However, Laffoy J also used several English cases in support of the proposition, despite the fact that those cases apply a more constrained interpretation of foreseeability of harm in cases of psychiatric injury than in cases of physical injury. The established principles of employers' liability assume the existence of a duty and focus purely on the standard of care. The English approach restricts the existence of a duty to cases where the individual susceptibility of the particular employee to the particular risk is known or ought to be known by the employer.[49] Laffoy J then actually applies that restricted view of foreseeability, despite the earlier assertion that the ordinary principles of employers' liability should apply. The question of the individual's susceptibility to harm is relevant to the magnitude of the risk in determining the appropriate level of precaution required of an employer to meet the standard of care, but it is surely an error to elevate it to being the central criterion in determining such cases. It would be better to regard it as one of several factors affecting the determination of appropriate precautions.

32 The ruling on statutory duty is also problematic. While Laffoy J is correct on the narrow ground that, absent a causal connection between breach of duty and the harm suffered, no liability can be imposed, the broader treatment of statutory duty is questionable. First, the plaintiff pleaded a breach of sec. 6 (2) of the 1989 Act, yet sec. 60(1)(a) of that Act precludes a civil action based on the duties in secs. 6–11. Secondly, the *dictum* that the high level of responsibility argued for by the plaintiff would place an unrealistic burden on employers is at variance with established authority that statutory standards in respect of occupational safety are generally higher than the reasonable care standard at common law.[50] There is little consideration given in the judgment to the details of the regulations raised by the plaintiff, particularly those related to risk assessment. Consequently, the precise level of protection afforded by the regulations is left unclear and the opportunity to provide some clarification has been missed.

[48] *Fletcher v Commissioners of Public Works* [2003] 2 ILRM 94; noted by E.Quill (supra fn. 1), at §§4–8; *McHugh v Minister for Defence* unrep HC, 28 January 2000; *Curran v Cadbury (Ireland) Ltd.* [2000] 2 ILRM 343.

[49] *Barber v Somerset County Council* [2004] 1 *Weekly Law Reports* (WLR) 1089; *Hatton v Sutherland* [2000] All ER 2, 1; *Walker v Northumberland County Council* [1995] 1 All ER 737.

[50] See G. Shannon, *Health and Safety: Law & Practice* (2002); E. Quill (supra fn. 15), at 142–148; B.M.E. McMahon/W. Binchy (supra fn. 15), at §18.23 et seq. and §21.42 et seq.

C. Literature

1. E. Quill, *Torts in Ireland* (2nd edn. Gill & Macmillan, 2004)

This is a student textbook on the Irish law of torts, providing an introduction to the main features of Irish tort law combined with a selection of comparative material. This edition incorporates the key changes in the law in Ireland over the five years since the first edition was published, many of which have been highlighted in the Yearbook reports over the past three years. It also incorporates a selection of new comparative material, mainly from Australia, Canada and England. 33

2. V. Corbett, *Tort* (Thomson Round Hall, 2004 (Round Hall Nutcases))

This is a student revision guide, containing a selection of extracts from Irish and English cases on key facets of tort law, accompanied by brief commentaries, placing the extracts in context and highlighting their relationship to general principles of tort law. 34

3. W. Binchy, Recent Developments in the Law of Torts, [2004] *Judicial Studies Institute Journal* 4:1, 8

This article reviews a wide range of Irish case law over recent years and notes a shift in emphasis in the SC towards defendants in tort cases, particularly in the reformulation of the general duty of care principle, a greater reliance on policy and pragmatic considerations to curb liability and large reductions in damages for relatively trivial instances of contributory negligence. The author points out that this shift has not been in evidence in the HC or CC decisions over the same period. He opines that the present trend in legislative reform, aimed at cutting the cost of insurance through reductions in the cost of the tort system, would be unlikely to meet significant judicial hostility in the SC. He notes that if such changes had been introduced a decade earlier, significant judicial concern over plaintiffs' constitutional rights, such as the right of access to the courts, the right to litigate and the guarantee of equality, could have been anticipated and a major constitutional clash between the legislative and judicial branches of government might have ensued. 35

4. K. Spencer, Tortious Liability for Private Security Services: Bouncers or Bullies? Parts I & II [2004] ILT 22, 30 and 46

Part I explains the law on assault and battery in Ireland and England, focusing on the defence of using reasonable force, but also briefly dealing with contributory negligence and private powers of arrest. It then goes on to deal with an employer's vicarious liability for illegal acts, focusing on the English decisions in *Lister v Hesley Hall*,[51] *Vasey v Surrey Free Inns plc*[52] and *Dubai Alu-* 36

[51] [2002] 1 AC 215.
[52] [1996] *Personal Injuries and Quantum Reports* (PIQR) 373.

minum Co. Ltd. v Salaam & Others.[53] Part II goes on to consider a more extended form of vicarious liability under the English decision in *Mattis v Pollock*,[54] where an employer was held liable for a violent attack on the plaintiff off of the employer's premises, following an altercation between the plaintiff and the member of the defendant's security staff responsible for the attack. The article suggests that Irish courts should follow the approach taken in *Mattis*. The remainder of the article considers administrative, regulatory and criminal aspects of liability for security services.

5. H.G. Kennedy, Limits of Psychiatric Evidence in Civil Courts and Tribunals: Science and Sensibility, [2004] *Medico-Legal Journal of Ireland* (MLJI) 10, 16

37 The author begins by discussing the role of expert witness in depth and proceeds to discuss aspects of the relationship between mental illness and the law. The nature of mental illnesses is outlined, focusing on particular facets of mental illness which have particular legal implications. The author then goes on to consider differences between scientific and legal views of causation, both in the role it plays in the respective reasoning processes and in methods of proof. This is followed by consideration of various aspects of tort law, such as the standard of care, capacity, consent, the duty of care in respect of providing safe systems of health care and compensation issues in respect of mental health.

6. M. Canny/A. Lowry, The European Convention on Human Rights Act 2003, a *Cause Célèbre* for Privacy Rights in Ireland, [2004] Bar Rev 9, 73

38 The authors argue for the 2003 Act to have horizontal effect so as to allow private parties, such as the media, to be accountable for the infringement of Convention rights, particularly the invasion of privacy. The authors also examine the action for breach of confidence to test its sufficiency in the protection of privacy. They focus in particular on English law and its attempts to stretch the action to fill the gap created by the lack of an independent privacy law and note that this threatens the doctrinal coherence of the action. They further note that even in expanded form the action cannot protect against republication of information already in the public domain. The article finishes by noting that the constitutional protection of privacy in Irish law could be used as a means to fulfil Ireland's convention obligations.

7. C. Murphy, 'Slopping out' and the European Convention on Human Rights, [2004] Bar Rev 9, 223

39 This article provides a commentary on *Napier v The Scottish Ministers*,[55] concerning an action against prison authorities for breach of the European Con-

[53] [2003] WLR 1913.
[54] [2003] *England and Wales Court of Appeal* (EWCA Civ.) 887.
[55] 26 April 2004 (Court of Sessions).

vention on Human Rights, arising out of the conditions in which the prisoner was kept. The article focuses on a breach of Article 3 in respect of inhuman or degrading treatment and Article 8 in relation to respect for private life. The author notes that the process of slopping out itself is not necessarily unlawful;[56] lawfulness depends on the individual circumstances of the individual prisoner. The author goes on to note other aspects of the prison regime relevant to the determination of breaches of Convention rights, in particular overcrowding in cells and the cramped facilities in the reception area in which prisoners going to court were kept before their departure and on their return.

8. R. Arthur, After Laffoy – What Remedies for Victims of Abuse, [2004] *Irish Journal of Family Law* (IJFL) 1, 3

The author notes the resignation of Miss Justice Laffoy from the Commission 40
on child abuse, due to a lack of sufficient government support in respect of compensation. The author notes the possibility of victims turning to tort law for compensation and examines developments in Canada, the United States of America, England and the jurisprudence of the European Court of Human Rights. He concludes that tort law does provide a viable option for victims and that the potential liability of the state is considerable. Consequently, he opines that the government would be better served by giving greater support to the commission, as government attempts to limit the cost of compensation are misguided.

9. W. Abrahamson, The Statute of Limitations and Discoverability, [2004] Bar Rev 9, 48

This is a case note on the SC decision in *Gough v Neary & Cronin*.[57] In that 41
case a majority held that the plaintiff's lack of knowledge that the hysterectomy performed on her was unnecessary was sufficient to delay the running of the statutory time limit, based on sec. 2(1) of the Statute of Limitations (Amendment) Act 1991. The author favours the dissenting view as being legally correct – that the plaintiff's lack of knowledge did not come within the parameters of sec. 2 (1) and so the plaintiff's claim should have been treated as statute barred. He suggests the introduction of a statutory modification to allow for the actual outcome reached in the case, by providing a judicial discretion to allow a case to proceed despite the time limit for instituting proceedings having elapsed.

[56] 'Slopping out' refers to the process whereby prisoners are provided with a bucket as a toilet in their cell, which is emptied in the mornings in a communal bathroom.

[57] [2003] 3 IR 92, noted in E. Quill (supra fn. 1), at §§22–28.

XIII. Italy

Emanuela Navarretta and Elena Bargelli

A. Cases

1. *Cassazione Sezioni Unite* (Plenary session of the Supreme Court, Cass. SS. UU.) 26 January 2004, no. 1338, 1339, 1340: Liability for Violation of Art. 6 of the European Convention of Human Rights – Doctrine of European Court of Human Rights as Legal Precedent[1]

a) Brief Summary of the Facts

1 The plaintiff claimed for the damage suffered for water infiltration in his flat. In his opinion, the trial had dragged on for an excessively long period of time. Because he had to wait a long time before winning the litigation, he sought damages for pain and suffering (15 million Lire, approx. € 7,500). He alleged that the sued court needed too much time to deliver the judgment. Therefore, it violated art. 6 ECHR (Right to a fair trial)[2] and art. 2 Law 24 March 2001, no. 89, which envisages compensation for pecuniary and non-pecuniary damage if the trial the plaintiff promoted has had an unreasonable duration. The Court of Appeal of Rome rejected the claim for two reasons. First, the judges argued that the original trial involved mere patrimonial interests of the plaintiff, and not fundamental rights or aspects of his affective life. Second, the plaintiff should prove his real loss, which could not be presumed by the mere duration of the trial. In fact, because the damages were very low, he should testify that his economic situation was so precarious to make even such a low sum of

[1] [2004] *Corriere giuridico* (CG), 600, with comment of R. Conti, *C.e.d.u. e diritto interno: le Sezioni Unite si avvicinano a Strasburgo sull'irragionevole durata dei processi.*

[2] It states: "1. In the determination of his civil rights and obligations or of any criminal charge against him, everyone is entitled to a fair and public hearing within a reasonable time by an independent and impartial tribunal established by law. Judgment shall be pronounced publicly but the press and public may be excluded from all or part of the trial in the interests of morals, public order or national security in a democratic society, where the interests of juveniles or the protection of the private life of the parties so require, or to the extent strictly necessary in the opinion of the court in special circumstances where publicity would prejudice the interests of justice."

money immediately necessary for him. The plaintiff appealed against the decision.

b) Judgment of the Court

The Supreme Court upholds the claim of the plaintiff. The judges remark that the European Court of Human Rights had already tried the present case, ascertained a violation of art. 6 ECHR and conceded damages for pain and suffering. Therefore, the Court of Rome was not allowed to refuse the damages, which on the contrary should rather be increased because, in the meantime, the original trial had continued and the violation of art. 6 ECHR had become more serious. Moreover, the small amount of the damages should not be considered enough reason to reject the claim, even in case of pain and suffering. In fact, the low level of pain could lead to a reduction of damages, but not to their exclusion. 2

c) Commentary

The present decision is relevant because it dictates the guidelines on how to solve two questions arising from L. no. 89/2001. First, how to prove pain and suffering deriving from the long duration of trials. Second, whether and how to take into account the rules expressed by the European Court of Human Rights for analogous cases. In order to answer these questions, the Plenary Session of the Supreme Court delivered three decisions together. They have the same date (that is, 26 January 2004), and progressive numbers: 1338, 1339 (that is, the commented judgment), 1340. 3

As regards the first question, until the present decision it had been disputed whether the mere violation of art. 2 L. no. 89/2001 could be enough to claim for damages for pain and suffering if the plaintiff has not proved a specific and concrete loss. The Supreme Court denied that the excessive duration of the trial could be considered as damage *in re ipsa*, that is a damage to be compensated as a consequence of the simple violation of the right envisaged by the cited statute. It adopted a quite rigorous position, and required, if not specific evidence of loss of amenities of life, at least circumstantial proof of it.[3] The court argued that the reasonable duration of a trial is not a fundamental right, but it is protected by a mere statute (that is, art. 2 L. no. 89/2001). In fact, the Supreme Court denied that both art. 6 ECHR and art. 111 subs. 2 of the Italian Constitution (Const.) (envisaging the right to the reasonable duration of trials) would be enforceable as between private parties. On the one hand, it emphasizes that art. 111 Const. would contain general guidelines for legislation, or principles to be used by the Constitutional Court to verify whether a statute is consistent or not with them (it means that art. 111 Const. is a so called *norma programmatica*).[4] On the other hand, it stated that Italian courts could not di- 4

[3] See *ex multis* Cass. 17 April 2003, no. 6168, [2003] *Giustizia civile* (GC), 2372.

[4] Cass. 2002, no. 11987, [2002] *Giurisprudenza italiana* (GI), 2039, with comment of A. Didone, *La Cassazione e l'equa riparazione per irragionevole durata del processo*.

rectly enforce the rights envisaged by the ECHR,[5] and were not obliged to follow the European Court of Human Right's doctrine, which allows compensation for damages as a consequence of the mere violation of fundamental rights. As a consequence, the victim could not invoke the disputed concept of "damage *in re ipsa*", which was supposed to apply only to fundamental rights.[6]

5 The present group of decisions of the Plenary Session of the Supreme Court seems to adopt a less rigorous rule, according to which non-patrimonial damages are presumed in case of violation of art. 2 L. no. 89/2001. They emphasize that the right to the reasonable duration of trials is protected by art. 6 ECHR. In the opinion of the court, damages must be awarded even if the plaintiff has not proved non-pecuniary losses, unless the defendant proves concrete and specific circumstances which exclude them. Even if this doctrine is formally expressed by the decision no. 1338, the rule dictated by no. 1339 is its coherent application. If the mere violation of art. 2 L. no. 89/2001 is enough to award damages, it is not significant whether the original suit concerned a low amount of damages.

6 This guideline seems consistent with the doctrine which identifies the concept of violation of someone's right and that of loss. In the Italian legal system, this theory has been developed by some courts and scholars in the field of personal damages.[7] However, it has been rejected by the most recent decisions of the Supreme Court[8] and of the Constitutional Court,[9] which have introduced a more rigorous rule. In fact, in order to award damages for non-pecuniary losses, they have required the proof of the concrete loss in case of violation of personal rights protected by the Italian Constitution. This recent opinion has been confirmed also by successive decisions of the Supreme Court[10] and of the

[5] See Cass. 29 October 2003, 15233, [2003] *Archivio civile* (Arch. civ.), 988.

[6] See, for example, Cass. 8 August 2002, no. 11987, [2003] GI, 579.

[7] See, as example, P.G. Monateri, La responsabilità civile, in: R. Sacco (ed.), *Trattato Diritto civile* (1998), 305 et seq.
See also Const. Court., 14 July 1986, no. 184, [1986] *Foro italiano* (FI) I, 2053, with comments of G. Ponzanelli, *La Corte costituzionale, il danno non patrimoniale e il danno alla salute,* and of P.G. Monateri, *La Costituzione e il diritto privato: il caso dell'art. 32 Cost. e del danno biologico („Staatsrecht vergeht, Privatrecht besteht").*

[8] Cass. 31 May 2003, no. 8827 and no. 8828, [2003] FI I, 2272, with comment of E. Navarretta, *Danni non patrimoniali: il dogma infranto e il nuovo diritto vivente*; [2003] *Danno e responsabilità* (DR), 816, with comments of F.D. Busnelli, *Chiaroscuri d'estate. La Corte di Cassazione e il danno alla persona*; of G. Ponzanelli, *Ricomposizione dell'universo non patrimoniale: le scelte della Corte di Cassazione*; and of A. Procida Mirabelli Di Lauro, *L'art. 2059 c.c. va in paradiso*.

[9] Const. Court, 11 July 2003, no. 233, [2003] FI, 2003, 2201, with comment of E. Navarretta, *La Corte costituzionale e il danno alla persona «in fieri»*; [2003] DR, 939, with comments of M. Bona, *Il danno esistenziale bussa alla porta e la Corte costituzionale apre (verso il "nuovo" art. 2059 c.c.)*, of G. Cricenti, *Una diversa lettura dell'art. 2059 c.c.*, of G. Ponzanelli, *La Corte costituzionale si allinea con la Corte di Cassazione*, of A. Mirabelli Di Lauro, *Il sistema di responsabilità civile dopo la sentenza della Corte costituzionale no. 233/03*, and of O. Troiano, *L'irresistibile ascesa del danno non patrimoniale*.

[10] See infra nos. 13 et seq.

courts of first instance.[11] While the Supreme Court has stated this strict rule about damages for violation of constitutional rights, Cass. SS. UU. N. 1338, 1339, 1340/2004 have set a different rule in case of violation of a fundamental right protected by the ECHR. This leads to an unreasonable incoherence of the tort law system.

The second question focuses on the influence of the European Court's doctrine on Italian decisions. As regards this point, the Plenary Session of *Cassazione* has introduced a far-reaching rule. In fact, before the present group of decisions, the Supreme Court had often stated that the doctrine of the European Court of Human Rights could not be held as binding for the national courts.[12] *Cassazione* argued that, while the Treaty of the European Union states that the decisions of the European Court of Justice are sources of law for national courts, there is no analogous provision as regards the statements of the European Court of Human Rights.[13] On the contrary, the Convention of Human Rights states that the citizen may bring a legal action before the Strassburg's court only if the protection offered by his State is either non-existent or insufficient.[14] According to this opinion, the ECHR would give a strictly subsidiary protection to the parties, and, as a consequence, Italian courts would not be subject to *stare decisis*. This doctrine allowed Italian courts to deny damages for violation of fundamental rights without at least a presumptive proof of the loss, even if the European Court of Human Rights had given or would give compensation in analogous cases. 7

Before the present decision, the Supreme Court had sometimes admitted the influence of the European Court's doctrine on Italian decisions. In fact, *Cassazione* had denied its role of judicial precedents, but had stated that it could be invoked as an influential argument or "hermeneutic guideline" in order to give a coherent enforcement to the human rights protected by the European Convention.[15] 8

The Plenary Session of *Cassazione* now states that Italian courts are compelled to follow the rules set by the European Court of Human Rights in order to determine damages. The criteria adopted by Italian courts must be consistent with those set by the European Court, otherwise the decision may be appealed for violation of legal dispositions. This statement is expressed by the decision no. 1340 of the Plenary Session, but it forms a unitary system with the rules provided by the others of the same date. *Cassazione* bases its *revirement* on a recent decision of the European Court of Human Rights, which has 9

[11] Trib. Roma, 16 January 2004, [2004] DR, 1107, with comment of F. Grimaldi, *Il nuovo art. 2059 c.c. e la giurisprudenza di merito*.

[12] Cass. 5 September 2003, no. 12935, [2003] *Massimario giurisprudenza italiana* (Mass. Giur. it.); Cass. 19 November 2002, no. 16262, [2003] Arch. Civ., 1372.

[13] Cass. 10 April 2003, no. 5664, [2003] CED *Cassazione*.

[14] Cass. 10 April 2003, no. 5664 (supra fn. 13).

[15] Cass. 14 April 2003, no. 5902, [2004] GI, 169; Cass. 19 November 2002, no. 16262 (supra fn. 12).

remarked upon the great discrepancy between its rules concerning determination of damages and the criteria adopted by Italian courts, and, as a consequence, admitted the claim of the plaintiff.[16]

2. Cass. SS. UU. 11 March 2004, no. 5044: International Crime – Damages for Pecuniary and Non-pecuniary Losses – Jurisdictional Immunity of the State in Foreign Country[17]

a) Brief Summary of the Facts

10 In 1944 the plaintiff was captured by the German army in Arezzo (Italy), deported to Germany and forced to work in German enterprises until 20 April 1945. In 1998 he claimed for damages from the Federal Republic of Germany. The defendant denied the competence of Italian jurisdiction. It invoked the Convention of Bruxelles of 27 June 1968, which grants immunity to one State from civil jurisdiction of another State if it was exercising its sovereignty while it provoked the harmful event. The Tribunale of Arezzo rejected the claim, and declared its lack of competence. This decision was confirmed by Florence's Court of Appeal.

b) Judgment of the Court

11 The Plenary Session of the Supreme Court admits the claim. The court states in advance that the principle of jurisdictional immunity of the State is still compelling. Its binding force, however, is restricted to activities which are "immediate and the direct expression" of the sovereignty of the foreign State. Germany, of course, was committing "*acta iure imperii*" when it captured and deported the plaintiff. Nevertheless, deportation is regarded as an international crime by the United Nation's Resolution of 11 December 1946. This crime, in fact, seriously violates freedom and human dignity, requires severe punishment, and, therefore, is indefeasible. In the opinion of the court, the jurisdictional immunity of the State which has committed such crimes would contradict these principles. In fact, it would obstruct not only the defence of human rights, but also the protection of the victim as regards compensation for damage. Furthermore, the court outlines that in tort litigations the role of the immunity principle and of *iure imperii* rule are going to decrease.

12 This tendency would not be contradicted by recent decisions which have reaffirmed the immunity principle even in case of international crimes. These litigations, in fact, concern harmful events which occurred in a State other than the one in which the claim has arisen. Instead in the present case the harmful act occurred in Italy, and the claim was brought before an Italian court.

[16] European Court of Human Rights, 27 March 2003, [2003] *Giornale diritto amministrativo*, 954.

[17] [2004] *Responsabilità civile e previdenza* (RCP), 1030, with comment of A. Viterbo, *I diritti fondamentali come limite all'immunità dello Stato.*

c) Commentary

The present decision introduces a far-reaching rule, as regards the supremacy of the human rights' protection on the sovereignty of the States. In particular, this statement is supposed to be based on the normative hierarchy theory.[18] The rule set by the Plenary Session is of course important in the context of international law, but it is also significant in tort law litigations. In fact, it leads to an increase in the protection of human rights, even if their severe violation is committed by a State in foreign territory. 13

3. Cass. 27 April 2004, no. 7980: Non-pecuniary Losses as a Consequence of Unlawful Dismissal; Constitutionally Oriented Interpretation of Art. 2059 cc

a) Brief Summary of the Facts

The plaintiff is a surgeon who was dismissed by the hospital (a public entity) and reinstated after eight years, as the dismissal was held as unlawful by the "administrative regional court" (TAR). Therefore, he sued the hospital before the "ordinary" court, and claimed for pecuniary and non-pecuniary damages (total: 5,000,000,000 Lire, approx. € 2,500,000) as a consequence of the unlawful act of the employee. The basic court (*Tribunale*) rejected the claim, arguing that the plaintiff had not proved the fault of the employee. This decision was confirmed by the court of appeal, but quashed by the Supreme Court, which ordered a retrial of the case before the basic court. This court partially upheld the claim and ordered the employee to compensate only for pecuniary damages. Instead, the court denied damages for non-pecuniary losses, and argued that the unlawful act could not be qualified as a crime. The plaintiff appealed against the decision before the Supreme Court, and asked to be compensated for personal damage as a consequence of the violation of the right to personal identity and dignity (art. 2 Const.), even if the unlawful act was not a crime. He quoted Cass. no. 8828/2003.[19] 14

b) Judgment of the Court

The commented decision acknowledges the constitutional relevance of the right to the free expression of the employer's personality. In the present case this right has been unlawfully violated, and, as a consequence, the victim must be compensated for non-pecuniary losses even if the tort is not held as a crime. The court follows the doctrine affirmed by Cass. no. 8828/2003, which had proposed a constitutionally oriented interpretation of art. 2059 cc. According to this theory, every violation of personal rights having constitutional relevance must be restored, even if compensation is not stated by a specific provision. Therefore, the claim must be upheld, even if the plaintiff has invoked art. 2043 cc as the legal provision concerning both pecuniary and non-pecuniary losses, instead of art. 2059 cc. 15

[18] A. Viterbo (supra fn. 17), 1037.
[19] Cass. 31 May 2003, no. 8828 (supra fn. 9).

c) Commentary

16 Cass. nos. 8827 and 8828/2003 are leading cases in the field of non-pecuniary losses. They have supported an extensive interpretation of art. 2059 cc, which is based on the indirect enforcement of constitutional principles in private law. As a consequence, while art. 2059 cc literally restricts damages for non-pecuniary losses to the cases envisaged by legal provisions, this doctrine extends them to every violation of constitutional rights concerning human persons. After these precedents, it is interesting to verify its impact on the jurisprudential debate, from at least two perspectives. First, which "personal" rights are supposed to have constitutional relevance. Second, which violation is required to justify a claim for damages, and how these should be quantified.

17 It is worth outlining that the courts have generally followed the cited doctrine. The above quoted decision is a coherent application of this tendency, as it upholds the claim for non-pecuniary losses even if the unlawful act is not held as criminal. The main argument of the court is based on the constitutional relevance of the employer's personality rights, which include the right not to be dismissed for unlawful reasons. This argument is not totally new. In fact, the courts had already held these rights to be protected by the Constitution before the *revirement* of Cass. no. 8288/2003, and conceded damages when, for example, an employer was compelled to work during holidays.[20]

18 The present decision, instead, does not set rules regarding determination of damages. It holds the court of appeal's quantification as lawful.

4. Cass. 25 May 2004, no. 10035[21]: Loss of Consortium – Damages for Pain and Suffering; Quantification

a) Brief Summary of the Facts

19 The wife of the victim who had died in a car accident sued the driver, and claimed for pecuniary and non-pecuniary damages. She alleged that the death of her husband had upset family life, above all that of her children. The courts of first instance upheld the claim, but, as regards non-pecuniary damages, compensated only for pain and suffering, and not for loss of consortium. In order to calculate the sum of money awarded as pain and suffering these courts adopted the method which calculates this sum on a fraction of *danno biologico* suffered by the "direct" victim. In the present case this damage was supposed to reach the percentage of 100% of invalidity, because the victim died. Damages for pain and suffering were calculated as a fraction of this percentage. The plaintiff appealed against this decision before the Supreme Court.

[20] Cass. 11 December 2001, no. 15580, [2001] DR, 587.

[21] [2004] DR, 1065, with comment of G. Ramaccioni, *La palingenesi dell'art. 2059 c.c.: dove conduce il (nuovo) diritto vivente?*

b) Judgment of the Court

The Supreme Court admits that the plaintiff is right. It reasons that quantification of damages for non-pecuniary losses requires taking into account every circumstance of the concrete case (the gravity of the violation, the suffering of the victim, and, in the present case, the effects of the harmful event on the life of the survivors and above all on the development of the children). The court argues that calculating pain and suffering as a fraction of *danno biologico* is not unlawful, because it pursues the purpose of avoiding the unequal treatment of equal situations. However, damages for non-pecuniary losses must not be standardised, because they must be the result of judicial *equitas*. As a consequence, the court must adapt the cited method of calculation to the concrete case, and show that it has taken its specificities into account. The appealed decision did not refer to the loss of consortium, which, in the present case, is considered relevant by the Supreme Court. Therefore it orders the retrial of the case before the basic court, which will have to judge whether the "tables" for calculating damages adopted by the quashed decision encompass loss of consortium or not. 20

c) Commentary

The present decision does not set a new rule as regards non-pecuniary losses. However, it is interesting for two reasons. First, it shows how the Italian method of determining *danno biologico* has influenced the system of quantification of pain and suffering and even other typologies of non-pecuniary damages. Second, it is consistent with the tendency to quantify non-pecuniary losses by equity rules, and, as a consequence, to take into account circumstances on a case by case basis. 21

The first method is widespread,[22] but not convincing, because damages are automatically deducted from *danno biologico*, and do not take into account the concrete and specific suffering of the victim. The doctrine which criticizes this method insists that non-pecuniary losses and pain and suffering require a case by case evaluation.[23] This is a typical *de facto* evaluation, which is a task of the basic courts, and may not be corrected by the Supreme Court.[24] The courts have often pointed out that the same damages for *danno biologico* must not be the simple result of the *tabellare* method,[25] but must also reflect the 22

[22] See Trib. Monza, 5 November 2004, in [2005] *Famiglia e diritto* (Fam. Dir.), 79, with comment of G. De Marzo, *Riconosciuto il risarcimento del danno al genitore non affidatario per l'interruzione di ogni relazione con il figlio*. The present decision awards damages for violation of the relationship between the mother and her son caused by unlawful behaviour of the father, and quantifies them taking into account the criteria to determine damages for loss of consortium as a consequence of relatives' death.

[23] E. Navarretta, Danni da morte e danno alla salute, in: M. Bargagna/F.D. Busnelli (eds.), *La valutazione del danno alla salute* (1995), 252 et seq.

[24] See Cass. 2 April 2004, no. 6519, [2004] *Repertorio Foro italiano* (RFI), voce Danni civili, no. 39.

[25] On this method see E. Navarretta/E. Bargelli, Italy, in: H. Koziol/B.C. Steininger (eds.), *European Tort Law 2002* (2003), nos. 1–5.

subjective situation of the damaged party. A recent decision of the *Giudice di Pace* (Italian first basic court) of Rome put forward this reasoning to argue the inconsistency of the recent statute on *danno biologico* with the Constitution[26], and sent the trial back to the Constitutional court.[27]

23 After the cited Cass. nos. 8827 and 8828/2003, the courts have again gone back to the topic of loss of consortium. The trend seems to be that of limiting damages for relatives' non-pecuniary losses to serious personal injury of the primary victim.[28] While the cited decisions have divided non-pecuniary losses into two figures (pain and suffering on the one hand, loss for violation of constitutional rights on the other hand), a recent decision of the Tribunal of Rome has put forward a different opinion. It has emphasized that damages for loss of consortium must not be added to that for pain and suffering, because the evaluation of non-pecuniary loss must embrace both of them as a whole.[29] Otherwise, the courts could run the risk of doubling victims' damages.

5. *Cassazione* 21 June 2004, no. 11488 A) and Cass. 19 May 2004, no. 9471 B)[30]: Medical Malpractice – Negligence of the Physician – Burden of Proof

a) Brief Summary of the Facts (A)

24 The plaintiffs are the parents of a severely handicapped child. In 1991 the mother attended a regular pre-natal check-up at the S. Giuseppe hospital in Milan, but the physician did not recognize the deformities of the foetus. As a consequence, the woman could not terminate the pregnancy within the legally final date. The plaintiffs brought an action against the hospital and the physician, and claimed for damages. The Tribunal of Milan and the Court of Appeal of Milan dismissed the claim, arguing that the plaintiffs did not prove the fault of the physician. In the opinion of the courts, in the present case the severe impairments of the foetus would have been difficult to recognize at the time of the pre-natal check-up. Therefore, art. 2236 cc should apply, and, as a consequence, the plaintiffs should prove the gross negligence (*culpa lata*) of the physician. The parents appealed the decision before the Supreme Court.

b) Judgment of the Court (A)

25 The Supreme Court upholds the claim. It argues that the court of appeal has not correctly justified its judgment. First, it has not shown why the recognition of the malfunction was particularly difficult in the present case. Moreover, it

[26] Giudice di Pace di Roma, 17 February 2004, [2004] DR, 863, with comment of G. Ponzanelli, *Micropermanenti nuovamente in attesa della Corte costituzionale*.

[27] The Constitutional Court has already expressed an opinion on this matter: see Const. Court, 21 February 2004, no. 64, [2004] DR, 863.

[28] Cass. 8 June 2004, no. 10816, [2004] RFI, voce Danni civili, no. 59.

[29] Trib. Roma, 16 January 2004 (supra fn. 11).

[30] [2005] DR, 23 et seq., with comment of R. De Matteis, *La responsabilità medica ad una svolta?*

has ruled that the burden of proof of the physician's gross negligence lays on the plaintiffs. The Supreme Court reasons that a physician's liability is contractual, and as a consequence, must be considered under art. 1218 cc. In fact, even if he has not drawn up a contract with the plaintiffs, a contractual relationship would arise from their "social contact". Art. 1218 cc states that the damaged party must prove only the non-fulfilment of the debtor, and that the defendant must prove his/her diligence. The Supreme Court points out that this rule is logical in medical malpractice. In fact, it would be difficult for the damaged party to prove the physician's gross negligence, as it requires technical knowledge in medical fields. As a consequence, the Supreme Court rules that the appealed decision has made a mistake in law.

c) Brief Summary of the Facts (B)

The plaintiff underwent an operation in order to change his sex. However, the 26
operation was not successful. He asserted that the hospital and the surgeon were jointly and severally liable, and claimed damages. While the Tribunal of Orvieto upheld the claim, the Court of Appeal of Perugia dismissed it, and argued that the plaintiff did not prove the surgeon's lack of skill. The plaintiff appealed the decision before the Supreme Court.

d) Judgment of the Court (B)

The court upholds the claim. It traces the evolution of medical fault in the ju- 27
risprudential debate, and outlines that courts have become more and more strict in ascribing medical liability. It starts from art. 2236 cc, which states that professional people are liable only for gross negligence when their activities are qualified as particularly difficult. The court outlines that jurisprudential interpretation has restricted the enforcement of this rule. First, the limitation of liability is held applying only to medical negligence, but not to lack of skill. Moreover, the operation is held as particularly difficult only when it has not been tested or studied enough yet. If the operation may not be classified as particularly difficult, the patient is required to prove only the causality link, while medical negligence is presumed as his health has got worse. In any case, in order to ascribe the liability to the surgeon the victim must not allege specific and technical signs of medical lack of skill. In the opinion of the court, it would be enough to give a presumptive proof of the medical lack of skill, and to base it on the common knowledge of a non-professional person.

e) Commentary (A and B)

Medical responsibility is situated in the borderline between contract and tort. 28
The cited decisions confirm the doctrine of Cass. no. 589/1999[31], according to which, medical liability is contractual even if the physician is an employee of

[31] Cass. 22 January 1999, no. 589, [1999] FI I, 3332 et seq., with comments of F. Di Ciommo, *Note critiche sui recenti orientamenti giurisprudenziali in tema di responsabilità del medico ospedaliero*, and of A. Lanotte, *L'obbligazione del medico dipendente è un'obbligazione senza prestazione o una prestazione senza obbligazione?*

the hospital, and the patient has not concluded an agreement with him, but only with the hospital. This doctrine upholds the theoretical concept of obligation from "social contact"[32], and pursues the purpose of facilitating the proof of medical liability. In fact, according to art. 1218 cc, the damaged party does not have to prove the negligence of the other party, but the defendant must prove that non-fulfilment is due to unforeseen circumstances. According to a widespread and traditional opinion, the defendant is also burdened by the proof of fulfilment if the victim alleges non-fulfilment; on the contrary, the victim who claims for damages caused by inexact fulfilment must prove this.[33]

29 Both decisions concern inexact fulfilment. The first decision sets a presumption of fault;[34] the second aims to ease the burden of proof for the damaged party. Their purpose is to burden with proof the party who has technical knowledge and is in possession of all the data necessary to defend himself/herself. In fact, the hospital and the surgeon may not avoid responsibility simply by proving their lack of fault, but they must show the fulfilment of medical duties required by *ars medica.*[35] This statement is in line with the doctrine stated by Cass. SS. UU. no. 13533/2001, which rules that the damaged party does not have to prove the inexact fulfilment of the physician, but the defendant must prove to have exactly fulfilled all the medical duties.[36]

B. Literature

1. M. Bona/P.G. Monateri, *Il nuovo danno non patrimoniale* (Ipsoa, 2004)

30 This book focuses on the evolution of the doctrine of non-pecuniary losses in the Italian legal system after Cass. no. 8827/2003 and no. 8828/2003, and Const. court no. 233/2003. The authors start from the division of non-pecuniary losses into three groups: *danno biologico*, damages for violation of other constitutional rights, and pain and suffering. This division was introduced by the cited decisions of the Supreme Court and the decision of the Constitutional Court. The authors deal specifically with non-pecuniary losses for violation of constitutional human rights: in particular, they outline their evolution in the legal debate; then, they analyse the question on how to prove the violations of those rights and how to quantify damages. Finally, the volume includes references to other European systems, to the doctrine of European Court of Human Rights and to European tort law projects.

[32] See C. Castronovo, L'obbligazione senza prestazione ai confini fra contratto e torto, in: *Scritti in onore di L. Mengoni* I (1998), 197.

[33] See A. Ciatti, *Responsabilità medica e decisione sul fatto incerto* (2002), 41 et seq.

[34] See also Cass. 28 May 2004, no. 10297, [2005] DR, 26, with comment of R. De Matteis, *La responsabilità medica ad una svolta?*

[35] R. De Matteis (supra fn. 30), 40.

[36] Cass. SS. UU. 30 October 2001, no.13533, [2002] GC I, 1934.

2. U. Izzo, *La precauzione nella responsabilità civile* (Cedam, 2004)

The cited volume deals with the questions on liability from contagion, especially as regards the role of the precaution principle. The author considers the impact of precaution on the concept of causality on the one hand, on the criteria to ascribe liability on the other hand. His research is based on a comparative method, including analyses of the French and German legal systems, and common law systems. 31

3. E. Navarretta (ed.), *I nuovi danni non patrimoniali. Lineamenti sistematici e guida alla liquidazione* (Giappichelli, 2004)

The cited book collects several articles of different authors, which are devoted to analysing the evolution of the doctrine of non-pecuniary losses after Cass. no. 8827/2003 and no. 8828/2003, and Const. court no. 233/2003. It is divided into two parts. The first is theoretical, and focuses on the impact of the new interpretation of art. 2059 cc on the Italian legal system. This part specifically analyses the new rule which allows damages for non-pecuniary losses in case of violations of fundamental rights, and considers its impact on tort liability, on contractual responsibility and on the public insurance system. In addition, the first part includes a chapter concerning trial questions, and another regarding the relationship between the Italian evolution of the doctrine of non-pecuniary losses and European tort law. 32

The second part contains a practical guide on the quantification of non-pecuniary damages. The authors have collected many decisions and catalogued them according to the nature of non-pecuniary loss. For every type of violation of personal rights they have made a "table" of pecuniary values, which are the result of the judicial precedents on that matter. This volume proposes a method of quantification, which is based on the average damages conceded by courts for every type of violation, and follows the example of the German *Schmerzensgeldtabellen*. The book addresses not only scholars, but also lawyers and judges, and is devoted to set rules to govern damages for non-pecuniary losses. 33

4. G. Ponzanelli (ed.), *Il "nuovo" danno non patrimoniale* (Cedam, 2004)

This volume deals with the topic of non-pecuniary losses. The authors trace a historical overview of the doctrine of non-pecuniary losses in the jurisprudential debate. Then, they concentrate their attention on the interpretation of art. 2059 cc which has been proposed by Cass. no. 8827/2003, no. 8828/2003, and Const. court no. 233/2003. The first five parts of the volume explore the meaning of the new doctrine and its impact on Italian tort law. The sixth part focuses on the main types of violation of personality rights or fundamental rights (defamation, wrongful birth, excessive length of trials, unlawful data transmission, lack of consent in medical treatment, violation of family duties). This part also includes an analysis of non-pecuniary losses in contract law. Moreover, the book contains comparative references to the French legal system as regards questions on non-pecuniary losses. 34

5. A. Procida Mirabelli Di Lauro, *La responsabilità civile. Strutture e funzioni* (Giappichelli, 2004)

35 In the first chapter the author explores the general concepts of unlawfulness and the pecuniary and non-pecuniary nature of damages in the tort law system. In the second part of the book he revises his view on the distinction between pecuniary and non-pecuniary damages. He supports the theory which holds art. 2043 cc as the general rule applying to pecuniary and non-pecuniary losses. The author concludes with the analysis of the impact of social security on tort liability. Particular emphasis is given to the role of strict liability.

6. M. Rabitti, *Rischio organizzativo e responsabilità degli amministratori* (Giuffré, 2004)

36 This book focuses on the liability of managers in corporate law. The topic has become relevant especially since the introduction of the corporate law reform act in 2003 (D.Lgs. 17 January 2003, no. 6). The author explores the relationship between the special rules on the responsibility of directors and the general tort law system. She concentrates specifically upon the concept of fault, the causality link, and the joint and several liability rule.

XIV. Latvia

Agris Bitāns

A. Legislation

1. Law on Compulsory Third Party Liability Insurance for Motor Vehicle Owners (*Sauszemes transportlīdzekļu īpašnieku civiltiesiskās atbildības obligātās apdrošināšanas likums*) (Latvian Herald (*Latvijas Vēstnesis*) No. 65, 27 April 2004)

On 7 April 2004 the Latvian parliament adopted a new Law on Compulsory Third Party Liability Insurance for Motor Vehicle Owners effective from 1 May 2004. The law includes provisions arising from the Directives 72/166/EEC, 84/5/EEC, 90/232/EEC, 92/49/EEC and 2000/26/EC. 1

This law replaces the previous law adopted on 13 March 1997. Substantial administrative changes have been made in the area of compulsory third party liability insurance for motorists. The Latvian Motor Insurers' Bureau is now responsible for the successful operation of the motor vehicle owners' compulsory third party liability insurance system[1]. The Bureau is no longer a state-owned entity. 2

Substantial changes have also been made in other areas. The law (sec. 15) now sets new limits on insurer's liability: 250,000 lats (approx. € 360,000) for indemnification of personal loss for each injured person and 70,000 lats (approx. € 100,000) for indemnification of property loss irrespective of the number of third persons. Previously the Cabinet of Ministers had established lower 3

[1] Sec. 43. Latvian Motor Insurers' Bureau
(1) The successful operation of the motor vehicle owners' compulsory third party liability insurance system in the country according to its purposes and objectives is ensured by the Latvian Motor Insurers' Bureau, which combines all insurance companies authorised to perform motor vehicle owners' compulsory third party liability insurance in Latvia.
(2) The activities of the Latvian Motor Insurers' Bureau are governed by this law, but its legal status is governed by the Societies and Foundations Act.
(3) If an insurer is excluded or withdraws from the Latvian Motor Insurers' Bureau, they will notify the Financial and Capital Market Commission.
(4) The Latvian Motor Insurers' Bureau shall perform green card office functions in Latvia.
(5) The Latvian Motor Insurers' Bureau independently makes decisions within its competence, performs assignments and is responsible for their fulfilment.

limits: 10,000 lats (approx. € 14,500) for indemnification of personal loss and 9,000 lats (approx. € 13,000) for indemnification of property loss.

4 The law permits a request for compensation (indemnification) from a third person in respect of losses which are not indemnified under this law or which exceed the insurer's liability limit, i.e. by filing a civil claim under general law.

5 A new progressive point in the law is the broadened definition of personal loss[2]. In addition to material losses caused to a person in a traffic accident, the new law permits compensation of non-material losses associated with pain and mental suffering. The law recognises non-material losses caused in a traffic accident associated with pain and mental suffering due to: 1) physical trauma to the injured person; 2) mutilation and/or disability of the injured person; 3) death of the breadwinner, dependent or spouse; 4) group I disability of the breadwinner, dependent or spouse.

6 This is not the best definition or description of non-pecuniary loss. The law demonstrates that the legislator did not quite understand the system and essence of personal injury and non-pecuniary loss. It should be noted, however, that this is the first time that the legislator has officially recognised that pain and mental suffering deserves legal compensation.

7 The Latvian Parliament has delegated the power to determine the scope of insurance indemnity and the procedure for indemnity calculations in respect of material and non-material personal losses to the Cabinet of Ministers. The Cabinet of Ministers has drafted a regulation setting a liability limit for pain and mental suffering at 1,000 lats (approx. € 1,430) for each injured person. There is much debate among legal professionals about the inadequacy of this liability limit.

2. Amendments to the Labour Code (*Darba likums*) (Latvian Herald (*Latvijas Vēstnesis*) No. 72, 7 May 2004)

8 New amendments to the Labour Code introduced on 22 April 2004 grant new safeguards for the employee against breach of the prohibition against differential treatment and the prohibition against causing adverse consequences.

[2] Sec. 19. Personal loss
(1) Material losses caused to a person in a traffic accident are losses associated with the following things of the injured person:
1) medical treatment;
2) temporary disablement;
3) loss of ability to work;
4) death.
(2) Non-material losses caused to a person in a traffic accident are losses associated with pain and mental suffering due to:
1) physical trauma to the injured person;
2) mutilation and/or disability of the injured person;
3) death of the breadwinner, dependent or spouse;
4) group I disability of the breadwinner, dependent or spouse.
(3) The scope of insurance indemnity and the procedure of its calculation for material and non-material losses to a person is determined by the Cabinet of Ministers.

9 The employee is now protected not only against direct and indirect discrimination but also against personal injury, because personal injury also qualifies as discrimination within the meaning of this law under sec. 29(4).

10 The amendments also entitle the employee to request compensation for loss and compensation for moral harm if the prohibition against differential treatment and the prohibition against causing adverse consequences is violated.

11 The court has discretion to award compensation for moral harm in case of dispute under sec. 29(8)[3].

[3] Sec. 29. Prohibition of Differential Treatment
(1) Differential treatment based on the gender of an employee is prohibited when establishing legal employment relationships, as well as during the period of existence of legal employment relationships, in particular when promoting an employee, determining working conditions, work remuneration or occupational training, as well as when giving notice of termination of an employment contract.
(2) Differential treatment based on the gender of employees is permitted only in cases where a particular gender is an objective and substantiated precondition, which is reasonable for the legal purpose reached as a result, for the performance of the relevant work or for the relevant employment.
(3) If in case of a dispute an employee indicates conditions which may serve as a basis for his or her direct or indirect discrimination based on gender, the employer has a duty to prove that the differential treatment is based on objective circumstances not related to the gender of the employee, or also that belonging to a particular gender is an objective and substantiated precondition for performance of the relevant work or the relevant employment.
(4) Injury to a person and instructions to discriminate against him or her shall also be deemed to be discrimination within the meaning of this Law.
(5) Direct discrimination exists if in comparable situations the treatment of a person in relation to his or her belonging to a specific gender is, was or may be less favourable than in respect of another person.
(6) Indirect discrimination exists if in comparable situations evidently neutral provisions, criteria or practice cause or may cause adverse consequences for persons belonging to one gender, except in cases where such provisions, criteria or practice is objectively substantiated with a legal purpose the achievement of which the selected means are commensurate.
(7) Injury to a person within the meaning of this Law is the subjection of a person to such actions which are unacceptable from that person's point of view, associated with his or her belonging to a specific gender, including acts of a sexual nature if the purpose or result of such acts is infringement of the person's dignity and the creation of an intimidating, hostile, humiliating, degrading or offensive environment.
(8) If the prohibition against differential treatment and the prohibition against causing adverse consequences is violated, an employee, in addition to other rights specified in this Law, has the right to request compensation for losses and compensation for moral harm. In case of dispute, a court at its own discretion shall determine the compensation for moral harm.
(9) The provisions of this Section, as well as Sec. 32, Paragraph one and Sec. 34, 48, 60 and 95 of this Law, insofar as they are not in conflict with the essence of the relevant right, shall also apply to the prohibition of differential treatment based on race, skin colour, age, disability, religious, political or other conviction, national or social origin, property or marital status or other circumstances of an employee.

3. Administrative Procedure Law (*Adminstratīvā procesa likums*) (Latvian Herald (*Latvijas Vēstnesis*) No. 164, 14 November 2001) and Amendments to the Law (Latvian Herald (*Latvijas Vēstnesis*) No. 12, 23 January 2004)

12 The present statute came into force on 1 February 2004. The law introduces a new era in the Latvian legal system – administrative procedure. The new law is based on principles typical for continental Europe[4], and is mainly influenced by German public and administrative law[5].

13 The law introduces many novelties such as a new Administrative court, the redefinition of legal principles in administrative processes, the requirements for an administrative act, the description of the obligations of subjects in administrative processes and the changing of burden of proof for institutions. The new law directly declared that any institution (state or local) is liable for losses and personal harm caused by it as a result of revocation of the administrative act (Clause 3 sec. 85)[6]. In addition, the mentioned law recognises a general right of private persons to claim from any institution compensation not just for financial loss but also for personal harm, including moral harm, caused by an administrative act or an actual action of an institution (sec. 92)[7]. This allows an award of compensation for non-pecuniary loss, which has been very limited in Latvian court practice so far.

4. Amendment to Law on the Bar (*Advokatūras likums*) (Latvian Herald (*Latvijas Vēstnesis*) No. 65, 27 April 2004)

14 New amendments to the Law on the Bar introduced on 27 May 2004 define more precisely when sworn advocates will be responsible for damage inflicted to the client from the legal assistance provided by an assistant sworn advocate. Besides the general obligation to compensate damage inflicted to the client by himself (sec. 110)[8], a sworn advocate shall be liable for losses caused to the client which have arisen from the legal assistance provided by an assistant sworn advocate not just only in his/her first year of practice, as was previously the case, but if an assistant sworn advocate has not passed the second exam for

[4] K. Dišlers, *Ievads adminstratīvo tiesību zinātnē* (2002), 252.

[5] F.J. Paine, *Vācijas vispārīgas administrīvas tiesības* (2002), XXII.

[6] Sec. 85. Revocation of a Legal Administrative Act
3) If the administrative act is revoked in accordance with Paragraph two, Clause 3 or 4 of this Section, the relevant public law legal person shall, in accordance with Chapter 8 of this Law, compensate the addressee for losses and personal harm caused to him or her as a result of revocation of the administrative act.

[7] Sec. 92. Right to Compensation
Everyone is entitled to claim due compensation for financial loss or personal harm, including moral harm, which has been caused to him or her by an administrative act or an actual action of an institution.

[8] Sec. 110. If the sworn advocate has permitted an infringement upon the right of a client which has resulted in some kind of damage for the client, then the client shall be entitled to demand compensation from the former, depending on the extent to which the former may be held responsible for this.

this profession[9]. That means, that a sworn advocate shall be liable for a longer period of time for losses caused to the client which have arisen from the legal assistance provided by his/her assistant if he/she does not successfully pass the second exam of this profession during his/her first year.

B. Cases

1. Riga Regional Court 13 October 2004, No. C04186703 (CA-916/04)[10]: Mass Media is not Liable for Information Received from Official Source and Small Disagreements Concerning Facts is no Base for Liability of Mass Media

a) Brief Summary of the Facts

On 5 September 2002 the national news agency distributed information that the medicine supervisory body had stated that the death of a patient was partially due to the fault of the surgeon during treatment. The surgeon was given a severe warning. On 2 October 2002 the news agency again reported on a new case, where the medicine supervisory body stated that the death of another patient was partially due to the fault of the same surgeon during treatment and the surgeon had to pay a fine of 100 lats (approx. € 150). National newspapers and national TV distributed this information to the public. The press published articles with such titles as "After patient death, doctor is severely warned", "For partial fault for patient's death – warning for doctor", "Doctor is blamed for patient's death and punished with a fine", "A doctor will pay 100 lats for death of patient", "Who killed the patient?" and "Price of life – 100 lats". 15

The surgeon initiated civil proceedings, because he was of the opinion that false information had been published and distributed concerning 1) that he is culpable (or partly culpable) for the death of the patients; 2) that he was administratively punished for his fault (or partial fault) in the death of the patients; 3) the amount of the fine – 100 lats. The claim was based on sec. 2352[a] of the Civil Code[11]. He considered that his reputation is injured as a result of 16

[9] Sec. 111. In the cases prescribed in Art. 110 of this Law, a sworn advocate shall be liable for losses caused to the client which have arisen from the legal assistance provided by an assistant sworn advocate who has not successfully passed the second exam of sworn advocate's assistant, as well as those losses caused as a result of a case conducted with the patron's permission.

[10] Not officially published.

[11] Sec. 2352a. Each person has the right to bring court action for the retraction of information that injures his or her reputation and dignity, if the disseminator of the information does not prove that such information is true.
If information which injures a person's reputation and dignity, is published in the press, then where such information is not true, it shall also be retracted in the press. If information which injures a person's reputation and dignity is included in a document, such document shall be replaced. In other cases, a court shall determine the procedures for retraction.
If someone unlawfully injures a person's reputation and dignity orally, in writing or by acts, he or she shall provide compensation (financial compensation). A court shall determine the amount of the compensation.

this untrue information and that the news agency is liable for damaging his reputation because all media received information from it.

17 He indicated that, as result of distributing false information, he lost his post as the head of department at the hospital where he was deputy. He also received a few nervous letters from his international partners regarding his ability to continue research in the S.T.I.C.H. project (Surgical Trial in Intracerebral Haemorrhage). The financial benefit he received from participating in that project was significant for him.

18 He demanded the retraction of the false information and 50,000 lats (approx. € 70,000) for non-pecuniary loss.

19 During the court procedure it was discovered that the plaintiff had been reprimanded only with a warning and that the fine was only 50 lats (approx. € 70). There were only formal breaches of medical procedure and there were no documents which stated that the surgeon was responsible for the death of the patients.

20 Representatives from the medicine supervisory body denied that they provided information regarding the culpability of the surgeon. The interview was not recorded. There were few breaches from a professional point of view although there had been some delays during treatment.

21 The news agency referred to the fact that they received information about the partial fault of the surgeon and the fact the he was punished from representatives of the medicine supervisory body. According to sec. 29[12] of the Law on the Press and other Mass Media, the mass media shall not be held liable for the dissemination of false information if it received such information from official authorities. The news agency pointed out that another journalist from a newspaper received similar information regarding the fault of the surgeon. Additionally they emphasized that, in point of fact, the information provided was correct containing only slight inaccuracies. The news agency also highlight the fact that they cannot be held liable for headlines, comments and reports made by the media, because they published their own interpretation of the facts.

b) Judgment of the Court

22 The court established that the plaintiff was indeed administratively punished for breaches in medical treatment on two occasions, receiving a severe warning and having to pay a fine of 50 lats. The judge stated that there was no dis-

[12] Sec. 29. Release from Liability
Mass media shall not be held liable for the dissemination of false information if it contains:
1) official documents of the State authorities and administrative bodies, announcements by political and public organisations;
2) announcements by official information agencies; and
3) publications by officials.

cussion that publications were addressed to the breaches during medical care (treatment) of the patients, who died during treatment. The court established that the plaintiff was involved in the medical treatment of the patients who later died. The court also pointed out that the surgeon was punished for permitted breaches during treatment of the patients.

The court established that it is impossible to evaluate the headlines of the articles independently from the context of the whole article and the information should be evaluated overall. 23

The court stated that it is irrelevant either that the incorrect amount of fine – 100 lats instead 50 lats – was published or that the surgeon received a severe warning instead of a warning, because such inaccuracy cannot injure the dignity and reputation of the plaintiff. 24

The court, taking evidence into consideration, stated that the medical supervisory body established the plaintiff's partial fault for the patients' deaths. The court also established that the medical supervisory body provided information to a reporter. Inasmuch as the information is true, there is no basis for holding the news agency liable. 25

The plaintiff did not appeal against the judgment. 26

c) Commentary

With the present judgment the court recognises four main principles regarding the protection of personal dignity and reputation. 27

Firstly, the media shall not be held liable for information received from an official authority. There is a possibility to prove that a journalist received information from an official authority with indirect evidence. 28

Secondly, culpability (partial or total) is not only a legal term. Using such a term is permissible in a publication if the patient died as result of the medical treatment and if it is stated that the doctor committed errors during the medical treatment of the patient, especially if he/she is punished for these errors later. 29

Thirdly, it is essential to evaluate the context of a whole article and not only part of it, for example, only the headlines. 30

Fourthly, irrelevant inaccuracies, for example, inaccuracy regarding the scale of punishment, cannot injure the dignity and reputation of the plaintiff if in point of fact the information is correct. 31

2. Senate of the Supreme Court, 25 August 2004, No. SKC-387[13]: Liability for Instructing another Person to Perform a Wrongful Act

a) Brief Summary of the Facts

32 A local authority allowed a road building company to mine for sand needed for building a local road on dredged sand in 1992. The dredged sand is located on some land owned by a private individual. The local authority restored ownership of the land during the denationalisation process in December 1991. The local authority neither requested nor received the landowner's consent to use the dredged sand located on his land.

33 After mining for sand from the dredged sand there was a pit seven metres deep and 0.5 hectares in area. The landowner concluded an agreement with entrepreneurs who calculated that the filling in of the pit and the recovery of the soil would cost 6,200.16 lats (approx. € 9,000). The landowner filed a civil claim against the local authority and the road building company and demanded compensation for damage.

b) Judgment of the Court

34 The court of first instance dismissed the claim but the Supreme Court satisfied the claim in part by recovering the amount from the local authority only. The court established that the local authority had instructed the road building company to mine for sand from the dredged sand located on the plaintiff's land. Sec. 36 of the Land use and Survey Act permits compensation to be claimed from the person who caused the damage[14].

35 The court concluded from the above that the local authority is liable for damage caused to the landowner and by reference to sec. 1779[15] of the Civil Code, the court decided that the claim should be satisfied in part.

36 The local authority filed a cassation appeal but the Supreme Court Senate upheld the decision of the Supreme Court in its decision of 25 August 2004 in the case SKC–387.

c) Commentary

37 In addition to the above-mentioned arguments, the court had the possibility of applying sec. 1781[16] of the Civil Code, which was directly applicable in the

[13] Not officially published.

[14] Sec. 36. Compensation of land users
Losses suffered by land users shall be fully indemnified by individuals or entities whose fault has caused such losses, including losses associated with the infringement of a land user's rights, expropriating or leasing his land and land quality deterioration.

[15] Sec. 1779. Everyone is liable to compensate for loss and damage he has caused by his acts or omissions.

[16] Sec. 1781. A person who has instructed another person to perform a wrongful act shall be liable for the action of the other person, notwithstanding that the acts of such person exceed the limits of the instructions. A person who has given another person cause for such action as results in losses to a third person, shall similarly be liable.

present case. The local authority gave wrong instructions to the road building company to mine for sand from the dredged sand.

The present judgment highlights an unacceptable practice regarding damage (loss). While sec. 1770 of the Civil Code states that a loss (damage) shall be understood to mean any deprivation which can be assessed financially, the courts usually neglect the provisions of sec. 1771, which clearly define two types of damage – already arisen and anticipated. Only arisen damage is compensable and in the case of anticipated damage only a right to security can be granted to the victim. From this we can conclude that an assessment of the necessary repairs in the future is not a sufficient ground for a court to grant compensation for damage. 38

C. Literature

1. A. Bitāns, Tiesas ieskats un svarīgi iemesli civiltiesisku strīdu izskatīšanā (Court discretion and good causes in resolving civil disputes), *Latvijas Universitātes Raksti* (Scientific Papers of University of Latvia) [2004] Law Volume 667, 107–132

This article is mainly concerned with the meaning and frontiers of judicial discretion and good cause in civil law. The author addresses a topical issue yet to be sufficiently explored, i.e. how the court should determine an adjudication of a civil dispute if the legislator has left it at the court's discretion by means of a special section of the Civil Code (i.e. sec. 5). The topicality of this question is confirmed by the increasing number of court claims seeking pecuniary compensation for moral injuries. 39

Despite the laconic style, applying sec. 5 requires the judge to have a wide knowledge of justice and general principles of law, as well as an ability to invoke these criteria as grounds in his judgment, in particular because the court has a duty to apply sec. 5 in statutory instances even if the plaintiff fails to refer to it in his claim. 40

The author points out the restrictions in applying this provision of substantive law. The notion of justice is examined from both historical and legal aspects, as well as with respect to civil law. 41

Sec. 5 of the Civil Code is not applicable as a general provision to all civil disputes but only in statutory instances. This provision of substantive law is not intended to create or interpret a new law or right but to protect infringed rights. 42

With respect to an awareness of justice, the court should be guided by the sense of justice which exists at the time of adjudicating the dispute, even if it differs from that prevailing at the date the law was enacted. Justice is not 43 something that may be described as subjective or abstract. Justice is rather an objective phenomenon that may be applied to each and every person. To pass a rightful judgment means to achieve the basic objective of civil law. The court should specify the principles of law applied in passing judgment, as well as the grounds which caused the court to hold that such judgment meets the sense of justice.

44 In analysing the court practice of applying sec. 5, the author points out the need to improve the quality of judgments in terms of reasonability, i.e. the courts are urged to set out in more detail the arguments of justice and principles of law serving as a basis for passing judgment. Likewise, the author urges the Senate not to be afraid of undertaking the review function.

2. A. Bitāns, Senāta loma CL 5.p. piemērošanā (The Senate's role in applying sec. 5 of the Civil Code), *Latvijas Vēstnesis*, vol. 117 (3065), 27 July 2004 and vol. 121 (3069), 3 August 2004

45 The author addresses the topical question of how the Latvian Supreme Court Senate should control the implementation of sec. 5 of the Civil Code, which requires the court to use discretion or invoke good causes in determining a case.

46 The author deals with an issue yet to be sufficiently explored, i.e. the role and responsibility of the Senate as a third-tier court. The topicality of this issue is confirmed by the increasing number of controversial court decisions, especially regarding the lawfulness of lower court decisions regarding pecuniary compensation for moral injuries.

47 The court should specify the principles of law applied in passing the judgment, as well as the grounds which caused the court to hold that such judgment meets the sense of justice and the Senate is under an obligation to review and control the implementation of general principles.

48 The existing court practice of applying sec. 5 is unsatisfactory and the author points out the need to improve the quality of court judgments in terms of reasonability. The Senate should demand that the court sets out in more detail the arguments of justice and principles of law serving as a basis for passing judgment.

XV. Lithuania

Herkus Gabartas and Milda Laučienė

A. Introduction

As this is the first Lithuanian contribution to the European Tort Law Yearbook, it is worth making several introductory comments on the Lithuanian tort law evolution over the period from 1990 (the year of Lithuania's restoration of its independence) until 2003. During this time the entire Lithuanian legal system was radically reformed, tort law being no exception. The most significant event of this period in the area of civil law, including tort law, undoubtedly was the adoption of the new Lithuanian Civil Code in 2001 that replaced the old civil code of 1964, which was a prototype of the Russian Civil Code. When drafting the new Civil Code, the codification experience of other western countries was followed – particular attention being paid to the Dutch Civil Code of 1992 and the Civil Code of Quebec (Canada) of 1991.[1] The new Lithuanian Civil Code has significantly modified formerly known institutes of civil law, introduced many new legal concepts and thereby opened a new page in the history of Lithuanian civil law. In addition, many other national tort-related laws have also been amended as a result of Lithuania's preparation for its membership in the European Union. 1

B. Legislation

1. *Lietuvos Respublikos pacientų teisių ir žalos sveikatai atlyginimo įstatymo pakeitimo įstatymas*, *Valstybės žinios* (Parliamentary Record, VŽ), 2004, No. 115-4284 (Law on the Rights of Patients and Compensation of the Damage to Their Health)

The Law on the Rights of Patients and Compensation of the Damage to Their Health (hereinafter – "the Law") has replaced the old law of 1996[2] in order to 2

[1] V. Mikelėnas/A. Vileita/A. Taminskas, *Lietuvos Respublikos civilinio kodekso komentaras. Pirmoji knyga. Bendrosios nuostatos* (1st edn. 2001), 11.
[2] VŽ, 1996, No. 102-2317, Law of 3 October 1996, with later amendments.

harmonise it with the Civil Code, the Law on Health Insurance and other Lithuanian legal acts. The new Law provides for essentially the same rights of patients as was formerly the case, however, the content and the order of implementation of these rights are considerably expanded.

3 One of the main novelties introduced by the new Law is the new regulation of compensation of damage caused to patients' health. The old Law distinguished two types of damage caused: (i) the damage suffered by patients as a result of the culpable actions of a physician or nursing staff member, which had to be compensated in accordance with the procedure established by the Civil Code, and (ii) the damage inflicted upon a patient's health through the legitimate actions (without fault) of the above-named persons. The new Law establishes tort liability, which is exclusively based on the fault of health care institutions or their employees. The Law defines the notion of "fault" in the above-mentioned context and indicates that the liability may be diminished depending on the degree of a patient's fault. In addition, the Law prescribes for compulsory civil liability insurance of health care providers, designating its minimal limit. Furthermore, the Law establishes absolutely new provisions – compensation of damage for non-pecuniary loss, the maximum level of compensation and adjustment criteria.

4 The new Law includes amendments on the procedure for the remuneration of damage indicated. A special pre-trial Commission shall assess the amount of damage in cases when disputes arise. The Law has two novel amendments that are worth mentioning. First, the Commission is now required to make a decision in two months (instead of the previously fixed three month period) from the date of receiving a complaint. Second, a person, not satisfied with the decision of the Commission may appeal against it by bringing a civil action before the court. As a result, the appeal procedure is two-chained instead of the former three-step procedure established by the old law. However, the old law failed to be properly enforced: although it included provisions that a pre-trial Commission for adjusting damages should be established and its decisions might be appealed to the Ministry of Health and then to the court, such Commission was actually not established at all.

2. *Lietuvos Respublikos transporto priemonių savininkų ir valdytojų civilinės atsakomybės privalomojo draudimo įstatymo pakeitimo įstatymas*, VŽ, 2004, No. 46-1498 (Law on Compulsory Insurance against Civil Liability of Vehicle Owners)

5 The new 2004 Law on Compulsory Insurance against Civil Liability of Vehicle Owners was inspired by Lithuania's obligation to harmonise its national law with European Union law. The new Law states that its provisions are aimed at the implementation of the EU acts, specified in the Annex to the Law. In comparison with the former law[3] many provisions have been amended and harmonised with respect to EU acts. Many definitions, specified in

[3] VŽ, 2001 No. 56-1977, Law of 14 June 2001, with later amendments.

Art. 2 of the Law, have been interpreted anew (e.g., the concept of insurance undertaking, the description of the categories of insurance contracts). The Law distinguishes two (instead of the previous four) types of insurance contracts – standard and frontier contracts. Rules on the duration and termination of insurance contracts have also been modified aiming at stricter time limits. Thus, it is indicated that the general duration of standard insurance contracts shall be 12 months, whereas for frontier insurance contracts – 15–90 days.

Substantial changes have been made in the regulation of insurance premiums. First, the amount of premiums has been clearly specified and the system of basic premiums has been abolished. Second, as the new Law provides for compensation of three types of damage (damage to persons, to property and non-pecuniary damage), it also establishes three types of insurance premiums. 6

The Law, as already mentioned, prescribes that three types of damage may occur in case of an insured event. Under Art. 14, it must be the duty either of an insurance undertaking or the Office of Vehicle Insurance Undertakings to adjust the pecuniary loss. The Law further enumerates the principles of assessing the amount of damages for impairment to human health or in case of death. It also lays down a novel provision that an injured person shall be entitled to claim non-pecuniary damages (the same right shall also be reserved for persons who lost the family member whose earnings were the primary source of support). 7

In addition, the Law on Compulsory Insurance has introduced two amendments of an institutional nature. First of all, the structure and activities of the Office of Vehicle Insurance Undertakings have been modified with a view to harmonisation with the respective EU rules. Secondly, the Law provides for the legal entities that are obliged to inspect if motor vehicles are insured. 8

3. *Lietuvos Respublikos moterų ir vyrų lygių galimybių įstatymo papildymo 24(1) straipsniu įstatymas*, VŽ, 2004, No. 171-6305 (Supplement to the Law on Equal Opportunities of Men and Women)

On 9 November 2004 an important supplement was made to the Law on Equal Opportunities of Men and Women. A new Art. 24(1) introduces a provision regarding compensation of damage: a person who suffered sexual discrimination or harassment shall be entitled to compensation of damage for both pecuniary and non-pecuniary loss under the rules of the Civil Code of the Republic of Lithuania. This new provision is important in one main aspect. Art. 6.250 of the Civil Code provides that "non-pecuniary damage shall be compensated only in cases provided for by laws", which means that the possibility to claim non-pecuniary damages shall be clearly indicated in either the Civil Code or in a special law. If the law contains no provision to claim non-pecuniary damage, the loss cannot be compensated.[4] Thus, the aforesaid amendment of the Law 9

[4] V. Mikelėnas, *Lietuvos Respublikos civilinio kodekso komentaras. Šeštoji knyga. Prievolių teisė. I tomas* (1st edn. 2003), 345. This book of Commentaries on the law of obligations under the Civil Code of Lithuania is also a useful source in tort law.

has legally embedded a person's right for the reparation of non-pecuniary damage in cases of sexual discrimination or harassment.

4. *Lietuvos Respublikos žalos, atsiradusios dėl valdžios institucijų neteisėtų veiksmų, atlyginimo įstatymo 1, 2, 3, 4 straipsnių pakeitimo ir papildymo įstatymas*, VŽ, 2004, No. 55-1888 (Supplement and Amendment to the Law on Compensation of Damage Caused by the Illegal Acts of State Authorities)

10 This amendment may be regarded as significant in the following aspect. The supplement establishes an additional basis for the compensation of damage caused by illegal acts of state authorities, i.e. the Ministry of Justice shall be entitled to implement decisions of international institutions such as the European Court of Human Rights or the United Nations Human Rights Committee concerning compensation of damage. The Law settles the procedures for implementing the decisions, as well as requirements for documentation and some other core aspects of compensation under the decisions adopted by the international institution as defined by the Law.

C. Cases

1. *Lietuvos Aukščiausiasis Teismas* (The Supreme Court of Lithuania, LAT), 18 February 2004, No. 3 K-3-16/2004[5]: Medical Negligence; Compensation of Non-Pecuniary Loss for the Bereaved

a) Brief Summary of the Facts

11 After treatment in two hospitals a woman died as a result of mis-diagnosis. The plaintiffs – close relatives of the deceased – argue that the woman's death was caused by medical malpractice as the doctors who treated the woman failed to take adequate measures to diagnose the disease that caused her death. The plaintiffs claim damages for their pain and suffering as well as compensation for loss of earnings that the deceased would have earned if she had been alive.

b) Judgment of the Court

12 The Court of Appeals had awarded the plaintiffs damages for non-pecuniary loss amounting to Lt 120,000 (€ 34,754) on the basis of negligence of medical staff. The damage was to be compensated by one of the hospitals that provided health care services to the woman.

13 The Civil Code prescribes that the damage suffered by patients as a result of the culpable actions of a physician or nursing staff member must be compensated. In its decision the Supreme Court stated that fulfilment of medical pro-

[5] The Supreme Court's decisions are available at http://lat.litlex.lt.

fessional obligations includes in itself not only legal but also moral aspects (as laid down in the Law on the Health System[6], the Law on Patients' Rights, Hippocratic oath). The conduct of a doctor should be judged considering conformity with legal rules regulating the provision of health care services without an emphasis on specific results of treatment. The doctor cannot guarantee any particular result, for instance, that a patient will be cured.

Regarding compensation of pecuniary damage in case of loss of income that 14
the deceased woman would have earned if she had been alive, the Supreme Court noted that compensation for loss of earnings could not be awarded to the plaintiffs as the Civil Code contains no provision establishing that loss of earnings includes the income which the deceased would have earned in case of absence of death.

The Supreme Court refers to an earlier case[7] concerning a description of the 15
criteria to be fulfilled in order to establish medical liability. The Court highlighted that, in assessing the professional liability of doctors, stricter standards of care, providence, advertence, deliberation and prudence must be applied. Moreover, professional doctors' liability may be established by any kind of fault.

The Supreme Court stated that the courts in providing adjustment as regards 16
the amount of damages for non-pecuniary loss shall take the financial status of a tortfeasor into account, as well as the severity of the tort, including its consequences and other significant circumstances. The Supreme Court ruled that courts of first instance and the Court of Appeals had exempted one of the defendants – the Hospital of Infectious Diseases – from civil liability without due reason. Therefore, the plaintiffs' claim is to be dealt with in the Court of Appeals anew.

c) Commentary

The Court made an important interpretation of rules related to medical liabili- 17
ty. The doctor has a duty to guarantee that treatment is carried out with the greatest possible effort and to ensure the highest level of care, prudence and advertence. From the point of view of civil professional liability, the conduct of a doctor shall be assessed considering conformation of certain treatment to health care legal acts and rules of professional medical ethics. As fault is the leading condition of medical liability, the Court elaborated that the lack of care, advertence, deliberation and prudence, as well as the violation of professional ethics' rules, should be treated as professional medical fault.

[6] VŽ, 1998, No. 112-3099, Law of 1 December 1998, with later amendments. Available at http://www.lrs.lt.

[7] LAT, 14 November 2001, *L.M.Sandienė v VšĮ Kauno Raudonojo kryžiaus ligoninė*, No. 3K-3-1140/2001.

18 The case at hand shows the growing tendency within Lithuania to claim for compensation of damage for pain and suffering in cases of medical negligence. Claims against the providers of health care services are increasing because, as the Lithuanian case law shows, patients are becoming more active in defending their rights. Another problem relates to the legal rules on compensation of damage caused by medical negligence that were quite vague and difficult to apply until the new edition of the Law on Patients' Rights entered into force as of 1 January 2005. The question of how this law will be enforced could be answered in the near future.

2. Lithuanian Court of Appeals, 30 November 2004, No. 2A-394/2004, *Zdaniai v VšĮ Marijampolės ligoninė* (*Zdaniai v Marijampolė Hospital*): Adjustment of Non-Pecuniary Damages

a) Brief Summary of the Facts

19 Two newborn twins were severely injured just after their birth in the provincial state-owned hospital. The newborns had been negligently swaddled with a warmer that was filled with hot water. As a result, 14% of the skin of one child, and 20% of the skin of his brother was burnt. Both newborns had to undergo numerous operations for grafting the skin donated by their father. All the family has suffered enormous physical pain and mental suffering. Several employees of the hospital were found guilty of the crime of medical negligence. The plaintiffs – the two newborns and their parents – initiated a separate civil case against the hospital claiming for non-pecuniary damages amounting to Lt 1 million (€ 290,000).

20 The lower court approved the claim in full and awarded the non-pecuniary damages amounting to Lt 1 million in favour of the plaintiffs. The treatment of the newborns was considered to be inhumane and unjustifiable. According to the court, the mental pain suffered by the plaintiffs was highlighted *inter alia* by the mass media. The defendant's argument regarding the hospital's potential bankruptcy was dismissed. The defendant filed an appeal.

b) Judgment of the Court

21 The Court of Appeals partially changed the decision of the court of first instance and decreased the amount of non-pecuniary damages by 50%, i.e. to Lt 500,000 (€ 145,000). The Court of Appeals did not agree with the lower court's findings that the treatment of the newborns was inhumane, because the hospital's employees were merely convicted of the crime of negligence. The increased attention of the media should also not influence the amount of non-pecuniary damages. Instead, the Court of Appeals emphasised that the defendant is a state-owned institution financed by the state budget. Thus, if the damage of Lt 1 million is to be paid by the hospital, then the interests of other patients who are living in that region would be undermined as they would not be able to receive a full scale of medical services from the hospital. Finally, the general subsistence level of society should also be taken into account when es-

timating the amount of non-pecuniary damages – the vast majority of the Lithuanian population would not be able to earn Lt 1 million even in their entire life.

c) Commentary

Though this widely-known ruling has been adopted by the Court of Appeals as a court of an appellate instance (therefore, the final word is still to be said by the Lithuanian Supreme Court), it illustrates the rule applied by judges all over the world, according to which the amount of non-pecuniary damages greatly depends on the social and economic conditions of the society to which the plaintiff belongs. In the authors' personal opinion, this case could be a potential multi-million dollar case in the USA and a case for a smaller amount of money in western European countries. However, due to comparatively low economic standards of the region where the Lithuanian plaintiffs reside, the Lithuanian Court of Appeals has considered the award of non-pecuniary damages in the amount of € 145,000 as matching the Lithuanian standard. On the other hand, the aforesaid award, to the best of the authors' knowledge, is the highest amount so far adjudged by Lithuanian courts for the compensation of non-pecuniary damage. Bearing in mind the rapid growth of economic welfare in Lithuania it is to be expected that the awards of non-pecuniary damages will increase accordingly. 22

3. LAT, 13 January 2004, No. 3K-7-24: Origin of Legal Relations between Health Care Institutions and Patients

a) Brief Summary of the Facts

The plaintiff – an outpatient clinic – applied to the court in order to terminate the contract on providing health care services to the defendant. The defendant – a six-year-old boy represented by his mother – was registered at the outpatient clinic as the user of health care services. The plaintiff claimed that the defendant's mother acted improperly by consulting other health care institutions, complaining about the services provided by the plaintiff and the incompetence of its doctors, thus causing damage to the reputation of the medical staff and the outpatient clinic. 23

b) Judgment of the Court

The Supreme Court annulled the decisions of the lower courts and denied the claim. It motivated its ruling using the following arguments. First of all, the Court emphasised that the provision of health care services by state or municipal health care services providers is not based on the contractual relationship between a patient and a health care institution, but instead is grounded on the rights and obligations arising out of laws and other legal acts. Further, the Court argued that since the above-mentioned relations do not have a contractual origin, the courts should not apply legal rules providing for termination of contracts. The Supreme Court expressly noted that the lower courts had to apply a principle of priority of the child's interests and, therefore, could not con- 24 sider the mother's improper behaviour as a legal basis for terminating the health care services contract.

c) Commentary

25 It is worth mentioning that the Supreme Court in its previous decision (*L.M. Sandienė v Kaunas Red Cross Hospital*) had provided a definition concerning contractual and delictual liability in cases of medical negligence. The courts dealing with cases of this category shall analyse whether the doctor or the health care institution is liable for damage suffered by the patient. The Supreme Court concluded that if medical services were provided by the state or a municipal health care institution and the costs for these services were reimbursed by the State Health Insurance Fund, then legal relations arise between the patient and a respective health care institution. Moreover, it would be the health care institution rather than the doctor who is liable for medical negligence. Thus such cases must be dealt with according to the rules of delictual liability.

4. LAT 29 September, No. 3K-3-475/2004: Traffic Accident, Compensation of Damage, Insurance Benefit

a) Brief Summary of the Facts

26 The plaintiff was injured by a car while crossing the road at a pedestrian crossing. As a consequence, the plaintiff suffered severe head trauma and various fractures that led to complex operations and treatment in hospital over a long period of time. Medical records state that in the post-operative period the plaintiff developed a depression syndrome and, as a result, she was forced to take a course of anti-depressants. The driver was sued and convicted of a crime. The plaintiff claims compensation for pecuniary and non-pecuniary loss.

b) Judgment of the Court

27 The Court of Appeals assessed the amount of Lt 25,000 (€ 7,240) for non-pecuniary loss in favour of the plaintiff. The car driver was obliged to cover non-pecuniary loss, whereas, the insurance company, which is the second defendant in the case, was to compensate pecuniary loss amounting to Lt 1,175 (€ 340). The Court of Appeals argued that, under the Civil Code, the insurer had an obligation to compensate pecuniary loss exclusively.

28 The Law on Compulsory Insurance against Civil Liability of Vehicles Owners[8] provides that the insurer, in case of an insured event, shall be obliged to pay the insurance benefit to the assured. Therefore, the defendant – the insurance company – was liable for the damage caused by the car driver. However, this obligation is limited to the liability insurance sum set out by law. At the time of the accident, the Law on Compulsory Insurance provided for

[8] VŽ, 2004, No. 46-1498, Law of 5 March 2004.

Lt 30,000 (€ 8,680) in personal insurance benefit and the same amount in property insurance benefit. The Civil Code establishes the principle of overall compensation of damage, thus, the car driver would have an obligation to compensate the loss if the damage exceeded the insurance sum. Within the stated benefit limits, the obligation of the insurer is restricted to covering for damage suffered by third persons.

The Supreme Court noted that compensation of damage to health also covers non-pecuniary loss as pain and suffering, due to its specific character, is closely related with a person's health. Art. 6.250 of the Civil Code prescribes that non-pecuniary damage shall be compensated in every case if damage occurred either as a result of a crime, or to one's health or causing a person's death. Thus, the insurer has committed itself to compensate non-pecuniary damage inflicted to third persons within the limits of insurance benefit. The value of non-pecuniary damage shall be determined by the court referring to the Civil Code Art. 6.250 § 2 which states as follows: in awarding non-pecuniary damages the court shall consider the consequences of the damage, the tortfeasor's fault, his financial status, the extent of material damage and other requisite circumstances as well as principles of honesty, justice and common sense. Therefore, the Supreme Court ruled that non-pecuniary damage amounting to Lt 25,000 (€ 7,240) shall be awarded by the insurance company. 29

c) Commentary

There is a tendency in Lithuanian tort law which is progressing towards the precise elaboration of criteria for compensation of non-pecuniary damage. It could be remarked that the number of claims for non-pecuniary damage in various types of categories is expanding fast. 30

5. LAT, 13 May 2004, No. 3K-7-298/2004: State Liability, Period of Detention, Compensation of Damage

a) Brief Summary of the Facts

The plaintiff sued the Ministry of Justice and the Office of the Prosecutor General for unlawful detention and claimed compensation. In his claim the plaintiff stated that on 21 March 1999 he was detained as a suspect in a criminal case for theft from an apartment of a well-known priest, Mikutavicius and for his murder. Ten days later a charge was brought against the plaintiff for the illegal keeping of explosives. The Court of first instance sanctioned his arrest and the term of detention was prolonged several times. On 1 May 2000 the criminal case with respect to the plaintiff was terminated as a result of lack of evidence of his participation in the crime. The plaintiff argues that he committed no crime; therefore, he was deprived of his liberty by arrest and detention for 187 days without legal grounds. Due to illegal detention and arrest the plaintiff suffered moral pain. He claimed for pecuniary damage – loss of earnings and Lt 100,000 (€ 29,000) for non-pecuniary damage. The plaintiff based his claim on the European Convention on Human Rights, as well as the Lithua- 31 nian Constitution, the Civil Code and the Law on Compensation of Damage Caused by the Illegal Acts of Governmental Authorities.

b) Judgment of the Court

32 The Court of first instance and the Court of Appeals dismissed the claim and ruled that the plaintiff's detention was in the public interest and that the duration of detention did not prove to be unduly long.

33 The Supreme Court in its ruling made reference to Art. 5 § 3 of the European Convention which states that everyone arrested or detained shall be entitled to trial within a reasonable time or to be released pending trial. The Court stated that judging the case of compensation for damage in the national judicial authorities, the obligation to pay compensation for damage occurs from Art. 5 § 5 of the Convention, whereas, the amount of damages shall be defined under the national laws.

34 In the previous case[9] between the same parties the Supreme Court ruled that, in analysing if the term of detention was reasonable, the courts shall apply criteria formulated by the European Court of Human Rights. The criteria include the factual period of detention or arrest, moral, financial and other consequences to the detained, behaviour of the detained, investigation procedure, complexity of the case and other significant circumstances. These criteria shall be applied by the court which deals with the case concerning compensation for damage. As the findings of the lower courts are unclear on this issue, the Supreme Court remitted the case to the Court of Appeals.

c) Commentary

35 The decision of the Court emphasises the criteria to be used when assessing the length of the detention in order that the compensation for non-pecuniary loss can be adjusted. The Supreme Court also points out that the lower courts should refer to the decisions of the European Court of Human Rights and base their rulings in accordance with the established practice of this Court. The decision shows the increasing number of claims against state institutions.

6. LAT, 8 March 2004, No. 3K-3-166/2004: Unfair Competition, Well-known Trademark, Compensation of Damage

a) Brief Summary of the Facts

36 The plaintiffs – three joint stock companies producing mineral water – sued a personal company for illegal usage of a well-known trademark, "Rasa" on its products. In the Supreme Court's ruling of 2001 between the same parties[10], the Court held that the Law on Competition[11] had been violated by the defen-

[9] LAT, 1 October 2003, No. 3K-3-895/2003.
[10] LAT, 1 October 2001, No. 3K–3–875/2001.
[11] VŽ, 1999, No. 30-856. Law of 23 March 1999, with later amendments.

dant and, thus, prohibited the defendant from labelling its products with the "Rasa" trademark as such activity constitutes unfair competition. Nevertheless, the defendant continued to label its products with the "Rasa" trademark which is identical to the plaintiffs' trademark. The plaintiffs invested approximately half a million Litas (€ 145,000) for advertising the "Rasa" trademark and the defendant enjoys the advantages resulting from the advertising of the product. Three companies were producing mineral water at that time, therefore, the plaintiffs' claim for material compensation amounting to one-third of the expenses incurred for advertising the label.

b) Judgment of the Court

The Court of Appeals failed to comprehensively analyse every circumstance of the case. Thus, the Supreme Court annulled the decision of the Court of Appeals and emphasised the following conditions. First of all, assessing the defendant's liability regarding unfair competitive acts, the Law on Competition should be referred to: unfair competition relates to the wilful usage of a label, therefore, the factor of *rationae temporis* is a significant condition in evaluating damage and its extent in case of unfair competition. Secondly, unfair competition can be proved only if labelling can be clearly defined. Thus, advertising a product labelled with a specific trademark must be treated as an important factor when analysing the defendant's liability. As may be clear in this case unfair competition was in particular characterised by using particular labels. 37

The Court further noted that the balance between manufactured and sold products by the defendant must be considered. Despite the fact that the plaintiffs claimed compensation amounting to one-third of the expenses spent on advertising the trademark, this requirement, however, would be logical only if the volume of production and sale of mineral water of all the three plaintiffs was equivalent. Moreover, the Supreme Court re-affirmed that all the four conditions must be proved in delictual liability: fault, wrongfulness, causation and damage. 38

c) Commentary

The Supreme Court noted that, when the aim to compete unfairly and perform actions restricting competition is identified, then this fact usually reveals the objective to gain profit unlawfully at the expense of third persons. Court practice in Lithuania is rather scarce in this category of cases. 39

7. LAT, 18 February 2004, No. 3K-3-124/2004: Shareholder's Liability for the Obligations of a Legal Entity

a) Brief Summary of the Facts

The plaintiff sued the defendants – a husband and wife each owning 50% of the shares of the company, "Baninis" – for the loss of goods. The lower court had satisfied the claim. The plaintiff argued that the defendants acted in bad 40 faith by reducing the property of "Baninis"; therefore, the company was unable to execute the court's decision. One of the defendants had established another company named "Transbaninis" with the same address, manager and similar activities. The "Baninis" company's rights had been transferred to the company "Transbaninis" leaving all the debts for "Baninis" exclusively. The plaintiff claimed that the defendants should be liable, in a subsidiary manner, for the debts of "Baninis" under Art. 2.50(3) of the Civil Code. The defendants lodged the cassation claim to the Supreme Court.

b) Judgment of the Court

41 The Supreme Court stated that the above-mentioned Art. 2.50(3) shall be applied and the liability of a shareholder of a legal entity shall arise in cases when a legal person fails to perform its obligations due to the acts in bad faith of a shareholder of that legal person. The Court emphasised that the aim of this provision is to establish a subsidiary liability for a shareholder in order to prevent him/her from having the opportunity to avoid liability under the pretext of a limited pecuniary liability in those cases when a legal person is not able to perform its obligations to the creditors and seeks to avoid the performance by unfair actions. When these actions are proved, the fault of a shareholder may be presumed. The Court ascertained that the defendants acted in bad faith since they put a lot of efforts into avoiding the execution of the lower court's decision and the fulfilment of their obligations towards the plaintiff by transferring the business to another legal person and leaving the company without assets. The Supreme Court noted that the defendants failed to perform a general duty established for all subjects of civil relations – to act according to the principle of good faith. Therefore the defendants, as shareholders of the legal company "Baninis", should be liable for the performance of its obligations. Thus, the cassation claim was denied.

c) Commentary

42 The case at hand is the first in the jurisprudence of the Supreme Court when the so-called doctrine of "lifting the corporate veil" has been invoked. The Court applied an exception to the general rule, which states that a shareholder of a legal person shall not be liable for the obligations of that legal person. The case emphasised that the liability of a shareholder of a corporation should not be limited when the actions of that shareholder were not performed in good faith. A person, being a shareholder of a corporation, who is not acting as a *bonus pater familias* shall be liable, in a subsidiary manner, for the obligations of that corporation. This case is both a good incentive for the courts to look at the issues of liability of this kind more thoroughly and more flexibly and also is a serious warning for unfair persons not to abuse their limited liability.

D. Literature

1. D. Ambrasienė/E. Baranauskas/D. Bublienė et al., *Civilinė teisė. Prievolių teisė: vadovėlis* (Civil Law. Law of Obligations) (Lietuvos teisės universiteto Leidybos centras, Vilnius 2004)

This book – a part of the series of the handbook, *Civil Law* – is dedicated to the "Law of Obligations" and consists of the general provisions on obligations and contract law, separate categories of contracts; much attention is also paid to the issues of civil – contractual and tort – liability. The institutes of civil law and various law theories are scrutinized by the method of comparative analysis. Most of the theoretical concepts are illustrated by practical examples and the respective Lithuanian jurisprudence. 43

As already mentioned the handbook deals, *inter alia*, with the topics of civil tort liability. General provisions on civil liability are discussed in subsection 26 of Section III. This section presents the notion of civil liability, the similarities and differences between contractual and tort liability, peculiarities of non-pecuniary damage and the grounds for non-application of civil liability or for exemption from it. Subsections 28, 29, 30 are exclusively dedicated to the issues of tort liability. First of all, the concept of tort liability is explored and further on various types of tort liability are scrutinized. As general provisions and grounds for civil liability are discussed in subsection 26, further subsections focus on certain peculiarities (e.g., subjects, grounds of liability, and conditions for the recourse) of each type of tort liability. The classification of tort liability into separate types is mainly based on the classification specified in the Civil Code and encompasses the liability of an employer for damage caused by the fault of his employees, liability of the owner (possessor) of buildings, liability arising from the exercise of hazardous activities, etc. Two final subsections discuss the specific features of two other types of tort liability: first, liability for damage caused by shortcomings of goods or services and second, the issue of compensation of damage resulting from misleading advertising. 44

2. A. Verikas, Darbdavio atsakomybė padarius žalą darbuotojo sveikatai (Employers' Liability for the Damage Caused to Employees' Health), [2004] *Jurisprudencija* 56(48), 61–68

In the article the author focuses his attention on the questions of employers' liability for the damage caused to employees' health as a result of accidents at work and occupational diseases. These issues are analyzed in the context of the Civil Code, as well as the Labour Code and the laws on social insurance. 45

The author points out two methods for compensation of damage caused to employees' health. According to the Law on Social Insurance of Occupational Accidents and Occupational Diseases[12], the employee who experiences an oc- 46

[12] VŽ, 1999, No. 110-3207. Law of 23 December 1999, with later amendments.

cupational accident or occupational disease, has the right to receive a social insurance payment. The compensation of damage caused to the employee's health is also regulated by the Civil Code and the Labour Code. According to the latter, in cases of occupational accidents, the employer shall be held liable for the damage which is not fully covered by the social insurance system, or when the damage is not compensated in accordance with the provisions laid down in the Civil Code. Thus the Law on Social Insurance of Occupational Accidents and Occupational Diseases ensures only partial compensation of damage: the social insurance system provides no compensation to the victim for non-pecuniary damage suffered and the expenses caused by the occupational accident or the occupational disease. The employer shall reimburse these expenses and non-pecuniary damage under the Civil Code and the Labour Code. Therefore, it is considered that employers' liability should entail complete compensation of damage suffered. For this reason, pecuniary liability should also be established as one of the disciplinary measures for ensuring that the employer will carry out the requirements of occupational safety.

47 The author also looks into the jurisprudence of the Supreme Administrative Court of Lithuania in cases concerning the investigation of occupational diseases. According to the case law, if an occupational disease is diagnosed when the person has already terminated work relations, he is not entitled to receive a social insurance payment because he is no longer considered to be insured by the social insurance against accidents at work and occupational diseases. In such cases the damage caused to health may be reimbursed under the provisions of the Civil Code, according to which the liability for restitution falls on the employer. The author of this article believes that the right to receive a social insurance payment under the Law on Social Insurance of Occupational Accidents and Occupational Diseases should not at all times be dependent on the fact that a person has to be insured at the moment when such a disease is diagnosed.

3. J. Kiršienė/A. Tikniūtė, Civilinė akcininko atsakomybė už bendrovės prievoles (Shareholder's Liability for Corporate Debts), [2004] *Jurisprudencija* 55(47), 68–77

48 The main issue of this article is a shareholder's tort liability for the obligations of a corporation. In the authors' opinion, the discussion on shareholder liability originated from the provision of the Civil Code (Art. 2.50(3)), representing the doctrine of "lifting the corporate veil", that rescinds an absolute limited liability protection, stated in the Lithuanian Law on Stock Companies. The authors offer two engrossing hypotheses at the beginning of the article and prove them at the end of it. The first hypothesis states that unlimited tort liability for corporative obligations may only be invoked if a shareholder has a decisive influence in the corporation concerned. The second hypothesis suggests that a shareholder in a position mentioned above shall be subject to the liability standards that are commonly applied to the managers of the corporation.

Whereas at the time when the article was in the process of being written it was a new topic in the Lithuanian jurisprudence, the authors present a comparative analysis of shareholder liability. The rationale and preconditions of this kind of liability are examined by analysing the purpose of limited liability. The objectives of the article are to provide a comparative overview of legal doctrines and case materials on shareholder liability in countries with civil and common law traditions, to define the main attributes of a corporation as a legal entity that determine the status of limited liability, to characterize the prerequisites of a shareholder as potential unlimited liability subject. The inference is drawn that the subject of an unlimited liability is only a controlling shareholder and "shadow director" of the corporation, and his duties towards the corporation and the creditors are the same as the fiduciary duties of directors. 49

XVI. The Netherlands

Michael Faure and Ton Hartlief

A. Introduction

1 In previous contributions to this Yearbook we already made clear that tort law is very actively followed in the Netherlands both at the legislative/policy level and in case law. Also for 2004 a number of interesting evolutions in the development of Dutch tort law can be mentioned. As far as the legislative level is concerned we can mention that a number of legislative proposals that we discussed in previous Yearbooks were either adopted or at least proceeded further at the legislative level. For instance, the new Act concerning the statute of limitations for personal injury claims entered into force on 1 February 2004[1]. We already discussed earlier a proposal pending in Dutch Parliament to regulate compensation for non-pecuniary losses and to award a compensation of € 10,000 to specific descendants or relatives[2]. Finally an already earlier discussed proposal to handle mass tort claims also came further during the parliamentary debate, although it has not been accepted yet. Many of these evolutions at the legislative level fit well into the tendency of the current Minister of Justice in the Netherlands (Donner) who is clearly afraid of a rising claim culture, and wishes to reduce the number of conflicts and the corresponding administrative costs of legal procedures[3]. At the policy level the tendency in the Netherlands today seems to be to strive to improve the position of victims on the one hand, but to keep liability risks manageable as well.

2 Indeed, nowadays there seems to be a high interest, also at the political level in the Netherlands, into the way in which accidents are dealt with, how damages are calculated and how the victim receives compensation. Critical issues that may affect the effectiveness of the claims handling procedure receive a lot of attention at the political level. An important aspect in this respect is the role

[1] For further detail see M. Faure/T. Hartlief, The Netherlands, in: H. Koziol/B.C. Steininger (eds.), *European Tort Law 2003* (2004), 280–281.

[2] See for an earlier discussion M. Faure/T. Hartlief, The Netherlands in: H. Koziol/B.C. Steininger (eds.), *European Tort Law 2001* (2002), 356–358 nos. 11–13.

[3] An interesting lecture of Minister Donner in which he develops his ideas has been published in [2003] *Verkeersrecht* (VR), 349–351.

of the medical expert in claims handling, which is especially receiving increased attention in the literature[4]. Politicians seem especially afraid of adverse actions that could be taken e.g. by attorneys, claims managers or insurers to negatively influence the effectiveness of the claims handling procedure[5]. In particular, there is criticism of the way in which personal injury claims are sometimes handled in practice. In that respect there is criticism both of victims who do not always show a very cooperative approach and of insurers who do not always show a cooperative willingness to come to an effective handling of claims. An issue that is raised in that respect is whether there should be fixed time limits for claims handling (in order to avoid insurers keeping victims waiting for compensation for many years). Also attention is given to the obligation of victims to cooperate in reducing the damage[6]. A strong discussion is in this respect also taking place concerning the question what precisely the goal of claims handling should be. In that respect the question has been addressed whether the traditional idea that the victim should always be put back in the situation that he would have been in had the accident not occurred can be upheld to the full extent today. It is sometimes suggested that a more positive approach would focus on what the current possibilities of the victim today still are instead of merely focusing on what the victim would not be able to do any longer[7].

B. Legislation and Evolutions at Policy Level

1. Collective Handling of Mass Claims

A first legislative proposal (which already originated in 2003) that surely deserves mentioning is a proposal concerning the collective handling of so-called mass tort claims[8]. In short the goal of this proposal is to make it possible for the judge that an agreement concerning compensation in case of a mass tort could be concluded between an organization representing the interests of the victims on the one hand and one or more liable parties on the other hand. 3

[4] Some of this literature will be discussed later.

[5] See in this respect documents of the Second Chamber of Representatives II 2003–2004, 29 200 VI, no. 168 and see more generally on the effectiveness of the claims handling procedure W.C.T. Weterings, *Efficiëntere en Effectievere Afwikkeling van Letselschadeclaims* (dissertation University of Tilburg, 2004), as well as R.M.J.T. van Dort/L.H. Pals, Rechtshulp bij letselschade anno 2004. De kwaliteit lijdt!, [2004] *Tijdschrift voor Vergoeding Personenschade* (TVP), 43–50.

[6] See in that respect an interesting contribution by Van Boom on the obligation of the various parties in handling claims resulting from labour related incidents: W.H. van Boom, [2004] *Nederlands Juristenblad* (NJB), 928–936.

[7] See in this respect the contributions in the proceedings volume of the Association of Personal Injury Lawyers (*Vereniging van Letselschade Advocaten* – LSA), *Schade: Vergoeden of Beperken?* (2004).

[8] See documents of the Second Chamber of Representatives, II, 2003–2004. 29 414, no. 1–2. For a comment on (various aspects of) this proposal see *inter alia* W.H. van Boom, [2004] *Weekblad voor Privaatrecht, Notariaat en Registratie* (WPNR) 6579, 384–387 and G.M. van Wassenaer, [2004] VR, 165–168.

The legislative proposal aims at creating the possibility that once this agreement is concluded, the judge could declare it generally binding for all victims or for a part of them. The direct reason for this legislative proposal were the problems that arose on the occasion of the handling of claims in the so-called DES daughters case[9]. However, the scope of application of the proposal is much wider: the new proposals could be applied as soon as catastrophic events occur where many persons are victims like with the explosion of a fireworks factory (in Enschede) or a café fire (in Volendam). But the new arrangement might equally be applicable when many individuals argue that they have suffered losses as a result of being wrongly informed concerning the possibilities of speculating on the stock exchange[10].

2. Liability Law or Insurance Solutions for Work-Related Injuries?

4 As we also mentioned in the previous edition of this Yearbook, an idea has been launched to replace the employers' liability for occupational diseases by a direct insurance scheme. The employer would then take out insurance coverage directly to the benefit of employees who are victims of occupational hazards[11]. However, in 2004 the Social Economic Council held that there are no good reasons to introduce a separate regime for disability caused by occupational health, so that this idea of a direct occupational hazard insurance was not pursued any further in 2004. However, it is interesting to mention that this interest in alternative compensation mechanisms fits into a general debate on the role of tort law in comparison with other compensation mechanisms[12]. However, some have also formulated criticism of this idea of a direct insurance for occupational health[13].

3. Statute of Limitations

5 Earlier we already indicated that the statute of limitations for personal injury claims (Art. 3:310 of the Dutch Civil Code) only applies from the moment that the victim has knowledge of the damage and of the liable injurer. In addition a twenty years term runs from the moment of the wrongful event. However, since 1 February 2004 a new fifth section has been added to Art. 3:310 as a result of which only a statute of limitations of five years will apply and no longer the absolute limit of twenty years[14]. The consequence for potential in-

[9] Many daughters of mothers who took the drug DES during pregnancy suffered serious personal injury as a result of which claims were instituted against the manufacturers of the particular drug.

[10] The case more particularly arises in the Netherlands because Dexia advised customers to lease substantial amounts of money to invest in stock. After the value of the stock market went down many of these people faced serious difficulties in paying back the loans they had taken out to buy the stock in the first place. These so-called "stock lease constructions" of Dexia have given rise to various claims being filed. Meanwhile these claims have been settled.

[11] See M. Faure/T. Hartlief (supra fn. 1), 279 nos. 5–6.

[12] See T. Hartlief/S. Klosse (eds.), *Einde van het Aansprakelijkheidsrecht?* (2003). See the discussion of this book in M. Faure/T. Harlief (supra fn. 1), 309, no. 96.

[13] See more particularly W.H. van Boom, [2004] TVP, 1–2

[14] For details see M. Faure/T. Hartief (supra fn. 1), 280–281, nos. 7–9.

jurers (and their insurers) is that they can be exposed to liability for a much longer term than under the old rule (where liability was in principle limited to thirty years after the event)[15]. Therefore there is much debate on the question when the short (five years) statute of limitation starts to run. Hence there is a lot of case law more particularly on this issue[16].

C. Case Law

1. Scope of Protection under Tort Law

Increasingly one can notice attempts of injurers (and their insurers) to find ways to limit their exposure to liability. One possible defence mechanism for a tortfeasor is to hold that he has indeed violated a duty of care, but that the damage of the plaintiff does not fall within the scope of protection of the particular norm that was violated. A recent case provides an interesting example of this and it may have implications for other domains of tort law as well[17]. The case deals with a barge called Linda. The buyer of the barge had the barge inspected within the framework of a regulation concerning the examination of ships on the river Rhine[18]. The specific certificate for the ship needed to be renewed and for that reason the ship was inspected by the Marine Inspection. The State renews the certificate for the Linda. Hardly a year later the Linda sinks as a result of which another boat owned by van Hasselt suffers damage. It appeared that the Linda sank as a result of rust in the bottom plates of the ship. Therefore water entered and the ship sank. Van Hasselt files a claim in tort law against the State arguing that if a more careful examination of the Linda had taken place, no certificate would have been issued. The Court of Appeals rejects the claim of van Hasselt on the basis of the relativity requirement in tort: violation of the norm does not lead to liability of the State since the third party is not protected under the particular norm. The *Hoge Raad* follows this reasoning and argues that the regulations concerned aim at protecting the safety of traffic by ship in a general manner. Of course the carefulness of the examination of a ship which will lead to granting or renewing the certificate will contribute to this general safety of marine traffic. However, the *Hoge Raad* argues that neither the specific regulations nor the duty of care have as specific object to protect the individual economic interests of third parties who suffer damage as a result of a (carelessly examined) ship causing damage. The involvement of the State in granting or renewing the certificate is the result of 6

[15] See for a comment on this new Dutch approach to the statute of limitations: E. de Kezel, in: *Liber Amicorum en Marcel Storme Tijdschrift voor Privaatrecht* (2004), 107–143.

[16] See M. Faure/T. Harlief (supra fn. 1), 304–306, nos. 78–84.

[17] *Hoge Raad* 7 May 2004, [2004] *Rechtspraak van de Week* (RvdW), 67. See on this case equally T. Hartlief, *Leven in een claimcultuur: wie is er bang voor Amerikaanse toestanden?*, lecture at the occasion of the 29th Dies Natalis of the University of Maastricht on 14 January 2005, University of Maastricht; 38–39 and see on these issues more generally I. Giesen, *Toezicht en aansprakelijkheid* (2005).

[18] *Reglement onderzoek schepen op de Rijn* – RosR.

the general responsibility of the State for the safety of ship traffic. However, this involvement of the State does not remove the fact that it is primarily the owner of the ship who is responsible for the maintenance and safety of the particular ship. Granting the certificate therefore does not guarantee that the ship is actually safe. The *Hoge Raad* in this respect also argues that if after an examination an accident occurs as a result of a ship failing to meet a specific safety standard that should have appeared after a careful examination, the liability of the owner of the ship against the third party is not based on the fact that he kept the ship in marine traffic notwithstanding the negligent character of the examination, but on the fact that it is the owner who is finally responsible for the safety of the ship. Therefore the *Hoge Raad* holds that the general responsibility of the State to proceed to an examination of ships in a careful manner does not have as a consequence that an in principle unlimited number of third parties would be protected against property damage or economic losses. As a result the State cannot be held liable when a negligent examination took place.

7 The *Hoge Raad* presents the reasoning very convincingly and as if there were no other reasoning possible, but of course this is hardly the case. The mere fact that the owner of the ship is liable because he is responsible for the safety of the ship and not because he kept a negligently examined ship in marine traffic of course does not remove the liability of the State for the negligently performed examination. In the literature it was therefore held that in fact two separate shortcomings existed that could be held against two separate injurers (the owner and the State respectively) and could hence lead to liability of both[19].

8 However, the policy reasoning behind the decision of the *Hoge Raad* may be clear. The *Hoge Raad* may have feared an, in principle, far-reaching liability for economic and property losses of an, in principle, unlimited number of third parties. Hence one has to consider this decision in the tendency of plaintiffs' attorneys to search for a solvent debtor other than the primary tortfeasor. Often this may be a public authority which for instance negligently omitted to intervene to prevent the damage. Van Boom and Giessen have, in a 2001 publication, argued strongly against a primary liability of these "secondary defendants" based on the idea that the primary tortfeasor should receive optimal incentives to avoid the harm[20]. Others have, on the other hand, argued that a potential liability also of these secondary defendants (as in this case the State) may particularly have as effect that pressure towards more care and safety will be exercised on the primary tortfeasors. Thus the argument used by the *Hoge Raad* that the goal of the certificate granted by the State is to promote the obligation of the owner of the ship to keep its ship in a safe state is hardly an argument

[19] For a critical review of this case see T. Hartlief, Kroniek aansprakelijkheids en schadevergoedingsrecht 2003 – 2004, [2004] *Nederlands Tijdschrift voor Burgerlijk recht* (NTBR), 462–475.

[20] See W.H. van Boom/I. Giesen, [2001] NJB, 1675–1685.

against liability. One could even hold that precisely liability of the State could have a positive effect on the incentives to prevent the harm[21]. Of course one could imagine that other limitations on liability are introduced more particularly for the case where the plaintiff is not a primary victim, but someone further down in the chain of distribution. However, the requirements of causation, absence of contributory negligence and the relativity requirement, could help to keep the liability in that respect within reasonable limits. The Linda case however shows that the *Hoge Raad* is probably too cautious since even a tort suit by primary victims against a secondary tortfeasor (the State) is excluded.

2. Increased Danger and Duty of Care

a) "Cellar Door" Factors

The case law of the *Hoge Raad* has often held that one is not supposed to expose a third party to a greater risk than would be reasonably justifiable under the given circumstances[22]. The *Hoge Raad* held in many decisions that various criteria and elements have to be weighed against each other in order to decide upon the liability. These criteria are often referred to as the "cellar door" factors since they were first established by the *Hoge Raad* in a case dealing with an incident where the victim fell into an open trap door of a cellar[23]. In a few recent cases the *Hoge Raad* has repeated the criteria formulated in the cellar door case law[24]. This is as such remarkable since also in the previous forty years since the *Hoge Raad* rendered its cellar door decision, there have been ample opportunities to refine the criteria for liability, which have not been used by the *Hoge Raad*. 9

Whether the creation of a danger for a third party is wrongful depends upon a variety of criteria that have to be balanced against each other. The starting point is usually that citizens are of course allowed to take a certain risk. Not every probability of damage obliges someone to take preventive measures[25]. Some risks constitute the unfortunate but unavoidable consequence of participating in social activities. This is in legal doctrine sometimes referred to as accidents as a result of coincidence or an unlucky course of events[26]. Hence, this considers cases where it is held that the defendant has not taken more risks than was reasonable given the particular circumstances. 10

21 So T. Hartlief, [2004] NTBR, no. 5.

22 See *inter alia Hoge Raad* 11 December 1987, [1988] *Nederlandse Jurisprudentie* (NJ), 393 with case note by W.C.L. van der Grinten and see *Hoge Raad* 23 June 1989, [1991] VR, 154 with case note by H.A. Bouman.

23 For a recent example of another accident with an open trap door to a cellar see Civil Court of Amsterdam 10 June 2003, [2003] VR, 174.

24 It concerns more particularly *Hoge Raad* 26 September 2003, [2003] NJ, 660 and *Hoge Raad* 28 May 2004, [2005] NJ, 105 with case note by C.J.H. Brunner, [2004] *Ars Aequi*, 866–873.

25 *Hoge Raad* 6 November 1989, [1989] NJ, 567 with case note by C.J.H. Brunner.

26 For the discussion of that case law see M. Faure/T. Hartlief, The Netherlands, in H. Koziol/ B.C. Steininger (supra fn. 2), 358–359, no. 16.

11 An important issue concerns the question in which context the cellar door criteria have to be weighed. It is indeed largely the context that will often be decisive for the applicable norm and hence for the scope of liability. A well-known example constitutes the incidents that occur within the private sphere[27]. Many types of behaviour of a daily nature are to some extent dangerous to others. When these normal acts cause damage there is, in principle, no liability, even though the damage that occurred is serious and the accident could probably have been avoided[28]. The reasoning behind this is that citizens should, in principle, be able to act as normal human beings[29]. Accepting liability in these kinds of situations would force people towards unnatural and hence abnormal behaviour. Nevertheless in some cases liability is accepted even in daily life situations like the moving of a washing machine[30]. But these decisions rather seem to constitute an exception to the general rule and are not in line with the case law of the *Hoge Raad*.

b) Sports and Games

12 Another example of the contextual character of the liability criteria can be found in case law concerning situations of sports and games. Generally one can notice that the case law seems to accept that within a sport or game situation another type of care can be required than in social life generally. In this respect the *Hoge Raad* refers to a higher threshold for liability[31]. These cases were discussed in the previous Yearbook[32]. Still the question arises of when precisely the higher threshold for liability applies. In a decision of 20 February 2004 the *Hoge Raad* had to express itself on this particular issue[33]. The case deals with an accident that occurred at a mini golf course. A group of youngsters were playing golf at the mini golf course in smaller groups. One of them was finished at a specific hole and was already walking to the next hole where another person was still playing. He watched how a girl hit the ball; she hit him in the eye with the golf stick as a result of which he lost his eye. The Court of Appeals considers the victim as a participant in the game and hence denies liability. The *Hoge Raad* upholds the decision. It makes clear that participation within a sport or game situation does not require that, at the specific moment of the accident, the injurer and the victim were in competition or that the victim was engaged in the behaviour which would be specific for the particular sport. The crucial issue in that particular case was hence whether the victim could be considered a participant or a bystander, suggesting that only if

[27] See on these issues also E.J. Dommering, [2004] NTBR, 72–79.

[28] See generally *Hoge Raad* 20 June 1986, [1986] NJ, 780, *Hoge Raad* 11 December 1987, [1988] NJ, 393 and *Hoge Raad* 9 December 1994, [1996] NJ, 403 with case note by C.J.H. Brunner.

[29] This was held by W.C.L. van der Grinten in his case note with *Hoge Raad* 11 December 1987, [1988] NJ, 393 and by J. Hijma in his case note with *Hoge Raad* 12 May 2000, [2001] NJ, 300.

[30] Court of Appeals of Leeuwarden 23 July 2003, [2004] VR, 24.

[31] See *Hoge Raad* 28 March 2003, [2003] NJ, 718 and 719 with case note by C.J.H. Brunner.

[32] See M. Faure/T. Hartlief (supra fn. 1), 282–284, nos. 16–21.

[33] *Hoge Raad* 20 February 2004, [2004] NJ, 238, [2004] NTBR, 250–251 with case note by P.L.P. Meiser, see on this issue also E.H. Hondius, [2004] *Ars Aequi*, 335.

the victim were a participant would the higher liability threshold apply. In this particular case the Court of Appeals and the *Hoge Raad* consider the victim a participant, so that he is confronted with the higher liability threshold. Moreover the question can be asked whether this difference between the participant and the bystander is indeed still that relevant in the light of the case law of the *Hoge Raad*. Also one could argue that bystanders should, under certain circumstances, expect that during the sports activity that they are observing mistakes are made as a result of which e.g. a ball could hit someone[34].

c) Specific Duties of Care

In some particular cases a specific duty of care is formulated by the *Hoge Raad*. This is for instance the case in the well-known Peat Heat Case concerning field management[35] as well as in the well-known Bus Lock Case with respect to traffic management[36]. The first case of interest, leading to a *Hoge Raad* decision of 26 September 2003[37], deals with an accident that occurred to a truck which was loaded with manure. Its weight was approximately 44 tons and the maximum breadth of the truck was 2.45 metres. The truck drove from a normal asphalt road onto a road covered with stones and gravel and subsequently sank into a ditch. The particular road was in the beginning approximately 2.50 metres wide, but further down it was considerably narrower. The accident took place in October at approximately 7 pm. The insurer of the truck started a recourse action against the authority liable for the management and maintenance of the road on the basis of art. 6:197 of the Civil Code which provides that in this particular case the general tort law regime of art. 6:162 needs to be applied. The plaintiff argues that the particular road was not suited for heavy traffic and this was not indicated through any particular sign. Both the Civil Court and the Court of Appeals accept liability in this particular case, probably also based on the relatively stringent case law of the *Hoge Raad* concerning liability of public authorities. The *Hoge Raad* however annuls the previous decision[38]. The motivation of the *Hoge Raad* seems to be inspired by the opinion of Attorney General Spier, holding that the case is clear and should not lead to liability. One can recognize here the idea that the victim was abnormally negligent in his behaviour and that the particular traffic manager should not expect such a careless behaviour of the particular truck driver. The *Hoge Raad* repeats in this respect the "cellar door" criteria for liability and indicates that this liability regime also applies to the liability of a traffic manager. The case also indicates in this respect that the traffic manager should in principle take into account potentially negligent traffic participants. This then becomes an important criterion for the care that can be expected from a traffic 13

[34] See T. Hartlief, [2004] NTBR, 464–465, no. 8.

[35] *Hoge Raad* 27 May 1988, [1989] NJ, 29 with case note by W.C.L. van der Grinten.

[36] *Hoge Raad* 20 March 1992, [1993] NJ, 547 with case note by C.J.H. Brunner. See in this respect also *Hoge Raad* 6 September 1996, [1998] NJ, 415 with case note by C.J.H. Brunner.

[37] It hence came too late to be discussed in the previous Yearbook 2003.

[38] *Hoge Raad* 26 September 2003, [2003] NJ, 660, [2004] *Aansprakelijkheid, Verzekering en Schade* (AV&S), 35–39 with case note by I. Giesen. See on this case also J.J. van der Helm, [2004] VR, 33–35.

manager. The traffic manager is apparently not liable when it should immediately be clear even for a not particularly attentive driver that this road is not suited for heavy traffic. In this particular case one can therefore hardly blame the traffic manager for not having put up a warning sign. Of course one can expect that the result of this case law will be that public authorities responsible for traffic management will increasingly simply put warning signs up in order to avoid liability. In the absence of signs they would be dependant upon the evaluation by the judge of what should be immediately clear even for a non-attentive driver.

14 The second case deals with the scope of the Peat Heat decision[39] and deals with a case that played on the island of Saint-Martin, a Caribbean island belonging to the kingdom of the Netherlands[40]. Mrs. Hartmann was standing on the extension of the runway in order to take a picture just as a Boeing 747 was taking off. As a result of the so-called "jet blast" she was thrown against the rocks and was injured. She found herself on public property at the site of Maho beach. She was separated from the runway by a public road and a fence. On the fence there were a number of signs indicating "warning low flying" and "departing aircraft blast can cause physical injury". Mrs. Hartman filed a claim in tort against the local airport. The Court of Appeals denies liability of the defendant because the airport had no power over the public property on which Mrs. Hartmann found herself and because the plaintiff, given the available signs, should have been aware of the danger. The *Hoge Raad* is of the opinion that the mere fact of the lack of power over the public property cannot be decisive in this respect. Decisive is that the airport can wrongfully handle also third parties who are not on the territory of the airport itself but in the close vicinity, more particularly at a place which can apparently also be endangered by a danger coming from the airport. Failure to take sufficient precautionary measures to avoid this danger could then lead to liability. This argument seems logical: the airport had created dangers outside of its sphere of influence. Hence the defence that they could not exercise power over the public property outside the airport was not very impressive given the fact that they apparently could create dangers on that territory.

15 Also the second argument, being that Hartmann could be informed of the danger to which she was exposed given the availability of the signs, does not help the defendant in this particular case. Being aware of the danger is apparently not sufficient to deny liability. With respect to the question of whether a warning is adequate, the crucial question is whether one can expect that the particular warning will lead to an act or omission as a result of which the danger is avoided. Hence the decision provides some important information with respect to the question of what should and can be expected from a warning[41]. A

[39] *Hoge Raad* 27 May 1988, [1989] NJ, 29 with case note by W.C.L. van der Grinten.

[40] *Hoge Raad* 28 May 2004, [2005] NJ, 105 with case note by C.J.H. Brunner, [2004] *Ars Aequi*, 866–873.

[41] A call in this respect had been formulated by C.E. Du Perron, [1996] *Bedrijfsjuridische Berichten*, 175–176.

problem in the particular case was that the airport could and should expect that the public would position itself in the close vicinity of the fence. Moreover, there was a high number of tourists who, despite the warning signs, all came to watch the airplanes taking off from the particular location where the accident occurred. Finally, the text of the signs did not clearly indicate what the specific danger was that could arise. A problem in this respect is that the sign, as is the case with many other signs, did not indicate what behaviour would then be expected from third parties. For instance it was not indicated what would be a safe distance to be taken into account by the public at large.

Whether a warning will be effective will depend *inter alia* upon the question 16 of whether the danger and the seriousness of the particular danger are made sufficiently clear. In that respect the question also arises to whom the particular warning is addressed: to children or for instance to grown-ups? Finally it will also play a role what the "creator of the danger" could expect from the behaviour of third parties in the specific case. In this case the airport was for instance aware of the fact that the warnings on the signs were largely neglected.

In fact the *Hoge Raad* case deals with a more general question, not only dealing 17 with warnings, but also with other preventive measures that aim at preventing victims from suffering harm as a result of a dangerous situation. Also as far as for instance a sign with a prohibition to enter or physical precautionary measures (like a fence) are concerned, one can ask the question whether they will effectively lead to an act or omission as a result of which the danger will be avoided. Dependant upon the specific situation this could for instance imply that:

- The warning mechanism chosen should be replaced by a more effective one;
- A sign indicating a clear prohibition might sometimes be preferred to a warning sign;
- Physical preventive measures (like fences which totally avoid certain behaviour) can sometimes be preferred to simple signs;
- Sometimes more extensive physical measures than the ones chosen should be taken[42];
- That the actor should abstain from the potentially dangerous activity altogether[43].

3. Liability of Public Authorities

Also in previous Yearbooks we reported on the relatively far-reaching liability 18 of public authorities in the Netherlands[44]. As we made clear in these previous

[42] See in this respect Civil Court of Amsterdam 10 June 2003, [2003] VR, 174, holding that simply placing a barstool close to an open trap door to the cellar is an insufficient precautionary measure.

[43] This solution is also suggested in *Hoge Raad* 20 March 1992, [1993] NJ, 547 with case note by C.J.H. Brunner, being the bus lock decision of the *Hoge Raad* with respect to the liability of the authority liable for traffic management.

[44] See for instance M. Faure/T. Hartlief (supra fn. 1), 288–292, nos. 33–42.

overviews, the *Hoge Raad* applies its case law with respect to the liability of public authorities based on the idea of the equality of citizens towards the public burdens, holding that disproportionate negative consequences that fall outside the scope of the normal social or corporate risks and hurt a limited group of citizens or institutions as a result of an act or a decision of a public authority should not be solely to the disadvantage of that particular group, but should be spread evenly over the community. This same idea has also been applied in a case whereby a convicted criminal, during his leave from detention, took two women hostage, assaulted them and took money from them. However, the case also showed the limitations of the mentioned equality case law. The Court of Appeals held that the State had not acted negligently in granting the convicted criminal the permission to leave, but nevertheless sustained a claim against the State based on the "equality" case law as it had been decided in the earlier decision of the *Hoge Raad* in the case of the State against Lavrijsen[45]. As mentioned above, the Court of Appeals holds that if disproportionate negative consequences of a government decision hit a limited number of citizens (like the as such lawful decision to grant a leave of absence to the criminal) based on the "equality" case law this can nevertheless be considered wrongful against that particular victim and hence give rise to liability of the State.

19 Both the State and the victim filed an appeal with the *Hoge Raad* against this decision of the Court. The *Hoge Raad* holds *inter alia* that the damage is the result of a wrongful act by the criminal (V.). However, within certain limits V. was entitled to a leave of absence from the detention institution. Within the framework of that decision a balance has then to be struck: on the one hand no certainty can be provided that V. would constitute no danger to others during the period of leave; on the other hand there needs to be a reasonable and justified expectation that this danger is so limited that granting the leave is acceptable with a view to the safety of third parties.

20 The judgment of the Court of Appeals concerning the carefulness of the decision to grant a leave of absence is therefore upheld by the *Hoge Raad*: the State did not act negligently in granting the leave. However, the argument of the State that the "equality" doctrine should not have been applied to the particular case is followed by the *Hoge Raad*[46]. In that respect the *Hoge Raad* points again to the fact that the damage is not the direct consequence of granting the leave of absence, but of the wrongful act by V. Crucial is however the idea that applying the "equality" doctrine is only possible if there has been an as such lawful act of the government that has led to a disproportionate damage for third parties. The *Hoge Raad* holds that the conditions are not fulfilled in the case at hand. First, there should have been reasonably foreseeable negative consequences for third parties. Given the fact that it was held that the decision to grant a leave of absence is as such lawful, that condition is not fulfilled. Second, the mere fact that V. would not have been able to act wrongfully if

[45] *Hoge Raad* 30 March 2001, [2003] NJ, 615 with case note by M. Scheltema.
[46] *Hoge Raad* 17 September 2004, C03/068HR.

the leave of absence had not been granted is not a sufficient reason to link the damage causally to the decision by the State, so that the damage could be attributed to the State. There is of course a connection between on the one hand the decision of the State to grant a leave of absence and on the other hand the damage, but that is as such not a justification for liability. Moreover, it cannot be held that the negative consequences of a decision which was taken in the public interest would disproportionately harm a limited number of citizens. The fact that granting a leave of absence to V. (or to anyone else in his situation) creates the possibility that serious damage is inflicted upon third parties, is a risk that in social life is suffered by anyone who comes into contact with V. When, however, the risk has materialised there is one individual citizen who suffers the harm whereas all the others who were potentially exposed to the risk remain untouched. There is in that sense still an inequality. This inequality is however not created through the granting of the leave of absence but through the fact that individuals other than the victim remain untouched.

Nevertheless criticism has been formulated on this case in the literature and 21
more particularly on the reasoning of the *Hoge Raad*[47]. The *Hoge Raad* indeed limits the application of the traditional "equality" case law, but that is not such a logical consequence from the facts of this case as the *Hoge Raad* suggests. The *Hoge Raad* regularly repeats that the damage has been caused by V. and that therefore liability should be primarily imposed upon him. On the other hand it can hardly be denied that the granting of the leave of absence was an essential element in the causal chain that led to the damage. Attorney General Spier held in his opinion before the decision that from a statistical point of view there are more or less inevitable consequences of acts of public authorities that play a role in this respect: on the one hand there is generally a reasonable likelihood of a repeat offence with a convicted criminal on a leave of absence and on the other hand there is the legal right of convicted criminals to a leave of absence. The mere fact that, for the damage finally to occur not only the government decision was essential, can of course hardly be decisive for the case. Also in other cases where the "equality" case law was considered applicable the damage was also not merely the consequence of a government decision[48]. The policy reasoning behind the decision of the *Hoge Raad* seems to be clear: it simply does not want to accept State liability in this particular case. This is a remarkable point of view given the fact that increasingly in legal doctrine calls are heard in favour of State liability for damage caused by previously convicted criminals[49]. The decision is more particularly remarkable since also the Dutch Government at one time considered that something "had to be done" for victims of previously convicted criminals. For instance in the well-known "Tjirk van Wijk" case, which considered a victim who was killed by a previously convicted criminal, the State paid € 10,000 to the descen-

[47] See particularly T. Hartlief, [2004] NTBR, 466–467, no. 12.
[48] See on these issues equally M.K.G. Tjepkema, Het referentiekader van het égalité-beginsel, *Overheid en Aansprakelijkheid* (2004), 12–22.
[49] See in this respect more particularly G.E. van Maanen, in: *Schadevergoeding bij Rechtmatige Overheidsdaad* (2002), 81 et seq.

dants[50]. It may be clear that this decision of the *Hoge Raad* will not be a great stimulus for further government action to provide compensation to victims of previously convicted criminals.

4. Employers' Liability

a) On the Way Back?

22 Already in the previous Yearbook we reported that there seems to be an end to the generally far-reaching employers' liability in the Netherlands. A certain restrictive trend in recent case law of the *Hoge Raad* concerning employers' liability based on Art. 7:658 of the Civil Code could be noticed[51]. Also in this respect one can notice a few remarkable tendencies. One of the worries of the government concerns the way in which the case law has interpreted Art. 7:658 of the Civil Code[52]. The *Hoge Raad* used this provision to introduce one of the most far-reaching liabilities that Dutch law knows today[53]. The crucial question still remains whether there is any shortcoming on the side of the employer. If that is the case, the victim is in principle entitled to 100% compensation. If there is no shortcoming on the side of the employer, the simple rule is that the employee is not compensated. It is precisely this "all or nothing" approach in employers' liability that has been criticized for instance within the framework of occupational diseases (more particularly the repetitive strain injury – RSI)[54]. The reason is that especially "modern" occupational diseases (like RSI) are often multi-causal. It is usually not only the shortcoming of the employer that caused the harm; the employee can have an influence as well[55]. As we indicated in earlier Yearbooks, the general tendency in case law was to accept a shortcoming relatively easily. The basic idea behind the far-reaching employers' liability was that Art. 7:658 also aimed at providing protection against the tendency of employees not always to take the necessary care and precaution during their work[56]. However, precisely in the latter respect there seems to be a different tendency now in the case law of the *Hoge Raad*.

[50] These descendants have moreover (unsuccessfully) tried to file a claim in tort against the psychotherapist to whom the convicted criminal would have told that he was planning to kill a specific person. See in this respect Civil Court of Assen, 16 July 2003, [2003] NJ, 585, [2003] NTBR, 601 and following with case note by E.F.D. Engelhard. See for a discussion of this case also J.K.M. Gevers, [2003] *Tijdschrift voor Gezondheidsrecht*, 523.

[51] See M. Faure/T. Hartlief (supra fn. 1), 294–298, nos. 49–61.

[52] See concerning the potential problems of insurability resulting from this case law E.J. Blom, De (on)verzekerbaarheid van werkgeversaansprakelijkheid, [2004] *Praktisch Procederen*, 67–72.

[53] As we have mentioned in previous Yearbooks the developments concerning the expanding employers' liability especially occurred very rapidly in the nineties. See in this respect for instance A.J.C.M. Geers, [2003] *Sociaal Recht* (SR), 396–400. Earlier we also discussed the case law of the *Hoge Raad* concerning work-related traffic incidents (M. Faure/T. Hartlief, The Netherlands, in: *European Tort Law 2002* (2003), 313–314, no. 17). For recent developments in this respect see E.J. van Sandick, [2004] VR, 197–202 and for the possible application of this case law to civil servants see J.J. Van der Helm, [2004] VR, 202–206.

[54] See for instance M. Cancian-van Ballegooijen, Alles of niets?! Werkgeversaansprakelijkheid en schuldverdeling bij beroepsziekten, *Arbeidsrecht*, 2004/4, 8–14.

[55] See in this respect B. Sorgdrager, [2003] TVP, 73–75.

[56] See for instance *Hoge Raad* 18 September 1998, [1999] NJ, 45 with case note by P.A. Stein and *Hoge Raad* 19 October 2001, [2001] NJ, 663.

In a few recent cases, some of which we already discussed in the previous Yearbook[57], liability of the employer was denied. Remarkable in that respect was that in the three cases the Attorney General had advised annulling the decisions of the Court (that had denied employers' liability) referring to the traditionally stringent case law of the *Hoge Raad* with respect to employers' liability. In all of these cases the opinion of the Attorney General was apparently not followed by the *Hoge Raad*[58]. Two of those cases were already discussed in the previous Yearbook, being: 23

- The case whereby employer's liability was denied after an employee had cut himself with a knife on the basis that the employee should know that one can cut oneself with a knife[59].
- The case where employer's liability was denied when an employee fell through a roof because he was standing on a dome which was not attached but simply deposited on a roof[60].
- A newer case (only briefly mentioned in the previous Yearbook) concerned the cleaning lady Peeters who fell on the occasion of the removal of a coffee stain[61].

In two out of the three cases the *Hoge Raad* stresses that Art. 7:658 of the Civil Code does not provide an absolute protection to employees. The fact that the *Hoge Raad* mentions this in an *Obiter Dictum* of course has its importance. Given the earlier case law in which the *Hoge Raad* required that employers also take into account the possible carelessness of employees, one could have expected a different outcome of these cases. One can therefore argue that the *Hoge Raad* has somewhat moved from the traditional, very protective approach[62]. The problem is, however, that neither the legal basis nor the underlying reasoning has changed. Therefore at this moment both academics and practitioners speculate on the precise consequences of this new tendency. More recent case law might provide further insight in this respect. 24

A recent case also sheds some light on the precise interpretation of Art. 7:658 of the Civil Code. The case deals with a relatively simple accident case: a truck driver slips on the occasion of the loading of a container with building waste and suffers an injury to his leg. Both in first instance and in appeal liability of the employer was denied. The *Hoge Raad* once more confirms that: 25

57 M. Faure/T. Hartlief (supra fn. 1), 294–295, nos. 49–52.
58 See on these issues more generally T. Hartlief, [2003] WPNR 6559, 933–934.
59 *Hoge Raad* 4 October 2002 [2004] NJ, 175.
60 *Hoge Raad* 16 May 2003, [2004] NJ, 176, [2003] SR, 228–231 with case note by C.J. Loonstra, [2004] TVP, 82–83 with case note by W.H. Bouman and [2003] VR, 369–370 with case note by L. Bier.
61 *Hoge Raad* 12 September 2003, [2004] NJ, 177 with case note by G.J.J. Heerma van Voss, [2003] NTBR, 538–539 with case note by E.F.D. Engelhard, [2004] AV&S, 82–83 with case note by C.J.M. Klaassen.
62 This is also what Attorney General Spier sees in his opinion before *Hoge Raad* 9 July 2004, [2004], *Jurisprudentie Arbeidsrecht* (JAR), 190.

- The employer is only held to take those measures that are reasonably necessary to prevent the harm;
- Art. 7:658 of the Civil Code imposes a duty of care on the employer, but not an absolute guarantee of safety towards the employee;
- It is a fact of general knowledge that during the daily course of work the necessary care of employees can be reduced and that this may especially be the case when the work performed by the employee may involve considerable risks[63].

26 With this point of view the *Hoge Raad* at least suggests that the applicable regime is not changed as far as the content is concerned. The *Hoge Raad* stresses, however, that it is important that the work may involve substantial risks. One can hold that this reasoning of the *Hoge Raad* implies that to decide upon liability the fact that daily work may involve substantial risks can be an issue. Only then would liability apply.

b) Issues of Proof

27 Case law with respect to employers' liability also deals with issues of proof. These issues of proof especially play a role with occupational diseases, even more than with the above discussions of accidents at work. Concerning proof of a causal relationship between the damage (personal injury) and a shortcoming of the employer, there is especially much debate in so-called repetitive strain injury cases[64] but also concerning asbestos-related injuries there is still much case law. A recent case deals with the question of whether, concerning the dangers of asbesto, it is relevant for the employer's duty of care what the particular type of asbestos is[65]. The case dealt with a claim of descendants of a mechanic who died of mesothelioma (cancer of the pleura) and whose task it was *inter alia* to remove brake linings which contained white asbestos. The claim was denied in the first two instances. The *Hoge Raad* confirms. The *Hoge Raad* holds that the court could, on the basis of the available documents, decide that the employer did not have to be aware of the dangers of mesothelioma in case of an exposure to white asbestos in the period 1965–1979.

c) Employment-Related Private Accidents

28 As far as employers' liability is concerned, we can finally also refer to the case law we discussed in the previous Yearbook concerning employment-related private accidents[66]. We already discussed the liability claim of a KLM pilot who, during a resting period between two flights, was involved in a serious

[63] *Hoge Raad* 9 July 2004, [2004] JAR, 190. However, in *Hoge Raad* 5 November 2004, liability of the employer is assumed again.

[64] See in this respect *inter alia* A.J.C.M. Geers/J.M. Ruijgrok/R. van de Water, [2003] NJB, 2034–2041 and see specifically concerning the burden of proof in these cases K. Kas/H.W. van Osch, [2004/3] *Arbeidsrecht*, 26–33 and H.J.W. Alt, [2004/6/7] *Arbeidsrecht*, 32–36 as well as M.S.A. Vegter, [2004] TVP, 3–10.

[65] *Hoge Raad* 4 June 2004, C03/034HR.

[66] M. Faure/T. Hartlief (supra fn. 1), 297–298, nos. 55–58.

traffic accident in the Ivory Coast. We mentioned that the *Kantonrechter* of Amsterdam denied liability of KLM *inter alia* based on the argument that KLM had sufficiently informed its staff of the possibilities of obtaining first party insurance for the risks connected to a stay abroad. In appeals, the court of Amsterdam, however, held KLM liable[67]. The court bases the liability on the changing specific risks to which an airline exposes its employees. The court hence holds that Art. 7:611 of the Civil Code does create a duty for the employer to limit these risks as much as possible or to take care of the consequences (for instance by concluding an insurance to the benefit of the employees). Recently liability was also accepted in the case of an accident that occurred during a balloon excursion which should have been the highlight of a company's day out[68].

5. Causal Uncertainty

In previous Yearbooks we already pointed towards a trend in the case law of 29
the *Hoge Raad* holding that in specific cases, where a violation of a specific norm is established, there is a presumption of causation. The case law of the *Hoge Raad* in this respect is referred to as the "reversal rule" (*omkeringsregel*), referring to the reversal of the burden of proving causal uncertainty[69]. Decisive in that respect were two cases of 29 November 2002 (both discussed in the Yearbook 2002) in which the *Hoge Raad* provided further details on the application of this reversal rule as a result of questions that had been raised in legal doctrine[70]. The reversal rule is only applicable, so the *Hoge Raad* held, when a norm has been violated that had as its goal the prevention of a specific danger from which damage could emerge and moreover that specific danger had to be substantially increased as a result of the violation of the norm. This tightening of the reversal rule by adding these new conditions of course makes clear that the scope of application becomes more restricted.

The consequences of this recent tightening of the reversal rule were discussed 30
in a few *Hoge Raad* cases in 2004[71]. In a first case of 9 April 2004[72] the application of the reversal rule was denied in a case in which the plaintiff suffers from so-called fibromyalgia. She claims that the particular injuries are due to a traffic accident in which she was involved. One can understand that the *Hoge Raad* denies the application of the reversal rule in this particular case. There was indeed uncertainty concerning the causes of this fibromyalgia and there was (especially) doubt whether the fibromyalgia could be caused by a traffic accident at all.

67 Court of Appeals of Amsterdam 11 December 2003, [2004] JAR, 25, [2004] SR, 106–107 with case note by M.S.A. Vegter.
68 Civil Court of Amsterdam 7 April 2004, [2004] JAR, 108.
69 See M. Faure/T. Hartlief (supra fn. 53), 315–316, nos. 19–20.
70 *Hoge Raad* 29 November 2002, [2004] NJ, 304 and 305 with case note by W.D.H. Asser.
71 In the most recent one (*Hoge Raad* 9 July 2004, see C03/081HR) the *Hoge Raad* upholds the decisions of the Court of Appeals to apply the reversal rule.
72 *Hoge Raad* 9 April 2004, [2004] NJ, 308 with case note by W.D.H. Asser.

31 The *Hoge Raad* case of 7 May 2004[73] dealt with apparent damage to various houses that, according to the owners, was due to the withdrawal of water by the province. The problem was however that the province did not keep precise track (through monitoring or documentation) of the specific works that had been undertaken. Hence, it was very difficult to prove a causal relationship between the works performed by the province and the damage to the houses and, precisely because of this negligent monitoring and documentation, the Court of Appeals had applied the reversal rule (hence leading to liability of the province). The *Hoge Raad*, however, annuls this decision. The *Hoge Raad* holds that the duty of care (concerning monitoring and documentation) aims at avoiding later problems of proof, but does not aim at preventing a danger of damage. The *Hoge Raad*, however, points at other possibilities for the victim to alleviate the burden of proof.

32 A remarkable case concerns a patient with cancer of the throat who had used Seresta and subsequently could not be woken up[74]. A general practitioner Dr. J was asked by Mrs. B to pay a visit to her husband K who had already slept for eighteen hours after taking two 50 mg tablets of Seresta. After an examination Dr. J informed Mrs. B that he expected Mr. K to wake up after a few hours. He, however, told her that if this were not the case or if his situation worsened, she would have to call either him or the next doctor on duty[75]. Mrs. B did not call anyone. The next morning she went to visit her own general practitioner (to buy diapers because of incontinence) who was alarmed by the announcement that Mr. K could still not be woken up. The general practitioner hence called for an ambulance but Mr. K had already died. A post-mortem examination was not performed. Dr. J was convicted by the medical disciplinary board. There was an unnatural situation in which a direct hospitalisation for observation should have taken place. In the subsequent civil lawsuit against Dr. J the issue of the causal uncertainty is the crucial one. The question of course arises what would have happened in case Dr. J had given better advice and who should prove what? The Civil Court holds the reversal rule applicable. The Court of Appeals holds that application of the reversal rule is as such correct, all be it that in this particular case the cause of death has not been established given the fact that no post-mortem examination took place. The Court of Appeals therefore holds that this brings Dr. J into difficulties regarding problems of proof (notably that he cannot prove any longer that his negligence did not cause the death) and this hence has to come for the risk of Mrs. B. The reversal rule is hence not applied by the Court of Appeals and Mrs. B is allowed to prove that the death of her husband K was a direct consequence of an act or omission of Dr. J.

[73] *Hoge Raad* 7 May 2004, [2004] NJ, 422 with case note by W.D.H. Asser.

[74] *Hoge Raad* 19 March 2004, [2004] NJ, 307 with case note by W.D.H. Asser, [2004] TBR, 289–292, with case note by E.F.D. Engelhard and see also C.H. van Dijk in [2004] TVP, 63–68.

[75] Dr. J was not the regular general practitioner of the family, but a doctor on duty.

The *Hoge Raad* takes the decisions from 2002 as a starting point and then stresses that the Court of Appeals did not make clear which norm that should have prevented a specific danger had been violated by the general physician. Apparently the Court of Appeals judged that it was impossible to indicate such a norm and probably even that it was not necessary to indicate this since it could anyway not be indicated that a specific danger materialised. Indeed, the cause of death was not established, which would have been necessary for the application of the reversal rule. This reasoning complies with the reversal rule. The *Hoge Raad* therefore clearly indicated that it would have been important to know what exactly the cause of death was. In an *Obiter Dictum* the *Hoge Raad* holds that, in many cases of medical malpractice, the norm that the physician would have violated can only be indicated in very general terms, like the norm incorporated in Art. 7:453 of the Civil Code holding that the physician has to act as a careful health care provider. In these cases there would be no room for the application of the reversal rule, but probably for other rules to alleviate the burden of proof for the victim. It is only "not excluded" that there would be a norm that aims at protecting the patient against a specific danger. That would be the case for instance when in a specific medical protocol behavioural norms are incorporated that have been violated[76]. In those cases of a violation of a specific norm the reversal rule can be applied. The message of the *Hoge Raad* seems to be clear: the general duty of care of health care providers incorporated in Art. 7:453 is too broad and too vague to justify the application of the reversal rule. With this judgment the *Hoge Raad* more or less renders the application of the reversal rule in cases of medical malpractice impossible. On an earlier occasion the *Hoge Raad* had indeed already decided that the reversal rule does not apply in case of a violation of a duty to inform[77]. The *Hoge Raad* now apparently holds the same in case of the violation of the general duty of care. 33

This ruling of the *Hoge Raad* concerning the general duty of health care providers stemming from Art. 7:453 of course also applies to other general duties of care, such as they apply for instance in cases of professional liability and for the general duty of care incorporated in Art. 6:162 of the Civil Code. Meanwhile it is well-known that those general norms are of course made specific in a concrete case. The concrete norm is of course often quite specific. The *Hoge Raad* is naturally aware of this and therefore still provides a theoretical opening for the cases where there would be a norm protecting a patient against a specific danger. However, the way in which it is formulated seems to be restrictive, so that one can assume that this would be more the exception than the rule. 34

It is hard to interpret this case other than as another attempt of the *Hoge Raad* to – once more – limit the application of this so-called reversal rule[78]. The 35

[76] The *Hoge Raad* refers in this respect to *Hoge Raad* 2 March 2001, [2001] NJ, 649.

[77] *Hoge Raad* 23 November 2001, [2002] NJ, 387 and 388 with case note by J.B.M. Vranken.

[78] So also T. Hartlief, [2004] NTBR, 470–471, no. 20 and see on the desirability of the reversal rule more generally P. Abas, [2003] NTBR, 448–450 and S.E. Lindenbergh, [2004] WPNR, 6580, 433–435.

practical consequence of this case law is anyway that it forces the parties involved and the judge to examine whether in this specific case a concrete norm can be found that has been violated. Only when that concrete norm can be considered specific enough can there be reason to justify the application of a reversal rule, according to this case law.

6. Damage

a) Assessment of Property Damage

36 As a general rule the damage should be assessed in a concrete manner. However, although this may be the case for personal injury, it does not apply for property damage. There case law holds that damage is assessed in a more abstract manner. As a general rule case law accepts that the victim has as a result of the damage to his property already suffered a loss equal to the reduced value of the specific property and this irrespective of the question whether reparation is possible. When reparation is possible, generally the reduction of the value is assessed on the basis of the repair costs that are assessed in an objective way. Moreover, in that case abstraction is also made of the question whether actual repair takes place.

37 The *Hoge Raad* added that as far as damaged buildings are concerned, that reparation can still be justified also in the case where the costs of repair are higher than the reduction in value[79]. Whether this is actually the case depends upon the specific circumstances. To this belong *inter alia* the specific functions of the object for the owner, the possibility to acquire a similar piece of property elsewhere that is similar to the damaged object and the amount by which the reparation costs exceed the loss in value. In the specific case at stake the costs to repair a few houses that had subsided were almost one million old Dutch Guilders whereas the loss in value was estimated at less than half a million. In that particular case the *Hoge Raad* nevertheless held that reparation was justifiable and reparation subsequently did take place.

38 A recent case deals with a similar question: is the reparation of a building justified in case the costs of reparation are almost 300,000 old Guilders, whereas the value of the building at the moment of the damage was only approximately 100,000 Guilders and what is the relevance of the circumstance that the actual repair did not take place[80]?

39 The case deals with a shed that was totally burned down in 1987. The parents of a few young children were held liable. Three years after the fire the former owner, Hiddema, transferred the shed to his son. At that time the shed was still burned down. The insurer of the building compensated (after a legal procedure) approximately 100,000 Guilders, being the estimated sale price of the

[79] See the case van Schravendijk/Den Haag (*Hoge Raad* 1 July 1993, [1995] NJ, 43 with case note by C.J.H. Brunner).

[80] See *Hoge Raad* 7 May 2004, [2005] NJ, 76 with case note by C.J.H. Brunner.

shed. Repair costs at the time were estimated at approximately 275,000 Guilders. Hiddema received the 100,000 Guilders from his insurer personally. Subsequently Hiddema started a claim in tort against the parents of the boys liable for the fire and claims the difference between the repair costs (275,000) and the amount he already received from his first party insurer (100,000). The parents of course replied that Hiddema is only entitled to the value the shed had before the fire took place. The Court of Appeals nevertheless sustained the claim of the parents.

A crucial element in the reasoning of Hiddema is that repair of the shed was justified. His reasoning is that the shed was previously used on a daily basis to store all kinds of agricultural tools and products and he claimed that it was impossible to find a comparable shed in the neighbourhood. Moreover it was held that the costs of repair were not unreasonably high compared to the sale price of the shed, so that the Court of Appeals held that it was not reasonable to pay Hiddema merely the amount based on the sale price of the shed. Hence, the Court of Appeals applies the criteria from the *Hoge Raad* decision of 1993 and Hiddema is subsequently entitled to the objectively estimated repair costs. In this abstract system of damage assessment it is not relevant whether Hiddema did indeed proceed to repair the shed. Hence, the mere fact that Hiddema did not rebuild his shed, but transferred it to his son does formally not affect his entitlement to repair costs. 40

The *Hoge Raad* first repeats the elements of its 1993 decision in the case of Schravendijk/Den Haag and subsequently upholds the decision of the Court of Appeals, being that in this specific case there was no reason to require from Hiddema to limit his claim to the loss in value, *inter alia* since Hiddema planned to rebuild his shed. The reason Hiddema did not rebuild the shed was also due to the fact that the province did not allow this repair at the same place and because a long procedure had taken place between Hiddema and his first party insurer concerning the scope of insurance coverage. Moreover, Hiddema meanwhile had reached the age of 65, so that he transferred the shed to his son who could therefore continue the same agricultural business and build another shed. However, all Hiddema's rights against third parties resulting from the fire remained with Hiddema. 41

Nevertheless the decision has led to serious criticism in the literature[81]. The question can indeed be asked why it is justified that Hiddema received almost three times the objective value of the shed, whereas repair of the shed was economically not justified and moreover was not even executed by Hiddema. Of course one can hold that in principle and under specific circumstances the owner should have the right to repair his building, even if repair costs exceed the loss in value. The reason is simply that the mere compensation of value loss does not give the owner his buildings back in the *status quo ante*. Still one has to keep in mind that this constitutes an exception to the general rule that 42

[81] See more particularly T. Hartlief, [2004] NTBR, 469–470, no. 19.

repair cannot be claimed by the victim when it is economically not justified. Therefore one could hold that more particularly in this case (where repair is economically not justified), one should require from the owner that repair actually takes place. It seems strange in this particular case that the Court of Appeals totally neglects the question of whether repair did in fact take place or not. It would have been more logical, so it is claimed in this criticism of the *Hoge Raad* decision, to hold that, if in this particular case the owner does not proceed to repair, he is not entitled to claim the repair costs either but will have to settle for the loss in value.

b) Psychological Damage

43 A difficult question in Dutch tort law remains the issue when there is psychological damage of such a nature that it gives an entitlement to compensation of this non-pecuniary loss. The *Hoge Raad* requires that the psychological damage should be established on the basis of objective criteria[82]. In practice, however, much discretion is left to the judge who has to form his opinion concerning the facts. The importance of the facts can of course be understood, but as a consequence one can notice that the results in seemingly similar cases in well-known decisions of the *Hoge Raad* diverge substantially without clear justification[83].

44 The reason victims often claim to have suffered psychological damage is that it is sometimes difficult to claim compensation in case of an infringement of personality rights. Hence one can predict that the more sympathetic case law is towards recognition of tort claims in case of a violation of personality rights, the more likely it is that victims will not have to file the tort claim under this category of "psychological damage"[84]. Many have held that a right to compensation for non-pecuniary losses in case of a violation of personality rights is quite important since it is probably the best (and perhaps only) way to enforce these personality rights. Without such an enforcement via tort claims, the recognition of personality rights would often remain a dead letter[85].

45 It is against this background that one has to consider a case which dealt with two persons who in the night of 30–31 December 1997 were assaulted in their house by a large group of youngsters who *inter alia* threw stones through their windows. The house was attacked three times in the course of the evening, the last time around midnight. The inhabitants of the house called the police at least five times and asked for help and protection. It was only around 2.30 am

[82] See for instance *Hoge Raad* 22 February 2002, [2002] NJ, 240 with case note by J.B.M. Vranken but also *Hoge Raad* 19 December 2003, [2004] NJ, 348.

[83] So also A.J. Verheij in his case note under *Hoge Raad* 9 May 2003, [2004] AV&S, 77–81.

[84] See in this respect more particularly S.D. Lindenbergh, De positie en de handhaving van persoonlijkheidsrechten in het Nederlandse privaatrecht, [1999] *Tijdschrift voor Privaatrecht* (TPR), 1665 et seq.

[85] See in this respect the extensive argumentation by A.J. Verheij, *Vergoeding van immateriële schade wegens aantasting in de persoon* (dissertation, Free University of Amsterdam, 2002), 445 et seq.

the next morning that the so-called mobile units of the police arrived in the neighbourhood. The house was then subsequently nailed down and the inhabitants could not return to their house anymore.

A tort claim was filed against both the community and the police authorities of Groningen where the incident occurred. The plaintiffs claimed compensation of the non-pecuniary loss they suffered as a result of the incident. They claimed that their personality rights were violated and that they suffered psychological damage as a result of the incident. The Civil Court in first instance sustained the claims. The Court held that the victims considered themselves endangered in their house for a much longer time than was necessary. The Civil Court sustained the claim on the basis of a violation of the personality rights as incorporated in Artt. 10 and 12 of the Dutch Constitution and Art. 8 of the European Convention on Human Rights. It holds that these are the most fundamental rights of the citizen in its relationship to the public authorities and that these rights therefore also form the contents of the personality rights in the private legal relationships. As a consequence of this, the Court did not have to address the issue of psychological damage. It simply held that the personality rights were seriously damaged, not only by the hooligans, but it equally held that the citizens in general should be able to trust that the government who is entrusted with law enforcement will, within a reasonable time, intervene to end those gross violations of their property rights. The claim for damages is therefore sustained on the basis of Art. 6:106 al. 1, b of the Civil Code. For the application of this article, the existence of psychological damage is not a requirement. It is sufficient that in this particular case there was a feeling of great insecurity and the shocked sense of justice of the citizen who did not receive adequate help and protection by the government in this particular case when he was assaulted by third parties in his house. 46

Before the *Hoge Raad* the defendants held that the violation of the right to respect the house does not constitute a violation of a personality right in the sense of Art. 6:106 al. 1, b. They argued that this is even not the case when a great sense of insecurity and a sense of injustice occur for the reason that the relationship with the personality rights is not sufficiently direct. The defendants held that this may be different when psychological damage has occurred, but the Court had not established that such psychological damage was actually suffered by the victims. 47

The *Hoge Raad*, however, sustains the judgment of the Civil Court[86]. It holds that the Court has apparently held that there was a very endangering situation whereby the victims waited in vain for help and assistance of the police. The Court clearly realised that the victims' fear was of course primarily caused by the hooligans. At the same time the Court apparently paid great attention to the fact that precisely in such a situation the sentiments of fear, insecurity and lack of safety with respect to health and property have largely increased as a 48

[86] *Hoge Raad* 9 July 2004, [2004] RvdW, 98.

result of the police failing to react to their repeated calls for help, help on which they could in the given circumstances have counted. The *Hoge Raad* therefore holds that the Court, taking into account the type and seriousness of this negligence which, according to the Court apparently led to a serious infringement of the personality rights and safety of the house, could judge that their personality rights were indeed infringed. In this case a proof of psychological damage is not required. The *Hoge Raad* only reforms the decision of the Civil Court as far as it had awarded non-pecuniary damages also to the youngest son of the family. It appeared that the youngest son was not at home during the incident and the parents had apparently called him and warned him not to come home and to sleep with friends. The Civil Court also awarded compensation for pain and suffering to him. That was, according to the *Hoge Raad*, not correct: the mere fact that someone's house is assaulted does not mean that that person is also violated in his personality rights.

7. Recourse Actions

49 In earlier Yearbooks we also pointed at the fact that there is much case law and legal doctrine on issues of recourse. Moreover we indicated that a dissertation was written dealing specifically with this topic[87]. An issue that is regularly dealt with, also in case law, is what the specific legal regime is that has to be applied in recourse actions. The general rule today is that the rules of the claim for damages that would apply to the claim of the victim should in the same way be applied to the recourse action as well, even though the recourse action is not a claim for compensation of damage. As a consequence, the *Hoge Raad* held that when, for instance, a health insurer of an employer starts a recourse action and claims compensation of internal administrative costs, the rules of Art. 6:96 al. 2 also apply. This means that, also in case of a recourse action, the plaintiffs seeking recourse can claim compensation of extra-procedural costs, in the same way as the victim could do so[88]. This means that, in as far as these costs would have been incurred by the victim and could be claimed by the victim, they can be claimed by the plaintiffs in a recourse action as well[89]. As a result of this, the rules of the law of damages are similarly applied to recourse actions as well. The reasoning is that on the one hand the injurer may not benefit from the fact that the victim had insurance; on the other hand the injurer should not be made worse off either by the simple fact that a party other than the victim himself files the tort claim.

50 Many problems also arise concerning the question of what type of statute of limitations applies to recourse actions. This is, in particular the case with

[87] See E.F.D. Engelhard, *Regres. Een onderzoek naar het Regresrecht van Particulieren en Sociale Schadedragers* (dissertation Maastricht University, 2003). See M. Faure/T. Hartlief (supra fn. 1), 314, no. 114.

[88] See on these issues of extra procedural costs M. Faure/T. Hartlief (supra fn. 1), 300–302, nos. 68–72.

[89] *Hoge Raad* 26 September 2003, [2003] NJ, 645 and *Hoge Raad* 9 July 2004, [2004] RvdW, 96.

claims based on the VOA (*Verhaalswet Ongevallen Ambtenaren*)[90]. As we explained in the previous Yearbook, in a *Hoge Raad* decision of 31 May 2002 it was decided that the five year statute of limitations of Art. 3:310 of the Civil Code had to be applied[91]. More recent case law deals with recourse actions of a guarantor. The Court of Appeals held that, in the absence of specific provisions, the general twenty year statute of limitations of Art. 3:306 of the Civil Code had to apply. Again the *Hoge Raad* holds that this is not correct and that the shorter (five year) statute of limitations of Art. 3:310 of the Civil Code had to be applied[92]. The *Hoge Raad* reaches this decision *inter alia* with a reference to the parliamentary history of the provision. The *Hoge Raad* holds that the goal of the recourse action of the guarantor who paid a debt is to prevent the debtor from being unjustifiably enriched by the fact that the guarantor has paid the creditor of the debtor. The *Hoge Raad* holds that the recourse action of the guarantor who paid is therefore to be considered as a "claim on compensation of damage" in the sense of Art. 3:310 of the Civil Code.

This decision probably has importance for other recourse actions also since in- 51
dependent recourse actions often have the same rationale as the recourse action of a guarantor. Hence it is reasonable to assume that also in these independent recourse actions the *Hoge Raad* will hold that the shorter five year statute of limitations of Art. 3:310 will apply. It is important to note in this respect that the statute of limitations for the recourse taker does not start at the same moment that the statute of limitations starts to run for the victim itself. The claim of the recourse taker indeed only emerges at the moment that the recourse taker pays the victim. That is hence the first moment that the statute of limitations can start to run. Moreover, also for the recourse taker the case law of the *Hoge Raad* may require that the statute of limitations only starts to run from the moment that the recourse taker is actually capable of filing a claim in tort. There can, for instance, be cases where the victim is aware of the damage and the identity of the injurer, but where that is not the case for the recourse taker. That can explain why in some cases the statute of limitations for the recourse taker starts to run later than for the victim.

8. Statute of Limitations

In the previous Yearbook we discussed at length the *Hoge Raad* decision of 52
31 October 2003 in the case of Saelman against the Academic Hospital of the Free University. One will recall that the *Hoge Raad* held in that case that the statute of limitations only starts to run the day after the moment at which the victim is really capable of filing a claim for compensation of the damage[93].

[90] The VOA is a statute that gives a right of recourse to the State for payments made to injured (or diseased) civil servants or their descendants.

[91] See M. Faure/T. Hartlief (supra fn. 53), 321–322, nos. 30–31.

[92] *Hoge Raad* 4 June 2004, [2004] RvdW, 80.

[93] See *Hoge Raad* 31 October 2003, [2003] RvdW, 169 and for a detailed discussion M. Faure/T. Hartlief (supra fn. 1), 304–306, nos. 82–84.

Meanwhile this case has been commented on extensively in the literature[94]. In these commentaries it is argued that it will often not be too clear at which moment the victim is really capable of filing a claim for compensation of the damage. One of the questions that arises in this respect is whether actual knowledge of the cause of the damage is necessary. A recent case of the *Hoge Raad* makes clear that that is not necessarily the case[95]. This particular case concerned water damage that was the result of negligence on the side of a constructor. For the possibility to file a claim for damages against the constructor it was, in the particular case, not relevant whether the water damage was caused by a leakage or by increased moisture in the house. In both cases it was clear against whom the lawsuit had to be filed. Hence there was at that moment the possibility to file a lawsuit and the statute of limitations started to run.

53 More complicated is the question whether the statute of limitations does not start to run as long as the plaintiff cannot file the lawsuit because of a lack of knowledge of the applicable law. One can indeed question whether the victim is capable of filing a lawsuit when the victim does know that there is damage and who is liable for the damage, but (given a lack of knowledge of the law) does not know that this person can actually be held liable as well. Meanwhile the *Hoge Raad* has clearly indicated that the ignorance of the law is no reason for the statute of limitations not to run.[96] More complicated are the cases where there is knowledge in the sense of the *Hoge Raad*, but the victim is not able to file a lawsuit for different reasons. There are well-known cases of the *Hoge Raad* concerning sexual abuse and child abuse. In those cases it was held that the victim could not file a claim earlier because of psychological circumstances that could more particularly be attributed to the injurer[97]. With the new formulation in the case law of the *Hoge Raad* concerning the moment at which the statute of limitations starts to run (the victim must be capable of filing a claim) the *Hoge Raad* suggests that also psychological circumstances which inhibit the victim from filing a lawsuit may be taken into account in this respect[98].

[94] See *inter alia* T. Hartlief, [2004] *Ars Aequi*, 266–275, J.L. Smeehuijzen, [2004] WPNR, 6572, 251–259 and P.C. Slangen, [2004] NTBR, 264–271.

[95] *Hoge Raad* 20 February 2004, [2004] RvdW, 37.

[96] *Hoge Raad* 26 November 2004, [2004] RvdW, 134.

[97] *Hoge Raad* 23 October 1998, [2000] NJ, 15 and *Hoge Raad* 25 June 1999, [2000] NJ, 16 with case note by A.R. Bloembergen.

[98] This was suggested by Attorney General De Vries Lentsch-Kostense in her opinion before *Hoge Raad* 17 September 2004, C03/134HR.

D. Doctrine

1. Doctrine with Respect to a Few Relevant Evolutions

a) Harmonization

As we already mentioned in the previous Yearbook[99] there is much debate on the benefits and possible dangers of harmonization of tort law in Europe. Also in the Netherlands the various works of the European groups on tort law receive a lot of attention. Some (more particularly Nieuwenhuis) have argued that the idea of a remaining diversity in Europe can be qualified as the "Romantic School of Maastricht"[100]. M. Faure and T. Hartlief wrote a reaction in which they analyzed the chances of survival of this romantic school which strongly believes in the praise of diversity in tort law in Europe[101]. In addition there is now an increasing awareness in the Netherlands that keeping track of European law is also necessary for those interested in tort law in the Netherlands, even if it were simply to be aware of evolutions concerning the use of tort law for violations of EC law[102]. 54

b) Defences

Some legal doctrine is very much occupied with the defences that could be used by a tortfeasor. Especially various scholars from the Nijmegen Law School have paid attention to this topic. It considers then more particularly the grounds of justification and excuse. Sieburgh draws a comparison between the use of defences in tort law and in criminal law[103]. Jansen addresses the defences of the tortfeasor from a legal historical perspective[104]. 55

c) Liability of Public Authorities

Above we already addressed that the liability of public authorities has led to a great deal of case law. Many publications have also again paid attention to this issue. For instance we can mention in this respect the monograph written by Scheltema & Scheltema[105]. Specific issues that were addressed concerning liability for public authorities are *inter alia* the insurance of this liability[106] as well as the liability of public authorities for rulings[107]. Also the question is in- 56

[99] M. Faure/T. Hartlief (supra fn. 1), 306–307, no. 87.

[100] J.H. Nieuwenhuis, *De Romantische Rechtsschool van Maastricht* (2003), 61–63.

[101] See M. Faure/T. Hartlief, in: *Liber Amicorum Tijdschrift voor Privaatrecht en Marcel Storme* (2004), 294–323.

[102] See on these issues *inter alia* the recent contributions by H.B. Krans, [2004] NJB, 571–576 and M.H. Wissink, [2004] AV&S, 145–156.

[103] C.H. Sieburgh, [2003] TPR, 647–683.

[104] C.J.H. Jansen, [2004] RM Themis, 120–126.

[105] M.W.& M. Scheltema, *Gemeenschappelijk Recht* (2003).

[106] See J.G.C. Kamphuisen, De verzekering van aansprakelijkheid van overheden, *Overheid en Aansprakelijkheid* (2003), 173–180.

[107] See in this respect the contributions of K.J. de Graaf and A.T. Marseille as well as from G.E. van Maanen in [2004] NJB, 779–784, 787–794. See also the contribution by R.J.N. Schlössels, 'Van Gog/Nederweert op de helling?', *Overheid en Aansprakelijkheid* (2004), 70–84.

creasingly asked whether a lack of monitoring control and enforcement could lead to liability of public authorities[108].

d) Employers' Liability

57 As we mentioned earlier, employers' liability is a topic that always leads to much debate in the Netherlands. Special attention in the legal doctrine is always given to the case law of the *Hoge Raad* and more particularly the way in which the employers' liability provision of Art. 7:658 of the Civil Code is interpreted[109]. As we mentioned earlier, employers' liability in the Netherlands would perhaps be in full evolution if a compulsory first party insurance for occupational risks were introduced. However, the Social Economic Council has, as we mentioned earlier, advised not to take any decisive steps in this respect at this moment. As a result, no further steps were taken by the government. Precisely that attitude has been criticized in a recent contribution by Van Boom[110].

2. Proceedings Volumes

a) J.M. Barendrecht/C.M.C. Van Zeeland/Y.P. Kamminga/I.N. Tzankova, *Schadeclaims: kan het goedkoper en minder belastend? Opties om de transactiekosten van het aansprakelijkheidsrecht te verlagen* (Boom Juridische Uitgevers, Den Haag 2004)

58 In this book the authors report on research they performed to examine whether the administrative costs of legal procedures, more particularly in liability law, could be reduced. They examine many instruments that could be used to reduce these costs, such as the introduction of alternative compensation mechanisms or standardization of amounts of liability and examine in what way these proposals could lead to a reduction of administrative costs.

b) W.H. van Boom/M.J. Borgers (eds.), *De rekenende rechter. Van „Iudex non calculat" naar actieve cijferaar?* (Boom Juridische Uitgevers, Den Haag 2004)

59 In this book various authors address the way in which lawyers and more particularly judges deal with numbers. Borgers discusses the way in which judges deal with statistical material; Nijboer addresses the role of statistics in criminal procedure and evidence and Van Boom addresses the importance of probability calculation in relation to damage suits. Barendrecht provides an example of a proportional division of liability in cases where accidents occur and Hammerstein analyses the use of statistical material from the perspective of the civil judge. Various other authors address similar issues, all related to the use of mathematics and more particularly statistical material by civil judges.

[108] This issue is more particularly addressed by C.L.G.F.H. Albers, Overheidsaansprakelijkheid voor gebrekkig toezicht en ontoereikende handhaving, [2004] *Nederlands tijdschrift voor bestuursrecht* (NTB), 201–211.

[109] See, with special attention to the potential problems of insurability, E.J. Blom, *Praktisch Procederen* (2004), 67 et seq.

[110] W.H. van Boom, [2004] TVP, 1–2.

c) P.J.M. Drion/J.H. Wansink/H.Th. Vos/B.K.M. Lauwerier (eds.), *Tussen persoon en recht. Afscheidsbundel Prof. Mr. J.G.C. Kamphuizen* (Kluwer, Deventer 2004)

This volume was drafted as a liber amicorum for the Nijmegen Insurance Law Professor Gerard Kamphuizen and contains many interesting contributions concerning insurance law, but also related to tort law. Well-known tort and insurance lawyers like Borgesius, Dorhout Mees, Cousy, Mendell and Wansink drafted contributions on a large variety of topics in insurance and tort law. 60

d) E. Engelhard/T. Hartlief/G.E. van Maanen (eds.), *Aansprakelijkheid in gezinsverband* (Boom Juridische Uitgevers, Den Haag 2004)

This volume contains various contributions that especially deal with the role of the family in tort law. Hartlief, for instance, deals with the question whether tort actions can be accepted in the context of family relationships. Cees van Dam deals with similar issues and adds the question what the consequences are for recourse actions by an insurer. Ten Hoopen and Verheij deal in their contribution with liability issues when a service to a friend has been performed. The issue of recourse is especially addressed in the contribution by Engelhard. The role of liability insurance in the family context is addressed in the contribution of Van Tichelen and Wansink. The interests of the unborn child are discussed by Forder whereas Hage discusses the wrongful life cases from a legal theoretical perspective. Koot addresses the role of contributory negligence in family relationships and Rutten addresses family relationships when other cultures are at stake. 61

e) A. Hartkamp/M. Hesselink/E. Hondius/C. Joustra/E. Du Perron/M. Veldman (eds.), *Towards a European Civil Code. Third fully revised and expanded edition* (Ars Aequi Libri, Nijmegen 2004)

This is the third edition of a volume dealing with various aspects of the European Civil Code. Although the setup of this volume is much broader than merely tort law, there is an entire chapter (pp. 607–724) that deals with tort. The chapters dealing with tort more particularly concern the general conditions of unlawfulness (David Howarth), product liability (G. Howells), the economic analysis of tort law and the European Civil Code (M. Faure), environmental liability (G. Betlem) and the frontier between contractual and tort liability in Europe (M. Bussani and V. Palmer). 62

f) Th. Veen/Ch.R. Coppens/G. Donker/S. Faber, *Prominenten kijken om. Achttien rechtsgeleerden uit de Lage Landen over leven, werk en recht* (Uitgeverij Verloren, Hilversum 2004)

In this proceedings volume interviews are published with eighteen lawyers from Belgium and the Netherlands who have played a major role in shaping the law in these countries. Although, again, the topics dealt with by these lawyers are broader than merely tort law, some of the issues are important for tort law as well. In this respect we can refer to the interviews with Schoordijk and Snijders who clearly deal with issues of private law and more particularly tort 63 law. The same is of course true for the interview with Van Gerven. But also some of the interviews with public lawyers such as Kortmann and Scheltema may have importance for tort law as well.

3. Monographs

a) M.W. Scheltema/M. Scheltema, *Gemeenschappelijk recht* (Kluwer, Deventer 2003).

64 This book pays attention to the division between private law and public law. It also deals with the liability of public authorities.

b) M. van Luyn/C.E. Du Perron, *Effecten van de zorgplicht. Klachten over effect en dienstverlening in de praktijk* (Kluwer, Deventer 2004)

65 This book deals with the duty of care of financial service providers dealing with stocks. Hence it addresses the amount of care that financial advisers and service providers should follow when advising and when transactions are executed. Moreover, the authors also address liability issues and more particularly the remedies (such as tort) that could be available when the duty of care is violated.

c) I. Giesen, *Toezicht en aansprakelijkheid* (Kluwer, Deventer 2005)

66 This book of the newly appointed Utrecht Professor Ivo Giesen provides a comparative overview of the liability in tort for public authorities with supervisory duties towards third parties. The liability of these public authorities, that have important controlling and supervisory duties, has become an increasingly important topic in the Netherlands. Often victims hold that the negligence in control and monitoring by supervisory authorities has caused their damage. Hence, Giesen addresses not only the positive Dutch tort law in this respect, but also the arguments in favour of and against an expanding liability in this domain, also using arguments from comparative law.

d) G.E. van Maanen/R. de Lange, *Onrechtmatige overheidsdaad. Rechtsbescherming door de burgerlijke rechter* (4th edn., Kluwer, Deventer 2005)

67 This is an important book that deals with the liability of public authorities towards third parties both from a public law and from a civil law perspective. All the actions a citizen could take to seek protection against wrongful acts of the government are discussed and the foundations of liability both in public law and in civil law are addressed. Also an overview of recent case law in this respect is given.

4. Dissertations

a) M.J. Kroeze, *Afgeleide schade en afgeleide actie* (dissertation Utrecht University, Kluwer, Deventer 2004)

This dissertation deals with a complicated topic, being the question whether the limited scope of the duty of care in tort law has a consequence that for instance an act that would be wrongful against the corporation would also be wrongful against the shareholders in such a corporation who can of course notice that the value of their stock will be reduced as a result of the wrongful act. The *Hoge Raad* is in principle very limited in awarding these more distant claims and it is more particularly this case law of the *Hoge Raad* that is the central topic in the dissertation of Kroeze. He in fact pleads strongly in favour of a right of action in tort law of shareholders. The advantage of such an action would be that they can recover their damage via such actions. 68

b) S. Lierman, *Voorzorg, preventie en aansprakelijkheid* (dissertation University of Antwerp, Intersentia, Antwerp 2004)

This book deals with an analysis of the precautionary principle and more particularly the application of the precautionary principle in medical liability for ionizing radiation. Moreover, Lierman examines whether the precautionary principle can be used to interpret the liability norm in tort law. 69

E. Concluding Remarks

Although also in the past period one could of course point at some cases and decisions of the *Hoge Raad* that may point in the direction of an expanding liability in tort, the best way to summarize the evolution of case law and at the policy level is probably to indicate the fact that the expanding liability in tort seems to be on the way back. In that respect we can point again at the fact that the recent cases concerning the application of the reversal rule seriously limit its application. Moreover, the case law with respect to employers' liability also points in the direction of more stringency instead of a further expanding liability. Some argue that this can be explained by the fact that the *Hoge Raad* stresses the individual responsibility of citizens and less the duty of care of various providers[111]. 70

One can however question whether that is really the case. For instance in the previous Yearbook we still discussed a case of the *Hoge Raad* where a far-reaching protection was awarded to citizens involved in the trade in stock options[112]. Those cases do not at all point in that direction, but still seem to stress the importance of duties of care. 71

[111] This was argued by W.J. Hengeveld/B.M. Jonk-van Wijk (de zorgplicht van de assurantie tussenpersoon), in: *Tussen persoon en recht* (2004), 107–135.
[112] See the discussion in M. Faure/T. Hartlief (supra fn. 1), 287–288, nos. 30–32.

72 However, one does indeed have the impression that the *Hoge Raad* does certainly not favour an expansion of tort suits against secondary tortfeasors such as public authorities or the State. Both the case of the barge, Linda and the case where the criminal on leave of absence caused damage concerned cases where someone other than the primary tortfeasor was addressed by the victim. In these cases the *Hoge Raad* clearly seems to be rather restrictive in allowing liability against those secondary tortfeasors. Nevertheless in legal doctrine the strong reservations formulated by the *Hoge Raad* are rather critically addressed as well[113].

73 Still more can be expected in the near future both from the legislator as well as from case law. As far as the legislator is concerned, several times we have referred to a draft act concerning the compensation for non-pecuniary losses. Notwithstanding severe criticism in the literature, it is likely that some legislative arrangement in this respect will come into being in the near future. As far as the "policy" of the *Hoge Raad* is concerned, one can clearly argue that certain cases that were rendered in this period (like the ones concerning the jet blast or concerning the barge, Linda) will have their influence on future decisions also. An important case that will be dealt with by the *Hoge Raad* in 2005 is the Kelly case concerning an issue of wrongful life. We already discussed the decisions of the Court of Appeals in that respect in a previous Yearbook. The decision of the *Hoge Raad* with respect to the wrongful life issue is expected to be very important since it may provide some insight into the question what, according to the *Hoge Raad*, the crucial functions of tort law in fact are. In that respect previous cases that we discussed in previous Yearbooks showed that there is still no clear line to be discovered. More certainty can therefore probably be expected from either the wrongful life or from other decisions that will be rendered by the *Hoge Raad* in the years to come.

[113] See particularly T. Hartlief, [2004] NTBR, 474–475, no. 31.

XVII. Norway

Bjarte Askeland

A. Legislation

There was no relevant legislation on tort law in 2004. 1

B. Cases

1. Norwegian Supreme Court, 30 January 2004, [2004] *Retstidende* (Rt.), 165[1]

a) Brief Summary of the Facts

A 22 year old man was found guilty of deliberately setting a home for elderly people on fire. He acted in this manner due to a sudden impulse in a state of confusion caused by his continuous use of drugs. The inhabitants were luckily saved but there was damage to property amounting to NOK 1.3 million. (approx. € 170,000). An insurance company paid for the cost of repairs and subsequently made a claim of recourse against the torfeasor. The primary issue the case dealt with was whether the facts of the case would qualify for an ad hoc reduction of the compensation sum. 2

b) Judgment of the Court

In § 5-2 *Skadeserstatningsloven* (Norwegian Compensation for Damage Act 1969, skl.) there is a legal basis for reducing the compensation sum after the use of ordinary assessment rules. The rule gives the judge a large margin of discretion although some guidelines are given. The judge shall put weight "on the extent of the damage, the financial abilities of the responsible party, the existence of insurance or insurance possibilities, gravity of fault and other relevant conditions". This is an exception from the general rule that a tortfeasor should restore the loss completely. The preparatory works to the act state that 3

[1] This Supreme Court case as well as the other cases referred to can be accessed in the internet: http://www.hoyesterett.no/4815.asp.

this exception is a narrow one and this is also emphasized by the Supreme Court.[2]

4 The court compared the case at hand to previous cases and found some differences. In earlier cases the lower courts had denied a reduction in compensation due to the gravity of the tortfeasor's act, namely that the acts were exercised with a determined criminal purpose. The court referred particularly to a case where a 20 year old man had deliberately set fire to a church because of his satanic beliefs. In considering the case at hand, the Supreme Court emphasised that the gravity of the tortfeasor was not as considerable as in the case mentioned. The court put weight on the fact that the tortfeasor had been influenced by drugs and the fact that he had acted on a sudden impulse. After a consideration of a totality of relevant factors, the court concluded ("having serious doubts") that the economic responsibility would be an unreasonable burden to the tortfeasor. Accordingly, the court reduced the sum of payment to NOK 700,000 (approximately € 85,000).

c) Commentary

5 The case illustrates how § 5-2 skl., a rule that is very similar to the ad hoc reduction rule in Art. 10:401 Principles of European Tort Law (PETL), is applied in Norwegian court practice. Although it is often emphasised that the rule in § 5-2 skl. is very narrow and is only applicable in exceptional cases, the referred case shows its application also where there is little cause for having sympathy with the torfeasor. The importance of the case lies within the fact that the court is willing to reduce the sum of payment even in cases where the plaintiff has intentionally committed a criminal act causing considerable danger to other people. It is hard to see how this could be an exceptional case where the facts comprised particularly mitigating circumstances in favour of the tortfeasor. Hence it is perfectly understandable that the judges hesitated in their finding, stating that they had serious doubts regarding their solution. Such a statement is very uncommon indeed for Supreme Court judges in Norway. The explanation of the result is probably that the judges simply felt sorry for the young man while at the same time they knew that it was an insurance company who would benefit from the full recourse. According to Norwegian law, the fact that the plaintiff was an insurance company is undoubtedly relevant when it comes to the question of ad hoc reduction, cf. § 5-2 skl.

6 The case shows the dangers of establishing a rule that makes the financial resources of the parties relevant. Such a rule will easily lead to a shifting of the loss from the poor to the rich. This may be a tempting solution in the case at hand, but such moves can lead to unwanted consequences for the tort law system taken as a whole. If one uses the intended exception rule to a large extent, there is a risk that the effect of all the other carefully constructed tort law rules will be undermined.

[2] E.g. Høyesterett (Norwegian Supreme Court, HR) 28 May 1997, [1997] Rt., 883.

2. Norwegian Supreme Court, 31 October 2003, [2003] Rt., 546

a) Brief Summary of the Facts

The plaintiff started smoking in 1953, and smoked on average 20 cigarettes a day throughout his life. He was diagnosed with lung cancer in 1996, and sued the tobacco company who was selling the brand of tobacco he preferred in 1999. He based his claim on the Norwegian rule of strict liability, holding that the selling of tobacco products was an activity that exposed the buyers to an extraordinary risk. The plaintiff died during the court proceedings, but his close relatives appealed his case to the Supreme Court. One should note that the basis of the claim was acts and omissions that took place a long time before *Produktansvarsloven* (the Norwegian act on product liability, pal.) of 1985, which today will apply to this kind of damage. 7

b) Judgment of the Court

The rule of strict liability under Norwegian law was developed by the courts in the aftermath of the industrial revolution in the last half of the nineteenth century. The rule applies when one can establish that there has been a "continuous", "typical" and "extraordinary" risk that has resulted in the harm at hand. However, even if one can determine that such characteristics are present in the factual situation in question, the courts will have a margin of discretion in deciding if liability should be attributed from more pragmatic points of view. One should note that the question of "extraordinary risk" depends on what is possible for the plaintiff to foresee, and the possibility he has to avoid the risk. 8

When applying the mentioned rule, the court placed weight on several pieces of evidence that served to prove that the dangers of smoking were known to "the plain and ordinary man" from 1964 onwards. The court then pointed out that the rule of strict liability in Norway first and foremost applies in situations where the victim is unable to guard himself against the risks, and that this was not the situation in the case at hand. The court then stated that information on the dangers in 1964 was such that an ordinary sensible man was able to take precautions. Accordingly, the plaintiff's continued smoking after the year of 1964 was an activity that he performed at his own risk. 9

The court then moved on to the situation before 1964. The court stated that common knowledge of the dangers of smoking was poorer at this stage, but nevertheless such that it was common knowledge that cigarette smoking could bring a risk of severe damage to one's health. The court then noted that it was doubtful whether the risk had all the characteristics which strict liability requires (cf. above). In addition, the court put weight on several arguments: 1) The case was not about errors in the manufacturing of the product; 2) the government had accepted the product as legal; 3) strict liability in this case would seem haphazard compared to the fate of many other people who had used tobacco before 1964 and had later died from smoking-related illnesses and 4) weight was put on the fact that the tobacco company had provided information 10 about the dangers of their products all along. Lastly, the court put weight on the fact that the smoker, in spite of all the risks and associated information, had made a personal, deliberate choice in taking up smoking. On these grounds the court found that there could be no strict liability in this case.

c) Commentary

11 The case is of importance as it puts an end to the discussion of the possibility of suing tobacco companies in Norway. It is likewise important because it delimits the range of the uncodified rule of strict liability in Norwegian law. The court's clear statement of the principle that the victim cannot claim compensation for damage he could have avoided is of interest to future cases. There has been a tendency to expand the limits of the rule of strict liability, and the mentioned statement can, in this respect, contribute to greater foreseeability.

12 Personally I agree with the result and the argument that strict liability should only apply when the victim has no possibility to foresee the risk. The last part of the judgment, which comprises a whole range of arguments, is less convincing. In my opinion, the judgment brought in a number of pragmatic arguments unnecessarily as the case could have been decided on the grounds of principles thus resulting in greater clarity. Additionally it is hard to see how the fact that the tobacco company had provided proper information about the dangers is relevant when the case is about *strict* liability.

3. Norwegian Supreme Court, 13 November 2003, [2003] Rt., 1601

a) Brief Summary of the Facts

13 In 1994 a 30 year old woman was badly injured in a car accident. The victim is now in need of help for eating and has no control of her bodily functions. The county council where the woman lived incurred a lot of expenses purporting to satisfy the needs of nursing and caring for the traffic victim. The county council estimated their costs in providing nursing and caring for the victim over the years 1995–2003 to be approximately NOK 7 million (approx. € 900,000). The claim for future losses was approx. NOK 12 million (approx. € 1.5 million). The county council claimed the right of recourse for these costs from the traffic insurer. It was held that the traffic insurer was the one that eventually should pay for all the costs caused by the accident, including those costs that the county council incurred. The legal basis of their claim was the Norwegian general principle of recourse: One who has covered a loss that the tortfeasor by law is obliged to pay, is entitled to a reimbursement paid by the tortfeasor.

b) Judgment of the Court

14 The claim for recourse was not granted by the Supreme Court. The reason for the judgment was a combination of a number of arguments, the most important mentioned below.

The court emphasized that the right to recourse for the municipality had never been mentioned in the preparatory works of statutes regarding tort law. Such claims had never been made except for one case in 1970 where a claim of recourse was dismissed. The plaintiff did not appeal the case, and the Supreme Court submitted that this was in accordance with the opinion in the county councils and in the insurance companies throughout the nation. The Supreme Court also referred to a statute in § 3–7 sec. 1. skl. This statute bars the social security institutions from having recourse for costs in providing the cost of living to Norwegian citizens. The court did not use this statute by analogy, because they stated that they had enough arguments to reach the conclusion that recourse should be denied. Instead the court pointed out some similarities between the social security institutions and the county councils. In this way the court was partially using analogical reasoning without the burden of openly admitting that they were building their result on an analogy from § 3–7 sec. 1. skl. Eventually the court submitted that recourse would change the legal framework that the insurance companies have been relying on for a number of years. 15

c) Commentary

In my opinion, the reasoning in this case is open to critique from two angles. Firstly, it is an unlucky turn to deny recourse on a number of pragmatic arguments. In this way one undermines the general principle of recourse and it remains uncertain to which degree such a rule exists in Norwegian law. Secondly, the result in the case could have been fully supported by relying on earlier decisions from the Supreme Court which presupposes that there can be no recourse. In several decisions the Supreme Court has made it clear that, regarding expenses related to nursing and care, the plaintiff has to settle for the help that is given from the public national health service. One is not entitled to make additional claims towards the tortfeasor or his insurer. The decisions state that the tortfeasor/insurance companies only have to pay for other expenses not related to treatment or maintaining health. When this kind of system (the system of reduction[3]) is established, it is evident that there can be no recourse claim from the county council. This critique of the decision is put forward in an article.[4] 16

4. Norwegian Supreme Court, 25 November 2004

a) Brief Summary of the Facts

One of the plaintiffs (A) owned 66% of the shares in a small limited company (B) that produced signs. He worked in the company and received an ordinary salary in return. A was a key worker and he therefore held that he generated income for the company on a higher level than his salary reflected. In 1997 A 17

[3] Cf. R. Lewis, *Deducting Benefits from Damages for Personal Injury* (1999), 43–47.
[4] Askeland, Regress og regress-avskjæring – Rt. 2003, 1601, [2004] *Tidsskrift for Erstatningsrett* (TfE), 43–60.

had a traffic accident and he lost his ability to work for the company. The traffic insurer agreed to pay compensation for A's loss of income as paid through his salary. A claimed in addition that he must be paid compensation that reflected the fact that the profit of his shares in the company was lowered because of the fact that he had stopped working for the company due to the accident. The other plaintiff was the company B, which also claimed compensation from the traffic insurer, holding that the company as a third party had suffered economic loss because of the accident.

b) Judgment of the Court

18 The court was divided in its decision. The three judges in the majority of the court stated that A could not claim any compensation in addition to his compensation for loss of salary. The court emphasized that the company was a legal personality separate from A. The loss that the personal injury had caused was therefore first and foremost a loss that was placed upon the company as a legal entity. The fact that the company's loss indirectly made the shares in the company less valuable, was an effect that in itself could not lead to compensation.

19 The majority then moved on to the question of whether the company B could claim compensation. Under Norwegian law, this question deals with remoteness in causation. It has been held in Norwegian doctrinal literature that the employer's loss stemming from his employee's illness in general is too remote to constitute a claim on the part of the employer.[5] The court built upon this theoretical statement and thus found that B had no claim. The fact that the employee owned 66% of the shares in B and that he was a key worker could not alter the principles that this solution rested upon, namely that the limited company in every way must be regarded as a legal person itself. When the owner of the shares, partly for tax reasons, had chosen to channel his income in an arrangement which comprised establishing a limited company, he must bear the consequences, also when they do not benefit him.

20 The minority of the Supreme Court (two judges) found that the traffic insurer had to pay compensation also for A's lost profit from his shares. The minority pointed to the fact that the statute that regulates the compensation for personal injuries, § 3-1 skl. does not exclude this kind of loss. Moreover, compensation for lost profit would be in accordance with the aim of the rules of compensation. Additionally, the profit channelled through a limited company was compared with profit channelled through a firm/enterprise with unlimited personal responsibility. The differences between these two arrangements were found not to be relevant to tort law and the question of compensation. Therefore, the minority of the court held that A should have been compensated. *Obiter dictum* the minority also stated that the company B should have the right to compensation because they had a close interest in their key workers' well-being. Hence B's loss was not regarded as too remote.

[5] N. Nygaard, *Skade og ansvar* (5th edn. 2000), 58.

c) Commentary

The decision is of great academic interest as it affects both the Norwegian doctrine of remoteness of damage and the question of whether one should respect the form of limited companies in relation to tort law. Both these questions have repeatedly been debated in legal theory and there have also been a number of cases which have left the overall picture quite blurred. As the judges disagreed on profound points, I am afraid that the last words on the issue have not been spoken. 21

The Norwegian approach to Supreme Court decisions in general is that they should be followed by the lower courts, also when there has been a judgment with a dissenting opinion. Accordingly, the lower courts should respect the majority decision and consequently respect the form of the limited company also when it comes to tort law. 22

Personally I agree with the majority of the judges mostly because otherwise great uncertainty would be brought into the picture of risks and the balance between possible tortfeasors and possible sufferers of damage. I do not believe in a sort of tort law-based "piercing the corporate veil" on the plaintiffs' side, as this would rock the principles of company law and the law of obligations. Moreover, there are good reasons for limiting compensation from the tortfeasor exclusively to the party who suffers personal injury. Otherwise the consequences are unpredictable. It should be sufficient to point to an imagined case of a severely injured football-star who indirectly generates large sums of money for his employer, the football club. Should the club have the opportunity to claim compensation for its losses when the famous footballer is injured in a traffic accident? Surely there must be limits to compensation here, and the limits must be based on principles, exactly those kinds of principles that the majority of the Supreme Court is applying. 23

5. Norwegian Supreme Court, 26 January 2004, [2004] Rt., 122

a) Brief Summary of the Facts

A dentist suffered from allergic reactions that stemmed from his use of a certain tooth maintaining material. The allergic reaction broke out in a rash on his hands. Later he experienced itchiness and sometimes pain in his fingertips. He also suffered from headaches and irritation in his breathing organs. The dentist had medical treatment but it eventually became clear that he could not continue working as a dentist using the mentioned material. The dentist sued the importer of the material under the Norwegian statute on product liability, *Produktansvarsloven* (pal.) which was enacted as an implementation of the EC Directive on Product Liability 85/374/EEC. 24

b) Judgment of the Court

According to § 2-1 pal., the court had to decide whether the product in question did or did not offer the security that a user reasonably could expect. In the 25 preparatory works of the act it was stated that the rule would not apply where the damage was caused by a risk that was known to the user and necessary for the function of the product. The court found that this description fitted the case at hand and they therefore acquitted the defendant. As an *obiter dictum* the Supreme Court pointed out that the plaintiff could not alternatively achieve compensation on the basis of strict liability because of the fact that Art. 13 Directive 85/374/EEC prevents the national legal orders from providing the consumers a more wide-ranging right to compensation than what is prescribed in the Product Liability Directive. In this respect the court referred to a decision from the European Court of Justice (ECJ) Case C-183/00.[6]

c) Commentary

26 The case is in itself not controversial as the solution had very strong support in the preparatory works. It is nevertheless interesting that a professional due to a product with a safety risk is forced to leave his occupation without compensation. The explanation of this seemingly unreasonable result lies within the fact that the dentist entered his occupation with knowledge of the risks connected with the material in question. One can, therefore, see the interpretation of pal. and the Supreme Court decision as connected with the principle of assumption of risk.

27 Of greater interest is the *obiter dictum* that limits the range of case-based strict liability in Norwegian law. Previously an uncodified basis of liability for dangerous products existed which, in principle, would apply even if pal. did not provide compensation for the damage. Now the Norwegian rule of strict liability has seemingly been narrowed through the referred case and its confirmation of the interpretation of Art. 13 85/374/EEC that was put forward in Case C-183/00. This is an example of how community law is affecting Norwegian tort law. The range of the EC influence has been debated by Norwegian commentators, a debate that will be outlined below.

C. Literature

1. Are Stenvik, Produktansvar for tobakkskader (Product liability for tobacco damage), [2004] *Lov og Rett* (LoR), 199–207

28 This rather short article is about the tension between the EC-initiated rules on product liability and the older uncodified rule of strict liability. The author points out that the tobacco case referred to above should have been solved in the light of the EC-rules on product liability even if the facts of the case mostly concerned acts which occurred long before the enactment of the product liability act in 1988. The author emphasises the importance of the three ECJ-decisions of 2002 concerning Art. 13 of the EC-directive on Product Liability

[6] Case C-183/00 *Sanchez v. Medicina Asturiana*, European Court Reports (ECR), I –3901.

85/374.[7] Because of these cases Stenvik maintains that the uncodified rule of strict liability in Norwegian law should be limited, and that no such rule can apply in the area of damage caused by products.

Moreover, the article stresses that Norwegian tort law should now be harmonised with European tort law also in the fields of law which are not yet regulated by the *acquis communautaire*. This view is founded in the general opinion that tort law, without harmonisation, may detrimentally affect European competition. The article is important since it is quite rare that a scholar proposes that Norwegian tort law should be harmonised even outside the areas that are regulated by EC directives. The article is additionally of great interest because the author states that Norwegian tort law can no longer maintain the uncodified rule of strict liability as long as the other European countries basically favour fault-based rules. 29

Lastly the author argues that tort law rules and product liability rules aim at inducing citizens to act in a safe manner. The tobacco companies and their selling of tobacco can, therefore, not be subject to tort law rules because it is not possible to make the product more secure or to replace it with a more secure substitute. One must, therefore, fight the damage to health that is caused by the use of tobacco through means other than tort law. 30

2. Asbjørn Kjønstad, Ulovfestet objektivt erstatningsansvar (On uncodified strict liability), [2004] *Tidsskrift for Erstatningsrett* (TfE), 99–122

This article is about the uncodified rule of strict liability in Norwegian law. The author goes through every aspect of the rule, and gives his personal comments on the more controversial issues regarding the rule of strict liability. Still it is fair to say that the article is more of an overview or an outline of the rule of strict liability than an innovative work. Despite this, the article is of a certain interest because it confirms the rule on strict liability as we know it, and does not take into consideration any of the aspects which are contemplated by Stenvik. In the article referred to below, Kjønstad discusses Stenvik's arguments on harmonisation with European tort law. 31

3. Asbjørn Kjønstad, Det nyeste rettskildematerialet om det ulovfestede objektive erstatningsansvaret (The latest development on uncodified strict liability), [2004] LoR, 579–605

In this article the author elaborates on the legal consequences of the two Supreme Court cases referred to above (supra nos. 7 et seq. and 24 et seq.). As mentioned above, the two cases both delimit the range of the case-based rule of strict liability under Norwegian law. The primary issue the article seems to defend is the Norwegian traditional rule of strict liability. The author both crit- 32

[7] Case C 52/00 *The Commission v. France* ECR 2002, I-3827, Case C 154/00 *The Commission v. Greece* ECR 2002, I-3879 and Case C 183/00 *Sanchez v. Medicina Asturiana*, ECR, I-3901.

icises the mentioned decisions and brings forward arguments in support of the traditional wide-ranging rule of strict liability.

33 Kjønstad disagrees with the result in the tobacco case and he holds that the judges were putting too much weight on the plaintiff's acceptance of risks. He supports this view by referring to other cases where the Supreme Court has granted compensation on the legal basis of the strict liability rule.

34 Furthermore Kjønstad attacks the assumption that Art. 13 Directive 85/374/EEC prevents Norway from applying the uncodified strict liability rule in the area of product liability. Kjønstad points out that § 1-1 pal. in its wording makes it clear that pal. does not delimit *other legal bases* of compensation. When the Norwegian state enacted this rule in 1992 it made a deliberate choice not to delimit the range of strict liability. Kjønstad maintains that the three 2002-cases of ECJ[8] therefore do not alter Norwegian tort law at this point. The argument is supported by references to the fact that Norway, when enacting the EØS-lov (the Norwegian Act on joining the EEA agreement), did not grant the future decisions of the ECJ binding force in relation to Norwegian law. The Norwegian Supreme Court has confirmed this by stating that a Norwegian statute that is impossible to interpret in accordance with the directive must apply even if it does not comply with an EC-directive.[9]

35 In this manner Kjønstad disagrees with Stenvik's assumption presented in supra no. 28. He maintains that the uncodified rule of strict liability applies even when a product causes harm, also in situations where the codified product liability rules in pal. do not apply. Kjønstad also embraces the traditional uncodified rule of strict liability more broadly.[10]

36 Kjønstad's and Stenvik's articles taken together form a very interesting debate on the subject of future Norwegian tort law and harmonisation with European law. The question of whether and to which degree the national tort law must be altered in order to comply with community law will certainly be raised again.

4. Morten Kjelland, Bråtane-dommen – Rt. 2002 p. 1436, [2004] TfE, 3–42

37 The article is a review of a 2002 Supreme Court decision on compensation for personal injuries. The case was about a girl who at the age of 11 collided with a car while riding a horse. As a result of the accident, she was disabled, but now, at the age of 22, she lives an active life as a student. She claimed compensation from the traffic insurance company to cover a full-time assistant helping her to lead "an independent" life. The case concerns the limits of com-

[8] Supra fn. 7.
[9] Cf. HR 16 November 2000, [2000] Rt., 1811.
[10] The content of the rule is explained in supra no. 8.

pensation for this kind of damage, and the article analyses the lines that are drawn by the court.

One point that is particularly interesting is that the court in the mentioned case based their assessment of damages on the fact that the plaintiff had an extraordinary ability and will to make the most of her situation as disabled. She did so by starting to study theology. In her daily life as a student she needed personal assistance that must be paid for. The court found that the costs of this assistance should be compensated. In this way the plaintiff's intellectual capacity in a way resulted in special expenses. The article analyses the principle that the judgment is based upon: The principle stating that compensation is given only as far as the expenses incurred are "necessary and reasonable". The investments one wants to be reimbursed for must accordingly be able to have a positive effect on the plaintiff's situation in terms of taking care of everyday needs. The author's point seems to be the idea that one who has great intellectual capacity should not get more compensation than someone who does not have the same use for assistance. Apparently the author considers granting different levels of compensation for the two victims mentioned to be unfair, because the plaintiffs should be treated equally. The author also emphasises that the assessment should not be done in such a manner that one implies that the plaintiffs could have a different human value. 38

Personally I do not agree with the author's criticism of the court's decision. There is, in my opinion, nothing peculiar in assessing damages based on the individual facts in the individual case. The fact that one disabled individual is passive, not trying to obtain an education while the other is trying hard to do so, is a factual difference that is simply important for making a precise assessment of damages. 39

XVIII. Poland

Ewa Bagińska

A. Legislation

1. Law on the Revision of the Civil Code of 17 June 2004 *Dziennik Ustaw* (Journal of Laws, Dz. U.) 2004, no. 162, at 1692

1 The amendments to the civil code (1964, KC) relate to public liability rules. Art. 417 § 1 KC in its new version provides for a general rule of liability for damage resulting from an unlawful exercise of public authority. New articles, 417^1 and 417^2 have been inserted into the code, and artt. 419, 420, 420^1 and 420^2 have been repealed. The latter related to the liability of local authorities, their associations and functionaries, and of public legal persons. Those persons' activities may now fall under the general rule of art. 417 KC. The law came into force on 1 September 2004 and applies to the facts and legal situations occurring after this date.

2 Art. 417 states that the liability for damage caused by illegal action or omission in the course of the exercise of public authority rests with the State Treasury, a local authority or other legal person who exercises authority conferred upon it by law. According to § 2, if the exercise of tasks falling within the scope of public authority was delegated to a local authority or other legal person by way of an arrangement, both the performer of the task and the State Treasury or the local authority who delegated the tasks are liable and their liability is joint and several.

3 If the damage has been caused through enactment of a legal act, compensation may be demanded only when in proper proceedings the legal act has been declared void on the ground of its unconstitutionality or non-conformity with an international agreement or a statute (art. 417^1 § 1). If the damage has been caused through rendering of a valid judgment or a final decision, compensation may be demanded only after having its illegality declared in proper proceedings. The same applies to a case where a valid judgment or a final decision have been rendered on the basis of a legislative act not conforming with the Constitution or an international agreement or a statute (art. 417^1 § 2).

If the damage resulted from omission to render a judgment or decision, when a provision of law provides for such a duty, compensation may be demanded only after having the illegality of the omission declared in proper proceedings, unless special rules provide otherwise (art. 417¹ § 3). 4

If the damage resulted from omission to issue a legal act, where there is a legal duty to issue such act, the court hearing the claims for compensation determines the illegality of the omission (art. 417¹ § 4). 5

If a lawful exercise of public authority brings about damage to a person, an aggrieved party may claim full or partial compensation including damages for non-pecuniary loss, when the circumstances, and in particular the inability of the injured person to work or a difficult financial situation, show that the considerations of equity (justice) so require (art. 417²). 6

The above-presented rules are not applicable if liability for damage resulting from the exercise of public authority is subject to special rules (art. 421), such as in the case of compensation for unjust detention and arrest, the liability of court enforcement officers and the liability for taxation decisions. The Act of 2004 repeals the relevant provisions of the code of administrative procedure (artt. 153, 160, 161 § 5) and by this move the legislator ensured that almost all cases of governmental liability are embraced by the rules contained in the civil code. As concerns fiscal organs, their liability is subject to art. 260 of the tax law, but damages are awarded according to the civil code rules (art. 4 of the Act of 2004). 7

The present revision of the civil code is meant to adjust the civil code to the new constitutional model of State liability[1]. It is the most significant change in tort rules since the enactment of the code in 1964. The new regime of public authority liability is liability without fault (strict liability). The most important novelties are: the introduction of the liability for legislative wrongs, liability for the omission to issue a jurisdictional act or a legislative act, putting all the persons exercising prerogatives on equal footing, irrespectively of the public/private ownership[2]. 8

Long awaited by the doctrine, the actual shape of the regime of public authorities' liability accepted by the parliament is not without flaws. The problems in the interpretation of the rules, already remarked by the doctrine (see the literature cited infra nos. 64, 67, 69, 70) are: the definition of the notion "exer- 9

[1] See the previous draft in E. Bagińska, Poland, in: H. Koziol/B.C. Steininger (eds.), *European Tort Law 2003* (2004), 329. About the constitutional model see E. Bagińska, Poland, in: H. Koziol/B.C. Steininger (eds.), *European Tort Law 2001* (2002), 382.

[2] See E. Bagińska, Liability of Public Authorities for Damage to Individuals: Is Article 77 of the Polish Constitution a Model Solution?, in: A. Bodnar/M. Kowalski/K. Raible/F. Schorkopf (eds.), *The Emerging Constitutional Law of the European Union – German and Polish Perspectives*, Beiträge zum ausländischen öffentlichen Recht und Völkerrecht 163 (2003), 185.

cise of public authority" and the relation of "contrary to law/illegality" to the civil wrongfulness.

10 The notion "exercise of public authority" refers to all kinds of activities, which usually, but not always, mean the ability to affect the rights, liberties or interests of individuals (*actes de pouvoir*). It also includes the judiciary, whose liability has rarely been admitted by the Supreme Court. Contrary to the previous position of the jurisprudence, the present wording of the civil code does not exclude the legislature from liability for damages. The change marks a milestone in the protection of individuals against unlawful acts of organs exercising legislative powers in Poland. Illegality of a public authority's conduct is to be regarded as a sole condition of liability, but it is disputable whether the common courts should follow the Constitutional Tribunal in its strict, constitutional interpretation of this notion (see also infra nos. 64, 70).

2. Act of 17 June 2004 on the claim for the violation of the right to judicial proceedings within a reasonable time, Dz. U. no. 179, at 1843

11 The law is designed to fulfill Poland's obligations of providing an effective means of ensuring that art. 6 of the European Convention on Human Rights is observed. A party to any court proceedings, including the enforcement proceedings, may file a claim for the violation of her rights due to an unreasonable delay of the proceedings, provided they have not ended. The court may order the trial court to take necessary measures in a given time framework and may award the plaintiff "an appropriate sum" not exceeding PLN 10,000 (€ 2,500). The compensation is to be paid by the State Treasury. A party whose claim was recognized may institute a separate legal action for the recovery of any damage, including non-pecuniary loss, that ensued from the unreasonable delay in court proceedings. The court hearing the suit for damages is bound by the judgment declaring the delay in the said proceedings. The statutory cause of action does not bar a claim for damages, based on art. 417 KC, filed after the ending of the proceedings.

B. Cases

1. *Sąd Najwyższy* (Polish Supreme Court, SN) 21 May 2003, IV CKN 378/01, [2004] *Orzecznictwo Sądów Polskich* (OSP) 4, at 55[3]: Tort Claims' Prescription

a) Brief Summary of the Facts

12 In 1964 the plaintiff was vaccinated with a vaccine whose validity had expired. As a result she suffered serious personal injury, for which she claimed compensation in 1965. In this lawsuit she seeks damages for non-pecuniary

[3] = [2004] *Orzecznictwo Sądu Najwyższego Izba Cywilna* (OSNC) 7–8, at 124.

loss she has suffered in the past three years. The plaintiff alleges that in 1998 she had to undergo heart surgery, during which she experienced a life-saving procedure. In the first two instances the courts dismissed the claim holding that all former and present claims resulting from the vaccination are time-barred.

b) Judgment of the Court

The main issue in the cassation is the interpretation of one of the two rules on time limits for the claims brought in tort, provided for in art. 442 KC. A claim for redress of damage caused by a tort is subject to limitation on the expiration of three years from the day on which the injured person learned of the damage and of the person obliged to redress it. In any event, however, the claim is subject to limitation after the passage of ten years from the day on which the event causing the damage occurred (art. 442 § 1 KC). 13

The Court observes the two possible ways of interpreting sentence 2 of art. 442 that have been offered in the case law since the introduction of the rule in the code of obligations (1933). The currently dominant case law and doctrinal positions hold that the ten-year period is a maximum and must always be counted from the day of the tort, and not from the day of the awareness of the damage.[4] This Court takes the opposite view, also found in the legal writing, according to which the time period begins to run from the day on which the damage occurred. 14

According to the Court, when interpreting art. 442 KC, one should not ignore the general rule of art. 120 § 1 KC stating that the period of limitation begins to run on the day the claim accrues. If the damage has not occurred, the claim for damages does not even arise. Thus, the literal interpretation of art. 442 KC would limit its application to typical situations where the time of the event and the time when the damage resulting from it occurs are the same or very close. The functional interpretation allows for the true right to demand compensation in cases where the damage occurred long after the event constituting its cause. It is also preferable in the light of art. 77 of the Constitution regarding claims brought against public authorities. 15

In contrast to the development and enlargement of the same injury, new losses have a separate existence and mark their own beginning of the limitation period[5]. The Supreme Court holds that the plaintiff's pain and suffering arising from the heart surgery could not be *a priori* rejected as a new damage. The lower courts should have examined the existence of the adequate causation between this new damage and the vaccination in 1964 and then whether the consequences of the vaccination, even those occurring in 1998, were reasonably foreseeable during the first lawsuit. The judgment was reversed and remanded. 16

[4] SN of 12 February 1969 [1969], OSN, 150.
[5] SN of 24 November 1971 [1972], OSN, 95.

c) Commentary

17 The decision is remarkable since it gives a new interpretation to art. 442 KC. This norm, although criticised by courts and doctrine, has not been changed since the 1933 code of obligations, with the exception of the shortening of the prescription period from 20 to 10 years in 1950. Hence, now not only is the prescription time shorter than in the main European codes (30 years), but also it puts at a disadvantage all victims whose damage occurred later than ten years after the tort. Dealing with the problem of time-prescribed tort claims, the Supreme Court admitted that the injured person could obtain a declaratory judgment stating a defendant's liability for future damage. Then, the limitation period for the new claims would begin to run on the day when the injured person learned of the new damage[6]. This solution has one flaw: it could not be used whenever the first damage did not occur until after ten years since the tort.

18 The commented judgment represents the second path of case law starting to gain more support in the doctrine[7]. It emphasises the prevailing role of the general rule of art. 120 KC. Thus, the claim for compensation will not arise until the damage actually occurs. Although one might say that the interpretation proffered by the Supreme Court is *contra legem*, this functional approach enhances the position of the injured. Nevertheless, the situation calls for the intervention of the legislator.

2. SN of 21 November 2003, VCK 16/03, [2004] OSNC 6, at 104: Wrongful Conception

a) Brief Summary of the Facts

19 The plaintiffs, a woman and her son, claim compensation for damage caused by the fact that the woman was "made to give birth to a child". In 1996, after having been raped, the plaintiff was referred to a public hospital for an abortion, to which she was entitled by law. It was based on a prosecutor's statement of the crime committed as well as on the medical examination of the state of her pregnancy (11 weeks). However, further examination in the hospital revealed that the plaintiff was in the 14th week of her pregnancy and, in addition, the woman did not provide the hospital with permission from a prosecutor for the abortion procedure (which was required by law). Thus, the hospital refused to perform the procedure because the pregnancy exceeded 12 weeks. When the plaintiff came to the prosecutor's office in order to obtain the permission, the latter decided to call an expert gynaecologist to determine the duration of the pregnancy and whether it was causally related to the rape. The plaintiff failed to show up for two appointments with the expert. As a consequence, she gave birth to a healthy child in due time.

[6] SN of 17 February 1972, [1972] OSN, 149.
[7] See M. Nesterowicz, Note to the judgment, [2004] OSP 55, 237.

The woman claims damages for non-pecuniary loss arising from the violation of her personality rights (making her give birth to a child conceived during a rape) as well as damages for the loss of income since the date of the visit in the hospital until the date of filing the suit. On behalf of her son she demands an annuity amounting to his monthly maintenance costs. The defendants are the local authority answering for the hospital (the defendant) and the State Treasury. 20

The Regional Court recognised that only the local authority has legal standing in the lawsuit. However, it dismissed the claim holding that a prosecutor is independent in establishing whether there is sufficient suspicion that a pregnancy has been caused by a rape. On appeal, the court of appeals held that the civil code provisions on personal injury do not embrace the birth of a child and there is no ground for the maintenance of the child by the community. 21

b) Judgment of the Court

There is no question that the law on family planning and abortion in art. 4a subparagraph 1[8] allows abortion to be performed when there is a justified suspicion that the pregnancy occurred as a result of a criminal offence. However, in such case, abortion is admitted (also in a private surgery, exclusively by a qualified physician), if the pregnancy is not older than 12 weeks. The circumstances that the pregnancy occurred as a result of an offence must be confirmed by a prosecutor's certificate. Under those conditions a woman may demand to have an abortion even in a public medical institution. Despite a prosecutor's certificate that the pregnancy occurred as a result of a criminal offence, the physician has no right to abort it when there are medical contraindications. 22

The Court recognises a distinctive character of the case and refers to foreign case law and doctrine concerning wrongful conception as well as to the jurisprudence of the ECHR in Strasbourg. The Court accepts in general that a right to plan a family is protected by the civil code (art. 23) as a personality right and by the Constitution as liberty. The violation of that right gives a ground for seeking compensation on the basis of art. 448 KC. However, the plaintiff's claim for compensation could not stand because at the time of an alleged violation art. 448 KC did not provide for damages to be paid to the party whose personality rights were violated. Art. 448 KC was altered by the Act of 23 August 1996 (Dz.U. no. 114 at 542)[9]. 23

The Court holds that a woman is entitled to recover identified pecuniary losses stemming from the failure to perform an abortion if she had a statutory right to 24

[8] 7 January 1993 *Law on Family Planning, Protection of a Human Foetus and Conditions for Abortion Admissibility* (*Journal of Laws* no. 17, item 78).

[9] Previously, an injured person whose personal interests have been infringed could demand that the wrongdoer pay an adequate sum for the benefit of the Polish Red Cross, provided there was an intentional fault.

this procedure. The damages would embrace the expenses linked to the pregnancy and birth, as well as the loss of income causally related to those events. Within the boundaries of the adequate causation test, the loss of income concerns damage suffered in a reasonable period of pregnancy and childcare.

25 In response to the defendant, the Court states that there is no duty to put an "unwanted" child up for adoption. Thus, if after the child's birth the plaintiff changed her primary intention to do so, it may not be alleged that she had not prevented the substantial part of the damage.

26 The local authority, which operated the hospital at the time, could be held liable for the physicians employed at the hospital. According to the Court, the management of health care services may be regarded as exercising public authority, thus in the light of art. 77 of the Constitution, no fault of the functionary needs to be proven.

27 Having ruled that the plaintiff (mother) has a right to compensation but her healthy born child has not, the Court reverses and remands the case for retrial because essential facts of the case were not established (the actual length of pregnancy, the causal link between the hospital examination and the refusal by a prosecutor to issue a certificate).

c) Commentary

28 Although in the case at hand the plaintiff could not succeed in claiming compensation for herself based on the violation of her right to planned procreation, this landmark decision has full effect in cases governed by current law. Previously the Supreme Court, in two judgments, accepted a woman's claim for compensation for the birth of a child, but both were medical malpractice cases. This decision makes clear that only a mother, and not her healthy though unwanted child, is entitled to both pecuniary and non-pecuniary damages. This judgment brings Polish law in line with the other European and American jurisdictions[10]. However, the Court's qualification of the right to planned family as a personality right met with some criticism, founded upon the assumption that there is no conflict between the right to live and the right to an abortion (the former prevails)[11].

3. SN of 13 June 2003, IV CZP 32/03, [2004] OSN 4, at 51: Indemnity from Insurer, Car Repair Costs

a) Brief Summary of the Facts

29 The plaintiffs were assignees of the claims against an insurer (the defendant) for the reimbursement of the costs of repair of the car damaged in a road accident for which the insurer bears liability. The amount of the sought claim is

[10] See M. Nesterowicz, Note to the judgment, [2004] OSP 10, 531; T. Justyński, Note to the judgment, [2004] *Państwo i Prawo* 9, 122.

[11] See S. Rudnicki, Note to the judgment, [2004] *Monitor Prawniczy* 10, 475.

the difference between the costs actually borne and the sum paid by the defendant as indemnity. The regional court filed a preliminary question with the Supreme Court as to whether the insurer is obliged to pay the actual costs of repair or the costs calculated by an expert according to the average prices of services necessary for the repair.

b) Judgment of the Court

Firstly, there was no disagreement between the parties about the necessity of the repair to the damaged car and about the scope and methodology of that repair. Secondly, the injured party chose the garage where he had his car restored to the previous technical condition necessary for using it and then presented the invoices for that service to the insurer for reimbursement. It is clear that the aggrieved party may elect where to have a car repaired, based on criteria such as high professional standard, authorised spare parts, etc. The Supreme Court has already explained that there is no duty to search for the cheapest service. However, the restitution should only cover the indispensable and economically justified cost of repair. 30

Servicing garages apply different prices and different methods of calculation. The prices in a garage are economically justified regardless of whether they deviate (in plus) from the average market prices of a certain type of services. If the right of the claimant to elect a garage has not been questioned, then the prices used by such garage should be the measurement of indemnity. 31

The Court rejects the average price approach to indemnity by insurer, but it still takes into account the aspect of territoriality. The prices (of labour, spare parts, materials used in the service) applied by a garage must reflect prices in a local market of car services, be it the place of residence of the claimant, or the place where the car was damaged. 32

Thus, the indemnity to be paid by the insurer covers the indispensable and economically justified cost of repair reflecting the prices applied in a local market. 33

c) Commentary

The judgment makes clear that the insurers' policy of unilaterally calculating damages for the losses suffered by car owners based on average prices of repair services and the practice of denying the reimbursement of any higher sums is not acceptable. Absent regulation in the civil code, the establishing of the criteria of measuring the costs of restitution rests with the courts. Any statements regarding the costs made to the aggrieved party who is not in a contractual relation with the insurer are of no significance. 34

4. SN of 26 September 2003, IV CK 8/02, [2004] OSN 11, at 180: Safety of Participants in Mass Events, Strict Liability of the Organizer

a) Brief Summary of the Facts

35 The plaintiff was badly beaten up by unidentified persons at the discotheque run by the defendants (a civil partnership). The administrative decision allowing for the operation of the club set out certain requirements to provide safety at mass events. A person responsible for the safety (obliged to attend organized events), named in the decision, was the owner of a security agency with whom the defendants concluded a contract for security services. The club has its by-laws that prohibit intoxicated, aggressive or vulgarly behaving persons from being present in the club.

36 On the night in question the person responsible for the security was absent, and the police who had been called to intervene refused to expel a group of aggressive clients for lack of grounds and claiming that the security is competent in such matters. The latter did not act and as a result the safety in the club got out of control. The group attacked the plaintiff and his partner. He claims compensation for serious personal injuries and trauma, resulting in permanent damage, including a complete disability to work.

37 The regional court awarded compensation on tort law basis finding that the defendants breached a duty to secure safety of a mass event envisaged in the law of 27 August 1997 on the safety of mass events[12], and that their employees were negligent in monitoring the club. It also declared the liability of the defendants for future claims arising out of the tort.

38 The court of appeals reversed and dismissed the claim on the grounds of art. 429 KC[13]. The defendants were not liable for the independent contractor (the security agency) because they chose a professional to perform the task of ensuring safety in the club.

b) Judgment of the Court

39 The Supreme Court observed that the plaintiff could have founded his claim on either a contractual or delictual basis, with the possibility of the concurrence of the two causes (art. 443 KC). However, once he chooses the tort ground, and the courts proceeded on it, he is not free to pick some elements of the claim from one and some from the other regime of liability.

[12] Dz. U. 1997, no. 106, at 680, with amendments.

[13] Art. 429 KC states that anyone who entrusts another person with the execution of a transaction is liable for damage caused by that person in carrying out the transaction entrusted to him, unless he is free of fault in his choice or he entrusted the execution of the transaction to a person, enterprise or institution which performs such transaction within the scope of their professional activity.

Art. 5 of the law on the safety of mass events provides for a duty to secure safety and order to the participants of mass events. The *ratio legis* of this act was to impose on the organizer the full liability for the safety of mass sport events, concerts and other entertainment events, which often create a serious risk of personal injuries. The duty is not fulfilled by formally contracting it out to other persons or institutions such as security agencies, or by using the help of police. 40

Breach of this duty results in strict liability of the organizer who has to undertake all material means to guarantee safety in the club. In consequence, art. 5 of the law on the safety of mass events, by introducing a stricter regime of liability, limits the possibility of exculpation under art. 429 KC. In art. 429 KC the liability is based on the presumption of fault in choosing the contractor. The Court states that art. 5 is *lex specialis* to art. 429 KC. 41

In addition, under the facts, the negligence of the defendants' employees and the agency was sufficient to hold them liable on the general basis of fault (art. 415 KC). The Supreme Court changed the judgment and reaffirmed the Regional Court decision. 42

c) Commentary

The judgment is significant because of the functional interpretation of law on the safety of mass events, which takes account of the aim of the statute. It underlines that the organizer of a mass event is solely responsible for the safety of such event. It may not discharge this liability by contracting out its duties to security agencies. 43

5. SN of 29 October 2003, III CK 134/02, [2004] OSN 12, at 200: State Liability for Failure to Act in a Bad Financial Situation of a Public Health Care Institution

a) Brief Summary of the Facts

The facts concern insufficient financing of a public hospital before the reform of the health care system effective as of 1 January 1999. The hospital (the plaintiff) received legal personality on 13 August 1998. Although the latter did not assign the hospital with sufficient resources on the said day, it performed all health care services. Now it claims the amount constituting its debt as of 1 January 1999. The lower courts ruled for the plaintiff, holding that the founding authority is obliged to wind up an autonomous medical institution or transform it into a budgetary unit if its annual balance is negative (art. 60 of the law on health care establishments of 1991, Dz.U. no 91, at 408 with later amendments). Failure to do so constitutes a tort. 44

b) Judgment of the Court

The Supreme Court rules that the head of the province should have issued a decree to wind up the plaintiff hospital or transform it into a budgetary unit 45 because he knew of the debt balance of the hospital. Failure to do so is wrongful and results in the liability for the hospital's loss. On a general level, the Court states that an organ founding a medical establishment should monitor the latter's activities and prevent the risks of its operation.

c) Commentary

46 In 1999, under the new scheme of the Universal Health Insurance Act, hospitals became independent from the State budget and gained more financial resources for their activities. Twice the legislator annulled all debts of all hospitals. The vast majority of public health care establishments were transformed into legally autonomous institutions (and got public assets under their management) on the day the reform entered into force. The plaintiff hospital, even though transformed earlier than others, had still been financed by the State budget by 1 January 1999, thus the correct basis for its claim should have been found in administrative or financial law rather than tort law[14].

47 Formulating its decision the Court, unnecessarily, went beyond the facts of the case. The Court's interpretation of art. 60 of the law on health care establishments, imposing a duty upon the local authorities to issue a decision on closing of an insolvent medical establishment or making it a *statio communis* cannot be approved of. The omission of such decision is usually justified by several arguments, not only those of an economic nature. Thus, it is questionable whether it should be assessed in the light of tort law.

6. SA in Poznań (Court of Appeals, SA) of 9 May 2002, ACa 221/02, [2004] *Prawo i Medycyna* 1, 116: Liability for Breach of Duty to Inform a Patient's Family of his Contagious Disease

a) Brief Summary of the Facts

48 The plaintiffs claim compensation for the infection with Hepatitis B, transmitted to them by the plaintiffs' husband and father (X), who had been diagnosed with the virus in the hospital (for which the State Treasury is responsible). The plaintiffs were not informed by the hospital personnel about X's infection, despite other detailed information about his condition. In consequence, they failed to take precautionary measures to avoid the infection and acquired hepatitis. The regional court dismissed the suit, and the plaintiffs appealed.

b) Judgment of the Court

49 The Court holds that medical personnel in a hospital have a duty to inform the relatives of a patient about his infection with a contagious virus. Such duty, if not stemming explicitly from legal provisions, arises from the general rule that servants in the public health care sector are obliged to undertake all possible actions, available according to the state of art, in order to prevent and reduce epidemiological risks. Such duty embraces, in particular, the obligation to in-

[14] See M. Nesterowicz, Note to the judgment, [2005] OSP 4.

form the family members, who in everyday life encounter the danger of infection. A spouse is most often endangered by Hepatitis B, since it is transmitted through intimate contact.

Simply giving to the patient his medical chart containing the results of medical tests does not discharge medical personnel of their duty. Medical language is too specialist and hermetic to be understood by an average person. Thus, the information must be given in a comprehensible manner, inducing the family members to undertake precautionary measures. This fact should be supported in writing. 50

The defence of the confidentiality of patient's data is not a defence in this type of case. The obligation to maintain the medical secret is not absolute, especially when maintaining the secret may pose a danger to other persons' health and life. 51

The breach of the duty to inform about a contagious disease constitutes a tort (artt. 415 and 417 KC). The plaintiffs' damage remains in adequate causation with the breach. The defendant did not prove that the plaintiffs' infection originated from other sources. 52

c) Commentary

The Court makes clear that when a patient was transmitted an infectious disease in hospital, the liability extends to all damage caused to him and his family. Although it was not established whether the hospital in fact informed the patient himself about the virus, the court of appeals did not consider it critical to the question of liability for the plaintiffs' injury. 53

The decision raises the question of the extent of the right of the patient's family to be informed of his condition. In general, the patient's consent is required. As Nesterowicz points out[15] the spouses are allowed to know more about each other's health state than other family members. However, in cases when the patient endangers the health of others, the requirement of his consent should be waived. Such interpretation of doctors' duties stems from the special character of the medical profession. 54

7. RC in Lublin (the Regional Court, RC) of 4 April 2002, IC 656/99, [2004] *Prawo i Medycyna* 3, 122: Public Hospital's Liability

a) Brief Summary of the Facts

The plaintiff sued a public hospital and its insurer for damages in the amount of 21,000 PLN (€ 500) for personal injury resulting from medical negligence. The defendant did not contest the facts. The plaintiff suffered burns on her feet due to a negligent after-surgery procedure. She had to undergo a skin trans- 55

[15] M. Nesterowicz, Note to the judgment, [2004] *Prawo i Medycyna* 1, 121.

plant and even though the treatment has been completed, further future complications are foreseeable.

b) Judgment of the Court

56 A public health care establishment is liable for damage caused by its physicians and medical personnel as a master for his servants on the basis of art. 430 KC. The plaintiff came to hospital for a surgical procedure. Services performed after the surgery belonged to the duties of medical personnel. Usually, the nurses and cleaning personnel are bound to follow the instructions of their principals. The notion of "acting in performance of the entrusted tasks" embraces not only instructions as to concrete acts, but also to all acts that belong to the entrusted functions. The instructions must be carried out in the purpose that may be objectively verified.

57 The Court established fault of the hospital personnel. It said that if a concrete person may not be pointed at, it is sufficient that a negligent act was authored by a person from the category of persons "subordinate to the management" (the theory of anonymous fault).

58 As to damages, the Court held that compensation for non-pecuniary loss must first of all compensate the victim's harm, thus its amount must not be symbolic, but have substantial economic value.

c) Commentary

59 The evolution of the liability for medical services has made a full circle[16]. For four decades artt. 417–420 (2) KC have been considered to form a special regime of State liability where the State is responsible for negligent acts committed by State functionaries. In medical malpractice cases the Supreme Court expressly rejected the division of liability according to the nature of the act: a hospital is liable for organizational acts and a physician for therapeutic and diagnostic acts. The Supreme Court "codified" the case law developments in the directive of 15 February 1971 (III CZP 33/70) [17], where it also ruled that general tort rules (artt. 415, 416, 427, 429, 430 KC) are not applicable to State liability. Thus, all physicians, nurses, technicians, cleaning personnel and others, regardless of their functions, became State functionaries, and thus were no longer treated as just organizationally subordinate.

60 By this case the Court returns to the applicability of art. 430 KC, though, as Nesterowicz put it: by "construing the liability 'on a higher level'"[18]. Thus, all physicians and medical personnel are regarded as "servants" due to their subordination to the general organizational authority of the hospital. In fact, a growing number of physicians are being employed as independent contrac-

[16] See M. Nesterowicz, Note to the judgment, [2004] *Prawo i Medycyna* 3, 126.

[17] Directive relating to the liability of the State Treasury and state legal entities for damage committed by state officials, [1971] OSN, at 59.

[18] See M. Nesterowicz, Note to the judgment, [2004] *Prawo i Medycyna* 3, 127.

tors. I believe that, in general, physicians employed by a hospital might be regarded as servants rather than independent contractors when it comes to the liability for low quality medical service, since they are dependent on the National Health Fund as to the organization and financing of the services. Those physicians who have contracted for services with a hospital (so they are registered entrepreneurs) may not be regarded as servants. They are independent contractors who provide services for the benefit of patients of that hospital. Their liability is joint and several with the hospital's liability (artt. 415, 441 § 1 KC).

However, the Court ignores the fact that since 1997 (art. 77 sec. 1 of the Constitution) public authorities' liability has been based on unlawfulness of its conduct. Thus, "regular" torts (not involving exercise of public authority) should be subject to the general principles of liability. The Court avoided the problem of qualifying health care services as acts of imperium. One can expect, however, future practice to evaluate each type of act individually (see infra no. 70). The change in positive law is generally criticised for deviating from the established case law and for worsening the situation of some victims, especially victims of medical malpractice in public health care institutions[19]. 61

C. Literature

1. M. Jagielska, *Podstawy odpowiedzialności za produkt* (C.H. Beck, Warsaw 2004)

The book surveys the bases of product liability in Polish law against the background of community law. A short history of the making of the Directive 374/85 is given first, then the implementation of the Directive in the Title VI[1] of the Book of Obligations KC. A detailed analysis of the rules, doctrinal views and court practice, including the case law of the ECJ, is supported by statistical data. 62

2. M. Nesterowicz, *Prawo medyczne* (Medical law) (6th edn. TNOiK, Toruń 2004)

The popular treatise on medical law is a thorough and comprehensive analysis of civil liability of physicians and hospitals and the guarantee and insurance liability for damage caused by medical malpractice and medical accidents, as well as of the regulation on health care activities. It deals in detail with liability for medical malpractice, lack of informed consent, and lack of safety during hospitalisation, as well as with medical experiments, cosmetic surgery etc. 63

[19] See G. Bieniek, Odpowiedzialność Skarbu Państwa za szkody wyrządzone przez funkcjonariuszy po wyroku Trybunału Konstytucyjnego z dnia 4 grudnia 2001 r., [2002] *Przegląd Sądowy* (The Judicial Review, PS) 4, 11; A. Górski, Artykuł 417 k.c. – przepis niewłaściwie interpretowany czy niekonstytucyjny, [2003] PS 1, 46 et seq., M. Nesterowicz, *Medical law* (2004), 293.

The author suggests that the liability for hospital infections, medical experiments, vaccinations and medical accidents should be detached from fault and borne by the State, perhaps by a guarantee fund.

3. M. Pyziak-Szafnicka (ed.), *Odpowiedzialność cywilna. Księga pamiątkowa ku czci Profesora Adama Szpunara* (Zakamycze 2004)

64 The book contains essays in honour of the late Professor Adam Szpunar, which were presented during the nationwide conference "Civil Liability" in Łódź on 4–5 December 2003. The authors are professors of law from almost all Polish universities and some foreign universities (L. Buriàn, P. Malaurie, G. Weick, G. Wiederkehr). The range of discussed problems includes: the tendencies in the evolution of civil liability, tort law issues (e.g. non-pecuniary loss, contributory negligence) and liability in specific contractual relations.

4. M. Safjan, *Odpowiedzialność odszkodowawcza władzy publicznej (po 1 września 2004 roku)* (Wydawnictwo Prawnicze Lexis Nexis, Warsaw 2004)

65 This short monograph covers the evolution, constitutional regulation and the interpretation of the new civil code rules on liability for exercise of public authority (see supra nos. 1–10). Safjan underlines the breakthrough in the field of public liability that took place after 17 October 1997 (the date of entry into force of the new Constitution). He seeks to explain several uncertainties about the premises of this liability as newly shaped in the civil code, in particular whether illegality should denote only acts violating the norms of positive law or relate also to conduct contrary to established customs and moral norms. The author supports the narrow understanding of unlawfulness, but admits that unlawful acts might be acts that simultaneously violate written norms and moral norms (the view supported by the case law of the Supreme Court). He also finds answers to the complicated problems of liability for legislative wrongfulness, legislative omission, liability for unlawful valid judgments and final decisions. Annexed are the relevant statutes, main decisions of the Constitutional Tribunal, of the Supreme Court (some of them not published officially) and of the ECJ.

5. E. Bagińska, Projekt unifikacji europejskiego prawa czynów niedozwolonych, [2004] *Państwo i Prawo* 6, 32

66 The article is devoted to the works of ECTIL concerning the European Tort Principles. It gives a presentation of the methodology of the Group, the scope of its harmonizing project and the contents of the Principles.

6. G. Bieniek, Cywilnoprawna problematyka ubezpieczenia OC posiadaczy pojazdów mechanicznych na tle nowych uregulowań, [2004] *Przegląd Sądowy* (The Judicial Review, PS) 5, 38

This article is a lengthy analysis of one aspect of the new insurance regulations – the civil liability insurance of possessors of mechanical vehicles. The author surveys the changes in insurance regulations and their practical impact on the interpretation of the relevant civil code provisions. 67

7. L. Bosek, Odpowiedzialność odszkodowawcza państwa za zaniechanie ustawodawcze (Uwagi na tle wyroku Sądu Najwyższego z 24 września 2003 r.), [2004] PS 11–12, 3

Taking as the background for the discussion the Supreme Court judgment of 24 September 2003 (unpublished), the author gives a thorough and interesting analysis of the problem of liability for legislative omission. He refers to the constitutional arguments, to the case law of the Supreme Court relating to the compensation of repatriated persons, and to the community legal system. He emphasizes that a positive duty to legislate is a condition of civil liability of public authorities for legislative omission as laid down in art. 417^1 § 4 KC. 68

8. J. Jastrzębski, Interferencje adekwatnej przyczynowości oraz winy przy odpowiedzialności za szkodę majątkową, [2004] PS 7–8, 26

The article is a comprehensive theoretical study of the relations between adequate causation and fault in cases of liability for pecuniary damage. In particular, the author examines a possible influence of degrees of fault or of the required standard of conduct on the selection of the consequences of the damaging event that should be borne by the wrongdoer. 69

9. M. Nesterowicz, Odpowiedzialność cywilna publicznego zakładu opieki zdrowotnej za wyrządzoną szkodę w świetle kodeksu cywilnego i art. 77 ust. 1 Konstytucji RP, [2004] *Prawo i Medycyna* 2, 52

The article deals with the problem of the basis of liability of public health care establishments in the light of the civil code and art. 77 sec. 1 of the Constitution. Public authorities have a duty to establish and realize health care services, but public medical establishments may not be regarded as organs of public authorities. Nevertheless, Nesterowicz advocates that liability without fault should be applied to public medical institutions since local authorities run most of them, and the contracting for services is a competence of the National Health Care Fund. Health care insurance premiums are deducted from citizens' income without any choice for any other public insurance scheme; moreover patients have to use the services of those public hospitals that have contracted for services (and within the contractual limits). In consequence, they are dependent to a high degree on organs of public authority. 70

10. Z. Radwański, Zmiany w KC dotyczące odpowiedzialności organów wykonujących władzę publiczną, [2004] *Monitor Prawniczy* 21, 971

71 The author describes and interprets the new rules on governmental liability (see supra nos. 1–10). He explains the meaning of unlawfulness, legislative wrongfulness, legislative omission, liability for unlawful valid judgments and final decisions, and particular problems of the relations of Polish rules with the principles of Member States' liability. Finally, the author briefly discusses the relation of art. 417^1 § 4 KC to the principle of the separation of powers, and concludes that there is no actual conflict between the two.

11. R. Stefanicki, Odpowiedzialność odszkodowawcza państwa wobec jednostki z tytułu niewypełniania prawa wspólnotowego, [2004] *Państwo i Prawo* 7, 41

72 The author analyses the rules of Member States' liability for the breach of European Community law. The author considers a number of issues, such as the place of the principle of State liability in the EU legal order, conditions and prerequisites of liability, and the limitation of claims.

12. M. Wałachowska, Wynagrodzenie szkód poniesionych na skutek doznania wstrząsu psychicznego spowodowanego śmiercią osoby bliskiej, [2004] PS 7–8, 45

73 The author surveys Polish practice relating to compensation of victims suffering a mental shock due to the death of a relative. It is interestingly presented against the background of French, German and English law. The author comes to the conclusion that the claim for compensation for this damage, based on art. 446 §3 KC[20] is dependent on the existence of some kind of a pecuniary loss, although the courts tend to mix pecuniary and non-pecuniary elements of damage. The author opines, however, that in case of a serious health disorder suffered by an injured person due to a mental shock resulting from his relative's death, a court might award compensation for non-pecuniary loss (art. 445 § 1 KC) although the pecuniary damage did not occur. In such case the injured person is not an "indirect" victim, but his injury is a direct one, but still causally linked to the event causing the relative's death.

[20] "In addition, a court may award the closest members of the family of the deceased an appropriate indemnity, if due to his death a considerable worsening of their material situation resulted".

XIX. Portugal

André G. Dias Pereira

A. Legislation

1. *Decreto-Lei* (Decree-Law, DL) no. 7/2004, of 7 January – Implements Directive on Electronic Commerce

This statutory instrument aims mainly at implementing Directive 2000/31/EC of the European Parliament and of the Council of 8 June 2000.[1] The Directive on electronic commerce does not regulate electronic commerce to the full extent: wide areas are left open, either because they are part of the contents of other directives, or because they were not deemed to be sufficiently consolidated for a Community harmonisation or rather because such harmonisation is not required. On the other hand, it governs issues such as contracts concluded by electronic means, the regulation of which only makes sense as a matter under ordinary law and not just under commercial law.[2] 1

One of the main purposes of the Directive is to ensure the exercise of the freedom of establishment and the freedom to provide information society services in the European Union, despite the limitations laid out. The scheme adopted consists in making service providers subject to the legal order of the Member State where they are established. This was thus provided for, clarifying as much as possible concepts that are expressed in general terms, though somewhat imprecise, such as "information society service". This is understood as any service provided at a distance by electronic means, in the scope of an economic activity at the individual request of a recipient of services – which excludes sound or television broadcasting. Recital 57) of Directive 2000/31/EC recalls that "the Court of Justice has consistently held that a Member State retains the right to take measures against a service provider that is established in another Member State but directs all or most of his activity to the territory of 2

[1] Portuguese legislation concerning information society can be found in English language at: http://www.anacom.pt/template2.jsp?categoryId=4600.

[2] A.L. Pereira, A Liberdade de Navegação na Internet: Browsers, Hyperlinks, Meta-tags, in: A. Pinto Monteiro (ed.), *Estudos de Direito da Comunicação* (2002), 227–260; Idem, Princípios do comércio electrónico, in: *Miscelâneas* (2004), 77–112.

the first Member State if the choice of establishment was made with a view to evading the legislation that would have applied to the provider had he been established on the territory of the first Member State".

3 Another strong purpose of this Directive is to determine the *liability regime of intermediary service providers*. The legislator aims more specifically at establishing the conditions of irresponsibility of these providers having regard to the possible illegal contents of messages they render available. The first step is to declare the absence of a general obligation on the part of the intermediary service provider to monitor the information that they transmit or store, or to which they provide access. A list of the common duties of all intermediary service providers is also presented. The legislator has followed the ruling of the specific liability regime of the activities provided by the Directive itself: "mere conduit", "caching" and "hosting". The opportunity was taken to provide also for the situation of intermediary providers of network content association services (such as search engines and hyperlinks), which assimilates the regime established for providers of hosting services. The resource to schemes for the provisional settlement of disputes that arise regarding the lawfulness of contents available on the network is introduced, having regard to the urgent nature that a settlement prima facie may present. This task is assigned to the respective supervision entity, without prejudice to the final decision of the dispute, which shall be a court decision.

4 The Directive also regulates the so-called commercial communications. It seems preferable to consider "network advertising communications", bearing in mind that only the advertising activity is concerned. In this scope the issue of unsolicited communications arises, which is, however, left open to a wide extent by the Directive. The approval in the meantime of Directive 2002/58/EC of the European Parliament and of the Council of 12 July 2002 concerning the processing of personal data and the protection of privacy in the electronic communications sector (Directive on privacy and electronic communications), the transposition of which is yet to be accomplished, was taken into account. Art. 13 of this Directive concerns unsolicited communications, establishing that messaging for the purposes of direct marketing is only authorised with regard to recipients who have given their prior consent. Within this context, this statutory instrument also represents the partial transposition of that Directive as far as art. 13 (unsolicited communications) is concerned.

5 The conclusion of contracts by electronic means is the most delicate matter of this Directive. It is explicitly stated that the provisions apply to all types of contracts, whether they are deemed as commercial contracts or not. The principle implemented is that of the free access to electronic means, so that the law does not create obstacles, with the exceptions pointed out. For this purpose, whatever opposes the conclusion of the contracts should be excluded. The written form requirement was deemed particularly important. The wording used in art. 4 of the Securities Code, which is broad and independent of technical considerations, is adopted: declarations issued by electronic means

shall meet the legal requirement of written form where they present the same guarantees of reliability, comprehensibility and storage. Another very critical issue is that of the moment of conclusion of the contract. The Directive does not rule on this point as it does not aim to harmonise civil law. Member States have taken very different positions. The legal significance of the acknowledgement of receipt is here under consideration in particular, as it may or may not be deemed as acceptance. The last position mentioned is adopted, being that of the majority, as the acknowledgement of receipt is intended to ensure the effectiveness of the electronic communication only, rather than to express a negotiating position. Nonetheless, it is also clarified that the online provision of products or services is deemed as a contract offer or invitation to treat, whether or not it includes all the necessary particulars for the contract to be concluded through the mere acceptance of the recipient.

The legislator also aims to regulate the conclusion of contracts by means of computers, that is, the fully automatic conclusion of contracts, without human intervention. It is established that to such contracts shall apply the common regime, except in cases where such regime suggests an action (human action). The framework for the application of the provisions on mistake is also determined. 6

Having regard to the fact that the Directive provides for the use of schemes for the out-of-court settlement of disputes, including through the adequate electronic channels, the legislator had to find the appropriate way to transpose this principle. The several functions assigned to public entities recommend the option for supervision entities. Where the responsibility is not upon special entities, an entity of central supervision shall operate: this task is performed by ICP-ANACOM. Supervision entities have functions in the fields of the investigation of breach proceedings, which are provided for, as well as the duty to apply the respective fines. The amount of the fines is set at very broad limits, in order to be discouraging, but at the same time, to adapt to the variety of situations that may arise. Additional sanctions may be associated to the breaches; however, the more serious additional sanctions shall be confirmed by court order, on the supervision entity's own motion. Provisional measures are provided for, and are to be applied by the responsible supervision entity, which may determine, modify or lift them at any moment. Lastly, this statutory instrument also intends to create schemes for the out-of-court settlement of disputes that arise in this field, avoiding impediments brought forth by general legislation, namely to the settlement of such disputes by electronic means. 7

Analysing in more detail the regulation of liability of networking service providers (Chapter III), it begins with the *principle of assimilation*: (Art. 11) "The liability of online service providers is subject to the common regime, namely in case of content aggregation, with the specifications arising from the following articles." Art. 12 establishes the *absence of a general obligation to monitor on the part of intermediary service providers*. However, art. 13 provides common duties of intermediary service providers, which are: a) to inform 8 them promptly when becoming aware of illegal activities undertaken via services rendered; b) to meet requests for the identification of recipients of their services with whom they have entered into storage agreements; c) to comply promptly with the instructions aiming to terminate or prevent an offence, namely to remove or disable access to a given information; d) to supply lists of owners of hosted websites, where requested.[3]

2. Decree-Law no. 26/2004, of 4 February – Establishes the *Estatuto do Notariado* (Notary Statute) and Decree-Law no. 27/2004, of 4 February – Creates the Notary Chamber (*Ordem dos Notários*)

9 In Portugal all notaries have been civil servants (functionaries of the State, Justice Department) since the 1940s. However a very important reform took place in 2004: A notary is now a *liberal professional*, but only those entitled by the State to practise (in a *numerus clausus* regime) are allowed to exercise this activity. The creation of the *Ordem dos Notários* (Notaries' Chamber) aims to establish disciplinary and deontological control in the exercise of this key function in the legal system. In the *Latin notary system*, that is here adopted, the notary has the privilege of "public faith" (*fé pública*). The professional

[3] Art. 14 concerning "*mere conduit*" states: "1. Where the intermediary service provider only pursues an activity that consists of the transmission of information in a communication network, or the provision of access to a communication network, not having initiated the transmission, nor modified the contents of the messages transmitted, nor selected either the information or the receivers, he shall not be liable for the information transmitted. 2. The exemption from liability shall also apply to the mere technological storage of the information transmitted, in so far as this takes place for the sole purpose of carrying out the transmission and provided that the information is not stored for any period longer than is necessary for the transmission."
Art. 15, concerning "*caching*" provides: "1. The intermediary provider of networking communication transmission services that does not modify the contents of the messages transmitted, nor selects either the information or the receivers, and that complies with the conditions on access to the information, shall not be liable for the automatic and temporary storage of that information, performed for the sole purpose of making more efficient and economical the information's onward transmission to recipients of the service upon their request. 2. The common regime of liability shall apply, nevertheless, where the provider does not comply with the usual rules of the sector regarding: a) the updating of the information, b) the use of technology, to obtain data on the use of the information. 3. The common rules shall also apply where the provider has obtained actual knowledge of the fact that the information has been removed from its initial source or access to it has been disabled, or that a court or an administrative authority with powers upon the provider who has originated the information has ordered an immediate enforcement action towards such removal or access disablement, and the provider does not act expeditiously to remove or disable access to the information."
Art. 16 regulates "*hosting*": "1. The intermediary provider of the server storage service shall only be liable for the information stored, under the common rules, where he has knowledge of an obviously illegal activity or information and does not act expeditiously to remove or to disable access to such information. 2. The service provider shall be civilly liable where, faced with his knowledge of circumstances, he is or should be aware of the illegal nature of the information. 3. The common rules on liability shall apply where the recipient of the service is acting under the authority or the control of the provider."
Art. 17 establishes "*liability of intermediary providers of content aggregation services*": "Intermediary providers of network content aggregation services, by means of search engines, hyperlinks or similar procedures that allow access to illegal contents, shall be subject to the liability regime that corresponds to that established in the preceding article."

must be registered in the Chamber. Artt. 35 et seq. regulate a notary's deontological duties, among others: loyalty and integrity, confidentiality, professional diligence and urbanity; it also prohibits publicity. The violation of these duties may generate disciplinary liability, which, however, does not exclude possible civil or criminal liability.

10 From 2005 notaries have become private professionals and citizens will be provided with a private legal service, which might in the future increase litigation in this field.[4] Art. 23 (1) (m) of DL 26/2004 obliges notaries to contract a liability insurance to the amount of a minimum of € 100,000.[5]

3. Decree-Law no. 59/2004, of 19 March – Strict Liability in Road and Train Accidents, Electricity and Gas: Amount of Damages in Case of Strict Liability

11 This Act changes Artt. 508 and 510 *Código Civil* (Portuguese Civil Code, CC), concerning the compensation caps in case of strict liability arising from road traffic accidents and electricity and gas accidents. Portuguese law concerning road traffic compulsory insurance (Art. 6 DL no. 522/85, 31 December, changed by DL no. 3/96, 25 January and DL no. 301/2001, 23 November) regulates the minimal amounts of coverage according to European Directives.[6] However, Art. 508 CC, which regulates the maximum amount of compensation in case of strict liability of the driver (or the car owner), established a different limit, which was considerably lower. This gave rise to an important discussion in literature and case law, that is, were the caps of Art. 508 CC in force or did DL 522/85 tacitly revoke that (part of the) norm? Should the minimal amounts of cover of compulsory insurance against civil liability in respect of motor vehicles be equivalent to the compensation caps in case of strict liability?[7]

12 The legislator solved this question by stating that the compensation cap in case of strict liability for road accidents is equivalent to the minimum amount of coverage of compulsory insurance. Thus, compensation caps in case of no-fault liability are automatically updated whenever the legislator changes the norms concerning compulsory insurance values (according to EU Directives). The same rule applies in case of public transport and in case of transportation by train.

[4] See J. Maia Rodrigues, Responsabilidade civil dos Notários, [2003] *Boletim dos Registos e do Notariado*, 2 (also in http://www.dgrn.mj.pt/brn-2003/brnfev03/opiniao_02-03.pdf).

[5] While a civil servant, a notary only responds in a *redress action* if he committed a tort with gross negligence or intention (Art. 2 DL 48051, 21 November 1967), and for this reason liability insurance was not so important. As a private professional, a notary is directly liable under any degree of fault, because ordinary civil law rules apply.

[6] Directives 72/166/EEC, 84/5/EEC and 90/232/EEC.

[7] See A. Pereira, Portugal, in: H. Koziol/B.C. Steininger (eds.), *European Tort Law 2003* (2004), 337–339.

13 Art. 509 and Art. 510 concern strict liability for damage caused by electricity or gas. According to DL 59/2004, the limit of compensation for each accident is the same as in case of Art. 508 (1), that is, the minimal amounts of cover of compulsory insurance against civil liability in respect of motor vehicles, except if a special Statute imposes compulsory insurance relating to electricity or gas use, in which case this compulsory insurance's minimal values apply.

14 The fact that the legislator solved this important question is to be applauded. For many years compensation for road accidents in case of strict liability was very low and there has been an intense debate in literature and case law concerning this issue. However, it did not resolve the problem concerning accidents that took place before 19 March 2004 and that have not been settled yet. The Supreme Court of Justice decided that matter on the *Acórdão de Fixação de Jurisprudência* no. 3/2004.[8]

4. Decree-Law no. 68/2004, of 25 March: Consumer Protection in Estate Acquisition

15 This DL provides consumer protection concerning real estate acquisition for family residence and transparency and fairness of the real estate market. It introduces several requirements concerning duties of information and regulates the publicity in this market. It also introduces an obligatory *habitation technical certificate* (*ficha técnica da habitação*) that describes in detail the immovable and its technical and legal characteristics. Art. 16 (1) establishes special norms concerning civil liability of the technician responsible for the construction (*técnico responsável pela obra*) and the estate agents: they are solidary liable for the damage caused to the *buyer* and *third persons*, if the *habitation technical certificate* contains untrue or false information.[9]

16 This norm creates an exceptional situation. First of all, it expands the scope of protection of the contract between the estate agent and the buyer and the contract between the buyer and the seller. It provides delictual protection of *pure economic interests* not only of the buyer but also of other relevant *third parties*. That is, not only the buyer (who is a party to the contract where the certificate is incorporated) but also third parties are protected by this element of the contract. Moreover, it states that the technician responsible for the construction is liable not only towards the owner of the construction, but also towards the buyer and even other third parties. It is also interesting to pay attention to the solidary obligation to compensate that is imposed on the "technician responsible" but also on the "estate agent".[10]

[8] Published in Official Journal (*Diário da República*) of 13 May 2004.

[9] Art. 16 (2) states that liability ceases in case the owner, at his own initiative, does modifications of the structure of the house, after receiving the "estate certificate".

[10] See infra (nos. 26 et seq.) the duties and the new liability regime that is imposed in general on the estate agent (Decree-Law no. 211/2004, of 20 August – Estate agents Statute).

5. *Lei* (Law) no. 18/2004, of 11 May: Equal Treatment of Persons Irrespective of Racial or Ethnic Origin

This *Lei* (Act of Parliament) implements into national law Directive 2000/43/ EC of 29 June 2000 implementing the principle of equal treatment between persons irrespective of racial or ethnic origin, which has the purpose of laying down a framework for combating discrimination on the grounds of racial or ethnic origin, with a view to putting into effect in the Member States the principle of equal treatment. 17

In the field of tort law, Art. 6 concerning *burden of proof* is relevant, since it states that persons who consider themselves wronged because the principle of equal treatment has not been applied to them have to establish facts from which it may be presumed that there has been direct or indirect discrimination; but it shall be for the defendant to *prove* that there has been no breach of the principle of equal treatment. This regime establishes a *"soft" inversion of the burden of proof*, which is imposed on the defendant in discrimination claims. This is an exception to the general rule on the burden of proof (Art. 340 (1) CC). These norms, combined with Art. 70 CC (general personality right), are legal grounds for tort liability. According to the aforementioned Art. 70, individuals may institute legal proceedings to protect themselves against any unlawful interference with their physical or psychological personality. Furthermore, victims are entitled to ask the courts to put a stop to such interference or, where there is a threat of such interference, to prevent it. 18

It is noteworthy to state that the implementation of the anti-discrimination Directives in Portugal, contrary to some other Member States, caused almost no political or academic debate, so that one may say that there is a general agreement on these new regimes. Moreover, Portugal already had an anti-discrimination statute in 1999: Law 139/99, of 28 August, which prohibited discrimination in the exercise of rights on grounds of race, colour, nationality and ethnic origin, applicable to public and private entities or persons.[11] Portugal has recently signed and ratified a large number of international legal instruments relating to the fight against racism and intolerance.[12] 19

6. Decree-Law no. 111/2004, of 12 May: Laboratories Licensing Statute

This DL regulates the licensing and activity of biomedical laboratories. Art. 35 imposes a compulsory civil liability insurance that covers liability of the professionals involved, as well as the liability of the institution. Art. 37 20

[11] For more details on this Act see: http://www.fd.uc.pt/hrc/network/ cfr_cdf_repportugal_ 2003.pdf.

[12] Portugal has ratified Protocol No. 12 to the *European Convention on Human Rights and the Framework Convention for the Protection of National Minorities* by Decree of 25 June 2001 and the *European Charter for the Protection of Regional and Minority Languages*. On 25 August 2001, Portugal issued a declaration under Art. 14 of the *International Convention on the Elimination of All Forms of Racial Discrimination* recognising the competence of the Committee set up under this Convention to receive and consider communications from individuals.

imposes the duty of storage for at least 5 years of some documents that are specified in this Act.

7. Decree-Law no. 124/2004, of 25 May: Leisure Boats Statute

21 This DL regulates leisure boats activity. Art. 41 imposes a strict liability regime for damage caused to third parties by the owners and the commanders of leisure boats, who are solidary liable. The only exception to strict liability is the *exclusive fault of the victim*. Therefore the owners of leisure boats (of certain categories described in the DL) are obliged to contract civil liability insurance.

8. Decree-Law no. 142/2004, of 11 June: Statute on Thermal Baths (spas)

22 This Statute regulates the activities of thermal baths and it includes some relevant norms in the field of tort law: Art. 16 imposes a compulsory civil liability insurance (for part or the totality of the liability) that covers professional liability and the spa. Art. 17 states the duty to store the files for at least 10 years. Finally, Artt. 28–30 state that a new therapeutic treatment with natural mineral water must be approved by the Ministry of Health and only after due investigation of a technical committee: the composition and the procedures are explained in the DL.

9. Law no. 35/2004, of 29 July – Regulates the Labour Code

23 This Act of Parliament regulates in detail Law no. 99/2003, of 27 August, the New Labour Code. It contains very important norms concerning personality rights of the worker, protection of private life, non-discrimination[13] and safety and hygiene in the workplace. Among many others[14], Directive 2000/78/EC, concerning non-discrimination in the working-place is implemented.

10. Decree-Law no. 202/2004, of 18 August: Hunting Act

24 Art. 114 of this Act regulates liability for damage arising from hunting. The owners of hunting fields are obliged to compensate the damage that activity causes to their neighbours. In the areas where hunting has been prohibited by the landowners (right to non-hunting), these are liable for damage caused by wild animals to their own property or to their neighbours.

[13] According to *Council Directive 2000/78/EC of 27 November 2000*, establishing a General Framework for Equal Treatment in Employment and Occupation.

[14] It implements (or re-implements) into national law several Directives (in short reference): Directive 75/117/EEC; Directive 76/207/EEC; Directive 2002/73/EC; Directive 80/987/EEC; Directive 2002/74/EC; Directive 89/391/EEC; Directive 90/394/EEC; Directive 97/42/EC; Directive 1999/38/EC; Directive 90/679/EEC; Directive 93/88/EEC; Directive 92/85/EEC; Directive 93/104/EC; Directive 2000/34/EC; Directive 94/33/EC; Directive 94/45/EC; Directive 96/34/EC; Directive 96/71/EC; Directive 97/80/EC; Directive 98/24/EC; Directive 2000/43/EC; Directive 2000/78/EC; Directive 2002/14/EC and Directive 2003/88/EC.

The State is liable for damage caused by wild animals in forests, agriculture or cattle breeding, as long as it did not authorize correction measures or had not caused the damage itself (Art. 115). 25

11. Decree-Law no. 211/2004, of 20 August: Estate Agents Statute

This DL regulates the activity of estate agents. In order to be authorised to exercise this activity, one has to fulfil several requirements. Among others, the estate agent (or *realtor*) must be (legally) a corporation (Art. 6 (a)) and civil liability insurance is compulsory (Art. 6 (e)). Art. 19 (d) also imposes that the contract of mediation (estate agent contract) provides an express reference to the existence of the compulsory insurance and its basic information. 26

Sec. III of this DL regulates civil liability. Art. 22 (1) reinforces the basic rule *pacta sunt servanda* and Art. 22 (2) states that the corporation is vicariously liable for the activities of its "independent agents" in relation to the contracts concluded between them. This norm has some importance, since according to the ordinary regime (Art. 500 Civil Code (CC)) some doubts could arise as to whether such "independent agents" (not functionaries or representatives of the corporation) should be included in the category of *comissários* (*commissioners*), which is now absolutely clear. Art. 22 (3) imposes solidary liability of the corporation and the agents in case of damage caused to third parties if the estate agents (realtors) did not respect the rules provided for in Art. 16 (1) a)-e) and Art. 16 (2) b) and c). Art. 16 expressly nominates some of the duties of the agents, which can be summarised as the duty to assure that at the moment of conclusion of the *estate agent contract* or mediation contract, a) the parties involved have legal capacity for the contracts they intend to promote; b) to analyse the characteristics of the immovable and to see if they are in accordance with those the seller announces and to check whether there is any burden (e.g., a security) on the immovable; c) to obtain accurate information concerning the characteristics, size, price, payment conditions, etc.; d) to communicate with clear language, so that the terms are comprehensible for the parties involved; e) to communicate immediately with the interested party whenever she has knowledge of any fact that might affect the envisaged contract. Art. 16 (2) prohibits the estate agent from receiving money from both parties interested in the same contract (except in case of Art. 18 (6)) and to take part as an interested party in the contract she is promoting, whether for herself or for a company for which she is a partner, or for her partners, administrators or managers, their husbands/wives, children or parents. The corporation is also prohibited (Art. 16 (2) c)) from participating in estate agent contracts when the circumstances of the case allow one to reasonably doubt the legality of the business. 27

Art. 22 (4) defines *third parties* as all those who in consequence of the mediation suffer pecuniary damage, even if they were not a party in the mediation contract. This rule extends the scope of protection of third parties since, according to ordinary civil law, it would be very difficult to obtain compensa- 28 tion according to the rules on contract, since third parties are not contractual parties (one could eventually apply the "contract with scope of protection for third parties"), as well as in tort law, since Portuguese tort law does not protect patrimony in itself, that is, pure economic loss is not compensable unless there is a violation of a "protective norm".[15] This DL creates and regulates these "protective norms" and the liability regime and extends the protection of third parties' pure economic interests.

29 Art. 23 creates a compulsory civil liability insurance that assures compensation for damage that emerges from a company's activity. This insurance shall cover liability for pecuniary damage caused to third parties from actions or omissions of the companies, their representatives or from the non-fulfilment of other obligations, as well as damage that arises from vicarious liability for the activities of the company's agents. Moreover, no company may start its activity without proving the existence and validity of the insurance contract (Art. 22 (3)).

12. Law no. 46/2004, of 19 August – Clinical Trials Act

30 This Act of Parliament implements into national law Directive 2001/20/EC, of 1 May 2001. Informed consent in clinical trials is regulated in detail, according to the rules of the Directive[16] and the violation of this right is an important source of civil liability.[17] DL 97/94, of 9 April, already established *strict liability*, supported by a *compulsory insurance scheme*. Therefore, Portuguese law already obliged the *promoter* to accomplish the requirement provided by the Directive (Art. 3(2) (f)). The new Law establishes the same regime in Art. 14 (1) and (2). It also states that the liability of the promoter and the professionals involved is *solidary*. Art. 14 (3) establishes a *presumption of causality* for the damage to health that arises during the clinical trial and one year after its termination. After that period, the claimant has the burden of proving that the damage was caused by the clinical trial. Art. 14 (4) leaves no doubt that the authorization to carry out the clinical trial by the competent administrative authority[18], as well as the opinion of the competent ethics commission do *not* exclude or reduce the liability of the promoter or the professionals involved.

[15] See J. Sinde Monteiro, Portuguese Report, in: J. Spier (ed.), *The Limits of Expanding Liability, Eight Fundamental Cases in a Comparative Perspective* (1998), 173–187.

[16] Portuguese law was more restrictive than the Directive in what concerns clinical trials with incompetent patients. On this issue and the influence of the Directive on national law in general see J. Loureiro/A. Pereira, Portugal, in: E. Deutsch/H.L. Schreiber/A. Spickhoff/J. Taupitz (eds.), *Die klinische Prüfung in der Medizin/Clinical Trials in Medicine – Europäische Regelungswerke auf dem Prüfstand/European Rules on Trial* (2004), 259–293.

[17] See A. Pereira, *O Consentimento Informado na Relação Médico-Paciente. Estudo de Direito Civil* (2004).

[18] INFARMED – National Institute of Drugs and Medicines.

13. Decree-Law no 229/2004, of 10 December: Lawyers' Corporations Statute

Lawyers' corporations are now regulated by this Act. Among many other relevant issues, it regulates in detail the rules concerning liability of the corporation and the partners and the right of recourse against the one who caused damage. Both *limited liability* and *unlimited liability* corporations are included (Artt. 33 et seq.). Corporation's liability includes debts emerging from activities of partners, associates or internship lawyers in the exercise of their professional duties. The corporations that opt for the *limited liability* regime must contract compulsory civil liability insurance (Art. 37). Otherwise, during the period the corporation did not fulfil such duty, partners have unlimited liability for the corporation's debts. 31

14. Decree-Law no. 238/2004, of 18 December: Statute Concerning Ultra Light Airplanes without Motor

The use of civil *ultra light airplanes without motor* is now regulated by this Act. It is not applicable to airplanes which are lighter than air (balloons and zeppelins). This activity was already regulated by DL 71/90, of 2 March. However, the legislator has the scope to adjust the legal framework to the technological evolution in this field. Concerning liability for damage, the legislator used the technique of combining strict liability with a maximal amount of damages and compulsory liability insurance. Thus, there is strict liability pending on the owner and the pilot for damage caused by the airplane, except if the accident was due to the exclusive fault of the victim (Art. 40 (1)); the maximum amount of damages (in case of strict liability) is the same as that applicable to civil aviation (Art. 40 (2)); Art. 41 imposes compulsory liability insurance for the damage caused by the airplanes. 32

B. Cases

1. *Acórdão de Fixação de Jurisprudência* no. 3/2004 of the Supreme Court of Justice (STJ), *Diário da República*, 112, Série I-A of 13 May 2004: Compensation Caps in Road Traffic Accidents

a) Brief Summary of the Facts

Mr. M. sued insurance company Z. claiming compensation of € 69,177.12 plus interest since the citation. He pleaded that the driver of the insured car is responsible for the damage he suffered. The Guimarães Court of Appeal Decision of 30 April 2003 ordered payment of € 35,706.75 (for non-pecuniary and pecuniary damages). The defendant appealed to the Supreme Court, claiming that, in case of strict liability for car accidents, the limit of compensation is € 19,951.92 (4 million escudos) according to Art. 508 CC. This article limits compensation to twice the *alçada* (value up to which a category of courts 33 judges without their decision being subject to an ordinary appeal) of the Court of Appeal, which was at the time of the accident € 19,951.92.

b) Judgment of the Court

34 The Supreme Court decided in "plenary court" in an "amplified trial", because there was a very important *divergence in case law* and in the national literature concerning this question.

35 In Portugal, road traffic accidents are subject to the regime of strict liability (Artt. 503–508 CC). As usual in strict liability regimes,[19] compensation caps are provided; and those were, according to Art. 508 CC, extremely low.[20] On the other hand, Art. 6 of Decree-Law (DL) 522/85, of 31 December,[21] which regulates motor vehicle compulsory insurance, provides a minimum amount of coverage of the compulsory liability insurance of € 600,000. This is in accordance with EC law.[22]

36 Directive 84/5/EEC, of 30 December 1983, on the approximation of legislations of Member States concerning liability insurance for road accidents imposed a minimal liability insurance capital and it also stated that "the amounts in respect of which insurance is compulsory must in any event guarantee victims adequate compensation irrespective of the Member State in which the accident occurred."[23]

37 In this respect, the European Court of Justice (ECJ) judgment of 14 September 2000[24] stated: "Articles 1(2) and 5(3) of Directive 84/5 on the approximation of the laws of the Member States relating to insurance against civil liability in respect of the use of motor vehicles, as amended by the Act of Accession of

[19] See B.A. Koch/H. Koziol, Comparative Conclusions, in: B.A. Koch/H. Koziol (eds.), *Unification of Tort Law: Strict Liability* (2003).

[20] These caps were associated to a criterion, which was the *alçada* (value up to which a category of courts judges without their decision being subject to an ordinary appeal) of the Court of Appeal. Thus, before DL 59/2004 of 19 March, Art. 508 provided the following limits: in case of death or injury to *one* person a cap of € 29,927.88 (the double of the *alçada* of the Court of Appeal); in case of death or injury to *several* persons in the same accident the cap was € 29,927.88 for each of the victims, with the maximum of 6 times the *alçada* of the Court of Appeal as a general cap (€ 89,783.64), and in case of damage to things, even if they belonged to different owners, the cap was equivalent to the *alçada* of the Court of Appeal, that is € 14,963.94 (as stated by Art. 24 of the Organic Statute on Activity and Organisation of Judicial Courts).

[21] Changed by DL 3/96, 25 January and later by DL 301/2001, 23 November.

[22] Directives 72/166/EEC, 84/5/EEC and 90/232/EEC.

[23] This Directive had to be implemented by 31 December 1987, but according to the Adhesion Treaties of Portugal and Spain to the European Communities (Annex I, Part IX, F), Portugal could implement it by 31 December 1995, however the Directive was implemented as early as 31 December 1985, by DL 522/85.

[24] Judgment of the Court (Fifth Chamber) of 14 September 2000, Reference for preliminary ruling*:* *Tribunal de Comarca* (first instance) *de Setúbal* (Portugal) (Case C-348/98, European Court Reports 2000, I-06711). See also *Order of the Court* (First Chamber) of 24 July 2003 (European Court reports 2003 I-07871).

Spain and Portugal, preclude domestic laws laying down maximum amounts of compensation that are lower than the minimum amounts of cover laid down by those provisions where, in the absence of fault on the part of the driver of the vehicle which caused the accident, only civil liability for materialisation of risk arises." It became clear that the caps provided for in Art. 508 were a violation of European law.[25]

In order to apply these amounts, some plaintiffs pleaded for the direct application of the Directive in *horizontal* relations. Case law was clear in the sense that Directives have no horizontal effect,[26] following thus ECJ's case law,[27] according to which the national judge is not obliged to overrule national legislation because the Member State did not correctly implement a Directive. Directives can only be applied in *vertical relations* and thus European courts (*Francovich* case) and national case law accept that the Member State may be considered liable vis-à-vis its citizens for non-implementation of a Directive. This solution however does not adequately satisfy claimants, since it involves more litigation (against the State). 38

Some doctrine and case law defended another possibility. They consider that Art. 508 had been tacitly revoked by DL 522/85, of 31 December. The existence of compensation caps prescribed in Art. 508 was not questioned. However, the limits of those caps should be equal to the minimum amounts of cover of the insurance established by the aforementioned Decree-law and its amendments. This thesis[28] places a strong emphasis on the principle of *interpretation in conformity with the Directive*.[29] 39

[25] See B.A. Koch, European Union, in: H. Koziol/B.C. Steininger (eds.), *European Tort Law 2003* (2004), 445–446.

[26] See, e.g., STJ 9 May 2002, [CJ-STJ, X, T-II, (2002), 55]; Porto Court of Appeal (CA), 14 March 2002, [CJ, XXVII, T-II, (2002), 183] and Guimarães CA, 9 October 2002 [CJ, XXVII, T-IV, (2002), 279]. The ECJ (Decision of 14 September 2000) also maintained its doctrine according to which Directives shall not be directly applied in litigation between private persons.

[27] See ECJ decisions on cases: *Marshall* (26 February 1986), *Faccini Dori* (14 July 1994) and *Arcaro* (26 September 1996).

[28] This thesis was defended by F. Matos, O contrato de seguro obrigatório de responsabilidade civil automóvel, [2001] *Boletim da Faculdade de Direito* (BFD), 77, 377 et seq.; Calvão da Silva, *Revista de Legislação e de Jurisprudência* (RLJ), ano 134, 112 (anotação ao Acórdão do Supremo Tribunal de Justiça de 1 de Março de 2001), Calvão da Silva, RLJ, ano 134, 197 (anotação ao Acórdão do Supremo Tribunal de Justiça de 13 de Fevereiro de 2003); A. Garção Soares, Seguro obrigatório de responsabilidade civil automóvel, [2003] *Cadernos de Direito Privado* II, 17–24; A. Garção Soares, A Evolução decorrente das Directivas comunitárias, in: A. Moreira/C. Martins (eds.), *III° Congresso Nacional de Direito dos Seguros* (2003), and P. Ferreira Dias, [2003] *Revista do Ministério Público* 93, 87. In case law, the Supreme Court has defended this thesis in some decisions: STJ 1 March 2001 (RLJ, ano 134, 102); STJ 13 February 2003 (RLJ, ano 134, 192) and STJ 27 March 2003. The same jurisprudence is to be found in the Porto CA 8 November 2001; Porto CA 9 July 2002, Porto CA 28 January 2003, Porto CA 18 February 2003.

[29] See ECJ decision on case *Marleasing* (13 November 1999).

40 This opinion was not consensual. Some authors and case law continued to maintain that, before the intervention of the legislator, the caps provided for by Art. 508 were still in force, and the citizen could only sue the State for non-implementation of the Directive.[30] The debate was intense and the case law and literature established a very interesting dialogue.

41 The Supreme Court of Justice decided the *vexata quaestio* in an "amplified trial",[31] which *harmonises* case law. According to the Supreme Court of Justice, the legislator, while enacting DL 522/85, intended to establish a *connection* between minimum amounts of cover and compensation caps. Moreover, the interpretation of the ECJ is "binding" for the national courts, in such a way that the national court shall interpret national law according to community law. Thus, although the prejudicial decisions of the ECJ have only relative effects (limited to the process), in practice they have a "precedent" effect. Thus, if the Directive is to be interpreted in a broad sense as the ECJ did (stating that the Directive aims to harmonise not only minimum amounts of cover of compulsory liability insurance but also the maximum amounts of compensation),[32] then also DL 522/85, which implements the Directive, shall be interpreted in national law in a *broad sense*. This results from the *principle of interpretation according to community law*, a principle that derives from the *primacy of community law over national law*. The STJ also mentions the recent DL 59/2004 and its preamble, and states that the legislator recognises, at least *tacitly*, the interpretation that considers that the first part of Art. 508 (1) CC had been tacitly revoked by Art. 6 of DL 522/85. In conclusion, the STJ adopted the following decision: "The part of the rule of Art. 508 (1) CC that establishes the maximal amount of damages that can be awarded to the victims in case of no-fault liability for road accidents was tacitly revoked by Art. 6 DL 522/85, 31 December, in its version of DL 3/96, 25 January."[33]

c) Commentary

42 The decisions in a plenary session have a high value in case law, since the lower courts shall obey them in future cases. The connection between com-

[30] This thesis was applied by: Porto CA 14 March 2002, Porto CA 10 March 2003 (CJ (2003) II, 170–173), Guimarães CA 2 October 2002, Guimarães CA 26 February 2003 (in [2003] *Scientia Iuridica* LII, 295, 157), Guimarães CA 29 September 2003 (CJ (2003) IV, 288–290); STJ 1 March 2001, STJ 18 February 2002, STJ 14 March 2002, STJ 9 May 2002, STJ 28 May 2002, STJ 19 September 2002 (in CJ-STJ, Ano X, III, 46), STJ 5 November 2002, STJ 18 December 2002 (CJ-STJ, ano X, III, 167), STJ 13 February 2003, STJ 18 February 2003. This thesis was supported in the literature by N. Oliveira, Revogação Tácita do Art. 508º do Código Civil?, [2003] *Scientia Iuridica* LI, 292, 97–109.

[31] *Acórdão de Fixação de Jurisprudência* no. 3/2004 STJ, *Diário da República*, 112, Série I-A of 2004-05-13. It is noteworthy that this type of decisions (harmonising case law) must be published in the Official Journal.

[32] The Directive, however, does not harmonise the liability regime, which is a matter left for national law.

[33] This decision was taken unanimously. However some judges stated that DL 59/2004 had *interpretative* character. The Public Prosecutor (at the Supreme Court) had also given the same opinion that was taken.

pensation caps and minimum amounts of coverage in road traffic accidents insurance was established by DL 59/2004, of 19 March. However this decision is of great importance for cases that occurred before the entry into force of that Act. This case is also a very impressive example of the growing importance of European community law in national private law. It concerns the implementation of Directives, the relationship between national courts and European Community Courts, the primacy of community law and the principle of interpretation according to community law.[34]

The STJ was impressed by the authoritative opinion of the ECJ and interpreted national law according to EC law. This solution also leads to a very interesting conclusion: the interpretation of national law in conformity with a Directive (or with the ECJ's interpretation of the Directive) leads, in this case, to a similar result as the direct application with horizontal effect of the Directive: that is, the adoption of the minimum amounts of coverage (provided for in the Directives) as the point of reference for compensation caps. As a consequence, this means that the Portuguese State had already duly implemented the Directive.[35] 43

In a tort law analysis one can say that the "round circle of strict liability" is now complete: (1) the prescription of *no-fault liability* that is followed by (2) a *compulsory liability insurance*, with a (3) *minimum amount of cover*; on the other hand (4) *caps on compensation* are established and, closing the circle (5) *these caps correspond to the minimum amounts of cover of the compulsory liability insurance.* 44

This whole situation shows that law develops from a dynamic and dialectic process where European instances as well as national "actors" play a role and is a good example of how European private law is being developed and harmonised. If apparently the leading role was played by the Portuguese legislator and the Supreme Court of Justice, the fact is – as both the legislator and the STJ recognise in the preamble of the Decree-law and in the arguments used to judge – that the ECJ was not only the harmoniser of European private law, but also the indirect "law-maker" of national private law. This also shows that harmonisation of private law very often comes from the existence and the activity of common European *jurisdictional* institutions. 45

As stated, the Supreme Court decided in "plenary court". Normally, the trial of the appeal of review is usually performed by three judges – a reporter and 46

[34] Against the decision see N. Oliveira, Responsabilidade pelo Risco: Limites Máximos de Indemnização. Anotação ao Acórdão de Uniformização de Jurisprudência n.º 3/2004, de 25 de Março de 2004, [2004] *Scientia Iuridica*, 369–405.

[35] One shall not forget that for almost 20 years many plaintiffs (victims of road traffic accidents that could not prove the fault of the wrongdoer) received "miserable" compensation, limited to the caps provided for in Art. 508. Should they sue the State for non-implementation of the Directive or for bad administration of the Justice? It seems like the State could escape liability in both situations!

two associate judges – although two more judges may be summoned in the case of abrogation of a judgment issued by the Court of Appeal, since three conforming votes are then necessary. However, and whenever necessary to *ensure the uniformity of case law*, the President of the Supreme Court of Justice may determine that the trial be conducted with the intervention of the whole of the Civil Chambers.[36] Such amplified trials only take place in the presence of at least *three quarters* of the judges practising in the Civil Chambers.[37]

[36] Also in order to ensure the *uniformity of Case Law*, appealing at the Supreme Court of Justice is admissible for an amplified trial, when against a judgment issued by the Court of Appeal which contradicts another judgment, issued by the same or another Court of Appeal, on the same fundamental question of law, and against which it is not possible to file an ordinary appeal due to reasons alien to the Court's jurisdiction. The exception to the latter is when the orientation followed by the judgment at issue is in harmony with the Supreme Court of Justice's previously established case law.

[37] "The other *types of appeal in Civil jurisdiction* are (1) the *Appeal of apelação* and (2) the *Appeal of review*. "The first (*Appeal of apelação*) is the appropriate way near a Court of Appeal, to dispute a first instance decision which considers the substance of the case. As grounds, one may invoke either a defect of substantive law or a question of procedural nature. In this appeal, the Court of Appeal has wide cognition powers, both in matter of law and in matter of fact. And, as regards the latter, the judgment may entail a re-weighting of the first instance decision on the basis of the same facts, the reconsidering of the decision with new data, or the decision's annulment. For the effectiveness of this double competence in matter of fact and in matter of Law, the Courts of Appeal are granted and ensured oral conditions and conditions of immediacy, as to ensure a true and complete control of the trial of fact. This aim has been deemed as achieved through the recording and transcription of the presentation of evidential elements. The *Appeal of review* is meant to be filed near the Supreme Court of Justice, and is firstly meant to review the judgments issued by the Courts of Appeal which decide on the substance of the case. The review appeal has a staying effect only in questions regarding the state of people. The great civil procedural reform of 1995/1996, which has been in force since January 1, 1997, introduced a *per saltum* appeal from the first instance to the Supreme Court of Justice, which may occur whenever the parties request it in the conclusions of the first instance appeal, if the value of the cause is above the *alçada* of the Court of Appeal, or when the value of the loss – the value of the part in which the decision is unfavourable to the appellant – is above half that same *alçada*, and the parties evoke only legal questions in their allegations. By allowing the decision of a first instance court to be a direct object of assessment by the highest Court in the judicial hierarchy, the legislator intended to introduce a simplifying and accelerating factor to the case, without emptying the role of the second instance courts, since the Supreme Court of Justice has the last word in matter of law. The specific ground for a review is the violation of substantive law, which may consist in a misinterpretation or misapplication of the applicable rule, as well as in a mistake in determining it. However and accessorily, one may also invoke the violation of procedural law. If the appellant disputes a decision on the sole basis of its nullity, he should then file an *appeal of agravo*. Since as a rule, the Supreme Court of Justice only considers matter of law, the mistakes in assessing evidence and establishing the material facts of the case's main issue cannot be the object of an appeal of review, except in the case of disregard of an express legal provision which demands a certain kind of proof of the fact, or which establishes the power of a certain evidence." (See www.stj.pt.)

2. Supreme Court of Justice, 31 March 2004 (CJ-STJ [2004], I, 158 et seq.): Liability of the State for Jurisdictional Function

a) Brief Summary of the Facts

Mrs. A. sued the Portuguese State for bad administration of justice. She claims that, in a court case concerning termination of a leasing contract, the court of first instance and the court of appeal decided against the law. Therefore, she suffered pecuniary damage arising from the non-termination of that contract, which she calculates at approx. € 100,000. The defendant (State) argues that the courts did not decide against the law, on the contrary they made the best interpretation of a difficult legal problem. Therefore the State should not be considered liable for that damage. The first instance and the court of appeal did not accept the plaintiff's arguments. She appealed to the Supreme Court. 47

b) Judgment of the Court

According to Art. 22 of the Portuguese Constitution, "The State and other public bodies shall be jointly and severally liable under the civil law, with the members of their organs, their officials and their personnel, for acts or omissions in the performance of their functions, or caused by the performance of their functions, which result in contravention of rights, freedoms or guarantees or in damage to another person." The main doctrine accepts that this includes civil liability for jurisdictional function in general, and not only in the specific cases mentioned in Artt. 27 (5) and 29 (6) (illegitimate imprisonment or criminal conviction). However, it is essential for the safeguarding of the principle of independence of judges to defend the "*autonomy of interpretation*", that is, each judge is independent and that includes the freedom to interpret the law; "the judge cannot be conditioned in his actions by the fear of being punished or with the hope of being rewarded by following one or another doctrinal perspective." Moreover, legal science is not exact and there are often several legal opinions for one certain case. Moreover, the legal order provides for a system of appeals that aims to avoid unbearable decisions, including *ordinary* and *exceptional* review procedures. 48

In other countries the judge is only blamed if he/she acted with gross negligence (the Court quotes an Italian Statute). In conclusion, in order to establish state liability for the jurisdictional function, it must be proved that an ordinary judge, with ordinary skills and dedication would never have achieved the solution under analysis.[38] In this concrete case the judges did not violate the law; they applied one of the doctrines accepted in the literature to the concrete case. Thus the STJ did not condemn the State. 49

[38] The Supreme Court of Justice already accepted State liability for jurisdictional function: see STJ Decision of 3 December 1998.

c) Commentary

50 This decision explains the limits of State liability for jurisdictional function. Liability is accepted in principle, but under very strict conditions. It is worth noting that the Supreme Court mentions Portuguese doctrine, as well as developments in comparative law.

51 The Constitution of the Portuguese Republic establishes the general principle that the access to law and courts is ensured to everyone, so that they may defend their legally protected rights and interests and that justice cannot be denied on the basis of insufficient economic means. To this effect, the law provides citizens with the adequate judicial proceedings. Therefore, the ordinary law establishes a system of appeals against judicial decisions, divided into two main categories: appeals in *ordinary* and *exceptional* review procedures.[39]

3. Supreme Court of Justice, 17 June 2004 ([2004] CJ-STJ, II, 90–92): Consent, Assumption of Risk, Football Game among Friends

a) Brief Summary of the Facts

52 During a football game among friends the claimant was severely injured by Mr. C. The injured sues the tortfeasor and insurance company G.A. claiming compensation for pecuniary and non-pecuniary damage. The defendants argue that the injured consented to participating in that activity.

b) Judgment of the Court

53 The Supreme Court of Justice explained that in a football match among friends the scope of consent does not include severe injuries that are not in accordance with the football rules and that are not usual in such a sport. Thus such a consent, even if it existed, would be a violation of *bonos mores* (Art. 340 (2) CC) and the injury is therefore wrongful.

c) Commentary

54 The circumstances of the case were very relevant for the argumentation of the Supreme Court of Justice. The fact that the kick was very hard and caused severe injuries, as well as the fact that it was a leisure game among friends and not among professionals were relevant criteria for the decision. The Court considered that when someone accepts playing football, that fact does not include consent to severe injuries. Or, in any case, consent is not valid because such consent to severe injuries would be a violation of *bonos mores* (Art. 340 (2) CC). The Court did not mention the defence "assumption of risk" in sport activities; rather it operated with the more traditional concept of consent.[40]

[39] For more details see: http://www.stj.pt/eng/index_eng.html.

[40] See on this issue A. Pereira, Portuguese case note, Handeln auf eigene Gefahr beim Fußballspiel aus Sicht des portugiesischen Rechts: assunção do risco, [2004] *European Review of Private Law* 1, 119–128.

4. Lisbon's Court of Appeal, 12 February 2004 ([2004] CJ (*Colectânea de Jurisprudência*)-I-112): Omission, Duty of Prevention of Danger, Causation, Damages

a) Brief Summary of the Facts

On 18 May 1996 Mr. X, married, 36 years old, with 2 children, died after being shot by a firework in a football stadium where a football match of *high risk* (the Final of the Portuguese Cup) was being played between two rival teams from Lisbon (Sporting and Benfica). The firework was shot by Mr. Y, a fan of the opposite team, who was standing approx. 200m. away. Before the beginning of the game, the tortfeasor had already shot a dangerous firework in the direction of the other team's fans, but it fell behind the Stadium and did not injure anyone. After the first goal, the tortfeasor shot the lethal firework in the direction of the other fans. The victim died soon after the brutal injuries; before dying he suffered extreme pain in a hostile and unknown environment, which caused him intense suffering. The tortfeasor was charged with reckless manslaughter (*homicídio com negligência grosseira*). The Stadium did not have a video surveillance system and the control that was done at the entrance was not very intense. The victim was a healthy man, he worked and enjoyed life. The victim had an income of € 5,000 a year, and 2/3 of his income was destined to his family. They lived in someone else's house, who let it in exchange for the maintenance and surveillance of the house. In that house the victim could plant vegetables and keep some animals (pigs, chickens, rabbits, and a calf), which helped the domestic budget. After his death, his family had to leave the house, because they could no longer perform the maintenance services. They live now with the grandmother, with no possibility of planting vegetables nor having animals. The wife and the children suffered severe psychological damage with the death and the extraordinary circumstances in which it happened. The wife and the children sued the tortfeasor as well as the Portuguese Football Federation for damages. The Court of first instance condemned both defendants to pay damages. The Football Federation appealed, claiming that it is not liable for the wrongful behaviour of a third person. The plaintiffs also appealed, claiming a higher compensation. 55

b) Judgment of the Court

The Court of Appeal mentions the phenomenon of violence in sport, especially in football. The Court quotes several Recommendations of the Council of Europe, including the European Convention on Spectator Violence and Misbehaviour at Sports Events and in particular at Football Matches (ETS No. 120 – Strasbourg, 19 August 1985), ratified by the Portuguese State and published in the Official Journal (*Diário da República* (DR)) of 10 March 1987. This document points towards several preventive measures that should be taken before a "high risk" football match, including the prohibition of dangerous objects, such as fireworks. The Court mentions other national legislation, which prohibits some dangerous behaviour in a football match and gives the tools for prevention of severe accidents (especially DL 270/89, of 18 August, 56 in force at the time of the damage). The Court considered that, although the Football Federation, the organiser of the match, took many preventive measures (increased the number of policemen, separation of fans, search controls at the entrance), the Act expressly mentions that in each concrete match the organiser shall evaluate the dangers and take special measures. In this case, the tortfeasor shot a firework before the beginning of the game, which was very dangerous behaviour and 10 minutes after the start of the match he shot the fatal firework. This proves that the organiser of the match – the defendant – did not "neutralize" the tortfeasor (first defendant). The Court of Appeal considers that in such a situation there should be preventive measures but also repressive or re-active measures, so that in case of dangerous behaviour the spectator is immediately removed for security reasons. The control and surveillance shall be exercised not only during the entry into the Stadium, but also during the match whenever it is appropriate. This omission of the organiser is negligent and is to be censured by the Court. The death of Mr. X. would have been avoided if the tortfeasor had been arrested immediately after the first shot of a firework, that is if the defendant (Football Federation) had established an organised system of surveillance and reaction to dangerous events. Thus, the Court establishes a *causal link* between the *omission* of the defendant and the *damage*. The Court recognises the cause is a "negative" activity, which is accepted in Art. 486 CC, since the duty to act was imposed by law (DL 270/89). Thus, the second defendant, the organiser of the football match (the Portuguese Football Federation) is liable for the damages in solidarity with the first defendant.

57 Concerning damage, the Court of Appeal firstly analyses the non-pecuniary damages issue. According to Art. 496 CC, the Court shall award compensation on the basis of equity (*equidade*) taking into consideration the common sense, the fault of the tortfeasor, the economic situation of the tortfeasor and the injured party and other circumstances of the case. In Portugal there is a particular compensation for the violation of the right to life (*dano da morte*), and the Court awarded, according to case law practice, € 25,000 for this damage (it corresponds to what the plaintiffs had demanded). Moreover, there is the pain and suffering of the victim between the moment of the injury and his death. Taking into consideration the violence of the attack, the extreme suffering of the injuries (the thorax was burned by the explosion of the firework and many other personal injuries), the fact that he was in an unfamiliar environment with hundreds of people in panic around him and his absolute shock at being so attacked, the Court decides to compensate this damage with € 25,000, as the plaintiffs demanded. Thirdly, there is the damage suffered by the plaintiffs (wife and two children of the victim). They gained knowledge of this terrible death from a neighbour whose husband, who was also at the Stadium, phoned. The victim participated actively in the education and the school activities of his children. After their father's death, the children suffered an emotional shock, and the young daughter had to seek psychiatric assistance. Moreover, such a tragedy was followed by intense media activity which increased the pain and suffering of the plaintiffs. Considering all these elements,

the Court of Appeal awarded € 35,000 for the non-pecuniary damage of the spouse and € 25,000 for the non-pecuniary damage of each of the children. The Court explained thereinafter the future pecuniary damage (loss of earnings). The victim was 36 years old, was active and industrious. He earned € 5,000 a year and it is adequate to suppose that he would have worked another 30 years. 2/3 of his income was devoted to the family. All in all, the Court decided to order the defendants to pay € 100,000 for loss of earnings, from which € 50,000 shall be paid to the wife and the other € 50,000 to the children. This is justified by the fact that the children would later become autonomous and the victim would not contribute to their maintenance. As the Court cannot calculate the amount of damages exactly, it is a decision based on equity (*equidade*), as established in Art. 566 (3).

c) Commentary

Liability for omission is provided when the law or a contract establishes the duty to act (in Art. 486). The Court decided there was a duty of prevention of danger that was not fulfilled. This case also provides a very clear example of how Portuguese courts calculate pecuniary and non-pecuniary damages. 58

5. Porto's Court of Appeal, 28 September 2004 (www.dgsi.pt): "Old Timer", Natural Restitution

a) Brief Summary of the Facts

B sued C, owner of a car purchase business, claiming compensation of approx. € 16,500 for damage caused to his car, when it was being removed to an upper floor in a lift. While moving the car to the upper floor, the elevator crashed and the car fell 3 metres and consequently incurred damaged in the chassis, suspension and mechanics. The plaintiff claims that he also suffered emotional distress. The claimant repaired the car (approx. € 7,500 + VAT). However, the market value of the car was € 3,000. The court of first instance awarded compensation of € 7,539.16 for pecuniary damages and € 498.80 for non-pecuniary damages, plus interest since the citation. The defendant appealed. 59

b) Judgment of the Court

The defendant states that the compensation should not exceed € 3,000, according to Artt. 562 and 566 (1) that prescribe that, if natural restitution is too onerous on the defendant, there shall be compensation in money. Otherwise there would be abuse of right or unjustified enrichment. The Court does not agree with this opinion. Indeed, natural restitution shall not be applied when there is a strong and disproportional difference between the interest of the plaintiff (victim) to repair the thing and the cost of repair for the defendant. However, following the jurisprudence of the Supreme Court of Justice,[41] this rule shall not become a "premium" to the tortfeasor in order to relieve him of 60

[41] STJ 7 July 1999, in [1999] CJ-STS, III, 16 et seq.

his duty to *compensate* the victim, that is, to put the victim in the position she would have been if there had been no tort.

61 An old vehicle loses market value. However, it may satisfy the personal needs of its owner, as the market value, often very low, may not compensate the damage. Thus, case law has been deciding that it is not sufficient to take into consideration the market value of the automobile, but also the *value of use* for its owner, the utilities that he enjoys from an old car.[42] What should not happen is that the victim becomes richer through the natural restitution. There is a big difference between the market value (€ 3,000) and the repair costs (€ 7,500 + VAT). However, the court took into consideration the following topics: a new car of the same brand (AUDI) is very expensive; the fact that the car was severely damaged; the fact that the car was in very good condition before the accident; and it is understandable that the victim went to the automobile repair centre authorised by the brand (which is more expensive), in order to ensure the best reparation. The Court added that after the repairs the *vehicle did not increase in value*. For all these reasons, the Court decided that natural restitution is not very onerous on the defendant and ordered the defendant to compensate the victim for the cost of repairs + VAT + interest.

62 Concerning non-pecuniary damages, the Court of Appeal agrees with the majority of case law, according to which non-pecuniary damages arising from violation of a contract[43] can be compensated.[44] That does not mean, however, that any damage shall be compensated. According to Art. 496 (1) CC, only severe non-pecuniary damage, *which deserves the protection of the law*, is to be compensated. This evaluation shall be made taking into account objective criteria and not subjective criteria. Mere "inconveniences" or "disturbances" do not demand the *protection of the law*. Although the plaintiff claims "emotional distress" (lack of sleep, stress, etc.), the Court does not find any *reasonable* cause for these consequences. Thus, contrary to the first instance, the Court of Appeal did not order compensation for non-pecuniary damages.

c) Commentary

63 Concerning non-pecuniary damages, the decision is wise and just: the destruction of a thing is traditionally not accepted as a reasonable cause for awarding non-pecuniary damages.[45]

64 The compensation for pecuniary damage seems to be excessive. In Germany the limit would be 30% over the market value of the car.[46] In this case it is approx. 150% higher! The Supreme Court jurisprudence is to give compensation

[42] The Court quotes decision STJ 21 November 2000 ([2000] CJ-STJ, III, 124–125).

[43] The claimant and the defendant had a contract of *depósito* (*Lagervertrag*).

[44] The Court quotes several scholars (Galvão Telles, Almeida Costa, Vaz Serra) and case law: STJ 17 January 93 ([1993] CJ-STJ, I, 61) and STJ 9 December 1993 ([1993] CJ-STJ, III, 175).

[45] M. Almeida Costa, *Direito das Obrigações* (9th edn. 2001), 549 et seq.

[46] See B. Markesinis/H. Unberath, *The German Law of Torts – A comparative treatise* (2002), 935.

not only taking into account the *market value* of the car, but also taking into consideration its *economic value for its owner*; that is, the amount of damages must be enough to buy a car that fulfils the same conditions as the damaged car, in spite of its age.[47] The Supreme Court does not require restoration of the damaged object as such but requires a restoration of the *situation* which would have existed had the harmful event not occurred. However, repair costs that are 150% higher than the market value of the car seem to be excessive and too onerous for the wrongdoer (Art. 562 (2)).[48]

C. Literature

1. Manuel Carneiro da Frada, *Teoria da Confiança e Responsabilidade Civil* (Almedina, Coimbra 2004)

Vertrauenstheorie and tort liability is the title of Frada's dissertation (*Habilitationsschrift*). In its more than 900 pages the book presents extensive comparative research in the field of liability between tort and contract, dealing especially with pure economic damages. According to the author, the dogmatic source of liability in this field is the theory of "reliance", where the principle of good-faith is of key importance. 65

2. Luísa Neto, *O Direito Fundamental à Disposição Sobre o Próprio Corpo (A Relevância da Vontade na Configuração do Seu Regime)* (Coimbra Editora, Coimbra 2004)

The book corresponds to a dissertation (*Habilitationsschrift*) defended at the University of Porto. Although it is primarily a Constitutional law thesis, it is important for tort law since it deals with important medical law issues. Its title: The fundamental right to dispose of one's own body (the relevance of the will in its regime) explains that it deals with the issue of consent in a broad perspective. It concentrates in the third part on the following subjects: the right to life (abortion); the right to physical integrity, health and intimacy (concerning the limits of the autonomy of consent) and finally the damage of death and the issue of euthanasia. 66

[47] Supreme Court of Justice, 27 February 2003 ([2003] CJ-STJ, I, 112–114), see A. Pereira (supra fn. 7), 31 et seq.

[48] The Principles of European Tort Law (PETL) state that "damages are a money payment to compensate the victim" (Art. 10:101), and admit that (Art. 10:104) "instead of damages, restoration in kind can be claimed by the injured party as far as it is possible and not too burdensome to the other party." As money payment is the rule, perhaps such a *disproportionate* "reinstatement or restitution" would not be accepted under the PETL.

3. Ana Gonçalves Moniz, *Responsabilidade Civil Extracontratual por Danos Resultantes da Prestação de Cuidados de Saúde em Estabelecimentos Públicos: O Acesso à Justiça Administrativa* (Coimbra Editora, Centro de Direito Biomédico, 8, 2003)

67 This book provides an analysis of the regime of civil liability of public health care services in Portugal. This liability is subject to the administrative jurisdiction and follows the rules provided in Decree-Law 48051, of 21 November 1967. The author especially concentrates on questions of procedural law of the administrative jurisdiction. The process of restructuring public hospitals led the government to create in more than 35 health care centres, corporations that administer the hospitals. These corporations are private law entities, although the State owns 100% of the shares. For that reason there are some doubts in the Portuguese doctrine on which jurisdiction is competent (administrative jurisdiction or common jurisdiction) and which substantive law applies (Civil Code or Decree-Law 48051). This book also provides important information on this issue.

4. André Gonçalo Dias Pereira, *O Consentimento Informado na Relação Médico-Paciente. Estudo de Direito Civil* (Coimbra Editora, Centro de Direito Biomédico, 9, Coimbra 2004)

68 Pereira's dissertation subject is informed consent in the physician-patient relationship. In 700 pages the author presents extensive comparative research on the issue (including several legal orders, especially Austria, Belgium, France, England, Germany, the Netherlands and Spain) on the doctrine of informed consent. Starting from the historical, philosophical and legal emergence of the principle of autonomy in bioethics and the doctrine of informed consent in law, he presents the basis of this theory in the Portuguese legal order.

69 In the second part he deals with the most important dogmatic questions. The first one is: which *protected interests* (*bens jurídicos*) are protected by criminal law and by civil law in Portugal? Portuguese criminal law, similarly to the Austrian criminal law, only aims to protect liberty; however, the author states that this solution would be inconvenient and inadequate for civil law. Thus also *physical integrity* (and *life)* are interests protected by tort law and both pecuniary and non-pecuniary damage shall be compensated in case of violation of informed consent.

70 Secondly the author defends a new comprehension of the capacity to act: the general and abstract concepts that are an inheritance of the *Pandekten* shall be substituted by a more concrete legal analysis which is closer to reality. Thus the capacity to consent to medical acts shall not be provided by the rules of the general part of the Civil Code, but shall be created *ad hoc* taking into consideration several elements of the legal order, especially the Criminal Code that points to 14 years as the age up to which one may legally consent and the Convention on Human Rights and Biomedicine (in force in Portugal since 1 December 2001) that defends more respect for the will of incompetent pa-

tients. It would be desirable to have a special Statute concerning patients' rights where the issue of capacity to consent should be ruled (similarly to Spain, France, Belgium and the Netherlands).

Thirdly, the author defends an inversion of the burden of proof in case of violation of informed consent: this is common in several European countries and is the best solution taking into consideration the rules of civil procedure and burden of proof. He states that the physician (or the hospital) bears the burden of proof in cases of informed consent. There are procedural reasons and substantive reasons. The first ones are that it is *easier* for the physician to prove the fulfilment of that obligation. The contrary solution (the burden lying on the patient) would lead to a burden of proving a negative fact: the patient would have to prove that he was *not* informed. The substantive reason is that informed consent is a justification ground, thus an impeditive fact, which – according to Art. 340 (2) CC – must be proved by the defendant (the physician). 71

The third part of his dissertation contains a very extensive analysis of the following issues: capacity to consent, the duty to inform and the rules concerning consent and refusal of treatment. Concerning capacity to consent, there is an analysis of the capacity of minors and adolescents, incompetent adults, and competent adults. Moreover he studies the regimes of living wills and healthcare proxies in foreign countries and proposes a statutory regulation for this in Portugal. The duty to inform includes risks, secondary effects, alternatives and many other subjects that are analysed in detail. He defends the *concrete patient* criteria. Therapeutic privilege and the right not to know are also provided in the Criminal Code and in the Convention on Human Rights and Biomedicine, ratified by Portugal in 2001. Consent and refusal of treatment are regulated in Portuguese criminal law and civil law: there is a right to refuse a treatment even if that leads to death. 72

Finally, he analyses the exceptions to informed consent, including emergency and legal authorisation (compulsory treatments (Hansen disease, tuberculosis), compulsory vaccination, feeding of detained persons, etc.). 73

Throughout the book one finds not only the general theory and rules concerning informed consent, but also a detailed analysis of special medical activities (e.g., clinical trials, sterilisation, human organs and tissues transplants, abortion, the end of life therapies, genetic and AIDS tests). Moreover he presents innovative research concerning medical files, telemedicine and the wrongful life/wrongful birth issue. 74

5. António Menezes Cordeiro, *Igualdade Rodoviária e Acidentes de Viação nas Auto-Estradas* (Almedina, Coimbra 2004)

Traffic accidents on motorways have been giving rise to much litigation and several difficult legal questions. Menezes Cordeiro publishes a thorough analysis of case law and doctrine. 75

76 In his opinion, there is no contract between the concessionaire and the "user" of the motorway.[49] The presumption of fault established in Art. 493 (1) CC does not apply to damage caused "in" the immovable, but only to damage caused "by" the immovable. Neither the "contract with effect of protection of third parties" nor the contract in favour of third parties applies in these cases. The adequate regime is extra-contractual liability for violation of a "protective norm" (Art. 493 (1) CC), and the "protective norm" is to be found in DL 294/97, 24 October, that regulates the duties of the concessionaire of motorways. The victim has the burden of proof of the violation of these norms, the connection between that violation and the damage and the fault of the concessionaire.

6. J. Cardona Ferreira, *Acidentes de Viação em Auto-Estradas – Casos de Responsabilidade Civil Contratual?* (Coimbra Editora, Coimbra 2004)

77 Traffic accidents on motorways: a contractual liability situation? With this title Cardona Ferreira, former Judge and former President of the Supreme Court of Justice, has written a book containing his opinions concerning this problem. Moreover this book has several appendices with the most important legislation and case law.

78 The author concludes: a) regarding the contracts between the State and the concessionaires of motorways, with or without payment of toll, there is a contract with norms in favour of the "user" (contracts in favour of third parties that are not individualized; b) the individualization of the users is done by the private autonomy, when one declares, expressly or tacitly by the payment of the toll of the motorway, or by entering the motorway when there is no toll, in both cases one demands the use of the high-way with safety, comfort and legal speed; c) the concessionaire is bound by this contractual relation vis-à-vis the user; d) if there is an accident caused by an abnormal circumstance in the motorway, the concessionaire is liable towards the user in contract; e) the concessionaire bears the burden of proving that it acted with all necessary diligence; f) the regime of contract liability applies which; g) includes compensation for non-pecuniary damage.

7. Nélia Daniel Dias, *A Responsabilidade Civil do Juiz* (Dislivro, Lisboa 2004)

79 Part one of this book presents extensive research on civil liability of the judge from a historical and comparative law perspective. Secondly the author analyses all the conditions of civil liability of the judge (especially causation, fault and damage). Furthermore the book discusses the regime of State liability for

[49] Case law's dominant position, nowadays, considers that there is a contract between the user and the concessionaire. See Supreme Court of Justice Decision of 22 June 2004 ([2004] CJ-STJ, II, 96 102). The Supreme Court makes a long exposition on this issue and concludes for the "contractual doctrine".

jurisdictional function. The last chapter concerns civil liability of arbitration tribunals and other entities.

8. Tânia Meireles da Cunha, *Da Responsabilidade dos Gestores de Sociedades perante os Credores Sociais: A Culpa nas Responsabilidades Civil e Tributária* (Almedina, Coimbra 2004)

This book concerns corporation managers' liability vis-à-vis the *creditors of* 80
the corporation and the *fiscal administration*. Its main focus of research is the requisite of fault, because there is an important difference between liability vis-à-vis the corporation's creditors and the fiscal administration: in the latter the law imposes a *presumption of fault* of the manager (Art. 24 (1) (b) of the Basic Tax Law (*Lei Geral Tributária*)). The author presents a critical opinion on these differentiated regimes.

9. Fernando Correia Gomes, *A Responsabilidade civil dos bancos pelo pagamento de cheques falsos ou falsificados* (Almedina, Coimbra 2004)

This book concerns civil liability of banks arising from the payment of false or 81
falsified cheques. It presents an analysis of literature and case law concerning this subject, concerning the problems of liability limitation or exemption clauses.

10. Fausto de Quadros, *Responsabilidade Civil Extracontratual da Administração Pública* (2nd edn., Almedina, Coimbra 2004)

This book deals with State liability. This issue is gaining increasing practical 82
importance. This second edition pays special attention to the problems emerging from the influence of international law and community law in the Portuguese legal order. It also contains a renewed very broad selection of case law.

11. Rui de Freitas Rangel, *A Reparação Judicial dos Danos na Responsabilidade Civil (Um Olhar Sobre a Jurisprudência)* (2nd edn., Almedina, Coimbra 2004)

This book provides a study and a systematised analysis of case law concerning 83
damages, in particular non-pecuniary damages. The second edition provides even more case law and searches for criteria used in Portuguese courts in the field of compensable damage, the nature of compensation and the burden of proof.

12. Ives Gandra da Silva Martins/Diogo Leite Campos (eds.), *O Direito Contemporâneo em Portugal e no Brasil* (2004)

This book provides several articles on several legal issues of private and pub- 84
lic law, written by Portuguese and Brazilian authors. It aims to increase comparative law studies between Portuguese and Brazilian academics. In the field of tort law, the book contains two very important articles. António Pinto Mon-

teiro, *A Responsabilidade Civil No Direito Contemporâneo* (Civil liability in contemporary law) and Paulo Mota Pinto and Diogo Leite De Campos, *Direitos Fundamentais 'de Terceira Geração'* (Fundamental Rights of "Third Generation").

13. *Estudos em Comemoração do Décimo Aniversário da Licenciatura em Direito da Universidade do Minho* (2003)

85 This collection of essays commemorates the 10th anniversary of the School of Law of the University of Minho (in Braga). In this book one finds two interesting articles concerning tort law: Heinrich Ewald Horster, *Esboço esquemático sobre a responsabilidade civil de acordo com as regras do Código Civil* (Tort law and the rules of the Civil Code) and Sónia Moreira, *O ónus da prova na responsabilidade pré-contratual por violação de deveres de informação* (Burden of the proof on *culpa in contrahendo* actions for lack of information).

14. Orlando Guedes da Costa, *Direito Profissional do Advogado – Noções Elementares* (2nd edn. 2004)

86 This book concerns the professional rules of advocates. It includes a chapter on the civil liability of lawyers.

15. João Loureiro/André G.D. Pereira, Portuguese Report, in: E. Deutsch/H.-L.Schreiber/A. Spickhoff/J. Taupitz (eds.), *Die klinische Prüfung in der Medizin/Clinical Trials in Medicine – Europäische Regelungswerke auf dem Prüfstand/European Rules on Trial* (Springer, 2004)

87 The authors analyse the influence of Directive 2001/20/EC in Portuguese law. Loureiro presents the Portuguese legal framework concerning "therapeutic cloning" (where the European Convention on Human Rights and Biomedicine is of paramount importance) and explains the regulatory proposals on this subject. Pereira describes Portuguese law relating to scientific research in general and the trial of medicinal products and the trial of medical devices. The issues of informed consent and civil liability are thoroughly explained, considering national law, the European Convention on Human Rights and Biomedicine, the Directive 2001/20/EC, and other international instruments (*maxime* the Helsinki Declaration and the CIOMS Guidelines).

16. Jorge Ribeiro Faria, O ónus da prova na responsabilidade civil médica – reflexões em torno do direito alemão, [2004] *Revista da Faculdade de Direito da Universidade do Porto*, Vol. 1, 117–195

88 Ribeiro Faria, Professor at the University of Porto, presents an extensive research study concerning the burden of proof in medical liability actions in German law, including literature and case law. The author discusses the arguments and the doctrinal disputes that have been taking place in that country.

He finishes with an important comparison with Portuguese law and discusses whether the jurisprudence of the BGH could be received in Portuguese law and presents several arguments and possible solutions to achieve a positive answer.

17. Andrea Pinna, Le nouveau droit français de l'obligation d'information sur les risques médicaux, [2004] *Lex Medicinae – Revista Portuguesa de Direito da Saúde*, no. 1, 83–96

This article analyses the recent French legislation concerning the duty of information of medical risks established in the *loi du 4 mars 2002*. This Act seems to contradict the evolution of case law (of the *Cour de cassation*). Independently of the quantity of risks that should be revealed, the author considers the method that should be used in order to determine this. The author provides a comparative analysis of the problem and concludes that there are other problems to be solved and not only the question of how many risks should be disclosed. 89

18. Rui Prista Cascão, A Responsabilidade Civil e a Segurança Sanitária, [2004] *Lex Medicinae – Revista Portuguesa de Direito da Saúde*, no. 1, 97–106

This article analyses the shifts in medical malpractice in recent years and criticises the dominant approach to prevention of medical injury based on deterrence on the provider level. After an introduction where the statistical relevance of the occurrence of adverse events in medical treatment is pointed out, section 2 illustrates the shifts in medical practice during the 20th century and shows the factors that caused the well-known and feared "malpractice crisis". In section 3, the author explains how adverse events happen and how human error and organisational faults contribute to their materialisation. Chapter 4 is a critique to the deterrence based approach to prevention of medical injury, and points out the advantages of a system's approach, where the cooperation of healthcare providers in the design of safety strategies achieves a more efficient and pro-active approach to prevent medical injury. Several successful examples of liability systems, such as the Scandinavian no-fault insurance schemes or French law after the 2002 reform, are presented to substantiate the advantages of prevention through risk management in a systems approach over preventive focus based on deterrence throughout provider specific liability in the context of a blame culture. 90

The author concludes by providing some guidelines that are essential to render concrete that model of prevention: 1) Shift from provider specific liability towards institutional liability of hospitals; 2) Strict liability in case of injury caused by technological risks or hospital-acquired infections and 3) Alternative resolution of disputes and non-litigious, non-adversarial settlement of claims. 91

19. João Maia Rodrigues, Responsabilidade civil dos Notários, [2003] *Boletim dos Registos e do Notariado,* no. 2

92 Although Portuguese notaries have always been members of the "Latin Notary system", the State "nationalised" this activity in the 1940s and since then a notary has been a civil servant. Thus, civil liability of the State or other public bodies Statute (DL 48051, 21 November 1967) and the administrative jurisdiction apply to cases concerning a notary's negligence. This article researches the notary function in the organisation of justice, analyses notary civil liability regimes in other countries, describes the main legal and deontological duties of the notary and concludes with a comprehensive analysis of civil liability of notaries, according to Portuguese law.

20. Princípios do comércio electrónico, in: *Miscelâneas*, no. 3, (IDET – Instituto de Direito das Empresas e do Trabalho, Almedina, Coimbra 2004), 77–112

93 This paper explains the basic principles that underlie the European legal framework of electronic commerce as well as their implementation into Portuguese national law, such as: the principle of freedom of exercise of economic activities on the Internet, articulated with the principle of the primacy of community law (1), the principle of transparency of the electronic market (2), the principle of the freedom to negotiate and conclude contracts by electronic means, and the protection of the consumer in e-shopping (3), the principle of freedom of communication and navigation on the Internet and the reinforcement of intellectual property rights (4), and the principle of adopting informal means of dispute resolution (5).

21. André Gonçalo Dias Pereira, Portuguese case note, Handeln auf eigene Gefahr beim Fußballspiel aus Sicht des portugiesischen Rechts: assunção do risco, [2004] *European Review of Private Law* 1, 119–128.

94 The author discusses the decision of *Cour de Cassation française, 2e chambre civile*, 4 July 2002, on the assumption of risk according to Portuguese law. In this case a young girl, aged 10, was taking part in a football training session within the framework of a team organised by an association. She was injured by a ball shot at her by her assistant trainer who had been charged with supervision. The doctrine of assumption of risk was discussed in French courts and the *Cour de Cassation* decided that the fact that the child was participating in a pedagogical activity under the authority and supervision of a trainer excluded the assumption of risk. This theory has thus a more limited scope in sports (it seems to be limited to competitive games).

95 In Portuguese law the doctrine of assumption of risk is accepted in sports,[50] as long as the players respect the rules of the sport. If there is a grossly negligent

[50] See B. Proença, *A Conduta do lesado como Pressuposto e Critério de Imputação do Dano Extracontratual* (1997), 619.

or intentional violation of the basis rules of the sport, this defence does not apply. Only contributory negligence (Art. 570 CC) or *ad hoc* reduction of damages (Art. 494) may be taken into consideration. The author also analyses the capacity to assume a risk according to the fundamental right to free development of personality (Art. 26 Portuguese Constitution) and concludes that a (10 year old) child can assume a risk that is in his/her sphere of action.

The author defends flexible criteria to evaluate the defence assumption of risk. 96
One shall take into consideration factors such as: professional sport vs. amateur sport, training for competition vs. playing among friends and practice of sport under regulation of a federation, existence of a first-party insurance or existence of compulsory medical exams. In case of sport among friends, without first-party insurance and without compulsory medical exams, the scope and limits of the assumption of risk shall be shorter.

XX. Slovakia

Anton Dulak

A. Legislation

1. Changes in Workers' Compensation – Compensation in Cases of Accidents at Work and Occupational Diseases

1 As of 1 January 2004 the methods of workers' compensation in cases of accidents at work and occupational disease have been significantly changed. Such compensation had been governed by labour law legislation, namely *Zákonník práce* (the Labour Code, Act No. 65/1965 Zb. as amended). The first significant change occurred in 2002 when the new Labour Code (Act No. 311/2001 Z.z.) entered into effect. The new Labour Code now stresses the private nature of employment relations. When compared to the Civil Code, the Labour Code is intended to be a special statutory regulation. The provisions of the Civil Code can be applied to employment relations only in the absence of specific regulation (§ 1(2) of the Labour Code).

2 The Labour Code still provides expressly for compensation arising from employment relations. In a separate part (Part Eight) of the Act, employees' general liability for damage is defined in §§ 179–181 and employers' liability is defined in § 192. There are significant differences in how liability of the employee and the employer arise. An employee is responsible to the employer for any damage caused by the fault of the employee, or resulting from a breach of duties during the performance of occupational tasks or any directly related activity; the burden of proof is on the employer (§ 179) except for some specific cases. For an employer's liability to arise, it is sufficient that, in the performance of official duties or closely related activities, the damage resulted from a breach of statutory duties or intentional conduct contrary to good morals [1].

[1] Employer's responsibility for damage caused to an employee is defined as employer's liability for the employer's unlawful conduct (§ 192 (1)) and also as liability for damage caused by an employee acting on behalf of the employer (§ 192 (2)).

In cases of accidents at work and occupational diseases, employers' liability is governed by §§ 195 et seq. of the Labour Code. Accident at work means any harm caused to an employee's health in the performance of his/her work tasks or directly related activities without his/her will or intention and resulting from immediate, sudden and violent external causes (§ 195 (2)). An employer's liability arises regardless of any fault on his/her part, and even in cases of compliance with the requirements of special rules and other safety and health regulations (see § 195 (6)). An employer will not be liable only where some strictly defined reasons can be proven. 3

Since 2004 the scope of compensation has been modified. Prior to 2004 the employer had the duty to compensate the loss of earnings, pain and social hardship, reasonable costs of medical treatment, material damage (§ 198 (1)), and also the loss of retirement benefit (§ 202). In cases of death, the employer was obligated to pay compensation for reasonable costs of medical treatment, expenses related to a funeral, costs in respect of survivors' maintenance, to pay a lump sum of damages to survivors and the material damage (§ 204). Since January 2004, the employer is liable only for the material damage resulting from an accident at work and occupational disease, (§ 198 (1)). The remaining claims of the injured party must be settled within the insurance system. 4

Compensation for pain and social hardship, reasonable costs and other benefits for the injured party have been transferred to the social insurance system. Accident insurance coverage, together with sickness and pension benefits, now form the basis of social insurance. The allowances paid under accident insurance are regarded as compensatory damages. Whenever paid together with sickness and/or pension benefits, they are entirely of a complementary and supplementary nature. 5

Social insurance law defines the terms "accident at work" and "occupational disease" (§ 11) in accordance with their previously defined meanings. The employer is required by law to be insured against risks of accidents at work and occupational disease (§ 17) from the date when at least one employee has been hired (§ 26)[2]. As defined by law, accident insurance covers accident allowance, accident annuity, lump sum settlement, survivors' accident annuity, lump sum compensation, work rehabilitation, rehabilitation benefits, re-training and re-training compensation, compensation for pain and suffering, compensation for social hardship, compensation for the costs related with medical treatment, and compensation of costs related to a funeral. For accident allowances, the individual terms, general terms and conditions and the amount of damages are specified by law (§§ 92 et seq.). 6

[2] Employer's responsibility to be insured against the above risks was generally formulated in the original version of the Labour Code (§ 210). Insurance covered by the Social Insurance established as of 1 January 1995 is provided under sickness and pension insurance, to which compensation for occupational accident and occupational disease was transferred from *Slovenská pois_ovòa, a.s.* (the Slovak Insurance Company) as of 1 January 2002.

2. Amended Civil Code

7 Act No. 404/2004 Z. z., by which the Civil Code was amended as of 1 August 2004, responds to changes in determining claims for accidents at work under Act No. 461/2003 Z. z. on social insurance. As a result of these changes it was necessary to harmonize the rights under §§ 446–448 of the Civil Code, i.e. compensation for the duration of incapacity to work, compensation after incapacity to work has terminated, disability compensation, compensation for survivors' maintenance with the compensation rules in accident insurance. The aim of the amended Act was to provide for a universal determination of average (so-called original) earnings as a "daily assessment basis applicable for the given period".

3. Act No. 541/2004 Z.z. on the Peaceful Use of Nuclear Energy (the Nuclear Act)

8 This law passed by the National Council of the Slovak Republic on 9 September 2004 regulates, *inter alia* the requirements of nuclear safety, emergency systems, and liability for damage caused by nuclear incidents. The law entered into force on 1 December 2004.

9 The law regulates nuclear energy used for beneficial purposes the benefits of which should outweigh any possible risks, particularly when compared to other methods by which a similar aim can be obtained (§ 3 (3)). In respect of nuclear energy, emphasis is placed on safety before any other aspects.

10 The special Part Seven (§§ 29 et seq.) deals with liability in cases of nuclear damage and its compensatory damages. For the purposes of liability for nuclear damage, primarily the international rules of the Vienna Convention on civil liability for any damage caused by nuclear incident (Notice No. 70/1966 Z. z.) and the Common Protocol on the Application of the Vienna and Paris Conventions (Notice NO. 71/1996 Z. z.) apply. The provisions on general statutory regulations will apply to determine the scope and type of compensation in cases of nuclear damage, (§ 29 (4)).

11 The right to compensation for any nuclear damage becomes statute barred after three years from the date when the injured person or the person liable for such damage learnt or may have learnt of the occurrence of such incident. The maximum period of limitation is 20 years from the date of the beginning of such incident. The period of limitation exceeding 20 years will apply to cases in which the term of insurance continues also after the expiration of the period of 20 years after the incident.

12 In addition, any loss incurred in an attempt to prevent or reduce radiation or to restore the environment that was impaired as a result of a nuclear incident to its former or similar quality can also be considered a nuclear incident if the merit of the incident so allows (§ 29 (5)).

The amount of compensation for nuclear damage is limited by law. In cases of nuclear power stations, such compensation for any single incident will not exceed € 75,000,000, in other nuclear plants and in the case of damage incurred during the transport of radioactive material, the limit is € 50,000,000. 13

Liability of licensees is strictly defined in § 29. Licensees are obligated to secure coverage of their liability up to a certain amount by means of insurance and other financial security. The duration of such liability coverage must coincide with the license period and continue for at least 20 years after any single nuclear incident. 14

Newly defined is the duty of the licensee to report any nuclear incident by publishing a notice for the general public on view in the licensee's premises, and announced through the Office for Nuclear Control and all municipal authorities within the area. 15

4. Act No. 437/2004 Z. z. Concerning Compensation for the Pain Suffered by an Injured Person and Resulting Social Hardship

The bill drafted at the end of 2003[3] dealt with compensation for pain and social hardship caused by accidents at work, occupational disease or other health impairment. There were three alternatives proposed in the bill[4]. 16

According to the current law (§ 5), the amount of compensation is determined from a point scale basis to be assessed by a medical expert. The amount of compensation per point should be 2%[5] of the average nominal monthly salary of the employee in the economic sector as determined by the Statistics Office of the Slovak Republic for the year preceding the one in which the accident occurred. 17

The possibilities to increase compensation determined in this manner are limited by law. A court can increase compensation for social hardship (but not compensation for pain and suffering) only in cases of special importance, e.g. in determining disability[6]. The maximum limit of increased compensation is 50%. 18

Newly defined is the possibility of an out-of-court settlement by a so-called settlement agreement (§ 6). The law makes it possible for the parties to agree in writing about compensation for social hardship also beyond the limit set by law. The agreed compensation, however, cannot be higher than the maximum limit of compensation that could be determined by a court. 19

[3] The draft of the new law concerning compensation for pain and social hardship of 19 December 2003 (No. 02321/2003-OAP).

[4] See H. Koziol/B.C. Steininger (eds.), *European Tort Law 2003* (2004), 359–361.

[5] The bill set the amount of compensation to 1.5% of the average nominal monthly salary.

[6] §§ 70–73 of Act No. 461/2003 Z. z. as amended.

20 The injured party can claim compensation for social hardship before a court where the injured party sought to make a settlement agreement under § 6(1) but no agreement satisfying the injured party's claims has been reached within three months.

21 The law became effective on 1 August 2004.

5. Act No. 420/2004 Z. z. on Mediation and the Amendment of other Laws

22 Mediation means an informal/out-of-court resolution of the parties' dispute arising from their contractual or other legal relations by a mediator. This law, applying to disputes based on civil, family business and employment relations[7], came into effect on 1 September 2004.

23 The parties can make a written agreement to resolve a dispute by mediation. Such written agreement can be replaced by a declaration of the parties to be recorded in the minutes taken by the mediator.

24 As established by law, the parties can agree that the settlement achieved by mediation will be binding on their legal successors (§ 7 (3)).

25 The result of mediation is a written agreement upon which the entitled party can seek enforcement or execution by a court order. Such agreement must have the form of a deed certified by a notary or a settlement to be approved by a court or arbitration tribunal (§15 (2)).

6. Act No. 382/2004 Z. z. on Experts, Interpreters and Translators, also Amending other Laws

26 This law, changing the law of 1967[8], sets the requirements and procedures for experts, interpreters and translators. One of the new requirements is the duty to hold an insurance policy against risks of liability for damage resulting from the activities of the profession in question. Such insurance must be maintained throughout the entire performance of their official duties.

27 Experts, interpreters and translators registered in the official list must hold insurance coverage with the liability limit set for experts at the minimum of SKK 1 million (approx. € 25, 000), and SKK 100, 000 (approx. € 2,500), for interpreters and translators.

[7] See also Act No. 550/2003 on probation and mediation officers. This law concerns probation and mediation matters dealt with in criminal proceedings. The task of a probation officer here is to make an agreement between the injured party and the defendant to compensate the damage caused by criminal activity, or to make good for the loss caused by the injury arising from a crime. The mediation officer acts upon a written action of a judge or a public prosecutor (in pre-trail proceedings).

[8] Act No. 36/1967 Zb.

7. Changes in the Limits of Compensation for Damage Caused by Defective Products

Act No. 294/1999 Z. z. governing liability for damage caused by defective products was changed on 1 September 2004[9]. Manufacturers are liable for damage arising from products other than defective products only where the damage exceeds SKK 20,000 (approx. € 500). Previously the limit was fixed at SKK 500 (approx. € 125) which was justified by the fact that the limit under the European Directive was too high for the Slovak Republic when considering prices of consumer goods and consumers' average income[10]. 28

8. Amended Consumer Protection Act

By Act No. 616/2004 Z. z., some fundamental consumers' rights have been included in the original regulation. These rights include the following: the right to good quality of products and services, the right to education, the right to information, the right to the protection of health, safety and economic interests, and the right to be compensated for damage (§ 2a). This amendment aims to eliminate the former insufficient regulation providing for such protection only indirectly by defining the powers of governmental authorities and prescribing some obligations for business associations. The amended law has expressly established some consumers' rights. 29

B. Cases

1. Judgment of *Najvyšší súd Slovenskej republiky* (Supreme Court of the Slovak Republic, NS SR) of 10 September 2002 (Case No. 2 Cdo 32/02), Published in the Collection of Supreme Court Decisions under No. R 29/04: Loss of Earnings of an Unemployed Individual

a) Brief Summary of the Facts

The plaintiff claimed compensation for damage caused by a gas explosion. 30

The appellate court upheld the decision of the court of first instance dismissing the claim of the injured party for compensation of the loss of earnings during her incapacity to work as unfounded. The appellate court held that the injured party was unemployed at the time of the damage (received unemployment benefits while looking for employment) and was not entitled to any wages during this incapacity to work. The courts concluded that the plaintiff incurred no loss of earnings during her incapacity to work. The courts did not think the plaintiff was entitled to compensation for the loss of wages after her incapacity to work terminated, although she has attended a training course on how to run a business. The appellate court also decided on the most important issue i.e. what 31

[9] Act No. č. 451/2004 Z. z. amending Act No. 634/1992 Zb. on consumer protection.
[10] See A. Dulak, *Liability for damage caused by defective products* (2002), 101.

basic earnings should be determined by the Court for the injured as compensation for the loss.

32 The Supreme Court of the Slovak Republic, as the court of special appeal, reviewed the judgment of the appellate court, and came to the conclusion that the decision of the appellate court had been wrong. The challenged decision of the appellate court was quashed and remanded for further proceedings during which the opinion of the Supreme Court was binding.

b) Judgment of the Court

33 The injured person is entitled to compensation for the loss of earnings after his/her incapacity has terminated also in cases when such loss occurred while he/she was unemployed and during which time the person received no wages or income other than unemployment benefit.

34 In such case the injured party must prove his/her intent to be involved in any gainful activity as soon as his/her incapacity to work has terminated, but he/she failed to do so solely because of the harm caused to his/her health.

35 In determining the amount of compensation for the loss of earnings after termination of incapacity to work, it is necessary to consider the possible earnings that could have been achieved if there had been no harm to health.

c) Commentary

36 In its opinion, the Supreme Court held that an equitable settlement for the damage caused to the injured party in contractual obligations could be reached only by absolute removal of any material disadvantage of the injured party.

37 The special nature of compensation for damage caused to health requires a special regulation in respect of the methods and amount of compensation. Therefore, the provisions of the Civil Code (§§ 445 et seq.) cannot fall under the definition of actual loss or lost profit.

38 In agreement with the Commentaries to the Civil Code (concerning the provisions contained in §§ 445 et seq.), compensation for the loss caused by harm to health is based upon the principle of material security of the injured party necessary for future life.

39 Loss of earnings as defined by §§ 445 et seq. of the Civil Code is a broader term than a wage loss or loss of other pay for work. Under this statutory rule, compensation for loss of earnings does not depend on the duration of gainful activity of the injured party (so-called employment or similar relation) at the time of the accident. Slovak legislation and the judicial practice, on the contrary, have always considered the possibility to compensate for the loss of earnings also during the time in which gainful activity could have been assumed, and which, if it were not for the accident and the related harm to health, would have been performed later.

2. Judgment of NS SR of 22 October 2002 (Case No. M Cdo 73/02), Published in the Collection of Supreme Court Decisions under No. R 45/2004: Payable Insurance Premium

a) Brief Summary of the Facts

The District Court/court of first instance bound the defendant to pay to the plaintiff SKK 24,700 (approx. € 618) plus interest of 17.6% for late payment and court costs. The District Court stated that the defendant obtained his car on 19 September 1995, paid the compulsory insurance in the morning of 3 October 1995, and on the same day (at 2.45 p.m.) a traffic accident was caused by this car. The Court maintained that the defendant was in default of insurance premium (due on 20 September 1995), therefore the defendant was obligated to pay to the plaintiff (the insurance company) a recourse compensation of 50% of the amount paid. 40

The Regional Court/appellate court upheld the decision of the District Court. 41

The Prosecutor General of the Slovak Republic challenged the judgments of the District Court and the Regional Court by lodging a special appeal, reasoning that both courts based their decisions on justly proven facts. The Prosecutor General, however, challenged the opinions of both courts as incorrect, disagreeing that late payment of insurance premiums did not constitute the right of the insurance company to require recourse compensation. The Prosecutor General held that although the premium was payable on 18 September 1995, after the defendant paid the premium amount on 3 October 1995, his debt was satisfied under § 559 (1) of the Civil Code. At the time of the accident the defendant was no longer in default and, therefore, the insurance company had no right to claim recourse compensation. 42

The Supreme Court of the Slovak Republic, as the court of extraordinary appeal, reviewed the case and concluded that the appeal was justified. Therefore, the judgments of both courts were quashed and the case was remanded to the court of first instance (District Court) binding it with this opinion. 43

b) Judgment of the Court

The insured, whose premium has been paid at the time of an insurance incident, is not in default in accordance with § 11 (4) of Regulation No. 423/1991 Zb., although the premium was paid after the due date. 44

c) Commentary

The Supreme Court of the Slovak Republic concurred with the opinion of the Prosecutor General holding that, by payment of the premium, the debt was satisfied. In the case in question the payment and the insurance incident occurred on the same day, and, therefore, in respect of compensation for the insurance company, the decisive factor was whether the premium payment was made before or after the accident. The burden of proof is on the defendant who 45 must show the exact time when he satisfied his debt against the insurance company.

3. Judgment of NS SR of 26 February 2002, (Case No. 5 Cdo 117/2000), Published in the Collection of Supreme Court Decisions under No. R 48/2004: Increasing Damages for Pain and Social Hardship

a) Brief Summary of the Facts

46 The plaintiff lodged a claim to a District Court for compensation for damage caused by an accident at work. He claimed compensation in the amount of SKK 1,168,160 (approx. € 29,204), an amount 70 times the basic point assessment for pain/suffering and social hardship. During the proceedings, and based on a new assessment of pain and social hardship, the plaintiff amended his claim by increasing the amount of compensation to SKK 7,208,250, (approx. € 180,206). He based his allegations on irreversible consequences of the accident, limited chances to engage in social, private and employment activities despite his young age, and continuing psychological suffering, all of which justified the extraordinary increase of compensation he was seeking to recover.

47 The District Court ordered the defendant to pay to the plaintiff compensation of SKK 1,004,775, (approx. € 25,119), dismissing the rest of the claim. The Court found the claim was justified within the limit of 20 times the amount corresponding to the basic point assessment of pain and social hardship. The Court held the rest of the claim to be unfounded, as "this was not a case of a top sportsman or an official involved in political or cultural matters of public interest".

48 The Regional Court as the appellate court changed the decision of the District Court and ordered the defendant to pay to the plaintiff the compensation of SKK 810,000 (approx. € 20,250), dismissing the rest of the claim, agreeing with the opinion of the District Court, according to which, 20 times the amount of the damages assessed was adequate. Unlike the District Court, the Regional Court maintained that compensation for pain and suffering must be distinguished from compensation for social hardship because these two categories of compensation are based on different criteria, and any compensation increased beyond the amount assessed by a medical expert can be justified only in exceptional cases, such as e.g. most severe suffering, which however, was not the plaintiff's case.

49 The plaintiff filed an extraordinary appeal against the decision of the appellate court to the Supreme Court. He maintained that the decision of the appellate court, by which the plaintiff's compensation was not granted in the amount of 20 times the basic point assessment, was incorrect. He disagreed with the opinion of the appellate (Regional Court) according to which a lump sum amount of increased compensation for pain was not possible and referred also

to judgments of other courts in which compensation for pain and social hardship was adequately and uniformly increased.

The Supreme Court of the Slovak Republic, as a court of extraordinary appeal, came to the conclusion that an extraordinary appeal was unfounded. 50

b) Judgment of the Court

Just reasons for increased compensation for social hardship as provided by § 7(3) of Regulation No. 32/1965 Zb. governing compensation for pain and social hardship as amended do not constitute just reasons for increased compensation for pain, or vice versa. 51

c) Commentary

In its opinion the Supreme Court held that compensation for pain and compensation for social hardship are two elements of compensation, relatively independent of each other, although they are governed by the same regulation. Regulation 32/1965 Zb. prescribes the requirements that must be met in claims for compensation for pain separately from those in claims for compensation for social hardship. Specifically defined are the assessment principles governing these two types of compensation. Compensation for pain relates to pain already suffered while compensation for social hardship relates to future pain. Where there are just reasons for increased compensation for social hardship, it does not follow that there are also just reasons for increased compensation for pain. 52

4. Judgment of NS SR of 24 November 2002 (Case No. 4 Sž 118/02) Published in the Collection of Decisions of the Supreme Court under No. R 36/2004: Driving under the Influence of Alcohol

a) Brief Summary of the Facts

The defendant sought to have a decision quashed through which he was discharged from his service in the Slovak police. The reason for his discharge was his driving under the influence of alcohol. The defendant argued, *inter alia*, he did not cause the accident, stressing that, according to an expert report, he minimized the accident consequences. The defendant contended that by his quick reaction to the given situation, he prevented more serious consequences although he did not prevent the accident itself. The defendant also argued that the Order of the Minister of Interior of the Slovak Republic, whereby a policeman under the influence of alcohol is liable for a gross misconduct is contrary to the Charter of Fundamental Rights and Freedoms, and the Constitution of the Slovak Republic, and places policemen in a more disadvantageous situation than other citizens. 53

The administrative authority under challenge dismissed his complaint as unfounded. The Supreme Court of the Slovak Republic reviewed the decision and concluded, concurringly, that the complaint was unfounded. 54

b) Judgment of the Court

55 Driving motor vehicles is, in essence, a dangerous operation as regards possible impact on property, health and life of others. This danger is even greater when a driver is under the influence of alcohol, i.e. in a condition significantly affecting and impairing his motor and reaction capabilities, his will and ability to follow the traffic rules and to respond quickly to traffic situations. The subjective feeling and the self-confidence of a driver under the influence of alcohol, who believes that his abilities remain unaffected, only further contribute to increased risks of dangerous driving.

c) Commentary

56 The opinion of the Supreme Court emphasizes, quite interestingly, the pledge taken by police officers as a prescribed procedure required in a service to the public. According to the Court, this pledge of service is not a hollow proclamation made in the solemn ceremonial act, it is a confirmation of official duties. By taking such a pledge, a person becomes an officer who, when acting in violation of legal rules, must be considered through the prism of such pledge. By driving under the influence of alcohol, the defendant acted in violation of the law and in breach of the pledge of his official duties, which may have a significant impact on the police authority.

C. Literature

1. J. Lazar et al., *Základy občianskeho hmotného práva* (Basic System of Civil Substantive Law) (2nd edn., Iura Edition 2004)

57 The second edition of the textbook covering civil substantive law reaches far beyond its original purpose as it is a book of authority of great significance in the given field. Written by a collective of authors, scholars from all public law schools in the Slovak Republic, this second modified edition describes all legislative changes of the period, 2000–2003. The book also presents the interpretations of E.U. Directives implemented into Slovak law and deals with some private attempts to create the principles of private European law. This book, therefore, is an important source of law not only for law students but also for all legal practitioners.

2. F. Miklík, Problémy zodpovednosti štátu za škodu pri výkone verejnej moci (Issues of Liability of the State for a Damage Caused in the Performance of Governmental Powers) – Part 1. [2004] *Justičná revue* 10, 1094 and Part 2 [2004]. *Justičná revue* 11, 1241 – 1251

58 This study deals with the newly passed law concerning liability of the State for a damage caused in the exercise of governmental powers and replacing the statutory regulation of 1969. The author comments on various legal provisions, criticizing the new law because it has not removed all of its former de-

fects. Without a definition of a wrongful conduct of official authorities, it is still not clear whether the Prosecutor General who has not made an appeal against a violation of law can also be liable for wrongful conduct. The author also comments on the right of the State to recover compensation from specified entities. Quite controversial is the issue of compensation required by the State from judges. However, not the judge but the court is the authority of governmental power. The author concludes that, because of significant limitations, compensation for damage by the State will not be applicable in many cases and the majority of compensation of recourse cases will not be applicable, and generally not recovered from the officials concerned. On the contrary, such compensation will be applicable only in exceptional cases. The State will not only be held liable for damage but the State will have to suffer and sustain the damage (s. 1251).

3. Ľ. Babjaková, O náhrade nemajetkovej ujmy alebo o ochrane osobnosti zase trochu inak (Some other Aspects of Non-material Compensation and Protection of Persons against Defamation), [2004] *Justičná revue* 12, 1373–1383

The article deals with the development of the concept of protection of persons 59
from defamation and the remedy of non-material compensation by monetary damages. The author refers to legislative differences between the Czech Republic and the Slovak Republic after they became independent, where the same provisions of §§ 11 et seq. of the Civil Code resulted in different practical applications. The author also refers to Act No. 514/2003 Z. z. on liability for damage caused in the exercise of governmental power, emphasizing, in particular, § 17 (2) of the Act, by which the current definition of the right to compensation of real material damage is also extended to cases of compensation as the right to "equitable satisfaction".

4. P. Kerecman, K úvahám o citovej ujme, jej odškodňovanie a ochrane osobnosti (Some Considerations Concerning Emotional Distress, Compensation and Protection from Defamatory Statements), [2004] *Justičná revue* 6–7, 783–789

The author reacts to some trends in the application of the provisions concern- 60
ing protection from defamation (§§ 11 et seq. of the Civil Code). By reference to some decisions made by the courts dealing with the issue, the author questions whether § 11 provides sufficient support for non-material compensation granted to surviving relatives of a killed person for interference with their rights to the protection of personal integrity, or whether non-material compensation can also be granted where other elements of personal integrity are involved.

XXI. Slovenia

Rok Lampe

A. Legislation

1 Due to the election year (European Parliament elections and National Assembly elections), the Slovenian legislator was not particularly active in 2004. In terms of statutory tort law the year was also relatively tranquil. The two statutes that must be mentioned, however, are the Data Protection Act and the Environmental Protection Act. Both statutes are the third in a row of their kind, which have been passed since 1991. If there are parallels between these acts, then it is perhaps their "lagging" behind the new technical achievements and developments. On the other hand, tort law in Slovenian court practice has been very vital. In particular, the Supreme Court dealt with many interesting cases which are highlighted in the following text. Tort law as well as civil law practice in general is still suffering under art. 6 of the European Convention on Human Rights syndrome. Civil litigation occurs over an unreasonably long period of time. One of the crucial issues is undoubtedly the complaint procedure which also takes an excessively long time.

1. Data Protection Act

2 The Data Protection Act[1] was passed on 8 August 2004 and has been valid since 1 January 2005. It is a modern data protection Act that follows new trends in data protection law as well as new scientific and technical achievements. The Act is a prolongation of art. 8 of the European Convention on Human Rights and the European Convention on data protection from 1981 which was ratified by the Slovenian parliament in 1994 and has also been valid since. Beside these international legal tools, the Act also follows EU-directives on data protection. The Act is designed to protect the individual from illegal invasions into his privacy. The right to privacy is protected in Slovenian law already with the Constitution (art. 35). This general rule protects individual's dignity in general, his physical and psychical integrity and privacy. Data protection is also specially guaranteed with a particular constitutional provi-

[1] Official gazette of the Republic of Slovenia, no. 86-3836/2004.

sion – art. 38. It states that the collection, use, monitoring and protection of personal data are regulated by special statutory law. Every person has the right to become acquainted with his stored personal data and has the right to legal protection from abuses of his personal data.

Data is also protected under criminal law, which consequently raises civil law consequences. The Penal Code incriminates misuses of personal data as a violation of one's privacy. It prohibits the illegal use of personal data which may be collected and stored only according to a special statute. It also incriminates invasion into an electronic data collection. These two crimes are qualified if committed by a public official. Such a qualified case was already registered when a police officer was found guilty of invading the police electronic data collection for personal reasons. An important legal tool for personal data and privacy protection in general is tort law. Slovenian civil courts have constantly based their decision on invasions of personality rights, including the right to privacy, on the Constitution. The direct effect (*unmittelbare Drittwirkung*) is characteristic also for Slovenian personality law. The Code on Obligations (art. 179) is the *causa remota* of civil liability for personality rights' violations. Slovenian civil courts have registered a number of cases of violations of the right to privacy, which seems to be the trend in respect of tort law practice in general. 3

The Data Protection Act includes general principles on personal data protection, which are already incorporated in various international documents (for example, the UN Guidelines on Computerized Personal Data Files[2]) and European ones, just to mention the European convention on data protection: principle of legality and fairness (art. 2, 8, 16), principle of proportionality (art. 3), accuracy principle of stored data (art. 18), prohibition of discrimination principle (art. 4), principle of free access (art. 29, 3), etc. Beside the general principles, the Act also includes a very important general rule on the limits of personal privacy. Art. 36 of the Data Protection Act, increases the limits of the right to privacy based on the European Convention on Human Rights, par. 2 of art. 8. According to this provision, one's privacy is limited due to reasons of national security and national defence; protection of constitutional order; political, safety and economic interests of the State; police competences; monetary and customary reasons; rights and freedoms of others. 4

The Data Protection Act defines a person's rights in respect of stored personal data – the right to examine the stored data; the right to be informed about stored data; the right to supplement, to correct, to block, and to demand cancellation of the stored data; and the right to judicial protection. The Act foresees a special administrative procedure for the implementation of these rights and a special administrative monitoring. Regarding the new technical trends, the Act defines and regulates the storage of highly sensitive data (data on racial or national origin, political, religious, philosophic belief, union member- 5

[2] UN Economic and Social Council, doc. E/CN.4/1990/72.

ship, health conditions, sexual life and criminal register) and data on personal biometry. Biometry data are such bodily, psychological or behavioural characteristics which are unique and permanent to each individual. With these data it is possible to identify an individual, as with finger prints, capillary lines on a finger, irises, retina, face, ears, DNA and characteristics of deportment.

2. Environmental Protection Act

6 The Environmental Protection Act[3], passed on 22 April 2004 and valid since 5 July 2004, is the key statute on the environment and its legal protection in general. Although specifically mentioned in the Constitution[4], the environment is still subjected to an anthropocentric approach. The Constitution guarantees everyone the right to a healthy environment. The Environmental Protection Act is designed to enforce this right. The Act is an administrative act, which includes some provisions that are also very important for civil law. Of prime importance is, of course, the polluter pays principle, which would also be one of the general principles of private environmental law. Civil/private environmental law is regulated partly with the Property Code and partly with the Code on Obligations.

7 The Environmental Protection Act foresees criminal and civil liability of the polluter as well. His primary duty is to remove the pollution source, to recover the pollution and to compensate the owner. The environment and private property within the environment must be used according to the principle of the ecological function of property.[5] The ecological function of property demands the use of property for the purpose of preservation and improvement of the quality of the environment, to foster natural values and biological diversity. The use and enjoyment of private property may be limited due to the protection of nature. Not only private property but also the public good must be used in such a manner as not to negatively influence the environment.

8 In terms of tort law, the following principles and provisions of the Environmental Protection Act are very important. Emission in private environmental law is defined as direct or indirect contamination of liquids, gases, heavy metals or energy (noise, vibrations, radiation, heat or light) from a source into the environment. An emission is legally permissible according to the Property Code if it is legally authorized or is within the customary limits of a certain commu-

[3] Official gazette of the Republic of Slovenia, no. 41-1694/2004.

[4] Art. 72 (Healthy Living Environment): "Everyone has the right in accordance with the law to a healthy living environment. The state shall promote a healthy living environment. To this end, the conditions and manner in which economic and other activities are pursued shall be established by law. The law shall establish under which conditions and to what extent a person who has damaged the living environment is obliged to provide compensation. The protection of animals from cruelty shall be regulated by law."

[5] This function of property is already defined in the Constitution – art. 67 (Property): "The manner in which property is acquired and enjoyed shall be established by law so as to ensure its economic, social and environmental function. The manner and conditions of inheritance shall be established by law."

nity. The administrative procedure for the environmental permit is regulated by the Environmental Protection Act.

One of the important civil law tools defined in the Environmental Protection Act is the environmental class action. Art. 9 foresees an environmental class action as a special action for citizens or associations to demand from the civil court that an intervention in the environment be stopped if such an intervention causes or could cause excessive burdening. Excessive burden is a direct threat to human life or health. A court can prohibit an international intervention if the applicant proves with a "high degree of certainty" that excessive burdening will be caused. 9

B. Cases

1. Judgment of the Supreme Court, II Ips 90/2003: Media Law

The first presented case is a media law case, which is becoming more and more frequent in Slovenian legal practice. The applicant *juge d'instruction* (*preiskovalni sodnik*, *Untersuchungsrichter*) allowed examination of a court record which was kept in his office. The judge instructed his secretary to open the locked writing table even if she had to use force. His secretary actually used force to open the locked table. A newspaper, the defendant, received an anonymous letter that drew attention to this unusual event. The defendant's employee, a reporter, interviewed the head of the "instruction/investigation department" as well as the head of the Court. Both neither denied nor confirmed the anonymous information. The head of the Court explained to the reporter that he had also received such a letter. He also commented that the accused or another party in the trial has the right to examine the court record, according to the Slovenian Act on Criminal Procedure. According to this gathered information, the defendant published an article entitled "Did they break into the judge's writing table?" in 1992. In particular, the Supreme Court considered the fact that the anonymous information was neither denied nor confirmed by the head of the investigation department or by the head of the Court to be an essential circumstance on which the reporter built his own opinion regarding its truthfulness. 10

The *juge d'instruction* filed a libel action which was rejected by the district court. The Court based its decision on the fact that the reporter examined the verity of the anonymous information according to the due standard of care. The Code on Reporters' Ethics namely demands that a reporter investigate and examine the authenticity and truthfulness of anonymous information. The decision of the district court, which was confirmed by the appellate as well as by the Supreme Court, found that the defendant did not intend to insult the applicant. He merely exercised his legitimate right to inform the public and to advise on conditions in the judiciary. 11

2. Judgment of the Supreme Court, II Ips 537/2003: Traffic Accident – Causality Issue

12 In 1998 the applicant, a moped rider, was injured in a traffic accident. He crashed with a car driver who was insured by the defendant. The applicant was 15 years old at the time of the accident. Because of the accident he had to use crutches for 12 months. During this time he fell because of using the crutches and suffered another fracture in the same spot that was injured in the traffic accident. He suffered a complicated fracture of his left thighbone, crumbled protuberance in his left knee and a disrupted wound to his left ankle.

13 The applicant underwent medical treatment continuously for 15 months. The treatment was performed partly on an in-patient basis, partly in a health resort and partly on an out-patient basis. The applicant underwent 3 operations, spent 38 days in hospital, received blood transfusions, was exposed to high doses of antibiotics, underwent a number of X-rays, used crutches for 12 months and constantly underwent various medical examinations. He suffered 2 months of severe physical suffering, followed by 2 months of middle physical suffering and 4 months of light physical pain. He will experience pain also in the future, the main reasons for this being burdening of his leg and bad weather changes. The district court awarded him € 11,000 for this type of non-pecuniary loss. The applicant was also exposed to a high level of fear, which in terms of the district court equaled horror. He was frightened before each operation and was exposed to secondary fear, which was present for at least a month. He was compensated on this basis with € 1,700. Because of the injury, the applicant will not be able to walk for long distances, uphill and downhill, will not be able to jump, to lift weights, to run, to knee down etc. Because of this he had to stop practising basketball and had to change his profession. He was awarded with € 17,000 for decreased life activities. His leg is disfigured and scarred. He received compensation in the amount of € 900 for fear.

14 The defendant challenged the decision at the appellate court, claiming that the applicant's second fracture is not in causal connection with the traffic accident. The defendant stressed that a medical expert witness is not competent to solve questions on a legally relevant causal connection. An insurance company is not liable for the damage that occurs to the applicant exclusively due to his own fault. It is apparently also not common that the use of crutches leads to such injuries and, because of this; the damage that occurred because of the traffic accident is the only object of this litigation. The lower courts have, according to the defendant's argumentation, exceeded the interpretation of legally relevant causality beyond reason. The defendant cannot be responsible for a fact that caused another fact, which led to the outcome.

15 The Supreme Court rejected the defendant's appeal and confirmed the decision and the argumentation of the appellate court. It found that the intermediate court correctly debated on the existing causal connection between the traffic accident and the fall with crutches. The lower courts correctly based their

decisions on the expert testimonies. The fall with crutches that caused the fracture of the plate thighbone occurred just two months after the operation of the thighbone fracture. An X-ray showed a fracture of the bone which was weakened because of the first fracture. The defendant was also misled in believing that the use of crutches does not normally lead to further fractions. Legal and medical practice register a number of cases where the use of crutches led to re-fracturing of the same bones. The defendant's argumentation that the second fracture was caused only because of the applicant's clumsiness is not correct due to given evidences.

3. Judgment of the Supreme Court, II Ips 56/2003: Traffic Accident

This is legally a very interesting case which highlights circumstances which, sadly, occur with increasing frequency nowadays. Both parties involved – the car driver as well as the motorcycle driver – in the accident were namely illegally intoxicated. They collided head-on on a 4-metre wide road. They filed civil actions against each other and the district court passed an intermediate judgment. The court found that the car driver drove outwith his "own" lane and drove on the motorcycle driver's left side. On the other hand, the motorcycle driver drove correctly, staying in his lane, however without his lights on. Art. 178 of the Act on Obligations (1978) foresees in case of vehicle collisions also shared liability. Based on this article, the district court found, after a very long litigation (the collision happened in 1989) shared liability. The motorcycle driver suffered total damage amounting to € 31,000 and the car driver in the amount of € 1,600. The district court decided that the car driver shared 75% of responsibility for the accident and the motorcycle driver 25%. Both parties appealed, the decision was confirmed by the appellate and the Supreme Court. 16

The Supreme Court, as mentioned above, confirmed the district court's judgment, highlighting the reasoning of the shared liability. The car driver was illegally intoxicated and his risky driving on the left side of the road contributed to a greater extent to the final damage. The motorcyclist was rather less intoxicated, able to control the machine and drove correctly. His share of the liability is based on the fact that his lights were off. He became an "invisible danger". Of course the judgment could be disputable. But, based on the evidence, the intoxicated car driver was held liable in proportion of three quarters because of the risky manoeuvre to the left side. 17

4. Judgment of the Supreme Court, II Ips 182/2003: Traffic Accident – Hitchhiking

The applicant was a hitchhiker who was given a ride by the defendant who was illegally intoxicated. He caused a traffic accident in which the applicant suffered severe pecuniary and non-pecuniary loss while sitting on the back seat. The district court awarded the defendant € 9,000 in damages and ordered the defendant to cover the applicant's litigation costs to the amount of approx. € 1,000. The defendant appealed and the appellate court decreased the amount 18 of damages awarded by the district court, explaining that the applicant contributed to the final damage. She namely failed to notice that the driver was illegally intoxicated! His blood/alcohol level was 3 times above the legal limit which, according to the appellate court's opinion, could be easily seen. The applicant could have foreseen such danger and could easily have prevented it and, because of this, the court decided that she contributed to the damage in the proportion of 10%.

19 The applicant appealed to the Supreme Court. It abolished the appellate decision, arguing that the applicant had not acted negligently. Her act did not violate any reasonable standard of care. She merely sat on the back seat and did not notice any strange or drunken behaviour while talking to the driver. The Supreme Court therefore overruled the appellate court's decision.

5. Judgment of the Supreme Court, II Ips 36/2003: Traffic Accident – Shared Liability

20 The applicant was a fifth-grade pupil who, in 1990, walked from the primary school to the nearby swimming pool to take gym lessons. He was hit by the defendant while crossing the road on a marked pedestrian crossing. He suffered severe pecuniary and non-pecuniary loss. His parents sued the driver and the school because of negligence. The district court ruled that the defendants have to cover € 57,000 for the applicant's non-pecuniary loss and € 2,000 for pecuniary loss. The court decided that the applicant contributed a share of responsibility in the amount of 10%.

21 The defendants appealed and the appellate court overturned the decision on the pecuniary loss. All parties challenged this decision in the Supreme Court. The first defendant, the car driver, argued that the applicant's act – crossing the road – contributed to the damage to a greater extent than decided by the district court. The boy was already 12 years old and educated enough to be able to cross the street. Instead he just ran across the pedestrian crossing, which was an unexpected and unforeseen act for the first defendant. Such an act, according to the first defendant's argumentation, contributed to the damage to at least 50%. The second defendant based his complaint on the Act on Safety in Road Traffic which allows children who are older than 12 to participate in traffic without supervision. The primary school did not have any obligations towards the applicant to supervise him crossing the road.

22 The Supreme Court rejected the first defendant's complaint. She namely exceeded the 50 km/h speed limit and drove at 59 km/h. She also noticed the applicant on the pavement but did not pay enough attention to the foreseeable act of him crossing the road. Traffic safety provisions require special attention especially towards children. Therefore, the Supreme Court affirmed the lower court's decision that the applicant contributed only 10% of responsibility to the final damage. Regarding the complaint by the second defendant, the Supreme Court accepted the argumentation. The Court considered that the lower

courts exaggerated the school's obligation towards children in traffic. The school is indeed responsible for children's education and upbringing. However, in this case, the applicant was 12 years old. This age allows him a certain grade of independence, especially as a pedestrian in traffic. He was also well-educated in this respect. He had passed the bicycle test and had sufficient knowledge of traffic safety. The school was not obliged to organize a supervised crossing over the road for every pupil. It is understood that such an obligation exists for younger children. Therefore the Supreme Court found that the factual situation was not clarified sufficiently and returned the case in this respect to the district court.

6. Judgment of the Supreme Court, II Ips 88/2003: Kindergarten

This case is also connected to liability for guardianship. The applicant is a child who fell and was injured while playing on a toboggan. The district court awarded him damages of € 3,500 for non-pecuniary loss for physical suffering, € 450 for fear experienced, € 650 for mental suffering and € 4,200 for decreased life activities. The defendant, a youth organization which organized sea-side camps, appealed against the judgment to the court of appeals. It attacked the judgment on the question of causal connection. 23

The district court namely found the guardian liable based on strict liability. The Act on Obligation Relations from 1978 foresees (art. 173) strict liability for an abnormally dangerous activity or thing. The district court found the defendant strictly liable and the appellate court agreed, because the applicant was injured while playing on an abnormally dangerous thing. The toboggan was 170 cm high and it was based on a concrete plate. The district court found that the applicant fell from a height of 50 cm while he climbed on the switchback's ladder. It reached this decision based on the given evidence. The applicant argued that he fell from 170 cm, i.e. from the top of the switchback. The court stressed that the applicant would have suffered the same damage even if he had fallen while standing on the ground. 24

The defendant challenged the decisions at the Supreme Court. He argued that strict liability may not be invoked in this case. It argued that the district court did not explain clearly why it considered the switchback a dangerous thing. In addition the defendant also argued that the switchback was not in his sphere of control. Therefore, he cannot be held liable even on fault-based theory. 25

The Supreme Court admitted the appeal. It stressed the essential elements of tortious liability (event, damage, causal link and fault). Fault is, according to the above quoted provision of the Act on Obligations, presumed. The defendant can exculpate himself if he proves that the dangerous thing was not the cause of the occurred damage. The Supreme Court held the following facts as crucial. Firstly, normally a switchback cannot be considered as a dangerous thing if used properly. This switchback, however, was dangerous because it was relatively high; it was not protected with a security fence or a security net. 26

However, in this case strict liability cannot be applied because this dangerous thing was not the cause of the applicant's loss. He fell from a height of 50 cm, but he might have suffered the exact same damage if he had fallen from the ground, regardless of the existence of a security fence. Because of this, the Supreme Court did not find any relative causal connection between the switchback and the applicant's damage. The Court decided that the lower courts misinterpreted the law. It returned the case to the district court, instructing it to reconsider on the basis of fault.

7. Judgment of the Supreme Court, II Ips 164/2003: Kindergarten

27 The applicant, an infant, was injured because she fell from a hydrant in the kindergarten playing-yard. The hydrant was erected on a concrete plate. The kindergarten was sued for non-pecuniary loss in the amount of € 13,000. The district court rejected the claim and the applicant appealed to the appellate court. The intermediate court overruled the prior judgment and awarded the demanded amount in damages. The defendant appealed to the Supreme Court arguing that the employees exercised all due care while taking care of the children. It highlighted all the safety measures regarding the number of children in the playing yard. They also had the safety certificate for the hydrant which was not even particularly high. Consequently a professional duty to build a safety fence around the hydrant did not exist. On the other hand the kindergarten's employee acted with due care. She even warned the applicant while she was playing on a climbing pole. Therefore the applicant's act was unpredictable and unexpected.

28 The Supreme Court rejected the complaint. It decided that the appellate court correctly decided on the question of liability. It agrees that the defendant's employee failed in her professional due care and is, therefore, responsible for the occurred damage. The Supreme Court did not follow the defendant's argumentation that all the safety measures were fulfilled. The arguments relating to either the number of children playing in the yard or safety measures taken on the hydrant are also irrelevant to this case because the applicant did not base his claim on a strict liability basis. The Supreme Court based its argumentation on the fact that the lower courts had already found that children used the hydrant as a playing tool constantly and, therefore, the applicant's act was not unpredictable and unexpected. The defendant's employee had not only to warn children, but also to prevent them from climbing on the hydrant. Such neglect is a violation of the professional due care, which was already found by the appellate court.

8. Judgment of the Supreme Court, II Ips 107/2003: Working Safety

29 The applicant, a warehouse worker, was injured while he loaded cargo with a loading machine. He suffered pecuniary and non-pecuniary loss because he suffered a fracture to his knee while he stepped approx. 80 cm down from the vehicle. The district court awarded him € 10,000 in damages. The applicant

and the insurance company appealed. The appellate court modified damages to the amount of € 11,000.

The defendant filed a revision at the Supreme Court. He claimed that the district court misinterpreted the law. According to the Safety at Work Act[6], employers are responsible to assure such safety measures which meet occupational safety standards. Such measures consequently lead to working safety but only due to worker's "normal" carefulness. The defendant's insurant took all the required safety measures and also adhered to the special Rules on the safe loading of motor vehicles.[7] Stepping down from a motor vehicle was in the exclusive sphere of the applicant. He had exercised such work for many years and was therefore exclusively liable for the damage that he suffered. The defendant's insurant cannot be reproached for not having taken all the safety measures also for stepping down from the vehicle. The applicant may also have used the so-called "self safeguard" measure, according to labour law provisions. He could have refused the concrete working duty and demanded removal of the danger. 30

The Supreme Court did not follow this argumentation and rejected the appeal. It stressed that the working safety provisions demand that the employer uses and imposes such measures that assure a safe working environment. It is not enough that such measures meet the safety regulations; they must actually guarantee safe working conditions. Rules on the safe loading of motor vehicles of course do not foresee each situation. However, they demand general safety measures. The employer would, therefore, have to build a new loading ramp on the same level as the existing loading surface. According to the opinion of the Supreme Court, the defendant did not contribute to the final damage. The crucial circumstance is that the employer did not assure a safe step down even though the applicant had performed such work for many years. The fact that the workers had to be fast in loading and unloading is another factor which led to the final damage. The argumentation that the worker could use the so-called "self safeguard" measure is misfounded. Labour law foresees such a measure only if the life or health of a worker is directly threatened. Taking a step down of approx. 80 cm cannot be interpreted as such threat. The applicant exercised all due care. Therefore, the Supreme Court confirmed the lower court's decision. 31

9. Judgment of the Supreme Court, II Ips 193/2003: False Imprisonment

The applicant was arrested for a crime and kept in jail for 10 months. During this time he was diagnosed with cancer and was operated on. His wife divorced him because of his arrest. Because of this, he suffered severe emotional distress. The criminal court decided that he committed the offence in an act of self defence. The time he served in prison was, therefore, illegal. The appli- 32

[6] Official gazette of the Republic of Slovenia, no. 32/94.
[7] Official gazette of the Republic of SFRY, no. 17/66.

cant sued the State for illegal arrest based on the Act of Obligations (art. 200). He demanded € 33,300 in damages. The district court awarded him the complete amount. It based its conclusion on the fact that his personality rights were violated and the awarded amount is a fair compensation. The appellate court did not support this argumentation. It reduced the awarded damages to € 9,000, explaining that the applicant had already served time in prison. He finished serving his sentence just before he was arrested once again. During his first term in prison, he was already suffering from cancer. The appellate court argued, in a rather unusual argumentation, that the applicant's personality rights were not so much at stake after all: "imprisonment environment, because of his earlier sentence, was not foreign to the applicant and did not present a serious situation and stigma in the eyes of the public". Consequently the appellate court did not base its decision on regular court practice to the usual extent.

33 The applicant appealed to the Supreme Court which accepted the appeal. It argued that the argumentation of the appellate court cannot be acceptable. The applicant undoubtedly suffered an enormous pecuniary loss because of the violations of his personality rights. However, the damages awarded by the lower courts were not justified. The Supreme Court weighted the characteristics of this individual case in the frame of continuous legal practice. It decided that an amount of € 13,000 would compensate the violations of personality rights in this particular case.

10. Judgment of the Supreme Court, II Ips 84/2003: Women's Soccer

34 The applicant was injured in a women's soccer match between the Slovenian A-team and the Slovenian junior team. During the game, while tackling, she stepped into a hole in the pitch (15 x 10 x 3cm) and injured her knee. She sued the organizer based on the strict liability theory. The district court decided that there is no support in Slovenian law that a soccer match could be considered as an abnormally dangerous activity. On the other hand, the district court also found no support for the tortious liability of the defendant. The organizer exercised all due care and met all the safety measures in organizing such a match. The court stressed that soccer is played in all weather conditions, small holes in the soccer field are therefore customary. The soccer field was registered as appropriate by a special commission and, therefore, no tortious liability can be imposed on the defendant.

35 The same argumentation was followed by the appellate court. After the appeal the Supreme Court also confirmed the earlier decisions. It also highlighted that the Act on Obligational Relations (art. 181) foresees strict liability for the organizer of an event (according to legal practice also sport events) only in relations to those who gather in an increased number and are therefore endangered. Strict liability does not focus on active athletes. This was also the case in this accident. The applicant's injury is a result of a coincidence which does not exceed the frame of a normal risk in sport activities. There are always var-

ious risks inherent in soccer, in particular. The burden of such customary risks is on the injured, except when the injury was caused by another athlete.

11. Judgment of the Supreme Court, II Ips 86/2003: Asbestosis

This case is a transparent example of compensation for asbestosis. Slovenia regulated the question of compensation for asbestosis with a special Act on the Prohibition of the Production and Trade of Asbestos Products[8] and with Rules on the determination of professional diseases exposed to asbestos.[9] The Act on the Prohibition of the Production and Trade of Asbestos Products allowed workers exposed to asbestos a transfer to another working position, not exposed to asbestos or the possibility to take early retirement. The applicant, a 47-year-old employee, freely decided on early retirement. The responsible State institution (Institute for retiring allowance and disability insurance) confirmed his decision with an administrative decision. 36

The applicant contaminated with asbestos was diagnosed with an infection of the pleura and retired in 1997 at the age of 47. The above mentioned Act assured him full pension. He also sued his employer for damage suffered because of the exposure to asbestos, demanding compensation for pecuniary and non-pecuniary loss which would be compensated as annuity on a monthly basis. The district court awarded him € 6,300 for physically suffering, € 21,000 for fear (he actually demanded € 50,000) and for mental suffering € 12,500. The court rejected the applicant's demand for compensation for pecuniary loss. 37

Both parties appealed to the appellate court. It decided that such amount of compensation for non-pecuniary loss is not provided for in legal practice. It reduced the awarded compensation by € 16,000. The appellate court also rejected the claim on compensation for pecuniary loss. The applicant objected to this decision, arguing that he had been exposed to asbestos since his 15th birthday when he was employed by the defendant. He lives in constant fear of his health condition; he also constantly experiences the deaths of his former colleagues. He suffers enormous mental distress for being "at the bottom of society, because he is unable to work". The applicant demanded full compensation for non-pecuniary loss as awarded by the district court and compensation for pecuniary loss. 38

The Supreme Court rejected the appeal stating that the difference between the applicant's salary and his pension is a result of his early retirement. This decision was taken by him alone. The defendant cannot be held liable for the difference. The applicant had a free choice of being transferred to another working position with full salary or taking early retirement with full pension. As proven by the decision of the Institute for retiring allowance and disability in- 39

[8] Official gazette of the Republic of Slovenia, no. 56/96, 35/98, 86/2000.
[9] Official gazette of the Republic of Slovenia, no. 26/97.

surance, he took the second choice. The Supreme Court also rejected the applicant's argumentation on non-pecuniary loss. It stated that the medical record shows that he is contaminated with the weakest type of asbestosis (infection of pleura). His health condition is now stable, but he is unable to work in an environment that is contaminated with asbestos, fibrogenic and carcinogenic substances which demand intensive need for oxygen. The decision of the appellate court was confirmed, based on the argumentation that it followed legal practice and awarded fair compensation for non-pecuniary loss.

12. Judgment of the Supreme Court, II Ips 76/2003: Toxic Torts

40 Environmental issues are rarely discussed at the Supreme Court. I would like to use the opportunity here to present another environmental-toxic tort case. The district court rejected a demand for injunction relief for nuisance. The applicant demanded the closure of a bakery that presumably produced illegal emissions. The court also rejected the applicant's claim for compensation for non-pecuniary loss. He argued that his health condition has been aggravated – she suffers from asthma – since the defendant started his bakery production. The defendant presumably produces toxic substances (suphloreted hydrogen, nitric oxides etc.) above the legally permissible level and above the community customs.

41 The appellate court confirmed the district court's decision, highlighting that the applicant failed to prove the existence of a causal link between the bakery's emissions and the applicant's health. It also rejected the appeal on injunction relief and the decision became final, according to the Act on Civil Procedure. The applicant challenged the appellate decision at the Supreme Court. She argued that her worsened health condition was caused by legally permissible emissions. She apparently did not suffer from asthma before the bakery started its production. She also stressed that lower courts reached their decisions contrary to the testimonies of expert witnesses. One of them apparently testified that flour contains one of the irritants that caused the applicant's health deterioration. If she was allergic to another irritant, then she would have suffered deterioration earlier. The Supreme Court did not follow this argumentation and rejected the appeal. It stressed that the crucial question would be whether the emissions produced by the defendant are above the legal limits. Expert witnesses testified negatively. They also could not establish with certainty that irritants contained in the bakery's emissions caused the applicant's health condition. Therefore, the applicant failed to prove the existence of a causal link between emissions and the applicant's health deterioration. It is impossible to conclude that one of the irritants was the cause, even if the applicant's state of health became worse at the time when the production started. The Court stressed the following formula on discovering causal links in toxic tort cases – if it is not possible to single out at least one of the factors among internal and external causes (emissions) which would cause the existing health condition, then the causal link is not proven. In this particular case the expert witness voiced a possibility that one of the irritants contained in the

defendant's flour could, among other internal and external factors, cause the applicant's state of health. He was not sure, though, if this irritatant was the actual cause.

C. Literature

1. R. Lampe, *The System of the Right to Privacy* (*Sistem pravice do zasebnosti*) (Bonex, Ljubljana 2004)

The central theme of this work is the right to privacy as a fundamental human right. This right is recognized and safeguarded in international law as well as national law, contained in the Constitutions of most States. The right to privacy is also safeguarded in civil law as a "right to personality". It is one of the indispensable elements that legally protects the individual against the might of the public authority, general public and individuals. It is the right to be left alone with minimum interference. 42

The book is divided into two basic chapters – civil law and public law aspects of the right to privacy. The first chapter is further divided into two major sections; the right to privacy in common law and the more extensive section on the right to privacy in civil law. The legal protection of the right to privacy in the USA common law is considered to be one of the most efficient and complete legal protections today. It is for this reason that the author devotes special analysis to American legal theory and its practice. Warren, Brandeis and especially Prosser are those scholars whose contributions have contributed greatly to the development of the legal theory concerning the right of privacy. Prosser introduced four special torts, being the Intrusion upon Seclusion, Appropriation of Name and Likeness, Public Disclosure of Private Facts, False Light in the Public Eye. 43

The second section is concerned with the analyses of the civil law regulation of the right to privacy in the province Québec. Special attention is given to the "general right to personality" in German and Swiss Civil Law. These legal systems, although on different premises, developed through the legal practice and the legal theory the protection of the general right to personality whose "outflow" is also "the private sphere". Close analysis of these legal systems is also crucial for the development of the concept of the right to privacy in Slovenian civil law. However it must be pointed out that the concept of the rights of personality in Slovenian Civil Law is also influenced by the legal principles of the Romanic civil law "family", especially France. 44

The basic legal provision of the right to privacy in Slovenian civil law is found in art. 35 of the Constitution. This article guarantees the so-called principle of the "*Drittwirkung*" or the direct applicability of the Constitutional provisions concerning rights of personality. The right to privacy protects in its legal application a variety of personal rights. These rights relate to the following 45 areas: proprietary privacy (inviolability of ones' home), psychical privacy (under which the following rights are implemented: the right to sexual integrity, the right of inviolability of one's personal and family life, "right to image", right to name and the right to respect the secrets of private life) and informational privacy.

46 The second chapter deals with the public aspects of the right to privacy. This chapter starts with the analysis of the development of the right to privacy in American Constitutional law. The right to privacy is not expressly stated in the Bill of Rights. Its "existence" is a result of a long evolution of the Supreme Court's practice. The current law recognizes the "penumbras" of the right of privacy in its 1st, 4th and 14th Amendments. The right to privacy is also included in various international human rights documents and the last chapter analyses the Public International Law aspects. Special attention is paid to the European Convention on Human Rights (art. 8), because of its direct implementation into the national systems and especially because it provides efficient international legal protection. This provision also defines, although abstractly, the limitations of the right to privacy. Those limitations are crucial for the determination of the exact limits of the individual's right of enjoyment of privacy. The Convention determines the legal grounds for the right to interfere with one's right to privacy. Those legitimate grounds are: the prevention of disorder or crime, protection of health and morals, protection of the rights and freedoms of others. The interference with one's privacy must pursue the legitimate aims in accordance with the internationally recognized "civilized" standards. The Convention lays down that there shall be no interference by a public authority with the exercise of this right, except in accordance with the law and as necessary in a democratic society in the interests of national security, public safety or the economic well-being of the country.

47 The author concludes the work with a definition of the right to privacy as one of the important factors in the development of one's personality and as one of the crucial elements of one's existence and one's pursuit of happiness. The "general" right to privacy assures a minimal interference of the public authority as well as of other individuals into one's enjoyment of decisional, physical, proprietary and informational privacy.

2. R. Lampe et al., *Human Rights Protection in Legal Procedures* (*Človekove pravice v pravnih in sodnih postopkih*) (Legalia, Slovenia 2004)

48 The work is divided into various chapters on human rights protection in legal procedures. The part necessary to highlight in the frame of tort law is Lampe's contribution on data protection and its civil law protection. The author focuses on the new Slovenian Data Protection Act and existing tort law practice. The first was briefly described at the beginning of this article, whereby legal practice focuses on the invasion of privacy. The author highlights a case where two public officials were unveiled by the media as agents of the former Yugo-

slav and Slovene secret service. In this extremely sensitive case, the Supreme Court affirmed the decision of the lower courts that, in this concrete case, their privacy had been violated and that such invasion into personality rights constituted a libel.

3. L. Koman-Perenič, *Damage and Compensation* (*Škoda in odškodnina*), (DZS, Slovenia 2004)

Supreme Court judge Lidija Koman-Perenič gives us in this systematic handbook an overview of Slovenian tort law in general. She bases her work on the new Code of Obligations which annulled the old federal Act on Obligational Relations. The author focuses primarily on the two main institutes of her book – damage and compensation. The book also includes a short introduction to foreign tort law systems, focuses however specifically on the Slovenian system. The book is an excellent guide for practitioners as well as for law students. 49

4. A. Polajnar-Pavčnik, Americanization of Tort Law (*Amerikanizacija odškodninskega prava*), [2004] *Journal Podjetje in delo* 7, 1158

The author critically analyses implementations of foreign legal principles into the national law. She understands a national legal system as a coexisting unity which has to be analyzed and debated in a certainly limited frame. The author is critical especially in respect of million-dollar compensation awards that are awarded in the US on a daily basis, especially in medical malpractice or producer's liability cases. 50

This social phenomenon is, in her opinion, the result of a much less sufficient social security system in the US compared to European ones. The other reason for this phenomenon is to be traced in collective consciousness. She quotes B.S. Markesinins and S.F. Deakin[10] that no American can experience five minutes of frustration without thinking of a tort action. The third reason could be traced in the social function of compensation and tort law in general. American tort law also incorporates the penalty function, which should be concentrated, in the author's opinion, only in criminal law. She states that European tort law systems have kept the sharp distinctions between these disciplines, while in US tort law these two functions have began to unify. 51

[10] *Tort Law* (1994), 2.

XXII. Spain

Jordi Ribot

A. Legislation

1. Tort Law

a) Road Traffic Liability Act

1 Together with other important texts in the field of Insurance Law, in 2004 the Spanish Government approved a new consolidated text of the Road Traffic Liability Act[1] (hereafter LRCSCVM). This version replaces that formerly in force, which dated back to 1968. Since then, the Act had undergone a number of substantial amendments[2], most of them in order to implement European directives on liability insurance of motor vehicles[3].

2 Authorization for consolidating the statute included regulating, clarifying and harmonizing its provisions. Several inconsistencies have thus been ironed out, and some controversial issues settled.[4] Moreover, the Government has brought the wording of the Constitutional Court's decision on the tariffication scheme

[1] *Ley sobre responsabilidad civil y seguro en la circulación de vehículos a motor* consolidated text approved by *Real Decreto Legislativo* 8/2004, of 29 October. The consolidated legislation on the ordering and supervision of private insurance undertakings and the consolidated version of the *Estatuto Legal del Consorcio de Compensación de Seguros* have been approved by *Real Decreto Legislativo* 6/2004 and 7/2004, respectively. All three texts were published in *Boletín Oficial del Estado* (BOE) no. 267, 5.11.2004. In addition *Real Decreto* (RD) 297/2004, of 20 February (BOE no. 45, 2.2.2004), modified the regulation on the ordering and supervision of private insurance undertakings currently in force, which was approved by RD 2486/1998, of 20 November.

[2] *Decreto* 632/1968, of 21 March, approving the consolidated text of Act 122/1962, of 24 December, on the Use and Circulation of Motor Vehicles. Regarding amendments introduced in 2003 in this Act see J. Ribot/A. Ruda, Spain, in: H. Koziol/B.C. Steininger (eds.), *European Tort Law 2003* (2004), 387.

[3] Directives 72/166/EEC of 24 April 1972, amended by Council Directive 72/430/EEC of 19 December 1972, 84/5/EEC of 30 December 1983, 90/232/EEC of 14 May 1990 and 2000/26/EC of 16 May 2000. The last one motivated an amendment of the *Reglamento* (regulations) of LRCSCVM, by RD 299/2004, of 20 February.

[4] See a comprehensive and updated overview in F. Reglero Campos, *Accidentes de circulación: responsabilidad civil y seguro* (2004).

for personal injuries and death resulting from traffic accidents into the act[5]. A new legal provision stipulates that the scheme is not to be applied in cases of temporary incapacity when "the relevant fault of the tortfeasor is established and, where appropriate, declared by the courts"[6]. In fact, however, the Constitutional Court allowed the judges to depart from the legal scheme only when the harm resulted from the *exclusive fault of the tortfeasor* and the compensation envisaged by the scheme would not completely repair the damage proven by the claimant. Some scholars argued that so far the decision of unconstitutionality did not put the scheme at risk. Others tried to play the wording of the decision down and advocated giving the legal scheme up in cases involving contributory conduct of the victim.[7] Apparently, the consolidated text endorses that view, thereby giving the judges wider discretion as to the amount of damages they can award when the harm suffered by a contributory negligent claimant is attributable to a faulty tortfeasor and is not fully compensated.[8]

b) Liability Regime of Clinical Trials on Medicinal Products

On 1 May 2004 a new regulation on clinical trials on medicinal products entered into force[9]. It provides that a clinical trial may be undertaken only when all the legal requirements are met and the sponsor has either taken out liability insurance or made any other financial provision to indemnify the trial subject for any damage resulting from the clinical trial[10]. These guarantees shall cover 3

[5] *Sentencia del Tribunal Constitucional* (STC [Constitutional Court Decision]) 181/2000, of 29 June. On this decision, among others, see M. Martín-Casals, An Outline of the Spanish Legal Tariffication Scheme for Personal Injury resulting from Traffic Accidents, in: H. Koziol/J. Spier (eds.), *Liber amicorum Pierre Widmer* (2003), 235–251 at 245–6. The amounts included in the scheme were last updated by a decree of the General Directorate of Insurances and Pension Plans issued on 9 March 2004 (BOE no. 83, 6.4.2004).

[6] See section II, Table IV, Annex to the LRCSCVM.

[7] On the different positions in legal writing see J. Ribot, La culpa "relevante" como culpa "adicional": la STC 181/2000 a la luz de la interacción entre responsabilidad objetiva y culpa, in: A. Cabanillas Sánchez et al. (eds.), *Estudios Díez-Picazo*, vol. IV (2003), 2868–2898 at 2875–8.

[8] Recent decisions of the Constitutional Court do not even mention the exclusivity requirement of the tortfeasor's fault. See decisions 15/2004, of 23 February and 222/2004, of 29 November.

[9] RD 223/2004, of 6 February, laying down the regulation as regards clinical trials on medicinal products (BOE no. 33, 7.2.2004). This regulation overides that formerly in force since 1993 (RD 561/1993, of 16 April), which will govern clinical trials commenced before the new regulation's entry into force (cf. Transitory Provision 2). Clinical trials are governed by Title III of Act 25/1990, of 20 December, on medicinal products (BOE no. 306, 22.12.1990). See M. Martín-Casals/J. Solé/J.C. Seuba Torreblanca, Liability for and Insurability of Biomedical Research Involving Human Subjects under Spanish Law, in: J. Dute/M.G. Faure/H. Koziol (eds.), *Liability for and Insurability of Biomedical Research with Human Subjects in a Comparative Perspective* (2004), 264–296 at 267. This act was amended by art. 125 Act 53/2002, of 30 December, in order to adapt it to the Directive 2001/20/EC, of 4 April 2001, on the approximation of the laws, regulations and administrative provisions of the Member States relating to the implementation of good clinical practice in the conduct of clinical trials on medicinal products for human use.

[10] The minimum amount covered by the insured is € 250,000 for each trial subject and € 2,500,000 for each clinical trial per year (cf. art. 8.6). Previously, the insurance coverage was € 180,000 per trial subject. See P. Rodríguez Fernández, Legalidad y deontologia en la realización de los ensayos clínicos, [2004] *Revista de Responsabilidad Civil Circulación y Seguro* (RRCCS) 7, 13–19 at 16.

the liability of the sponsor, the main researcher and his or her collaborators and the owner of the hospital or centre where the clinical trial is carried out.[11] When by any circumstance the insurance policy does not offer full coverage, those persons will be held solidary liable in tort although "fault cannot be established". In addition, there is a rebuttable presumption of the causal link between the trial and "the damage related to the health of the trial subject, suffered while she is undergoing this experimentation and during the year following its termination".[12] At any rate, the defendants may prove that the impairment to the health of the trial subject is a) inherent to the pathology under study; b) can be included in the side-effects associated with the medication prescribed for that sort of pathology or c) belongs to the regular evolution of the illness resulting from the inefficacy of the treatment (art. 8.5).

2. Insurance Law

4 In the aftermath of September 11 the insurance coverage by the public entity *Consorcio de Compensación de Seguros* of extraordinary risks such as terrorism was broadened to include loss of profits resulting from damage to persons and to property[13]. Nevertheless, both the extent and the limits of the new coverage were to be established by a future regulation.

5 This regulation was finally passed last year[14]. The definition of loss of profits included therein seeks to limit the extension of coverage. It thus relies implicitly on the distinction between *consequential* and *pure* economic losses.[15] Furthermore, the new regulation lays down new definitions for certain extraordinary risks, thereby extending the coverage provided by the *Consorcio*[16]. It also makes far-reaching amendments to the thresholds and periods of time uncovered that have been applied so far. On the other hand, however, it does not elu-

[11] Art. 28 RD 223/2004 lays down rules with regard to the "exclusive" liability of physicians for *compassionate use* of medicinal products still in clinical trials.

[12] See M. Martín-Casals/J. Solé/J.C. Seuba Torreblanca (supra fn. 9), 269.

[13] This damage used to be covered by private insurers. See M. Martín-Casals/J. Ribot, Liability for Acts of Terrorism under Spanish Law, in: B.A. Koch (ed.), *Terrorism, Tort Law and Insurance. A Comparative Survey* (2004), 88–117 at 90–2. Art. 6 *Estatuto Legal del Consorcio de Compensación de Seguros*, as amended in 2002.

[14] RD 300/2004, of 20 February, approving the regulation on extraordinary risks insurance (BOE no. 47, 24.2.2004; rect. BOE no. 80, 2.4.2004). The regulation lays down two transitional periods: 18 months to adapt the terms of the existing policies and 6 months for the new ones (Transitory Provision RD 300/2004).

[15] This conceptual dividing line is alien to Spanish tort law. See more recently M. Martín-Casals/J. Ribot, Compensation for Pure Economic Loss under Spanish Law, in: W.H. van Boom/H. Koziol/C.A. Witting (eds.), *Pure Economic Loss* (2004), 62–76. In fact, the borrowing of legal concepts from the common law is quite usual in insurance practice. Sometimes, however, practitioners are not fully aware of how to handle the technical devices borrowed. Indeed, to make the distinction clear, the new regulation provides some examples (art. 6 I: "losses suffered as a consequence of a cut off or an alteration in the external supply of electricity, gas, water, fuel-oil or any other fluid, or [losses consisting in] any other indirect loss or damage … even if these are due to a circumstance included within the extraordinary risks coverage").

[16] For instance, the legal notion of "atypical cyclonic storm", which did not allow the cover of damage caused by extraordinary winds or tornados. Or the legal notion of "floods", which used to exclude damage caused by tide waves.

cidate the controversial question of whether the concept "acts of terrorism" embraces damage resulting from riots and disturbances by supporters of terrorist organizations or not.[17]

3. Alternative Compensation Schemes

a) The "Prestige" Oil Spill Compensation Scheme

In our report last year we pointed out that funds available for victims from the "Prestige" Oil Spill Compensation Scheme were quite limited. Nevertheless, we also stressed that it was very likely that many victims would apply for the benefits and sign the so-called "compromise settlement" in return for payment of them.[18] Now we know that € 160 million were insufficient even to fulfil the agreements already reached upon. This situation prompted the new Government formed after the elections held in March 2004 to adopt emergency measures[19] whose main goal was to overide the above mentioned cap and to remove the legal constraints that prevent the competent State agency from distributing the allowances between the beneficiaries or reaching new settlements with victims without compensation. Moreover, compensation for loss of profits due to an evident fall in catch or in production of fish farms "directly attributable to the oil spill" is extended by one year (art. 2.1)[20]. At any rate, amendments introduced by the new Government did not challenge the controversial principles upon which the scheme was set up. Applications shall refer thus only to limited types of damage, a prior waiver of any action against the Spanish State is required and the Spanish State is subrogated in any action that the applicant might have against third parties.[21] 6

b) New Compensation Scheme for Spanish Citizens Killed or Injured while Taking Part in International Peace and Security Operations

As a result of public outrage subsequent to a plane crash that caused the death of 62 Spanish soldiers assigned to a peace operation in Afghanistan, the new Government has decided to set up a new compensation scheme[22]. In this case, 7

[17] See B. Arquillo Colet, Anotaciones al Reglamento de seguro de riesgos extraordinarios. Comentario al Real Decreto 300/2004, de 20 de febrero, [2004] *InDret* 3 (www.indret.com).

[18] J. Ribot/A. Ruda (supra fn. 2), 386.

[19] *Real Decreto-ley* 4/2004, of 2 July, laying down certain measures as regards the damage caused by the "Prestige" incident (BOE no. 160, 3.7.2004). Validated by decree of the Parliament issued on 21 July 2004 (BOE no. 178, 24.7.2004).

[20] The amended regulation covered this sort of damage only up to 31 December 2003. As to the current limitation to financial year 2004 see the criticisms raised by J.R. Pardo Gato, La indemnización civil de los daños causados a los particulares en el caso Prestige. Las actuaciones gubernativas, [2004] *Aranzadi Civil* 15, 9–10.

[21] Concerning the unconstitutionality of this requirement, see M.P. García Rubio, El caso *Prestige* un año después de la tragedia. Algunos apuntes en torno al Real Decreto-ley 4/2003, de 20 de junio, [2003] *La Ley* 5893, 3. More recently see J.M. Busto Lago, Pago de "indemnizaciones" por el Estado Español a los afectados por el siniestro del *Prestige* y renuncia de acciones (algunos aciertos del legislador y algunas dudas de constitucionalidad), [2004] *Revista Práctica Derecho de daños* 18, 6–14.

[22] *Real Decreto-ley* 8/2004, of 5 November, laying down compensations to participants in international operations of peace and security (BOE no. 271, 10.11.2004; rect. BOE no. 280, 20.11.2004).

the scheme covers personal injury to and death of Spanish military personnel, members of the police or civil servants (art. 2) that are assigned or stay abroad taking part in peace operations, humanitarian missions or any kind of international operation that has Government approval (art. 1 I)[23]. Benefits granted are in keeping with other schemes currently in force[24]. Unlike these, however, they are fully compatible with any other compensation or payment that the beneficiaries may obtain (art. 6.1).[25]

4. Prescription

8 The recently enacted *Catalan Civil Code* (hereafter CCCat)[26] has laid down new rules on prescription. They entered into force on 1 January 2004. Among these rules, the code stipulates a three-year prescription period for claims in tort (see art. 121-21 CCCat). Moreover, new rules on commencement of prescription make it dependant upon knowledge of both the grounds of the claim and the identity of the defendant (cf. art. 121-23 CCCat).[27] These rules are to be applied only to tort claims governed by Catalan law[28]. They entail a substantial change, though, especially if compared with the one-year prescription period still provided for in art. 1968.2 Spanish Civil Code (hereafter CC), which runs from the moment the claimant knew about the harm.

B. Cases

1. European Court of Human Rights (ECtHR) Decision, 16 November 2004, *Moreno Gómez v. Spain*: Interferences due to Night-time Disturbances

a) Brief Summary of the Facts

9 Ms Pilar Moreno Gómez had lived in a flat in a residential quarter of Valencia since 1970. Since 1974 the Valencia City Council had allowed licensed premises such as bars, pubs and discotheques to open in the vicinity of her home. Several reports commissioned by the City Council found that the noise levels were unacceptable and exceeded permitted levels. Indeed, following a resolu-

[23] Exceptionally, certain benefits to victims involved in operations organized by NGOs are recognised and also to Spanish journalists authorized by the competent Spanish authorities (see Additional Provision 1).

[24] For a comprehensive outline of the existing compensation schemes see M. Martín-Casals/J. Ribot/J. Solé, Non-Pecuniary Loss Under Spanish Law, in: W.V.H. Rogers (ed.), *Damages for Non-Pecuniary Loss in a Comparative Perspective* (2001), 202–207.

[25] With the exception of benefits granted to the victims of terrorist attacks (see art. 6.2).

[26] Final Provision 2 § I Catalan Act 29/2002, of 30 December, First Act on the Civil Code of Catalonia (*Diari Oficial de la Generalitat de Catalunya*, no. 3798, 13.1.2003).

[27] The new rules also include a so-called *preclusion period* of thirty years whose completion bars any kind of action regardless of whether the claimant could not get knowledge of any of the above mentioned circumstances (artt. 121–24).

[28] Transitional Provision Catalan Act 29/2002 deals with claims that were actionable before its entry into force.

tion of the Valencia City Council, the area in which the claimant lived was designated an "acoustically saturated zone" (*zona acústicamente saturada*), i.e. an area in which the large number of establishments, the activity of the people frequenting them and passing traffic expose local residents to high noise levels that cause them serious disturbance.[29] Complaining of inaction on the part of the local authorities, Ms Moreno Gómez sued the Valencia City Council, for having failed to put a stop to the night-time disturbances. She relied on art. 15 (*right to life and to physical integrity*) and art. 18.2 (*right to privacy and inviolability of the home*) of the Spanish Constitution (hereafter CE) and sought € 3,907 for the non-pecuniary loss she had sustained and the cost of installing double glazing. The *Tribunal Superior de Justicia* of Valencia dismissed the claim. The Constitutional Court did the same with regard to the *amparo* appeal lodged by her.[30]

Although the Constitutional Court referred to ECtHR case-law and submitted 10
that "in cases of exceptional gravity, repeated damage to the environment could infringe the right to respect for private and family life … even if it did not endanger health", the court unanimously held that the claimant had not established the existence of a nuisance in her home that amounted to a violation of her fundamental rights. In any event, she had not established a direct link between the noise and the damage.[31]

b) Judgment of the Court

The claimant alleged a breach of her right to respect for her home contrary to 11
art. 8 ECHR. She claimed that although the Valencia City Council was not the direct source of the noise pollution, it had caused the acoustic saturation by issuing an unlimited number of licences, without taking measures to comply with the law. The Spanish Government submitted that the noise came from private activities and that there had not been direct interference by the public authority in her right. It also recalled that court decisions noted that she had failed to establish that she had been exposed seriously enough to noise emanating from night-time disturbances.

The court recalls that the object of art. 8 is essentially that of protecting the indi- 12
vidual against arbitrary interference by public authorities. Nevertheless, it may also involve the authorities adopting measures designed to secure respect for private life even in the sphere of relations of individuals between each other. It unanimously holds that there has been a violation of art. 8 ECHR as long as this

[29] Although the consequences entailed a ban on new activities (such as nightclubs and discotheques) that led to acoustic saturation, on 30 January 1997 the City Council granted a licence for a discotheque to be opened in the building she lived in. The licence was subsequently declared invalid by a judgment of the Supreme Court of 17 October 2001.

[30] See decision 119/2001, of 24 May.

[31] "[t]he appellant has confined herself to making a general complaint by stating that the origin of the noise was diffuse and not restricted to a single source of production, and that the acoustic saturation resulted from a combination of noises. … on the contrary, her entire case is based on a few sound-level readings taken inside her home which gave disparate results … and do not establish that there has been a violation of the right relied on".

provision protects not just the right to a physical area where private and family life develops, but also the quiet enjoyment of that area. Breaches of the right to respect of the home include therefore those that are not physical, such as noise, emissions, and smells or other forms of interference, provided that they are serious enough to prevent a person from enjoying the amenities of her home.

13 *In casu*, the court concedes that the claimant lives in an area that is indisputably subject to night-time disturbances. Concerning whether the nuisance caused by the noise attained the minimum level of severity required for it to constitute a violation of art. 8, the court relies on its volume – at night and beyond permitted levels – and the fact that it continued over a number of years. By so doing, it disagrees both with the Spanish Government and the national courts. It considers that to require the claimant to establish the noise levels inside her home has been "unduly formalistic" once the City authorities had already designated the area an "acoustically saturated zone". Moreover, infringements of maximum permitted noise levels had been confirmed on a number of occasions by council staff. Consequently, there is no need to require a person living in such a zone to afford evidence of a fact of which the municipal authority is already officially aware.

c) Commentary

14 It is ironic that the Kingdom of Spain has once again been held liable for an infringement of art. 8 ECHR in a nuisance case.[32] As already explained in last year's report[33], one of the most apparent trends of recent case-law has been that courts are more prone to grant relief to the victims of interferences resulting in environmental pollution, especially in cases of nuisances consisting in acoustic interferences. Indeed one may talk of an incorporation of the ECtHR case law.[34]

[32] ECtHR, Decision 9.12.1994. Case *López Ostra v. Spain.* Commented on by J. Egea Fernàndez, [1996] *Derecho Privado y Constitución* (DPyC) 6, 323–364.

[33] See J. Ribot/A. Ruda (supra fn. 2), 396–7, commenting on the decision issued on 29.4.2003 (*Actualidad Civil* 2003, 524). In this decision, the *Tribunal Supremo* relied upon the view held by the Constitutional Court in the *obiter dicta* of the decision under comment. On the importance of this judgment, see J. Egea Fernàndez, Relevancia constitucional de las inmisiones por ruido ambiental procedente de una zona de ocio nocturno. Recepción de la jurisprudencia del TEDH, [2001] DPyC 11, 69–105.

[34] It is worth mentioning that courts other than civil courts have invoked similar arguments to compel public bodies to effectively apply the noise statutory standards. For instance, by imposing on them a penalty until they can reduce or eliminate the source of noise. Moreover, the Criminal Chamber of the *Tribunal Supremo* has held that a serious nuisance consisting in acoustic pollution may amount to a crime against natural resources and environment according to art. 325 Penal Code (STS [= Administrative Chamber] 24.2.2003 [*Repertorio de Jurisprudencia Aranzadi-Westlaw* (RJ) 2003, 950]). Eventually, this judicial activism prompted the legislator to pass the Noise Act (*Ley 37/2003, de 17 noviembre, del ruido* [BOE no. 276, 18.11.2003]) establishing a general statutory framework for administrative control of noise and the corresponding penalties in case of infringement. The decision of the Constitutional Court 16/2004, of 23 February has used the same rationale to uphold the penalties imposed by a municipality on a very noisy disco-club, in spite of the fact that a specific legal ground for those penalties was lacking at the time of the facts (but see immediately afterwards decision 25/2004, of 26 February, holding an inconsistent view).

The broad construction of the constitutional protection of home (see art. 18.1 CE) in connection with the protection granted to family and personal privacy (see art. 18.2 CE) is widely accepted and applied by Spanish courts[35]. In the case at stake, however, the Constitutional Court found first that no infringement of the right to life and to physical integrity had taken place. It argued that a violation of art. 15 CE purports a serious and immediate damage to health and that the claimant could not provide enough evidence of having suffered regular insomnia. One of the concurring opinions considered that the requirements of the court were unreasonable. As shown by the decision under comment, such a criticism makes no difference as to the final outcome for the protection offered to the victim of the interferences on the basis of art. 8 ECHR (or art. 18 CE) is enough to overcome the limits of the protection on the basis of the right to physical integrity. Moreover, this outcome is fully consistent with the fact that, under Spanish law, compensation for non-pecuniary losses does not require a bodily or mental injury. On the contrary, it covers damage that does not medically qualify as an illness[36]. In nuisance cases Spanish courts have even admitted compensation for harm consisting only in the "environmental detriment that impairs *the quality of life of the claimants*".[37] 15

The Spanish Constitutional Court emphasized the difference between environmental acoustical pollution resulting from noisy activities undertaken in the area in which the claimant lived and her situation at home. The ECtHR holds instead the opinion that environmental acoustic pollution may also impinge on the claimant's right to respect for her home. This has an immediate impact on the burden of proof of both the level of acoustic pollution and the seriousness of the interferences suffered by the claimant at home. In the case at stake, evidence collected while investigating the level of noise produced by the licensed premises is deemed sufficient both to establish the infringement of her rights and the right to claim compensation for the damage sustained.[38] This is fully consistent with the way ordinary courts usually decide these types of cases. Whereas proof of the interferences and of their seriousness shall lie with the claimant, providing objective proof is often difficult. Courts then use other means of proof that are assessed according to common sense and that may lead to the conclusion that the interference is unlawful.[39] Sound level mea- 16

[35] As a matter of fact, the approach based on fundamental rights allows claimants and courts to overcome some procedural and substantive restrictions through specific civil remedies and faster proceedings.

[36] In this sense, see M. Martín-Casals/J. Solé Feliu, El daño moral, in: S. Cámara Lapuente (ed.), *Derecho Privado Europeo* (2003), 879.

[37] Emphasis added. See STS 2.2.2001 (RJ 2001, 1003) quoted by M. Martín-Casals/J. Solé Feliu, Comentario a la sentencia de 31 de octubre de 2002, [2003] *Cuadernos Cívitas de Jurisprudencia Civil* (CCJC) 61, 260. In the same sense, see F.J. Fernández Urzainqui, *La tutela civil frente al ruido* (2003), 92. An unconvincing criticism of this trend may be found, most recently, in A. Macías Castillo, *El daño causado por el ruido y otras inmisiones* (2004), 407 et seq.

[38] In the domestic proceedings before the Constitutional Court, the *Ministerio Fiscal* (General Attorney) did not consider it necessary to require the claimant to provide additional evidence and suggested that in the present case a reversal of the burden of proof should apply.

[39] See STS 29.4.2003 (RJ 2003, 3041).

surements or other technical tests are not deemed conclusive or even necessary. Besides, the decision under comment supports the practice of courts whereby the proof of a concrete harm is not required once the seriousness of the interferences is ascertained.[40]

17 Up to now, most of the claims have been filed against public bodies. *López Ostra* and now *Moreno Gómez* have made it clear that public bodies cannot contend that interferences originated in premises owned by private individuals.[41] At any rate, however, the reasoning based on art. 8 ECHR (and its counterpart art. 18 CE) can also be applied in private litigation. Preferring to sue public authorities may be due to practical difficulties in meeting causation requirements. As a matter of fact, acoustic environmental pollution is produced by a number of sources of noise that operate at the same time and which often concur with traffic and other activities of daily life in squares and streets. It may be arguable whether a causal link exists between any of the activities (or even all of them) and the damage sustained by the claimant.[42]

2. Constitutional Court Decision 15/2004, of 23 February[43]: Application of Compulsory Tariffication Scheme for Personal Injuries Resulting from Road Traffic Accidents

a) Brief Summary of the Facts

18 On 3 July 1996 two policemen suffered a traffic accident when a lorry crashed against their car. Both were injured, one of them suffering very serious injuries that eventually led to him giving up the service and becoming qualified for a permanent total incapacity benefit. The driver of the truck was held to be both criminally and civilly liable. The court awarded the two policemen amounts that were fitting to their injuries in accordance with the tariffication scheme of the LRCSCVM. The spouse of the severely handicapped policeman had taken part in the criminal proceedings as claimant in her own name. Nevertheless, she was denied compensation for the non-pecuniary losses she asked for, on the basis that the tariffication scheme did not consider her to be a victim. As a matter of fact, she asked for compensation for "moral damage" related to the suffering she experiences because of her husband's mood changes and the permanent assistance she must afford him. This decision was upheld in appeal and the claimants subsequently lodged an *amparo* appeal with the Constitutional Court. The policemen contended that the damages awarded

[40] In these sorts of cases it is simply assumed that damage exists. See P. Cillero de Cabo, La prueba del daño y de la relación de causalidad en el ámbito de la tutela frente al ruido: estudio jurisprudencial, [2004] *Aranzadi Civil* 14, 8 et seq., with more references therein. Among many others, see the decisions of Provincial Court [hereafter, SAP] of Córdoba 27.4.2004 (*La Ley* 2004, 1597) and Valladolid 20.7.2004 (JUR 2004, 211055).

[41] STS 29.5.2003 (RJ 2003, 5366).

[42] F.J. Fernández Urzainqui (supra fn. 37), 286.

[43] Commented on by M. Medina Crespo, Una nueva cata en el cajón de las sorpresas. La STC de 23 de febrero de 2004: el caso de la esposa del lesionado que, sin sufrir una gran invalidez, padece una discapacidad importante, [2004] RRCCS 40, issue 6, 14–22.

to them were insufficient. The spouse challenged the decision because it excluded her from receiving any kind of compensation.

b) Judgment of the Court

Firstly, the Constitutional Court recalls its own doctrine on the constitutionality of the legal tariffication scheme laid down in LRCSCVM[44]. Accordingly, starting out from the premise that the legislator has the constitutional power to set up different regimes of civil liability in relation to specific areas of social life, the above mentioned act neither infringes the equal treatment clause (art. 14 CE) nor the fundamental rights to life and physical integrity (art. 15 CE).[45] 19

The Constitutional Court then dismisses the *amparo* appeal lodged by all applicants. As regards the alleged infringement of art. 24 CE (*right to an effective judicial protection*), it argues that the policemen did not provide any evidence that the trial court, by applying the legal tariffication scheme, had been prevented from awarding them full compensation for their damage. The rejection of the *amparo* appeal of the spouse relies upon the idea that the main characteristic of personal injury cases is that the direct victim is the only beneficiary of any amount awarded as damages in accordance with the legal tariffication scheme. 20

c) Commentary

The *amparo* appeal lodged with the Constitutional Court not only sought the nullity of the previous judgments issued by the ordinary courts, but also a declaration of the unconstitutionality of the rules preventing or limiting the rights of certain indirect victims to obtain compensation in cases of personal injuries sustained in road traffic accidents. *In casu*, this refers to the compensation for the painful life that the spouse of one of the direct victims had to endure due to the resulting disability of her husband. Nevertheless, the Constitutional Court dismisses the *amparo* appeal without making any statement regarding the constitutional validity of a legal provision that may lead to a limitation of both the number of claimants in tort in this sort of case and the requirements they have to meet to obtain a damages award. 21

[44] Decision 181/2000, of 29 June.

[45] Among many others, see decisions 242/2000, of 16 October and 49/2002, of 25 February. This statement has led the civil courts to consider that the tariffication scheme was not intended to be applied to personal injuries other than those suffered in traffic accidents. The Civil Chamber of the *Tribunal Supremo* expressly rejected its application even if for guidance only, since this could be detrimental to the plaintiff (STS 20.6.2003 [RJ 2003, 4520]); an approach that is in striking contrast with Administrative and Criminal courts' practice. These apply the legal scheme of tariffication of damages to all kind of situations involving personal injuries. See the accurate account of S. Ramos González/A. Luna Yerga, Los baremos como paradigma de valoración de daños personales, [2004] *InDret* 1 (www.indret.com). See also P. Sebastián García, La aplicación extensiva del baremo contenido en la Ley 30/1995, de 8 de noviembre, de Ordenación y Supervisión de los seguros privados, a supuestos ajenos a la circulación de vehículos de motor, [2004] *Revista de Derecho de los Seguros Privados* 11, issue 1, 7–12.

22 The reason for dismissing the *amparo* appeal is a formal one: the applicants did not mention the legal provision they intended to challenge.[46] Anyhow, the court afterwards embarked on a restrictive construction of the provisions of LRCSCVM and held, first, that the "moral damages of near relatives" referred to by the act were to be limited to cases of "great disability" (*gran invalidez*).[47] In the case at stake, the disability only amounted to a permanent total disability. The second and most important statement of the decision is that, in any case, the only person allowed to claim such a damages award is the direct victim, not her relatives. Surprisingly enough, the LRCSCVM itself links the damage with the relatives. Indeed, the act even clarifies the head of damage: i.e. the "substantial alteration of the life and personal relationship as a consequence of permanently caring and supporting [the disabled person]". The Constitutional Court thus endorses a view held only by a minority of ordinary courts, and one which considers that head of damage to be a part of the condition of the disabled person[48]. Although open to criticism from a theoretical point of view, this construction has the positive effect that awarding compensation to the direct victim prevents the spouse or the relatives from getting the money and deserting her.[49]

3. *Tribunal Supremo* (Civil Chamber) 31 December 2003, RJ 2004, 367[50]: Accident in the Workplace

a) Brief Summary of the Facts

23 On 26 June 1995, a maintenance work team of the defendant company was sent to an electric transformer belonging to a third party. Before beginning to work, personnel of both the defendant company and the owner of the equipment demarcated the restricted area with plastic ribbon and danger posters. The team leader subsequently went to the control site to sign the permission of entry to the working area. At the same moment and for unknown reasons, one of the members of his staff entered the restricted area to start working. As he put a ladder next to a device that was still plugged in he suffered an electric shock that eventually caused him to die the day after. The employee had been hired by the defendant company only six months before, yet he had substantial experience in this kind of job and specific training in electric installations. Apart from social security benefits, his wife and minor child received € 45,000 from a first-party insurance taken out by the defendant. Nevertheless, they sued the enterprise claiming compensation for damage amounting to € 100,000.

[46] See the criticisms raised by M. Medina Crespo (supra fn. 43), 18.

[47] With regard to other issues previously tackled with by the court it showed reluctant to apply analogically the provisions of the LRCSCVM. See J. Ribot/A. Ruda (supra fn. 2), 391.

[48] M. Medina Crespo (supra fn. 43), 19.

[49] Later on the Constitutional Court used the same rationale to uphold the legal rule that estipulates the award of a unique compensation for all indirect victims in cases of death, regardless of whether they are one or several (see decision 105/2004, of 28 June).

[50] Commented on by E. Rubio Torrano, Responsabilidad civil por accidente laboral, [2004] *Aranzadi Civil* 12, 1–3.

b) Judgment of the Court

The *Tribunal Supremo* shares the view held by the trial court that the claimants did not afford any proof of faulty behaviour attributable to the defendant enterprise. Quite the contrary, both courts argue that the company complied with all safety measures required by the type of activity. Evidence provided in the proceedings showed that the workers developed their tasks following the common procedure which all of them were familiar with, especially as regards the prohibition not to enter the restricted area until the team leader had received the installation and had given permission to start working. The court argues that to require the team leader to permanently supervise the workers would be inappropriate. From this standpoint, since the victim was a qualified and experienced worker, his conduct is seen as unforeseeable and the defendant is blameless for his death. 24

c) Commentary

Beyond the case in itself, the decision under comment is significant because it encloses several general statements on employer's liability that may shape future development in case-law in this field. The court recalls first that victims may ask for compensation on the basis of an employer's civil liability regardless of whether they have a right to social security benefits. In that respect, it stresses that civil courts hold their competence when the grounds of the tort claim are artt. 1902 or 1903 CC, i.e. the general rules on civil liability. Conversely, labour courts are to be deemed competent when the claimant relies upon the infringement of the safety measures required by the labour contract or by specific legislation. The court concludes that such criteria are justified on the basis that a "legislative amendment clarifying the issue" is lacking and that "labour law alone does not grant full compensation" to the victim. Secondly, damages awarded by civil courts are compatible with social security benefits. Nevertheless, this fact does not allow the accumulation of both amounts, and the trial court must undertake a careful analysis that all the requirements of fault liability provisions are met. The reversal of the burden of the proof of fault, which is applied in many settings by Spanish courts, is not available here. In addition, the claimant is required to afford substantial evidence as to the causal link. Finally, defences like contributory negligence can be opposed. 25

The decision seems to endorse a trend whose main goal is to reach more predictable and fairer decisions in the field of accidents in the workplace.[51] In that sense, it concurs with the idea – occasionally held by some writers – that the conditions for the employer to be liable in tort should be influenced by the fact that a no-fault system integrated in social security provides benefits to injured workers and their relatives.[52] This decision, however, cannot be seen as final 26

[51] E. Rubio Torrano, [2004] *Aranzadi Civil* 12, 3. As to the Social Chamber of the *Tribunal Supremo* see decisions 30.9.1997 (RJ 1997, 6853) and 20.7.2000 (RJ 2000, 6754).

[52] See L. Díez-Picazo, *Derecho de daños* (1999), 178. See also J.R. Mercader Uguina, *Indemnizaciones derivadas del accidente de trabajo. Seguridad Social y Derecho de daños* (2001), 132–3.

for it cannot be ruled out that other decisions regarding similar cases will take the opposite view.[53] These decisions are likely to apply stricter liability tests arguing, for instance, that it "is in harmony with social trends … and with the idea of justice that always underlies tort actions and especially in accidents in the workplace, unfortunately so common today".[54] Both the fact that social security benefits provide for a low coverage and that civil courts tend to undercompensate damage for personal injury and death may explain why these kinds of considerations still enjoy wide acceptance among Spanish courts and scholars.[55]

4. *Tribunal Supremo* (Civil Chamber) 23 January 2004; RJ 2004, 1[56]: Civil Liability of the Magistrates of the Constitutional Court

a) Brief Summary of the Facts

27 The claimant filed two appeals with the Administrative Chamber of the *Tribunal Supremo*. He challenged a decision of the Constitutional Court regarding the appointment of clerks assigned to the court. He accused its members of pulling strings in order to have their protégés appointed. Both appeals were dismissed by a decision of the *Tribunal Supremo*. The applicant then lodged an *amparo* appeal with the Constitutional Court. However, the appeal was addressed to the Constitutional Court "made up of new members capable of coming to an impartial decision". He asked for a) the abstention of all current members of the Constitutional Court, since they had a direct interest in the lawsuit; b) that the court should request the President to start the legislative proceedings in order to promote the passing of an Act that could guarantee him the right to an impartial examination of his case; and c) the declaration of nullity of the appealed decision "by the [new] court appointed in accordance with the said act". On 10 July 2002 the Constitutional Court decided unanimously not to admit such appeal. It held that "the appeal does not address this court but another hypothetical one that ought to replace it". A new appeal against that decision was also dismissed by the court. When the admission decisions of the Constitutional Court became final the claimant sued its members before the Civil Chamber of the *Tribunal Supremo*. He blamed them for having "intentionally or at least negligently" infringed his right to a fair judi-

[53] E. Rubio Torrano (supra fn. 51).

[54] STS 29.4.2004 (RJ 2004, 2092); previously see STS 22.4.2003 (RJ 2003, 3545), 1.10.2003 (RJ 2003, 6206) and 17.10.2001 (RJ 2001, 8642). A good overview on the state of the art by N. Álvarez Lata, in: L.F. Reglero Campos (ed.), *Lecciones de Responsabilidad Civil* (2002), 463–4. More recently see L.F. Reglero Campos, Responsabilidad del empresario por accidentes de trabajo: jurisdicción competente y título de imputación, [2004] RRCCS 10, 8–23.

[55] For instance, see more recently B. Gutiérrez-Solar Calvo, *Culpa y riesgo en la responsabilidad civil por accidentes de trabajo* (2004), *passim* and 289–306. From an economic standpoint see the criticism of this approach offered by M. Faure/T. Hartlief, Economic Analysis, in: U. Magnus (ed.), *The Impact of Social Security on Tort Law* (2003), nos. 67 and 72.

[56] Commented on by G. Escobar, [2004] RRCCS 4, 26–29 and P. Salvador Coderch/A. Luna Yerga/S. Ramos González, Diseño institucional defectuoso. Comentario a la STS, 1ª, de 22.1.2004, [2004] *InDret* 1 (www.indret.com).

cial protection and claimed € 11,000 as a compensation for the ensuing "moral" damage.

b) Judgment of the Court

The claimant based his action on art. 441 Organic Act on Judicial Power[57], which lays down the conditions of civil liability of judges. The *Tribunal Supremo* considers that this provision "cannot be applied to magistrates of the Constitutional Court", for this court does not belong to the judiciary. Nevertheless, it subsequently holds them liable in tort on the basis of the general rule on fault liability (art. 1902 CC) because the *amparo* appeal lodged by the claimant was dismissed without adequate reasoning, thereby incurring a reproachable *non liquet*. This fact led to a blatant contravention of the duty to justify the decision, and infringed the claimant's right to an effective judicial protection harming "his faith in a social and democratic State, subject to the rule of law". 28

c) Commentary

The main problem of the existence of two types of courts dealing with issues involving fundamental rights consists in the fact that on many occasions the Constitutional Court has turned down decisions of the ordinary courts because they had infringed a fundamental right of one or more of the parties.[58] This situation – that is common to other jurisdictions, especially those that allow lodging individual appeals with the Constitutional Court against decisions of the ordinary courts[59] – has amounted to a very serious power conflict in Spain. This conflict has been shaping the relationship between both courts during the last few years[60]. The last(?) chapter of this sad story[61] is the unfortunate decision under comment, which may well be seen as a sort of reappraisal of the *Tribunal Supremo* against the members of the Constitutional Court. 29

As stressed by the only dissenting opinion, the petition enclosed in the claimant's *amparo* appeal was simply untenable. The criticisms addressed to the 30

[57] *Ley Orgánica 6/1985, de 1 de julio, del Poder Judicial*) (as amended by Organic Act 6/1998, of 13 July).

[58] The reasons can be either a different construction of the legal rules applicable to the case under the light of the fundamental rights involved, or the infringement of the procedural guarantees that are recognised as well as fundamental rights in the Spanish Constitution (namely, those contained in art. 24: the right to a fair process and the right to an effective judicial protection, among others). On the issue see A. de la Oliva Santos/I. Díez-Picazo Giménez, *Tribunal Constitucional, Jurisdicción ordinaria y derechos fundamentales* (1996).

[59] P. Salvador Coderch/A. Luna Yerga/S. Ramos González, [2004] *InDret* 1, 4.

[60] In this sense, P. Salvador Coderch/C. Gómez Ligüerre/A. Luna Yerga/S. Ramos González, Libertad de expresión y luchas de poder entre tribunales, [2001] *InDret* 4 (www.indret.com). See also M.P. García Rubio/J. Lete, Spain, in: H. Koziol/B.C. Steininger (eds.), *European Tort Law 2001* (2002), 419–420.

[61] The Constitutional Court issued an official statement on 3 February 2004 declaring that the decision of the *Tribunal Supremo* infringed its jurisdiction. Besides that, the magistrates lodged an *amparo* appeal with the Constitutional Court.

members of the Constitutional Court lack therefore any grounds.[62] In that respect, it must be borne in mind that applicable procedural rules allow the dismissal of any request lodged with the Constitutional Court that does not comply with the legal requirements, without special justification. That was clearly the case and it should be dismissed. As a consequence, holding the magistrates liable in tort for issuing a lawful decision within its competence is utterly wrong.

31 Moreover, the decision under comment applies the liability criteria in a dubious manner, since its reasoning appears in striking contrast to the conditions usually posed by case-law to declare the civil liability of magistrates and judges belonging to the judiciary. Indeed, only a patent infringement of law due to gross or inexcusable negligence makes an ordinary judge liable.[63] Moreover, to be held liable he must have directly caused the claimant a pecuniary loss. The decision under comment, on the contrary, makes each magistrate of the Constitutional Court pay a damages award of € 500 on the questionable basis that they caused the claimant a personal disappointment by their decision not to admit a groundless appeal. Needless to say, taking this head of damage seriously would entail opening doors to an infinity of claims filed by disappointed users of the judicial machinery. [64]

5. *Tribunal Supremo* (Civil Chamber) 9 July 2004, RJ 2004, 5121: Legal Malpractice; Heads of Damage

a) Brief Summary of the Facts

32 The claimant worked as a secretary to the sales manager of a retail chain. She was notified that she was going to be transferred to another section, thereby changing her timetable and working conditions. As she was a member of a trade union, she decided to request the legal aid of the union. One of the attorneys working for the union under a labour contract took charge of her case but failed to lodge her claim with the labour court within due time. As a consequence, the action brought on her behalf was dismissed. She then sued both the lawyer and the trade union seeking compensation for the psychological harm resulting from the change in her working conditions and the economic loss consisting in the likely award of damages for breach of the employment contract and the subsequent unemployment benefits she would have been entitled to had the action been successful. The court of first instance upheld the claim against both defendants. However, it awarded only € 12,000 as compensation for non-pecuniary losses. The trial court rejected the appeal lodged by the claimant and the trade union.

[62] See M. Pulido Quecedo, El debido respeto al Tribunal Constitucional, [2003] *Repertorio Aranzadi del Tribunal Constitucional* 20, 1 et seq.

[63] Recently see J.I. Álvarez Sánchez, La responsabilidad civil de jueces y magistrados, abogados y procuradores, in: *La responsabilidad civil profesional* (2004), 24.

[64] Cf. M. Pulido Quecedo, [2003] *Repertorio Aranzadi del Tribunal Constitucional* 20, 4. See also G. Escobar, [2004] RRCCS 4, 28.

b) Judgment of the Court

The *Tribunal Supremo* quashes the decision of the trial court with regard to the trade union. The court shares the view of the appellant and contends that the error leading to the dismissal of the claimant's action is attributable only to the lawyer. It points out that although the lawyer was its employee, the trade union did not act with fault, as required by art. 1903 CC, since it had "entrusted the task to defend its member to a person who, according to his academic degrees and his affiliation to the bar association, furnished sufficient proof of his knowledge and skills". On the other hand, the court confirms the decision of the trial court that considered that the claimant was not entitled to compensation for what she might have obtained if the claim had been successful, and awarded damages only for the non-pecuniary loss resulting from not having been able to pursue her claim in court. 33

c) Commentary

This judgment follows a view held in previous decisions of the *Tribunal Supremo* according to which damages for pecuniary loss are not available in legal malpractice suits that involve an uncertain outcome. In this sort of case only the "unlawful loss of procedural opportunities" may be compensated. This head of damage is a multi-faceted concept embracing a range of different situations, such as, for instance, the failed possibility of appealing or of being able to provide certain evidence during legal proceedings. In fact it works as a minimal compensation whose amount is assessed freely by the court, no matter what the probabilities of success are. The *Tribunal Supremo* has even said that it allows it to be presumed that damage exists once the negligent infringement of the claimant's legal interests has been established. 34

Notwithstanding this trend, in a recent decision the *Tribunal Supremo* was prepared to allow compensation of both pecuniary and non-pecuniary losses. In this decision the court held that a "qualified probability test" should be applied with regard to the probability of success of the claim had the lawyer not been negligent[65]. Accordingly, only if the claimant had not much chance of success could damages for pecuniary loss be ruled out. Both points of view might not be as necessarily inconsistent as they appear to be. In the case at issue, for instance, the trial court had emphasised that the claimant had little chance of success. As a matter of fact, the change in the claimant's working conditions took place after an agreement was reached between the unions and the employer. This agreement enabled her to keep both her position and her salary. 35

Finally, the *Tribunal Supremo* applies a quite lenient test in order to free the defendant union from liability. The lawyer was its employee. It is thus correct to apply art. 1903 CC, which refers to the employer's liability and lays down a rebuttable presumption of fault. Nevertheless, the court argues that it is 36

[65] See STS 28.7.2003 (RJ 2003, 5989).

enough to prove that the legal aid was entrusted to a person holding the relevant academic degrees and who was affiliated to the bar association. It stresses as well that he conducted the cases assigned to him with autonomy. It is worth mentioning that this outcome, even if reasonable, is in striking contrast to the criteria currently applied by case law with regard to insurance companies that offer health services through a catalogue of independent health providers from which the insured chooses.[66]

6. *Tribunal Supremo* (Civil Chamber) 22 September 2004: Non-Pecuniary Loss

a) Brief Summary of the Facts

37 On 15 October 1973 a factory was completely destroyed by fire. As a consequence, the workers lost their jobs. Inquiries were made to determine the circumstances of the fire. Its general manager was prosecuted, but he was eventually discharged without trial. More than twenty years later, in 1995, several employees brought a claim in tort against him and his son, who formerly acted as head of the health and safety committee. The court of first instance dismissed the claim. This decision was confirmed in appeal. The trial court held that the action against the second defendant had prescribed. As regards the general manager, the court exonerated him arguing that "the moral damage for which compensation is sought has not been proven". At any rate, this damage would be embedded in the economic loss that the claimants allegedly also suffered – the reduction of income due to forced termination of their contracts – but which they did not manage to demonstrate.

b) Judgment of the Court

38 Starting from the fact that the destruction of the factory gave rise to the termination of the employment contracts, the *Tribunal Supremo* holds it irrelevant that the defendant was released without charges from criminal proceedings and that no infringement of safety regulations was ascertained. The notion of "enterprise risk", which purports "a sort of liability for risk attributable to the enterprise", justifies the duty to compensate for the damage caused to the workers.

39 The compensatable damages are both pecuniary losses, related to forced inactivity after being dismissed, and non-pecuniary losses, the latter consisting in the fear and worry linked to the uncertainty about finding a new job. The court quashes the trial court decision stressing that the burden of proving and assessing this damage is not to be placed upon the claimants. Once the causal link between the fire and the termination of their contracts is established, the emotional impact suffered by them may be presumed and its assessment falls to the court's discretion.

[66] See infra fn. 86.

c) Commentary

The facts in the decision under comment are far from clear. Apparently, the lawsuit only involved the former employees as claimants and the general manager and his son, as defendants. This leads one to think that when the claim was finally brought against them, the company that owned the factory had ceased to exist. No mention is made either of the circumstances of the fire or of how the defendants contributed to it. 40

In any event the reasoning developed by the decision is odd and unconvincing. It is submitted that the court relies upon a vague notion of "risk liability" which will trigger liability without any need to establish fault on the part of the defendant and on the basis of operating an element that may harm the protected interests of third parties in one's own interest. What is more striking is that this notion is used to make the former manager liable, not the company. Besides that, the decision makes no effort to link the grounds of liability to the activities carried out in the factory (whether they were particularly dangerous or not) or to the conduct attributable to any of its employees. The decision apparently accepts that it could have been due to acts attributable to third parties or even to *force majeure.* All this was done to grant the former employees compensation for a non-pecuniary loss that the Court simply presumes from the factual situation.[67] 41

This decision is to be considered in the light of the circumstances of the case. Presumably the fire brought about the end of the company as a whole. Moreover, the facts carry us to a period of a deep economic crisis. In all probability the workers were fired without receiving a penny of indemnification, and it is possible that the defendants had a personal link with the property of the factory. The judgment under comment, however, makes no effort to elucidate any of these items although they might have had influence in the final outcome of the case. From a technical standpoint, the decision can be seen as an extreme illustration of how courts make use of damages for non-pecuniary loss to indemnify economic losses not fully demonstrated in the proceedings.[68] In this case, this is done with regard to a type of damage that is normally left uncompensated for either on the basis of a rough application of the requirement of determination – as contended by the trial court[69] – or by arguing that a causal link between the tortfeasor's conduct and the damage is lacking.[70] 42

[67] The *Tribunal Supremo* awards a lump sum of € 6,000 to each claimant.

[68] See F. Gómez, Daño moral, [2000] *InDret* 1 (www.indret.com).

[69] "The claimants had not provided any proof that they had tried to overcome the economic impact of the closing of the factory by taking positive steps to find a new job instead of receiving all the unemployement benefits that they were entitled to".

[70] See M. Martín-Casals/J. Ribot (supra fn. 15), 65. For instance, STS 28.2.1983 (RJ 1983, 1079) (involving the destruction of rented premises that caused the end of the contract of lease; causal link between the defendant's behaviour and the damage not proven). But see STS 30.5.1986 (RJ 1986, 2918) (physical harm caused to a factory that resulted in temporary dismissal of the workers; causal link established).

7. *Tribunal Supremo* (Administrative Chamber) 11 October 2004, RJ 2004, 6822 (= *La Ley* 2004, 2499): State Liability

a) Brief Summary of the Facts

43 The Registry of Wills (*Registro de Actos de Última Voluntad*) – an administrative unit answerable to the Ministry of Justice – issued a certificate in 1982 declaring officially that the last will of the claimant's uncle was one made on 23 September 1977. Following this will, the brothers of the testator took possession of his estate and sold most of the assets. In 1993, while the process of computerization of the Registry of Wills was being carried out, notice of a will made by the testator on 8 March 1979 appeared. In this will the claimant was the heir. By chance he knew about the finding and made several enquiries that led him to ask the Registry to issue a new certificate. This was issued on 1 December 1995 and declared that the last valid will made by the testator was the one dated on 8 March 1979, which was missing due to an error eventually amended in 1993.

44 The real heir filed an application with the competent administrative authorities to obtain compensation for damage ensuing from the mistake of the Registry of Wills. Following the advice of the Council of State, the Minister of Justice refused any compensation for economic loss and only agreed to pay € 6,000 as compensation for non-pecuniary loss. The *Audiencia Nacional* turned down this decision and awarded € 90,000 instead. The court deemed "within the more perfect logical order of things that the claimant was suffering from an extremely poor psychiatric condition and alcoholism" as a result of the irregular service provided by the Registry of Wills. The court rejected awarding compensation for the value of the estate. It argued that before asking for compensation from the State, the claimant should have initiated a civil action against the false heirs and tried to obtain the assets or their current value from them. Until then the pecuniary damage was deemed to be not fully determined for its amount was dependent on how successful these claims would have been.

b) Judgment of the Court

45 The Administrative Chamber of the *Tribunal Supremo* quashes the decision of the trial court and declares the right of the claimant to receive compensation on account of the negligent functioning of the Registry of Wills. Moreover, together with damages for non-pecuniary losses already granted by the trial court, the *Tribunal Supremo* awards an amount of € 1,260,096 as compensation for pecuniary losses. The court holds that forcing the claimant to seek the restitution of the estate by means of a civil action whose probabilities of success are uncertain and that in fact would postpone the resolution by ten, fifteen or twenty years, amounts to a violation of the right to an effective judicial protection laid down in art. 24 of the Constitution.

c) Commentary

The claimant had little chance of obtaining the restitution of his uncle's estate or of being paid back its current value. When he first sought compensation from the Ministry of Justice fifteen years had already passed and most of the assets of the estate were in the hands of *bona fide* third parties, who had acquired the pieces of land under the protection of the Registry of Property. The *Tribunal Supremo* probably took this into account as well as the fact that the Registry of Wills did not take any steps after acquiring knowledge of the mistake that harmed the claimant's interests. Had the Registry acted otherwise perhaps the real heir would have been in a better position to assert his rights in the civil courts. It took almost three years until the Registry issued a correct certificate at the claimant's request, and three more years to respond to the compensation he asked for. 46

The pointlessness of the claimant's civil actions might explain why the *Tribunal Supremo* agrees to concede the whole amount of damages he had asked for. At the same time, in a remarkable and probably technically wrong decision, the court says that the judgment means that the claimant's rights to his uncle's estate are to be transferred to the State. By so doing the decision seems to treat the tort action as a compulsory purchase, justified by the fact that the claimant still holds a right (although ineffective due to the negligence of a public service). This option may be seen as the alternative to postponing the awarding of the compensation and having to indemnify afterwards for the total value of the estate and all non-pecuniary losses and further expenses related to the claimant having had to pursue his rights in vain. 47

The decision also deals with the issue of prescription. Apparently, the negligence of the public service caused the harm many years before the victim lodged his application for compensation. In the case at stake, however, all courts ruled out the defence of prescription raised by the State. The rationale was that, as regards State liability, the one-year prescription period runs either from the time when the harmful event occurred or from the moment where its effects are apparent. The courts drew the conclusion that the right was still actionable from the fact that the estate had not been transferred yet in accordance with the testator's will. That the claimant knew about the will three years before lodging his claim is deemed immaterial "because a lay person may not derive from that mere fact that a public service has caused damage to his legally protected interests". It is submitted that the same result could have been achieved by applying a subjective test of knowledge of both the grounds of the claim and the person against whom to bring it.[71] 48

[71] See supra fn. 26.

8. *Tribunal Supremo* (Civil Chamber) 2 November 2004, RJ 2004, 6864: Liability for Animals; Alternative Causation

a) Brief Summary of the Facts

49 As a result of a cow injuring him, a 53 year old man died while he was going for a walk in the countryside. There were no witnesses to the accident. It was thus unclear which cow injured him because there were cows belonging to two different owners. One was the defendant, who was the owner of the land where the cattle had been grazing. The other owner was the brother of the victim, who was one of the claimants who sued the defendant and his insurance company. The claim was dismissed by the court of first instance on the basis of contributory negligence. In appeal, however, the claim was upheld and the defendants were made liable following art. 1905 CC, which lays down a strict liability of the possessor of an animal causing damage to a third party.

b) Judgment of the Court

50 The *Tribunal Supremo* partially upholds the decision of the trial court. It rejects the argument raised by the defendant that the claimants were responsible for taking care of the cattle, and that accordingly they should bear the harm suffered by their brother. The defendant blamed them for letting their brother be present at the place where the cows were. To rule out both arguments the *Tribunal Supremo* relies on the fact that the claimants were simply "*servidores de la posesión*", that is instruments of the possession of the cattle for the defendant. On the other hand, the appeal is upheld regarding the complaint that one of the claimants himself owned some of the cows involved in the fatal accident, which were in the same grazing area with the permission of the defendant. Since it was unknown which cow attacked the victim, the court concludes that this claimant "cannot recover anything on account of his brother's death, since he can be held accountable for the damaging event and his own liability was insured by the same company".

c) Commentary

51 The special feature of the case is the complex situation of some of the claimants with regard to the defendant and the damaging event. Some of them were his auxiliaries and were responsible for the cattle involved in the accident. Moreover, one of them had several cows in the defendant's grazing area when the accident took place. Both he and the defendant had their liability insured with the same insurer.

52 As to the grounds of the decision, in the case at issue the distinction between possessors or persons who use an animal[72] and persons who are simply an in-

[72] In the sense of the person who obtains a service or a benefit from the animal, even without being its possessor. See I. Gallego Domínguez, *Responsabilidad civil extracontractual por daños causados por animales* (1997), 61 and A. Ramos Maestre, *La responsabilidad extracontractual del poseedor de animales* (2003), 123 et seq.

strument of the possession for another (*servidor de la posesión, Besitzdiener*) seems immaterial. The latter is certainly not liable in accordance with art. 1905 CC[73]. Liability on the basis of his or her negligent conduct cannot be ruled out, though. For the very same reason, it is submitted that the decision under comment should have allowed the defendant to contend either that the claimants had infringed their contractual duties toward him with regard to the custody of the cattle or that he could at any rate recover their contribution to the damage.

The second issue dealt with by the decision is alternative causation. The decision is consistent with previous case-law on the issue, which makes all alternative tortfeasors solidary liable for the damage sustained by the claimant.[74] Moreover, in this case there is more room for analogy with regard to the only legal provision dealing with the issue in Spanish law: art. 33.5 *in fine* Hunting Act[75]. A specific feature of the case here is, however, that both alternative tortfeasors were insured by the same company, although they held different policies. The court refuses to grant any damages to the claimant who simultaneously might be held liable for the same damaging event. The court agrees with the insurance company that the latter is discharged because the right of the claimant to be compensated for his brother's death merged with his own duty to compensate arising from the accident and which is covered by the liability insurance.[76] 53

9. *Tribunal Supremo* (Civil Chamber) 17 November 2004, RJ 2004, 7238: Liability of a Hospital

a) Brief Summary of the Facts

The claimant underwent a hysterectomy to remove a mioma in a private hospital in the Canary Islands. Five days later, during the post-operative period, she became unconscious and suffered from light tachycardia. These symptoms continued over the next day. It was decided to transfer her to another hospital for an assessment of her cardiac condition. Immediately after being admitted, the patient experienced non-sustained ventricular tachycardia and was prescribed *Propafenoma*. Several incidents of this type took place over the next 54

[73] I. Gallego Domínguez (supra fn. 72), 67.

[74] A recent account of the case-law may be found in M. Martín-Casals/A. Ruda González, Comentario de la sentencia de 26 de noviembre de 2003, [2004] CCJC 65, 843–859. In legal writing see L. Díez-Picazo (supra fn. 52), 166 and R. de Ángel, Indeterminación del causante de un daño extracontractual, [1983] *Revista general de legislación y jurisprudencea,* 23–76.

[75] Act 1/1970, of 4 April. This provision establishes that if when hunting with firearms a person is injured and it cannot be assessed which hunter caused the injury, all the members of the hunting party will be held solidary liable. To this end art. 35.6.b) Hunting Compulsory Insurance Regulation, provides that "those hunters who have practised the activity of hunting on the occasion and in the place where damage has occurred and who have used a firearm of the same sort as the one that caused the harm will be the only ones that will be considered members of the hunting party".

[76] On the difficulties of the recoupment action against a joint tortfeasor when only one of them is sued see M. Martín-Casals/J. Solé, Multiple Tortfeasors under Spanish Law, in: W.V.H. Rogers (ed.), *Unification of Tort Law: Multiple Tortfeasors* (2004), 203.

few hours. The medical staff thought that the patient was at risk of sudden death and decided to start treatment with *Amiodarona* in high doses. The patient continued to suffer from ventricular fibrillation and tachycardia. An increase in the *Amiodarona* dosage was then ordered. Eventually the patient had a cardiac arrest that led the medical team to think about the need to implant a pacemaker, which would have required an electrophysiology test in a hospital in Madrid previously. When the drug treatment was discontinued to perform this test, however, the heart activity returned to normal. Moreover, the test showed that the patient had no kind of cardiac anomaly or disease. From this time she has not experienced any further incident. As a consequence of the cardiac arrest suffered while she was at the second hospital, however, her brain was severely damaged and she is in need of permanent assistance. Her husband sued the two hospitals and the insurance company that managed the healthcare provided to her. The court of first instance held them all solidary liable and awarded the patient € 720,000 as compensation. In appeal, the provincial court exonerated the first hospital and declared that the insurance company was only subsidiary liable. The second hospital appealed to the *Tribunal Supremo*.

b) Judgment of the Court

55 The appeal argued that the trial court had applied artt. 25 and 28 General Consumer Protection Act 1984 (hereafter LGDCU)[77], which lay down a strict liability regime for certain services. The *Tribunal Supremo* dismisses the appeal and confirms that these provisions refer expressly to "health services" and that they are applicable to the case. Once the harm arises during the provision of health services this fact triggers the liability of the hospital in spite of the fact that fault is not established. In addition, the court also mentions the doctrine of "disproportionate damage", which allows the existence of fault to be presumed from the fact that the magnitude of the harm suffered by the patient allows it to be qualified as an illogical and completely unusual outcome of the medical treatment or intervention undergone by her.

56 As regards the insurance company, the *Tribunal Supremo* turns down the subsidiary liability and justifies holding it solidary liable due to the fact that the claimant had taken out health insurance including the hospitals involved in the treatment. Relying on prior case-law, the court considers that liability for others may be established on the grounds that the insurance company and the hospitals were bound by a contractual relationship. Although this relationship does not imply that the health provider is subordinated to the insurance company, the latter performs its contractual duties vis-à-vis the insured person by means of the services supplied by the former. The insurance contract requires then that the company guarantees efficient and safe medical aid by allowing the client to choose among appropriate healthcare providers included in the catalogue of services.

[77] *Ley 26/1984, de 19 de julio, General para la Defensa de los Consumidores y Usuarios* (BOE no. 176, 24.7.1984).

c) Commentary

Medical liability cases have increased dramatically over the last ten years. In 2004 this was evident. Many cases concerning either private or public healthcare providers have been dealt with by the different chambers of the *Tribunal Supremo*, which correspond to hundreds also being tried by provincial courts or administrative instances.[78] 57

The case-law of the *Tribunal Supremo* continues to state that individual health providers, such as physicians or nurses, are only liable when their fault is established[79]. Nevertheless, several devices are also used to ease the proof of fault by the victim or distribute the burden of the proof between the doctor and the patient. On the other hand, private hospitals and healthcare centres are subject to a strict liability regime[80], as is the case for the public sector[81]. The legal grounds of liability are to be found in art. 28 LGDCU, which refers to "health services"[82]. As a consequence, in a case of damage suffered by a patient that is attributable to a mistake during the treatment, the hospital will be made liable for the malpractice attributable to its staff regardless of whether the specific error is never ascertained. Accordingly, it is not necessary to sue the physician involved in the case. Some decisions have even held the hospital liable despite freeing the physician due to lack of fault on his part.[83] 58

In the decision under comment the *Tribunal Supremo* does not declare the members of the medical team liable either. In addition, the court draws the conclusion that an improper performance of the health service took place due to the fact that the treatment was "clearly aggressive and unnecessary". To reach such an opinion, the fact that when the treatment discontinued the claimant recovered her normal heart condition, appears to be decisive. The *dicta* about the strict liability regime and the reference to the doctrine of "disproportionate damage" serve thus in fact merely as an argumentative tool whose aim is to reinforce the conviction held by the judge by other means that 59

[78] The current situation worries both the professionals and their insurers. Therefore, both cry out for legislative measures such as passing an act enclosing a legal tariffication scheme akin to the one applied to injuries suffered in road-traffic accidents. In November 2004 the Minister of Health declared to the press that together with the Ministry of Justice her department is considering a draft following this advice. The Minister announced that the bill will allow a "predetermination of damages that could be awarded as a result of medical errors", thereby stopping the "extraordinary increase that the lawsuits concerning liability for medical malpractice have experienced over the last few years".

[79] For instance, see STS 25.3.2004 (RJ 2004, 2149), 26.3.2004 (*La Ley* 2004, 1114) and 19.7.2004 (RJ 2004, 5128).

[80] Besides the decision under comment, see also STS 18.3.2004 (RJ 2004, 1823).

[81] A general overview of the liability regime of both public and private health institutions, in M. Martín-Casals/J. Solé Feliu/J.C. Seuba Torreblanca, Compensation in the Spanish Health Care Sector, in: J. Dute/M.G. Faure/H. Koziol (eds.), *No-Fault Compensation in the Health Care Sector* (2004), 334–66, and more references therein.

[82] About the possibility of applying such liability regime to doctors and other health professionals see J. Ribot/A. Ruda (supra fn. 2), 391–3, commenting on STS 31.1.2003 (RJ 2003, 646).

[83] For instance see STS 18.2.2004 (RJ 2004, 1193), 20.5.2004 (RJ 2004, 3249) and 7.10.2004 (RJ 2004, 6229) (all of them regarding public healthcare).

the treatment was inadequate and caused the severe injuries suffered by the claimant.[84]

60 Following a trend of recent case-law the *Tribunal Supremo* holds solidary liable the hospital and the insurance company. In fact the contract binding the patient and the insurance is a first-party insurance contract whose main feature is that, instead of recovering the costs of medical services, it allows them to be directly provided by doctors and hospitals included in a catalogue of services managed by a specialised insurance company and among which the insured patient chooses freely[85]. In the decision under comment, the court holds the insurance company liable with a blurred line of reasoning. Apparently the court argues that the contract guarantees the patient assistance free from mistakes and medical errors. The court recalls some dicta of a prior judgment involving an insurance company that had chosen both the physician that prescribed a certain procedure and the surgeon who performed it negligently. However, it is submitted that this doctrine is very difficult to apply as a general rule.[86] Usually, the provision of healthcare services will be supplied on the grounds of a free choice of the insured person from an extensive catalogue of health centres and professionals. In addition, these health providers perform their services toward the insured person with autonomy and without interference from the insurance company.

61 Finally, a similar problem may affect hospitals that make their equipment and installations available to physicians and surgeons for performing interventions or for treating their private patients, offering them hospitalization services during the post-operative period. For the time being, in these sorts of cases the hospital would not be liable for damage flowing from malpractice of the physicians responsible for the treatment.[87] One recent decision of the *Tribunal Supremo*, however, declares a hospital solidary liable together with a surgeon for having allowed him to carry out a surgical intervention without executing a pre-operative test on the patient that would have indicated the risk of cardiac arrest that in fact took place during the post-operative period[88].

[84] See also STS 22.6.2004 (RJ 2004, 3958).

[85] See previously STS 19.4.1999 (RJ 1999, 2588), 2.11.1999 (RJ 1999, 7998) and 19.6.2001 (RJ 2001, 4974).

[86] See M. Martín-Casals/J. Solé Feliu, Comentario de la sentencia de 10 de junio de 2004, [2004] CCJC, 65 (forthcoming). The likely outcome of this trend is the increase in the number of recoupment actions between the health insurance company and the physician's liability insurer (for instance see STS 31.3.2004 [RJ 2004, 2024]).

[87] For instance, see STS 4.10.2004 (RJ 2004, 6066).

[88] STS 12.3.2004 (RJ 2004, 2146).

C. Literature

1. Yolanda Bustos Moreno, *La responsabilidad civil en la navegación aérea: los daños a terceros* (Dykinson, Madrid 2003)

This volume is a well-documented book on civil liability *within* air traffic activities. From the very beginning, its title shows the goal of the work: to deal with the subject-matter extensively, considering all possible points of view. Needless to say, the strict liability regime of air carriers and operators according to the special set of rules laid down in the Air Navigation Act is studied in the light of the corresponding international conventions (pp. 69 et seq), including liability for damage to persons or to property located on the ground by the action of an aircraft or by any objects detached or that are thrown out of it (pp. 247 et seq.). Special attention is paid to the relationship between the strict liability regime and the general rules on fault liability (artt. 1902 and 1903 CC) (pp. 94–115)[89]. Furthermore, the book offers a comprehensive examination of other interesting issues as well, such as the liability of the producer of airplanes (pp. 151 et seq.) or cases where the liability of a public body is at stake on account of its responsibility for supervising the activities of the producers of airplanes (pp. 182 et seq.), for controlling the air traffic (pp. 220 et seq.) or for preventing terrorist attacks (pp. 247 et seq.). A final appendix of more than 200 pages rounds off the book including an extensive index of relevant international, European and Spanish provisions, a reprint of the main regulations examined by the book, and even a catalogue of aircrafts and their main features. 62

2. José María Pena López (Dir.), *Derecho de responsabilidad civil extracontractual* (Cálamo, Barcelona 2004)

This is a new "handbook" on tort law, written by a group of scholars of the University of La Coruña under the direction of Professor Pena López. Although published within a series named "basic texts" the book is lengthy (410 pages). It aims to be comprehensive and its 22 chapters are grouped in three very different parts: an *introduction*, which the reader can easily do without, a *general part*, some pieces of which are very well written, and a *special part*. In general terms, the book offers no special interest. Most chapters are short versions of previous works published by its authors. That would certainly have been positive had the desirable combination of in-depth analysis and concision been achieved. On the other hand, case law is cited randomly, and a selection of relevant bibliography is lacking. In conclusion: whereas as an introduction to tort law the book seems too much, for tort lawyers it is elementary. 63

[89] On this question see M. Martín-Casals/J. Ribot/J. Solé, Spain, in: B.A. Koch/H. Koziol (eds.), *Unification of Tort Law. Strict Liability* (2003), 313–4.

3. Ricardo Juan Sánchez, *La responsabilidad civil en el proceso penal* (La Ley, Madrid 2004)

64 This publication reports on a comprehensive in-depth study of procedural aspects of tort actions brought as ancillary claims within criminal proceedings. It must be stressed that a substantial part of all tort claims are dealt with in Spain by the criminal courts. These have jurisdiction, not only to decide the question of criminal responsibility arising from a crime or a misdemeanour, but also to make an award for civil damages arising from such an offence to any person who has been injured or has suffered damage as a result of the accident. The Spanish legal system follows the French pattern and starts from the principle of accumulation of the civil action and the criminal one, unless the victim expressly decides to bring a separate and distinct civil action before a civil court.[90] The book examines the different elements of this model: its *subjective* and *objective* requirements, applicability of the civil procedural law in criminal proceedings, limitations imposed on criminal courts because of the requirement of consistency with the *petitum* of the civil action, and the legal regime of exceptional cases where criminal courts are allowed to decide on the civil liability without criminal conviction. Finally, the last part of the book is devoted to insurance issues, to the execution of the judgment of the criminal court and to the legal effect of this judgment upon subsequent civil claims based on the same cause of action.

4. Álvaro Luna Yerga, *La prueba de la responsabilidad civil médico-sanitaria. Culpa y causalidad* (Thomson Cívitas, Madrid 2004)

65 This is an important book stemming from a PhD thesis on medical liability written by the author. It seeks to assess the most recent trends of case-law as regards the liability of healthcare providers[91], focusing on certain keynotes of medical malpractice litigation: how to establish the doctor's fault, how do courts deal with causation issues, and so on. Specific attention is paid to criteria laid down in the new procedural law in order to ease the burden of proof that as a rule falls with the claimants. A powerful case against the way in

[90] See the recent account of J.M. Busto Lago, El responsable civil en el proceso penal en la perspectiva de la reforma de la justicia penal: modelos comparados y problemas del vigente sistema de acumulación potestativa, [2004] *Aranzadi Civil* 17, 1 et seq.

[91] Further references include, among others: a) Medical liability: J.J. Bonilla Sánchez, *La responsabilidad médica extracontractual*, (2004); P. Gómez Pavón, *Tratamientos médicos: su responsabilidad penal y civil* (2004); J. Guerrero Zaplana, *Las reclamaciones por la defectuosa asistencia sanitaria. Doctrina, jurisprudencia, legislación y formularios* (3rd edn. 2004); P. Rodriguez López, *Responsabilidad médica y hospitalaria* (2004), and *Nuevas formas de gestión hospitalaria y responsabilidad patrimonial de la administración* (2004). b) Informed consent: P. González Salinas/E. Lizarraga Bonelli (eds.), *Autonomía del paciente, información e historia clínica. (Estudios sobre la Ley 41/2002, de 14 de noviembre)* (2004); J. Guerrero Zaplana, *El consentimiento informado. Su valoración en la jurisprudencia* (2004); J. Sánchez-Caro, Consentimiento informado y salud, in: J. Guerrero Zaplana (ed.), *Salud pública y derecho administrativo* (2004). c) Other issues: J. Sánchez-Caro/J. Abellán, *Atención farmacéutica y responsabilidad profesional* (2004).

which courts make use of devices like *res ipsa loquitur* or the doctrine of "disproportionate damage" is made.[92]

5. Miguel Ruiz Muñoz, *Derecho europeo de responsabilidad civil del fabricante* (Tirant lo blanch, Valencia 2004)

In the light of ECJ case-law on the product liability directive, the author puts forward an in-depth analysis of the issues raised in each decision and casts doubt on the capacity of the directive to advance towards the harmonisation of that field of tort law.[93] 66

6. Xabier Basozábal Arrue, El artículo 76 LCS: una invitación a legislar, [2003] *Revista Española de Seguros*, no. 113–114, 87–115

This is an interesting essay on the *acción directa* (direct claim) against the liability insurer granted to the victim by art. 76 Insurance Contract Act. Special attention is paid to the so-called victim's "immunity", which sets an uncertain limit to the defences that the liability insurer may invoke against the direct claimant. After a brief overview of the endless academic debate and how courts have coped with the problems posed by the *acción directa*, the author divides defences between those that arise from the policy as a "legal act" and those that purport an infringement of the "contractual rule". The former could be invoked against the victim whereas the latter not. This framework may be conceptually fruitful for future legal reform and, most important, is consistent with court practice. Furthermore, it provides an explanation of current case-law forbidding insurance companies from refusing the victim compensation when the tortfeasor acted with intent or in a very dangerous way.[94] 67

[92] See also M. Navarro Michel, Sobre la aplicación de la regla *res ipsa loquitur* en el ámbito sanitario, [2004] *Anuario de Derecho Civil*, 1197–1230.

[93] As to Spanish law, 10 years after the enactment of the act transposing the product liability directive, many works deal with the application of the act by the courts. Especially see P. Gutiérrez Santiago, *Responsabilidad civil por productos defectuosos: cuestiones prácticas* (2004). Further references: I. Zurita Martín, Evolución jurisprudencial en materia de responsabilidad civil por productos y servicios defectuosos, [2004] *Revista de Derecho Patrimonial* 12, 533–555 and A.J. Vela Sánchez, *Criterios de aplicación del régimen de responsabilidad civil por productos defectuosos* (2004). Specifically devoted to liability for medicinal products see S. Ramos González, *Responsabilidad civil por medicamento. Defectos de fabricación, de diseño y en las advertencias o instrucciones* (2004).

[94] This is one of the main reasons why insurance companies cry out for an amendment of the Insurance Contract Act (see C.I. López-Cobo, Seguro de Responsabilidad Civil: Hacia la reforma de la Ley de Contrato de Seguro, [2004] RRCCS 40, issue 4, 4–15). More recently, on insurer's coverage of intentional acts of the insured person or of those for whom he may be held liable see the decisions of the Criminal Chamber 22.4.2002 (RJ 2002, 5454) and 4.2.2004 (RJ 2004, 2113).

7. Alejandro Ferreres Comella, Carlos Viladàs Jené, Algunas reflexiones en torno a las reclamaciones por daños y perjuicios derivados del consumo de tabaco en España y en Europa, [2004] *La Ley*, 6123, 1–9

68 The article provides a brief overview of tobacco litigation in Spain[95]. The authors are the legal counsel of Philip Morris and therefore the paper includes valuable information as to the types of claims brought against tobacco producers before Spanish courts. It offers a synthesis of the main arguments raised by claimants and defendants and a selection of holdings of the decisions issued up to now. The authors stress that no claim has been successful yet. In their opinion, the onus of providing convincing evidence of the product's defectiveness[96] and about the causal link between the defect and the harm hinders claimants from receiving compensation. Furthermore, they recall that "assumption of risk" is also brought into play by a number of decisions dismissing the actions of former smokers.[97]

8. Eduardo Gamero Casado, Los seguros de responsabilidad patrimonial de la Administración: recientes pactos y reformas, [2004] *La Ley*, 6044, 1–5

69 The author briefly comments on the amendments brought in the relevant legislation at the end of 2003.[98] These legal reforms tried to overcome existing conflicts between courts on the jurisdiction that should deal with tort claims filed against public bodies when their liability is covered by private liability insurance. The author believes that this reform is completely flawed and cries out for the enactment of a comprehensive set of rules on liability insurance for public bodies. Lack of such a regulation has prompted legal actors to sign odd gentlemen's agreements that involve insurance companies, public bodies, bar associations … and judges! The author's suggested solution would be to quali-

[95] Besides individual claims brought by former smokers, Spanish courts have considered civil actions lodged by associations of laringotomized patients and a claim brought by the Regional Government of Andalusia to be compensated for healthcare costs related to diseases due to smoking. A common feature of these lawsuits is that they have been dismissed *a limine* because the court deemed it necessary to sue the State, thereby referring the claimants to a new procedure before the administrative courts.

[96] As to the defectiveness based on misleading information on the risks involved in smoking, see I. González Barrios, La falta de información como fundamento de la responsabilidad civil de las empresas tabaqueras, [2004] RRCCS 40, issue 5, 17–29. Courts tend, however, to rule out such an argument (see SAP Barcelona 1.12.2003 [AC 2003, 1897]).

[97] On the dividing line between contributory conduct of the victim and that she had assumed the risk of being harmed, see J. Solé Feliu, Los perfiles borrosos de la asunción del riesgo en el derecho comparado, in: *Estudios Díez-Picazo*, vol. IV (2003), 3097–3123. For a recent overview about assumption of risk under Spanish Law, see M. Medina Alcoz, *La asunción del riesgo por parte de la víctima. Riesgos taurinos y deportivos* (2004).

[98] See J. Ribot/A. Ruda (supra fn. 2), 383–85. Further references: A. Huergo Lora, El seguro de responsabilidad civil de las Administraciones Públicas y la doctrina de la "vis attractiva", [2004] *Revista española de Derecho administrativo* 122, 199–222, and C. Gómez Ligüerre/S. Ramos González/A. Luna Yerga, Todos a una. Jurisdicción competente para condenar a la Administración pública y a su compañía aseguradora, [2004] *InDret* 1 (www.indret.com).

fy the insurance contract taken out by public bodies as an "administrative contract", thereby routing all claims against the insurance companies through the special procedure established to determine the liability of public bodies.

9. Miquel Martín-Casals/Josep Solé Feliu, Contributory Negligence under Spanish Law, in: Ulrich Magnus/Miquel Martín-Casals (eds.), *Unification of Tort Law: Contributory Negligence* (Kluwer, The Hague/London/New York 2004), 173–195

The Spanish contribution to the research conducted on contributory negligence by the European Group on Tort Law deals mainly with an accurate analysis of existing case law, and demonstrates that in some substantial points Spanish law is quite far from the criteria that prevail in most European legal systems. For instance, rules derived from case-law show that Spain does not follow the "mirror image rule"[99]. Therefore, persons with no tortious capacity are held contributorily negligent. Moreover, courts tend to identify fault of the parents or guardians in the performance of their duty to supervise and the contributory negligence of their children or pupils. 70

[99] See Art. 8:101 (1) Principles of European Tort Law.

XXIII. Sweden

Håkan Andersson

A. Introduction

1 Concerning Swedish tort and insurance law, one could say that 2004 was not exactly an eventful year, at least not on the surface. No revolutions, no genuine evolutions and no exceptionally interesting beginnings. However, in order not to give an impression that 2004 were a dull year, some comments on underlying tendencies in the legal discourse will follow. Therefore, the title – or subheading – of this article should read *Tort Law Development – In a Silent Way*.

B. Legislation

1. Legislative Proposal

2 There was no relevant legislation on tort and insurance law this year. However, a proposal (Proposition 2003/04:150) for a new Insurance Contract Act was – after a very long journey[1] – finally presented to parliament. It is expected that this proposal, with some alterations, will become law in 2005. A main idea, which characterises this proposal, is to provide a stronger protection for policyholders in all types of insurance contracts. Therefore, the new legislation will cover consumer and company insurances, individual and group insurances and even insurances based on collective agreements. The proposal can be described as a balance between the insured's interest of protection and the interest of the insurance companies to develop their products; a consideration regarding economic consequences for the collective is also part of the balancing act. The legislative approach is therefore not to regulate the contents of the terms in binding rules. Instead, rules about mandatory information to the insured are suggested in order to give them the opportunity to obtain insurance which covers their individual needs. If the insurance company fails to

[1] See SOU 1977:84; SOU 1986:56; SOU 1989:88; Ds 1993:39. Cf. B. Bengtsson, *Försäkringsteknik och civilrätt* (1998), 57 et seq.

give the prescribed information, the company may not be allowed to invoke the term in question (a limitation, a qualification, etc.). Among the new developments in the proposal, the extended compulsory contracting, including that of personal injury, should also be mentioned.

C. Cases

1. Supreme Court, *Högsta domstolen*, 25 May 2004, [2004] *Nytt Juridiskt Arkiv* (NJA), 279: Reconsideration of Life Annuity According to Altered Circumstances

a) Brief Summary of the Facts

According to the Swedish Tort Liability Act (ch. 5, sec. 5), a life annuity can be reconsidered in court if the circumstances upon which the amount of the compensation was based have altered.[2] Regular cases involve changes in health development or in the effect of the injury on the working capacity. In this case, however, the plaintiff did not argue that her medical condition had worsened. Instead, she claimed that the increase of wages in her former profession exceeded the amount upon which the parties had based their calculation when stipulating her life annuity. As a result, the annual amount she received was lower than the salary she would have obtained if she had not been injured. Therefore, she sued the tortfeasor (the insurance company) six years after the agreement was made (and 11 years after the accident). According to admission during the trial, the divergence between the amount of the life annuity and the alleged payment in her former profession was set to 12%. However, the insurance company argued that a future salary increase was not a circumstance that provided a right to reconsideration. Accordingly, the company claimed that only alterations of those facts about the injury (and its consequences) which are decisive when calculating an annuity would be considered as such "circumstances" as referred to in the Tort Liability Act. Increased salary and such would instead be considered as a general improvement of the standard of living and, as such, not an alteration in relation to those facts which the annuity amount was based upon. In this context, it may also be worth mentioning that life annuities, according to Swedish legislation, are raised annually in relation to the general increase in the costs of living. However, this case did not involve these kinds of increases. 3

b) Judgment of the Court

The Supreme Court decided in favour of the plaintiff. The Court found that, among the circumstances on which the stipulation of compensation for future income loss was based, was the assumption of future development if the plaintiff had not been injured. The salary increase in her previous profession was 4

[2] B. Bengtsson/E. Strömbäck, *Skadeståndslagen* (2002), 256 et seq.

therefore regarded as a circumstance which may allow a right to reconsideration.

c) Commentary

5 If one just reads the wording of the Tort Liability Act and the judgment, it may not seem surprising that the altered salary level can be determined as an actual change, and hence give the plaintiff an opportunity to have the amount corrected. However, for the Swedish insurance companies it came as an unpredicted setback. Due to the examples in the preparatory works, they had no doubt assumed that economic alterations concerning costs of living, welfare and level of income were only to be considered by way of the annual general increase of annuities (during the last few years, this increase has been about 2%).[3] All of the examples in the preparatory works and in earlier case law, when individual circumstances served as a basis for a new calculation of the case, have consistently dealt with a worsening of initial injuries or their effect on the individual's working capacity.[4]

6 If the judgment were to be interpreted in such a way that everybody always can claim reconsideration if the wages in the plaintiff's former profession exceed the annual increase of annuities due to general legislation, then this case would lead to a great insecurity among insurance companies. There would be difficulties in evaluating the economic situation and calculating the correct premiums – and there would be much duplication of work when the same case must be dealt with once again. Furthermore, hypotheses are always uncertain. After ten years, when introducing a factual change (such as salary level) and assuming permanence among all other factors, one gets into considerable difficulties. The negative effects that these facts have had on the insured may, after such a long time, be balanced or weighed against other changes which have occurred during the same timeframe. For example, why should it be assumed after ten years that every individual would still be working in the same sphere? Should we in such cases make deep penetrating surveys concerning statistics, so that we can have a hypothesis about how many (10%, 50%, 90%) employees would have continued working in their occupation? Should we then have different rules for law professors (who are likely to continue their interesting vocation) and toilet guards (a livelihood where the prognosis perhaps indicates that very few would have continued their position for more than 2–3 years)?

7 These, and other, problematic questions for practising lawyers are nevertheless not a necessary outcome of this judgment. There are some limitations to be observed; some theoretical and practical restrictions can be noted if one thoroughly reads the case. One important expression in the decision may be emphasized: The circumstances that have changed should have been consid-

[3] Cf. *Regeringens* Proposition 1975:12, 79 et seq.; *Regeringens* Proposition 2000/01:68, 39.

[4] Cf. *Regeringens* Proposition 1975:12, 170 et seq.; *Regeringens* Proposition 2000/01:68, 72 et seq.; B. Bengtsson/E. Strömbäck (supra fn. 2), 262 et seq.

ered when determining the amount of the life annuity, i.e. the amount should have been "based upon" those circumstances. This can be interpreted as a necessary requirement, i.e. the future development of this profession's wages should unequivocally have been considered during the previous calculation. Otherwise, it is not – with a restrictive interpretation – an important circumstance that has subsequently changed. If no explicit assumptions about the future salary level were made at the time of the initial settlement, later discrepancies cannot be regarded as a "change" in the strictly legal sense of the notion. Due to the legal procedure in this particular case, both parties gave the Court the impression that these facts had actually been considered in the initial calculation. Therefore, the Court had to regard this circumstance in this way and, under such conditions, the outcome could not have been any different. Nonetheless – and this is the practical message to insurance companies – in future cases one can be more strict in pointing out the facts that really are part of the agreement. The working methods of Swedish insurance companies, when deciding on life annuities, hardly ever include specific hypotheses about the future development of the specific wages of the specific profession. The future modifications of annuities are rather seen as a more or less automatic business in accordance with the legislation on annual increase of annuities.[5]

An important feature to emphasize is that – if, after all, we can argue that a future development was actually considered initially – the deviation from the hypothesis must refer to the injured person's specific profession. There is no possible lawsuit if the litigant is just referring to the general development. Therefore, the litigant must show a specific fortunate growth of her specific profession in order to succeed in court; she has to establish as a fact that her former profession had an extraordinary salary increase compared to other groups. 8

In other words: The case illustrates that litigants can get their life annuities reconsidered in court even with reference to later development of salary levels (i.e. not only – as customary – with reference to changes in the health situation and its consequences for the working capacity). However, the case also displays that insurance companies can avoid this situation by taking a different procedural approach. The message to both parties is that they should explicitly state the considered facts so that they later – in these kinds of lawsuits – can produce their respective relevant evidence. 9

The commentary above is an interpretation of the judgment, and an effort to show the legal requirements upon which the outcome may have been based. Interpreted in that way, the judgment "makes sense" and is in accordance with traditional tort law. It also does not pave the way for future exaggerated and troublesome reconsideration cases. However, this interpretation is a kind of rationalization. The Supreme Court did not explicitly elaborate on all these re- 10

[5] Cf. B. Bengtsson/E. Strömbäck (supra fn. 2), 153; J. Hellner/S. Johansson, *Skadeståndsrätt* (2000), 387.

quirements, but given the claims and facts of the case, including the procedural admissions, the interpretation and conclusions can be defended as a restricted rule of reconsideration. If no restrictions were to be interpreted, the judgment could be considered as an open invitation to unlock the floodgates for litigants.

2. Supreme Court, *Högsta domstolen*, 14 October 2004, [2004] NJA, 566: The State's Compensation Claims Due to Precautionary Measures by Public Authority after Traffic Accident

a) Brief Summary of the Facts

11 As a result of a traffic accident, fuel was spilled out on the roadway. To restore traffic safety, the National Road Administration cleared the roadway of oil. These precautionary measures cost about 5,000 Swedish kronor (approx. € 550). The State (the National Road Administration) sued the car owner who caused the collision. According to the Swedish Motor Traffic Damage Act, third parties who are injured by cars have a right to compensation regardless of negligence. In this respect, there is a strict liability, and the compulsory insurance covers the damages.

12 Two main issues appeared as decisive in determining this case: 1) Was there any property damage? The roadway was not destroyed, but the authority had to pay the costs of the precautionary measures. According to the Motor Traffic Damage Act, pure economic loss is not covered, but only losses caused by injury to the person or property. The preliminary problem was, therefore, to decide if the spillage could be considered as "damage to property" or if the expenses only constituted "pure economic loss".

13 The next question (if the first one is answered affirmatively) is: 2) Should the authorities have a right to compensation for costs related to measures that are imposed on them by legislation?

b) Judgment of the Court

The Supreme Court answered the questions with "yes" and "no", respectively:

14 1) Yes – the state of affairs in the case was considered as damage to property. The Supreme Court laid down two requirements: a) There must be some "physical influence" on the property, i.e. the oil must in some way have affected the roadway; b) The actions taken to deal with the physical influence must go beyond the degree of "none or merely insignificant" measures. Since the fuel had this physical influence and since the clearing of oil was not an insignificant measure, the criterion of "damage to property" was fulfilled.

15 2) No – since the clearing of oil from the roadway was among those "measures of safeguarding character which are normally imposed upon the authority" (the National Road Administration), the authority could not claim com-

pensation for damage from the individual road-user. This second question was answered through the application of two negative requirements, i.e. criteria of non-compensation: a) A situation where the above-mentioned safeguarding measures are normally imposed upon the authority; b) Measures that do not surpass the "proportions which are normal in cases of traffic accidents". In this case, the authority had an obligation to undertake these precautionary measures, which did not exceed the normal proportions in cases of traffic accidents. Therefore, the Supreme Court denied the authority a right to compensation.

c) Commentary

1) The concept of property damage: The borderline between damage to goods and pure economic loss has been subjected to intense discussion in the last decades. Since the general rule of negligence (and also the different rules of strict liability, for example the Motor Traffic Damage Act) presupposes damage to person or property, there will always be controversy around the issue of what should be considered as "property damage", and what should be considered as purely economic losses (and, therefore, be placed outside the area of compensation).[6] The Supreme Court has rarely dealt with this matter, but over a time span of twenty years, we can see tendencies of a widening of the concept of property damage.[7] However, this development of the concept is not explicit, but rather by way of gradually allowing further borderline situations to be covered. The same "physical" requirement is emphasized, but more situations of a non-physical character are labelled as damage to goods. In Sweden, we consequently have had a discussion about the "functional property damage concept".[8] The problematic cases are, for example, (as this) when the property in question has not been damaged in a literal sense, but the owner has had costs or losses due to the hindered or obstructed use of the property. In such cases, the courts sometimes have decided in favour of the plaintiff, but, as previously mentioned, the phraseology applies the same words, such as "physical effect" or "physical influence". The traditional concept has consequently not been challenged. 16

In this new case, the roadway was not destroyed by the car collision or by the fuel spill; there was no need for reparation, only for removal of the fuel by cleaning measures. In order to evaluate the judgment's novelty value, we can label the above-mentioned two criteria as a) "qualitative requirement" ("physical influence" on the property) and b) "quantitative requirement" (measures of more significant degree). The wording of these two requirements gives an impression of a restrictive rule but, by its argumentation, the Court is in fact 17

[6] Concerning the traditional "physical" property damage, see *Regeringens* Proposition 1972:5, 579; B. Bengtsson/E. Strömbäck (supra fn. 2), 290 et seq.; J. Hellner/S. Johansson (supra fn. 5), 98 et seq.

[7] [1990] *Nytt Juridiskt Arkiv* (NJA), 80; [1996] NJA, 68.

[8] H. Andersson, *Skyddsändamål och adekvans* (1993), 538 et seq.; J. Kleineman, *Ren förmögenhetsskada* (1987), 153 et seq.

extending the concept. Previous cases involved goods that were used in production processes; when the usage in such cases was hindered, the result could more easily relate to a pecuniary loss. On the other hand, the National Road Administration would never receive an income from the roadway. In other words, the case demonstrates that the "functional" approach to defining property damage has taken a new direction.

18 Moreover, from a discursive viewpoint, the judgment raises some interesting legal matters. The qualitative and quantitative requirements are applied as constraining factors, and the reader should consequently not get the impression that the Supreme Court has given up the traditional concept. Nevertheless, this "limited rule" somehow seems as a disguise, since the actual result is an apparent widening of the scope of compensation for damage to goods. If this "physical influence" of fuel being spilled over a roadway is enough, what about ordinary cleaning situations when an area has been littered with trash and lumber? Could we really argue for different solutions in cases when ground is covered with 1) oil or sand (which in a way can be "attached" to the ground) and 2) when the ground is covered with trash (which can only be "placed" on the ground)? Besides, if there was a "physical influence" in the first situation, how could we sort out the "significant" degree of measures when the trivial amount of € 550 was sufficient in this case? Should we even set a limit in clear-cut cases, so that the tortfeasor would not have to carry any liability for costs, when, for example, they are below € 100 or € 200? These questions are not raised in order to criticize the Court. Instead, they exemplify the understanding that the explicit limitations of the decision's basis will not affect future cases in a restrictive manner. Therefore, the conclusion may be that the Supreme Court made a lasting *de facto* broadening of the concept of property damage, while the wording of the case gives a formal *de jure* restriction of the concept.

19 2) The restrictions with regard to claims by the State for compensation: The Supreme Court maintained the principle that costs for society's obligations cannot be met by compensation under Swedish tort law.[9] Also this part of the judgment can be interpreted as a rule with a) a "qualitative requirement" (the character of the authority's safeguarding measures) and b) a "quantitative requirement" (the proportions of measures). The first part is in accordance with earlier case law; the fire department, for example, has not been recognized a right to compensation to cover the expenses for a turnout.[10] Up to this point, there is no apparent new development in this case. However, if one seriously considers the quantitative aspect, it may pave the way for future openings to the already established legal arguments. The facts of another case can perhaps reveal a situation where the authority's measures are of a magnitude way beyond the "normal". Thus, the quantitative requirement may provide an argu-

[9] Regarding this principle, see H. Andersson, *Trepartsrelationer i skadeståndsrätten* (1997), 133 et seq.

[10] [1950] NJA, 610. Cf. also [2001] NJA, 627.

ment that will allow compensation. In such a situation, difficulties will naturally appear with regard to what is to be considered as a "normal" quantity of measures. Should a turnout of the fire brigade be considered as "normal" when the fire was set to a single house, but "extraordinary" when a whole block is burning? The future will tell how lawyers decide to use this new opening.

3. Supreme Court, *Högsta domstolen*, 27 October 2004, [2004] NJA, 609: Third Party Losses

a) Brief Summary of the Facts

A car was damaged in a traffic accident. The owner of the car (A) had given his father (B) the right to use the car. B claimed compensation for the losses he suffered because of the accident. He incurred travel expenses and income losses relating to a period when he organised the transactions of purchasing a new car. 20

b) Judgment of the Court

The Supreme Court described B as a third party who had not showed a sufficiently close relationship to the damaged goods. He had "as a matter of fact" used the car, and paid expenses. This situation was nevertheless "not sufficient" to recognize an independent claim. The Court emphasised that B had not demonstrated that his agreement with A was such that it gave him a right "with such contents" to give him a right to compensation as a third party. 21

c) Commentary

The case deals with a "classical" problem in tort law – third party losses. Within this field of discussion, Swedish tort law (which is in line with international tendencies) stipulates a strong "Bright Line Rule" of non-compensation, with some vague exceptions.[11] Actually, there are many situations when third parties are awarded compensation and the tortfeasor has ultimately to stand for the costs, and to pay either directly to the third party or indirectly through compensation to the immediate victim who transfers the compensation to the third party. Cases of contractually based chains and third parties' interest in other's goods and individuals present a pattern of more or less strong connections of interests. 22

Among the contractual relationships with a pronounced interest, we find the third party's right to use someone's property.[12] This case with B's use of A's car matches this group of exceptions to the main rule of non-compensation. Nevertheless, no compensation was awarded to B. Should we, therefore, interpret this case as a negative and restrictive deviation from the positive excep- 23

[11] J. Hellner/S. Johansson (supra fn. 5), 364 et seq; A. Peczenik, *Causes and Damages* (1979), 259 et seq. The monograph on the topic is H. Andersson (supra fn. 9).

[12] H. Andersson (supra fn. 8), 137 et seq.

tion which bestows users an independent right to claim compensation for losses? Probably not. Some particular circumstances may explain why the rule of exception did not apply. 1) B was only the "main user" of the car, i.e. it would have been closer to an exception if he had been the exclusive user (then he could have "taken the place" of the owner regarding the interest in the car); 2) B had "not demonstrated" that his right to use the car was of "such contents" that it would motivate third party compensation, i.e. it would have been better for him if the contractual arrangement had explicitly shown his independence to A; 3) Moreover, although the Court did not overtly say so, the problem of contractual relations among family members may serve as an explanation. To counteract the possibility that family members afterwards give an account of the facts that will suit their claims, the rules regarding submission of evidence must be strictly upheld.

24 In short, no restriction of earlier case law rules is to be interpreted in this decision. There are still some exceptions to the principal rule of non-compensation for third party losses, and an exception can be considered when the third party has a right to use another person's property for his own purposes. However – and this is the message of this case – the third party has to give substantial evidence of his concrete and close interest (an interest that in some sense sets aside the owner's interest); he cannot just merely display an ordinary situation where a father borrows his son's car.

4. Supreme Court, *Högsta domstolen*, 26 November 2004, [2004] NJA, 662: Compensation Due to Failed Implementation of European Standards

a) Brief Summary of the Facts

25 Prior to the entrance into the European Union, Sweden was a member of EFTA (European Free Trade Association) and bound to the EEA Agreement (European Economic Area) as a sort of preliminary stage to full membership of the EU. The EEA Agreement states that its articles (when identical to articles in the EC Treaty) should be interpreted according to relevant decisions from the European Court. The famous *Frankovich* judgment (Cases C-6, 9/90 ECR L-5327) has paved the way for governmental liability for non-implementation of EC directives. In this new case (where the situation took place some years before the Swedish entrance into the Union), precisely as in *Frankovich*, there was a directive intended to ensure payment of salary when the employer becomes insolvent. This directive had not been fully implemented in Sweden. The question was if the EEA Agreement could generate the same governmental liability as the EC Treaty had given rise to.

b) Judgment of the Court

26 In *Frankovich*, no specific article in the EC Treaty established tort liability. Instead, the treaty was interpreted as a whole, and by its general system and fundamental principles, such a liability could be inferred. In the new Swedish

case, the Supreme Court declared that the EEA Agreement was not as far-reaching, regarding the establishment of a judicial system, as the EC Treaty was. Nevertheless, the EEA Agreement was considered as extending beyond the scope and aims of an ordinary international treaty. The Supreme Court referred to two cases from the EFTA Court (1998 E-9/97 and 2002 E-4/01) where the EEA Agreement had been interpreted in this way, and hence called for tort liability to be based upon the system and purpose of the Agreement (not a specific article). Although the judgments by the EFTA Court are not binding, the Swedish Supreme Court found that great attention should be paid to the judgments, especially since a harmonized interpretation was highly valued. The Court consequently concluded that the State was liable for not implementing the directive.

The Court, however, was not unanimous. The minority emphasized that judgments from the EFTA Court were not binding. Consequently, the minority pointed out that a Swedish court has both a right and an obligation to evaluate all the conditions of a case. The minority interpreted the *Frankovich* case as a manifestation of the specific legal order of the European Union, and those distinctive features were not, according to the minority, characteristic of the EEA Agreement. 27

c) Commentary

Since Sweden is now a member of the European Union, this case as such is not of any great importance, Of some relevance, however, is the pattern of reasoning which can be noticed, particularly when we compare the majority's and the minority's different approaches to the values of harmonization. The minority was apparently striving to uphold the banners of national independence. This style of reasoning demonstrates greater restriction in interpreting systematic teleological ends; instead, explicit rules are favoured. In turn, the majority upholds a more positive attitude to harmonization, and accordingly, the absence of an explicit rule may be compensated by the underlying purposes and intentions of the European project. When the less unifying EEA Agreement could be teleologically interpreted as recognizing tort liability without specific rules, we can expect even greater liberty in interpreting harmonizing European standards when interpreting the EC Treaty. 28

5. Supreme Court, *Högsta domstolen*, 15 December 2004, [2004] NJA, 746 I-II and T 1399-03: Liability for Passengers in a Stolen Car Due to the *Casus Mixtus* Principle

a) Brief Summary of the Facts

The two cases concern youngsters who, without permission, used another individual's car. In one case the car was stolen, in the other case a car belonging to the father of one of the participants was illicitly used. In both cases, a traffic accident occurred and the car was damaged. Moreover, in both cases a person in the backseat was sued for compensation. Since the "back-seat driver" him- 29 self had not been negligent as a driver, the legal issue was to consider how he could be made liable.

b) Judgment of the Court

30 The Supreme Court regarded the initial illegal conduct (when the boys took possession of the car) as a "joint activity", and viewed that event as the "starting point" for the course of actions which eventually led to the car being damaged. The foreseeability of causation, it was argued, could be questioned. However, a person who has illicitly taken possession of someone's property must "undertake the responsibility for accidental consequences". The *casus mixtus cum culpa* principle was consequently invoked as a justification for tort liability.

c) Commentary

31 The applied technique of legal reasoning, i.e. the *casus mixtus* principle, is in Swedish tort law traditionally concerned with the question whether a tortfeasor who has committed a prohibited action (*culpa*) should be liable for subsequent effects of an accidental nature (*casus*).[13] The principle explains, for example, why a thief will be held responsible if the stolen property is destroyed by a fire in the building where the thief keeps the property, even if he did not cause the fire. The two cases are not at the centre of the principle's field of applicability, since the car was damaged (by negligence, as far as one can understand) during the actual illicit use, and not because of an unrelated accident which occurred afterwards. Therefore, the liability could also have been based on joint liability for illegal and negligent action.

32 Nevertheless, one has to interpret what novelty value the judgment has for the explicitly upheld *casus mixtus* principle. In an earlier case from 1961,[14] a person was not found liable when he borrowed a stolen moped and thereafter returned it to the thief, instead of handing it over to the owner. The two new cases show that tort liability presupposes something more than the mere keeping of goods, and that something more is required than just being a passenger in a stolen car. That the user can return the property to the legitimate owner is not sufficient for liability when no damage has been done to the goods during the activity. The new cases inform us under what circumstances several individuals' actions should be regarded as a joint action. The youngsters in these cases had planned the car trip together, and therefore even the boy (who was an accessory to the crime plan) they picked up in the stolen car was held responsible. In addition, if an accident occurs during the period of illicit use, the possessor will be held responsible. However, the new cases do not challenge the above-mentioned decision of 1961, i.e. there will be no joint liability for a person who has taken no part in the original crime plan, but has only been a passenger or just used and returned the goods.

[13] On this principle, see H. Andersson (supra fn. 8), 393 et seq; J. Hellner/S. Johansson (supra fn. 5), 213 et seq; A. Peczenik (supra fn. 11), 88 et seq. and 264 et seq.

[14] [1961] NJA, 518.

6. Concluding Remarks

So far so good … so what? As was initially mentioned above, the year 2004 will not go down in history as an extremely exciting year in Swedish tort law. However, and as a matter of fact, with lower expectations regarding "new developments" on a larger scale, one can focus on interesting details and examine argumentative and justifying processes as well as theoretical concepts and practical requirements in case law. All of this is in a constant state of change – as the moon turns the tides … gently, gently away. In the light of this process, the year 2004 in Swedish tort law may show some interesting features. You do not see them in the single cases, but you can see these cases from the horizon of an ongoing history. 33

"*Kindness tendency*". The case concerning reconsideration of life annuity (supra nos. 3–10) can give rise to some reflections on the issue of "kindness". As was mentioned above, if there were no restrictions to be interpreted, the judgment would be a bare invitation to open the floodgate for litigants. Perhaps that is not all too wrong, since one can often sense an underlying tendency in Swedish case law that in "hard cases" or in "borderline cases" the Court will support the injured party, particularly in situations of personal injuries. In a single case, that should not be a problem, but if the borders were always transgressed in the same direction in "hard cases", we would eventually have difficulty in establishing any borders – or rules – at all. This "kindness tendency" can, at least, be pointed out and discussed. Regardless of any accusations of cruelty, an author of legal science can continue bestowing upon himself the task of penetrating this trend and looking for criteria that will give more specific (and sometimes restrictive) requirements in accordance with a theoretical and practical understanding of tort law. 34

"*Surface and deeper levels*". The criteria brought into play by the Supreme Court in the case about precautionary measures by public authority (supra nos. 11–19) generate some deliberation on the topic "words on the surface" compared to "deeper levels of connections to values and reasoning processes". From an argumentative point of view it is worth noting that both questions in this case – 1) the concept of property damage and 2) the restrictions on tort claims from the State because of costs for precautionary measures – are answered with related criteria in two parts, i.e. "qualitative" and "quantitative" requirements. With regard to the first issue, the Supreme Court gives, on the surface of the words, new restricting rules through the new quantitative requirement. However, at the same time the Court expands the concept of property damage when the physical impact of the qualitative requirement is used in a case where the property is not of an economic "productive" character, as was the situation in earlier judgments. À propos the second issue, the Supreme Court is, on the surface, sticking to the traditional rule of non-compensation (the qualitative character of the measures), but adds novelty value by the extra quantitative factor regarding normal proportions. If that later requirement should have any relevance – and we assume that every step in a Supreme Court 35 judgment really means something – it could be transformed into an argument for compensation in cases where the scope of measures is exceptional. This possible novelty is tacitly made in the judgment. That trait can be regarded as a common feature of legal argumentation, i.e. not to show the news explicitly and at once, but letting the old words gradually acquire new meanings.

36 “*Principal rules and the other side – deconstruction*”. When a legal sphere is described in terms of a strong Bright Line Rule and some vague exceptions – as in the case of third party losses (supra nos. 20–24) – we often get the result that the exceptions do not develop to an explicit and positive stage of recognition. Instead, the negative principal rule will define the whole problem. However, if the “other side” of the line could be thoroughly investigated, we would see something more articulated coming out of the shadows. In all countries there are some exceptions to the rule of non-compensation for third party losses in case law, and if we compare those situations we can – instead of just seeing the negative main rule “as a principle” – take note of positive arguments for compensation, not only positive arguments for the main rule. From a theoretical point of view, the case highlights the urgent task of finding patterns of legal argumentation.[15] Instead of merely seeing the one and only third party case, we – in legal science – could “deconstruct” the alleged unity on the surface.[16] The positive presence of the principal rule can be challenged when the “other side” of the binarism is revealed as something more than a negative and diffuse valley of shadows. If we are increasingly able to see specific circumstances and relations that can motivate a positive outcome, we will be able to establish concrete and positive rules allowing compensation for third party losses. That is, we would not only have the traditional negative Bright Line Rule. The more we learn to see beneath the surface, the more there is to discuss. Otherwise, we will merely see the one and only principle in a principled way – and that would ultimately lead us to seeing nothing at all.

37 “*European harmonization*”. The judgment about failed implementation of European standards (supra nos. 25–28) inevitably – as it happens, at least – brings various modes of reasoning to mind. Sweden, as a relatively new member of the European Union, is apparently demonstrating a profound inclination to harmonizing interpretations. With a liberal portion of irony, we can perhaps say that this teleological reading is akin to the old Jesuit theological device, “The end justifies the means”.

38 “*Crucial choice of reasoning pattern*”. The two cases regarding *casus mixtus* (supra nos. 29–32) make obvious that the legal style of argumentation can often choose between different patterns. Moreover, the chosen path governs how the facts, values and arguments are displayed. For instance, the circum-

[15] H. Andersson (supra fn. 9) is a monograph attempting to achieve that goal.

[16] H. Andersson, Constructive Deconstruction, in: M. Andenas/N. Jareborg (eds.), *Anglo-Swedish Studies in Law* (1998), 356 et seq; H. Andersson, Diversity and Unity. In Search of a Pluralistic View on Problems in Tort Law, [2001] *Scandinavian Studies in Law* 41, 11 et seq.

stances in these two cases could have led to legal reasoning concerning joint liability, causation and remoteness, duty of care and so on. Each of the just mentioned issues would have highlighted different aspects of the facts and focused on different arguments. Thus, applying law is always a discursive activity, and not just a representation of unambiguous facts and meticulous rules. Legal language, with its use of words, terms, wordings, signs and significations has an inherent tendency to maintain a surface with unequivocal denotations. However, beneath the surface, the structures of reasoning and justification constantly change. New values and factual circumstances influence how traditional concepts are being interpreted. Gradually the concepts, rules and descriptions of facts acquire new meanings. Thus, both the view of the normative level and the factual level are in a constant – but slowly evolving – flux. In legal reasoning, therefore, a rule, principle, concept, word or a factual circumstance is never permitted to establish a conclusive representation of anything outside language. Accordingly, a task for legal science will always be to look for new patterns and the ways language uses them. Moreover, the greatest challenge will be in private law (and in other areas of "down-to-earth" law) with its concrete knowledge of the legal background – not in jurisprudence with its general view. A theorist in the post-modern era must have the ability to combine general trends with specific explanations to the development of specific legal issues.

D. Literature

1. M. Radetzki, *Skadeståndsberäkning vid sakskada* (Establishing Compensation for Damage to Property) (Svenska Försäkringsföreningen, 2004)

The book covers a wide area of interesting issues concerning establishing 39
compensation for damage to property. It is a survey of the concepts and methods that have been discussed and practised in Sweden. One chapter deals with a development tendency, which has frequently occurred in Swedish case law during the last decades, that is the borderline between economic and non-economic consequences of damage to property; according to the main rule, no compensation can be awarded for non-economic consequences, but in certain cases a trend can be seen where such values have given rise to compensation. Among other issues in the book that could be mentioned are third party losses, causation and foreseeability, the obligation of the victim to minimize the damage and, finally, issues concerning legal procedure (burden of proof, etc.).

2. Articles

A few articles on tort law were published in the Swedish law reviews in 2004. 40
The Chancellor of Justice, G. Lambertz, discusses some recent trends and possible developments in tort law relating to the State's liability (*G. Lambertz, Det allmännas skadeståndsansvar i framtiden – trender och utvecklingsmöjligheter*

[Tort Liability for the State in the Future – Trends and Prospects of Development], *JT 2004–05, 3*). Among the issues examined can be mentioned the influence of the European Community and the European Convention. Yet another article deals with the tendency of increased number of compensation claims against the authorities (*W. Warnling-Nerep, Skadeståndstalan mot staten – en allt vanligare företeelse?* [Tort Claims Against the State – A More and More Common Phenomenon?], *JT 2004–05, 181*). An account of the prehistory and contents of the above-mentioned proposal for a new Insurance Contract Act is presented in an article (*E. Strömbäck, Något om den renoverade försäkringsavtalslagen* [About the Refurbished Insurance Contract Act], *JT 2004–05, 352*). There is also a survey of tort law cases from the years 2001–03 (*B. Bengtsson, Skadestånd utom kontraktsförhållanden 2001–03* [Tort Law in Non-contractual Relations 2001–03], *SvJT 2004, 829*). Last, and maybe least, it can be mentioned that a series of articles about new cases from the Supreme Court – including theoretical framework and practical consequences – as always (the same procedure as every year) was published by the author of this Yearbook article, *H. Andersson*, at the web site *www.pointlex.se*.

XXIV. Switzerland

Peter Loser

A. Legislation

1. Revision and Harmonization of Swiss Tort Law: Progress Report

For several years, a total revision of tort law in Switzerland has been planned and detailed reports appeared in the Yearbook 2002.[1] The expert draft dating from 2000 was the object of discussion at the Convention of Swiss Lawyers (*Schweizerischer Juristentag*) on 23 September 2003, where a resolution demanding the revision's pursuance was adopted. 1

However, the revision draft received substantial criticism in its public consultation from political, economic and academic groups when it was presented to the public: 2

A) The business sector is against either any intensification of vicarious liability within companies or the general clause of strict liability. Also, the suggested possibility for courts to award damages according to the degree of probability is criticized. 3

B) The cantons, on the other hand, especially oppose a federal regulation of liability for state actions. 4

C) From an academic perspective, the extension of tort law to issues previously covered by contractual liability is criticized. Many authors are furthermore not convinced by the draft's provision that a violation of the rule of good faith may lead to unlawfulness and thus liability. 5

The Swiss government has not yet given an opinion in substance regarding the fate of the draft. For now, the issue has been postponed as the revision of tort law has not been included in the Federal Council's legislative programme of 2003–2007. 6

[1] Cf. the Swiss Report in the Yearbook 2002: P. Loser-Krogh, Switzerland, in: H. Koziol/B.C. Steininger (eds.), *European Tort Law 2002* (2003), nos. 1 et seq.

2. Revision of the Swiss Statute on Insurance Supervision (*Versicherungsaufsichtsgesetz*, VAG)

7 The Swiss parliament adopted the completely revised Statute on Insurance Supervision at the end of 2004.[2] In alignment with the development within the EU area, there is now state supervision of independent insurance agents. This affects about 3,000 people. Around another 10,000 insurance agents working in the field service of insurance companies have the right to be registered.

8 During the statute's implementation regulated in the executive order on supervision, the definition of independence gave rise to criticism. For according to the executive order, an agent is no longer seen as independent if he has entered into cooperative arrangements or other agreements with insurance companies possibly "impairing his free choice of an insurance company". Most insurance agents have entered into agreements with different insurers, though, securing them compensation in the form of brokers' fees. The agents argue that this does not impair their independence.[3]

B. Cases

1. Swiss Federal Court, 27 April 2004, Decision of the Swiss Federal Court (BGE) 130/2004 III 417:[4] No Liability for Stolen Travellers' Cheques/Contributory Negligence

a) Brief Summary of the Facts

9 Businessman X, originating from India, travelled to New Delhi, where he visited a bazaar and, in a simple travelling bag, carried his travellers' cheques worth USD 20,300 (€ 16,400) with him. While buying new shirts, he put the bag down between his feet for a moment. Shortly after, the bag was stolen by strangers.

b) Judgment of the Court

10 X demanded replacement of the stolen cheques from American Express. American Express did not issue new cheques arguing that X did not keep them safe as outlined in their terms of business. The Federal Court agreed: The keeper has to store the cheques in a way a prudent person would store an equal amount of cash.

[2] For the draft version, cf. the Swiss Report in the Yearbook 2003: P. Loser-Krogh, Switzerland, in: H. Koziol/B.C. Steininger (eds.) *European Tort Law 2003* (2004), nos. 15 et seq.

[3] Cf. M. Kuhn, Unabhängige Versicherungsvermittler und neues Aufsichtsgesetz, [2004] *Haftpflicht und Versicherung* (HAVE), 320 et seq.

[4] Also to be found at: http://www.bger.ch/jurisdiction-recht.

2. Swiss Federal Court, 23 December 2003, Decision of the Swiss Federal Court (BGE) 130/2004 III 193:[5] No Liability for Unsafe Skiing Slopes (1)

a) Brief Summary of the Facts

The claimant X was on vacation and had bought a weekly season card for the ski lifts of company Y. X fell in the lower, steep part of one of the slopes and lost conscience hitting the icy ground. Consequently, he slid roughly 75 metres down the slope and about 12 metres beyond the edge of the slope where he hit his head on a pipe. The accident resulted in a long stay in hospital and a walking disability likely to remain. 11

b) Judgment of the Court

The courts found that on alpine ground, the risk of falls has to be reckoned with at all times. The obligation to secure principally only exists for the slope itself as well as a strip roughly two metres wide bordering the slope. The operator of a slope is not liable for a whole skiing area. In principle, the user of a slope is liable for the risks himself, even if he is not going down the slope at an excessive speed or keeps away from icy slopes. 12

c) Commentary

The decision shows, as well as the judgments discussed in the following, the courts' effort to limit the liability for risks and not to minimize self-responsibility. This tendency is to be fundamentally welcomed, for the functioning of society can hardly be ensured without self-responsibility. 13

3. Swiss Federal Court, 1 June 2004, Decision of the Swiss Federal Court (BGE) 4C.54/2004:[6] No Liability for Unsafe Skiing Slopes (2)

a) Brief Summary of the Facts

A, together with a group of "freeriders", left the marked slope to ski down to the valley in deep snow, parallel to the cable railway. After a few curves A fell and hit her head on a rock covered under the snow. She has been paralyzed since and claims legal redress in the amount of CHF 150,000 (€ 97,000) from the cable railway operator. 14

b) Judgment of the Court

The courts deny that the accident occurred on a "factual" slope. Neither was it a subsidiary area of the slope for which special obligations to secure would exist. It is rather open ground which the cable railway operator does not need to free from obstacles. On an unprotected slope stones have to be reckoned with at all times. 15

[5] Also to be found at: http://www.bger.ch/jurisdiction-recht.
[6] Also to be found at: http://www.bger.ch/jurisdiction-recht.

c) Commentary

16 The decision in principle can be supported, but it also shows the starting points of liability. It especially cannot be excluded that actual usage may establish a factual slope.

4. Swiss Federal Court, 8 July 2004, Decision of the Swiss Federal Court (BGE) 130 III/2004 571:[7] No Liability for Accidents on a Toboggan Run

a) Brief Summary of the Facts

17 Company Y operates a summer toboggan run. In September 1996, the toboggan of the two children S and T (twelve and nine years old at that time) collided from behind with the toboggan of X on the last stretch of the course. The collision catapulted X and her son out of the toboggan onto the lawn, with X suffering contusions to the head.

b) Judgment of the Court

18 First, the court states that the toboggan run does not represent a railroad, where strict liability applies. It is irrelevant whether the toboggan runs on tracks. Rather, it is decisive that the toboggan run does not serve public traffic.

19 In addition, the court finds that the warning with signs is sufficient. With minimal attention that may absolutely be expected from every user of the facility, the ride is possible without colliding with the previous driver. Safety measures are thus sufficient and liability has to be denied.

c) Commentary

20 In my opinion, the judgment is not convincing as it does not take into consideration that users of toboggan runs may act carelessly themselves. Especially with young people targeted by such facilities, irresponsible behaviour is not unusual. The connected risks for other users should be prevented or be paid for if necessary by the operator.

5. Swiss Federal Court, 8 September 2004, Decision of the Swiss Federal Court (BGE) 130 III/2004 736:[8] No Liability of the Owner of a Pathway

a) Brief Summary of the Facts

21 A, a three-and-a-half year old girl, was visiting an aunt in a rural area with her father. During the visit, A left together with an older child, without the parent's knowledge, to go to the bathroom. Consequently, she did not come back

[7] Also to be found at: http://www.bger.ch/jurisdiction-recht.

[8] Also to be found at: http://www.bger.ch/jurisdiction-recht.

to her father but went playing in the neighbourhood. She fell into a canal without any gates next to a small road and was injured.

b) Judgment of the Court

The Federal Court states that it cannot be expected from the road proprietor to maintain every road in such a way that it provides the highest degree of transport safety possible. It is sufficient if the street may be used safely when applying common care. Primarily, it is up to the individual road user to apply all due caution and to adapt his behaviour to the circumstances. Additionally, it has to be evaluated in every individual case whether the road proprietor was able to ensure safety according to the temporary, technical and financial circumstances. 22

As an exception, though, the proprietor of a work has to take special safety measures to prevent inappropriate behaviour of children. This especially holds true if risks exist that, when not applying due responsibility, could lead to serious damage or if the work leads children to an inappropriate use because of its appropriation. 23

In the case discussed here, the courts denied liability because the scene of the accident was not close to the house but on the access road. 24

c) Commentary

The reasoning of the judgment rightly puts the considerations in the "toboggan run judgment" (supra nos. 17 et seq.) into perspective. Especially convincing is the demanding of special safety measures to prevent irresponsible behaviour of children if the facility leads them to such behaviour. This may be the case for example in a "fun bath".[9] 25

6. Swiss Federal Court, 23 December 2003, Decision of the Swiss Federal Court (BGE) 130 III/2004 345:[10] No Liability of an Assessor towards Third Parties

a) Brief Summary of the Facts

In his appraisal report, an expert failed to realize some defects in real property. The report did not mention the scope of the valuation (which the client used toward a bank in order to receive a higher loan). Two years later, the expert's opinion was also used in negotiations for the sale of the house. The new owner, after discovering the defects, sues the expert for damages. 26

[9] See the decision of the Swiss Federal Court (BGE) 116/1990 II 442.

[10] Also to be found at: http://www.bger.ch/jurisdiction-recht; cf. the article of A. Koller, Haftung einer Vertragspartei für den Schaden eines vertragsfremden Dritten, in: A. Koller (ed.), *Neue und alte Fragen zum privaten Baurecht* (2004) (described infra no. 44); J.S. Plotke, Entscheidungen, Vertrauenshaftung, [2005] *Aktuelle Juristische Praxis* (AJP), 350 et seq.

b) Judgment of the Court

27 The Federal Court denied an unlawful behaviour because the loss at hand was purely economic (pure economic loss). Also, any protective character towards third parties was ruled out.

28 In contrast, the Federal Court examined a so-called liability based on reliance. The Federal Court found that, in order to impose this kind of liability, a special relationship needs to have been formed, which must not be based on coincidence. Liability based on reliance takes effect if the assessor knows or should have known that the client would hand the appraisal report on and, according to content and use, a risk of liability could materialize. It is not decisive whether the expert knows the third party, for the risk of liability depends on criteria such as the report's content and its use.[11] It is thus sufficient that the person sued declared – explicitly or silently, but in a legally relevant manner (*normativ zurechenbar*) – to "vouch" for the correctness of specific statements and the claimant then made arrangements duly relying on these statements, leading to his loss.

29 Nonetheless, the Federal Court dismissed the claim for it was not foreseeable to the property's owner that the appraisal report would be used for subsequent sales negotiations with the claimant.

c) Commentary

30 The Federal Court rightly denied the appraisal report's protective character towards the buyer of real property for the buyer's interests are contrary to the ordering client's interests (so-called "counter interests").[12]

31 The Federal Court also rightly confirmed the concept of a liability based on reliance[13] as an alternative way of establishing responsibility. Concerning this newly recognized kind of liability, the court correctly examined first whether the property assessor, at the time of writing the appraisal report, knew about the buyer and his intentions to buy, and thus about the use of the report for the property sale. This was not the case, as the report had been written two years before the sale. The initial use (raising of a mortgage loan with a bank), however, was not evident from the report in any way. Thus, from the perspective of the information's user, the appraisal report presented by the seller was very well suited as a basis of reliance.

[11] The Swiss Federal Court cites the article of C.-W. Canaris, Die Reichweite der Expertenhaftung gegenüber Dritten, [1999] *Zeitschrift für das gesamte Handelsrecht und Wirtschaftsrecht* (ZHR), 224 et seq.

[12] See C.-W. Canaris, Schutzwirkungen zugunsten Dritter bei „Gegenläufigkeit" der Interessen, [1995] *Deutsche Juristenzeitung* (JZ), 441 et seq.; H.-P. Walter, Vertrauenshaftung im Umfeld des Vertrages, [1996] *Zeitschrift des Bernischen Juristenvereins* (ZBJV), 291 et seq.; P. Loser-Krogh, Schutzwirkungen zugunsten Dritter, in: *Privatrecht und Methode, Festschrift für Ernst A. Kramer* (2004), 579, 586 et seq.

[13] For a general overview of the concept of liability based on reliance, see the Swiss Report in the Yearbook 2002: P. Loser-Krogh (supra fn. 1), nos. 32 et seq.

Hence it had further to be examined whether the assessor was responsible for the impression created, i.e. whether he had to expect a later use during sales negotiations. In that respect, the Federal Court decided all too restrictively.[14] Particularly the argument that the inspection of the valuation by that particular claimant in the course of a sales contract two years later should have been foreseeable is not convincing. However, the foreseeability of a use in the course of later negotiations concerning the sale of the property in general was not to be excluded and, according to the lower court's opinion, even obvious. In addition, an attribution of the created reliance and liability would in this case also have been arguable as the appraisal's re-use in the property sale did in no way double the risk of liability. For with the high selling price, the loan could have been reduced and the bank's potential damage thus been removed; and with the buyer taking over the mortgage debt and later on disposing of the pledged property, the damage claimed from the bank would have had to be set-off against the loan. 32

Affirming liability in this case thus would not have denaturized (*denaturiert*) liability based on reliance to a responsibility towards all people coincidentally touching on the appraisal report (*erga omnes*). It remains to be pointed out that it would have been easy for the assessor to state the purpose in the report and thus deprive later users of any basis for reliance. 33

C. Literature

1. Stephan Weber et al. (eds.), *Retouchen oder Reformen? Die hängigen Gesetzesrevisionen im Bereich Haftung und Versicherung auf dem Prüfstand* (Touching up or reforming? Putting the pending legal revisions in the field of liability and insurance to the test) (Schulthess Juristische Medien AG, Zürich 2004)

The book's emphasis is placed on the revision of tort law as well as the revision of the law concerning insurance contracts.[15] In the part on tort law, Felix Schöbi portrays the results of the public consultation. Helmut Koziol looks at the revision from the perspective of a foreign observer. Pierre Widmer, as one of the draft's authors, explains the revision's basic ideas. Markus Müller-Chen examines the possibility to limit liability and Hardy Landolt gives a broad overview on the historic development of the various forms of compensation for damage (including state systems for compensation and insurance). 34

[14] See also the criticism by A. Koller (supra fn. 10), nos. 76 et seq.

[15] For the Revision of the Swiss law concerning insurance contracts, see the Swiss Report in the Yearbook 2003: P. Loser-Krogh (supra fn. 2), nos. 10 et seq.

2. Bénédict Foëx/Franz Werro (eds.), *La réforme du droit de la responsabilité civile* (The reform of tort law) (Schulthess Juristische Medien AG, Zürich 2004)

35 This book's theme is also the revision of Swiss tort law. It contains the papers which were delivered at a convention at the end of 2001.

3. Thomas Sutter-Somm et al. (eds.), *Risiko und Recht, Festgabe zum Schweizerischen Juristentag 2004* (Risk and Law, An anthology in honour of the Convention of Swiss Lawyers 2004) (Helbing & Lichtenhahn und Stämpfli Verlag AG, Basel und Bern 2004)

36 This anthology examines the legal system's function to reduce risks or at least to distribute the responsibility for risks. In the private law part, mostly questions concerning tort law are investigated. The contributions of Stephan Fuhrer on the revision of tort and insurance contract law, of Ernst A. Kramer on liability for IT services, of Markus Müller-Chen on liability for genetic engineering as well as of Beat Schönenberger on the general clause of strict liability deserve to be highlighted.

4. Susan Emmenegger/Franz Werro (eds.), *Straßenverkehrsrechts-Tagung* (Convention on road traffic law) (Universität Freiburg, Freiburg 2004)

37 The report of a convention held by the University of Freiburg shows the latest development in road traffic law. It particularly contains contributions on tort law in relation to road traffic, to adventure sports, to injury of animals and to insurance law as well as a valuable overview of the latest court decisions.

5. Walter Fellmann/Tomas Poledna (eds.), *Die Haftung des Arztes und des Spitals* (Medical practitioners' and hospital liability) (Schulthess Juristische Medien AG, Zürich 2003)

38 This convention report gives a detailed overview of the latest developments in the area of medical practitioners' and hospital liability. In particular, it investigates the question whether court decisions concerning the duty to disclose risks of treatment and to inform the patient of the intended treatment's nature and gravity are reasonable and describes the development of the relationship between physician and patient, characterized today by the patient's right to self-determination. The contributions of Antoine Roggo as well as of Monika Gattiker on the duty to disclose risks and to inform of the treatment, of Walter Fellmann on private physicians' liability and of Thomas Sutter-Somm/Brigitte Spitz on evidential issues in medical tort law deserve to be pointed out especially.

6. Franz Werro (ed.), *La fixation de l'indemnité* (The determination of compensation for damage) (Verlag Staempfli AG, Bern 2004)

Even if the extent of the loss is known, this does not mean that the wrongdoer has to compensate the whole damage in every case. The contributions in this book investigate the question based on what criteria has the extent of liability to be determined? The book shows that Swiss law provides, from an international point of view, a flexible solution for determining compensation. 39

7. Corinne Widmer, *Umfang des Schadenersatzes bei nicht zur Perfektion gelangten Verträgen* (Extent of damages in the case of contracts not fulfilled to perfection) (Helbing & Lichtenhahn, Basel 2003)

The author investigates important questions in the borderline field of contractual liability and tort law. She questions the so far leading opinion that fault prior to the conclusion of a contract *(culpa in contrahendo)* usually results in compensation to the extent of the negative interest only. Widmer demonstrates with the examples of erroneous expression of intention and of breaking off of negotiations, taking into consideration foreign developments, that a violation of pre-contractual duties may also lead to a claim for compensation to the extent of the positive interest. 40

8. Martin Petrin, *Fortentwicklung der Geschäftsherrenhaftung in der Schweiz* (Continued development of vicarious liability in Switzerland) (Schulthess Juristische Medien AG, Zürich 2004)

Petrin examines the development of vicarious liability in Swiss tort law. He criticizes the provision in art. 55 of the Swiss Code of Obligations (OR), based on the principal's breach of the duty of care. The author, on the other hand and in alignment with foreign legal regulations, postulates a more strict liability for a third party's misconduct. 41

9. Oliver Waespi, Organisationshaftung – mit ungleichen Ellen gemessen (Organizational liability – judged by different standards), [2004] *Haftung und Versicherung* (HAVE), 271–281

Unlike the publication of Petrin, Waespi criticizes the growing intensification of vicarious liability according to art. 55 OR by actual practice and doctrine. The author also demonstrates that the new interpretation of art. 55 OR contradicts the interpretation of structurally related rules also providing a liability of the management based on failure to provide proper organizational channels. Waespi suggests distinguishing the principal's duties of care gradually and thus to limit liability. To keep the balance, a general clause of strict liability should *de lege ferenda* be embodied in a statutory law. 42

10. Beat Zirlick, *Freizeichnung von der Deliktshaftung* (Exemption of liability in tort) (Stämpfli Verlag AG, Bern 2003)

43 In Swiss law, claims under contractual liability and tort law exist next to each other. In his book, Zirlick examines whether the regulations of tort law are compulsory or whether the wrongdoer may exclude or limit his liability in advance just as he could do so in a contract. The author answers this question, which is disputed in the doctrine, in the affirmative. He demonstrates where the limits of a limitation of tort liability need to be drawn. In particular, he suggests a differentiated treatment of limitations in respect to personal injuries.

11. Alfred Koller, Haftung einer Vertragspartei für den Schaden eines vertragsfremden Dritten (Liability of a party to a contract for damage caused by a third party not participating in the contract), in: Alfred Koller (ed.), *Neue und alte Fragen zum privaten Baurecht* (Verlag Vereinigung für Baurecht V.BR, St. Gallen 2004), 1–62

44 Starting from two Swiss Federal Court decisions, the author discusses the question whether one party to a contract is liable for damage caused by a third party not participating in the contract. Koller answers this question in the affirmative according to current law and puts down an unwritten rule: If someone, within the scope of legal relations, faultily creates or maintains a wrong impression, he then becomes liable for damages towards third parties who have thus been misled. According to Koller, for this liability based on reliance[16] (*Vertrauenshaftung*) – compared to common tort liability – stricter rules of liability, partly assimilated to contractual liability, apply.

12. Caroline Flühmann, *Haftung aus Prüfung und Berichterstattung gegenüber Dritten* (Liability for auditing and reporting towards third parties) (Haupt Verlag, Bern 2004)

45 Flühmann investigates the same problematic issue as Koller in a special field of application. She examines whether an auditor, auditing a joint-stock company and handing in an incorrect report, becomes liable also towards third parties. The work of Flühmann goes to show that a difference needs to be made between an audit ordered by law and other, voluntary reports although in both cases tort liability may be considered in addition to the legal regulations.

13. Beat Schönenberger, Die dritte Widerrechtlichkeitstheorie (The third theory of unlawfulness), [2004] HAVE, 271–281

46 The article deals with a theory of unlawfulness deviating from the past Swiss understanding. The author demonstrates that the linking of unlawfulness to the success of a behaviour, i.e. the occurrence of a legally protected interest's

[16] For a general overview of the concept of liability based on reliance, see the Swiss Report in the Yearbook 2002: P. Loser-Krogh (supra fn. 1), nos. 32 et seq.

violation, is not convincing. The relevant factor is in his opinion – and increasingly in the opinion of others – the breach of a duty to act in a certain way.[17] According to Schönenberger, this action should not be confused with the precondition of fault but be defined in a more abstract form.

[17] See also V. Roberto, *Haftpflichtrecht* (2002), nos. 42 et seq., 258 et seq.; P. Loser-Krogh, Kritische Überlegungen zur Reform des privaten Haftpflichtrechts – Haftung aus Treu und Glauben, Verursachung und Verjährung, [2003] *Zeitschrift für Schweizerisches Recht* (ZSR), volume II, 141 et seq.

XXV. European Union

Bernhard A. Koch

1. Introduction

1 In the year 2004, several legislative projects presented in earlier reports in this series[1] were concluded by the adoption of a piece of legislation. In the following, these final documents will be presented in overview only to the extent more detailed information has already been presented before.

2 The proposed regulation on the law applicable to non-contractual obligations ("Rome II")[2] presented in last year's report[3] did not see any publicized progress in 2004 apart from the European Economic and Social Committee's adoption of a highly favourable opinion, suggesting only rather technical modifications.[4]

3 Further indications[5] that the Commission has re-embarked on the project of harmonizing the liability of service providers have become apparent with the publication of a highly interesting comparative study sponsored by the Commission.[6] It remains to be seen whether the carefully drafted conclusions by the authors[7]

[1] See my European Union reports in H. Koziol/B.C. Steininger (eds.), *European Tort Law 2001* (2002), 473; H. Koziol/B.C. Steininger (eds.), *European Tort Law 2002* (2003), 432; H. Koziol/ B.C. Steininger (eds.), *European Tort Law 2003* (2004), 435. These reports will be referred to as EU Report 2001, EU Report 2002 and EU Report 2003 respectively in the following.

[2] COM(2003) 427 final, 22.7.2003. This document as well as other COM or SEC documents cited in the following are available via the PreLex homepage http://europa.eu.int/prelex/rech_simple.cfm?CL=en. Press Releases (PRES) can be found with the Rapid search service under http://europa.eu.int/rapid/start/cgi/guesten.ksh. COD documents and further legislative referrals can be obtained on the Legislative Observatory search page (http://wwwdb.europarl.eu.int/oeil/oeil4.FR212_en) by entering the reference numbers cited below.

[3] EU Report 2003, nos. 1–17.

[4] *Official Journal* (OJ) C 241, 28.9.2004, 1 (see in particular the conclusions on p. 7).

[5] See already a statement made by a Commission representative at the occasion of a colloquium honouring Hans Claudius Taschner, [2002] *Zeitschrift für Europarechtliche Studien* (ZEuS), 74.

[6] U. Magnus/H.-W. Micklitz, Comparative Analysis of National Liability Systems for Remedying Damage Caused by Defective Consumer Services, http://europa.eu.int/comm/consumers/cons_safe/serv_safe/liability/reportabc_en.pdf.

[7] U. Magnus/H.-W. Micklitz (fn. 6), Part D (http://europa.eu.int/comm/consumers/cons_safe/serv_safe/liability/reportd_en.pdf).

will be used to start a new initiative after the failure of the Commission's first efforts in this field.[8]

It was also interesting to note in the most recent communication by the Commission on European Contract Law that the Commission now expressly rules out any plans to introduce a European Civil Code[9], which of course also has its impact on the development of tort law in Europe. 4

2. Environmental Liability

This series of reports has already served as a forum to criticize the downfall of a once rather promising project on environmental liability[10]. The following overview of its feeble remains as adopted at the end of April 2004 shall therefore serve as an obituary. 5

The "Directive 2004/35/CE of the European Parliament and of the Council of 21 April 2004 on environmental liability with regard to the prevention and remedying of environmental damage"[11] is claimed to be based on the "polluter pays" principle (Art. 1) and therefore wishes to go after those who have already caused harm to the environment or who are highly likely to do so in the near future. In practice, this wish will hardly ever be fulfilled but in clear-cut, self-evident cases, as the Directive does not foresee any alleviation of the burden of proof (apart from certain duties to cooperate in the assessment), in particular not with respect to causation, which is of course required for any preventive or remedial action (Art. 4 para. 5). 6

The Directive does not seek to address all negative consequences of harm to the environment, and certainly not those beyond damage to the environment as such, so that harm to individuals remains outside its scope (Art. 3 para. 3). Apart from land contamination that might be harmful to human health, only damage to certain feathered species and habitats protected under the 1992 Habitats Directive as well as pollution of water falling under the 2000 Water Framework Directive are covered (Art. 2). 7

Furthermore, the whole concept of collecting payments in response to harmful activities has been shifted from tort law to administrative law (though still retaining tort law terminology, which is why this Directive is still presented here for warning purposes). Not courts of law, but certain administrative bodies identified by the Member States (Art. 11) will be in charge of executing the vague concepts of this Directive. 8

[8] Proposal for a European Parliament and Council Directive on the Liability of Suppliers of Services, COM(90) 482 final, OJ C 012, 18.01.1991, 8; officially withdrawn four years later: COM(94) 260 final.

[9] COM(2004) 651 final, 11.10.2004, 8. See also the summary of a workshop held on 3 December 2004 (http://europa.eu.int/comm/consumers/cons_int/safe_shop/fair_bus_pract/cont_law/workshop_summary.pdf), 3.

[10] EU Report 2001, nos. 6–14; EU Report 2002, nos. 1–5; and EU Report 2003, nos. 18–24.

[11] OJ L 143, 30.4.2004, 56.

9 Two mechanisms for collecting refund payments (erroneously called "liability regimes") have been incorporated into this Directive:

- Enterprises who pursue activities which are likely to result in harm to the environment can be forced by the administrative body in charge to take preventive or remedial measures or to at least finance such action (Art. 3 para. 1 lit. a). Unfortunately, this rule has been linked to an enumeration of certain specific activities in Annex III to the Directive. Of course, this makes it impossible to get a hold of polluters whose activities have simply been forgotten (be it by way of lobbying of their respective representatives in Brussels), let alone those who have been innovative enough to create a new risk to the environment previously unknown.
- All other professional activities not covered by the Annex III enumeration can theoretically also be called in, but only if pursued at fault (Art. 3 para. 1 lit. b)[12].

10 Enterprises can avoid payment obligations by claiming *force majeure* (Art. 4 para. 1). They can also raise the equivalent of a development risk defence or point at an express authorisation of their activity[13].

11 International conventions as well as existing national legislation aiming at the protection and restoration of the environment are left untouched by this Directive (Art. 16).

12 Though it has been vividly demanded by the EESC[14] (and rightly so), the Directive fails to foresee any duty to take out insurance or to provide for any other financial cover in advance, claiming that this were not yet available on the market. The weakness of this argument is self-evident – if the Directive had produced a demand for an insurance product (be it in the form of a certain minimum coverage), it would most certainly have been offered on the market. For the time being, the Commission merely claims to watch the market until the year 2010 when the first report on the application of the new regime will have to be produced (Art. 14).

13 In light of all this, it comes as no surprise that the Directive was not given retroactive effect, not even with respect to those harmful activities already identified as such (Art. 17).

[12] See EU Report 2003, no. 19 at fn. 23, on the, well, interesting wording used in the English text ("whenever the operator has been at fault or [*sic!*] negligent") and how this message was understood by the translators.

[13] These latter two defences are only optional under the Directive and were left for the Member States to decide (Art. 8 para. 4).

[14] Opinion of the Economic and Social Committee on the Commission's proposal, OJ C 241, 7.10.2002, 162 (para. 4.4).

3. Motor Vehicle Insurance

As expected in last year's report on the status of the Commission's project to introduce a "Fifth Motor Insurance Directive"[15], the Council adopted a favourable Common Position on 26 April 2004[16]. It therefore seems to be only a matter of time until the proposal will become law. 14

After rather diverging proposals by the various institutions[17], the draft Directive, as modified by the Common Position, intends to raise the minimum insurance amount for personal injuries to € 1 million per victim, coupled with a € 5 million cap per accident. Property damages arising out of traffic accidents shall be covered by an insurance of at least € 1 million (though only after a five year transitional period, which is also the interval at which these amounts shall be revised in the future according to the European Index of Consumer Prices). 15

Another controversial aspect of the proposal[18] is the inclusion of pedestrians and cyclists into the regime by introducing a new Art. 1a into Directive 90/232/EEC, which initially meant to cover all their losses suffered from an accident involving a motor vehicle under the latter's compulsory insurance policy[19]. This has been modified by the Council by adding the requirement that these non-motorised users of the roads have to be entitled to compensation according to their respective national tort law. 16

4. Liability and Insurance for Aviation Accidents

A 2002 Commission draft on insurance requirements for air carriers and aircraft operators as amended[20] became law in 2004 as Regulation (EC) No. 785/2004[21]. 17

The new regulation introduces minimum insurance requirements for aircraft flying into, out of or within Community airspace, irrespective of their country of origin (Art. 1). Certain small or non-motorized aircraft is excluded from its scope, as is aircraft used in military, customs and police services (Art. 2). 18

[15] COM(2002) 244 final, 7.6.2002, OJ C 227, 24.9.2002, 387; see EU Report 2003, nos. 25–28; see already EU Report 2002, nos. 35–46.

[16] COM(2004) 351 final.

[17] On the alternative figures considered in the course of this legislative process see EU Report 2003, no. 27 (including fn. 30).

[18] On further details see the earlier reports quoted in fn. 15.

[19] See in particular J. Fedtke, Strict Liability for Car Drivers in Accidents Involving "Bicycle Guerrillas"? Some Comments on the Proposed Fifth Motor Directive of the European Commission, [2003] *American Journal of Comparative Law*, 941–957.

[20] The original proposal can be found under COM(2002) 521 final 24.9.2002, OJ C 20, 28.1.2003, 193. On earlier stages of the legislative process, see EU Report 2002, nos. 19–34, and EU Report 2003, nos. 29–32.

[21] Regulation (EC) No. 785/2004 of the European Parliament and of the Council of 21 April 2004 on insurance requirements for air carriers and aircraft operators; OJ L 138, 30.4.2004, 1.

19 The mandatory insurance shall cover aviation-specific liability in respect of passengers, baggage, cargo, but also third parties. It thereby presupposes liability of the air carrier or operator, though without prejudice to its legal basis – be it international conventions, Community or national laws (Art. 4 para. 3). A highly interesting extension of the compulsory insurance cover is the second sentence of Art. 4 para. 1, which reads: "The insured risks shall include acts of war, terrorism, hijacking, acts of sabotage, unlawful seizure of aircraft and civil commotion."

20 As far as passengers are concerned, the insurance shall cover at least 250,000 SDRs[22] per passenger[23]. Insurance for baggage must cover at least 1,000 SDRs, the minimum insurance for cargo is 17 SDRs per kilogram. The latter two figures correspond to the liability caps of Art. 22 para. 2 and 3 of the Montreal Convention. These insurance requirements do not extend to non-EU aircraft flights merely passing through EU territory without landing (Art. 6 para. 4).

21 In respect of tort liability for third parties, the minimum insurance cover depends upon the category of the aircraft as defined by its maximum take-off mass (MTOM). The range goes from 750,000 SDRs for aircraft with a MTOM less than 500 kilograms up to 700 million SDRs for aircraft whose MTOM exceeds 500 tons[24].

22 The regulation already foresees scenarios such as the immediate response of insurers to the World Trade Center attack by including clauses for "insurance-market failure" (Art. 5 para. 5) and unavailability of insurance "due to risks of war or terrorism" (Art. 7 para. 1).

23 Further provisions deal with the enforcement of the insurance requirements and sanctions for failure to meet such standards.

5. Compensation for Crime Victims

24 Irrespective of possible doubts concerning the legitimacy of such legislation, the Council has passed a Directive on Compensation to Crime Victims[25] following a proposal by the Commission in 2002[26].

[22] This amount corresponds to the insurance requirements currently foreseen by the European Civil Aviation Conference (ECAC). See Resolution ECAC/25-1 on minimum level of insurance cover for passenger and third-party liability (as modified by DGCA/117 on 27 November 2002), available on the ECAC website under https://ecac-ceac.org/file_pub/get_file_o.php?idDoc=190.

[23] For non-commercial operations of aircraft with a maximum take-off mass (MTOM) of 2.7 tons or less, the Member States may lower this amount, but not below 100,000 SDRs, which is the no-fault liability cap of Art. 21 Montreal Convention.

[24] The latter will be true for the new Airbus A380-800, whereas an average long-distance airplane such as the Airbus A340 or the Boeing 747-400 would fall under the second-highest category of aircraft with an MTOM between 200 and 500 tons, whose insurance for third-party losses has to be at least 500 million SDRs.

[25] Council Directive 2004/80/EC of 29 April 2004 relating to compensation to crime victims, OJ L 261, 6.8.2004, 15.

[26] COM(2002) 562 final, 16.10.2002, OJ C 45 E, 25.2.2003, 69. See EU Report 2002, nos. 47–54; EU Report 2003, nos. 33–36.

The new Directive (merely) aims at facilitating access to compensation for crime victims, ensuring that the latter will be protected irrespective of the actual place where the crime was committed. For that purpose, a system of cooperation between the Member States has been introduced, so that victims can now turn to an authority in their own country of residence, even if the crime was committed elsewhere in the Union. This merely changes the addressee of an application, however, whereas the ultimate payer of compensation will always be the country on whose territory the crime had been committed (Art. 2), and whose laws define the availability of compensation in the first place. 25

The only remains of the initial intention to harmonize the compensation regimes in all Member States is Art. 12 para. 2: 26

> "All Member States shall ensure that their national rules provide for the existence of a scheme on compensation to victims of violent intentional crimes committed in their respective territories, which guarantees fair and appropriate compensation to victims."

The entire Section 1 of the initial draft, however, which was meant to introduce minimum standards for compensation to crime victims, was deleted due to objections by Germany and the UK[27], thereby taking the sting out of the proposal by reducing it to merely administrative matters. 27

6. Equal Treatment Between Women and Men

While the original proposal of a directive aiming at promoting gender equality wanted to ban different insurance premiums and benefits for men and women[28], the finalized text of the Directive adopted on 13 December 2004[29] was softened in light of the uproar that this proposal had caused in some countries. The new wording takes into account (and thereby acknowledges) concerns that such differences may be based on different risk assessment. Art. 5 para. 2 of the Directive therefore allows Member States "to permit proportionate differences in individuals' premiums and benefits where the use of sex is a determining factor in the assessment of risk based on relevant and accurate actuarial and statistical data". They may do so until 21 December 2007 if they "ensure that accurate data relevant to the use of sex as a determining actuarial factor are compiled, published and regularly updated". However, "costs related to pregnancy and maternity" must never account for such differences (para. 3). 28

[27] See PRES/2004/76, 30.3.2004, 8.

[28] COM(2003) 657 final, 5.11.2003. Cf. EU Report 2003, no. 37.

[29] Council Directive 2004/113/EC of 13 December 2004 implementing the principle of equal treatment between men and women in the access to and supply of goods and services, OJ L 373, 21.12.2004, 37.

29 The new Directive also makes sure that all Member States provide for appropriate compensation mechanisms for losses sustained as a result of sex discrimination (Art. 8 para. 2) and aids victims in obtaining such relief by promoting the application of the *res ipsa loquitur* rule (Art. 9[30]).

[30] Art. 9, whose header reads "Burden of proof", provides in para. 1 that "Member States shall take such measures as are necessary, in accordance with their national judicial systems, to ensure that, when persons who consider themselves wronged because the principle of equal treatment has not been applied to them establish, before a court or other competent authority, facts from which it may be presumed that there has been direct or indirect discrimination, it shall be for the respondent to prove that there has been no breach of the principle of equal treatment."

XXVI. Revision of the Japanese Civil Code

Kunihiko Okubo

The Japanese Civil Code (JCC) was revised completely on 25 November 2004. The new law was enforced on 1 April 2005. 1

The modernization of the Japanese Civil Code is the main purpose of this revision, without adding substantial changes to the contents of the current law. Titles have also been attached to the provisions. Furthermore some established judicial precedents and accepted theories, which were not shown in the wording of the old provisions clearly, have also been incorporated in regulations. In tort law, the following articles have been revised. 2

First, Art. 709 JCC, the key regulation of tort liability, has been revised as follows[1]. 3

> (the previous provision[2]): A person who violates intentionally or negligently the right of another is bound to make compensation for damage arising therefrom.
>
> (the new provision): A person who violates intentionally or negligently the right <u>or the legally protected interest</u> of another is bound to make compensation for damage arising therefrom.

In addition, the same revision is made in Art. 720 (1) JCC which shows the requirements for legitimate self-defence. 4

> (the previous provision): A person who, in order to protect his own right or that of a third person against the unlawful act of another, unavoidably commits a harmful act is not liable in compensation for damage; however this shall not preclude a demand of compensation for damage by the injured party against the person who committed the unlawful act.

[1] Regarding judicial precedents and theories of Japanese tort law, see K. Okubo, Compensation for Pure Economic Loss Under Japanese Law, in: W.H. van Boom/H. Koziol/C. Witting (eds.), *Pure Economic Loss* (2004), 56 et seq.

[2] Translations of the old provisions are taken from *The Civil Code of Japan*, EHS Law Bulletin Series, EHS Vol. II (1992).

(the new provision): A person who, in order to protect his own right or the legally protected interest or that of a third person against the unlawful act of another, unavoidably commits a harmful act is not liable in compensation for damage; however this shall not preclude a demand of compensation for damage by the injured party against the person who committed the unlawful act.

XXVII. Comparative Remarks

Meinhard Lukas

1. Preliminary Remarks

The bases for this comparison are reports from 24 European countries with a volume of several hundred pages. Obviously, it is not possible to deal with all aspects of the documents presented and, therefore, a selection had to be made, which was arbitrary to some extent. The main focus will be put on those issues which were dealt with in several countries since this report aims at identifying current trends in the European law of damages. The reports presented give a most excellent overview of the extent to which national legal systems have already grown closer to each other with respect to the law of damages, be it regarding legislation or court decisions. 1

However, the reports presented this year also show very impressively the difficult value judgments the highest courts have had to make in some cases. In this respect I would like to mention a case in Poland, where a raped woman was refused an abortion[1]. In this case the problem of wrongful births, which seems hardly solvable anyhow, has come to a head because the woman had been raped. Difficult questions also arose with respect to the Greek case where a father of an Albanian family was killed in a car accident[2]. Although the man had worked in Greece, he had not held the necessary working permit. When his wife and daughters claimed lost maintenance payments, the offender pleaded that the working contract, i.e. the only source of income of the deceased, had been null and void. Also the Supreme Court in Slovenia had to render a delicate value judgment[3]. A defendant who had already served a sentence in the past was arrested once more. In the course of the criminal proceedings it turned out that he was innocent. He claimed compensation for deprivation of liberty, which was dismissed by the statement that there had been no impairment of his interests as there would have been in the case of a person having a clean record. This case, as well as the two cases mentioned before, show the limits of generally accepted principles of the law of tort. They con- 2

[1] Poland nos. 19 et seq.
[2] Greece nos. 35 et seq.
[3] Slovenia nos. 32 et seq.

cern value issues which cannot be answered exclusively on the basis of the law of damages.

2. Employment Relationships

3 It is striking that the country reports contain a large number of decisions concerning employment relationships. In this field accidents at work play an important role. In case of physical injury, liability is often not (or not exclusively) based on the employment contract but on the law of tort. The employer's liability for fault depends partly on specific employee protection regulations and partly on general duties to exercise care. In some countries, as, e.g., in England[4], employer's strict liability applies if employee protection regulations are not observed. When analysing relevant decisions rendered in 2004, considerable differences become obvious:

4 Decisions of the Greek Supreme Court are especially restrictive, as can be seen from a decision rendered regarding an accident at work sustained by an engineer on a vessel[5]. According to the applicable provision of Greek maritime law, an injured employee may claim damages if s/he is injured as a consequence of a violation of employee protection regulations. According to the Greek Supreme Court, this provision only applies if a specific employee protection regulation has been violated. Since in the present case only a violation of the employer's general duty to exercise care was alleged, the Greek Supreme Court denied the employer's liability. A Danish case also concerned a violation of the employer's general duty to exercise care[6]. A construction worker suffered a herniated disc on a construction site because his work consisted, *inter alia*, in carrying considerable amounts of cement up to the first floor of a building without a lift being available to him. The worker then claimed damages on grounds of disorganisation of the work flow. The Danish Supreme Court did not agree. Although – unlike the Greek court – it admitted that an employer is subject to a general duty to exercise care, it denied any negligence of the employer in view of the many years of working experience of the worker concerned. The court held that the employer had been justified in assuming that the worker would organise the necessary activities on his own. The Spanish Supreme Court argued very similarly when a worker suffered an accident at work because he had entered a closed area[7]. According to the *Tribunal Supremo*, an employer cannot be asked to permanently supervise an experienced worker.

5 In comparison thereto the Slovenian Supreme Court was of the opinion that an employer's duty to exercise care goes much further. The decision concerned an accident at work suffered by a warehouseman who had worked for the company for many years[8]. He injured his knee when getting off a lorry. The

[4] England and Wales no. 21.
[5] Greece nos. 11 et seq.
[6] Denmark nos. 2 et seq.
[7] Spain nos. 23 et seq.
[8] Slovenia nos. 29 et seq.

accident was caused by a difference in height of 80 cm between the loading floor of the lorry and the loading platform, which the worker had obviously overlooked. According to the Slovenian Supreme Court, the difference in height between the loading floor and the loading platform alone constituted a violation of the employer's duty to exercise care. According to the court, the fact that the injured person was an experienced worker would not change this either.

These considerations of the Slovenian Supreme Court remind me of court 6
practice of the Dutch *Hoge Raad*, on which we have reported several times in the past few years[9]. The *Hoge Raad* already assumes that an employer is liable if a defect can be detected in his sphere. According to a decision rendered in 2004, the employer, however, is not liable for all risks of a working process[10]. The *Hoge Raad* denied a claim for compensation of an employee who had slipped due to inattentiveness when loading a container and had injured himself. In a current decision the House of Lords also limited the employer's liability. Although the House of Lords recently also confirmed the employer's strict liability in case of a violation of employee protection regulations, the majority of the finding judges held that liability only applies if the regulation concerned aims at preventing such damage or injury as was suffered by the employee. The protective purpose of an employee protection regulation is referred to. Thus, an analogy exists between liability for fault and strict liability.

3. Compensation for Non-Pecuniary Loss

In the present context another decision should be taken note of, which is of great 7
importance even beyond labour law. In Italy a surgeon was dismissed by a hospital without legal cause and was employed again after eight years of labour law proceedings[11]. Consequently he claimed compensation for pecuniary losses and non-pecuniary losses. The lower courts denied compensation for non-pecuniary losses because no provision was violated that would provide for payment of compensation for such a damage. The Italian Supreme Court, however, did not follow this opinion. The Supreme Court rather assumed that a personal right of the surgeon, secured by the Constitution, had been violated. This is of importance because after two fundamental decisions rendered in 2003 compensation for non-pecuniary loss was granted for violation of rights guaranteed by the Constitution. Against this background the Italian Supreme Court also held that compensation was to be paid for the non-material damage suffered by the surgeon. However, for this purpose the Supreme Court had to assume that an employee has a constitutional right to not be dismissed without legal cause.

[9] See M. Faure/T. Hartlief, The Netherlands, in: H. Koziol/B.C. Steininger (eds.), *European Tort Law 2001* (2002), 365–369, nos. 29–37; M. Faure/T. Hartlief, The Netherlands, in: H. Koziol/B.C. Steininger (eds.), *European Tort Law 2002* (2003), 311–315, nos. 15–18; M. Faure/T. Hartlief, The Netherlands, in: H. Koziol/B.C. Steininger (eds.), *European Tort Law 2003* (2004), 294–295, nos. 49–52.

[10] The Netherlands nos. 25 et seq.

[11] Italy nos. 14 et seq.

8 This decision confirms a trend already pointed out by H. Koziol last year[12]: not only physical integrity but also personal rights are being asserted in order to justify payment of compensation for non-pecuniary loss. This fact is also confirmed by the report from the Netherlands. There, in many cases a violation of personal rights in addition to mental detriment is asserted[13]. An example thereof is a case where two persons were attacked by adolescents in a house[14]. At night the teenagers repeatedly threw stones at the windows, frightening the people who lived in the house. Due to the fact that the police intervened much too late, the persons affected subsequently claimed compensation for non-pecuniary loss (caused by fear) from the relevant authorities. In this respect the plaintiffs, *inter alia*, alleged a violation of their personal rights. The *Hoge Raad* confirmed such argument. Not only the teenagers but also the competent police officers were held responsible for the violation of central personal rights. Accordingly, the *Hoge Raad* held that compensation for the non-pecuniary-loss suffered was justified without proof of a specific mental detriment being necessary.

9 The special importance of personal rights with respect to non-material damage is also shown by a Hungarian case[15]. The Hungarian Supreme Court denied compensation for non-material damage in connection with a failed abortion as allegedly no personal right is violated if a child is born even though the child was unwanted. In contrast thereto compensation for non-material damage was deemed to be justified in a case where a training contract was breached because the plaintiff affected, according to the Supreme Court, suffered a disadvantage with respect to her personal right to education/training[16].

10 As was the case in previous years, this year the issue of compensation for mental strain is also of particular importance. If a person is killed, damages for the mental strain are increasingly claimed by the person's close relatives. In this connection in several countries the question arose whether contributory negligence of the killed victim is to be imputed to the relatives. This question is of special interest because it is closely linked to the issue of the cause of liability. In this respect there are two alternatives. The claim of the relatives may be deduced from the offender's culpable conduct vis-à-vis the direct victim. In such a case it is obvious that a relative has to accept that contributory negligence of the victim has to be attributed to him/her. The situation is totally different if the relative affected is granted a direct claim against the offender. Such a case deals with attribution of the conduct of a third party as contributory negligence.

[12] H. Koziol, Comparative Remarks, in: H. Koziol/B.C. Steininger (eds.), *European Tort Law 2003* (2004), 463–465, nos. 2–7.
[13] The Netherlands nos. 43 et seq.
[14] The Netherlands nos. 45 et seq.
[15] Hungary nos. 1 et seq.
[16] Hungary nos. 23 et seq.

The Austrian Supreme Court answered this question in the affirmative[17]. This decision is remarkable because, according to court rulings, in Austria relatives affected are considered to be directly harmed and are, therefore, allowed to assert a claim of their own. However, since according to Austrian court rulings such a claim is defined by the close relationship to the person killed, contributory negligence of the person killed should also be taken account of by reducing the amount claimed. In order to support its arguments the Austrian Supreme Court also took considerations into account which were based on a comparison of laws and referred to the development in Germany, Switzerland and France. 11

The Belgian Supreme Court arrived at the same result in a similar case[18] although the Austrian and Belgian Supreme Courts have different approaches with respect to liability: whilst the Austrian Supreme Court considers relatives to be directly harmed parties, the decision in Belgium obviously speaks of the moral damage of a relative suffered "by repercussion". In both decisions, however, family ties are considered to be a material reason for imputation. Against this background it would also be advisable to take into consideration the contributory negligence of the person killed. 12

In a Greek decision the claim for compensation was reduced because of an existing relationship[19]. However, in that case the relation to the offender is referred to. Thus, the facts and circumstances differ decisively from the Belgian and the Austrian decision: A father of a Greek family caused a traffic accident, in which his wife was killed. Their common children claimed, *inter alia*, compensation for mental strain. According to the Greek Supreme Court, compensation for relevant damage is not excluded due to the relationship between the offender and the persons harmed, however, the claim is to be reduced for this reason. This comes down to a privilege of the offender based on his status as a relative. 13

All three cases mentioned do, however, have in common that the relationship is seen both as a cause for a claim and as a reason for a reduction of a claim. 14

With respect to compensation for mental strain, a decision rendered in Finland[20] should also be taken note of. It deals with the killing of a parent who left a five-month-old baby behind. The baby's claim for damages was based on a statutory provision of the Finnish law of tort which, in case of the killing of a person, provides for compensation for mental strain to close relatives. The Finnish Supreme Court, however, negated the claim of the baby affected because a child of this age would suffer other non-material detriments than those stated in the cited provision. The court also excluded liability for future men- 15

[17] Austria nos. 51 et seq.
[18] Belgium nos. 41 et seq.
[19] Greece nos. 46 et seq.
[20] Finland nos. 12 et seq.

tal strain of the child. This decision at least causes a feeling of unease. However, the Finnish Supreme Court at least admitted that an infant is physically, mentally and emotionally tied to its parents. Against this background the following conclusion may perhaps have been drawn: if adults are allowed compensation for mental strain in case a close relative is killed, the non-material interests of a baby are to be protected as well, although they may be impaired in a different way. But perhaps the baby did not succeed before court for procedural reasons. The claim, for example, was obviously only based on the above-cited provision of Finnish law without other bases for the claim being asserted at the same time.

16 In the present context I would finally like to briefly mention another decision rendered in Austria[21]. Also in this case a specific emotional bond between the plaintiff and the person killed was presented for discussion. According to the Austrian Supreme Court, an offender may try to prove that, despite a close family relationship, no considerable emotional bond existed. In such a situation compensation for mental strain cannot be granted. The applicable arguments could be that in such a case the relative concerned did not suffer a considerable non-pecuniary loss.

4. Assumption of Risks

17 In the field of strict liability the Norwegian decision on compensation for damage caused by smoking[22] is particularly interesting. This decision could serve as an example for other European countries. The plaintiff had smoked cigarettes of a tobacco company for more than forty years. In 1996 he fell ill with lung cancer. The decision rendered by the Norwegian Supreme Court in this case was not based on the Norwegian Act on Product Liability of 1985 but strict liability was assumed, the principle of which had been developed in Norwegian court rulings long before. Strict liability applies when a continuing, typical and extraordinary risk is created. However, liability is denied if such risk was foreseeable for the harmed person and if s/he could have protected him/herself from such risk. Against this background liability of the tobacco company was denied in this case because the plaintiff had acted on his own risk. This decision is convincing in the light of the principles on strict liability developed in Norway.

18 However, it is questionable whether the argument brought forward by the Norwegian Supreme Court would also exclude the tobacco company's liability for fault. After all one could argue that the tobacco company did not fulfil its general duties of care because they of course knew about the harmful consequences of smoking. This gives rise to the question of whether liability for fault is in fact always excluded already if the harmed person knew about relevant risks of a harmful product. Does this also apply if severe harm or even

[21] Austria nos. 25 et seq.
[22] Norway nos. 7 et seq.

the death of a person are to be feared? This question should not be answered in the affirmative without giving it profound thought. Liability for fault of the tobacco company should, therefore, rather be denied primarily for a different reason: since the sale of cigarettes is accepted in our society (at least to date) and is not prohibited by law, the conduct of the tobacco company cannot be considered illegal. In this connection the phenomenon of social adequacy, which is becoming more and more important, is referred to. Harmful conduct does not trigger liability because it is socially accepted. This argument was mainly developed for criminal law; it can, however, also be applied to civil law *mutatis mutandis*[23].

The phenomenon of assumption of risk referred to by the Norwegian Supreme Court played an important role in a variety of decisions in the field of sports and leisure accidents in 2004: according to the German *Bundesgerichtshof*, guests of a public swimming pool cannot expect that a water slide which is equipped according to the relevant technical safety regulations is, in addition, permanently monitored by the swimming pool staff[24]. The Swiss *Bundesgericht* is of the opinion that a skier must expect dangers of falling anywhere in the Alpine area[25]. Accordingly, the court denied liability of a ski lift operator in a case where a skier hit a pipe twelve metres away from the ski piste after he had fallen. According to the Swiss Supreme Court, liability is also excluded if a skier falls onto a stone after he has left the marked piste with a group of free riders in order to ski downhill off-piste and parallel to the cable railway in deep snow[26]. According to the Swiss Supreme Court also, the users of a summer toboggan run assume specific risks which may result, in particular, from their own failure to take care as well as from other users' failure to take care[27]. Accordingly, the court denied liability of the toboggan run operator vis-à-vis a customer who was crashed into by two minor users of the toboggan run. The court stated that the relevant warning signs that had been put up along the run had been sufficient. This case shows most clearly that courts demand less stringent requirements to exercise care with respect to sporting activities. 19

The Dutch *Hoge Raad* went even further when it denied liability of a mini golf player who hit the eye of a golf player next to her, who lost his eye as a consequence thereof[28]. Although the other golf player had only been watching the offender play when the accident happened, the *Hoge Raad* considered him to be a participant in the game. Accordingly, he was subject to the increased liability threshold. In another case the *Hoge Raad* decided totally differently, when a woman was injured near the airport by a jet blast[29]. She was there to 20

[23] See J. von Hein, Neutrale Beihilfe im Zivilrecht, [2004] *Archiv für die civilistische Praxis*, no. 204 761 et seq.
[24] Germany nos. 43 et seq.
[25] Switzerland nos. 11 et seq.
[26] Switzerland nos. 14 et seq.
[27] Switzerland nos. 17 et seq.
[28] See The Netherlands no 12.
[29] See The Netherlands no 14.

take photos of the airplane taking off. Although there were numerous warning signs of this kind of injury, the *Hoge Raad* held the airport operator to be liable. In the court's opinion, the operator had to assume that tourists would not observe the sign. This decision confirms that which I have already pointed out with respect to the Norwegian decision regarding the tobacco company's liability[30]; even if a harmed person knowingly exposes him/herself to a risk, the person causing such risk may still be liable.

5. Medical Liability

21 In the field of medical liability once more the burden of proof played a central role. First of all an Italian case is to be mentioned in this respect, in which the parents of a handicapped child had brought an action against both a hospital and the physician in charge at the hospital[31]. During a gynaecological examination of the pregnant mother the physician did not recognise a dysfunction of the foetus. However, it is doubtful whether the physician acted negligently. The Italian Supreme Court assessed the claim against the hospital and the claim against the physician on the basis of contractual principles. Even if no contract was concluded with the physician, a relationship similar to a contractual relationship existed due to the specific social contact between the physician and the plaintiffs. Based on this fact the Italian court applied the burden of proof principle, which is applicable in cases of breach of contract. According to this principle, the plaintiff only had to prove non-performance; the hospital and/or physician, however, had to prove that due care was exercised.

22 According to a decision of the Polish Supreme Court a harmed patient is not required to prove which staff was actually responsible for a wrong treatment[32]. Also the German *Bundesgerichtshof* showed much sympathy for harmed patients. I am referring to a decision concerning an incomplete diagnosis of the physicians who treated a patient after a traffic accident[33]. In the beginning the physicians overlooked a fracture of the pelvis. This injury caused considerable pain to the patient. If the diagnosis and the treatment had been made or commenced early, the probability that the healing process would have been the same increases to ninety per cent. Nevertheless the German Supreme Court assumed that the diagnostic error had been the cause of the pain suffered by the patient. Due to their obviously negligent conduct, the physicians had to bear the burden of proof for lack of causality. The only case where the burden of proof is not shifted is if it is very improbable that causality exists or if the risk of a wrong treatment (diagnostic error) has not become reality. Based on this opinion of the German Supreme Court, the physicians were held to be liable in the present case despite the fact that causality was very uncertain.

[30] See no. 19.
[31] Italy nos. 24 et seq.
[32] Poland nos. 54 et seq.
[33] Germany nos. 46 et seq.

Also one of the English cases concerned the tricky issue of causality[34]: a surgeon carried out a neurological operation without explaining to the patient the risk that this operation could cause symptoms of paralysis. Due to the fact that this risk became reality, the patient sued the surgeon for damages. The court of first instance ascertained that the patient would have asked other physicians for their opinion if the surgeon had duly informed her about the risk. However, there were no indications that the patient would have cancelled the operation if she had known about the risks. The House of Lords, however, thought that this fact was not to be considered and that the only relevant fact was that the specific operation would not have been carried out. The Lords stated that for reasons of justice and public policy there was no room for further considerations regarding causality. Otherwise the physicians' duty to inform the patient would be undermined, i.e., considerations of general prevention stood against a strict examination of causality in the end. 23

An Irish decision rendered in 2004 also concerned a tricky problem of causality[35]: in a hospital a patient's cancer was diagnosed too late although the patient showed clear symptoms. Consequently the necessary operation was also delayed. In his claim the patient asserted that his life expectancy had decreased due to the delayed diagnosis. The court did not hold this fact as proved since it was not certain that the plaintiff would immediately have undergone an operation if the diagnosis had been made earlier. However, the negligent conduct of the treating physician had deprived the patient of his chance to be treated early. The plaintiff was awarded an amount of € 45,000 on this ground alone. 24

Thus, the German, English and the Irish Supreme Court finally affirmed liability (based on the proven fault of the treating physician in each case) although in all three cases causality was doubtful. 25

6. Public Liability

As last year, public liability plays a major role in the country reports. Due to the fact that this topic was dealt with thoroughly last year[36], I will only refer to a few especially remarkable decisions of this year. First of all it is good to hear that the House of Lords did not hold an entity that is responsible for maintenance of roads liable only for failing to mount a warning sign for speeders on a road that is difficult to oversee[37]. It is likewise comforting that in Italy a party to court proceedings was awarded damages because they had to wait for a decision by the competent civil court for an unreasonably long period of time[38]. The Italian Supreme Court, however, did not give an answer to the question raised by the appellate court in the public liability proceedings, 26

[34] England and Wales nos. 4 et seq.
[35] Ireland nos. 21 et seq.
[36] See H. Koziol (supra fn. 12), 468–469, nos. 20–25.
[37] England and Wales nos. 12 et seq.
[38] Italy nos. 1 et seq.

namely what was the causality between the delay of the proceedings and the damage asserted? For Spanish heirs it is positive to hear that, according to a decision of the *Tribunal Supremo*, the state is liable for malfunctions of the Registry of Wills even if the presumptive heir's claim could also be possible[39].

27 Two decisions rendered in the Netherlands should also be mentioned. The first decision concerned a prisoner who had been released on parole[40]. He took two women as hostages, attacked them and stole their money. Although no duty to exercise care was violated in connection with the parole the appellate court admitted a liability of the state. The reason given for rendering this decision was the extraordinary public burden which the victims had to bear due to the prisoner's release. The appellate court based its decision on decisions rendered by the *Hoge Raad*. The Dutch Supreme Court had assumed that the state was liable because individual citizens had to bear an extraordinary burden, which should actually be split among the general public. In the present case, however, the *Hoge Raad* refused to apply this principle because there was no direct interference of the state. By rendering this decision the *Hoge Raad* denied strict liability of the state in connection with release of prisoners. In another, completely different decision the *Hoge Raad* also limited the state's liability[41]. The case concerned an inspection of a vessel prescribed by law. Despite renewal of the necessary certificate by the Marine Inspection the vessel sank one year later and damaged the plaintiff's boat. The *Hoge Raad* denied liability of the state by stating that the statutory inspection only served marine safety. Individual financial interests of third parties would, however, not be protected by such inspection. This consideration of the Dutch Supreme Court is not quite unproblematic because the plaintiff's property was quite obviously damaged.

[39] Spain nos. 43 et seq.
[40] The Netherlands nos. 18 et seq.
[41] The Netherlands no. 6.

Other Contributions

I. Tort Law in the Irish Legal System

Denis N. Kelliher

1. Introduction

1 Irish law derives primarily from four sources:[1] the Constitution, legislation, the common law, and E.U. law. These four sources of law have each played a part, albeit to differing degrees, in shaping current Irish tort law.

2 The Constitution is the basic law of the State and it is from the Constitution that all other sources of law derive force. The common law has been carried forward by the Constitution, the Oireachtas[2] has been vested with the power of enacting legislation, European law is now an established part of Irish law, and the Constitution itself has substantial provisions, all of which have contributed to the development of Irish tort law.

2. Common Law

3 All laws in Ireland prior to the Irish Free State coming into being were carried forward by Article 73 of the 1922 Constitution. On the enactment of the 1937 Constitution, Bunreacht na hÉireann, an almost identical article, Article 50, provided that:

4 "Subject to this Constitution and to the extent to which they are not inconsistent therewith, the laws in force in Saorstát Éireann immediately prior to the date of the coming into operation of this Constitution shall continue to be of full force and effect until the same or any of them shall have been repealed or amended by enactment of the Oireachtas."

5 It is accepted that the common law which was in force in Ireland at the time of the enactment of the Constitution was carried over and is of full force in Ireland except where it is inconsistent with the Constitution. A question arose as to whether only the actual common law rules at the date of the carrying over of the laws were carried over into the new legal system or whether the 'common law system' was carried forward, which would allow judges to 'push for-

[1] See generally, R. Byrne/J.P. McCutcheon, *The Irish Legal System* (4th edn. 2001), 5–9.
[2] National parliament.

ward' or 'develop' the law, by means of interpretation, analogy and distinction of prior case law. Hogan & White posit that it could be argued that "the interpretative power, from which whole new structures of law have emerged, is itself part of the common law, and just as much carried over by the old Article 73 and the present Article 50 as any other part"[3]. This would appear to be the tacitly accepted view.

Thus, as issues in tort had been primarily dealt with by the common law prior to the coming into being of the Irish Free State, the common law is the primary source of tort law in Ireland today. Whilst the Irish courts will often look to the development of the common law in England in determining issues, the courts have been vigilant in stating that decisions of English courts are of persuasive value only and are not binding on the Irish courts,[4] and the courts will resort to basic first principles and have regard to the provisions of the Irish Constitution in reaching decisions. 6

As is the way of the common law, the legal principles of tort law in Ireland have been enunciated by way of decisions rather than by reference to an authoritative code. The principles developed prior to the coming into being of the Irish Free State still apply therefore and thus familiar common law tests are still employed in the Irish courts. Principles familiar to the common law that are employed in Ireland include the "but for" test,[5] the determination of legal causation,[6] and the concept of remoteness.[7] 7

The cornerstone of negligence for common law countries is the case of *Donoghue v. Stevenson,*[8] often referred to as the "Case of the Snail in the Bottle". Here, a woman drank ginger beer from a coloured bottle which had been purchased for her by a friend. After having consumed most of the contents of the bottle, she allegedly discovered the decomposed remains of a snail in the bottle. She became ill. However, as she was not party to the contract between the purchaser and the vendor, she was unable to sue for breach of contract. She therefore sought to bring an action against the manufacturer of the product. Her case came before the House of Lords, where the neighbour principle was enunciated. Lord Atkin stated: 8

"The rule that you are to love your neighbour becomes in law, you must not injure your neighbour; and the lawyer's question, Who is my neighbour? re- 9

[3] G. Hogan/G. Whyte, *Kelly: The Irish Constitution* (4th edn. 2003), 2151–2152.
[4] See, in particular, the decision of McCarthy J. in *Irish Shell Ltd. v. Elm Motors Ltd.* [1984] *Irish Reports* (I.R.) 200.
[5] See, for example, *Kenny v. O'Rourke* [1972] I.R. 339, *Collier v. Earl of Mountcharles* (Unreported, Supreme Court, 19 December 1969), *CIE v. Carroll & Wexford County Council* [1986] *Irish Law Reports Monthly* (I.L.R.M.) 312.
[6] B. McMahon/W. Binchy, *Law of Torts* (3rd edn. 2000), 65 quote Street, *The Law of Torts* (8th edn. 1988), 224: "There is no precise legal rule, but common sense and law unite in looking for the abnormal or the deliberate human act, and regarding that as 'the cause'."
[7] See, in general, B. McMahon/W. Binchy (supra fn. 6), Chapter 3.
[8] [1932] *Appeals Cases* (A.C.) 562.

ceives a restricted reply. You must take reasonable care to avoid acts or omissions which you can reasonably foresee would be likely to injure your neighbour. Who, then, in law is my neighbour? The answer seems to be – persons who are so closely and directly affected by my act that I ought reasonably to have them in contemplation as being so affected when I am directing my mind to the acts or omissions which are called in question."[9]

10 From this dictum exploded the law of negligence which would develop rapidly and expansively in the following years.

11 A similar case, a number of years later, came before the Irish courts.[10] Here, a woman had purchased a pot of jam which was consumed by her husband and children, although she herself did not consume the product. Her family became ill, and an action was brought against the manufacturer of the product. Whilst the court refused to follow *Donoghue v. Stevenson* explicitly (being at best only of persuasive authority in Irish courts), a similar result was reached. The court reverted to first principles and having referred to O.W. Holmes's The Common Law[11] Gavan Duffy J. stated:

12 "That master of the common law shows that the foundation of liability at common law for tort is blameworthiness as determined by the existing average standards of the community; a man fails at his peril to conform to those standards. Therefore, while loss from accident generally lies where it falls, a defendant cannot plead accident if, treated as a man of ordinary intelligence and foresight, he ought to have foreseen the danger which caused injury to his plaintiff."[12]

13 In Irish courts, in order to succeed in an action in negligence, it is necessary to prove, on the balance of probabilities, that a duty of care existed, that this duty was breached, and that the defendant caused the damage that resulted.

3. Legislation

14 Although tort law in Ireland is primarily derived from the common law, legislation is also significant. The legislature has introduced a number of pieces of legislation dealing with tort law issues. Indeed, one piece of legislation was introduced primarily as a response to the development tort law had taken in the courts.

15 At common law, occupier's liability dealt with four categories of entrant. Contractual entrants were afforded a duty of care as determined by the contract; where the contract was silent on this, a duty of reasonable care to make the premises safe for the contemplated purposes was implied into the con-

[9] *Donoghue v. Stevenson* [1932] A.C. 562, 580.
[10] *Kirby v. Burke & Holloway* [1944] I.R. 207.
[11] (London, 1887).
[12] *Kirby v. Burke & Holloway* [1944] I.R. 207, 214.

tract.[13] Invitees (such as a shop customer) were afforded a duty of "reasonable care by the occupier to prevent damage from unusual danger"[14]. Licensees onto a property, where there was no material benefit to the occupier but implied/express permission to enter, were afforded a duty to be warned of concealed dangers of which the occupier was aware. In the case of the fourth category, trespassers, occupiers were under a duty not to injure intentionally and not to act recklessly.

The situation at common law was radically altered in Ireland in the case of *McNamara v. E.S.B.*[15] where an eleven-year-old boy was seriously injured whilst trespassing on an electricity power plant. On appeal of the decision in the High Court, the Supreme Court stated that a duty of reasonable care was owed to trespassers who could be reasonably foreseen. Walsh J. noted: 16

"The known physical facts were the condition of the fence, its proximity to the building, and the habit of the local children to play around the immediate area of the fence. In those circumstances it was the duty of the defendants to take reasonable steps to ensure that the children, or any of them, would not be able to enter the danger area. In a case such as the present, that means taking reasonable steps to prevent the children trespassing."[16] 17

Although the duty owed to trespassers was clearly elevated by the court, none of the judgments delivered in the case dealt with whether the other categories of entrants were thereby also afforded a higher duty of care than had been afforded previously or whether an anomalous situation now existed whereby trespassers who could be reasonably foreseen were afforded a higher duty of care than invitees and licensees. 18

Due to the legal uncertainty resulting from the decision in *McNamara*, and the new higher level of duty of care owed to trespassers, political lobbying, by especially farmers' interests groups, ensued to which the legislature responded. Farmers in particular had been anxious that they could be held liable for damage caused to persons who were not authorised to enter their land, such as tourists and hill walkers. As these entrants could be reasonably foreseen, it was thought the higher duty of care, that of reasonable care, would apply as opposed to a duty not to injure intentionally and not to act recklessly as had applied prior to the decision in *McNamara*. 19

The Occupier's Liability Act, 1995 changed the categories of entrant and the duty of care to be afforded to each category of entrant as defined under the Act. "Visitors" are to be afforded a duty of reasonable care; "recreational users" and "trespassers" are to be afforded a duty not to injure intentionally or to 20

[13] See McMahon & Binchy, (supra fn. 6), 300.
[14] *Indermaur v. Dames* (1866) *The Law Reports* (L.R.) 1 *Common Pleas* (C.P.) 274, 287.
[15] [1975] I.R. 1.
[16] [1975] I.R. 1, 15.

act with reckless disregard. In the recent case of *Weir-Rodgers v. S.F. Trust Ltd.*[17] the Supreme Court overturned a judgment of the High Court awarding the plaintiff, who claimed to be a recreational user on the land, damages when she fell from the edge of a cliff; the Supreme Court took the view that the occupier had not acted in reckless disregard in not erecting a notice warning of the inherent dangers associated with the cliff.

21 Whilst the legislature has been slow in introducing legislation dealing with substantive areas of tort law, it has been more active in the area of adjectival law, especially as of late. The legislature has set up a number of tribunals of compensation to compensate victims who the legislature deemed should be spared the burdens and anxieties of having to bring an action in the courts for damage suffered. Such tribunals included the Stardust Tribunal, which compensated victims of a fire in a nightclub after which there was a significant outpouring of public sympathy, the Hepatitis C and HIV tribunal, to compensate victims of contaminated blood products provided by the State, and the Residential Institutions Redress Board, which was established to determine the level of damages which should be awarded to victims of abuse whilst resident in specified institutions in the State.

22 The most significant procedural change introduced by the legislature was the introduction of the Personal Injuries Assessment Board. The Personal Injuries Assessment Board Act, 2003 established the Board in April 2003 with, *inter alia*, a view to decreasing the caseload of the courts by facilitating the settlement of disputes at an earlier stage. On 1 June 2004 all employment liability cases and since July 2004 all personal injuries cases (except where the claim is one of medical negligence) came within the remit of the Board.[18] Now, in order to initiate an action for personal injuries in the courts, it is first necessary to follow certain prescribed procedures. A claimant must now first make a claim with the respondent. If a settlement is not agreed, a claim is made to the Board. The claim must provide a brief description of the accident, the nature of injury suffered, losses suffered (such as wages and medical expenses), and a medical report. Where liability is not contested, the Board will determine the level of damages to be awarded. If liability is contested, the Board will issue an authorisation to bring the action in the courts. If, having made an assessment of damages, either party is not satisfied with the assessment, the award can be rejected, and the Board will issue the authorisation for the plaintiff to bring the action before the courts. In assessing damages, the Board has regard to a Book of Quantum which provides figures indicating the amount of damages to be awarded generally. The Book of Quantum, independently compiled after a survey of awards in the courts, takes into account compensation for pain and suffering. Financial losses are also compensated. The Board uses the Book of Quantum as a guide only and

[17] (Unreported, Supreme Court, 21 January 2005).

[18] Section 4(1) also excludes actions in respect of breaches of a provision of the Constitution, actions to be pursued under sec. 3 of the European Convention on Human Rights Act, 2003, and applications for compensation under the Garda Síochána (Compensation) Acts 1941 and 1945 from the ambit of the Board.

has stated that "... full recognition of how an injury has affected a claimant personally will always be considered and reflected in any assessment made ..."

An even more recent example of legislative intervention in tort law is the Civil Liability and Courts Act, 2004. Here, the legislature changed the limitation period for bringing a personal injuries action from three years to two years.[19] A further requirement, imposed by sec. 8 of the Act, is that a letter of claim should be served on a wrongdoer stating the nature of the wrong alleged to have been committed by him or her within two months from the date of the cause of action. A failure to do so is not likely to be fatal to a claim, but the court can draw inferences from the failure to do so and a plaintiff may be penalised, if ultimately successful in the action, when costs are being awarded. The Act also provides that if false or misleading evidence is given in a personal injuries action this is a criminal offence and can result in the dismissal of the action. The penalty for conviction of the criminal offence is a fine of up to a maximum of € 100,000 and/or 10 years imprisonment.[20] 23

The Act of 2004 also introduced specific provisions on the calculation of damages where a charitable gift has been received by the plaintiff. In the event of a fatal injury, a charitable gift will not be accounted for unless it is made by the defendant and, at the time, the defendant donor stated that on an award of damages application would be made to reduce the award by the amount of the gift. The same is provided in the case of a non-fatal injury. However, in the case of a non-fatal injury, it is also provided that if an employer makes a gift consisting of a "series of payments that resemble, in amount and frequency, the normal remuneration that the plaintiff would be entitled to receive from the defendant in the course of his or her employment", this shall be excluded from the calculation. 24

4. European Dimension

As the Constitution provides that it is the basic law of the State and it is from the Constitution that laws derive force, it was necessary for Ireland to amend its Constitution when joining the E.E.C. in 1973. Where any amendment is 25

[19] Time runs from the date of knowledge as defined in sec. 2 of the Statute of Limitations (Amendment) Act, 1991. The date of knowledge is the date on which the plaintiff first had knowledge of the following facts:
(*a*) that the person alleged to have been injured had been injured,
(*b*) that the injury in question was significant,
(*c*) that the injury was attributable in whole or in part to the act or omission which is alleged to constitute negligence, nuisance or breach of duty,
(*d*) the identity of the defendant, and
(*e*) if it is alleged that the act or omission was that of a person other than the defendant, the identity of that person and the additional facts supporting the bringing of an action against the defendant.
There is no prescribed outer time limitation period within which an action must be brought, but it is open to a defendant to apply to the court to exercise its inherent jurisdiction to dismiss proceedings on the grounds of inordinate and inexcusable delay.

[20] It should be noted that there is a constitutional requirement that all penalties be proportional.

made to the European treaties, it is necessary to go to referendum, except where "such amendments do not alter the essential scope or objectives of the communities"[21]. Thus any tort law emanating from the European legal order will become part of Irish law in the normal course.

26 Ireland, also, recently transposed the European Convention on Human Rights into Irish law by way of the European Convention on Human Rights Act, 2003. This Act requires the Irish courts to take judicial notice of the Convention and case law of the European Court of Human Rights. The Convention is, however, subject to the provisions of the Irish Constitution. Whilst the Irish courts had adopted a deferential approach to the jurisprudence of the European Court of Human Rights,[22] the Act provides a legislative basis for now so doing. Whilst it is expected by some that the incorporation of the Convention will have significant effects on certain areas of Irish law, the effect it will have on Irish tort law remains to be seen.

5. Constitution

27 Whilst the Constitution sets out a number of fundamental rights which have tort law implications, the effect on established tort law has been somewhat limited. Article 40.4 of the Constitution provides that no person may be deprived of his or her liberty save in accordance with law[23] and Article 40.5 provides that the dwelling of every citizen is inviolable and may not be entered forcibly, save in accordance with law.[24] Article 40.3 provides for the protection of personal rights of the citizen, in particular the life, person, good name and property rights of every citizen and this article has been interpreted by the courts to include protection for unenumerated personal rights. Unenumerated rights have been held to include the right to bodily integrity,[25] the right to marital privacy,[26] and the right to individual privacy.[27] Whilst the courts had been particularly active, especially since the 1960s, in developing the scope of Article 40.3, it has been recently questioned by the then Chief Justice, Mr. Justice Ronan Keane, whether it was a function of the courts to declare what unenumerated rights were protected by the Constitution.[28]

28 Whilst certain rights enjoy constitutional protection, the courts have declined to change the nature of a cause of action in tort which involves these rights. In *Hanrahan v. Merck Sharp & Dohme (Ireland) Ltd.*[29] Henchy J. stated:

[21] *Crotty v. An Taoiseach* [1987] I.R. 713, 767.
[22] See, in general, Byrne & McCutcheon (supra fn. 1), Chapter 17.
[23] Cf. the tort of false imprisonment.
[24] Cf. the tort of trespass to property.
[25] *Ryan v. A.G.* [1965] I.R. 294.
[26] *McGee v. A.G.* [1974] I.R. 284.
[27] *Kennedy v. Ireland* [1987] I.R. 587. It should be noted that some commentators posit that this case recognises only a right to privacy in one's telephone communications; however, the case is often proffered as illustrating a more general constitutional right to privacy.
[28] *T.D. v. Minister for Education* [2000] 3 I.R. 62.
[29] [1988] I.L.R.M. 629.

"So far as I am aware, the constitutional provisions relied on have never been used in the courts to shape the form of any existing tort or to change the normal onus of proof. The implementation of those constitutional rights is primarily a matter for the State and the courts are entitled to intervene only when there has been a failure to implement or, where the implementation relied on is plainly inadequate, to effectuate the constitutional guarantee in question. In many torts for example, negligence, defamation, trespass to person or property a plaintiff may give evidence of what he claims to be a breach of a constitutional right, but he may fail in the action because of what is usually a matter of onus of proof or because of some other legal or technical defence. A person may of course in the absence of a common law or statutory cause of action, sue directly for breach of a constitutional right[30] but when he founds his action on an existing tort he is normally confined to the limitations of that tort. It might be different if it could be shown that the tort in question is basically ineffective to protect his constitutional rights."[31] 29

This was reaffirmed in a later case where Costello J. stated: 30

"There is therefore no need to construe the Constitution as conferring a new and discrete cause of action for damages in those cases in which the acts or omissions which constitute the alleged infringement also constitute an actionable wrong at law for which damages are recoverable."[32] 31

This can be evidenced by the reluctance of Geoghegan J. in *Foley v. Independent Newspapers*[33] to shift the action for defamation from tort law to constitutional law. One area however where a right afforded by the Constitution came into its own which is relevant to tort law is that of privacy rights. At common law, there was a marked reluctance to afford a general protection to privacy. Neither had there been legislation introduced in Ireland to deal with the area. Thus, where a violation of privacy is alleged an action for infringement of the constitutional right to privacy is the more appropriate recourse. This can be contrasted with the approach of the English courts to develop a right to privacy through the machinery of the European Convention on Human Rights as incorporated into English law by the Human Rights Act, 1998 and the action for breach of confidence. 32

6. Jury Trial

The right to a trial by jury for personal injuries and fatal injuries actions was abolished by the Courts Act, 1988 largely as a response to a perception of overly generous awards by juries. Anecdotal evidence suggests, however, that judges may be even more generous in their awards than juries had previously 33

[30] Citing *Meskell v. C.I.E.* [1973] I.R. 121.
[31] [1988] I.L.R.M. 629, 636.
[32] *W. v. Ireland (No. 2)* [1997] 2 I.R. 141, 167.
[33] [1994] 2 I.L.R.M. 61.

been.[34] The right to trial by jury in the High Court remains in actions for false imprisonment, intentional trespass to the person, and defamation.

7. Damages

34 The principle of *restitutio in integrum* is central to the awarding of damages in Irish tort law. Damages are intended to be compensatory in nature and seek to place the plaintiff in the position prior to the suffering of the wrong. Of course in situations involving, for example, the loss of limbs, damages are accepted as being "notional or theoretical compensation to take the place of that which is not possible, namely, actual compensation"[35].

35 Whilst the courts are hesitant to award exemplary or aggravated damages, it is permissible, and considered appropriate in certain circumstances, that they be awarded. Where a constitutional right is violated, exemplary damages may be awarded. In *Garvey v. Ireland*,[36] the State was ordered to pay exemplary damages, for breach of fair procedures, in an action for wrongful dismissal. Also, in *Kennedy v. Ireland*,[37] where the State had tapped the telephones of journalists, exemplary damages were awarded for the violation of the constitutional right to individual privacy[38] by the State. The Supreme Court stated in *Conway v. Irish National Teachers Organisation*[39] that, in order to protect and vindicate constitutional rights, it would be necessary to be able to award exemplary damages.

36 Of course, this gives rise to a difficulty as to the nexus between tort law and the Constitution. Whilst generally common law principles for determining the level of damages to be awarded are employed by the courts, and the decision in *Hanrahan* stated that an action in tort should be confined to the limitations of that tort (and thus common law principles on level of damages), it seems unreasonable that a different scope for damages is available if the action is couched in terms of infringement of constitutional rights as opposed to being an action in tort. This specific aspect of the relationship between tort law and constitutional rights remains yet to be conclusively determined by the courts.

[34] Section 22 of the Civil Liability and Courts Act, 2004 now ties awards of damages in the courts to the levels specified in the Book of Quantum of the Personal Injuries Assessment Board. The courts are however permitted to have regard to matters other than the Book of Quantum in awarding damages. It remains to be seen, however, how much deference the courts will be willing to afford the Book of Quantum, or whether the courts will consider it an encroachment on their judicial independence. Recently, however, in *Nolan v. Murphy* (Unreported, Supreme Court, 18 March 2005) Denham J. had regard to the Book of Quantum in considering, on appeal, the appropriateness of the level of the award of damages to a plaintiff, in a case involving an action for damages for sexual assault and for actions calculated and intended to cause emotional suffering, by a jury.

[35] *Rushkin v. National Coal Board* [1953] 1 *Queen's Bench* (Q.B.) 495, 502.

[36] [1981] I.R. 75.

[37] [1987] I.R. 587.

[38] See fn. 27.

[39] [1991] 2 I.R. 305.

II. Portuguese Tort Law: A Comparison with the Principles of European Tort Law

André G. Dias Pereira[1]

A. The Portuguese Civil Code of 1966

If geography and linguistic family alone influenced law, no doubt one could include Portuguese civil law within the Romanistic legal family. Indeed, the modern Codification movement started in Portugal at the beginning of the 19th century and it was most influenced at that time by French law. 1

Not surprisingly, commercial law was the first branch of private law to be codified. The first Commercial Code dates from 1833; Ferreira Borges was its main mentor and it had a particular national character, it codified the national customs of the *lex maercatoria* and previous legislation. In 1888 it was replaced by a new code, which took account of the Commercial Codes of Italy and Spain, which had followed on the *Code de Commerce*. 2

1. From "L'école de l'Exegèse" to "Die Pandekten"

In 1867 the first Portuguese Civil Code was enacted[2]. Prof. Seabra, influenced by the *Code Napoleon*, wrote the whole Code alone. Other Codifications were also studied and taken into consideration, especially the *Allgemeines Landrecht* (Prussia), the *ABGB* (Austria) and the *Sardinian Civil Code*. But he was able to create a very peculiar style: the systematisation is different from the French Code[3]. The Civil Code, as the Code of the person, should follow "the personal biography" of the citizen. Naturally, it was meant the citizen of the 19th century, that is to say, a Code thought for the bourgeois and the landowner. 3

[1] This paper was presented on 20 October 2004 at ECTIL. I would like to thank Prof. Koziol for the important suggestions for this article and his kind invitation to do research at ECTIL in the period of October, November and December 2004 as well as the Austrian Academy of Sciences for the financial support.

[2] On that same date (1 July 1867) the death penalty was abolished in Portugal.

[3] Our first Civil Code of 1867 results from the movement of Codification and was also influenced by *L'école de l'Exegèse* (19th Century). See L. Menezes Leitão, *O Ensino do Direito das Obrigações* (2001).

4 In 1966, after more than 20 years of preparation, the new *Código Civil* (CC) was enacted (entered into force on 1 June 1967). Zweigert & Kötz[4] comment that this Code "is remarkable for the intelligent attention it pays to foreign legislation – especially German, Swiss, and Italian – to the point where *one may wonder whether Portuguese private law ought still to be included in the Romanistic legal family.*" We will briefly analyse its structure and we will conclude that Portuguese civil law has, over the last century, jumped over the Rhine and the Alps to establish a fruitful dialogue with German, Austrian, and Swiss as well as with Italian law.

5 First of all, one should note that the Portuguese legislator opted for the solution of keeping labour law and commercial law out of the CC, although it may be subsidiarily applicable. Thus, only "classical" private law will be found in its 2334 articles. In this respect the German model of 1900 (BGB) was followed, rather than the Italian *Codice Civile* of 1942. Another commission intended to simultaneously revise the entire commercial law but it was considered more appropriate to leave this aside.

6 Secondly, the Pandectistic divisions of the BGB and much of its conceptual apparatus were strictly followed. Thereinafter, the CC is divided into 5 books: Book I – General part (*Allgemeiner Teil*), Book II – Law of Obligations (*Schuldrecht*), Book III – Property Law and other rights *in rem* (*Sachenrecht*), Book IV – Family Law (*Familienrecht*) and Book V – Law of Successions (*Erbrecht*).

7 In Book I (General Part) one finds the following issues: Sources of law and Interpretation of law; Private international law; Law of natural persons; Legal persons (Corporations and Foundations); Things (*res*); Rules relating to acts in law (contract law); Law of proof (which follows the Romanistic tradition).

8 Within the law of natural persons, one shall stretch the Chapter concerning personality rights: Artt. 70–81 were a space of freedom within the dictatorship that was keeping Portugal in the darkness. It is fair to say that civil law was the guardian of the liberties until the 1933 Constitution of the Corporative-Fascist regime was replaced by the Democratic 1976 Constitution. In this respect, the general personality right (*Allgemeines Persönlichkeitsrecht*) was established in Art. 70[5] and it has played a significant role in protecting the rights of persons against unlawful conduct.[6] This is a so-called *Rahmenrecht,* to be fulfilled by particular rights to be found elsewhere. We can find specific per-

[4] K. Zweigert/H. Kötz, *An Introduction to Comparative Law* (3rd edn. 1998), 108. For a different perspective of the legal families see J.M. Rainer, *Europäisches Privatrecht: Die Rechtsvergleichung* (2002), 57.

[5] Art. 70 (General protection of the personality): "The law protects individuals against any unlawful offence or threat of offence to his physical or moral entity."

[6] See R. Capelo de Sousa, *O Direito Geral de Personalidade* (1995). A. Menezes Cordeiro, Os Direitos de Personalidade na Jurisprudência Portuguesa, [2001] *Revista da Ordem dos Advogados* (ROA), 1229–1256.

sonality rights, like name; honour, reputation and credit; image; privacy and publication of one's picture or private letters in Artt. 72–80 CC, and many other recent personality rights like protection of genetic data, confidentiality of medical data, the right not to know, etc. in other legal sources such as the Constitution, Penal Code, International Conventions and case law. The remedies are not only *damages*, but also *restoration in kind* and *injunctive relief* (Art. 70 (2)).[7]

Artt. 217 et seq. (Subtitle III) provide rules relating to "acts in law" (*factos jurídicos*). The Portuguese legislator uses the concept of *Rechtsgeschäft* (*negócio jurídico*) and *Aussage* (*declaração negocial*), which proves the strong German-Pandectistic influence in the first half of the 20th century. Among others, there are rules concerning error, deceit, duress, form, agency, conditions, legality and immorality, and usury[8], which are the core of contract law elsewhere. 9

Book II – Law of Obligations – makes a distinction between (Title I) *Law of Obligations in General* (i.e., creditor-debtor relationships in general) and (Title II) *Special Types of Contract* (Sales contract; Donation; Partnership of civil law; Lease; Cattle breeding Partnership; Borrowing; Labour contract; Services Contract; Mandate; Deposit; Building contract; Rent (Perpetual rent and Life long Rent); Gambling and Transaction). 10

We will further concentrate on the law of obligations in general. The legislator enounces and regulates the sources of obligations: contract; unilateral legal acts (*einseitiges Rechtsgeschäft*); torts; *negotiorum gestio* and law of unjustified enrichment. Moreover this Title regulates the types of obligations, the transmission of credits and debts and security rights such as surety, the transfer of securities, pledges, mortgages, rights of priority, and also the oblique action of a creditor are dealt with in the general law of obligations. In fact, security rights ("lease-income consignment", pledges, mortgages, priority rights, retention rights), although considered as rights *in rem*, have an instrumental character: they only exist as long as the credit exists, and therefore it is dogmatically adequate to regulate these rights *in rem* in the Book of the Law of Obligations. The very important Chapter on performance and non-performance of an obligation is regulated in Artt. 762–816 CC. It is interesting to note this issue is not regulated as a specific contract law problem, but a general problem of the law of obligations, independently of its source: contract, unilateral legal act, tort, *negotiorum gestio* or unjust enrichment. However, the Chapter on performance and non-performance of obligations is indeed a core 11

[7] Art. 829-A regulates a private pecuniary sanction for every day or every event the tortfeasor breaches his duties. This is similar to the French *Astreinte* and it can be very important for avoiding continuous violation of personality rights.

[8] Art. 282 states that a contract concluded under usury can be declared *void*. Alternatively, Art. 283 allows *modification* of the contract according to "equity" in case of usury, that is when one party takes advantage of the other's necessity, inexperience, dependency, deftness, psychological weakness and obtains excessive or unjustified benefits.

area of contract law. The chapter concerning judicial fulfilment of the obligations (which establishes a bridge towards civil procedural law) is regulated in Artt. 817–836. Finally, this Title also regulates other ways of extinguishing an obligation rather than the performance of the duty (*Dação em cumprimento* [alternative payment]; consignment; set-off; novation, remission; confusion).

12 Book III regulates possession, ownership and other real rights. Its norms apply (except when otherwise provided) both to movable and immovable things. Intangible property is regulated elsewhere[9], but the Civil Code may apply when appropriate. The three main principles of Portuguese property law are: (1) Principle of "*numerus clausus*" of the rights *in rem* (Art. 1306); (2) Principle of consensual transfer of ownership (Art. 408 (1))[10]; and (3) Principle of Publicity.[11] In this field, especially considering the *consensual principle* (Art. 408), Napoleonic influence is obvious. In this important aspect of civil law, one can say that Portuguese law indeed follows the Romanistic legal family.

13 Family law and the law of succession are regulated in Books IV and V, respectively. There were great modifications in 1977, when the Civil Code was reformed so that it would be in accordance with the new democratic Constitution of 1976. Thus, equality between husband and wife, non-discrimination of children born out of wedlock, divorce also for Catholic marriages (since 1975), and a very strong inheritance position for the surviving spouse are some of the paramount modifications that brought Portuguese family law back to European standards.

14 In conclusion, the main influences of Portuguese civil law are *German* (in the structure of the Code, the existence of a General Part, including abstract concepts, the regulation of the law of obligations) and *French-Italian* in the field of property law. Moreover, the Portuguese legislator took into consideration other modern civil codes, like the Swiss Code of Obligations[12] and the Greek Civil Code.[13]

15 When analysing a legal system, one should look not only at the legal texts, but also at the law in action and other sources of law. The influence of German speaking countries has also been important regarding advanced academic works (PhDs and habilitation theses). In fact, academics pay attention to the

[9] Code of Intellectual Property (2003), Copyright Act, etc.

[10] Art. 408: "the creation or transfer of real rights to a specific thing occurs *simply by virtue of the contract* (…)." This rule is similar to the French and the Italian and different from the German, the Austrian or the Spanish one, as well as from Roman law.

[11] See the Land estate registry Code (1984) for immovable things. Registry is not mandatory, nor a condition to acquire ownership, it has merely declarative effects (i.e., not constitutive) and is a condition of publicity, which protects the acquirer against third parties who acquire later from the same *tradens*. In the field of movable things, publicity is achieved through possession. However, in Portugal the rule *possession vaut titre* does not apply.

[12] For example Art. 494 provides limitation of damages (*ad hoc*), like Art. 43 (1) of the Swiss Code of Obligations from 1911 (entered into force in 1912).

[13] Art. 334 on Abuse of a right was influenced by the Greek Civil Code.

doctrine in those countries and sooner or later this trend has some influence in the courts. On the other hand, there are strong Portuguese legal traditions that are really "autochthonous".

B. Portuguese Tort Law: A Comparison with the Principles of European Tort Law

Presenting a national legal system, which is rather unknown to many, might be more appealing if a comparison with another normative system is established. The comparative law studies and the tentative efforts for the harmonization of private law, notably tort law, have been a very important contribution towards the emergence of common Principles and a common *Grammatik* of a truly European private law. In this respect the *Principles of European Tort Law* of the *European Group on Tort Law*[14] is an outstanding legal work. Therefore, I will compare Portuguese tort law with the *Principles*. At the same time this exercise allows an explanation of national law and a test of the aforementioned *Principles*. 16

At a first glance, we can observe that the *Principles* are sometimes broader, sometimes narrower, than the CC. They are *broader* in Chapter 3 (Causation) and Chapter 9 (Multiple tortfeasors). The last set of problems is regulated very briefly in Art. 490[15], all the questions concerning solidarity of the tortfeasors are rather established on general rules concerning solidary *obligations* and solidary credits (Artt. 512–533) that may apply independently of the sources of obligations (tort, contract, unjust enrichment, etc.). The first group of norms is more impressive. In fact, the Portuguese CC does not have such a set of norms regulating causation such as provided by Chapter 3 of the *Principles*. As we shall see, there is only one rule concerning causation (Art. 563) and some reference is made to the problem of *potential causes* in Artt. 491, 492, 493 (1), 616 (2) and 807 (2). The *Principles* are sometimes *narrower*; because they regulate neither all situations of strict liability nor limitation of action, deliberately leaving this to national law.[16] 17

Portuguese tort law is divided into three sets of norms.[17] The first one is on Artt. 483–510 concerning extra-contractual liability. In our law, besides the general clause of liability (Art. 483 CC), there are two particular cases: offences 18

[14] Published in H. Koziol/B.C. Steininger (eds.), *European Tort Law* 2002 (2003), 562 et seq. *Principles of European Tort Law* as of 3 May 2003. See the most recent and definitive version at http://www.egtl.org/Principles/index.htm.

[15] Art. 490 CC: "If there are multiple actors, instigators or collaborators of the wrongful act, all of them are liable for the damage caused by them."

[16] Art. 498 CC establishes a general rule of limitation in tort law of 3 years after knowledge of the right, even though without knowledge of the tortfeasor or the full amount of damage.

[17] See, in German, J. Sinde Monteiro/R. Moura Ramos/H. Hörster, Portugal, in: C. von Bar (ed.), *Deliktsrecht in Europa* (1994).

against consideration and credit (Art. 484 CC) and damages caused by advice and recommendations[18, 19]; Art. 486 (Omissions); Artt. 487–489 (Fault and capacity to commit torts); Art. 490 (Multiple tortfeasors); Artt. 491–493 (Inversions of the burden of the proof); Art. 494 (Limitation of damage); Art. 495 (Compensation in case of death or physical injury); Art. 496 (Non-pecuniary losses); Art. 497 (Solidary liability);[20] Art. 498 (Limitation); Artt. 499–510 (Strict liability). Another set of rules is to be found in Artt. 562–572 (obligation to compensate), because these rules are common to tort and contract liability[21]. Here one finds the rules about damages, causation and contributory negligence: Art. 562 (General principle) – *restitutio in natura*; Art. 564 (Causation); Artt. 564–569 (Damages); Artt. 570–572 (Contributory negligence). Thirdly, norms regulating defences are to be found in Artt. 334 et seq., especially: Art. 336 (self-help), Art. 337 (self-defence), Art. 339 (necessity) and Art. 340 (consent).

1. Basic Norm

19 The Basic Norm of the *Principles* states: (1) "A person to whom damage to another is legally attributable is liable to compensate that damage. (2) Damage may be attributed in particular to the person (a) whose behaviour constituting fault has caused it; or (b) whose abnormally dangerous activity has caused it; or (c) whose auxiliary has caused it."

20 The basic norm establishes very clearly the old principle *casum sentit dominus*.[22] This principle is obviously recognised by Portuguese law as well, in

[18] Art. 484 (*Action injurious to personal standing or good name*): "Whoever affirms or disseminates a fact capable of prejudicing the credit or good name of any person, private individual or legal person, is responsible for the damage caused." Art. 485 (*Advice, recommendations or information*): "(1) Mere advice, recommendation or information do not confer liability on whoever gives it, even though there may be negligence on their part. (2) The obligation to compensate exists, however, when the responsibility for damage has been assumed, when there is a legal duty to give advice, recommendation or information and this has been done with negligence or intent to harm, or when the behaviour of the agent constitutes a punishable act."

[19] Recent special torts are related with the certification service providers and online service providers (the Directive 2000/31/EC: Directive on electronic commerce). Decree-Law 62/2003, 3 April implements EC Directive EC/1993/93 on Digital Signature. Art. 26 establishes civil liability of the certifying entity towards the certificate titular and third parties for non-accomplishment of legal duties. See J. Sinde Monteiro, Assinatura electrónica e certificação (A Directiva 1999/93/CE e o Decreto-Lei n.° 290-D/99, de 2 de Agosto), [2001] *Revista de Legislação e Jurisprudência* (RLJ), 261–272.

[20] Tortfeasors are liable *in solidum*, according to Art. 497 (1) CC. The definitive apportionment of compensation between several tortfeasors depends on the degree of fault and the consequences of their acts (Art. 497 (2) CC).

[21] The main differences between contractual liability and non-contractual liability in Portuguese law are the following: (1) the debtor is presumed to have acted in fault in case of non-performance or defective performance of a contractual duty (Art. 799 (1)); (2) Limitation period in tort law is 3 years (Art. 497) and 20 years in contract (Art. 309). The *cumul* of contractual and extra-contractual liability (*Anspruchsnormenkonkurrenz*) is accepted by literature and case law, and plays an important role in cases of medical liability and transport liability. Case law accepts that non-pecuniary damages may be compensated under contract law.

[22] See H. Koziol, Die „Principles of European Tort Law" der „European Group on Tort Law", [2004] *Zeitschrift für Europäisches Privatrecht* (ZeuP), 237.

Art. 483, because compensation is only possible if all the conditions are fulfilled.

The *Principles* start by a dynamic and plural source of tort liability, which indeed reflects the reality of our times. Perhaps in a still romantic way, the Portuguese CC concentrates the *General Principle* (Art. 483) on the individual person, who acts with fault and causes damage to another. Art. 483 (1) CC states, "Whoever, whether by wilful misconduct (*dolus*) or by negligence unlawfully infringes the rights of another person or any legal provision intended to safeguard the interests of others, must compensate the injured party for damage arising from such violation." Strict liability, liability for dangerous activities and liability for auxiliaries are seen as a deviance from the main rule. Art. 483 (2) confirms this idea by stating: "an obligation to pay compensation when there is no fault shall arise only in cases specified by law." Thus, fault liability is the principle and strict liability is an exception. Neither analogical application, nor a general clause is accepted. This might seem to be only a question of style, but I suppose it shows that the *Weltanschauung* of the Portuguese legislator of the 50s and 60s was quite different from that of the drafters of the *Principles*. An urban society of risk, rather than a rural society; an economy based on enterprises, rather than on individual entrepreneurs, might well be the explanation why the drafters of the *Principles* gave fault a place which is at the same level as an "abnormally dangerous activity" or the liability for the "auxiliary". 21

This is indeed not a matter of drafting style, since this will have effects in the whole structure of the tort law presentation. The Portuguese CC structures the whole question on the basis of the General Principle of a faulty and wrongful behaviour of a person with capacity to commit torts and from then on inserts exceptions, inversions of the burden of the proof, or particular regimes. 22

The Portuguese CC distinguishes between *liability for wrongful acts* (Subsection I: Artt. 483–498) – where one also finds general rules about non-pecuniary losses, multiple tortfeasors, solidarity, limitation – from *strict liability* (Subsection II: Artt. 499–508). On the other hand, rules concerning damages, causation and contributory negligence are common to contract law and, thus, are provided in another section of the CC (Artt. 562–572). 23

The *Principles* follow another structure: there a title (I) on the *General Conditions of Liability* (damage and causation); one (II) on the *Bases of Liability* (Liability based on fault, Strict Liability, and Liability for Others); another (IV) on *Defences*; another one (V) on *Multiple tortfeasors* and finally one title (VI) on *Remedies*. 24

Summarizing, some of the substantial differences we have already mentioned are: the *Principles* are an isolated body of norms on tort law, and thus have to regulate some issues that in a Civil Code could be regulated elsewhere (solidarity, causation, damages, contributory negligence, defences). The division 25 between liability for wrongful and faulty acts on the one hand, and strict liability on the other is a signal of a rural and less dynamic society of the 50s in Portugal.

2. General Conditions of Liability

a) Damage

26 As a general comment, one can observe that, although the *Principles* accept the concept of wrongfulness, they avoid the use of such "name".[23] That is understandable in an effort to conjugate different European traditions. For the CC wrongfulness is also a basic concept in tort law. Art. 483 (1) enounces two types of wrongfulness: (1) violation of "rights of another" (*erga omnes* rights) and (2) violation of legal provisions intended to protect the interests of others ("protective norms"). Moreover, the literature agrees that there is a third type of wrongful behaviour: intentional damage *contra bonos mores* (*Gute Sitten*) that is to be found in Art. 334 – abuse of a right (*Rechtsmissbrauch, abuso do direito*).

27 As Koziol states, "in essence, the European Group's *Principles* acknowledge wrongfulness as one decisive factor."[24] In that respect, the *Principles* describe the scope of protection of interests (Art. 2:102). The most extensive protection to *life, bodily or mental integrity, liberty and dignity* (Art. 2:102 (2)) is guaranteed by the *Principles*. So does the CC. In fact, Art. 483 (1) protects "rights of another", which include *personality rights*. Artt. 70–81 CC provide an extensive protection of personality rights, including the General Personality Right (*Allgemeines Persönlichkeitsrecht*).[25] Thus the CC provides an extensive protection to personality rights. The enumeration of protected rights in the *Principles* is only indicative; however the catalogue of personality rights may be considered short, taking into account European case law.

28 Property rights' protection (including rights over intangible property) seems to be narrower than that of personality rights. That may well be the case also in court practice in Portugal. But technically, no distinction is made between the protection provided to personality rights and rights *in rem*, since the law states that it is wrongful to violate (absolute) "rights of another" (Art. 483 (1)).[26]

[23] See R. Zimmermann, Principles of European Contract Law and Principles of European Tort Law: Comparison and Points of Contact, in: H. Koziol/B.C. Steininger (eds.), *European Tort Law 2003* (2004).

[24] H. Koziol, The concept of wrongfulness under the Principles of European Tort Law, in: H. Koziol/B.C. Steininger (supra fn. 14), 552 et seq.

[25] Some authors (Oliveira Ascensão, Carvalho Fernandes) do not accept the concept of a general personality right. They state that Art. 70 provides a general clause, where one can include the fundamental rights provided by the extensive catalogue of our Constitution or by the European Convention on Human Rights or even the European Charter of Fundamental Rights (especially after the approval of the Constitutional Treaty).

[26] See R. Zimmermann (supra fn. 23), 12.

But the most important difference – at least in style – lies in paragraph (4) of Art. 2:102. The *Principles* protect, to some extent, as a starting point, pure economic interests and contractual relationships (Art. 2:102 (4)).[27] This has been subject of a hard discussion in Portugal. In fact, Art. 483 (1) establishes an obligation to compensate for damage caused whenever the "rights of another" have been unlawfully violated. According to the intent of the author of the preparatory work on the Civil Code[28], as well as the doctrine and prevailing jurisprudence, only the "absolute rights" (*erga omnes*) are to be protected by tort law, and that is the traditional solution in Portuguese law. There was some influence from the German law and doctrine in the preliminary work of the current CC, although the formulation of Art. 483 (1) is considerably more open than the corresponding § 823 I of the BGB.[29] Thereinafter, the main doctrine and case law state that *relative rights* deserve no protection under tort law.[30] 29

Exceptionally, an action grounded in Art. 483 and Art. 334 (abuse of a right, intentional behaviour *contra bonos mores*) may be accepted in an intentional case of *inducement of breach of a contract*.[31] Another possibility may be the existence of *culpa in contrahendo*[32] or other legal instruments, such as, "contracts whose protective scope extends to certain third parties" (*Verträge mit Schutzwirkung zugunsten Dritter*). But at this point, we are already outside tort law. 30

Portuguese tort law can be considered as following a "middle road". It follows the recent tendency to avoid a general and virtually unlimited scope of 31

[27] See the critics of R. Zimmermann (supra fn. 23), 13–14. However, the intention of the drafters is not to provide such an extensive protection as Zimmermann states, as explains H. Koziol (supra fn. 22), 243. The correct interpretation of the whole Art. 2:102 leads to a scarce protection of pure economic loss or contractual relationships under tort law.

[28] A. Vaz Serra, Responsabilidade Civil (Requisitos), [1960] *Boletim do Ministério da Justiça* (BMJ), no. 92, 37 et seq. (122, no. 13) and Responsabilidade de Terceiros no Não-Cumprimento das Obrigações, [1959] BMJ, 85, 345 et seq.

[29] See J. Sinde Monteiro, Manuel de Andrade und der Einfluss des BGB auf das Portugiesische Zivilgesetzbuch von 1966, in: E. Jayme/H.P. Mansel (eds.), *Auf dem Wege zu einem gemeineuropäischen Privatrecht – 100 Jahre BGB und die lusophonen Länder* (1977), 41.

[30] See J. Sinde Monteiro, Portugal, in: J. Spier (ed.), *The Limits of Expanding Liability, Eight Cases in a Fundamental Perspective* (1998). See also M Almeida, *A Responsabilidade Civil do Banqueiro Perante os Credores da Empresa Financiada* (2003) and M. Frada, O problema e os limites da responsabilidade dos auditores, [2002] *Direito e Justiça*, 159–169.

[31] See the recent work of S. Júnior, *Responsabilidade Civil de Terceiro por Lesão de Direito de Crédito* (2003). This dissertation deals with the question of liability of third parties that cause damage to a credit right of another. The traditional Portuguese doctrine advocates that a credit right only has *inter partes* effects, and thus – except in cases of abuse of right – a third party may not be held liable for violating it. On the contrary personality rights, real rights or intellectual property rights are absolute rights, with efficacy *erga omnes* and their violation might be argued against any wrongdoer. The author, however, after a comprehensive analysis of comparative law, defends that Portuguese law should follow the North-American (e.g., *tort of interference with contractual relations)*, French and Italian doctrine, which accepts, under some circumstances, that a third party might be held liable when breaching a credit right.

[32] See E. Silva, *Da Responsabilidade Pré-Contratual por Violação dos Deveres de Informação* (2003).

Artt. 1382 and 1393 Code Civil,[33] as well as the overly compartmentalized model of the BGB and the piecemeal approach of the English law of torts.[34]

32 Preventive expenses as recoverable damage were accepted by some Portuguese courts. These cases deal with accidents with public transport buses, which had to stop running for some time due to necessary repair work. The bus company had replacement buses that were used and the Court awarded compensation for a proportion of the costs of maintenance and even a proportion of the costs of the replacement buses.[35]

33 Art. 2:103 (legitimacy of damage) cannot be found in the aforementioned Portuguese rules. However, Art. 334 CC, which forbids the exercise of a right against the *Gute Sitten*, leads to the same conclusion, i.e., "losses relating to activities and sources which are regarded as illegitimate cannot be recovered."

34 The *Principles* state that the court may estimate the extent of damage where proof of the exact amount would be too difficult or too costly. Such a rule does not exist in Portugal. However Art. 566 (3) accepts a calculation of damage according to *equity* if the exact extent of losses cannot be proved, and Art. 564 (2) allows forwarding to an ulterior decision when a future damage is not yet possible to calculate.

b) Causation

(i) Conditio sine qua non

35 The *Principles* depart from the *conditio sine qua non* theory, the "but-for test". This seems the logical solution. Portuguese CC (tries to) escape from this starting point, and rather adopts adequacy theory as the *moto* for all causation problems.[36]

[33] For a complete overview of the question in Portugal, see C. von Bar, *The Common European Law of Torts* I (1998), 22 et seq.

[34] W. van Gerven/J. Lever/P. Larrouche/C. von Bar/G. Viney, *Tort Law – Scope of Protection* (1997), 55. This recent trend is also followed by the Dutch, Swiss, Italian and Greek codifications. They take as a "starting point a general provision founded on sufficiently flexible concepts to adjust to new situations, while at the same time limiting or excluding certain heads of damage." See also D. Moura, *Da Responsabilidade Pré-contratual em Direito Internacional Privado* (2001), 188.

[35] Awarding compensation for a proportion of the costs of the replacement buses is, however, already outside the scope of protection of the rule concerning "preventive expenses". See A. Abrantes Geraldes, *Indemnização do dano da privação do uso* (2001), 42 et seq. The author quotes a decision of the Lisbon Court of Appeal (9 March 1989), and decisions of the Court of Justice of Lisbon from 31 October 1994 and 7 March 1996. More recently the Lisbon Court of Appeal decision of 21 January 1999 denied this damage.

[36] This is beginning to be criticized, See A. Menezes Cordeiro, *A Responsabilidade dos Administradores das Sociedades Comerciais* (1997), who defends a return to *conditio sine qua non*, complemented, in a second step by the *protective purpose of the rule theory*. His theory is in accordance with the *Principles* in what a return to *conditio sine qua non* would concern, but the over-consideration of the protective purpose of the rule theory and the "abandonment" of the adequacy theory is a little too exaggerated. The *Principles*, on the contrary, do take into consideration the adequacy theory (Art. 3:201 a)).

And indeed, as Varela[37] states, *conditio sine qua non* is sometimes too broad (leading to liability for unforeseeable or unpredictable damage),[38] sometimes too narrow (as in the cases of potential causes). The *Principles* also deviate from the *conditio sine qua non* in a number of cases: Art. 3:102 Concurrent causes, Art. 3.104 (1) Potential causes, and Art. 3.105 (uncertain partial causation or minimal causation).

The *Principles* regulate in detail the delicate problems of causation (Chapter 3. of Title II) and the connected problem of multiple tortfeasors (Title V); on the contrary, the Portuguese CC only provides two articles concerning these problems (Artt. 563 and 490). Art. 563 states that: "the obligation to compensate only exists in relation to damage that the injured *probably* would not have suffered had he not suffered harm". Literature and case law agree that the theory of adequacy has been adopted and they normally omit the reasoning of the "but-for test".[39] On the other hand, if the damage was caused by several tortfeasors, be they joint tortfeasors or instigators, the solution is considered to be the following: the victim shall have the right to demand full compensation from any of the tortfeasors who are liable *in solidum*;[40] redress action, thereinafter, shall be decided upon according to each of the tortfeasor's participation in the damage; but there is a *presumption of equal shares* in that liability (Art. 497 (2) and Art. 516 CC). 36

The *Principles* offer solutions to some very delicate problems on causation that are not definitively solved under Portuguese law (concurrent causes, alternative causes, potential causes and uncertain partial causation). The solutions proposed are very progressive and are not to be found in Portuguese literature. However, since there is no mainstream doctrine in these issues, the *Principles* might be well-accepted in the future. As Zimmermann acknowledged "the chapter on causation breaks new ground."[41] An example of an innovative proposal is Art. 3:106. Koziol states the solution proposed is important in order to recognise the theory of "loss of a chance".[42] Portuguese case law recognises this theory and has applied it.[43] 37

[37] J. Antunes Varela, *Das Obrigações em Geral* (1996).

[38] This critic to *condition sine qua non* theory is only valid if it were the only criterion of causation. However, the *Principles* use some other "normative" criteria.

[39] However, one could argue that Art. 562 is normally considered as establishing the principle of natural restitution. Nevertheless, one can read it as a statement of the *conditio sine qua non*. It says that one shall reintegrate the situation that would exist if the damaging event had not taken place. Moreover, Art. 483 imposes liability for damage that "results" (*resultantes*) from the activity. To *result* from an activity leads us to the 'but-for test' reasoning.

[40] J. Antunes Varela (supra fn. 37).

[41] R. Zimmermann (supra fn. 23), 27.

[42] H. Koziol (supra fn. 22), 246.

[43] Lisbon Court of Appeal decision of 8 July 1999, in [1999] *Colectânea de Jurisprudência* (CJ), IV, 97–104. The decision was taken on the basis of "equity", and it is stated in Art. 566 (3) that damage may be calculated that way, when there are no other solutions.

38 Our literature and case law state that since an activity has *definitely and irreversibly* led the victim to suffer damage, a *subsequent* activity or occurrence or other circumstance, including natural events, which alone would have caused the same damage, is to be disregarded even if it lies within the victim's sphere. In Portuguese law the rule is that the *potential* cause (*causa virtual*) is irrelevant. However, in exceptional cases the legislator attributed relevance to the *potential* cause, excluding liability if that is proven. This happens in Artt. 491 (liability for damage caused by incompetent persons), 492 (ruined buildings), 493 (1) (liability for detention, surveillance or maintenance of immovable or movable things or animals), 493 (2) (liability for dangerous activities),[44] 616 (2) (third party liability in case of "paulianus action" [oblique action of a creditor]) and 807 (2) (delay on the part of a debtor). In these cases there are *presumptions of fault* (or for other reasons an aggravated liability) and the legislator tries to "compensate" that "hard regime" giving the possibility to escape liability by proving that such damage would have occurred for a different reason, that is, the damage would have occurred even if the wrongdoer had not breached any duty of care.[45] In all other cases, the potential cause is disregarded.

(ii) Scope of Liability

39 The *Principles* list in detail several criteria and theories that might be used in order to determine the scope of liability (Art. 3:201). The inclusion of this Section on the Chapter concerning causation is due to a "compromise"[46] because some legal systems do not make the separation between causation and scope of liability. The Portuguese legal system is in fact one of these. This list is also welcome in Portugal, where adequacy dominates and the protective purpose of the rule theory is sometimes adopted. But under "adequacy" Portuguese courts sometimes apply some other policies although not expressly recognized. For example some scholars and some courts defend that, in the field of wrongful acts, the scope of liability should be broader than in the field of strict liability,[47] which is in accordance with Art. 3:201 (c).

40 As I previously said, both scholars and courts defend that Art. 563 adopts the *Adäquanzlehre* elaborated by Von Kries.[48] Art. 563 departs from the *Äquivalenztheorie* (theory of equivalence), however the adverb "*probably*" is understood by the literature as consecrating the *adequacy* theory. The fact must not only be a *conditio sine qua non*, it must also be adequate, i.e., the probable cause of damage.[49] Recently, the adequacy theory has been challenged in Por-

[44] Liability for damage caused by things and dangerous activities is similar to Artt. 2050 and 2051 *Codice Civile* – see C. von Bar (supra fn. 33), 118.
[45] I. Galvão Telles, *Direito das Obrigações* (7th edn. 1997), 410 et seq.
[46] H. Koziol (supra fn. 22), 244.
[47] See J. Antunes Varela (supra fn. 37).
[48] M. Andrade, *Teoria Geral das Obrigações* (3rd edn. 1966), 351 et seq.; J. Antunes Varela (supra fn. 37), 916; L. Menezes Leitão, *Direito das Obrigações* (3rd edn. 2003), 346.
[49] L. Menezes Leitão (supra fn. 48), 347.

tuguese literature by the protective purpose of the violated rule theory (*Schutzzweck der Norm*).[50] This theory is applied and complements the reasoning of the adequacy theory avoiding establishing causation in some cases. Portuguese courts are beginning to accept the method of interpreting the law according to its purpose ("teleologische Interpretation").[51]

3. Bases of Liability

The *Principles* distinguish conditions of liability based on fault (Chapter 4), strict liability (Chapter 5) and liability for others (Chapter 6). 41

a) Liability Based on Fault

In Portugal, one distinguishes two categories of fault: intent (*dolus*) or negligence. The required standard of conduct is abstract (objective standard on the assessment of fault), as prescribed in Art. 487 (2) taken "by reference to the diligence expected of a dutiful *pater familias*, having regard to the circumstances of each case." The burden of proof lies on the plaintiff.[52] There are no main differences between this norm and the *Principles*, except that these are much more detailed in the description of the criteria to assess the required standard of conduct (Art. 4:102). Moreover, the *Principles* suggest some interesting criteria such as the foreseeability of the damage, the relation of proximity or special reliance between those involved, and the availability and the costs of precautionary or alternative methods. According to Portuguese law, a "higher" standard is demanded in case of professionals. For example, a physician must act according to his skills and mainly according to his field of activity. The reasonable person is not the "person in the street". 42

Koziol[53] explains that the goal of paragraph (2) of Art. 4:102 is to avoid liability of persons with below-average abilities (such as children, incompetent adults, etc.). Under Portuguese law, Art. 488, regulating the capacity to commit torts (*Deliktsfähigkeit*), achieves the same objective: "1. A person who, when the event occurred, was incapable for any reason of understanding or of forming intent shall not be liable for the consequences of the injurious event, unless he wilfully caused himself to be in that condition, and that condition was temporary[54]. 2. Persons who are aged less than seven years or are subject to a psychiatric disorder shall be deemed not to bear liability." Persons with disabilities, children and the elderly are subject to a comparison where the model becomes "a reasonable person with disabilities, a reasonable child of 43

[50] See: L. Menezes Leitão (supra fn. 48), 348; L. Menezes Leitão *Responsabilidade do Gestor*, 281 and A. Menezes Cordeiro (supra fn. 36), 532 et seq.

[51] H. Koziol, Austria, in: J. Spier (ed.), *Unification of Tort Law: Causation* (2000), 12.

[52] Art. 487. *Fault*. 1. It shall be incumbent on the injured party to prove the fault of the person who caused the injury, unless there was a legal presumption of fault. 2. Fault shall be assessed, in the absence of any other legal criterion, by reference to the diligence expected of a dutiful *paterfamilias*, having regard to the circumstances of each case."

[53] H. Koziol (supra fn. 24), no. 16.

[54] This second part recognises the rule *actio libera in causa*.

that age, a reasonable old person of that age with that kind of problem". However, Portuguese doctrine defends that, "except for children, a new requisite is added in order to avoid the judgment of fault: these kinds of persons must act taking into consideration their own limits, which may lead to *abstentions* from acting in extreme cases."[55]

44 Art. 4:102 (3) of the *Principles* states, "Rules which prescribe or forbid certain conduct have to be considered when establishing the required standard of conduct" and Portuguese doctrine also defends that when someone violates a protective rule, she shall be considered liable in fault for the damage caused. A judicial presumption of fault follows the violation of a protective rule. In fact, "if causing damage when performing a dangerous activity was sufficient for the legislator to establish a presumption of fault [Art. 493 (2) CC], it seems even more convincing that a presumption also exists whenever a rule that aims in abstract to avoid certain danger is infringed, and the danger becomes a reality".[56] In case law, this viewpoint has been accepted[57], even if not always supported by a tenable argumentation. Case law is giving more attention to literature that defends the existence of a "judicial presumption of fault".[58] Nowadays, it is said to be one of the most interesting and practical features of the Portuguese tort law system. Legal provisions such as safety regulations (on lifts, for instance), a significant set of traffic rules or criminal rules and rules commanding professional good practice can be regarded as "protective rules".[59]

45 There is no specific norm imposing a duty to protect others from damage but Art. 486 (omissions) states, "Mere omissions shall give rise to an obligation to make reparation for the damage where, regardless of any other legal requirements, there was a duty, by *law* or by virtue of a *legal act*, to take the action which was not taken." Thus, if a law or a contract imposes the duty to protect others from damage, that action is required. For example, Art. 200 Penal Code imposes a duty to rescue; Art. 284 of the Penal Code imposes the duty of the physician to treat patients in a severe condition. In the field of family law, spouses have the duty to protect the other from damage (Artt. 1672 and 1674 CC) and parents are obliged towards their children (Art. 1878 CC). The doctrine also considers the case when the actor creates or controls a dangerous situation. Other situations like the special relationship between the parties or dis-

[55] J. Sinde Monteiro/M. Veloso, Portuguese report, in: P. Widmer (ed.), *Unification of Tort Law: Fault* (2005). H. Koziol (supra fn. 24), 556, seems to defend a different position. He states, "their [persons with below-average abilities] mere existence, which inevitably implies their participation in social intercourse, cannot be sufficient reason for establishing liability, even if their unavoidable behaviour does not comply with objective standards."

[56] J. Sinde Monteiro, *Responsabilidade por conselhos, recomendações ou informações* (1989), 264; M. Teixeira de Sousa, *O concurso de títulos de aquisição da prestação* (1988), 319.

[57] *Supremo Tribunal de Justica* (Supreme Court of Justice, STJ) 21 February 1961, in J. Sinde Monteiro (supra fn. 56), 267 and fn. 305.

[58] Évora Court of Appeal 9 December 1977, [1977] CJ IV, 90; Porto Court of Appeal 11 December 1981, [1981] CJ V, 274.

[59] See J. Sinde Monteiro/M. Veloso (supra fn. 55).

proportion between the seriousness of the harm and the ease of avoiding it are still being discussed in the literature. Thus, Art. 4:103 of the *Principles* is indeed a step ahead from the individualistic regulation of the CC.[60]

The *Principles* prescribe an inversion of the burden of proving fault in case of dangerous activities (Art. 4:201) as does Portuguese law (Art. 493 (2)). In this case the defendant has to provide positive proof that he used all necessary preventive measures required by the circumstances. Potential cause does not exclude causation. 46

The CC has some other situations of reversal of the burden of proof. Art. 491 on liability for minors or mentally disabled persons will be analysed later. Art. 492 (1) imposes liability on the owner or the tenant of a building or other facility if it falls down due to a construction or maintenance defect and causes damage to another. However, if the damage is caused by a maintenance defect, only the person obliged, by law or by contract, to preserve the building is liable, according to paragraph (2). Art. 493 imposes liability on the person who possesses a movable or immovable thing, as well as on the persons who are in charge of surveying animals for the damage they (the things or the animals) cause. In all these cases the defendant may prove he acted in accordance with the required standard of conduct or that a potential cause would have also caused the damage. A similar solution (inversion of the burden of the proof of fault) can be found in the *Principles* for situations like ruined buildings or detention of animals, as these normally involve an increased risk. 47

Enterprise liability is an "innovative proposal"[61] of the *European Group on Tort Law* and as such is not to be found in the CC. However, the CC provides strict vicarious liability and there is no-fault product liability. However, the scope of enterprise liability is clearly broader, although its regime consists only in an inversion of the burden of the proof. But from a careful analysis, we can conclude that it does not enlarge liability that much compared with Portuguese law. Under "Enterprise Liability" we can find cases concerning liability for: (1) auxiliaries; (2) technical equipment; (3) products; and (4) services. 48

Under Portuguese law there is strict liability for the acts of auxiliaries (Art. 500 and Art. 800 CC). Technical equipment may fall under the inversion of the burden of the proof of Art. 493 (1) CC. Product liability is strict, according to the European Directive. Concerning liability for services, the parties to the contract are protected by the contract law regime, which also provides an inversion of the burden of proof (Art. 799 (1) CC). Thus, Portuguese law only offers less protection than the proposed Enterprise Liability of the *Principles* to third parties who suffer damage arising from a service. 49

[60] H. Koziol (supra fn. 22), 249: "Die Principles gehen weiter als die meisten Rechtsordnungen (…)".

[61] R. Zimmermann (supra fn. 23).

b) Strict Liability

50 On this issue there is also a basic difference: the *Principles* accept a general clause of strict liability for abnormally dangerous activities[62] and accept analogical application of strict liability legal categories. The CC prescribes that there is only strict liability when the law so provides (Art. 487 (2)).

51 The most important cases of "liability without fault" in the CC are[63]: vicarious liability (Art. 500 CC); liability of the holder of an animal (Art. 502 CC); liability of the keeper of a car (Art. 503 CC); liability of the keeper of gas or electric energy structures (Art. 509 CC), and liability for damage caused to immovables in the neighbourhood (such as damage caused by nuisance or by excavations) (Artt. 1346–1352 CC).

52 Some of the most important supplementary statutes imposing strict liability are: Product Liability Act (DL 131/2001, 24 April); State Liability Act (Decree 48051, 21 November 1967); Environmental Basic Law 11/87, 7 April 1987; Clinical Trials Act (Law 19/2003, 19 August); Organ Donation Act (Law 12/93, 22 April); Activities with radioactivity sources (Decree-law 153/96, 30 August [with amendments]); protection of people exposed to ionising radiation (Decree-law 348/89, 12 October [with amendments]).

c) Liability for Others

(i) Liability for Minors or Mentally Disabled Persons

53 There are very strong similarities between Art. 6:101 of the *Principles* and Art. 491 CC. The small difference is that the CC only directly applies when the obligation to take care of others derives from *law* or *contract*. The *Principles* do not have such a positivist perspective. Nevertheless the practical results may be the same, since some non-legal or non-contractual relations could – according to some doctrine – lead to the obligation of surveillance of another who is a minor or subject to mental disability if the principle of *good faith* and *bonus morus* so imposes. Both under Portuguese law and the *Principles*, is this not really a case of strict liability[64], since the defendant may prove that "he took all proper care to prevent it [the damage]."

54 "Art. 491 CC establishes a presumption of fault of supervisors of persons lacking natural capacity for the damage caused to others. "Natural incapacity" is a concept different from tortious incapacity. It means the incapacity of self-determination. A conspicuous example of this difference would be the case of minors. Minors of seven or more, although incapable of ruling their own lives, are, nevertheless, tortiously liable (in general). Amongst other features of this

[62] Art. 927 of the Brazilian Civil Code introduced a general clause of strict liability for *dangerous activities*. See A. Pereira, Brazil, in: H. Koziol/B.C. Steininger (supra fn. 23), 457.

[63] See also the special cases of: Emergency situation (Art. 339 (2) second part CC); Liability based on equity of incapable agents (Art. 489 CC).

[64] See H. Koziol (supra fn. 22), 253.

kind of liability[65], we would like to enhance the fact that it has been deemed as a case of liability for one's own act[66]. Another interesting dimension of supervisor's liability (in particular, parental liability) is the fact that the courts accept the idea of a *culpa in educando,* which shows that the judgment of fault might in some cases take into consideration facts previous to the act (of the direct agent, the minor)."[67]

(ii) Liability for Auxiliaries

55 The rule provided by Art. 6:102 of the *Principles* is similar to Art. 500 CC, which prescribes *vicarious strict liability.* Also in contract law, Art. 800 CC imposes liability of the debtor for acts committed by helpers or representatives.

56 A possible defence, accepted by Portuguese case law, for the principal is to prove that the auxiliary caused damage outside the scope of his functions, even if the action took place during the time schedule of the service. On the other hand, Art. 500 (2) expressly considers the principal liable even if the auxiliary acted intentionally or against his instructions (but within the scope of her functions). Portuguese literature considers that the dogmatic ground for this strict liability lies in a "guarantee theory", rather than in the "risk theory". That is, the principal is an economic guarantor of the victim, since he has the right of redress towards the auxiliary (Art. 500 (3)).[68]

4. Defences

a) Defences in General

57 Defences are regulated in the General Part of the CC (Artt. 336–340). There we find *self-help, self-defence, necessity* and *consent*[69]. The CC tries to define the defences; the *Principles* leave it to the courts and the doctrine. Furthermore, the Principles state: "(2) Whether liability is excluded depends upon the weight of these justifications on the one hand and the conditions of liability on the other. (3) In extraordinary cases, liability may instead be reduced." This solution is in accordance with Portuguese law where Art. 339 (necessity) imposes an obligation to compensate if the tortfeasor was the only individual responsible for the danger; in other cases the court may, according to equity, impose compensation as well. On the other hand, in case an individual acts in

65 For a detailed explanation of supervisors' liability, see H. Sousa Antunes, *Responsabilidade civil dos obrigados à vigilância de pessoa naturalmente incapaz* (2000).

66 R. de Alarcão, *Direito das Obrigações* (1983), 227.

67 J. Sinde Monteiro/M. Veloso (supra fn. 55).

68 Each one's contribution depends on their faults. Often the auxiliary is the only one who acted with fault.

69 Art. 81 CC concerning voluntary limitation of personality rights is also to be taken into account when discussing consent and personal values are at stake. It states: "(1) All limitation to the exercise of personality rights is void if it is against the principles of *ordre publique.* (2) The voluntary limitation, when legal, is always revocable, even though with the duty to compensate damage to other party's legitimate expectations."

self-defence or on the basis of self-help, when they in fact have no right to do so (Art. 338), there might be a duty to compensate, depending on fault.[70]

58 Portuguese doctrine considers that there is no "*numerus clausus*" of justifications.[71] The same shall naturally be valid in the interpretation of the *Principles*. I could mention, for example, the *exercise of a right* (the exercise of the right of retention, for example), the *accomplishment of a duty*, the *prosecution of a legitimate right* (so relevant in the field of the media), or *acting within allowed risk*.

b) Defences against Strict Liability

59 The *Principles* accept only two defences against strict liability: force of nature and conduct of a third party (Art. 7:102). Thus, the fault of the victim or the conduct of the victim is not regarded as a defence.

60 The CC has no general rule concerning defences against strict liability. However, we find those defences in some particular no-fault liability provisions: Art. 505 on traffic accidents accepts: *force majeure*, act of third party and act of the victim as defences; Art. 509 (2) on damage caused by electric energy or gas accepts alone *force majeure*; and Art. 7 of the Product Liability Act makes reference to *force majeure*, act of third party and act of the victim.

61 The *act of the victim* is thus mentioned in Art. 505 CC, leading to the exclusion of (strict) liability of the holder of a car. A traditional and prevailing opinion accepted that also the non-faulty activity of the victim would lead to the exclusion of liability[72]. However, some authors do not agree with such a solution, because they state there is the aim of protecting the victim (especially in case of compulsory insurance, as is the case). The solution of Art. 7 (1) of the Product Liability Act has been pointed out as an example to follow in strict liability cases.[73]

c) Contributory Conduct or Activity

62 Artt. 570–572 regulate contributory negligence in a very similar way to the *Principles*. The main difference is that the CC puts more emphasis on the contributory *negligence* and *its consequences*, and the *Principles* have a broader perspective ("*fault and any other matters*") but this may be only a matter of style. A substantial difference is to be found concerning the relation between contributory negligence and presumed fault. According to Art. 570 (2) CC,

[70] Art. 338 excludes compensation in case of error about the conditions of direct action and self-defence if the error is "excusable".

[71] The same rule applies in penal law (see Art. 31 Penal Code).

[72] See, for example, STJ 31 March 1993 (www.dgsi.pt). The Court disregards the fact that the victim was a three year old child and excluded liability of the holder of the car who ran over the child.

[73] This provision states: "If a faulty act of the victim also caused the damage, the Court may reduce compensation or exempt from liability the defendant, taking into consideration all circumstances".

contributory negligence excludes liability if it were based on a presumption of fault.

5. Multiple Tortfeasors

Art. 490 states: "If there are multiple actors, instigators or collaborators of the wrongful act, all of them are liable for the damage caused by them." Art. 497 prescribes the solidary regime in tort law. Details over solidarity are in Artt. 512 et seq, which prescribe norms very similar to Art. 9:102. The difference is that Art. 9:101 (3) accepts a hypothesis of *several liability*, when there is a basis for attributing only part of the damage to each of a number of persons liable to the victim. Under Portuguese law, this is debatable.[74] Varela states that the victim shall always be protected by the solidarity regime in cases of joint tortfeasors, cumulative causation or mere coincidence of causes of different nature. In the internal relations, there may be "perfect solidarity" or only "apparent solidarity". The regime prescribed by the *Principles* seems more fair towards the tortfeasors. Why should they bear the risk of the other's insolvency in cases when "there is reasonable basis for attributing only part of the damage to each of a number of persons liable to the victim?" 63

6. Remedies

a) Remedies in General

Remedies are ruled in a Chapter that applies both to contractual and non-contractual obligations. This is the advantage of a complete regulation of patrimonial civil law. Remedies are reinstatement or restitution (Art. 562). Monetary compensation is ordered whenever reinstatement or restitution is not possible, does not fully repair the damage or is excessively costly. Thus, there is an important difference of approach in the field of remedies. Under Portuguese law (Art. 563), *restitutio in natura* (*Naturalherstellung*) is the primary solution,[75] and pecuniary compensation shall only be awarded when restoration in kind is not possible or too burdensome to the other party. However, in practice, money payment is the rule. On the contrary, the *Principles* state that "damages are a money payment to compensate the victim" (Art. 10:101), and admit that (Art. 10:104) "instead of damages, restoration in kind can be claimed by the injured party as far as it is possible and not too burdensome to the other party." Moreover, Portuguese law also accepts periodical payments (See Art. 565 CC and Art. 10:103). 64

Considering the benefits gained through the damaging event is a consequence of the *Differenztheorie* that is adopted in Art. 566 (2) Civil Code. The main relevance of Art. 10:103 is its last part: "unless this cannot be reconciled with the purpose of the benefit." This is a very fair proposal that is not to be found expressly in the CC. One could defend such result only through a *teleological reduction* of Art. 566 (2). 65

[74] J. Antunes Varela (supra fn. 37), 954.
[75] See R. Zimmermann (supra fn. 23), 18.

b) Pecuniary Damage

66 Art. 10:201 of the *Principles* states that, "recoverable pecuniary damage is a diminution of the victim's patrimony caused by the damaging event." This includes *damnum emergens* and *lucrum cessans*, as well as provided by Art. 564 (1), and Art. 566 (2), which adopts the *Theory of Difference*. The *Principles* explicitly prescribe that: "such damage is generally determined as concretely as possible but it may be determined abstractly when appropriate, for example by reference to a market value." This is not expressly stated in the CC, but it is the practice of our case law.

67 In the case of *personal injury and death*, pecuniary damage includes loss of income, impairment of earning capacity (even if unaccompanied by any loss of income) and reasonable expenses, including cost of medical care. Most of these items fall within the general clause of Art. 564 (1): the duty to compensate includes not only the loss that was caused, but also the benefits that the victim did not obtain because of the injury. Moreover paragraph (2) of the same Art. 564 states that future damage may be compensated if it is *predictable*. Thus, under Portuguese law, it is not clear if, for example, a housewife could obtain compensation for pecuniary damage, since there is no "predictable" loss of income. This has been under discussion.[76]

68 In the *case of death*, Portuguese law has a victim-friendly statutory provision, since it does not establish a closed list of persons to whom compensation may be provided, on the contrary it even converts natural obligations into civil obligations. In fact, Art. 495 (Compensation for third parties in the event of death or bodily injury) paragraph (3) states "The right to compensation shall also be available to those entitled to require maintenance (alimony) from the injured party and to those to whom the injured party paid maintenance in fulfilment of a natural obligation." This rule is not as broad as the *Principles*, since it does not always include the persons the deceased "would have maintained if the death had not occurred" (Art. 10:202 (2) of the *Principles*).

69 On the other hand, paragraphs (1) and (2) provide: "1. Where an injury leads to death, the person responsible shall be obliged to pay compensation for the costs incurred in seeking to save the injured party, and all other expenses, not excluding funeral expenses. 2. In any such case, and in all other instances of bodily injury, a right to compensation shall be available to those who tendered help to the injured party, and to hospitals, doctors or other persons or entities which took part in treating or assisting the victim."

70 Loss, destruction and damage of things give rise to some very debatable questions. The Supreme Court of Justice (27 February 2003) decided, in case of a road accident that destroyed an "old-timer" in very good condition, that the defendant had to pay not only the *market value* of the car, but also the *economic value* the owner of the car obtained from his car: that is the compensa-

[76] About this issue, see J. Dias, *Dano Corporal* (2001).

tion must be enough to buy a car that fulfils the same conditions as the destroyed automobile. According to some doctrine, there is not only one "market value" and accepting that compensation should be equal to the "market value" would mean that tort law is "a kind of private expropriation by the market value" which would be undesirable.[77] Such a solution is not to be found directly in Art. 10:203 (1) of the *Principles*. However, its last sentence may be interpreted in such a way as to accept this decision.

Compensation for *loss of use* is also accepted in Portuguese case law and doctrine. Consequential losses may be compensated as far as they are "predictable" (Art. 564 (2)). 71

c) Non-Pecuniary Damage

Art. 10:301 (1) provides compensation for non-pecuniary damage. In order to understand clearly the important differences between the *Principles* and the CC, we should distinguish between: 72

(a) non-pecuniary damage in general;
(b) personal injury (including injury to liberty or other personality rights);
(c) non-pecuniary damage suffered by persons having a close relationship with a victim suffering a fatal injury;
(d) non-pecuniary damage suffered by persons having a close relationship with a victim suffering a very serious non-fatal injury.

(i) Non-Pecuniary Damage in General

Non-pecuniary damage is regulated in Art. 496 CC. It is an apparently simple norm that states: "For the determination of compensation, regard must be had to *non-pecuniary damage* which, due to its *seriousness, deserves protection of the law.*" Thus, the legislator left to the courts the decision on what "deserves the protection of the law". The *Principles* appeal to the notion of *scope of protection of the interest* (Art. 10:301). 73

The norm under analysis does not exclude the possibility of awarding non-pecuniary damages in case of the destruction of a *pet* or a *thing* (for example: a family treasure or souvenir), but Portuguese case law has been very conscious and careful on deciding what "deserves the protection of the law". 74

On the other hand, case law accepts that non-pecuniary damage may be compensated also in the field of contractual liability. The literature has been divided concerning this question.[78] 75

[77] J. Gomes, Custo das Reparações, valor venal ou valor de substituição? – Anotação ao Acórdão do Supremo Tribunal de Justiça de 27.2.2003, Ver. 4016/02 [2003] *Cadernos de Direito Privado* I, 52–62.

[78] See J. Antunes Varela (supra fn. 37); A. Pinto Monteiro, *Cláusula Penal e Indemnização* (1990).

(ii) Personal Injury (Including Injury to Liberty or other Personality Rights)

76 Personality rights have played a very important role in this field. In the absence of a limited enumeration of protected rights in the general provision of Art. 483 (1) CC or in Art. 496, Portuguese courts have included personality rights in the scope of protection of tortious liability rules and award compensation for non-pecuniary damage when those rights are violated. Menezes Cordeiro states that, "the XXth Century was the period of the contracts and its refinement, through "*Treu und Glauben*", the 21st century can well be the time of the *rights of the person* ..."[79] For the past 20 years there has been an increasing study and implementation of tort liability for the violation of personality rights in Portugal. We can find sentences recognising: the right to life, namely to compensate the death (a); the consecration of the right to a good environment (b); the right to health, to rest and to tranquillity (c); and the reinforcement of right to honour, reputation and credit, mostly by offences perpetrated by the mass media (d).[80]

77 In conclusion, I suppose that, in respect to problems (a) and (b), the *Principles* are in accordance with Portuguese law.

(iii) Non-Pecuniary Damage Suffered by Persons Having a Close Relationship with a Victim Suffering a Fatal Injury

78 On the contrary, concerning question (c) and (d) we will find some differences.

79 Art. 496 (2) states: "Where a victim dies, the right to compensation for non-material damage shall be available, jointly, to the spouse who is not legally separated ... and to the children or other descendants; failing the latter, to the parents or other ascendants; and, finally, to the brothers and sisters or nephews and nieces representing them. (3) The amount of compensation shall be fixed equitably by the court, having regard in any event to the circumstances mentioned in Art. 494; *in the event of death*, regard may be had not only to non-material damage *suffered by the victim* but also to such damage *suffered by the persons* entitled to compensation by virtue of the foregoing paragraph." These quite difficult norms are interpreted as follows. There are two different kinds of non-pecuniary damage: one that is suffered by the relatives described in paragraph (2); the other that is "suffered" by the deceased himself. This is a peculiarity of Portuguese law. The ground for this norm is that if all personality rights deserve protection and deserve compensation (for non-pecuniary damage), the same shall apply for the most important of all the personality rights (life).[81]

[79] A. Menezes Cordeiro (supra fn. 6).
[80] A. Menezes Cordeiro (supra fn. 6).
[81] It is discussed in the literature, whether this compensation shall be received by the heirs or by the persons referred to in paragraph (2) of Art. 496.

Thus, on the one hand, Portuguese law concedes more protection than the *Principles* since it compensates the "death damage" (*dano da morte*). On the other hand, it is quite restrictive, since only close relatives referred to in the norm may receive compensation for their non-pecuniary damage. The *Principles* allow the compensation to any person "having a close relationship with a victim". 80

In brief, it shall be made clear that, concerning non-pecuniary damage, in case of death three (possible) losses shall be compensated: (1) "loss of life" of the victim; (2) the damage suffered by the victim before dying; and (3) damage suffered by the relatives. 81

There is some debate in the doctrine concerning the amount of damages that shall be awarded in case of death (in respect to the specific "death damage"). Some authors state it should be equal for everyone (arguing with the constitutional principle of equality)[82]; others claim general rules of assessing damage should apply. The Supreme Court of Justice decided on 25 January 2002[83] that, when establishing the amount of damages for loss of life, the concrete circumstances of the life of the deceased person are relevant. The fact that the victim was 24 years old "with a long life expectancy and a promising future in front of her" was taken into consideration.[84] 82

A right of a non-married partner to compensation in case of death of the partner has been an issue of lively debate in Portuguese case law. In 2002 the Constitutional Court decided this norm unconstitutional in one particular case;[85] one year later the Supreme Court decided that the non-married partner had no right to receive compensation for non-pecuniary damage.[86] If the *Principles* were to apply, no doubt he/she would have that right. The sentence of the Constitutional Court was a ground-breaking decision in the direction of recognizing some rights to unmarried couples. As we saw, according to Art. 496 (2) CC, compensation for non-pecuniary damage in case of death is 83

[82] See D. Leite de Campos, "A vida, a morte e a sua indemnização", [1987] BMJ, 365, 15, and J. Dinis, Dano Corporal em acidentes de Viação, [2001] CJ-STJ, 7.

[83] [2002] CJ-STJ I, 62.

[84] Similarly R. Dworkin, *Life's Dominion: an argument about abortion and euthanasia* (1993), 86 et seq.: "I am now asking, then, not about justice or rights or fairness, but about tragedy and the waste of life, and therefore the insult to the sanctity of life, on different occasions? (...) ... the death of a young woman in an airplane crash is worse than the death of an old man would be. The young woman would probably otherwise have had many more years left to live. (...) But how bad this is – how great the frustration – depends on the stage of life in which it occurs, because the person has made a significant personal investment in his own life, and less if it occurs after any investment has been substantially fulfilled, or as substantially fulfilled as is anyway likely." See in Portuguese Case-law: STJ, 3-2-1976 (BMJ 254, 180); STJ 8-2-1969 (BMJ 184, 267); STJ 4-5-1971 (BMJ 207, 155); STJ 6-7-1971 (BMJ, 209, 102); STJ, 1-4-1975 (BMJ, 246, 126); STJ, 225–1979 (BMJ 287, 287); STJ, 7-5-1971 (BMJ, 207, 149).

[85] Decision of the Constitutional Court no. 275/2002, in *Diário da República* (DR) II, 24 July 2002. See A. Pereira, Portugal, in: H. Koziol/B.C. Steininger (supra fn. 14), 346.

[86] Supreme Court of Justice decision of 4 November 2003. See A. Pereira, Portugal, in: H. Koziol/B.C. Steininger (supra fn. 23), 343.

restricted to the spouse, the offspring or other descendents, subsidiary to the ascendants, and at last to the siblings or nieces/nephews of the deceased person. Thus, the traditional jurisprudence did not concede any compensation to a partner in a *de facto* marriage.[87] This Constitutional Court decision, on the contrary, considered this norm as unconstitutional, since Art. 36 of the Constitution protects all kinds of families. Art. 496 Civil Code should not exclude partners (who have lived together for more than 2 years) from the right to be compensated for non-pecuniary damage for the death of their partner.[88]

(iv) *Non-Pecuniary Damage Suffered by Persons Having a Close Relationship with a Victim Suffering a very Serious Non-Fatal Injury*

84 The *Principles* are also more generous than the CC in case of serious non-fatal injury. Non-pecuniary damage suffered by third parties (even close relatives) is normally not compensated by Portuguese courts, except in the aforementioned case of death. However, recently we can find some decisions that accept what the French doctrine calls *dommage par ricochet*. That was the case decided by the Oporto Court of Appeal on 29 June 2003 and a Supreme Court decision of 25 November 1998.

85 In the first case (Oporto Court of Appeal decision of 29 June 2003)[89], due to a car accident Mr. X suffered several injuries, including impotence. The plaintiff, his wife, sued the insurance company of the tortfeasor claiming compensation for her non-pecuniary damage (consisting of being unable to have sexual intercourse with her husband). The Court considered that this is a *direct* damage, since the wedding contract creates the mutual *duty of cohabitation* (Art. 1672 Civil Code), including having a *regular sexual life*, which is now impossible. The wedding creates also the *duty of fidelity* (Art. 1672 CC). Moreover, at the time of the accident, the wife could still have been a mother biologically, which means that another "right" was affected (Art. 68 of the Constitution: protection of motherhood). In short, the Court considered that there is a *right to marital sexual life* according to the norms of family law and the general personality right (Art. 70 CC), and ordered the insurance company to pay compensation for non-pecuniary damage of the "injured" woman.

[87] See, e.g., Supreme Court of Justice, 13 January 1994, [CJ (STJ), I, 2000]; Supreme Court of Justice 23 April 1998, CJ (STJ); Lisbon's Court of Appeal, 17 March 1992, CJ, II, 167; and Supreme Court of Justice, 20 January 1994. In the doctrine, J. França Pitão, *União de Facto no Direito Português* (2000), 30, argues against this conservative jurisprudence. It is also interesting to observe that the new Civil Code of Macao (that was created under the Portuguese sovereignty) attributes a right to be compensated for non-material damage also to the *partner* (in a *de facto* marriage).

[88] Moreover, sociological empirical data show that *common law marriage* is becoming more frequent. Most of the births occur within a marriage (76.2%); however births outside marriage are increasing steadily. They represented 23.8% in 2001. Of those, 17.8% of the parents live together, and 6% do not. Single parent families represent 12% of the total of families with children. Source: Ministério da Justiça – Gabinete de Política Legislativa e Planeamento, *Estatísticas da Justiça (Justice Statistics) Portugal 2000*, 19. See also www.ine.pt.

[89] See A. Pereira (supra fn. 86), 345.

In the second case (Supreme Court of Justice decision of 25 November 1998)[90] a child was severely injured. The parents claimed compensation for their own non-pecuniary damage. The Supreme Court awarded them compensation, arguing that there is a family law relationship of parental power, which includes "the right to see the young child grow up healthy." 86

According to the *Principles*, one would probably achieve the same result in the second case; the first case however is more dubious. 87

(v) Paragraph (2) and (3)

Paragraph (2) of Art. 10:301 provides criteria for the assessment of non-pecuniary damage. Similar criteria are to be found in Art. 496 (3) and Art. 494: "degree of fault, the economic situation of both the defendant and the victim and other circumstances of the case." 88

Paragraph (3) prescribes that "in assessing damages (...) similar sums should be awarded for objectively similar losses." This derives from the principle of equality (Art. 13 of the Portuguese Constitution) and case law normally justifies the amount awarded by reference to previous case law. There is still no system of *barêmes* in Portugal, but a significant part of the doctrine defends such solution.[91] 89

d) Ad hoc Reduction

The Portuguese legislator introduced in 1967 the limitation of compensation in cases of mere fault (Art. 494): "Where liability is based on mere fault, compensation may be fixed equitably to an amount *lower* than that corresponding to the damage caused, provided that the degree of fault of the wrongdoer, the financial situation of the wrongdoer and of the injured party as well as the other circumstances of the case so justify." A similar rule is to be found, among other legal systems, in Swiss law or in the very recent Art. 944 of the Brazilian Civil Code (which entered into force in 2003).[92] In case of negligence, the court might decide the defendant is not liable for full compensation. The degree of fault, the economic situation of both the defendant and the victim and other circumstances of the case are the criteria the court shall take into consideration. Pointed out as a "spectacular turning point" in the Portuguese Civil Code, the idea to shape compensation according to the degree of fault in case 90

[90] *Boletim do Ministério da Justiça* 481, 470.

[91] See J. Dias, *Dano Corporal – Quadro Epistemológico e Aspectos Ressarcitórios* (2001) and J. Dinis, Dano Corporal em Acidentes de Viação, [2001] CJ (STJ), 5–12.

[92] See A. Pereira, Brazil, in: H. Koziol/B.C. Steininger (supra fn. 23), 458. A. Tunc, *La Responsabilité Civile* (1981), 73: "la diminution des dommages-intérêts quand la partie responsible est un individu et non une organisation est tout-à-fait courante dans nombreux pays socialistes, y compris la Chine, ainsi qu'au Portugal. Elle est couramment acceptée pour les dommages causes par un malade mental, et elle est maintenant prise sérieusement en consideration ou meme partiellement introduite en Allemagne, aux Pays-Bas et en Scandinavie." In fact the new Dutch Civil Code (BW, *Burgerlijk Wetboek*) introduced in Art. 6:109 such a provision (see E. Hondius/C. van Dam, Niederlande, in: C. von Bar (ed.), *Deliktsrecht in Europa* (1994), 20.)

of non-intentional fault was warmly welcomed by private lawyers. Before the Code, supplementary statutes imposed that solution, but it was not a general rule. Still, the provision should not be seen as an automatic right of the defendant. Full compensation is the scope of liability, according to Art. 562 CC. Deviations of that basic rule in the law of damages must be applied with reserve and must be justified. The prevailing opinion in Portugal undermined the field of application of the moderation "clause", discarding the same solution in contractual liability[93] and in cases of strict liability[94]."

C. Conclusion

91 There are some important differences in structure and in dogmatic background between the *Principles* and the CC, of which one can point out the following: (1) The CC adopts the principle of fault, the *Principles* offer the same dogmatic level to fault, strict liability and liability for others. (2) The definition of wrongfulness and the protection of pure economic interests and contractual relationships is broader in the *Principles* than in the Portuguese CC. (3) The regime on enterprise liability and (4) the chapter on causation of the *Principles* are very innovative. (5) Concerning remedies, the *Principles* provide compensation for non-pecuniary damage for anyone having a "close relationship" with the injured, which is opposed to the enumeration of *relatives* and (6) the *Principles* provide compensation of non-pecuniary damage suffered by persons having a close relationship with a victim suffering a very serious *non-fatal* injury.

92 In general, the practical results are frequently similar but, perhaps, the regime provided in the CC is stricter and is possibly more efficient in "keeping the floodgates shut."

[93] See A. Pinto Monteiro (supra fn. 78), 95, fn. 182. See also STJ [2003] CJ-STJ, 17 June 2003: the Court did not apply Art. 494 CPC, not because there was contractual liability, but because the agent had acted with gross negligence.

[94] Accepting it instead J. Antunes Varela, Rasgos inovadores do código civil português de 1966, [1972] *Boletim da Faculdade de Direito* (BFD), 100–104. See: J. Sinde Monteiro/M. Veloso (supra fn. 55).

Contributors

Håkan ANDERSSON

Uppsala University,
Faculty of Law
P.O. Box 512
SE-751 20 Uppsala
Sweden
Tel.: (+46) 18 471 2001
hakan.andersson@
jur.uu.se

Håkan Andersson is Professor of Private Law at Uppsala University. After graduating (LL.D, Dr juris) in 1993 on a thesis in tort law (Purpose of Protection and Adequacy. On the Limits of Liability in Tort Law) he has developed his interest in constructive use of newer philosophy in the field of private law, especially tort law. His research project "Transformation of the Legal Argumentation in Late Modernism" is developing discourse theory and philosophy of language in direct contact with private law. He has written more than 50 opus.

Bjarte ASKELAND

Faculty of Law
University of Bergen
Magnus Lagabøtes
plass 1
5010 Bergen
Norway
Tel. (+47) 55 58 95 84
Fax: (+47) 55 58 95 71
bjarte.askeland@
jur.uib.no

Bjarte Askeland studied law at the University of Bergen and finished as cand. jur. in 1991. From 1992–1994 he worked as an assistant judge and as a judge in Jæren district county court, Norway. He later worked at the Faculty of Law, University of Bergen as assistant professor, as research fellow and from 2001 as associate professor. After finishing his thesis on vicarious liability, he became doctor juris in 2001. He has written a number of articles, mainly within tort law and legal theory.

Ewa BAGIŃSKA

Uniwersytet Mikolaja
Kopernika
ul. Gagarina 15
87-100 Torun
Poland
Tel.: (+48-56) 662 3296
Fax: (+48-56) 611 4005
baginska@uni.torun.pl

Ewa Bagińska holds a PhD in law and is Assistant Professor in the Department of Civil and International Commercial Law, Faculty of Law and Administration, Nicholas Copernicus University (UMK), Torun. Fulbright Visiting Scholar (1998/1999) and NATO Science Fellowship grantee (2000/2001) at The Catholic University of America, Columbus School of Law, Washington, DC.

Areas of expertise: civil and commercial law – civil liability, contracts, consumer protection, products liability, unfair competition, health law, e-commerce, harmonisation of Polish laws with the EU legal system. Author of the book *Odpowiedzialnosc za produkt w USA* (Products liability in the USA), Torun 2000, and several articles.

Elena BARGELLI

Facoltà di Economia
Universitá di Pisa
Via C. Ridolfi, 10
I-56124 Pisa
Italy
Tel.: (+39-050) 94 53 37
Fax: (+39-050) 54 03 40
e.bargelli@ec.unipi.it

Elena Bargelli is currently lecturer in Private Law at the Faculty of Economics (University of Pisa), and is teaching Private Law at the Faculty of Political Science (University of Pisa). She graduated in Law at the University of Pisa, and got a PhD in Private Law in 1999. She is author of a book on Property and Tenancy Law, and has written several articles concerning Tort Law (with particular regard to non-pecuniary losses), Contract Law and Family Law.

Agris BITĀNS

University of Latvia,
Lecturer at Faculty
of Law,
Attorney at Law
Kr. Valdemara iela 19,
Riga, Latvia, LV 1010
Tel.: (+371) 7280102
Fax: (+371) 7504566
agris.bitans@
baltmanebitans.com

Agris Bitāns graduated from the Faculty of Law at the University of Latvia with a Bachelor's degree in law in 1993 and with a Master's degree in law in 1995. Apart from practising as an attorney at law, he continues his academic studies at the University of Latvia for a Doctor's degree. He is also a lecturer at the Civil Law Department, Faculty of Law, University of Latvia. His area of expertise is obligations law, with a focus on contract law and civil liability, tort law, intellectual property law. He is a co-author of the commentary on the Latvian Civil Code. He is the author of the book "Civil liability and its kinds" (Civiltiesiskā atbildība un tās veidi) and of many articles relating to law issues.

He is a member of the Latvian Bar, International Bar Association and AIPPI (International Association for the Protection of Industrial Property).

Since his admittance to the Latvian Bar in 1998, he has been practising mostly in civil (contracts and tort), intellectual property, commercial and administrative matters. His fields of legal research include contract and tort law, personality law, medical law and media law. He is also a regular participant at international conferences and workshops dealing with intellectual property law, civil law, litigation and arbitation.

Eugenia G. DACORONIA

Attorney-at-Law
Lecturer of Civil Law
at the Athens University
Department of Law
312, Patission Str.
GR-11141 Athens
Greece
Tel.: (+30-1) 201-0011
Tel./Fax:
(+30-1) 223-7150
Dacoronia@yahoo.com

Eugenia Dacoronia was born of Greek nationality in Cairo (Egypt) in 1958. She graduated with excellence in 1979 from the Athens Faculty of Law, where she also received her doctorate with excellence in 1994. She has attended several courses abroad (Amsterdam, King's College London, Tulane University).
Since 1980, Eugenia Dacoronia has worked as an assistant at the Athens University Department of Law. Since her admittance to the Athens Bar in 1981, she has been practising mostly in civil (contracts and real property), intellectual property, commercial and administrative matters. She is also a European Patent Attorney.
Eugenia Dacoronia has also been a lecturer of civil law at the Athens University Department of Law since 1995. She teaches, among others, General Principles of Civil Law, Real Property Law, Law of Environment, Torts in the legal system of the U.S.A.
She has participated in International Congresses as a National Representative and published various articles and notes on Court decisions in Greek legal periodicals and in the European Review of Private Law. Eugenia Dacoronia participates in the Trento Common Core project as well as the Study Group on a European Civil Code as a member of the Advisory Council on: a) Torts and b) Lease of movables.

Anton DULAK

Univerzita Komenského v Bratislave
Právnická fakulta
Šafárikovo nám. 6
818 05 Bratislava
Slovakia
Tel./Fax:
+421 2 434 26 611
Anton.Dulak@flaw.uniba.sk

Anton Dulak was born in 1963 in Košice. After graduating in law in 1985, he started to work at the Department of Civil Law at the Commenius University Bratislava as an assistant. In 2001 he obtained his PhD degree. In 2003 Anton Dulak habilitated with a thesis on Product Liability Law and was promoted to an associate professor.
His main fields of research include Tort Law and Consumer Protection Law.

Isabelle C. DURANT

Université catholique de Louvain
Faculté de droit
Place Montesquieu 2/38
B-1348
Louvain-la-Neuve
Belgium
Tel.:
(+) 32 (0)10 47 47 41
Fax:
(+) 32 (0)10 47 47 32
isabelle.durant@obli.ucl.ac.be

Isabelle Claire Durant studied law at the Université catholique de Louvain (UCL), where she was a teaching and research assistant from 1991 until 2004. She got her PhD Degree in law in 2003 from this university and is currently Visiting Professor in the Department of Private Law. She teaches contract and real property law and mainly publishes in the areas of contract and tort law. She also contributes to several research projects for the Austrian Academy of Sciences' Research Unit for European Tort Law and for the European Centre of Tort and Insurance Law in Vienna where she was on leave for work from October 2004 to March 2005.

Michael FAURE

METRO, Faculty of Law
Maastricht University
P.O. Box 616
6200 MD Maastricht
The Netherlands
Tel.: (+31-43) 388-3028
Fax: (+31-43) 325-9091
Metro.Institute@facburfdr.unimaas.nl

Michael Faure studied law at the University of Antwerp (licenciate in law 1982) and criminology at the University of Gent (licenciate in criminology 1983). He obtained a Master of Laws from the University of Chicago Law School (1984) and a doctor iuris from the Albert Ludwigs Universität Freiburg im Breisgau.

He was first a lecturer and then a senior lecturer at the department of criminal law of the law faculty of Leiden University (1988–1999) and became academic director of the Maastricht European Institute for Transnational Legal Research (METRO) and professor of Comparative and International Environmental Law at the law faculty of Maastricht University in September 1991. He still holds both positions today.

In addition, he is academic director of the Ius Commune Research School and member of the board of directors of Ectil.

Since 1982 he is equally attorney at the Antwerp Bar.

He publishes in the areas of environmental (criminal) law, tort and insurance and economic analysis of (accident) law.

Jörg FEDTKE

University College London
Institute of Global Law
Faculty of Laws
Bentham House
Endsleigh Gardens
London, WC1H OEG
United Kingdom
Tel.:
(+44-20) 7679-1474
Fax:
(+44-20) 7679-1502
j.fedtke@ucl.ac.uk

Jörg Fedtke obtained a doctorate at the University of Hamburg in 2000, where he worked as a researcher at the Seminar für ausländisches und internationales Privat- und Prozessrecht in 2001 and 2002.
He currently teaches at University College London, where he is Reader in Law and the Director of the Institute of Global Law. Since 2003 he also holds a post as Visiting Professor at The University of Texas.
He publishes in the areas of tort, constitutional and comparative law.

Herkus GABARTAS

Mykolas Romeris University Department of Finance and Tax Law
Ateities st. 20
LT-08303 Vilnius
Lithuania
Tel.: (+370 5) 263-9321
Fax: (+370 5) 269-1993
gabartas@legalservices.lt

Herkus Gabartas obtained his doctorate degree from Mykolas Romeris University (Vilnius, Lithuania) in 2004, where he currently teaches the course on EC Finance and Tax Law. He is also a graduate of Vilnius University, Lithuania (Master's degree, 1999) and the University of Florida, USA (LL.M. in Comparative Law, 2001).
Herkus Gabartas is also a practising attorney at the Lithuanian Bar. The areas of his particular interest are: EC Tax Law, Private International Law, Tort Law.

Israel GILEAD

The Hebrew University of Jerusalem,
Faculty of Law
Mt. Scopus
Jerusalem 91905
Israel
Tel.: (+972-2) 882-526
msigms@mscc.huji.ac.il

Israel Gilead is Bora Laskin Professor of law, Faculty of Law, The Hebrew University of Jerusalem. He graduated from the Faculty of Law of The Hebrew University of Jerusalem in 1979 (LL.B.), in 1983 from the Faculty of Economics (B.A.) and in 1984 he obtained his LL.D. Israel Gilead held various academic positions at the Hebrew University where he was Dean of the Faculty from 1999–2002. Israel Gilead has been a member of Codification Committees in Israel, a member of the European Group on Tort Law and of the European Centre of Tort and Insurance Law since 1999, and since 2004 a member of the American Law Institute. His major fields of research and teaching have been tort law, limitation of civil actions and economic analysis.

Suvianna HAKALEHTO-WAINIO

University of Helsinki
Department of Public Law
P.O. Box 4
FI-00014
Finland
Tel. +358 44 344 7768
hakaleht@mappi.helsinki.fi

Suvianna Hakalehto-Wainio was born in Helsinki in 1966. She works as a lecturer in administrative law in the Department of Public Law, Faculty of Law, University of Helsinki. She has been working there in various research projects since 1996. Suvianna Hakalehto-Wainio spent the academic year 1994–1995 in Estonia lecturing at the University of Tartu (Eurofaculty program). She is currently working on her PhD on the tort liability of public authorities. Suvianna Hakalehto-Wainio's main fields of interest are tort law, administrative law, education law, child law and human rights.

Ton HARTLIEF

University of Maastricht
Postbus 616
NL-6200 MD
Maastricht
The Netherlands
Tel.: (+31-43) 388-3104
Fax: (+31-43) 325-8981
t.hartlief@pr.unimaas.nl

Ton Hartlief is professor of private law at the University of Maastricht.

Jiří HRÁDEK

Jáchymova 2
110 00 Praha 1
Czech Republic
Tel.: (+420) 728 228224
Fax: (+420) 224235450
j.hradek@seznam.cz
hradek@prk.cz

Jiři Hrádek graduated in law from the Charles University in Prague in 2002. He studied at the University of Hamburg (2000–2001) LL.M. programme at the University of Tübingen (2002–2003) and is currently working on his PhD at the Charles University in Prague. Since 2003 he has been an associate at the Czech law firm, Procházka/Randl/Kubr, in Prague.

Jiři Hrádek's current research focuses on the area of EC law, particularly in relation to liability issues and conflict of laws. He is a regular participant in international conferences and workshops dealing with EC law and civil law.

Denis N. KELLIHER

Research Unit for European Tort Law
Landesgerichtsstraße 9a-11
A-1080 Vienna, Austria
Tel.:
(+43-1) 40127-1691
Fax:
(+43-1) 40127-1685
denis.kelliher@oeaw.ac.at

Denis N. Kelliher is a first class honours graduate of the National University of Ireland, Galway where he obtained the degrees of Bachelor of Corporate Law (2001) and Bachelor of Laws (2002). He subsequently spent two years at the Honorable Society of King's Inns in Dublin where he qualified with the degree of Barrister-at-Law and was called to the Irish Bar (2004). He has worked as a judicial research assistant for the judges of the High Court and Supreme Court in Ireland in the Judges' Library, Four Courts, Dublin and as a researcher in the Office of the Ombudsman and in the Office of the Information Commissioner in Dublin. He is currently employed as a research assistant in the Research Unit for European Tort Law of the Austrian Academy of Sciences in Vienna. Denis Kelliher is researching his Ph.D. on the personality rights of a deceased at University College Cork, a constituent university of the National University of Ireland.

Bernhard A. KOCH

University of Innsbruck
Innrain 52,
A-6020 Innsbruck
Austria
Tel.:
(+43-512) 507-8110
Fax:
(+43-512) 507-9885
bernhard.a.koch@uibk.ac.at
http://www.zivilrechts.info

Bernhard A. Koch was born in 1966 in Feldkirch (Austria). He studied law in Innsbruck (Mag. iur. 1989), Tübingen (Germany, Dr. iur. summa cum laude 1992), and Michigan (USA, LL.M. 1993). He completed his habilitation for private law and comparative law in 1998.

Bernhard A. Koch started to work as an assistant at the University of Innsbruck in 1985, where he was awarded tenure in 1999. After two years on leave for work at ECTIL and the Austrian Academy of Sciences, he returned to Innsbruck, where he holds a chair in civil law. Since 2004, Koch is the Vice Director of the Austrian Academy of Sciences' Research Unit for European Tort Law.

Bernhard A. Koch's main fields of research are tort, contract, real property and family law. He is a member of the European Group on Tort Law.

Helmut KOZIOL

European Centre of Tort and Insurance Law and Research Unit for European Tort Law
Landesgerichtsstraße 11
A-1080 Vienna, Austria
Tel.:
(+43-1) 40127-1680
Fax:
(+43-1) 40127-1685
koziol@ectil.org
and helmut.koziol@oeaw.ac.at

Helmut Koziol is currently Executive Director of the European Centre of Tort and Insurance Law as well as Director of the Research Unit for European Tort Law of the Austrian Academy of Sciences. He was born in 1940 in Vienna and, after graduating (Dr. iuris) from the University of Graz in 1963, he worked as an assistant at the Law Faculty in Bonn. Helmut Koziol returned to Austria in 1967 when he became Professor of Private Law at the University of Linz (1967–1969), subsequently being offered a chair at the University of Vienna which he held until 2000.
His main fields of legal research include Tort Law and Banking Law.

Irene KULL

University of Tartu
Faculty of Law
Näituse 20
50416 Tartu
Estonia
Tel.: + 372 7 375 385
Fax: + 372 7 375 983
www.iuridicum.ee
www.ut.ee
Irene.Kull@ut.ee

Irene Kull obtained her PhD in Civil Law at the University of Tartu in 2002. She is currently assistant professor of civil law and holder of the chair of Contract Law. Since 1995 she has worked as an advisor to the civil chamber of the Estonian Supreme Court. Irene Kull participates in the Study Group on a European Civil Code as an advisor on the Working Team on Rental of Movable Property. She was a member of the group working on the draft of the Estonian Law of Obligations Act. Among her publications there are two textbooks and a variety of journal articles on issues in contract law and the harmonisation of private law. She lectures on contract law, law of obligations and European commercial law. Her main interests include the law of obligations, contract and tort law, harmonisation of European private law, comparative law and family law.

Fabien LAFAY

Institut de Droit Comparé Edouard Lambert
Université Jean Moulin Lyon 3
6, cours Albert Thomas
B.P. 8242
F-69355 Lyon Cedex 08
France
Tel.:
+33 (0) 4 78 78 71 41
Fax:
+33 (0) 4 78 78 75 00
fabienlafay@voilà.fr

Fabien Lafay was born in Lyon in 1973. He obtained a "DEA" in ethic and medical law and a diploma in comparative law at the Institut de droit comparé Edouard Lambert. He is currently completing his PhD thesis in private and criminal law at the University Jean Moulin Lyon 3 on "le pouvoir modérateur et modulateur du juge en droit privé français". In his capacity of teaching and research assistant, he teaches French law of obligations and company law. He already has made several contributions in tort law, insurance law and family law, mainly for ECTIL.

Rok LAMPE

University of Primorska
Faculty of Management
Cankarjeva 5
6105 Koper
Slovenia
Tel.: +386 2 2512 024
+386 40 84 66 21
rok.lampe@uni-mb.si

Rok Lampe is currently lecturer of law at the University of Primorska. He was born in 1973. He graduated from the Faculty of Law – University of Maribor (Slovenia) and obtained an LL.M. from the University of Utah. He defended his PhD thesis at the Faculty of Law, University of Maribor where he worked as an assistant.
Research Stays: 1996 – European Law at University of Amsterdam, Tempus scholarship programme. 1999 – Governmental scholarship of the Czech Republic for PhD research at the Charles University in Prague.
2001 – Visiting researcher at Yale Law School under tutorship of Prof. Anita L. Allen for the PhD thesis "The Right of Privacy, In Defence of a Broad Concept of the Right of Privacy".
His fields of legal research include tort law, personality law, medical law and media law.

Milda LAUČIENĖ

Health Policy Centre
Erfurto 6-11
LT-04117 Vilnius
Lithuania
Tel: +370 686 93581
Fax: +370 5 260 8559
advokate@spc.lt

Milda Laučienė was born in 1975 and graduated from the University of Vilnius, Faculty of Law (Lithuania) in 2000. In 1997 she received a bachelor in English at the Faculty of Philology of the same University.
She is a practising attorney-at-law at the Lithuanian Bar and her areas of expertise include medical law and civil liability.
She is a founder of the public institution, Health Policy Centre, that takes an active part in the process of healthcare reform in Lithuania.

Peter LOSER

University of St. Gallen
Dufourstraße 50
CH-9000 St. Gallen
Switzerland
Tel.: (+41-71) 222-3033
peter.loser@unisg.ch

Peter Loser was born in 1964. He studied law in St. Gallen and Lausanne, Switzerland (University of St. Gallen, lic.iur. 1990; Dr.iur. summa cum laude 1994). He was a visiting scholar at Yale University in 1992/93 and did research at the UNIDROIT in 1999 and at the University of Oxford in 1999.
Currently Peter Loser teaches private, company and tort law at the Universities of St. Gallen and Lucern and is completing his habilitation for private and comparative law. His main fields of research are contract, tort and company law. He is an active participant of the project "The Common Core of European Private Law" (University of Trento, Italy).
Peter Loser has also worked as a lawyer since 1995 and is legal counsel of a bank.

Meinhard LUKAS

University of Linz
Altenberger Straße 69
A-4040 Linz
Austria
Tel.:
(+43-732) 2468-8464
Fax:
(+43-732) 2468-9841
www.zivilrecht.jku.at
meinhard.lukas@jku.at

Meinhard Lukas was born in 1970 in Linz (Austria). He studied law in Linz (Mag. iur. 1992, Dr. iur. 1998). He completed his habilitation for private law in 2004. Meinhard Lukas started to work as an assistant at the University of Linz in 1993, where he became associate professor of private law in 2004. From 1996 to 1998 Meinhard Lukas worked at a law firm in Linz. He is a member of the Institute of Banking Law in Linz. He has repeatedly represented Austria at the United Nations Commission on International Trade Law (UNCITRAL). His main fields of research are law of obligations, tort law, banking law and international private law.

Attila MENYHÁRD

ELTE Faculty of Law,
Civil Law Department
Egyetem tér 1-3
H-1364 Budapest
Hungary
Tel.: (+36-1) 411 6510
menyhard@ajk.elte.hu

Attila Menyhárd was born in 1968. He works at the University of Eötvös Loránd, Faculty of Law, Civil Law Department (Budapest) and he is also a practising lawyer. Special research fields are: contract law, tort law and property law. Participant in several international projects on contract and tort law. Promoted with PhD degree in 2003.

Olivier MORÉTEAU

Paul M. Hebert Law Center
Louisiana State University
W323 Law Center
Baton Rouge, LA 70803
United States
Tel.: +1 225 578 1126
Fax: +1 225 578 3677
moreteau@lsu.edu

Olivier Moréteau was born in 1956 in Lyon. He studied law at the Université Jean Moulin Lyon 3 where he completed his doctorate in comparative law (Estoppel and protection of reliance), after research in Cambridge with a British Council scholarship. He worked as an assistant and then lecturer at the Université Jean Moulin Lyon 3. He was appointed professor (agrégation de droit privé) at the University of Grenoble 2 and then Lyon 3. He served as a Director and Vice-President for International Relations at Université Jean Moulin Lyon 3 (1993–1999) and as the Director of the Edouard Lambert Institute of Comparative Law (Deputy Director 1985–2000, Director 2000–2005). He was visiting professor at the University of Minnesota (1992), Boston University (almost every year between 1993 and 2004) and the University of Melbourne (2002, 2004). He publishes books and articles on English law and comparative law. He is a member of the International Academy of Comparative Law and of the European Group on Tort Law. In 2005, he was appointed Professor of Comparative Law on the newly created Russell Long Chair of Excellence, at Louisiana State University where he is Director of the Center for Civil Law Studies. He teaches comparative law and the law of obligations.

Emanuela NAVARRETTA

Università di Pisa
Palazzo della Sapienza
Via Curtatone e Montanara 15
I-56100 Pisa
Italy
navarretta@ddpriv.unipi.it

Professor of Private Law at the Faculty of Law of the University of Pisa. Professor of Civil Law at the post-graduate course for forensic professions at the University of Pisa. Professor of Person and Family Law at the post-graduate course for notaries of the Council of notaries in Florence. Member of Board of Directors of the journal "Responsabilità civile e previdenza" ("Tort Liability and Insurance"). Member of Board of Directors of the journal "Rivista di Diritto Civile" ("Civil Law Review"). National coordinator of the research study "Non-pecuniary losses in recent laws and judgments" financed by the Ministry of Scientific Research. National coordinator of the research study "The harmonization levels in European contract law: a study concerning types and groups of contracts" financed by the Ministry of Scientific Research. Member of the parliamentary commission for the reform of the law on the protection of privacy. Author of books and several essays on tort law, contract law and human rights.

Kunihiko OKUBO

Konan University Law School
8-9-1 Okamoto,
Higashinada-ku,
Kobe, Hyogo, 658-8501
Japan
Tel.:
+81-(0)78-435-2615
Fax:
+81-(0)78-435-2760
http://www.lawschool-konan.jp/
kunihiko@center.konan-u.ac.jp

Kunihiko Okubo was born in 1963 in Osaka. He graduated in law from Kyoto University in 1991 (LL.M.). He started to work as an assistant at Kyoto University (1991–1993). He became lecturer and then associate professor at Kobe Gakuin University (1993–2003). From 1999–2001 he worked as a guest researcher at Vienna University under tutorship of Prof. Helmut Koziol. Since 2003 he is Professor at Konan University.
His main interests include system and principles of private law, particularly of tort and contract law.

Ken OLIPHANT

Cardiff University, Law Building
Museum Avenue
Cardiff CF10 3XJ
United Kingdom
Tel.:
(+44-29) 2087-5365
oliphantka@cf.ac.uk

Ken Oliphant was born in Glasgow but educated in England. He is now a senior lecturer at Cardiff Law School, Cardiff University. Previously he lectured at King's College London (1988–99). He has written extensively in the fields of tort law and compensation for incapacity. He is the joint author of Tort Law: Text & Materials, Oxford University Press, 2nd edn., 2003 (with Mark Lunney) and Torts, Palgrave MacMillan, 3rd edn., 2003 (with Alastair Mullis), and a contributing editor of the practitioners' reference work, Tort Law, Butterworths, 2002 (general editor: Andrew Grubb). He is also currently an assistant editor of the Journal of Law and Society and UK correspondent for the Torts Law Journal.

Caroline PELLERIN-RUGLIANO

Institut de Droit Comparé Edouard Lambert
15 quai Claude Bernard
69007 Lyon, France
Tel.: (+33) 4-78-78-71-94
perugline@free.fr

Caroline Pellerin was born in Lyon (France) in 1977 but grew up mainly in Reunion Island where she started her law studies. She graduated in Lyon after specialising in Fundamental private law for which she wrote a small dissertation on the meaning of tort from a comparative view, which was given an award by the Centre Français de Droit Comparé in 2001. As teaching and research assistant in the Law faculty, she is currently working on her doctoral thesis under the supervision of Prof. O. Moréteau ("La notion de délit civil en droit comparé") within the Center of Law Theory and the Institute of Comparative Law Edouard Lambert. Her main fields of research are tort law and linguistics for which she contributes to various projects within European networks.

André G. Dias PEREIRA

University of Coimbra
P-3004-545 Coimbra
Portugal
Tel.: (+351) 239-859801
Fax: (+351) 239-821043
andreper@fd.uc.pt

André Gonçalo Dias Pereira studied law at the University of Coimbra (awarded Prof. Manuel de Andrade Prize for best student). He has attended several courses abroad in Göttingen, Utrecht and Helsinki and has been abroad doing research as invited Scholar at the Roger Williams University School of Law (Rhode Island – USA), at the European Centre of Tort and Insurance Law/Research Unit for European Tort Law of the Austrian Academy of Sciences in Vienna and at the Faculty of Law, University of Salzburg. He wrote the thesis "Informed Consent on the Patient-Doctor Relationship", obtaining the highest mark and published it in 2004 (700 pp.). He has also published several articles in Portugal and abroad (in some European countries and in Brazil). He is presently Assistant Professor at the Faculty of Law of the University of Coimbra (Department of Civil Law) and lectures Medical Law in several Academic Institutions. He is the Scientific Secretary of the Centre for Biomedical Law. He is involved in several international research projects, especially in the fields of tort law, biomedical law and human rights. Pereira has been invited internationally for papers, lectures and seminars. He has given papers in Brazil, Austria, England, Estonia, Germany, Greece, Netherlands, Spain and in Israel. He is Vice-President of an Institutional Review Board of a Health and Research Institution in Coimbra and member of the National Council on Forensic Medicine.

Eoin QUILL

University of Limerick
School of Law
Limerick
Ireland
Tel.: (+353-61) 20-2220
Fax: (+353-61) 20-2682
Eoin.Quill@ul.ie

Eoin Quill was born in Limerick in 1965. He studied law at University College Cork, a constituent college of the National University of Ireland, between 1982 and 1988 obtaining two bachelors and a masters degree – BCL; LLB; LLM.
He lectured at the School of Professional and Management Studies in Limerick from 1988–1990 and has been lecturing in the University of Limerick since 1991 in a variety of subjects including Tort, Commercial law and Comparative Civil Obligations. His publications include a textbook – Torts in Ireland (Gill & Macmillan 1999, 2nd edn. 2004) – and a variety of journal articles on issues in tort and contract. He was treasurer of the Irish Association of Law Teachers from 1997 to 2000 and is currently an examiner in Tort for the Law Society of Ireland.

Jordi RIBOT

University of Girona
Facultat de Dret
Campus de Montilivi
E-17071 Girona
Spain
Tel.: (+34-972) 418 140
Fax: (+34-972) 418 146
ribot@elaw.udg.es
Website: civil.udg.es/members/Pages/jribot.htm

Jordi Ribot was born in 1966. He graduated from the Autonomous University of Barcelona in 1989 and obtained his PhD in 1993. He became lecturer in Civil Law at the Autonomous University of Barcelona in 1994 and at the University of Girona in 1996, where he currently teaches Spanish and Catalan Civil Law.
Member of the "Observatory of European and Comparative Private Law" of the University of Girona and of the "International Society of Family Law", he cooperates on a regular basis with the Catalan Government in legal drafting of civil law legislation. Fellow of ECTIL, his main fields of research are tort law, family law and contract law.

Geneviève SCHAMPS

Catholic University of Louvain (U.C.L.)
Faculty of Law
Place Montesquieu 2
B-1348 Louvain-la-Neuve
Belgium
Tel: +32 10 47 46 71 – +32.486.33.87.00
Fax: +32 10 47 46 77
schamps@pen.ucl.ac.be

Geneviève Schamps is professor at the Faculty of Law at the Catholic University of Louvain. She was visiting professor at the University of Paris II (Pantheon-Assas) in 2004. In 1997 she obtained a PhD in Law at the Faculty of Law of the Catholic University of Louvain (U.C.L., Louvain-la-Neuve). In her doctoral thesis on comparative law she proposed the creation of a general principle based on a specific risk for the compensation of victims. This thesis received two awards: the quinquennial prize of the Revue Critique de Jurisprudence Belge (2000) and the quinquennial prize of Baron E. van Dievoet (2000). Her main fields of research and teaching are tort law, criminal law, biomedical law, comparative law and nuclear law. She is co-founder of the interdisciplinary Research Center "Sciences, Techniques et Société" ("Cites", U.C.L.). She is a promoter for PhD students in nuclear, genetic and biotechnological fields (civil law, criminal law and biomedical law). She is vice-president of the Belgium federal Commission "Patient's rights". She is a member of the U.C.L. Commission of ethics. She is also a member of the editorial board of several reviews: the Revue générale de droit civil (civil law), the Greifswald (medical law) and the Revue de droit pénal et criminologie (criminal law). She is President of the Bachelor's Commission of the Faculty of Law of the U.C.L. She has been a lawyer at the Brussels Bar and legal translator in Dutch.

Barbara C. STEININGER

Research Unit for European Tort Law
Landesgerichtsstraße 9a-11
A-1080 Vienna, Austria
Tel.: (+43-1) 40127-1610
Fax: (+43-1) 40127-1685
barbara.steininger@oeaw.ac.at

Barbara Steininger was born in Feldkirch (Austria) in 1977 and was brought up bilingually (German/Dutch). Between 1998 and 2000 she worked as a student assistant at the Institute of Roman Law, University of Vienna. She completed her law studies in Vienna in 1999. From 1998 to 1999 Barbara Steininger gained experience of a foreign university when she completed two terms at the University of Leiden, the Netherlands. Barbara Steininger has worked at the European Centre of Tort and Insurance Law in Vienna since its beginnings in 1999. She is now a staff member of the Research Unit for European Tort Law of the Austrian Academy of Sciences. In 2002 Barbara Steininger spent time at the Maastricht European Institute for Transnational Legal Research (METRO) in Maastricht and at the Institut Suisse de Droit Comparé in Lausanne in order to conduct research. From June to December 2004 Barbara Steininger was on leave for work at the University of Geneva. She finished her doctoral thesis under the supervision of Prof. Helmut Koziol ("Verschärfung der Verschuldenshaftung") in 2005 and is currently doing a court internship.

Vibe ULFBECK

University of Copenhagen
Studiegaarden,
Studiestraede 6,
1455 Copenhagen,
Denmark
Tel.: 35323148
Vibe.Ulfbeck@jur.ku.dk

Vibe Ulfbeck was born in 1966 and graduated as a lawyer at the University of Copenhagen in 1990. In 1991 she obtained an LL.M. degree at the University of Cambrigde, UK. From 1991–1992 she was employed in the Danish Justice Department and since 1993 she has been at the University of Copenhagen where she obtained her doctorate in 2000. In 2004 she was appointed professor of private law.

Index

The numbers refer to the marginal notes and the letters refer to the country reports; A stands for Austria, B for Belgium, CH for Switzerland, CR for the Comparative Remarks, CZ for the Czech Republic, D for Germany, DK for Denmark, E for Spain, EST for Estonia, EU for European Union, EW for England and Wales, F for France, GR for Greece, H for Hungary, I for Italy, IRL for Ireland, LT for Lithuania, LV for Latvia, N for Norway, NL for the Netherlands, P for Portugal, PL for Poland, S for Sweden, SF for Finland, SLO for Slovenia and SK for Slovakia.

act of God, see *force majeure*
adequacy PL 16, 24, 52
administrative acts, see public liability
administrative law A 33, 37; CZ 110; EU 8, 9; GR 1; LV 12, 13; NL 64, 67; P 67; PL 46; SF 31, 34; SLO 5, 6, 8
affection damage, see psychological harm
AIDS, see HIV
animals B 15, 106; CH 37; CZ 29–41; D 22; E 49–53; F 52; N 37; P 24, 25; SF 25–34
asbestos B 114; NL 27; SLO 36–39
assessment of damages, see damages, calculation of
associations PL 1
aviation A 75; CR 20; D 4, 22, 58; E 62; NL 14–17, 28; P 32; SF 21

bank A 55, 66; DK 20; GR 24, 57–59; IRL 5; P 81
bankruptcy DK 5; GR 64; LT 20; PL 47
boni mores A 66; EST 4; GR 9, 38, 57, 63; P 53, 54
burden of proof A 57–61, 68, 69; B 15; CR 21, 22; D 8, 48–50, 56; DK 15, 16, 18; E 16, 58; EST 18, 23; EU 6; EW 20; F 47; GR 43, 45; I 29; LV 13; NL 33; P 18, 30, 71, 76, 78, 85, 88; SF 23, 24; SK 2, 45
    reversal of the ~ E 25; P 18; SF 23

caps A 1, 2; E 6; EU 15, 20; LV 3; P 11, 12, 35, 37, 39, 40, 42; SF 5
causation A 7, 23, 40, 55–61, 68–70; B 22, 54, 57, 58, 62, 63–70, 80, 92, 94, 105, 106, 113; CR 22–26; CZ 53, 54, 56, 64–66, 80, 94, 104; D 49, 50, 53, 55; E 42, 68; EST 4, 6, 18, 23, 34, 36; EU 6; EW 4–11; F 54, 63, 66–68; GR 25, 26, 64; H 7, 21, 22, 28–31, 34, 38; I 27, 36; IRL 32, 37; LT 38; N 19; NL 8, 29–35; P 30, 56; PL 16, 24, 27, 52, 69; SF 38; SK 53; SLO 14, 23, 26, 41
    alternative ~ E 49–53
    hypothetical ~ A 70
    proof of ~ DK 15, 16
children, see minors
cohabitants EW 1
compensation, see damages
compensation funds PL 63
confidentiality EW 24–29; PL 51
consent A 60; B 2; D 18, 19; EW 5, 11; IRL 37; P 4, 72, 73; PL 54, 63
constitution A 13, 34–37, 39, 40; CR 7; D 9, 15, 38; E 2, 9, 15, 18–22, 27, 29, 30; F 3, 75; GR 2, 61, 62; H 4, 42; I 4, 6, 17, 30; IRL 26, 27, 35, 38; LT 31; PL 3, 8, 10, 23, 26, 61, 65, 68, 70; SLO 2, 6, 42, 45, 46
constructions B 71–83; EST 24; LT 44; LV 32–44; NL 37; SF 21

consumer protection CZ 22; D 1; F 23; GR 42, 43, 45; N 25; P 15, 16, 93; SF 37
contract A 66, 67, 71–73; B 19, 22, 79, 97–104; CH 44; CR 21; CZ 8, 11–23, 28, 70–72, 75, 76; D 8, 61; DK 20; E 37–39, 56, 60; EST 1, 2, 5, 12, 30, 34, 35; EW 21, 35; F 9, 11, 20, 40, 60, 65; GR 3–8, 57; H 10–13, 19, 26–34, 38; I 25, 28, 32; LT 43; P 1, 5, 6, 10, 16, 26–29, 47, 62, 65, 78; PL 34, 35, 39, 64; S 2, 23, 40; SK 29, 36
  breach of ~ B 77–80, 83; CR 9; E 32; EW 31; H 19, 29–31; IRL 28
contractual liability B 9, 71–83; CH 5, 40, 43; D 44; EST 2; LT 24, 25; P 28; PL 60; SF 1, 38
contributory negligence A 51–54; B 32, 41–45; CR 10–12; D 30, 55, 56; E 2, 25, 70; EST 37; F 43, 44; GR 21, 49; H 7; IRL 35, 36; LT 43, 44; NL 8; PL 64; SF 35, 36; SLO 16–19
court expert, see expert, court
crime victims EU 24–27; H 20; IRL 40; LT 31; SF 3–6, 35, 36
criminal law A 18–24, 41, 51, 66; B 53, 56, 91, 93, 94; CR 2, 18; CZ 5, 42; D 5, 24, 35, 37–39; E 18, 38, 64; EST 14, 38; EW 7, 35; F 5, 13, 18; GR 64; H 10, 17, 20–22, 35; IRL 8, 14, 18, 19; LT 19, 21, 26, 29, 31; N 2, 4, 5; NL 18, 21, 55; P 9, 55, 69, 70, 72; PL 22; S 31, 32; SF 3–5, 12–19, 35, 36; SLO 3, 5, 7, 10, 32, 51

damage
  actual ~ B 77; CZ 15, 36–38, 41, 94; IRL 26; PL 29
  direct ~ B 5, 77, 79; DK 9–10; EST 16, 31; EW 37; PL 73
  future ~ GR 40, 41; IRL 2; LV 38; PL 37, 55; S 3–10; SF 17
  indirect ~ B 5; DK 10; EST 31; EW 37; N 18, 23; PL 73
damages
  adjustment of ~ DK 18, 19
  aggravated ~ EW 25
  calculation of ~ A 70; B 19, 56, 84–89; CZ 30, 86–94; D 31–33; DK 5–7; EW 7; I 9; IRL 2, 27; LT 4, 7, 26–30; N 38, 39; NL 40; PL 29–34
  exemplary ~, see punitive damages
  general ~ IRL 2, 18
  nominal ~ IRL 26; PL 58
  punitive ~, see punitive damages
  quantum of ~ A 5, 8, 19, 26, 30, 44, 55, 62; B 71–83; CH 14; CR 24; CZ 8, 42, 44; D 4, 21–27, 43, 46, 48; E 23, 31, 32, 44, 45, 54; EST 13, 17, 20, 24, 25; EU 15, 20, 21; EW 1, 2, 25; GR 39, 42, 50, 57, 62; H 24, 36; I 1, 2, 5, 14, 18; IRL 2; LT 12, 19–22, 31, 33; LV 3, 7, 18, 19; NL 21, 38, 39; P 11, 13, 32, 33, 39, 41–44, 47, 55, 57, 59–64; S 11, 18; SF 1, 3, 5, 10, 38; SK 13, 17, 18, 27, 28, 37, 40, 46–49; SLO 13, 16, 18, 23, 27, 29, 32, 33, 37, 38, 50, 51; see also damages, calculation of
danger A 67; B 52; CR 19; CZ 77–85; E 67; EST 6; EW 15, 16; F 11, 18, 51, 63; GR 18; N 27; NL 11, 14–17, 19, 29, 31, 33, 34; P 55–58; SK 55; SLO 18, 24, 26, 30, 34
danno biologico I 20–22, 30
death A 26, 51; B 41, 84; CR 10, 18; CZ 8, 10, 64; D 5; E 7, 23; EST 5, 6; EW 1; GR 15, 22, 35, 36; H 8, 29; I 19; LT 11–18, 31; LV 15, 16; N 7, 10; NL 32, 33; P 55–58; PL 73; SF 12–19
defamation A 11, 16, 41–50; B 14; D 62; EST 3, 9, 20–23; H 14–16; I 34; IRL 5–8, 12–16; LT 23; LV 5, 15–31; SK 59, 60; SLO 10, 11
defect A 68; B 30, 31, 46–50, 105, 106; CH 26; CZ 101; D 51; EST 2, 7; EW 20–23; F 20, 51, 60, 62, 64, 67, 69, 70, 76; GR 43; N 10; SK 28
defences B 67, 76, 106; D 28, 30; EW 26, 29; IRL 6–8, 36; NL 55; SLO 4
development risks DK 20; F 69
difference theory B 26
disability A 5; B 2; CH 11; D 6, 8; E 21, 22; GR 15, 39–41; H 42; I 24; IRL 2; LV 5; N 37–39; NL 4; PL 36; SK 7
disclaimer DK 20
discrimination D 6–10; LV 8–11; P 17–19, 23; SF 7–10; SLO 4
drugs N 2
duty A 38, 40, 61, 65, 67; B 31, 35, 37, 39, 40, 101, 102, 111; CH 15, 46; CZ

4, 12, 65, 68, 86, 98, 106, 107; D 38, 39, 45; E 28; EST 4, 11, 13, 19; EU 6, 12; EW 4–13, 15, 17, 20, 21, 29; F 9, 17, 20, 40, 62, 65; GR 4, 13, 15, 32; I 29; IRL 18, 28, 29, 30–32; LT 17, 41, 49; LV 40; NL 34; P 3, 7–9, 20, 22, 27, 31, 60; PL 4, 25, 47, 56, 68, 70; SK 2, 4, 56
legal ~ CZ 61
to inform A 40, 55–57, 59–61; CH 38; CR 23; D 2, 43, 56; EW 4, 5, 8, 10, 11; H 11–13, 17–19, 29–31, 38; IRL 22; N 9, 10, 12; P 8, 15, 72, 89; PL 49, 50, 52, 54
to mitigate the loss B 115; IRL 8
to protect D 44; PL 35, 37, 38, 40–43
to supervise DK 2–4; F 39
to warn A 55; B 28, 29; CH 19; CR 19, 20; D 51; EW 4–11
duty of care A 23, 38, 59, 61, 66, 67, 69; B 102; CH 42; CR 3–5, 18, 21, 27; D 51; EST 29; EW 8, 13, 15, 30; GR 45; IRL 29, 35, 37; NL 6, 13–17, 25, 31, 33, 34, 65, 68, 70, 71

earning capacity DK 2–7; GR 49; N 17–23; PL 6, 36
ECHR, see human rights
e-commerce CZ 24–28; F 1–19; P 1–8, 93
emotional harm, see psychological harm
employees' liability A 11; PL 60; SK 2
employers' liability A 11, 76; B 17; CR 3–6; CZ 77–85; D 25; DK 2–4, 22; E 25, 36, 40–42; EST 2; EW 18, 23; GR 11–15; H 8–10, 19; I 14; IRL 1, 17, 28–32; LT 3, 44–47; LV 8–11; NL 4, 22–28, 57; PL 26, 37, 42, 60; SK 1–7; SLO 31, 37
environment B 14; CZ 109, 110; E 10, 16; SK 12; SLO 1, 6–9, 40
environmental liability EU 5–13; EW 36; NL 62
equal treatment of men and women D 6, 8, 9; EU 28, 29; LT 9
expert D 63; EST 35; IRL 11, 22, 37; SK 26, 27
court ~ A 18–24

family of the victim, see persons close to the victim
fault A 49, 63, 68; B 5, 21, 32, 53, 58, 59, 61–70, 72, 74, 78, 79, 85, 86, 93, 94, 96, 99–101, 103, 113, 116; CH 40, 44, 46; CR 3, 6, 18; CZ 17; D 23, 24; E 2, 24–26, 28, 58, 62, 70; EST 3, 4, 6, 9, 13, 37, 38; EU 9; EW 14, 16; F 17, 26–40, 45, 49, 54, 59, 62, 63; GR 16–23, 31, 43, 44, 56, 57; H 39; I 24; LT 3, 13, 15, 29, 38, 41, 44; LV 15, 16, 21, 25; N 3; P 21, 32, 37, 80, 90; PL 57, 69; SK 2; SLO 14, 25
intentional ~, see intent
financial law PL 46
force majeure EU 10; F 57
foreseeability A 37; B 12, 14, 100; CH 29, 32; CR 17; CZ 55, 65, 66; D 44; DK 10, 16; F 9; GR 51; I 28; IRL 29, 31; N 8, 11, 12; PL 16, 55; SLO 18
freedom
of expression A 47, 50; EW 26, 27, 29; F 3
of the press D 11–20
funeral costs SK 6

genetic engineering CH 36; D 66
good faith B 90; CH 5; GR 9, 45; LT 41, 42; P 65

harmonization of tort law LT 5, 8; N 29, 31, 36
hepatitis PL 48–54
HIV P 74
human rights A 35, 36, 42, 47; B 111; CR 7; CZ 7; D 9, 11, 12, 19; E 9–17, 19, 29; EW 17, 26, 29, 31, 34; F 3; GR 61; I 1–9, 11, 13, 30; IRL 35, 38–40; LT 31–35; NL 46; P 70, 84, 87, 95; PL 11, 23; SK 53; SLO 1, 2, 4, 42, 46, 48

imprisonment CR 2; P 48; SF 5, 12; SLO 32
indirect loss, see damage, indirect
information A 32, 38, 41, 47, 63; D 15, 19, 38, 56; EST 21; EW 24, 26–29; F 1, 5, 7, 69; H 6, 26–31, 32–34; IRL 22, 38; LV 16, 17, 20, 25, 31; N 9, 10, 12; NL 3; P 2, 8, 15, 85; PL 48,

53, 54; S 2; SF 31, 34; SK 29; SLO 10, 11; see also duty to inform
injunction A 10–17, 41, 44, 47–49; D 8; SLO 40
insurance A 71; B 4, 6, 16–21, 33–40, 64–70, 90, 91; CH 7, 8, 34, 36, 37; CZ 11–23; D 7, 31–33, 46; E 4, 36, 53, 54, 56, 60, 64, 69; EU 12, 17–23, 28; EW 6, 31, 35, 36; F 16, 26, 30, 43; GR 18, 51; H 11–13, 17–19, 26–34; IRL 20, 35; LT 2, 5–8, 25, 27, 28; N 3, 5, 13–16; NL 2, 4–7, 13, 39, 49, 51, 57, 60, 61; P 11–13, 30–32, 39, 96; PL 30, 32–34, 55, 63, 67, 70; S 2, 3, 5, 6, 9, 40; SK 5, 40–45; SLO 14, 30
  liability ~, see liability insurance
intent A 25, 31, 66, 67, 69; B 96; D 39–41; E 27, 67; EST 4, 18; F 17; IRL 26; LT 37; N 5; SF 9; SK 2
interest D 12, 15, 19; EW 3; LT 32
internet A 77; CZ 24–28; EU 3; F 1–19; GR 61; P 1–8, 93

jurisdiction B 9, 10
jury IRL 5, 8
justification, see defences

lawyers E 32–36; EW 2; LV 14; P 85
legal person D 7; F 10; N 17–23
liability
  contractual, see contractual liability
  for legislative acts A 37
  insurance A 1–4; CZ 15–19; E 3, 53, 67; EST 19; LT 3; LV 1–7; NL 61; P 10, 20–22, 26, 29, 31, 32, 36, 41, 44
  joint ~ B 75, 91; S 31
  joint and several ~ GR 20; H 20; I 26; P 48; PL 2, 60
  limited ~ LT 42, 48, 49
  solidary ~ P 15, 16, 21, 27, 30, 56
liberty EST 3, 9, 14; LT 31–35; PL 23
limitation A 62–65, 70, 72; B 15, 82, 114; CZ 13, 14, 68, 69, 73, 74; D 56; DK 20; E 8, 48; GR 51, 53; IRL 3, 4, 41; NL 5, 50–53; PL 13–18, 72; SK 11
loss
  of amenities of life I 4; IRL 2, 18
  of chance A 70; B 22, 51, 105; D 53; IRL 24, 25; P 37
  of consortium I 19–23
  of earnings A 62; B 17, 22–27; CZ 5, 38; DK 2, 5–7; E 37; EST 9; EW 3; IRL 2; LT 11, 14, 31; N 17; PL 20, 24; S 3–10, 20, 25; SK 4, 30–39
  of pension B 98; SK 4, 5; SLO 39
  of profit B 77; CZ 36–39, 41, 51–66, 104; DK 8–10, 11, 13; E 6; EST 16; GR 38, 57; IRL 26; N 17, 20
lump sum B 109; CZ 8, 9, 18, 102; SK 4, 6, 49

maintenance CR 2; CZ 18; N 16; P 55–58; PL 20, 21; SF 2, 15; SK 4, 7
manager's liability I 36; LT 48; P 80
media A 41, 42, 62; B 111; D 11–17, 62; EST 20, 22; EW 2, 24–29; F 7; GR 61, 62; LV 15–31; SLO 10, 11, 48
mediation SK 22–25
medical expenses B 17, 35, 40; DK 5
medical liability A 5–9, 62–65; B 108, 109; CH 38; CR 21–25; D 25–27, 46–50, 53, 56, 65, 68; E 54–61, 65; EW 4–11; H 38, 42; I 24–29; IRL 9–11, 21–24; LT 2–4, 11–22, 25; LV 15; N 24–27; NL 69; P 66–74, 87–91; PL 12–18, 48–61, 63
medical treatment A 62; B 33; D 40, 46; EW 4–11, 26; IRL 11, 21, 22; LT 11, 13, 17, 26; LV 22; N 13–16, 24; SK 4, 6; SLO 13
mental shock CZ 64; PL 73
military service E 7; EU 18; SF 8
minors A 26, 28, 30, 32, 68; B 2, 33–40, 64–70, 112; CH 17–25; CR 2, 8, 13, 15, 19, 21; CZ 8; D 18–20, 25, 30, 40–42, 43, 70; EST 33; EW 1; F 31, 32, 34–40, 64, 72, 74; GR 16, 35–37, 46–48; H 2, 8, 42; I 24; IRL 2, 40; LT 19, 23, 24; N 37; NL 12, 16, 39, 45; P 27; S 29–32; SF 12–19; SLO 12, 20–28
misstatement A 41, 42, 47, 48, 50; EW 26, 31, 37
motor insurance B 18, 33–40; CZ 1–11; D 31–33; EU 14–16; IRL 20; LT 5–8, 26–30; N 13–23, 37; PL 67; SK 40–45
multiple tortfeasors A 69; B 96; GR 20; H 20–22

negligence A 18, 25, 49, 70; B 52, 57; CR 4, 10; D 22, 24, 28–30, 35, 39, 41, 42; DK 3, 4, 8–10, 17, 22; E 27, 31, 35, 48; EST 4, 29; EW 4–11, 15, 16, 31, 37; F 17, 26–33, 65, 69; GR 16, 17, 19, 49; I 24, 25, 27, 28; IRL 9–11, 22–24; LT 12, 18, 19, 21, 25; NL 6–8, 20, 31, 52; P 92; PL 37, 42, 55, 57, 59; S 11, 16, 31; SF 9, 26; SLO 19
gross ~ A 25, 31; D 39; DK 8–10; E 31; EST 4, 18; I 24, 25, 27; P 49; SF 13
nervous shock, see mental shock
noise E 9–17
non-pecuniary loss A 5–9, 25–32, 51–54; B 41–45; CR 7–16; CZ 5, 7; D 5, 21–27, 43, 46, 55, 102, 103; E 9, 18, 33, 39, 41, 42, 44, 45, 47; EST 3, 16, 20–27; EW 3; GR 3, 8, 20, 42, 43, 48; H 3, 4, 8, 14, 23–25, 35–38; I 1, 5, 6, 10–19, 23, 30, 33–35; LT 3, 6, 7, 9, 12, 16, 19–22, 26, 27, 29–31, 35, 44, 46; LV 5, 6, 7, 11, 13, 18; NL 1, 43, 44, 46, 47, 73; P 52, 57, 58, 59, 62, 63, 69, 83; PL 6, 11, 20, 28, 58, 64, 73; SF 15; SK 59, 60; SLO 18, 20, 27, 29, 37–40
notaries A 72; D 51; EST 17–19; P 9, 10, 92; SK 25
nuclear liability A 78; GR 61; SK 8–15
nuisance E 10, 14; EW 2; F 72, 73; SLO 40

occupational diseases EW 30; LT 45–47; NL 27; SK 1–7, 16
occupational safety D 1; DK 2–4; IRL 30, 32; LT 46; P 23; SLO 29–31
omission A 59, 60, 70; B 57, 59, 61; EST 4; GR 4, 11, 21, 58, 59; H 35–37; IRL 2; N 7; NL 32; P 29, 48, 56, 58; PL 2, 4, 5, 8, 68, 71

pain and suffering A 7, 62; CR 22; CZ 10; D 8, 13, 21–27, 42, 43, 46, 48, 71; GR 16, 17, 19, 20, 22, 43, 47; I 1–3, 19–23, 30; IRL 2, 18; LT 11, 18–20; LV 5, 6; N 24; NL 48; P 55; PL 16; SF 2, 5; SK 4–6, 46–52; SLO 13
parents' liability B 64, 112; E 70; F 31, 32, 36; NL 39
pecuniary loss CR 7; D 43, 55; E 35, 44; EST 16–19, 21; EW 3; GR 8, 41; H 8; I 10–14, 35; LT 7, 9, 14, 26, 27, 31, 41; LV 39, 46; P 28, 29, 47, 52, 58, 59, 64, 69; PL 24, 28, 69, 73; S 11, 17; SF 15; SK 4, 36; SLO 18, 29, 33, 37, 38
personal injury A 5–9, 25, 26, 32, 51, 60; B 14, 15, 17–21, 33–45, 51, 109; CH 11, 14, 43; CR 4, 5; CZ 5, 7, 81; D 4, 21, 25–27, 40, 41, 43, 46–50; DK 2, 5; E 2, 7, 15, 18–26, 54–61, 62, 64; EST 2–6, 10; EU 7, 15; EW 2–12, 18, 20, 21, 23; F 14, 26–44, 60–71; GR 29, 35, 39, 49; I 14, 23; IRL 1–4, 9–11, 17–20; LT 6, 7, 26–30; LV 6, 7, 13; N 13–23, 37–39; NL 1, 14, 25, 27; P 52–58, 90; PL 6, 21, 36, 40, 55; SF 1, 2, 5, 20–24; SK 31, 38; SLO 12–19, 20–28, 29–31, 34, 35
personality rights B 14; CR 7–9; CZ 5; EST 3, 4, 21, 22, 26, 27; GR 61, 62; H 3, 4, 14, 15, 24, 25, 35, 37; I 15, 16, 34; NL 44, 46–48; P 18, 23; PL 20, 23, 28; SK 59, 60; SLO 3, 33, 44, 45
persons close to the victim A 25–32, 51–54; B 33–45, 84; CR 2, 10–13, 15, 16; CZ 8, 10, 102, 103; EW 1; GR 15, 16, 20, 22, 35–37, 46–48; H 29; I 19, 23; LT 7, 11, 19; N 7; NL 1, 21; P 55–58; PL 48–54, 73; SF 6, 12–19; SK 60
police CR 8; E 7, 18–22; EU 18; H 8, 35; NL 45, 48; SK 53–56
post-traumatic stress disorder IRL 9; PL 36
precautionary principle IRL 31; PL 48, 50
predisposition DK 14–16
prescription, see limitation
press, see media
presumption B 15
of causation NL 29
of fault I 29; LT 41; PL 41
prevention B 15; CZ 109; DK 22
Principles of European Contract Law EST 2
Principles of European Tort Law EW 33; F 75; I 30; N 5; NL 54; PL 66
privacy A 79; B 14; CZ 7; D 5, 11–20, 73; E 9–17; EW 24–29; GR 61; IRL 38; P 4, 23; SLO 1–5, 42–48

privilege A 71; D 29, 30, 40
product liability A 68, 80; B 14; CR 17; CZ 108; D 1–6, 52, 74; DK 14–16, 20, 21; E 3, 62, 66; EST 2, 7, 32; EW 35; F 20–25, 60–71; GR 43; N 7, 10, 24–27, 28, 30, 34, 35; NL 62; PL 62; SF 37, 38; SK 28, 29; SLO 36
product safety D 1, 51; N 25, 26
professional liability DK 20
property damage B 14, 15, 64; CZ 5, 32, 37, 38, 41, 51, 52, 54–56, 65, 67, 86–94; D 75; E 62; EST 9–11, 16; LT 6, 28; LV 3; N 2; NL 6, 8, 36–42; S 12, 14, 16, 35, 39
protective norm D 76
psychological harm A 25–32, 51–54; E 32; IRL 23, 24, 28–32, 37; NL 43–48; P 55–58, 59, 62; SK 46; SLO 32, 38
public liability A 10–17, 33–40, 72, 83; B 51–63, 97–107, 116; CH 4; CR 26, 27; CZ 31, 32, 36, 86–96, 105; D 34–39, 42, 51, 54, 78, 82; DK 22; E 69; EST 8–12, 14–16, 24; EW 31, 34; GR 1; H 37, 40, 41; LT 10, 31, 35; NL 6, 7, 13, 18–21, 56, 66, 72; P 47–51, 79, 82; PL 1–10, 15, 26, 59, 61, 65, 68, 70–72; S 40; SF 25–34; SK 58
punitive damages IRL 26
pure economic loss A 67, 70; CH 27; E 5; EW 37; P 16, 28; S 12, 16

railways CH 15, 18
recourse NL 49–51
redress, see recourse
reduction clause N 2–6
reliance CH 31–33, 44; P 65
remoteness N 21
restitution in kind D 32; P 59–64
reversal rule, see burden of proof, reversal of the
risk B 54; CH 12, 13, 20, 23, 28, 36, 38; CR 17, 19, 20, 23; D 22, 39, 44; E 4, 41; EST 2, 13; EU 9, 10, 19, 22, 28; EW 2, 4–11, 13, 16, 19, 20, 22, 23, 36; F 30, 33, 69, 73, 75; H 3, 11, 32–34; IRL 19, 31, 32; N 6, 7–10, 11, 23, 25, 26, 33; NL 1, 10, 18, 25, 26, 32; P 54, 56, 90, 94–96; PL 40, 45, 49; SF 38; SK 6, 9; SLO 17
    assumption of ~ CR 17–20; E 68; N 26

salmonella DK 14–16
satisfaction B 23, 34, 99; D 22, 24, 26
secret PL 51
service providers, see internet
sexual abuse D 77; NL 53
ski resorts CH 11–16; CR 19
social hardship SK 6, 16, 18–20, 46–52
social insurance A 33; D 42; I 32; LT 25, 45–47; SK 5–7
social services B 97–104; D 80; N 15
sports A 86; CH 37; CR 19, 20; D 1, 81; F 26–33; IRL 26; NL 12; P 52–58, 94–96; PL 40
standard of care D 2; DK 2; IRL 10, 11, 18, 19, 31, 32, 37; LT 15; SLO 11, 19
state liability, see public liability
statutory duty D 53; EW 13, 15, 21, 31; SK 2
stock options LT 40–42, 48, 49
strict liability A 1–4; B 5, 32, 47; CH 3, 18, 36, 41, 42; CR 3, 6, 17, 27; CZ 31, 40, 50, 72, 83; D 21–24, 30, 45, 54, 83; DK 4, 22; E 49, 55, 58, 59, 62; EST 6, 9, 14, 32; EW 20, 21, 31, 35; F 38; GR 31; IG 1–73; N 7–12, 25, 27, 28, 29, 31–35; P 11–14, 21, 30, 32, 35, 44, 91; PL 8, 26, 35–43, 70; SK 3; SLO 24, 25, 28, 35

tax D 31–33, 84; N 19
tender DK 11–13
terrorism EU 19, 22; GR 61
third party D 46; DK 20; EST 13, 35; EU 19, 21; F 22; GR 51, 56; LV 1–7; N 17; NL 6, 14, 15, 20, 46; P 16, 21, 27–29, 76; S 21–24, 36, 39
tobacco A 68, 69, 85; CR 17, 18, 20; E 68; N 7–12, 28, 30, 33
traffic liability A 1–4, 26, 51, 52, 67; B 11, 14, 17–21, 28–45, 109; CH 37; CZ 1–10, 19, 67–75, 102, 104; D 21–24, 28–33; E 1, 2, 18–22; EST 6; EW 2, 12–17, 18; GR 14, 16, 18, 21, 49, 62; H 26; IRL 17–20; LV 1–7; N 13–23; NL 6–8, 13, 14, 25, 30; P 11–14, 33–46, 59–64, 75–78; S 11–24, 29–32; SK 53–56; SLO 12–19
transplant PL 55

unfair competition B 14; LT 36–39
unjust enrichment EST 2; P 60

vicarious liability B 106; CH 3, 41, 42; EST 33; EW 31; GR 29–34; H 8–10, 19, 37; IRL 36; P 27, 29; PL 56, 60; SF 28
vis maior, see *force majeure*

whiplash D 87
work accidents B 17–21; CR 3–5; DK 2–4; EW 18, 23, 35; GR 11–15; LT 45–47; NL 4; SK 1–7, 16, 35
wrongful birth B 113; CR 2, 9; CZ 28; GR 61; H 2–4, 42; I 34; PL 19–28
wrongful life B 113; NL 61, 73
wrongfulness A 42, 68, 69; CH 5, 27, 46; CR 18; CZ 53, 106; E 16; EST 2–4, 9, 11, 13, 14, 16, 18, 23, 29; F 5; GR 4, 8–10, 38, 54–56, 58, 59, 63; H 38; LT 38; LV 32–44; NL 14, 20, 62, 68; P 55; PL 2–5, 9, 10, 45, 61, 65, 71; SK 58

Publications

Principles of European Tort Law

Volume 1: *The Limits of Liability: Keeping the Floodgates Shut.*
Edited by Jaap Spier.
Kluwer Law International, The Hague. Hardbound.
ISBN 90-411-0169-1. 1996, 162 pp.

Volume 2: *The Limits of Expanding Liability. Eight Fundamental Cases in a Comparative Perspective.*
Edited by Jaap Spier.
Kluwer Law International, The Hague. Hardbound.
ISBN 90-411-0581-6. 1998, 244 pp.

Volume 3: *Unification of Tort Law: Wrongfulness.*
Edited by Helmut Koziol.
Kluwer Law International, The Hague. Hardbound.
ISBN 90-411-1019-4. 1998, 144 pp.

Volume 4: *Unification of Tort Law: Causation.*
Edited by Jaap Spier.
Kluwer Law International, The Hague. Hardbound.
ISBN 90-411-1325-8. 2000, 161 pp.

Volume 5: *Unification of Tort Law: Damages.*
Edited by Ulrich Magnus.
Kluwer Law International, The Hague. Hardbound.
ISBN 90-411-1481-5. 2001, 255 pp.

Volume 6: *Unification of Tort Law: Strict Liability.*
Edited by Bernhard A. Koch and Helmut Koziol.
Kluwer Law International, The Hague. Hardbound.
ISBN 90-411-1705-9. 2002, 444 pp.

Volume 7: *Unification of Tort Law: Liability for Damage caused by Others*
Edited by Jaap Spier.
Kluwer Law International, The Hague. Hardbound.
ISBN 90-411-2185-4. 2003, 335 pp.

Volume 8: *Unification of Tort Law: Contributory Negligence.*
Edited by Ulrich Magnus and Miquel Martín-Casals.
Kluwer Law International, The Hague. Hardbound.
ISBN 90-411-2220-6. 2004, 300 pp.

Volume 9: *Unification of Tort Law: Multiple Tortfeasors.*
Edited by W.V. Horton Rogers
Kluwer Law International, The Hague. Hardbound.
ISBN 90-411-2319-9. 2004, 313 pp.

Volume 10: *Unification of Tort Law: Fault.*
Edited by Pierre Widmer.
Kluwer Law International, The Hague. Hardbound.
ISBN 90-411-2098-X.
2005, 393 pp.

Principles of European Tort Law. Text and Commentary
Edited by the European Group on Tort Law.
Springer, Vienna/New York.
Softcover, ISBN 3-211-23084-X.
2005, 282 pp.

Tort and Insurance Law

Volume 1: *Cases on Medical Malpractice in a Comparative Perspective.*
Edited by Michael Faure and Helmut Koziol.
Springer, Vienna/New York.
Softcover. ISBN 3-211-83595-4.
2001, 331 pp.

Volume 2: *Damages for Non-Pecuniary Loss in a Comparative Perspective.*
Edited by W.V. Horton Rogers.
Springer, Vienna/New York.
Softcover. ISBN 3-211-83602-0.
2001, 318 pp.

Volume 3: *The Impact of Social Security on Tort Law.*
Edited by Ulrich Magnus.
Springer, Vienna/New York.
Softcover. ISBN 3-211-83795-7.
2003, 312 pp.

Volume 4: *Compensation for Personal Injury in a Comparative perspective.*
Edited by Bernhard A. Koch and Helmut Koziol.
Springer, Vienna/New York.
Softcover. ISBN 3-211-83791-4.
2003, 501 pp.

Volume 5: *Deterrence, Insurability and Compensation in Environmental Liability. Future Developments in the European Union.*
Edited by Michael Faure.
Springer, Vienna/New York.
Softcover. ISBN 3-211-83863-5.
2003, 405 pp.

Volume 6: *Der Ersatz frustrierter Aufwendungen. Vermögens- und Nichtvermögensschaden im österreichischen und deutschen Recht.*
By Thomas Schobel.
Springer, Vienna/New York.
Softcover. ISBN 3-211-83877-5.
2003, 342 pp.

Volume 7: *Liability for and Insurability of Biomedical Research with Human Subjects in a Comparative Perspective.*
Edited by Jos Dute, Michael G. Faure and Helmut Koziol.
Springer, Vienna/New York.
Softcover. ISBN 3-211-20098-3.
2004, 445 pp.

Volume 8: *No-Fault Compensation System in the Health Care Sector.*
Edited by Jos Dute, Michael G. Faure, Helmut Koziol.
Springer, Vienna/New York.
Softcover. ISBN 3-211-20799-6.
2004, 492 pp.

Volume 9: *Pure Economic Loss.*
Edited by Willem H. van Boom, Helmut Koziol and Christian A. Witting.
Springer, Vienna/New York.
Softcover. ISBN 3-211-00514-5.
2003, 214 pp.

Volume 10: *Liber Amicorum Pierre Widmer.*
Edited by Helmut Koziol and Jaap Spier.
Springer, Vienna/New York.
Softcover. ISBN 3-211-00522-6.
2003, 376 pp.

Volume 11: *Terrorism, Tort Law and Insurance. A Comparative Survey.*
Edited by Bernhard A. Koch.
Springer, Vienna/New York.
Softcover. ISBN 3-211-01867-0.
2004, 313 pp.

Volume 12: *Abschlussprüfer. Haftung und Versicherung.*
Edited by Helmut Koziol and Walter Doralt.
Springer, Vienna/New York.
Softcover. ISBN 3-211-20800-3.
2004, 180 pp.

Volume 13: *Persönlichkeitsschutz gegenüber Massenmedien/The Protection of Personality Rights against Invasions by Mass Media.*
Edited by Helmut Koziol and Alexander Warzilek.
Springer, Vienna/New York.
Softcover. ISBN 3-211-23835-2.
2005, 713 pp.

Volume 14: *Financial Compensation for Victims of Catastrophes.*
Edited by Michael Faure and Ton Hartlief.
Springer, Vienna/New York.
Softcover. ISBN 3-211-24481-6.
2005, approx. 400 pp. (forthcoming)

Volume 15: *Children in Tort Law. Part I: Children as Tortfeasors.*
Edited by Miquel Martín-Casals.
Springer, Vienna/New York.
Softcover. ISBN 3-211-24480-8.
2005, approx. 600 pp. (forthcoming)

Volume 16: *Tort Law and Liability Insurance.*
Edited by Gerhard Wagner.
Springer, Vienna/New York.
Softcover. ISBN 3-211-24482-4.
2005, 361 pp.

European Tort Law Yearbook

European Tort Law 2001.
Edited by Helmut Koziol and Barbara C. Steininger.
Springer, Vienna/New York.
Softcover. ISBN 3-211-83824-4.
2002, 571 pp.

European Tort Law 2002.
Edited by Helmut Koziol and Barbara C. Steininger.
Springer, Vienna/New York.
Softcover. ISBN 3-211-00486-6.
2003, 596 pp.

European Tort Law 2003.
Edited by Helmut Koziol and Barbara C. Steininger.
Springer, Vienna/New York.
Softcover. ISBN 3-211-21033-4.
2004, 493 pp.

Springer and the Environment

WE AT SPRINGER FIRMLY BELIEVE THAT AN INTERnational science publisher has a special obligation to the environment, and our corporate policies consistently reflect this conviction.

WE ALSO EXPECT OUR BUSINESS PARTNERS – PRINTERS, paper mills, packaging manufacturers, etc. – to commit themselves to using environmentally friendly materials and production processes.

THE PAPER IN THIS BOOK IS MADE FROM NO-CHLORINE pulp and is acid free, in conformance with international standards for paper permanency.